SOCIAL ISSUES
AND CONTRADICTIONS IN
CANADIAN SOCIETY

SOCIAL ISSUES AND CONTRADICTIONS IN CANADIAN SOCIETY

SECOND EDITION

B. SINGH BOLARIA
UNIVERSITY OF SASKATCHEWAN

Harcourt Brace & Company, Canada

Toronto Montreal Fort Worth New York Orlando
Philadelphia San Diego London Sydney Tokyo

Canadian Cataloguing in Publication Data

Main entry under title:
Social issues and contradictions in Canadian society

2nd ed.
Includes bibliographical references and index.
ISBN 0-7747-3291-1

1. Canada - Social conditions - 1971- .*
I. Bolaria, B. Singh, 1936-

HN103.5.S623 1995 971.064 C94-931839-6

Publisher: Heather McWhinney
Editor and Marketing Manager: Daniel J. Brooks
Projects Co-ordinator: Megan Mueller
Director of Publishing Services: Jean Davies
Editorial Manager: Marcel Chiera
Supervising Editor: Semareh Al-Hillal
Production Editor: Celène S. Adams
Production Manager: Sue-Ann Becker
Production Supervisor: Carol Tong
Copy Editor: Margaret Hoogeveen
Interior Design: Dave Peters
Cover Design: Opus House
Typesetting and Assembly: Bookman Typesetting Co.
Printing and Binding: Data Reproductions Corporation

Cover Art: Glenn Priestley, *Winter Bus* (1993). 26-1/2" × 20". Oil over tempera on board. Photograph courtesy of the Mira Godard Gallery, Toronto. Reproduced with permission of the artist.

(∞) This book was printed in the United States of America on acid-free paper.
1 2 3 4 5 99 98 97 96 95

PREFACE

This second edition came about in response to a continuing demand for a text detailing the major issues and contradictions in Canadian society. With the exception of two new additions, the articles were original contributions written specifically for the first edition. These have all been revised and updated. Obviously this resource cannot cover an exhaustive list of topics but, rather, examines what the editor believes to be the most important issues affecting Canadian society today.

The social issues that concern the public change from time to time. Early sociologists were preoccupied, for the most part, with matters of social stability and social harmony. They focussed on issues of deviance and other behaviour patterns considered to be disruptive of social order. Issues of "morality," such as prostitution, homosexuality, and abortion, were topics commonly discussed in texts on social problems. One of the assumptions often made by early sociologists was that these problems resulted from "defective" individuals—mentally deficient persons or social misfits. While some of these issues are still included in texts on social problems, they are no longer analyzed solely in terms of the "personal deficiencies" of individuals. For example, the question of homosexuality has largely been transformed from one of "deviant" or "sinful" behaviour to an issue of human rights—of discrimination and oppression based upon sexual orientation.

The issues that receive the most attention at any given time are determined by many different causes, including shifts in the values and norms of the society and social and political movements. For example, environmental degradation and pollution have not always been major social concerns. Environmentalists have helped raise the public consciousness and heighten awareness of hazardous chemicals, carcinogens, and toxic waste. The civil rights and feminist movements that began in the 1960s have brought into focus the issues of racism and sexism. Currently, the issues of social, economic, and political inequality, based upon the status ascribed to attributes such as gender, race, or other criteria, are receiving considerable attention from the general public, politicians, and the academic community. First Nations land claims and demands for self-government have helped focus attention on the historical and contemporary issues now facing the indigenous population.

Empirical evidence indicates that many individuals and groups continue to encounter inequality of conditions (for example, differential distribution of income and wealth) and inequality of opportunity (for example, differential access to education and health care). Political, economic, and social stratification are fundamental aspects of Canadian society. Thus, a number of essays in this volume are devoted to the issue of inequality and its consequences.

Sociologists interested in this area approach and examine these essential topics and issues from various theoretical perspectives and paradigms, and use varying levels of analysis. Although the issues are diverse, the underlying contradictions of society are major determinants of all these issues and problems. Sociologists with critical orientation tend to focus on structural conditions and contradictions, and on the institutional arrangements that produce and perpetuate social problems. In short, the focus is on the social structure and its primary and secondary contradictions, rather than on the personal pathologies of the problematic populations. The social issues in this volume are analyzed largely in terms of various structural contradictions.

A final note may be added here. Critical sociology in its various forms—liberal or racial—has proved its utility in the analysis of a wide range of social phenomena. More recently, in the areas of gender studies and racial and cultural studies, the works of feminist scholars and racial minority scholars have made significant contributions to the literature in critical sociology, which is characterized by its focus on class relations and class contradictions under capitalism. These and other developments have helped "make the case" for critical social analysis. Critical sociology's contributions to a number of substantive areas in sociology are now well recognized and accepted, however grudgingly, by noncritical sociologists. It is hoped that the essays in this volume will make a contribution to the critical analysis of social issues and social problems.

Acknowledgements

A number of people have contributed to the completion of this book. First, I would like to express my appreciation to the contributing authors who accepted my invitation to write chapters for this volume or the first edition. I am also grateful to Michael Owen, director of Research Services, College of Graduate Studies and Research, University of Saskatchewan, for a grant from the President's Publication Fund to assist in the preparation of this book.

Of course, I wish to thank a number of people at Harcourt Brace & Company Canada, particularly Dan Brooks, Heather McWhinney, Marguerite Martindale, Megan Mueller, Semareh Al-Hillal, and Celène Adams, who, with their colleagues, bore the responsibility to see this book through to its completion. I am grateful to all of them for their professional guidance, enthusiasm, and support for this project. Finally, I wish to thank my family for their patience, understanding, and support—especially Rosemary, who provided considerable academic and intellectual support to clarify my ideas, and editorial assistance in completing this book.

B. Singh Bolaria
University of Saskatchewan
Saskatoon

A Note From the Publisher

Thank you for selecting *Social Issues and Contradictions in Canadian Society*, Second Edition by B. Singh Bolaria.

We want to hear what you think about *Social Issues and Contradictions in Canadian Society*, Second Edition. Please take a few minutes to fill out the stamped reply card at the back of the book. Your comments and suggestions will be valuable to us as we prepare new editions and other books.

CONTRIBUTORS

B. Singh Bolaria	University of Saskatchewan
Harold E. Bronson (now retired)	University of Saskatchewan
William K. Carroll	University of Victoria
Michael Clow	St. Thomas More College
Wilfrid B. Denis	St. Thomas More College
Harley D. Dickinson	University of Saskatchewan
Lawrence F. Felt	Memorial University of Newfoundland
James S. Frideres	University of Calgary
Karen R. Grant	University of Manitoba
Alison Hayford	University of Regina
Leslie J. Miller	University of Calgary
Alicja Muszynski	University of Waterloo
Herbert C. Northcott	University of Alberta
Leslie Samuelson	University of Saskatchewan
Vic Satzewich	University of Lethbridge
Peter R. Sinclair	Memorial University of Newfoundland
James Stolzman	Dalhousie University
Kathleen Storrie	University of Saskatchewan
Gary Teeple	Simon Fraser University
K. Victor Ujimoto	University of Guelph
Rennie Warburton	University of Victoria
Terry Wotherspoon	University of Saskatchewan

CONTENTS

CHAPTER 1

Introduction: Social Issues and Contradictions

B. Singh Bolaria

Introduction

The social issues and social problems that concern the public and the academic community change over time. Early sociologists concerned themselves mainly with issues of deviance and behaviour considered disruptive to social stability, social harmony, and the social and moral order (Coleman and Cressey 1984; Eitzen and Zinn 1989). It was commonly assumed that many of these problems resulted from maladjusted, abnormal individuals who had some mental deficiency or disorder, or social misfits who had been inadequately socialized into societal norms and values. The "medical model" of deviance, expressed in clinical language, was dominant in the analysis of social ills. Over time, there has been a shift in both the conceptualization and the analysis of social problems. These issues are no longer analyzed solely with reference to personal pathologies of individuals. Sociologists with critical orientation tend to focus on social, political, and economic conditions, and institutional arrangements, that produce social problems.

Changes in the social issues that receive the most attention have many different causes. These may include shifts in the values and norms of the society as well as social and political movements (Coleman and Cressey 1984). For example, environmental degradation and pollution have not always been important social issues. Environmentalists are largely responsible for heightened public awareness in this regard. The civil rights and feminist movements that began in the sixties have brought into focus the issues of racism, sexism, and racial and gender inequalities. Issues related to inequality, whether based on factors of social ascription such as gender or race, or on other criteria, have dominated public and academic debates in recent years. While there has been increasing awareness of these inequalities and a growing consciousness of the right to equality shared by all Canadians, many individuals and groups continue to encounter inequality of conditions and of opportunities. These inequalities create different opportunities and life chances for individuals, which are reflected in such measures as their level of education, health status, nutrition, and treatment by the justice system.

Because of the prominence of social, political, and economic stratification in Canada, the primary focus of this book is on inequality and its consequences. These and other issues are analyzed for the most part in terms of various systemic structural contradictions.

The purpose of this chapter is, by way of introduction, to outline some of the salient aspects of theoretical and conceptual debate in the study of social issues and social problems. More specifically, this chapter treats the topics of the definition and etiology of personal troubles and public issues, and individualistic and structural explanations. The fundamental question is, who or what is to be "blamed"—— "defective" individuals or "faulty" structures. Wherever appropriate, examples from various subdisciplines of sociology are used to illustrate the relative aspects of the debate. It is hoped that this discussion will put into context the analyses presented in various essays in this book.

Personal Troubles and Public Issues

Many people tend to individualize such issues as poverty and unemployment as personal problems of the poor and unemployed, rather than regarding them as social problems. This distinction between personal and social problems is a crucial one, since it is germane to the question of who or what is at fault (Lauer 1978; Eitzen and Zinn 1989). For instance, is poverty due to the laziness or other "defects" of the poor individuals? Or is it due to the maldistribution of wealth and differential opportunity structures in society? Lauer defines a personal problem as "one whose causes and solutions lie within the individual and the individual's immediate environment," and a social problem as "one whose causes and solutions lie outside the individual and his or her immediate environment" (1978, 3).

C. Wright Mills, in *The Sociological Imagination*, made a crucial distinction between "the personal troubles of milieu" and the "public issues of social structure." Mills (1959, 8) states: "Troubles occur ... within the range of [the individual's] immediate relations with others; they have to do with [individual] self and with those limited areas of social life of which [the individual] is directly and personally aware.... A trouble is a private matter." On the other hand, "issues have to do with matters that transcend these local environments of the individual and the range of his [or her] inner life. They have to do with the organization of many such milieux into the institutions of an historical society.... An issue is a public matter." Mills states further that "it is the very nature of an issue, unlike even widespread trouble, that it cannot very well be defined in terms of the immediate and everyday environments of ordinary men [or women]. An issue, in fact, often involves a crisis in institutional arrangements, and often too it involves what Marxists call 'contradictions' or antagonisms" (1959, 8-9).

Mills provides a number of illustrations of the difference between the two. If an individual is unemployed, that is his personal trouble. The individual may lack skills, have flaws in his character, and may lack motivation. But if millions of workers are unemployed and high unemployment rates persist year after year, then it is a public issue, not just a question of immediate opportunities for an individual.

Mills (1959, 9) states: "The very structure of opportunities has collapsed. Both the correct statement of the problem and the range of possible solutions require us to consider the economic and political institutions of the society, and not merely the personal situation and character of a scatter of individuals." Similarly, inside a marriage a couple may experience personal troubles and ultimately get a divorce. If this couple is only one of the very few marriages that experience such problems then one may conclude that the couple has entirely personal problems or troubles. But if the divorce rate is high and millions of marriages break up, affecting millions of couples and children, it is no longer a "personal trouble." Then the question is not what is wrong with a particular couple but rather what has happened to the institution of marriage and the family. According to Mills, "this is an indication of a structural issue having to do with the institutions of marriage and the family and other institutions that bear upon them" (1959, 9).

If the current economic arrangements produce high unemployment and cyclical boom and bust periods, then the problem of unemployment becomes incapable of personal solutions. However, sociological discussions often lack analysis of the economic institutions and the way they affect other areas of social and individual life. In part, sociologists continue to have difficulty appreciating the connection between personal troubles and public issues (Fry 1984).

In one sense, to those who are affected, it makes no difference whether a particular situation is defined as a personal or a social problem. The consequences for the unemployed and the divorced are still the same in terms of individual suffering. But in other respects, whether a problem is defined as "personal trouble" or a "social issue" is of crucial significance. This distinction determines the causes, consequences, and solutions to the problems (Lauer 1978).

"Defective" Individuals or "Faulty" Structures

In their study of social issues and social problems, generations of sociologists have used different conceptual frameworks and perspectives. Also, a debate continues over the unit of analysis, that is, whether the focus of analysis ought to be the individual or the social structure. A corollary of this is the matter of who is to be "blamed" for such issues as poverty, and for race, class, and gender inequalities. There is continuing debate as to whether these inequalities emanate from the personal pathologies and inadequacies of the individuals (individualistic explanations)—or from structured inequalities of the system (structural explanations)—in other words, whether minorities or other disadvantaged groups are themselves the problems or victims of the system. A discussion of selective examples helps to illuminate the basic arguments involved in the study of social issues.

Why is there poverty in the midst of plenty? Explanations of poverty tend to fall within three areas: personal, cultural, and economic.

One persistent element in our ethos is the belief that everyone in this society has equal opportunities. Consequently, success or failure is thought to depend upon individual characteristics. Belief in the value of hard work and competition tends to promote the thinking that each individual is responsible for his or her destiny. Joe

Feagin (1975, 91–92) has summarized the basic contents of what he characterizes as the "ideology of individualism" as follows:

1. Each individual should work hard and strive to succeed in competition with others.
2. Those who work hard should be rewarded with success (seen as wealth, property, prestige, and power).
3. Because of widespread and equal opportunity, those who work hard will in fact be rewarded with success.
4. Economic failure is an individual's own fault and reveals lack of effort and other character defects.

Poverty, then, is a consequence of "defective" personal traits of individuals. People are poor because of some personal deficiency, which is either innate inferiority (biological or intellectual) or cultural inferiority (the culture of poverty). Proponents of Social Darwinism, like the nineteenth-century sociologist Herbert Spencer, have argued that the poor are unfit: "Poverty was nature's way of 'excreting' ... unhealthy, imbecile, slow, vacillating, faithless members of society in order to make room for the 'fit'" (Eitzen and Zinn 1989, 178). Arthur Jensen (1969, 1980) and Richard Herrnstein (1971, 1973) have argued that certain groups lack intellectual endowment—for instance, blacks as compared to whites—and that intelligence is primarily inherited. Poor performance in school and subsequent failure are attributed to low intelligence rather than the differential educational opportunities, culturally biased IQ tests, and advantages and disadvantages of class background and inheritance (Eitzen and Zinn 1989, 179). William Ryan (1976, 54) states: "Arthur Jensen and Richard Herrnstein confirm regretfully that Black folks and poor folks are born stupid, that little rich kids grow up rich adults, not because they inherited Daddy's stock portfolio, but rather because they inherited his brains."

While the personal approach locates the source of poverty within the individuals themselves—"defective" individuals—the "culture of poverty" hypothesis locates poverty in poor people's way of life—"defective" culture. Poverty in both instances is a consequence of "defective" behaviour of the individuals. Anderson and Gibson (1978, 168) state:

> The cultural account is similar to the personal account in that both attribute the causes of poverty to the defective behaviour of the individual, but differs in that the cultural account, rather than tracing the deficiencies of the poor individual to independent sources within the individual, explains poverty-producing deficiencies as originating in a lower class way of life.

The "culture of poverty" was given its most systematic treatment by Oscar Lewis (1966). Cultural traits he attributes to the poor include low aspirations, impulsiveness, lack of moral values, present orientation, resignation, and fatalism. Others, such as Banfield (1977), Kluckhohn and Strodtbeck (1961), and Sowell (1981), add to the list of cultural traits with which they explain the disadvantaged status of some groups; they cite devaluation of education, present time orientation, low motivation, language difficulties, dependency, and lack of achievement orientation.

Because poor individuals are blamed for their condition, a stigma is attached to being poor (Coleman and Cressey 1984, 166). They get labelled as "disreputable" (Matza 1966). This stigmatization and labelling further strengthens negative images of the poor, such as lazy, unwilling to work, and "welfare bums." Poor parents are also blamed for the poverty of their children, through the transmission of defective "culture of poverty" traits to the next generation. In other words, it is the "culture of poverty" that is the cause of the cycle of poverty rather than the economic system and the differential opportunity structures. However, opponents of this thesis, such as Anderson and Gibson (1978), have argued that the economic system that has made one generation of individuals poor will usually do the same kind of job on their children. Mills (1956, 111) states: "The accumulation of advantages at the very top parallels the vicious cycle of poverty at the very bottom." Liebow, in his attempt to clarify the distinction between culturally transmitted poverty and poverty produced anew in each generation, explains that

> the son goes out and independently experiences the same failures, in the same areas, and for much the same reasons as his father. What appears as a dynamic, self-sustaining cultural process is, in part at least, a relatively simple piece of social machinery which turns out, in rather mechanical fashion, independently produced look-alikes. (1967, 223)

The "culture of poverty" thesis is criticized on other grounds as well. Valentine (1968) argues that the conditions of the poor described by Lewis are imposed on them from outside rather than being the product of the "culture of poverty." Lifestyles of the poor, Roach and Gursslin (1967) argue, are an adaptation to poverty rather than the cause of poverty.

Whether the poor are defined as poor because of "defective" individual traits or their "defective" way of life, in either case they are objects of what Ryan (1971) has called "blaming the victim." Parenti (1978, 24) comments: "Focusing on the poor and ignoring the system of power, privilege, and profit which makes them poor, is a little like blaming the corpse for the murder."

This focus on individuals and their way of life is not confined to the analysis of poverty alone. Individual lifestyles and consumption patterns are widely invoked to explain the increase in many diseases. The inadequate or improper use of medical services by the poor is often attributed to their lack of knowledge, lack of readiness to use services, lack of positive values toward health, and cultural impediments to the use of services. Though it is phrased somewhat differently, again the analysis shifts the responsibility for not benefiting from services onto the individual—it blames the victim (Bolaria 1988). This focus on individual lifestyles and self-imposed risks tends to downgrade the importance of social and environmental factors in the production of illness and the differential availability of health services to different groups.

With few exceptions, sociological studies of racial minorities are guided by the traditional "race relations cycle" perspective and its many present-day variations of assimilation theories. One can hardly avoid the literature dealing with cultural distinctiveness, cultural patterns and orientations, adaptation, integration, accommodation, identity, assimilation, and so forth. In addition, the tendency has been to examine the "problems" of non-Europeans. Studies of racial minorities, for the most part, tend to degenerate into more-or-less socio-psychological examinations of "ethnic problems" or "identity crises," of "adaptation problems" or "assimilation problems," of "race problems" or "family problems." In short, they highlight personal and social pathologies of racial minorities and their institutions (Bolaria 1983; Bolaria and Li 1988). The disadvantaged position of racial minorities is often explained by biological and cultural deficiency theories in which the organization of the society along racial lines, institutional racism, and differential power relations are typically overlooked (Eitzen and Zinn 1989; Bolaria and Li 1988).

The sociology of deviance has often concentrated on what Davis (1980) characterizes as the unconventional and problematic aspects of life (for example, crime, alcoholism, and prostitution) and other social and personal "failures." Davis (1980, 9) further observes: "In its unreflective form, the field has focused exclusively on the victims of social change, rather than on the structural sources of change and social problems, thus turning human tragedy into the bread and butter issues for sociologists of deviance."

Many studies in this area focus on the "antisocial" individuals and their maladjustments, personal failures, and pathologies, rather than on social conditions and class, race, and gender inequalities in the legal structure and the justice system (Davis 1980; Eitzen and Zinn 1989).

Another illustration of the debate in sociology comes from the study of gender inequality. In this area, two approaches can be identified: the gender-role socialization approach and the structural approach. The first approach focusses on individuals and the characteristics they acquire in the process of socialization (for example, masculine–feminine roles, independent and dependent behaviours); the second one focusses on factors external to the individuals, such as differential opportunity structures for men and women, inequality of power, and so forth (Eitzen and Zinn 1989; Glazer and Waehrer 1977). While socialization may "produce differences in the personalities, behaviors, and motivations of women and men, essentially gender stratification is maintained by societal forms" (Eitzen and Zinn 1989, 250). Uncritical use of the socialization perspective, Peterson and Enarson (1974) contend, diverts attention from the structured inequalities of the system: "Misuse of the concept of socialization plays directly into the Blaming the Victim ideology, by focusing on the victim; responsibility for 'the woman problem' rests not in the social system with its sex structured distribution of inequality, but in socialized sex differences and sex roles" (1974, 8).

The individualization of social problems and its accompanying focus on the personal pathologies of the victim are prevalent in numerous areas of study. As Ryan (1971, 5) states,

> the miserable health care of the poor is explained away on the grounds that the victim has poor motivation and lacks health information. The problems of slum housing are traced to the characteristics of tenants who are ... not yet "acculturated" to life in the big city. The "multiproblem" poor, it is claimed, suffer the psychological effects of impoverishment, the "culture of poverty," and the deviant value system of the lower classes; consequently, though unwittingly, they cause their own troubles.

This focus on "problematic individuals" or "problematic groups" and on "blaming the victim" tends to strengthen " the ideological construct of bourgeois individualism by which one is responsible for one's own wealth or lack of it, for one's own work or lack of it, and for one's own health or lack of it" (Navarro 1978, 206). Thus it masks the structural conditions in the society that produce inequality, unemployment, and ill health. Among other consequences, the "blaming the victim" approach—what Eitzen and Zinn refer to as the person-blame approach—absolves institutions of any blame and justifies Social Darwinism (Eitzen and Zinn 1989, 18).

The structural approach, or what Eitzen and Zinn refer to as the system-blame approach, tends to focus on "system pathologies" rather than individual pathologies.

In contrast to the individual and cultural deficiency approaches, a structural explanation of poverty, for instance, locates its causes in the social-structural conditions that produce high unemployment, low-paying jobs, and unequal opportunity structures. Michael Harrington, in his book *The Other America*, states that "the real explanation of why the poor are where they are is that they made the mistake of being born to the wrong parents, in the wrong section of the country, in the wrong industry, or in the wrong racial or ethnic groups" (1963, 21). He points to the social-structural conditions in capitalist society that produce inequality.

The basic tenet of capitalism—the profit motive—produces inequality and poverty in several ways. To maximize profits, capitalists use every means to reduce labour costs. Such reductions are accomplished by maintaining a surplus of labour, which depresses wages, allowing employers to benefit from paying workers the lowest possible wages, and from the rotation of labourers and other measures (Eitzen and Zinn 1989, 185).

Labour market characteristics are particularly important in any discussion of poverty because a vast majority of Canadians earn their income in the form of wages from employment (Osberg 1981). Therefore, the type of job, the pattern of demand for workers in it, and their bargaining power vis-à-vis their employer are very important in relation to earnings. For instance, those in managerial and professional jobs are less likely to be poor than are workers in service industries and fishing. It should be noted that service industries are heavy employers of women (National Council of Welfare 1988). Moreover, the Canadian labour market is segmented along occupational, gender, ethnic, and racial lines. Many women and minorities end up in secondary and marginal sectors that offer poor working conditions and low wages.

Illustrations from other areas illuminate the distinction between individualistic and structural explanations. In medical sociology, rather than focussing on individual lifestyles, behaviour, and consumption patterns, recent studies from the perspective of historical materialism have focussed on illness-generating conditions. Several social conditions that generate illness and are associated with high levels of mortality are the focus of this approach. Social class, economic cycles, socially produced stress, production processes, the nature of work, and measures taken to increase profits are all analyzed (Waitzkin 1983; Navarro 1986). It is well known that cancer and other chronic diseases are related to environmental factors and the workplace. Evidence also links incidence of illness to economic cycles and levels of employment. Disruption of stable community relations has consistently led to an increase in rates of hypertension.

Rather than focussing on the individual life cycle and its relation to stress, "historical materialist epidemiology shifts the level of analysis to stressful forms of social organization connected to capitalist production and industrialization" (Waitzkin 1983, 63). Studies in the area of occupational health and safety provide persuasive evidence that links work environment to illness and disease, and points to basic contradictions between profit and safety. If it is expected to interfere with profits, a health- or safety-related improvement in the workplace is not likely to be implemented. Waitzkin (1983, 9) writes:

> Safety in the workplace, in almost all instances, means increased cost of production and, as a result, decreased profits. The technical improvements necessary to protect workers from dust, fumes, radioactivity, accidents, and stress entail inevitable expenses.... The constraint of private profit is a structural basis for resistance to changes in production that would assure occupational health and safety.

The contradiction between profit and safety also accounts for environmental degradation. The safe disposal of the waste products of industrial production would be costly indeed. Profit considerations encourage dumping of hazardous waste without regard to the environment or the health and safety of the public. The analysis of illness, work, and the environment in the light of these and other features of capitalism (for example, class conflict and exploitation) points to the fact that inequalities in health are closely linked to the structural contradictions of the system. The focus on individuals' lifestyles, behaviours, and their "accident proneness" tends to obfuscate the social causes of disease. As well, it diverts attention from unhealthy and unsafe workplaces and environments, obscures the extent to which health and illness depend upon socially determined ways of life, shifts responsibility for health and illness back onto the individual, and so individualizes the problem of inequality in health status.

Similarly, in contrast to the biological and cultural deficiency theories that put the blame on racial minorities, and others that blame individual racism for the disadvantaged position of minorities, the structural theories focus on institutional patterns and structural inequalities, which perpetuate racial inequality and racial oppression independently of prejudicial attitudes. Carmichael and Hamilton (1967, 4–5) discuss both types of racism. Individual racism "consists of overt acts by individuals, which cause death and injury, or the violent destruction of property," and institutional racism "originates in the operations of established and respected forces in the society."

The normal daily operations of our respected institutions continue to perpetuate racial inequality. Racial ideology and practices reach far back into the Canadian past. Colonization of the Native population, racist immigration policies and practices against Chinese and South Asians, internment of Japanese—all attest to the racist policies and practices of the Canadian state and other institutions. These past policies and practices continue to affect the current status of racial minorities in this country. Institutional inequality and racism are manifested in various exclusionary practices in the social, political, and economic spheres. While patterns and practices of discrimination have changed over time, racial domination and racial discrimination remain a permanent feature of Canadian society (Bolaria and Li 1988).

Like the racial minorities, a large proportion of women face discrimination in the workplace and end up in dead-end jobs and low-paying segments of the labour market. Their location in the labour market primarily accounts for their poverty and social subordination. Women of colour face both racial and gender discrimination and exploitation (Bolaria and Li 1988).

Because institutions are interrelated, exclusion of minorities from one institution is likely to influence their opportunities in other institutions (Eitzen and Zinn 1989). Inadequate income and poverty, for instance, affect individual life chances as manifested in health status, nutrition, and educational levels, which in turn will affect job opportunities and income levels. These inequalities are cumulative. Inequality of conditions produces differential opportunity structures, which in turn produce differential conditions. As Benokraitis and Feagin (1974, 6) put it, "unequal resources will produce unequal qualifications to compete for goods and services, unequal qualifications will limit access to goods and services and unequal access to goods and services will result in unequal resources."

In summary, an analysis of social institutions and of the structural contradictions inherent in the current political-economic and social arrangements illuminates how these institutions and arrangements cause and perpetuate inequalities and differential opportunity structures. This approach locates the cause of the "problems" in the defective system rather than in the deficiencies of the individuals and their "defective" way of life.

Individual and Social Structure

The division into an individualistic structural dichotomy may be a simplification of a complex phenomenon, but it does allow for some enlightening perspectives on social issues. It also helps clarify the distinction between the types of explanations used by sociologists and others. Whether social problems are considered to emanate from the personal "pathologies" of individuals or from systemic structural contradictions has important consequences for the individual (Lauer 1978). For example, if we define a "personal situation" as one that is due to our own failure or inadequacies, we are likely to blame ourselves and perhaps even passively accept the situation. Sennett and Cobb, in *The Hidden Injuries of Class*, tell of the "self-accusation ... of a nearly illiterate" garbage collector, who states: "Look, I know it's nobody's fault but mine that I got stuck here where I am, I mean ... if I wasn't such a dumb shit ... no, it ain't that neither ... if I had applied myself, I know I got it in me to be different, can't say anyone did it to me" (1973, 96). This self-blame is not surprising in the face of the dominant ideology of individualism, equality of opportunity, and fair competition. It is an ideology that tends to promote the idea that only individual qualities such as hard work, motivation, initiative, and intelligence determine one's station in life.

While this ethos is used to justify the inequalities in our society, the empirical reality is quite different. One's location in the social structure has important bearing on one's opportunities in life. Max Weber saw class position as closely linked to people's life chances, that is, their chances to acquire material goods and other amenities (Gerth and Mills 1958). As noted above, a number of studies indicate that economic inequalities produce inequalities in opportunities and life chances, which are reflected in such measures as education, health, and consumption patterns (Wotherspoon 1987; Bolaria and Dickinson 1988; Chossudovsky 1983). Racial ascriptive status continues to be an important determinant of the life chances of racial minorities (Bolaria and Li 1988). A recent royal commission report, *Equality in Employment*, says of Canada's Native people that

> their economic plight has taken its inevitable toll on social conditions. Native people are angry over the disproportionate numbers of native people who drop out of school, who are in prison, who suffer ill health, who die young, who commit suicide. They are saddened by the personal, communal, and cultural dislocation of their people (Abella 1984, 33).

Other factors of social ascription, such as gender, continue to be Important determinants of inequalities of conditions and opportunities (Abella 1984). These examples signify the importance of structural analysis in the study of gender and racial inequality and the link between individuals' location in the social structure and their life chances.

The analysis of the social system and structured inequalities, and their impact on individuals, is the appropriate domain of sociology. The insights of the "sociological imagination" have been increasingly significant in understanding institutional structures and how they interrelate, and the connection between personal troubles and social issues.

Organization of the Book

Despite the optimistic prognosis by some social thinkers that with industrialization and modernization the traditional social ascriptive bases for systems of inequality, such as gender and race, would no longer be relevant, empirical reality indicates that they continue to be important determinants of social, political, and economic inequalities in Canada. These inequalities produce differential access to opportunity structures, and hence different life chances for various social groups in this society.

In Part 1, entitled "Gender, Class, and Family," three essays address the issues of gender relations and gender inequality, encompassing both the domestic and public spheres. With varying degrees of emphasis, these essays present an analysis of the historical and contemporary structural basis of gender inequality. The underlying theme of these readings is that gender inequality is rooted in the ideology and social construction of patriarchal gender relations, the cult of domesticity, the bourgeois family ideal, and capitalist class relations. These readings elaborate on specific processes that place women in subordinate social roles, both in the public sphere (the world of work) and in the private sphere (the family), and the structural barriers that produce and reproduce gender inequality.

Like gender, racial ascriptive status forms another important basis of social, political, and economic inequality. Essays in Part 11 address the issues of racism, racial inequality, economic exploitation of racial minorities, and the institutional and structural arrangements and social contradictions that continue to sustain these inequalities. The underlying theme of these essays is that racism and racial inequality are structural aspects of both the past and the present operation of Canada as a capitalist society. Specific processes involved in the racial subordination and economic exploitation of racial minority immigrant groups and the First Nations are discussed here. Other subjects discussed in this section pertain to multicultural policy and its limitations, and French and English language rights and constitutional issues, both in historical and in contemporary eon texts.

Part 111 examines health, illness, and the health care system. Issues that it treats include differential health status and differential accessibility and utilization of health services according to socio-economic status and age; environmental pollution and hazardous work environments, and the linkages between environmental degradation and illness; and the study, diagnosis, and treatment of mental disorders.

In Part IV, entitled "State, Capital, and Labour," a number of issues are discussed regarding the contradictions of economic and social relations of production, class contradictions, and the state's role in the structuring and mediation of capital–labour relations and regulation of the labour market. The underlying theme of these essays is that unemployment, capital–labour relations, and conditions of work are all social issues when seen from the workers' point of view, and that the capitalist state structures and mediates capital–labour relations in the interest of the class it represents. These themes and issues are highlighted in the discussions on postwar restructuring of industrial production, transfer of production to low-wage areas, and the procurement and use of foreign labour to meet the labour-force needs and capital accumulation in Canada.

The Free Trade Agreement (FTA) and the North American Free Trade Agreement (NAFTA) brought into sharp focus the issues of Canadian political, economic, social, and cultural sovereignty. These issues cannot be divorced from internal contradictions of regional inequality, and rural–urban disparities and problems. These issues and contradictions are examined in Part V. The underlying theme of these essays is that the corporate market strategies and capital investment decisions, primarily guided by profit motives, produce a number of structural contradictions and have numerous economic, political, and social consequences for Canadians. Many of these contradictions are likely to intensify as corporate investment decisions and market strategies become more international in scope, and thus further exacerbate the internal contradictions of regional inequality and rural–urban disparities.

Part Vl examines the impact of structured inequalities on the life chances of individuals and social groups. Differential access to opportunity structures and life chances is reflected in unequal education, health, consumption patterns, nutrition, and involvement in and treatment by the justice system. These inequalities are correlated with gender, class, and race. This section concludes with a discussion of the development of the welfare state and its current contradictions. The welfare state, which was at one time viewed as the most important institution for solving social problems, has itself become a problem that requires fixing. The confrontation between social welfare policy and the politics of deficit can be expected to produce unfavourable reduction changes in state policies and priorities. The social welfare constraints that result are likely to sharpen social contradictions and escalate social problems.

The concluding chapter in this book, entitled "Social Issues and Social Policy," examines the policy implications of interpreting and analyzing social problems within individualistic or structural frameworks. It is argued that a strictly individualistic approach absolves the political, economic, and social structures and other institutions of any responsibility for social ills; its consequence is the orientation of policy toward changing the individuals and their "defective" ways of life. In contrast, within a structural framework the solutions are seen to lie in transforming the basic structures and institutions that produce and reproduce deleterious social conditions.

References

Abella, R.S. 1984. *Equality in Employment.* Ottawa: Minister of Supply and Services.

Anderson, C.H., and J.R. Gibson. 1978. *Toward a New Sociology.* 3d ed. Homewood, IL: Dorsey Press.

Banfield, E. 1977. *The Unheavenly City Revisited.* Boston: Little, Brown.

Benokraitis, N., and F.R. Feagin. 1974. "Institutional Racism: A Review and Critical Assessment of the Literature." Paper presented at the American Sociological Association, Montreal, August. Cited in Eitzen and Zinn, *Social Problems.* 217–18.

Bolaria, B.S. 1983. "Dominant Perspectives and Non-White Minorities." In *Racial Minorities in Multicultural Canada*, ed. P.S. Li and B.S. Bolaria. Toronto: Garamond Press. 157–69.

———. 1988. "The Politics and Ideology of Self-Care and Lifestyles." In *Sociology of Health Care in Canada.* Ed. B.S. Bolaria and H.D. Dickinson. Toronto: Harcourt Brace Jovanovich. 537–49.

Bolaria B.S., and H.D. Dickinson.1988. *Sociology of Health Care in Canada.* Toronto: Harcourt Brace Jovanovich.

Bolaria, B.S., and P.S. Li. 1988. *Racial Oppression in Canada.* 2d ed. Toronto: Garamond Press.

Carmichael, S., and C.W. Hamilton. 1967. *Black Power: The Politics of Liberation in America.* New York: Vintage.

Chossudovsky, M. 1983. "Underdevelopment and the Political Economy of Malnutrition and Ill Health." *International Journal of Health Services* 3, no. 1: 69–87.

Coleman, J., and D. Cressey. 1984. *Social Problems.* 2d ed. New York: Harper and Row.

Davis, N.J. 1980. *Deviance.* 2d ed. Dubuque, IA: Wm. C. Brown.

Eitzen, D.S., and M.B. Zinn. 1989. *Social Problems.* 4th ed. Boston: Allyn and Bacon.

Feagin, J.R. 1975. *Subordinating the Poor: Welfare and American Beliefs.* Englewood Cliffs, NJ: Prentice-Hall.

Fry, J.A. 1984. *Contradictions in Canadian Society.* Toronto: John Wiley and Sons.

Gallup Report. 1985. "Poverty." No. 234 (March): 21–25.

Gerth, H.H., and C.W. Mills. 1958. *Max Weber: Essays in Sociology.* New York: Galaxy.

Glazer, N., and H.Y. Waehrer, eds. 1977. *Women in a Man-Made World.* Chicago: Rand McNally.

Harrington, M. 1963. *The Other America: Poverty in the United States.* Baltimore: Penguin Books.

Herrnstein, R. 1971. "1.Q." *Atlantic* 228 (September): 43–64.

———. 1973. *I. Q. in the Meritocracy.* Boston: Little, Brown.

Jensen, A.R. 1969. "How Much Can We Boost IQ and Scholastic Achievement?" *Harvard Educational Review* 39 (Winter): 1–123.

———. 1980. *Bias in Mental Testing.* New York: Free Press.

Kluckhohn, F., and F.L. Strodtbeck. 1961. *Variations in Value Orientations.* New York: Harper and Row.

Lauer, R.H. 1978. *Social Problems and the Quality of Life*. Dubuque, IA: Wm. C. Brown.
Lewis, O. 1966. *La Vida*. New York: Random House.
Liebow, E. 1967. *Tally's Corner*. Boston: Little, Brown.
Matza, D. 1966. "The Disreputable Poor." In *Class, Status, and Power*. 2d ed, ed. R. Bendix and S.M. Lipset. New York: Free Press. 289–302.
Mills, C. 1943. "The Professional Ideology of Social Pathologists." *American Journal of Sociology* 49, no. 2: 65–180.
———. 1956. *The Power Elite*. New York: Oxford University Press.
———. 1959. *The Sociological Imagination*. New York: Oxford University Press.
National Council of Welfare. 1988. *Poverty Profile 1988*. Ottawa: Minister of Supply and Services. (April)
Navarro, V. 1978. "The Crisis of the Western System of Medicine in Contemporary Capitalism." *International Journal of Health Services* 8, no. 2.
———. 1986. *Crisis, Health, and Medicine*. New York: Tavistock Publications
Osberg, L. 1981. *Economic Inequality in Canada*. Toronto: Butterworths.
Parenti, M. 1978. *Power and the Powerless*. 2d ed. New York: St. Martin's Press.
Peterson, L., and E. Enarson. 1974. "Blaming the Victim in the Sociology of Women: On the Misuse of Concept of Socialization." Paper presented at the Pacific Sociological Association Meetings, San Jose, California, March. Cited in Eitzen and Zinn, *Social Problems*. 259–60.
Roach, J.L., and O.R. Gursslin. 1967. "An Evaluation of the Concept 'Culture of Poverty.'" *Social Forces* 45: 383–92.
Ryan, W. 1971. "Postscript: A Call to Action." *Social Policy* 3 (May–June).
———. 1976. *Blaming the Victim*. New York: Random House.
Sennett, R., and J. Cobb. 1973. *The Hidden Injuries of Class*. New York: Vintage Books.
Sowell, T. 1981. *Ethnic America: A History*. New York: Basic Books.
Valentine, C.A. 1968. *Culture and Poverty: Critique and Counter-Proposals*. Chicago: University of Chicago Press.
Waitzkin, H. 1983. *The Second Sickness*. New York: The Free Press.
Wotherspoon, T., ed. 1987. *The Political Economy of Canadian Schooling*. Toronto: Methuen.

PART I

Gender, Class, and Family

INTRODUCTION

Canada is a "vertical mosaic" of different social groups and categories. These groups are not equal in income, power, and status. While there has been an increasing awareness of these inequalities and a growing consciousness that all Canadians possess the right to equality, many groups continue to encounter unequal opportunities and differential life chances. These inequalities and life chances are correlated with gender, class, and race.

Essays in this section address the issue of gender inequality and gender relations encompassing both the public and the private spheres. Alicja Muszynski, in the chapter entitled "Social Stratification: Class and Gender Inequality," provides a comprehensive discussion of structural gender inequality and its origins, and of the continued position of women in Canadian society as a disadvantaged and subordinate group.

Muszynski notes that, while the Charter of Rights and Freedoms proclaims the principle of equality before the law regardless of factors such as race, gender, or age, the reality is that inequalities based on gender and race, structured into society itself, prevent people from participating as equal members of Canadian society. Beginning with legal contradictions, this chapter explores the various structural barriers to gender equality.

Gender inequality, Muszynski points out, is rooted in a history that includes legal inequalities, feudalism, gender stereotyping, capitalist class relations, and patriarchal gender relations. The subordinate position of women in the public and private spheres is one of the reinforcing systems of capitalism and patriarchy. Muszynski provides a detailed discussion of the historical development and transformation of the policies, processes, and practices that confine women to subordinate positions and roles, and of their ideological justification. While the nature of exploitative relations and the patterns of exploitation have changed over time, the basic inequality, subordination, and oppression remain.

Muszynski notes that, while women have made significant gains in abolishing discriminatory laws, the economic reality has been much more difficult to change. Class relations continue to embody patriarchal principles. Her chapter concludes with empirical evidence that shows the growing proletarianization of women and their increasingly disadvantaged position in economic relations—the "feminization of poverty." In conclusion, Muszynski argues that redressing gender inequality and the wrongs suffered by women will require an economic and ideological restructuring of Canadian society.

While women's right to equality is seen as desirable and progressive by many, others see it as a threat to the "traditional" family and hierarchical gender relations. In the chapter by Kathleen Storrie, a social movement led by conservative Protestants is examined. She finds that it constitutes a protest by husbands against what they perceive as a threat to their exclusive access to their wives' time and labour. This threat, Storrie argues, stems from the increased employment of married women that began in the 1950s, largely as a result of the expansion of capitalism and of the state in the postwar years. This development was seen by Evangelicals as endangering a moral and spiritual order in which the male as sole wage-earner, supported by the full-time "homemaking" activities of his wife, symbolizes a divine hierarchy.

Although paid labour has been a necessity for many working-class women from the start of capitalism, the bourgeois pattern of the non-employed wife has become the ideal for families of all classes. This chapter traces the origins of the bourgeois family to people acting out of economic and religious interests. Storrie examines its beginnings in the Puritan reconstruction of the family "as a little church and a little state," and compares it to a later religious reconstitution of the family by a group of Evangelicals (the Clapham Sect) in the nineteenth century. She argues that the Clapham Sect was responding to social and economic changes created by capitalist relations and also to the feminism of the time. Industrial capitalism deprived women of their productive activities within the household; as a result, this space became designated as a private sphere, women's labour within it was defined as a personal service to husbands (and children), and women's economic dependence on their husbands increased. Through the "Cult of True Womanhood," a series of religious legitimations accentuated these developments, strictly confining women to the private realm and thereby inadvertently reinforcing the double standard of morality by making femininity (but not masculinity) virtually synonymous with morality.

In these ways, the bourgeois form of the family became "sacralized" as "Christian" by conservative Protestants. Not surprisingly, such Christians reacted in the 1960s and 1970s, when they perceived this "sacred" form of the family to be imperilled. They launched a massive campaign, the "submission-of-women movement," to reinforce hierarchical marital relations and in so doing preserve "the integrity of society." Furthermore, instead of criticizing the increasing penetration of capitalist relations into their lives, as represented by the increasing paid labour of women, these Evangelicals scapegoated certain social movements of the 1970s and mobilized themselves politically by launching a counter-movement in the 1980s. The rest of the chapter reviews briefly the developments of this so-called New Christian Right in the United States and in Canada and identifies the various contradictions and ironies entailed in this attempted entrenchment of a specific form of religiously legitimated gender inequality.

While Storrie analyzes how the political and religious right have relied on domestic ideology drawn from the submission movement to mobilize themselves politically as a counter-movement to "protect" the "ideal traditional family" and hierarchical gender relations, Leslie J. Miller shows how the emergent bourgeois family ideal—the patriarchal "cult of domesticity"—provided the standard against which all familial arrangements have come to be measured. She suggests that the family problems (and the "problem families") of the nineteenth and much of the twentieth century—from the "slum" family to the "blended," homosexual, or communal one—are precisely those whose arrangements appear to diverge from the ideal. Miller's discussion is informed by insights emerging from the fields of feminist scholarship and the sociology of deviance and social control.

In the first part of the chapter, Miller outlines the historical roots of the modern ideal family and the picture of the "fit" family it implies, and reviews attempts to enforce it by regulating alternative or "unfit" forms. Different mechanisms have been used to reform the "unfit" family over time. Still, it is considered necessary to invoke the image of the "normal" family regularly to justify the social control of a whole range of more-or-less discredited alternatives. The discredited family types discussed in this section are the "slum" family, the family with a "working" (i.e., employed) mother, and the lesbian family. Despite the variety of alternative domestic arrangements that have emerged in the recent past, the ideal family type is still held up as the norm against which these alternative forms should be judged. Feminist scholars have argued that the labelling of such alternative arrangements as immoral, evil, or unhealthy be abandoned. As Miller notes, however, such core images in the culture cannot simply be argued away; they demonstrate a remarkable persistence, and various formal and informal mechanisms are used to enforce their moral authority.

One consequence of the rise of the domestic ideal was to focus attention on families that failed to measure up. A second important consequence was the protective cloak of secrecy that enclosed modern family life. This norm of privacy obscured not only women's contributions, but also the inequalities and abuses they and their children suffered. Miller emphasizes that these long-hidden aspects of family life represent forms of conduct that are now in the process of being "problematized"—that is, "discovered" as social problems. Such family realities as the unrecognized and unpaid labour of housewives, the "normal" violence of routine family life, and the structural impoverishment of women are being targeted by various groups wanting to raise their visibility and thus their recognition as urgent social problems requiring intervention and social control. Miller discusses some of these not-yet-problematized or newly problematized aspects of the family and the various socio-cultural factors that have kept them beneath the threshold of attention for so long.

In the concluding section, Miller notes some of the contradictions and ambiguities associated with the demand for social intervention into family life. If the families that fail to measure up to the bourgeois ideal can be thought of as constituting the family problems of yesterday and today, then the inequalities hidden by this same ideal are the problems of tomorrow. For feminists, the first set of problems has suffered from too much intervention; the second set, *too little*. Though not always consistent, feminists generally aim to shift the state's power, so that it may be used not to perpetuate the injustices of patriarchy but to redress them.

CHAPTER 2

Social Stratification: Class and Gender Inequality

Alicja Muszynski

Learning Objectives

The objective of this chapter is to demonstrate how and why women in Canadian society are not treated as the equals of men. The argument identifies structural barriers to full equality between men and women. That is, we cannot simply look to changing individual attitudes; in addition we must look at how Canadian institutions are implicated in constructing and perpetuating gender inequality. Women's subordinate position in this society is rooted in capitalist class relations and patriarchal gender relations. Students are encouraged to become aware of the complexities surrounding class and gender inequality and consider the contradictions between our liberal democratic tradition, which espouses the freedom and rights of the individual regardless of race, class, or gender distinctions, and the current reality. Not only have Canadian women suffered discrimination, exploitation, and oppression, but their situation is worsening. This is the feminization of poverty.

Introduction

As Canadian citizens, we live in a liberal democracy. We are guaranteed certain fundamental rights, which, in 1982, were entrenched in the Canadian Charter of Rights and Freedoms. Fundamental to the legal rights of citizens living in a liberal democracy is equality before the law. Article 15 (subsection 1) of the Charter of Rights and Freedoms states: "every individual is equal before and under the law and has the right to the equal protection and equal benefit of the law without discrimination and, in particular, without discrimination based on race, national or ethnic origin, colour, religion, sex, age or mental or physical disability." This subsection, however, is immediately qualified by the following: "(2) Subsection (I) does not preclude any law, program or activity that has as its object the amelioration of conditions of disadvantaged individuals or groups including those that are disadvantaged because of race, national or ethnic origin, colour, religion, sex, age or mental or physical disability" (reproduced in Berger 1982, 280-81). Subsection 2 acknowledges that individuals and groups have suffered discrimination. While the principle of equality is now embodied in the Canadian Constitution, so is the recognition of its uneven application within the Canadian population. That recognition, however, was not readily acknowledged by those who drafted the Charter. Rather, it was the result of hard-won struggle by the groups who suffered discrimination.

Inclusion of the word sex in these two subsections was the result of an organized campaign by women's groups across the country, who "reacted with enthusiasm to the suggestion that women's rights to equality might be enshrined in fundamental law" (Prentice et al. 1988, 401). It was not an easy battle, as witnessed by the complaint of Senator Harry Hays (the legislative committee's co-chairman), who asked "who would take care of the children while 'you girls' were out running the country" (1988, 401). Nor was it an easy battle for Canada's aboriginal peoples. They failed to have the word *existing* removed from article 35, referring to the recognition of "existing" aboriginal and treaty rights, thereby omitting those claims that were still outstanding. In 1981, however, the prime minister and the premiers decided to delete the entire provision. The word *existing* was a necessary concession in order to have the rights of aboriginal peoples recognized in the Charter at all. As Mr. Justice Berger (1982, 250) notes: "None of the other measures in the Constitution is limited in this way."

The reluctance of political leaders and legislators to formally recognize that people suffer discrimination because of their gender, race, age, and other characteristics, indicates the existence of structural barriers to the full realization of equality in Canadian society. That is, individuals suffer discrimination not because of who they are as individuals, but because they are assigned to a group that is stereotyped in negative ways. That is, the colour of a person's skin as well as her gender influence the way others treat her, both in her everyday encounters with individuals and in her dealings with institutions—for example, in courts of law, places of work, and schools.

The lack of equal treatment because of one's race or gender points not only to the existence of individual prejudiced attitudes against, for example, Natives or women, but also to *institutional* racism and sexism.[1] The very institutions that are supposed to enforce equality, which include our legal and parliamentary systems, often serve in practice to perpetuate inequality. This is a fundamental contradiction in our society. It can be traced to the incorporation in the British North America Act (BNA Act) of legal principles developed in Great Britain.

Origins of Structured Gender Inequality in the Emergence of the Canadian State

Confederation did not extend the privileges of citizenship equally to all. For example, in the second half of the nineteenth century, Chinese male labourers helped establish the British Columbia fishing industry through their work in the fish plants, and laboured and died in the construction of the Canadian Pacific Railway. Not only were they denied the right to become citizens, but once the CPR was completed, their further entry into Canada was restricted by the imposition of head taxes. Then, in 1923, the Exclusion Act virtually stopped further immigration from China. Other groups denied citizenship until after the end of the Second World War were status Indians (as defined in the Indian Act) as well as Japanese and South Asian Canadians.[2]

Race has been one means of excluding people from the rights attached to citizenship. Another has been gender. While some women in New France, under the French regime, had been able to vote, this right was taken from them when the Act of Union joined Upper and Lower Canada: "In 1849 a Reform government finally passed a law specifically excluding women from the franchise in both of the Canadas" (Prentice et al. 1988, 99). It was not until 1918, after many decades of struggle organized by the suffragists, that women were finally given the vote with the passage of the federal Women's Franchise Act.

> The logic of political liberalism demanded that all citizens, female and male, have the right to vote. But women everywhere waited long and lobbied hard before they were granted this right.
>
> Nineteenth-century logic required that women be excluded from politics. When the parliamentarians of Lower Canada revealed their desire to exclude women from the voters' list in 1834, they were attempting to correct a historical anomaly and acting in character for their time. (The Clio Collective 1987, 122)

Even with the right to vote, however, women were still not equal before the law. Women could not be appointed to Senate positions under the terms of the British North America Act of 1867 because women were not deemed to be "qualified persons" in the legal sense. Judge Emily Murphy appealed to the highest court in Canada and lost her case. She then appealed to the Judicial Committee of the Privy Council in England, and in 1929 it "unanimously reversed the judgment of the Supreme Court of Canada and held that the word 'persons' in section 24 of the BNA Act did ... include women as well as men" (Prentice et al. 1988, 282).

That is, women, regardless of their race, entered Confederation without what are today considered to be fundamental freedoms. Because they could not vote, they could not run for political office. They were barred from entry into certain professions. And marriage laws restricted their right to hold property.[3] Under the law, they were regarded as dependents of first their fathers, and, upon marriage, their husbands.

It is important to keep in mind, however, that while Canadian women were denied certain legal privileges, when it came to penalties they did not suffer the same discrimination. Emily Murphy discovered that, under British Common Law, "women are persons in matters of pains and penalties, but are not persons in matters of rights and privileges" (quoted in Wilson 1986, 134).

Class Inequality

While Canadian laws have excluded women from enjoying what are today considered to be fundamental rights, the legal structure itself mirrors deeper divisions in Canadian society. Politically, Canada is a liberal democracy; economically, it is an advanced capitalist state. Here we find a third set of contradictions that undermines the principle of equality. Class relations characterize a capitalist economy. Certain groups, or classes, control the means of production (the resources necessary to realizing one's livelihood) through the institution of private property, encoded in the Canadian legal system and enforced by the Canadian state. Private property does not simply consist of material assets such as land, buildings, or tools. It also involves relationships between and among groups of people (Macpherson 1978, 3).

Relations involving notions of property are subject to changing interpretations. Engels (1981, 120) situates the emergence of private property relations with"the world historical defeat of the female sex." That is, he connects the emergence of private property relations with changing family and household relations, whereby women and children became subordinated legally to the authority of the husband or father. The head of the household controlled the labour of the members who comprised his household, including the reproductive power of his wife. Engels argues that monogamy was necessary for the emergence of the bourgeoisie, because it allowed men to pass on their wealth to their biological progeny—specifically, their sons. While Engels's analysis has been severely criticized, he does make clear the connection between individual rights to property and the emergence of capitalism. Further, he links this historically to the dispossession of women from rights over their own labour: their work and their children.

Thus, paradoxically, the individual/citizen emerges in a capitalist economy after women and children have lost their legal rights. Superimposed on the transformation of labour power into a commodity that is sold in the marketplace like any other is the legal subordination of women and children through marriage laws to the husband or father. While men are exploited in and through their productive capacity for labour and their need to sell this capacity for a wage, women and children are oppressed through unequal relationships tied to familial property relations. Gender and class inequality can be seen here to be in operation simultaneously. While class inequality in its present form is tied to the emergence of Canada as a capitalist economy, gender inequality has an even older history, which goes back to the establishment of Western civilization, of Western patriarchy. At the root of women's oppression is the very conceptualization of gender itself as a dichotomous category.

Constructing Gender

In our day-to-day lives, we tend to take the reality of gender for granted. When we meet someone for the first time, we immediately establish that person's gender identity. We ask ourselves: "Am I speaking to a boy or a girl, a man or a woman?"

Even when we encounter babies, we find it difficult to talk about the child unless we know the name, which then allows us to speak of "it" as a "he" or a "she." The English language forces us to speak to and about individuals in a gendered way.[4]

Is gender typing natural? Is there something in our genetic make-up that predisposes us to "become" male or female and to remain the sex assigned to us at birth throughout our lives? There is a branch of sociology, called ethnomethodology, that questions what we take as given in our daily lives. In other words, ethnomethodologists study how people construct their everyday lives and how they come to accept certain attitudes and behaviours as "natural," unchanging, and therefore unchangeable. While Harold Garfinkel (1967) developed this approach, Suzanne Kessler and Wendy McKenna (1978, vii) applied it to gender construction in everyday life: "Our theoretical position is that gender is a social construction, that a world of two 'sexes' is a result of the socially shared, taken-for-granted methods which members use to construct reality."[5]

Kessler and McKenna argue that scientists who investigate the connection between physiological sexual characteristics and behaviour (for example, whether the male hormone testosterone makes men more aggressive and competitive than women) have already accepted the "natural attitude"; that is, they assume that there are two and only two sexes.

> In the natural attitude, there is reality and constancy to qualities like race, age, social class, and, of course, gender, which exist independently of any particular example of the quality. It is a fact that there are two genders; each person is a mere example of one of them; and the task of the scientist is to describe, as accurately as possible, the constant characteristics that define male and female, for all people and for all time. This is reality in Western society. (1978, 4 5)

What this suggests is that what we take for granted as normal, as real, as factual, in Western society is already socially constructed and passed on to us (for example, in the way we are socialized by our parents, teachers, friends, and the mass media), such that we take a whole breadth of complex social constructions as immutable. There is no change possible because this is the way things are and always have been. Inherent in this cultural baggage that we as Westerners inherit is a tendency to think in dualistic or dichotomous terms—for example, in terms of male/female, black/white, positive/negative, good/evil. We even think of our brains as having two sides, left and right.

We also think of values in dichotomous terms. It is "good" for a little boy to be competitive, but not "good" for him to cry. Only girls cry. Thus crying is attached to girls, and both are judged to be negative. Boys don't want to be "sissies," a girl categorization. In other words, the dichotomy masculine/feminine splits values into masculine and feminine. While girls and women are expected to possess the "feminine virtues," to be female is not generally considered to be "good" in itself. Simone de Beauvoir, in *The Second Sex* (1970, xv-xvi), asks the question, What is a woman? And she answers that woman is defined as "Other," as not man. She quotes Aristotle: "The female is a female by virtue of a certain *lack* of qualities ... we should regard the female nature as afflicted with a natural defectiveness" (emphasis in original). Thus, the very values that serve to define the feminine, which we can argue are *human* values, are judged to be "defective" *because* they are female.

Times have changed since Aristotle, and since Simone de Beauvoir wrote her book in France in the late 1940s. Consider, however, the results of a poll conducted between March 7 and 24, 1988, by Environics Research Group for Canada's "national newspaper," *The Globe and Mail*. It asked 2046 adult Canadians this question: "In your opinion, is it better to be a man or a woman in our society?"

What is particularly surprising, and disturbing, is that half of those surveyed in the eighteen-to-twenty-nine age group thought it better to be a man, while the percentage went down somewhat (44 percent) for those aged sixty and over. And while people with little education (zero to eight years) were split fairly evenly among the three categories (better to be a man, better to be a woman, makes no difference), 55 percent of those with a university degree thought it better to be a man, while only 12 percent thought it better to be a woman. The results indicate that men and women are still perceived to be different, and that being a man is generally perceived to be "better" than being a woman.

Such an idea—that men and women are dichotomous and unequal categories—is a feature of Western society that does not extend to all human societies. This has proved to be difficult because many anthropologists have been raised and trained in Western countries. Many, especially those trained when the discipline was still new, did not question their own "natural attitudes." Like some scientists, they assumed certain characteristics (like the *fact* of two, and only two, genders) to be universal and thus transcultural.[6] However, as Kessler and McKenna point out, there is evidence in other cultures that people do not think of gender in dichotomous terms. They give as an example some Native American societies of about a hundred years ago where, if there was a shortage of men or women to perform certain gender-typed tasks, boys or girls would be reassigned genders. Certain rituals were performed in this reassignment, but the child would henceforth be treated as belonging to the new gender. In these cases, gender did not attach as much to the individual as to the work that had to be performed in order for the group to survive (a gendered division of labour).

And there is the institution of the *berdache*. The term was used to refer to the North American aboriginal practice whereby social sanctions existed permitting a person to assume the gender opposite to that originally assigned. But this practice has also been found in many other cultures. There is evidence that the person may not necessarily assume a specific gender identity. That person may be seen as non-gendered, or as both male and female (especially in those cultures where these people play important roles as leaders or sages). Unfortunately, anthropologists did not have the conceptual tools to think of this institution in the way the people they studied did. The berdache were often simply characterized as homosexual, but

> the term homosexual only makes sense here if we assume that the berdache were only acting like the other gender. If we assume that berdache became the other gender, or were members of a third category, then what may have seemed homosexual to the ethnographer, would actually be heterosexual and vice versa. The categorizing of berdache as

> homosexual or heterosexual by ethnographers does not imply that the berdache's culture considered this distinction meaningful.
> (Kessler and McKenna 1978, 28)

If we are prepared to accept evidence from other cultures that thinking of gender as dichotomous is an approach rooted in Western thinking, then we can also ask how such thinking originated. This is difficult because the earliest written records already embody such thinking. Feminist historians suggest that the definition of history as a record of "man's" progress through time from the establishment of Western civilization (measured on a scale whose pivot is the birth of Jesus Christ, or the establishment of Christianity—a religion that celebrated a monotheistic trinity with God the Father at its head) represents the historic defeat of woman and the establishment of patriarchy.

Time itself thus acquires a dichotomous dimension. The bulk of the period before Christ (BC) is often characterized in negative terms: the period of barbarism and savagery. The period after Christ (AD) represents "civilization," humans emerging from prehistory and becoming properly "human." We often find the term *man* associated with the events occurring on this side of the dichotomy. In fact, most of recorded history has to do with men, especially with warfare. Much of the history we learn in school has to do with the deeds of great men who won battles and conquered "barbaric" peoples, bringing their territories into civilization. Or we learn of battles fought among the great men themselves for domination within Europe.

This history thus reconstructs for us a certain way of seeing ourselves as human.[7] At the same time, it renders invisible the majority of people and daily events. This type of history, then, is ideological, and not merely factual. It celebrates and justifies the right of certain individuals to hold power over the majority through the control of those institutions that organize our daily lives, ultimately through force (institutionalized in the army and the police).[8]

History is thus a recording of events that are deemed worthy of being preserved and passed on to future generations. It has its own history, connected to the emergence of patriarchy and Western civilization.

> History-making ... is a historical creation which dates from the invention of writing in ancient Mesopotamia. From the time of the king lists of ancient Sumer on, historians, whether priests, royal servants, clerks, clerics, or a professional class of university-trained intellectuals, have selected the events to be recorded and have interpreted them so as to give them meaning and significance. Until the most recent past, these historians have been men, and what they have recorded is what men have done and experienced and found significant. (Lerner 1986, 4)

Patriarchy and Class

A number of ideas and institutions are associated with the emergence of Western civilization. Chief among these is the celebration of reason as the guide for human activity. The use of reason is seen as the organizing principle behind the formation of the state. Political theorists have linked the two and traced their roots to the Greeks arid the establishment of the city-states, especially that of Athens. The ideas that were formulated by Plato and Aristotle are acknowledged to be the foundation of Western political thought.

Hannah Arendt is a political theorist who examines the idea of the Athenian polis, the creation of a public realm in which citizens come together to act on the basis of reason. She argues that the public realm is a space that is man-made and inserted into daily life. She begins with the premise that humans are caught in the circle of necessity, that they are subject to the laws of nature. That is, they must eat, clothe themselves, find shelter, and reproduce if they wish to survive and to perpetuate themselves in the next generation. For Arendt, then, nature is cyclical and humans are but an insignificant part of the world of nature.

But, she argues, humans also possess consciousness and reason, and these are part of human nature. They wish to separate themselves from the natural world over which they have no control, and they wish for immortality as men. As Arendt states,

> immortality is what nature possesses without effort and without anybody's assistance, and immortality is what the mortals therefore must try to achieve if they want to live up to the world into which they were born, to live up to the things which surround them and to whose company they are admitted for a short while. The connection between history and nature is therefore by no means an opposition. History receives into its remembrance those mortals who through deed and word have proved themselves worthy of nature, and their everlasting fame means that they, despite their mortality, may remain in the company of the things that last forever. ([1954] 1987, 48)

Nevertheless, in a later work, Arendt argues that political life requires a separation from "the limitations imposed upon us by the needs of biological life, which are the same for the human animal as for other forms of animal life" (1958,24). Historically, then, the polis, the realm of the public, emerged in conjunction with the patriarchal household, the private sphere. Political life represented a freeing of the citizen from necessity. This was made possible because the citizen was the head of a household, in which family members and slaves laboured. These people (women, children, and other men who were denied citizenship) were seen as tied to nature, little better than other animals. But their labour was the basis of the freedom of the head of the household, who alone could qualify for citizenship.

> What all Greek philosophers, no matter how opposed to polis life, took for granted is that freedom is exclusively located in the political realm, that necessity is a prepolitical phenomenon, characteristic of the private household organization, and that force and violence are justified in this sphere because they are the only means to master necessity—for instance, by ruling over slaves—and to become free. Because all human beings are subject to necessity, they are entitled to violence toward others; violence

> is the prepolitical act of liberating oneself from the necessity of life for the freedom of world. (Arendt 1958, 31)

Arendt's analysis makes clear the establishment of a fundamental dichotomy between the private world of the household and of necessity and the public world of ideas, of history, and of reason. The latter is founded on the former through violence, by the dominance of certain men over women, children, and other men. Because force is involved, the polis must also establish ways of ruling over others. Mary O'Brien (1983, 103) criticizes Arendt for her claim that violence has nothing to do with politics:

> Violence is needed to overcome the imperiousness of biological necessity. From this axiom emerges [Arendt's] odd and ahistorical contention that violence has nothing to do with politics, but belongs exclusively to the private realm. She simply does not see that the violence needed to maintain the separation of public and private in both the reproductive and productive spheres must have a political component. Paterfamilias, to preserve his freedom, requires family law, fraternal co-operation and ideological legitimization. He also, then as now, retained the option of brutality to enforce his domestic power.... Patriarchy and the doctrine of potency are the products of political power, the creations of a brotherhood of fathers acting collectively to implement their definitions of manhood in social and ideological forms.

Thus, O'Brien argues Western civilization was founded on patriarchy. We can further argue that the foundation of the concept of the state in Western civilization is based on the elaboration of a public realm, not only divorced from, but also with the power over the private. At the heart of the public/private dichotomy is the further separation of the rulers (of households, who thus qualify for membership in the public spheres) from the ruled (all women, all children, and most men).

But the dichotomy does not end here. For the emergence of the state also coincided with the emergence of class society. Those who rule in the public realm (the political sphere) control the labour of those whom they rule (beginning with the household). But households are themselves organized around economic relations of subsistence. Western civilization also marked a transition toward settled agriculture and a feudal mode of production. Those who laboured produced a surplus above and beyond the means necessary to sustain the household. This surplus was appropriated, in the first instance, by the household head. But household heads themselves were implicated in a set of power relations whereby those at the top could appropriate the surplus from those below them in a whole series of stratified relations.

However, to rule by virtue of the exercise of violence is never sufficient. Those who are subjugated must accept their powerlessness. The force of patriarchal thinking is that it renders half of humanity invisible. That this did not happen naturally, quickly, or without resistance is now being made clear by feminist anthropologists, archaeologists, and historians. Gerda Lerner (1986) argues that recorded history was necessary in order to reconstruct a different vision of humanity. Previously, women had occupied central and important positions; for example, many of the deities were female. Western patriarchy, then, was a long, drawn-out process in the course of which those attributes previously valued and seen as feminine were reconstructed not only as negative, but as invisible. Greek philosophers such as Aristotle came to see women as animal-like. Only men could possess reason (second nature) and could qualify to rule in the man-made public realm.[9] At the same time, women continued to resist, and thus the ideology had to be continually reaffirmed.

Samir Amin (1980) characterizes European feudal society as belonging to the tributary mode of production. This mode has taken various historical forms in different parts of the world, but in essence it is based on the extraction of tribute. While force has often been used, far more important has been the legitimation of the extraction of surplus through various ideological practices (Christianity being one, absolute monarchy another). "In tributary formations, ideology is dominant" (Am in 1980, 69). The exercise of power by the few had to be legitimated.

Patriarchy was central in this ideological formation. But patriarchy is not simply ideological or political, it also has an economic component, as we have seen in Arendt's discussion of the freeing of the citizen from necessity by providing him with control over the labour of the members of his household. Systems of stratification emerged from the household, where the father ruled as head and represented the household in the public realm. His wife, on the other hand, often ruled the internal household economy, and exercised power over children and slaves in the name of her husband. Further divisions, based largely on the size and complexity of the household economy, were possible. This represented a transition from previous modes of production based on kinship relations. The transition marked the severing of power (of ruling) from kinship in the direction of class relations, although kinship still organized the household economy (of production). What changed was the manner of surplus appropriation.

Although women have been subordinated to men socially, economically, and ideologically, their subordination is as a *category*. "Woman" is barred from ruling and from the public realm. However, individual women have been able to acquire power. Women married to upper class men rule over the private domain of the household, which can be very extensive. They thus have power over not only their own children, but also over other women, and over men.

Rendered invisible in political thought, the historical reality has been that women have exercised considerable power at different periods in Western society. The extent to which particular women have exercised power in the political and economic realms is tied to the history of changing class relations. Opportunities open to women have been most numerous in periods of transition and societal upheaval.[10] The consolidation of a new economic or political system, however, has generally been accompanied by the suppression of the gains women made in the transitional period. Thus, Monique Saliou (1986, 192) argues that the transition to Athenian democracy represented a debasement of women's status.

> "Democracy" could not accept the status of women who had "a right to speak up" because it would have had to extend it to all citizens' wives. It is significant that women's status in Sparta during the classical period

> was far higher than in Athens: Sparta had kept an aristocratic government. Similarly, the French Revolution of 1789 deprived all women of political rights, whereas the old regime accepted women holding fiefs and the rights that derived from it.

What Saliou's analysis suggests is that, paradoxically, historical periods of transition toward democratic forms of government in the West have been accompanied by the legal subordination of women, such that women belonging to the upper classes are stripped of their wealth and power. Their dispossession, however, does not involve them as individuals or even as classes. Rather, women as a category are legally reconstructed, in that *all women* are deprived of what come to be defined as universal rights. The emergence of Canada as a democracy and a capitalist economy can be inserted into this history.

The capitalist mode of production initially emerged from European feudalism. In capitalism, it is economic relations that predominate between individuals, while labour is divorced from the means of production. The products of labour are similarly separated from labour and from the means of production, and become commodities. Commodities are exchanged in the marketplace and produced in workplaces divorced from their ancient basis, the household. What we find in capitalism is a new articulation between the private and the public spheres. While the private sphere continues to be the household, the latter is deprived of the basis upon which it survived in the tributary mode of production, the employment of labour to produce the means of subsistence. These are produced in the economy, which has now become part of the public realm. Labour now acquires a value on the basis of its exchangeability in the marketplace, where labour power becomes a commodity with a price, which is its wages.

Although the structure of the household economy is fundamentally transformed under capitalism, it does not disappear. Labour continues to be performed within the household, but is now further devalued because it has no monetary worth. And most of the work (Engels distinguishes between paid labour and unpaid work)[11] within the household is now "women's work." Men's labour is reconceptualized economically with the emergence of a class of proletarians. While women also work for wages, their class position is mediated through their legal subordination to their fathers and husbands.[12] Thus patriarchy survives within capitalism, in law, ideology, and practice, and it modifies the new set of class relations. At the same time, the new capitalist relations render some of the patriarchal forms obsolete and they also provide women with new sets of opportunities to emancipate themselves from oppressive patriarchal relations, if not from exploitative class relations.

The Position of Women in Canadian Society

The foregoing has been a very global and general discussion meant to demonstrate the historical development of patriarchal and class relations in Western civilization. Canada, because it emerged as a nation by means of its colonial subordination to Great Britain and to France, inherited the legal structures that had evolved from

Greek and Roman times. Economically, it became tied to the global expansion of capitalism. Politically, it emerged as a liberal democracy.

But liberal democracy is necessary in the creation of the wage labourer as an individual freed from feudal ties to his community, where he had historically realized his means of subsistence.[13] The contradiction lies in the fact that his means of production and reproduction as an individual continue to be realized in the household, which becomes increasingly dependent on the capitalist economy for its survival. While the position of men as proletarians changes, the position of women, in the ancient division of labour by which women were responsible for household work and child care, is still based on patriarchal legal principles, which define their economic place as dependants of men and as wage labourers in their own right.

Thus, we see that the position of women in Canadian society is a complicated one. Legally, women have used the rights elaborated within the liberal democratic tradition to redress their position. While they have made significant gains in abolishing discriminatory laws, the economic reality has been much more difficult to change.

Some women have made significant gains since the women's movement regained momentum in the 1960s, for example, in the professions, in the business world, and in politics. While women have not generally become the true equals of men in these areas, there has been a growing acceptance of the entry of women into fields previously denied them. But here class distinctions become important, as well as racial discrimination. If some women have realized significant gains, they are very much in the minority, and many come from privileged class backgrounds.

Further, it must not be forgotten that it is in the interest of a liberal democratic state to allow limited entry into positions of at least some power to members of groups that suffer discrimination, for these few can then be seen as proof that the system works. This is called *tokenism*. Structural barriers are such that only a minority of individuals from the group that is discriminated against can gain access to positions opened, for example, by affirmative action plans. They are perceived to have gained their positions not by their own hard work but by means of special privilege. And frequently they are not treated as individuals but as members of the minority group they represent.[14]

The record of affirmative action programs has been abysmal. For example, the city of Regina adopted an affirmative action plan in 1987. But a report received in May 1988 and published in a Regina newspaper showed that minor gains had been made in its first year of operation. The three target groups were women, Native peoples, and the physically challenged. Women made up 16 percent of Regina's work force, the same proportion in 1988 as in 1986. "Native representation" was up slightly, to 3 percent of the workforce, while physically challenged people represented 6 percent of city employees, a gain of 2 percent from 1986 (*The Leader Post*, 15 June 1988: A3).

And this is not abnormal for the success rate of such programs. The May 2,1988, edition of *The Globe and Mail* carried a story (page A8) entitled "Affirmative Action a Failure, Professor at Western Reports." A report submitted to the president of the University of Western Ontario noted that a voluntary affirmative action plan, in place for three years, had not increased the ratio of women faculty members at this university, the third largest in Canada. And a report released the previous week by the Council of Ontario Universities demonstrated that only 5.7 percent of full professors and 14.4 percent of associate professors in Ontario universities were women.

Table 2.1 indicates that the situation of faculty women in universities across Canada had not improved significantly by 1989–90. Only 17.2 percent of tenured appointments and those leading to tenure in Canada as a whole (except for Quebec) were held by women. Table 2.1 first appeared in the Canadian Association of University Teachers' 1991 *Status of Women Supplement* in which positive action programs to improve the status of women in Canadian universities are discussed in considerable detail. What is evident from the table is the large proportion of women concentrated in the lower ranks, those of assistant professor and lecturer. It remains to be seen whether these proportions will progress through the ranks to eventually equalize the ranks at all levels and finally redress the current imbalance.

The numbers and composition of women who work for wages has changed dramatically in the past 30 years. The most significant feature is the large number of married women with young children who now work for wages. Table 2.2 shows the increased participation of women in the labour force from 1921 to 1985. In 1921, the total percentage of women in the paid labour force was only 18 percent, and it had risen only 6 percentage points by 1951. However, the same increase again was realized by the next decade, and by 1985 55 percent of Canadian women were in the paid labour force. The largest increase by age group was among women in the childbearing years (15 to 44 years of age).

In 1993, Statistics Canada published a second edition of *Women in the Workplace*, authored by Nancy Zukewich Ghalam. This report uses statistical informa-

TABLE 2.1: Proportion of Tenured and Leading to Tenure Appointments Held by Women by Province and Rank, 1989–1990

	Full	Assoc.	Asst.	Lect.	Total
Newfoundland	7.2%	20.1%	32.4%	55.6%	19.6%
Prince Edward Island	5.3	13.0	24.2	0.0	13.5
Nova Scotia	7.8	18.2	43.6	56.3	20.8
New Brunswick	8.6	21.0	30.7	50.0	17.4
Ontario	6.5	18.0	34.2	52.0	17.3
Manitoba	6.7	19.1	29.5	25.0	15.6
Saskatchewan	4.6	19.5	27.3	57.1	13.5
Alberta	8.6	19.7	36.8	64.3	17.4
British Columbia	5.4	17.6	29.3	40.0	16.3
Canada (excluding Quebec)	6.8%	18.5%	33.6%	52.4%	17.2%

Note: Data for Quebec were not available.

Source: Statistics Canada, *Canadian Association of University Teachers Bulletin: Status of Women Supplement,* Vol. 38, No. 4 (Ottawa: Minister of Industry, Science and Technology, 1991), p. 13. Reproduced by permission of the Minister of Industry, 1994.

TABLE 2.2: Long-Term Trends in Participation in the Labour Force of Women Age 15–64: 1921–1985

Year	Ages:	15–24 %	25–34 %	35–44 %	45–54 %	55–64 %	TOTAL: All Ages %
1921		29	17	11	11	10	18
1931		33	24	13	13	13	20
1941		41	25	16	13	10	21
1951		42	24	22	20	14	24
1961		41	30	31	33	24	30
1971		49	44	44	44	34	39
1981		61	66	64	56	42	52
1985		71	69	69	60	34	55

Source: Canadian Congress for Learning Opportunities for Women, *Decade of Promise: An Assessment of Canadian Women's Studies in Education Training and Employment, 1976–1985* (Toronto: Avebury Research and Consulting Limited, 1986).

tion available for the year 1991. In the "Highlights" it is noted: "The employment rate of women with children, even those with pre-school-aged children, has increased dramatically since 1981. In 1991, 63% of mothers with children less than age 16 were employed, versus 50% ten years earlier. Similarly, the percentage of women employed whose youngest child was under age 6 rose from 42% in 1981 to 57% in 1991." And, in the first edition of this chapter, Table 3 indicated a dramatic increase of the labour-force participation of women with children under the age of 16 for the ten-year period 1971–81. Unfortunately, differences in the data collection techniques show some differences in percentages and thus do not allow detailed comparison for the period 1971–91. While the latest statistics are more conservative in the percentages of women indicated as employed in the 1980s, they do corroborate the upward trend in women's involvement in the paid labour force. In fact, while 5.6 million women, "representing 53% of all women aged 15 and over," were employed in 1991, "male employment fell from 74% to 67% over the same period" (1993, 5). Table 2.3 shows the percentage of women and men in the paid labour force, by marital status, for the period 1981–91.

The reasons for this massive entry of married women into the paid labour force are many and complex. The primary reason has probably been declining living standards since the 1960s, meaning that a husband's income is no longer sufficient to provide for a nuclear family with the wife as full-time mother and homemaker. But to look no farther than this assumes a nuclear family household as the norm.

In 1968, passage of the federal Divorce Act made it easier and less costly to obtain a divorce. It became somewhat easier, at least legally, for women caught in abusive relationships to leave their spouses. Their economic situation, however, was precarious. It has proved extremely difficult for women with custody of their children to collect child support payments.

TABLE 2.3: Percentage of Women and Men Employed, by Marital Status, 1981–1991

Year	Single		Married		Separated/ Divorced		Widowed		Total	
	F	M	F	M	F	M	F	M	F	M
1981	58.1	61.8	46.8	79.7	58.9	72.1	17.5	24.8	47.4	72.9
1985	58.1	58.8	49.6	75.1	56.5	65.6	15.0	24.7	48.8	68.7
1991	59.0	60.2	55.9	71.4	56.1	65.2	12.2	19.7	52.6	66.7

Source: Nancy Zukewich Ghalam, *Women in the Workplace,* 2nd edition, Cat. no. 71-534 (Ottawa: Statistics Canada, 1993), Table 1.2, p. 18. Reproduced by authority of the Minister of Industry, 1994.

While women find it easier to obtain a divorce, they are still made responsible for the care of their children. For example, in 1980, custody of dependent children was granted to wives in 78.2 percent of the 59 600 cases reported in Canada, while husbands received custody in only 16 percent of the cases (in the remaining cases, there was no award or the children went to a third party) (Eichler 1983, 215). With the great increase in the number of divorces since 1960 (from 39.1 per 100 000 people in 1960 to 259.1 per 100 000 in 1980) (1983, 48), we see that women have a much heavier economic responsibility in providing for their children both within the nuclear family household and outside it.[15]

Table 2.4 indicates that women with children under the age of 16 years tend to be employed whether they are the lone heads of their families or in two-parent families. In fact, women in two-parent families show a higher rate of full-time paid employment (64.6 percent) than women who are lone parents (52.2), while female lone parents show a much higher rate of unemployment.

In 1991, far more employed women (26 percent) worked part-time than did employed men (9 percent). "In fact, women have consistently accounted for at least 70% of the part-time workforce in Canada over the past fifteen years" (1993, 5). It is further noted in the report that while "36% of female part-time workers indicated a preference for part-time employment in 1991, another 27% were unable to find full-time positions." And women continue to fill the "traditionally female dominated occupations. In 1991, 71% of women versus just 30% of men were employed in five occupational groups—teaching, nursing or related health professions, clerical, sales, and service." Women accounted for "80% of all unpaid family workers." "The earnings of women employed on a full-time, full-year basis in 1991 were just 70% those of comparable men. In fact, there has been little improvement in this earnings ratio since 1980, when women earned 64% as much as men." And Ghalam notes that women are less likely than men to be covered by pension plans. Finally, despite the large proportion of women with children in the paid labour force, most of the child care was arranged informally. "Organized or regulated care services were the main form of care for only 11% of children."

TABLE 2.4: Labour Force Characteristics of Women With Children, by Age of Youngest Child, 1991

	Youngest child less than 3 years	Youngest child 3–5 years	Youngest child 6–15 years	Total with children less than 16 years
% employed				
Lone parents	30.8	47.4	62.2	52.2
Women in two-parent families	56.9	62.3	70.3	64.6
% unemployed				
Lone parents	25.5	20.4	13.8	16.8
Women in two-parent families	10.9	10.4	8.7	9.6
% not in the labour force				
Lone parents	58.6	40.7	28.0	37.4
Women in two-parent families	36.1	30.1	23.1	28.5
% employed part-time[a]				
Lone parents	25.8	23.3	16.4	19.4
Women in two-parent families	32.4	32.0	26.4	29.1

Note: [a] Expressed as a percentage of total employed.
Source: Nancy Zukewich Ghalam, *Women in the Workplace,* 2nd edition, Cat. no. 71-534 (Ottawa: Statistics Canada, 1993), Table 1.4, p. 19. Reproduced by authority of the Minister of Industry, 1994.

Tables 2.5 and 2.6 present statistical information on average earnings of men and women by education and by occupation, respectively. In Table 2.5, the earnings ratio between men and women in the category "all earners" is only 61.5 percent although the ratio for full-time, full-year workers climbs to 69.6 percent. While increased levels of education improve the situation for women, the ratio increases less than 5 percent for full-time, full-year workers from an educational attainment of less than Grade 9 to the possession of a university degree. Of note in Table 2.6 are the differences in the earnings ratio by occupation. Men earn the highest incomes in medicine/health, where the ratio of women's earnings to those of men is the lowest at 49.3 percent. The report *Women in the Workplace* (1993, 35) points out that employed women in Canada earn considerably less than their male counterparts and that the situation has not changed much in the last decade (from 64 percent for full-time, full-year workers in 1981 to 70 percent in 1991).

Finally, it is worth mentioning that the recessions of 1981–83 and the early 1990s appear to have had especially negative effects on the employment opportunities of "female lone parents." As noted in Table 2.4, these women are the least likely, among women with young children, to be employed full-time. "As well, the proportion of female lone parents currently with jobs (52%) is actually about two percentage points lower than it was in 1981 when 54% of these women were employed" (Ghalam 1993, 11).

TABLE 2.5: Average Earnings of Women and Men, by Education, 1991

	Full-time full-year workers			Other workers			All earners		
	Women	Men	Earnings ratio[a]	Women	Men	Earnings ratio[a]	Women	Men	Earnings ratio[a]
	$	$	%	$	$	%	$	$	%
Educational attainment:									
Less than grade 9	18 138	27 116	66.9	6 545	13 076	50.1	11 476	21 030	54.6
Some secondary school	20 709	32 348	64.0	6 050	9 193	65.8	11 060	20 652	53.6
High school diploma	23 265	33 583	69.3	9 034	13 288	68.0	17 013	27 179	62.6
Some post-secondary	24 891	35 845	69.4	7 706	10 354	74.4	14 826	23 595	62.8
Post-secondary certificate or diploma[b]	26 951	37 887	71.1	10 966	15 790	69.4	20 062	31 587	63.5
University degree	40 537	56 522	71.7	14 028	18 054	77.7	31 233	49 231	63.4
Total	**26 842**	**38 567**	**69.6**	**8 890**	**12 539**	**70.9**	**18 050**	**29 328**	**61.5**

Notes: [a] Represents women's earnings as a percentage of those of men.[b] Includes trades certificate.
Source: Nancy Zukewich Ghalam, *Women in the Workplace,* 2nd edition, Cat. no. 71-534 (Ottawa: Statistics Canada, 1993), Table 3.3, p. 41. Reproduced by authority of the Minister of Industry, 1994.

Conclusions

The empirical evidence indicates that the economic situation of women, despite some improvement in their legal status, has deteriorated. A term that has come into the literature to refer to this trend is the "feminization of poverty." It almost seems that as soon as women organized to overthrow the oppression they suffered during the long history of Western patriarchy, capitalist class relations reintegrated that oppression through economic class exploitation. Increasingly, the poor in Canada (and elsewhere) are women and the children for whom they are made responsible. Women are participating in ever greater proportions in the paid labour force but in a disadvantaged position. They occupy jobs in segregated spheres of work that pay wages a fraction of those that men receive, and in the worst conditions of work.

Since the end of the Second World War, the state has assumed increased social service responsibilities. But in the 1980s, with the election of conservative governments in Canada, Great Britain, and the United States, those services were cut back or eliminated altogether, at a time when working women have increasing need of

TABLE 2.6: Average Earnings of Women and Men, by Occupation[a], 1991

	Women	Men	Earnings ratio[b]
	$	$	%
Managerial/administrative	32 299	51 173	63.1
Natural sciences	37 544	46 535	80.7
Social sciences/religion	37 015	53 507	69.2
Teaching	39 723	51 115	77.7
Medicine/health	32 155	65 175	49.3
Artistic/recreational	28 006	33 017	84.8
Clerical	23 771	32 097	74.1
Sales	23 970	34 339	69.8
Service	18 146	29 152	62.2
Agriculture	12 558	18 010	69.7
Processing	23 499	34 076	69.0
Product assembly/fabrication/repair	20 666	34 763	59.4
Transport equipment operation	23 311	34 029	68.5
Material handling	22 134	30 153	73.4
TOTAL	26 842	38 567	69.6

Notes: [a] Includes only full-time, full-year workers. [b] Represents women's earnings as a percentage of those of men.

Source: Nancy Zukewich Ghalam, *Women in the Workplace,* 2nd edition, Cat. no. 71-534 (Ottawa: Statistics Canada, 1993), Table 3.4, p. 41. Reproduced by authority of the Minister of Industry, 1994.

them. The deficit-cutting mood of the 1990s is having its effect as well. The evidence is visible all around us. Children go to school hungry. The homeless have proliferated, and women and children swell their ranks.

There are other aspects of the feminization of poverty that have not been covered here, but that is not because they are insignificant. While poverty increasingly wears a gendered face, the further aspect of racial discrimination makes the lot of Native and Métis women as well as immigrant women especially difficult.[16]

The mushrooming of transition houses for battered women and their abused children, despite government cutbacks, testifies to the extent of violence within families. Wife battering and child abuse were taboo subjects two decades ago, and little research took place in the area. They were invisible problems. Today they have become a field of study in their own right. Family violence is now widely acknowledged, but, unfortunately, little is being done to efface it. Most of the resources to help battered women and children are organized in and through the community, by groups that have little funding. This is but another aspect of patriarchal relations.

We have seen that patriarchy is an ancient—many would claim an outmoded—concept. But it is clear that it still organizes relations between men, women, and children in the 1990s in Canada. The wealth often associated with capitalism (related to a large increase in productive forces available in the economy) has not improved the lot of those who occupy the bottom rungs in our society. Increasingly, these people are women, children and the elderly—the majority of whom are also women.

The redressing of the wrongs suffered by women requires a fundamental restructuring of Canadian society, not only at the economic level but also ideologically. We must rethink the categories we use so unreflectively, beginning with gender construction. We must also rethink how, as humans sharing nature with each other and with the creatures around us, we can construct a public realm in which we can all come together and reason in a truly rational, humane, and egalitarian fashion.

Study Questions

1. Are women the "equals" of men in Canadian society? How would you go about measuring equality? What sources would you use? Finally, how would you define equality"?

2. Are women a class? What arguments would you employ to support the answer Yes? What arguments to support the answer No?

3. How has the political, as opposed to the economic, reality in Canada located women in contradictory class location?

4. How are class and poverty relations connected within a capitalist mode of production? How have women been historically disadvantaged in this respect?

5. What is gender? Use your definition to demonstrate that woman is "constructed" unequally to man.

6. How does the public/private dichotomy change in the transition from feudalism to capitalism and with what consequences for the concept of "labour"?

Recommended Reading

Barret, Michele. *Women's Oppression Today: Problems in Marxist Feminist Analysis*. London: Verso, 1985.

Coontz, Stephanie, and Peta Henderson, eds. *Women's Work, Men's Property: The Origins of Gender and Class*. London: Verso, 1986.

Kessler, Suzanne J., and Wendy McKenna. *Gender: An Ethnomethodological Approach.* Chicago: The University of Chicago Press, 1985.

Lerner, Gerda. *The creation of patriarchy.* New York: Oxford University Press, 1986.

National Council of Welfare. 1990. *Women and Poverty Revisited.* Ottawa: Supply and Services Canada.

National Council of Welfare. 1992. *Poverty Profile, 1980–1990.* Ottawa: Supply and Services Canada.

O'Brien, Mary. *The Politics of Reproduction.* Boston: Routledge and Kegan Paul, 1983.

Prentice, Alison, Paula Bourne, Gail Cuthbert Brandt, Beth Light, Wendy Mitchinson, and Naomi Black. *Canadian Women: A History.* Toronto: Harcourt Brace Jovanovich, 1988.

Notes

1. Bolaria and Li (1985, 21) distinguish between the terms "institutional" and "individual" as applied to the concept of racism. This distinction is also relevant to the concept of sexism. For a classical sociological treatment, see C. Wright Mills's discussion of private troubles and public issues in *The Sociological Imagination* (1969).
2. Peter Ward discusses the discriminatory policies and racial hatred expressed toward Chinese, Japanese, and South Asian immigrants in British Columbia in *White Canada Forever* (1978). He notes:

   > The federal government repealed the Chinese Immigration Act in 1947, although sharp limitations on the number of entrants were to continue for years. Of greater symbolic significance was the removal of the franchise restrictions which had long been imposed on all Asiatics. Chinese and South Asian Canadians gained the vote both provincially and federally in 1947. After a further 2 year delay, symptomatic of greater white prejudice, Japanese Canadians were also given the franchise. (165)
3. The history of women's property rights as they relate to marriage is complex. For example, prior to the Act of Union, Quebec women had dower rights under French law, which gave them property rights upon the death of their husbands. For a fuller discussion, see The Clio Collective's *Quebec Women: A History* (1987, 123–27).
4. Even the recurrent fashion among rock stars to adopt androgynous dress does not belie the necessity of establishing gender identity. "Boy George" consciously strove for an androgynous look that crossed conventional gender-assigned clothing and hair styles, as well as make-up, mannerisms and general behaviour. But his very name established that he was a male who was deliberately "crossing over" in certain ways.
5. There is some debate among feminists about the use of the term *gender*. Mackie provides the standard distinction between the terms *sex* and *gender*: "Sex is the biological dichotomy between males and females. It is determined at conception and is, for the most part, unalterable. Gender, on the other hand, is what is socially recognized as femininity and masculinity" (1983, 1). *Sex* refers to a biological feature of the individual that is given at birth whereas *gender* refers to a cluster of qualities that are associated with masculinity and femininity. Just which qualities are regarded as masculine or feminine varies considerably from one society to another. Masculine and feminine behaviours do not appear to follow automatically from one's biology, they are learned through socialization.
6. Here they showed themselves open to the classic charge of ethnocentrism, within which a further charge of androcentrism can be laid.
7. Dorothy Smith (1974) develops this idea further in her analysis of the "reality" and "factuality" of documentary evidence. While it is socially constructed, as a finished product it attains scientific validity and comes to be seen as objectively true. She extends the discussion of history as "man-made" to the discipline of sociology in *The Everyday World as Problematic: A Feminist Sociology* (1987).
8. Since the 1960s, there has been considerable research done on the history of women in various countries. A now classic treatment is Sheila Rowbotham's *Hidden From History* (1976), a history of women in Great Britain. Canadian feminist historians have also been productive. Two historical overviews that are used in this chapter are *Canadian Women: A History* (1988) and *Quebec Women: A History* (1987).
9. This analysis already takes for granted a masculine/feminine dichotomy. To trace its history requires an examination of the gendered division of labour. For an account that explores the *lack*

of such a division of labour in hominid societies, see Lila Leibowitz (in Coontz and Henderson 1986, 43–75).

10. Marilyn French (1985) develops the same general point. That is, when patriarchal power is relaxed, women take advantage and take up creative pursuits wherever they can. She argues this holds true historically, although the specific activities in which women engage change in various periods of time.
11. "The English language has the advantage of possessing different words for the two aspects of labour here considered. The labour which creates Use-Value; and counts qualitatively is *Work*, as distinguished from labour; that which creates Value and counts quantitatively, is *Labour* as distinguished from Work" (note by Engels in Marx, *Capital*, vol. 1: 47, fn. I, emphasis in original).
12. The private/public split within capitalism has been extensively analyzed within the domestic labour debate. Various analysts have taken sides as to whether or not there is a domestic mode of production. The analysis developed in this chapter points to the social construction of the public and private spheres and argues that the dichotomy changes and assumes different forms under tributary as opposed to capitalist modes of production. The split itself is linked to patriarchal relations rather than to class relations in a strictly economic sense. For a summary of the various positions adopted within the domestic labour debate, see Hamilton and Barrett, eds., *The Politics of Diversity* (1986, 139–254).
13. In his early writings, Marx examined the role played by the state within capitalism; see, for example, his review article entitled "On the Jewish Question" (in Marx 1977, 39–62).
14. For a fascinating discussion of tokenism as it applies to women working in corporations, see Rosabeth Moss Kanter's case study, *Men and Women of the Corporation* (1977).
15. The courts' practice of awarding custody to mothers rather than to fathers is a fairly recent historical development. It was the result of organised women's struggles in the temperance and suffragist movements. Before then, children were assumed to be the private property of men (Gloria Geller, personal communication, 26 May 1989).
16. The 1989 *Annual* of the Society for Socialist Studies is devoted to the study of the interconnections between feminism and racism. The articles explore the situations of Native, Métis, and immigrant women as well as women of African descent in Canadian society. Many question whether the women's movement is addressing the particular oppression and exploitation suffered by these groups of women, or whether it has become elitist, universalizing the experiences of white middle class women to all women.

References

Amin, S. 1980. *Class and Nation, Historically and in the Current Crisis*. New York: Monthly Review Press.

Arendt, H. [1954] 1987. *Between Past and Future: Eight Exercises in Political Thought*. Harmondsworth, England: Penguin Books.

———. 1958. *The Human Condition*. Chicago: University of Chicago Press.

de Beauvoir, S. 1970 [1949]. *The Second Sex*. New York: Alfred A. Knopf.

Berger, T. 1982. *Fragile Freedoms: Human Rights and Dissent in Canada*. Toronto: Clarke, Irwin and Company.

Bolaria, B.S., and P.S. Li. 1985. *Racial Oppression in Canada*. Toronto: Garamond Press.

The Clio Collective. 1987. *Quebec Women: A History*. Toronto: The Women's Press.

Coontz, S., and P. Henderson, eds. 1986. *Women's Work, Men's Property: The Origins of Gender and Class*. London: Verso.

Eichler, M. 1983. *Families in Canada Today: Recent Changes and Their Policy Consequences*. Toronto: Gage.

Engels, F. 1981. *The Origin of the Family, Private Property, and the State*. New York: International Publishers.

French, M. 1985. *Beyond Power: On Women, Men, and Morals*. New York: Summit Books.

Garfinkel, H. 1967. *Studies in Ethnomethodology*. Englewood Cliffs, NJ: Prentice-Hall.

Ghalan N.Z., *Women in the Workplace*. 2d ed. Statistics Canada, Housing, Family and Social Statistics Division, Ottawa, Ontario, March 1993.

Hamilton, R., and M. Barrett, eds. 1986. *The Politics of Diversity: Feminism, Marxism and Nationalism.* Montreal: Book Center.

Kanter, R.M. 1977. *Men and Women of the Corporation.* New York: Basic Books.

Kessler, S.J., and W. McKenna. 1978. *Gender: An Ethnomethodological Approach.* Chicago: University of Chicago Press.

Labour Canada. Women's Bureau. 1987. *Women in the Labour Force.* 1986–87 ed. Ottawa: Supply and Services.

Lerner, G. 1986. *The Creation of Patriarchy.* New York: Oxford University Press.

Mackie, M. 1983. *Exploring Gender Relations: A Canadian Perspective.* Toronto: Butterworths.

Macpherson, C.B. 1978. *Property: Mainstream and Critical Positions.* Toronto: University of Toronto Press.

Marx, K. 1967. *Capital: A Critique of Political Economy.* Vol. 1. New York: International Publishers.

———. 1977. *Karl Marx: Selected Works.* Ed. David McLellan. London: Oxford University Press.

Mills, C. 1969. *The Sociological Imagination.* London: Oxford University Press.

O'Brien, M. 1983. *The Politics of Reproduction.* Boston: Routledge and Kegan Paul.

Prentice, A., P. Bourne, G. Cuthbert Brandt, B. Light, W. Mitchinson, and N. Black, eds. 1988. *Canadian Women: A History.* Toronto: Harcourt Brace Jovanovich.

Rowbotham, S. 1976. *Hidden From History: Rediscovering Women in History from the 17th Century to the Present.* New York: Vintage Books.

Saliou, M. 1986. "The Processes of Women's Subordination in Primitive and Archaic Greece." In Coontz and Henderson, *Women's Work.* 169–206.

Smith, D. 1974. "The Social Construction of Documentary Reality." *Sociological Inquiry* 44, no. 4:257–67.

———. 1987. *The Everyday World as Problematic: A Feminist Sociology.* Toronto: University of Toronto Press.

Ward, P. 1978. *White Canada Forever: Popular Attitudes and Public Policy Toward Orientals in British Columbia.* Montreal and Kingston: McGill–Queen's University Press.

Wilson, S.J. 1986. *Women, the Family, and the Economy.* 2d ed. Toronto: McGraw-Hill Ryerson.

CHAPTER 3

Gender Inequality: Political and Religious Conservatism, and Counter-movements

Kathleen Storrie

Learning Objectives

This chapter discusses how the political and religious right have relied on domestic ideology drawn from the submission movement to mobilize themselves politically in order to protect their ideal of the traditional family and hierarchical gender relations, and to oppose the feminist movement and gender equality. Students are encouraged to consider why these Christians have identified as their "enemies" the leaders of social movements such as feminism, and not the effects of capitalist dynamics such as the increased employment of married women, and why these religious groups have become politicized and have launched counter-movements against these "enemies." Students are also encouraged to understand the many contradictions and ironies involved when Evangelicals condone and legitimate the very economic system, which, as is argued in this chapter, is subverting their own cherished values and their vision of a "proper" moral order.

Introduction

This chapter focuses on a social movement that, in advocating female submission to men, exemplifies the relationship between people's religious beliefs and their material conditions. This relationship has long been a source of interest to social scientists. For example, Max Weber is perhaps best remembered for a treatise on the connection between what he called "the spirit of modern economic life" and "the rational ethics of ascetic Protestantism" (1958, 27). In his analysis, Weber ignored the work of women for reasons that will be made clear later in this chapter. I intend to show that women's work both in and outside the home also constitutes a historical case of dynamic interplay between people's economic and religious interests.

The chapter examines what has happened in recent times when economic and social changes have impinged on a specific religious and moral order, namely that of conservative Christianity in which the domesticity of women under the control of men symbolizes a divinely ordained order. In the 1960s and 1970s, conservative Christians (Evangelicals) came to the conclusion that male hegemony in the home, which for them represented God's order in the form of a chain of command, was being threatened by the increasing employment of women and by other social changes. These Evangelicals responded by launching a massive campaign to reinforce hierarchical relations within marriage and the family and by so doing to preserve "the integrity of society." As Lechner (1985, 245) has noted, "the perceived loss of the social canopy or of solidary community may become the focus of revitalization efforts." The submission movement, however, contains a paradox: On the one hand, its leaders support capitalism whole-heartedly, and its particular form of gender relations fits some aspects of capitalism rather well. On the other hand, I argue, the material and religious interests of these conservative Christians begin to be undermined when capitalists (and agents of the state) threaten a central symbol in conservative Protestantism—the ethic of the male as sole breadwinner.

The increasing entry of married women into the labour force that began in the 1950s was due to a number of factors, including inflation and a growing response to massive advertising of consumer goods. But larger numbers of married women could not have taken paid jobs without the tremendous expansion of capitalism that occurred in the years following the Second World War (Armstrong and Armstrong 1984).

Instead of criticizing this increasing penetration of capitalism into their lives, however, conservative Christians have scapegoated certain social movements of the 1970s, including the renewed women's movement and the lesbian and gay rights movement, and other perceived enemies such as "radical secularists" in the media and the state. These Christians, with some allies in other faiths, launched a countermovement, beginning in the 1980s. They mobilized themselves politically in order to oppose these perceived threats, through the so-called New Christian Right. I shall review these developments briefly as they have occurred in the United States and in Canada.

Evangelicalism

Who are the Evangelicals and how many of them exist in North America? Considerable disagreement surrounds the defining of "Evangelicalism," and varying operational definitions produce different statistics. Bibby and Brinkerhoff (1973, 1983) base their count on denominational affiliation and include the following denominations as "Evangelical": Christian and Missionary Alliance, Baptist, Nazarene, Salvation Army, Pentecostal, and Plymouth Brethren. This procedure, with the addition of the Mennonites and other independent churches, produces a figure of 7 percent of the Canadian population (Bibby 1987, 27).[1]

But James D. Hunter (1981) criticizes this approach based on denominational affiliation, along with other approaches, arguing that since self-defined Evangelicals exist in the mainline churches, too, the only valid criteria are theological ones. He advocates using as criteria "personal adherence to the core doctrines of biblical inerrancy,[2] the divinity of Christ and eternal salvation through the redemptive act of God through Christ" (1981, 371). This theological operational definition produces a figure of 31.7 percent for Evangelicals in North America (Hunter 1987, 5). Finally, a Gallup–*Christianity Today* survey (1979), which employed a mixture of doctrinal and behavioural criteria, has found that 20 percent of Americans (thirty-one million) are Evangelicals.

"Fundamentalists" are a faction within Evangelicalism; briefly, they are distinguished by their stress on moral absolutes and on the universality of sin, and an even greater emphasis on biblical inerrancy than is typical of the average Evangelical (Carpenter 1984; Marty 1984, Hunter 1983). It is important to note, as Carpenter (1984, 260) has done, that "Fundamentalists are Evangelicals but not all Evangelicals are Fundamentalists." In this chapter, "Evangelical" is used in the theological sense, that is, as denoting those who hold to the doctrines specified by James D. Hunter (1981), and thus the term will not be limited to denominational affiliation.

We need to note also that Evangelicals hold differing views on a number of issues, including gender relations (Hunter 1987). Indeed, the early 1970s saw the renaissance of "biblical feminism" in North America, a movement among Evangelicals that claims biblical authority for its advocacy of egalitarian gender relations in church and society (Bendroth 1984; Mollenkott 1977a; Hardesty and Groh 1984; Scanzoni 1984). This movement parallels, in some aspects, nineteenth-century feminism, whose roots can be traced to the revivalism of Charles G. Finney and that movement's reform activities (Dayton 1976; Rossi 1974). Evangelicalism, therefore, should be seen as a spectrum rather than a monolithic bloc. Nevertheless, because feminists constitute a minority within this tradition, it is accurate to characterize the submission movement as Evangelical, provided one bears in mind that not all Evangelicals support female subordination. This point can be illustrated by the satirical view taken of *The Total Woman* by the editors of *The Wittenburg Door*. *The Total Woman* by Marabel Morgan constitutes an Evangelical marriage manual on how wifely submission, if combined with continuous hard work to appear always glamorous and sexy, can ensure a husband's fidelity. The depiction of a "totaled woman" reprinted here suggests that at least some Evangelicals are prepared to treat Morgan's prescriptions with considerable irreverence. *The Wittenburg Door*, in fact, is an Evangelical magazine that specializes in the humorous handling of notable Evangelical personalities and events.

The Submission-of-Women Movement

The term "social movement" may be used in the sense of a collective attempt to promote, maintain, or resist social change (Wood and Jackson 1982). One of the features of a social movement is its non-institutionalized activity, which develops because its interests are not met through the routine operations of society's established institutions and conventions (Fitzsimmons-LeCavalier and LeCavalier 1986). Beginning in the 1960s and gaining momentum in the 1970s, a massive volume of material—literature, films, tapes, seminars, and TV and radio programs—

FIGURE 3.1: *The Wittenburg Door* Cover

Source: *The Wittenburg Door*, 1224 Greenfield Dr., El Cajon, CA 92021, Issue No. 26 (August–September 1975): 1.

began to promote "domestic ideology" in a new and vigorous way as part of a new concern about the family as "a symbol of social stability and traditional moral virtue" (Hunter 1987, 76). Authors have included Helen Andelin, whose *Fascinat-*

ing Womanhood, published first in 1963, had sold 400 000 copies by 1975;[3] Marabel Morgan, whose *Total Woman* was *the* bestselling non-fiction book in the United States in 1974; Bill Gothard, founder of the Institute in Basic Youth Conflicts, whose mass seminars were attracting 200 000 annually by 1973 and 330 000 in 1982;[4] and other writers too numerous to list here.

This movement has diverse roots; its members include adherents of the Mormon church and of the Charismatic movement,[5] whose members attend mainline churches, and some Episcopalian groups, but Evangelical/Fundamentalist Christians predominate. In Canada they have produced such organizations as "Woman Alive," "Woman Aglow," and "Winning Women," and in the United States, "Total Woman" seminars, "Successful Fulfilled Womanhood," and "Enriched Living." Most of the American organizations have also operated in Canada.

Although its leaders are white and middle class, the movement's vocabulary and style are essentially populist, designed for mass appeal. Its detailed prescriptions are expressed in simple, "folksy" language and are vividly supported with anecdotal evidence that such straightforward formulas do indeed work. A central perception is that "God's order" in the public domain cannot be separated from "God's order" in the private domain. This is the case in terms of both the crucial task of socializing children and male dominance over women. Thus, ironically, there is a sense in which these Christians would support the feminist dictum: "The personal is political." Of course, unlike feminists, they express this in the belief that the Christian home should exemplify a divinely ordained hierarchy. To understand more fully this world-view, we need to look briefly at two earlier Protestant responses to social and economic change, the seventeenth-century Puritan and the nineteenth-century Evangelical reconstruction of gender and its relation to the material world.

Historical Contexts

Weber's thesis arising from his study of seventeenth-century Puritans is well known: the character traits of the ideal-typical Puritan, such as self-control, discipline, frugality, and rationality (an "inner-world asceticism") had an affinity with the developing social formation of capitalism, and eventually they gained cultural ascendancy in the form of "the Protestant ethic" (1958). What has not been so well understood is that Weber, like other early sociologists, such as Durkheim and Marx, assumed that male dominance and female subordination were "natural," that is, rooted in women's reproductive role (Sydie 1987). Consequently, Weber did not conceptualize the sexual division of labour as a sociological problem to be investigated and explained. This meant that the domestic role of women and its connections to capitalism were invisible to Weber, because he simply took women's domestic labour for granted. Indeed, Morgan (1981, 93) argues that "it is possible to see Weber's *Protestant Ethic* as a study of masculinity [only]."

Weber's lack of attention to the role of women has been remedied to some extent by such studies as Hamilton's analysis of the interacting effects of capitalism and Puritan ideology on gender relations in seventeenth-century England (1978). Hamilton argues that the patriarchal ideology of that time was transformed by two central Protestant beliefs—the priesthood of all believers, and one's "calling," as a commitment to godly behaviour in every aspect of living. As a consequence of these beliefs, Protestant reformers rejected all forms of ecclesiastical mediation, including the celibate priesthood. Married life, regarded by the Catholic Church as inferior to celibacy, was redefined as the key to success in one's calling. Marriage, as the means of both the procreation and the proper godly nurturing of children, was viewed as the location of a new familial patriarchy. Drawing on the patriarchal models of the Old Testament, the Puritans constituted the husband/father as the "high priest" of the family, replacing the dethroned priests and saints in assuming responsibility for the spiritual wellbeing of wife and children. The Catholic conception of woman as the source of evil was rejected and a new image was substituted, that of the good, hardworking, loyal "help meet," firmly enclosed within the home.[6]

By reconstituting the family as "a little church and a little state," the Protestant preachers continued the Catholic doctrine of wifely subordination (Morgan 1966), but they also insisted somewhat contradictorily that this male dominance was to be informed by love (Haller and Haller 1942; Frye 1955). As Hamilton (1978,10) notes, "perhaps if any one idea of the Protestants contributed to keeping women in the home ... it was their marrying of spiritual and conjugal love."[7] Nevertheless, the main substance of Protestant marriage was the newly defined religious and economic partnership of wife and husband, and so the work of women became an intrinsic part of capital formation.

This marital partnership broke down in response to the complex changes produced by the emergence of industrial capitalism. These included the separation of work from home, of the public from the private sphere, and of production from consumption, with men being associated with paid work in the public and productive sphere and women being confined to unpaid work in the home, which was then defined as a private sphere (Hamilton 1978). The domestic labour of women, which under feudalism had been inseparable from the general productive activity of the household, eventually was reduced to a wife's personal service to her husband and defined as one of the most important means of expressing love—now the only legitimate basis of marriage. In this way, the so-called bourgeois family—that form of family typical of the middle and upper industrial classes—became institutionalized, and eventually came to constitute the ideal even for the working class (Ariès 1962; Lasch 1977).

It would be misleading, however, to imply that only changes in material conditions produced this type of family with no corresponding ideological development. Once again, Protestants, this time a group of Evangelicals within the Church of England known as the Clapham Sect, responded to economic and social changes by contributing significantly to an ideological reconstruction of gender relations, this time in the nineteenth century.

Members of the Clapham Sect became deeply concerned about three developments: notions of female equality being promoted by the feminists of the day, such as Mary Wollstonecraft;[8] what they perceived as the general licentiousness and immorality of the late eighteenth century, and what they saw as the frivolous use to which aristocratic and bourgeois women were putting their new-found leisure and affluence. From 1780 to 1840, these Evangelicals conducted a systematic campaign to transform British national morality, using all the means of mass communication available to them, including books, meetings, and cheap tracts, or pamphlets (Hall

1979). Among the assumptions they inherited from their Puritan forebears were that religion should be a daily rule of life as a defence against the universality of sin, and that the home should be the primary arena in this spiritual and moral struggle.

Unlike prosperous Puritan women, however, well-to-do Evangelical women of the late eighteenth century had been stripped of their direct economic roles. The Clapham Sect developed a comprehensive strategy to fill this void through what became known as "the Cult of True Womanhood" (Ruether 1973). This ideology redefined the position of women in the spiritual and moral realm (Roberts 1834; Gisborne 1801; More 1799). As "Angels of the Home," women were given a major role in regenerating the nation morally, although their power to do so was strictly defined and limited to the following duties: supporting and influencing their husbands, whose morals they were to sustain and even improve; making the home a haven (in modern terms, managing the tensions of the family); socializing children into Christian virtues; and engaging in philanthropic activity—their one legitimate public role (Hall 1979).

This domestic ideology crossed the Atlantic in the late eighteenth century. In Canada, it came with the arrival of British women related to influential and prominent male colonists, such as Elizabeth Simcoe, wife of the first lieutenant governor of Upper Canada (Errington 1988). In the United States, the doctrine of women's separate and distinct sphere entered first via literature imported from England, and was later spread through books published in New England (Easton 1979). In both societies, this bourgeois family-type clashed with and began to replace the interdependent gender relations of pioneering communities. Within the frontier family, women played a major part in the common enterprise of subsistence and survival (Errington 1988; Prentice et al. 1988). However, the frontier society was by definition temporary, and its levelling effect on female–male relations was resisted by the colonial elite in Canada and by the capitalist elite in the United States. Eventually, it was these elites' definition of "true womanhood" that prevailed, although less so in Canada than in the United States.[9]

The split between the public and private spheres created already by industrial capitalist relations was accentuated by the ideological efforts of Evangelicals. This division became, in Hall's words, "a split between the sexes of a peculiarly exaggerated kind" (1979, 24), which left a legacy of sharply delineated gender expectations. These were legitimated on both religious and supposedly "biological" grounds, for succeeding generations to inherit, including the advocates of the present domestic ideology.

However, the Evangelical forms of behaviour created for one purpose were shaped eventually for another (Hall 1979). The members of the Clapham Sect redefined the role of women in response to economic changes and as a vital part of their strategy to reform the nation's "manners and morals." But, ironically, this reconstruction of "femininity" contributed ultimately to the defeat of their campaign for public morality. Since women had been so closely identified with morality and with the private sphere, this Evangelical redefinition of gender relations contributed to a subsequent "privatizing" of religion. That is to say, a cultural norm developed, aided by secular liberalism, that was well suited to capitalist interests: it held that religion and morality are ultimately "feminine" matters, which not be allowed to interfere with the competitive, tough world of business where men spend most of their time. As Dorothy Sölle (1984, 30) has pointed out, the great commandment of Judaism and Christianity, "Love your neighbour as yourself," became a diminished one: "Love your neighbour but not in public." The privatizing of morality not only contributed to the failure of the Evangelical goal of national reform, but also left Christian families in danger of being undermined by an "unregenerate" society and of being penetrated by the "contaminating" policies of civil authorities. These two tensions would confront Evangelicals for decades thereafter.

Furthermore, the Evangelical ideal of the non-employed wife could be readily put in place only by the middle and upper classes. At the time this ideal was being entrenched in Britain in the mid-nineteenth century, at least a quarter of the British female population over the age of fifteen was employed outside the home for the purpose of sheer survival. Many of them worked as domestic servants for these "Angels of the Home" (Wilson 1986, 73). Yet this need for women to labour outside the home obviously threatened the exclusive control by husbands of their wives' reproductive labour inside the home (childbearing, child caring, housework, and personal services to husbands) (Luxton 1980). The work of women both inside and outside the home has thus constituted an area of struggle between competing masculine interests from the beginning of capitalism. For example, working-class men, facing the threat that cheap female labour posed both to their own jobs and to their exclusive access to women's labour (in the home), supported state intervention in at least two areas: protective legislation restricting female work hours and the types of jobs available to women, and the notion of a "family wage"—an income sufficient for a man to support his children and a non-employed wife (Hart Mann 1976, 1981). Eventually, the ideal of the husband as sole breadwinner became intrinsic to the dominant cultural definition of masculinity (Carrigan et al. 1987; Tolson 1977).

In these various ways, through ideology, legislation, and restrictive practices, men of different classes with different material and ideological interests at stake succeeded in keeping female participation in the labour force at relatively low levels (except in times of war) until the rapid expansion of the economy and of state bureaucracies in the late 1950s and early 1960s (Armstrong and Armstrong 1984; Braverman 1974; Wilson 1986). In Canada, for example, in 1931 only 3.5 percent of married women were in the labour force; the Second World War increased this by only 1 percent.

The Modern Context

As urbanization grew and monopoly capital and the state expanded in the 1950s and 1960s, social and geographic mobility increased, as did the divorce rate, particularly in the United States (Bendroth 1984) and in Canada after the liberalization of the divorce laws in 1968 (Wilson 1986, 21–22). Isolated in the newly built suburbs and geographically more separated than ever from the public realm, many women became increasingly alienated by male dominance and by their own domestic roles—a situation dramatically documented in Betty Friedan's *The Feminine Mystique* (1963). The percentage of married women in paid jobs more than doubled in the decade ending in 1951 (to 11.2 percent) and doubled again to 22 percent by 1961 (Connelly 1978, 64). In 1941, only slightly more than 10 percent of all employed women were married (during the later war years, this proportion did increase, but dropped again when the war ended), but by 1961 nearly 50 percent of all female workers were married (Prentice et al. 1988, 312).[10]

Confronted by this new fluidity in family life, and particularly by the challenge to the status of husbands as sole breadwinners, Evangelical theorists have found the legitimations of female subordination inherited from their Puritan and nineteenth-century Evangelical forebears to be inadequate. Modern submission advocates do draw upon these arguments. They include biological claims (female subordination is "natural") and a dualistic world-view (the "pure" home exists in contrast to the "sinful" world). But these contemporary advocates have escalated the level of rhetoric by appealing to no less than cosmic principles, such as the divine "order of creation"—an ancient idea now put into modern dress.

Writers such as Ryrie (1968) and Christenson (1970) argue that male hegemony is rooted in a divinely instituted hierarchy, often termed "the chain of command," a fundamental principle of creation unaffected by Christ's work. " In the words of Elizabeth Elliot (1976, 132–33), "A Christian home ... is a world in itself, a microcosm, representing—as the church itself represents—the hierarchy of the cosmos itself." This cosmic chain of command—"a great chain of being" (Scanzoni 1976)—extends to the Godhead itself. It is claimed that God rules over Christ and so the husband should rule over the wife—and, indeed, this hierarchy should be mirrored in society as a whole (Cooper 1974; Christenson 1970; Bockelman 1976).

The submission literature contains many other legitimations for its hierarchical prescriptions. The rest of this chapter will focus mainly on those relating to the wife's role, including her importance in the realm of morality. Since the wife's domestic work is perceived to be threatened, the overall strategy of this movement is to reinforce already existing norms of female behaviour that are of specific material interest to men. The traditional "helpmeet" role is raised to new heights as a sacred duty. Miles (1975, 99–103), for example, invokes John the Baptist's dictum that he must decrease so that Jesus could increase and translates it into the "Joan the Baptist" principle, whereby the wife decreases so that the husband's career can increase.

Although such a prospect would appear at first glance unappealing to many women, particularly when put in these terms, sociologists have documented the numerous structural and cultural supports for "a hierarchy of priorities in which the needs of the husband's work are accorded top priority, followed by those of the family ... with the wife's paid work, actual or potential, coming a very poor third" (Finch 1983, 134). These structural and cultural supports include the disadvantaged status of female wage-earners and state (as well as business) policies that constitute the male wage as a family wage and fail to provide adequate child-care services (see, e.g., Eichler 1983; Dineen and Johnston 1981).A number of studies have documented the widespread practice whereby many wives do not merely support their husbands' jobs in a general sense but are actually incorporated into them in various ways (Finch 1983).

The movement's vehement stress on the theological importance of women's work in the home is accompanied by equally or even more vehement denunciation of the employment of wives outside the home, usually for three major reasons. Employment outside the home causes wives to desert their "God-given" primary vocation, domesticity; it erodes the wife's dependence on her husband; and it undermines the man's sense of masculinity and his authority in the home. Miles (1975, 125–26) castigates employed wives for acting like Eve—seeking knowledge for themselves and deserting or delegating their primary tasks. LaHaye (1968, 29) is typical of submission writers when he declares that the employment of wives "breeds a feeling of independence and self-sufficiency which God did not intend a married woman to have." He goes on, "I am convinced one of the reasons young couples divorce so readily today is because the wife is not economically dependent upon her husband."

Frequent analogies made between God (or Jesus) and the husband also serve to strengthen the legitimacy of masculine authority. Maleness and divinity are fused, in that God is viewed as masculine and the husband is to be treated as if he were God. Bob Johnston (1986, 10), a Canadian author, states that "all three Persons of the Holy Trinity are unalterably masculine." Some in the movement portray the husband as God. One of many examples is Handford (1972, 29), who states: "A woman is to obey God himself. She can be as certain of God's will when her husband speaks as if God has spoken audibly from heaven."[12] Underlying these claims is the Puritan view of the husband as priest to the wife, so representing God to her (Christenson 1970).

As one might expect, the doctrine of female submission appears frequently in sermons preached at Evangelical weddings. The following excerpt from such a sermon, videotaped in December 1982 at a Baptist wedding, illustrates not only the stress on submission but also the association of masculinity with divinity. Also noteworthy are the minister's assumptions that a single woman's relative freedom of action constitutes a privilege and that female self-sacrifice is normative. (The names of the bride and bridegroom have been changed.)

> Until now, Mary, you've been free and on your own and you've been, in a sense, privileged to do many things you wanted to do. When you share your vows, you are cutting some of those paths of freedom and you are committing yourself to Jim. When you share your vows, you are saying you are going to submit yourself to him. In other words, you are going to meet his needs. You will find, Mary, that it seems that the cost is too high, that there are needs of your own crying out to be met. But you are there trying to meet the needs of your husband. One of the many needs that a husband has is that of dignity.... Men don't always feel good about themselves. When we look in the mirror, we are supposed to be able to say we look like God because God made us and ... we are made in the image of God. But because of many things, Mary, we don't always feel that way about ourselves and ... we don't treat others as we should and we certainly don't treat ourselves the way we should. You can help Jim to have the dignity that God wants him to have.

Long before this modern submission movement, Milton stated poetically "Thee for God only, shee for God in him" (quoted in Hamilton 1978, 58). Sennett (1980) argues that a paternalistic metaphor that fuses love and power when applied to any superior greatly magnifies the superior's potency. Jay Adams (1972) seems to agree when he claims that a woman fully loved by her husband is fully under his control. Another metaphor for masculine hegemony, this time derived from capitalist relations, is that of president. Morgan (1973, 82) states, "God ordained man to be the head of the family, its president and the wife to be the executive vice-president.... Allowing your head to be president is just good business."

Not surprisingly, the nineteenth-century "Angel of the Home" reappears, and is linked firmly with the double standard and with biology. Miles, for example, claims that "what we know of peace, order, cleanness, purity, virtue we know primarily from woman and secondarily from men who learned it from their mothers.... The old double standard of morality is deeper than cultural: it is recognition of innate qualities" (1975, 25–26). The theme of female responsibility for male behaviour recurs constantly; Miles goes on to argue that "without a beloved, incarnate model of submission and loyalty, males ... will not understand how to submit themselves ... to God" (1975, 151). George Gilder, who became a conservative Christian after writing *Sexual Suicide* (1973) and was one of President Reagan's advisers, defines men as "sexual barbarians" who need to be reformed through fidelity in marriage to women who, he claims, are innately moral (see also Gilder 1986). It becomes clear that the "traditional" family, which these Evangelicals are defending as "Christian," is in fact the prototypical nineteenth-century bourgeois family. Virtually all of its Evangelical advocates seem unaware of how recently this type of family has come into existence (for additional examples equating "Christian" with bourgeois, see Falwell 1980; LaHaye 1981; Brown 1983). The alleged female abdication of domesticity, and innumerable other ills, predictably are blamed on the women's movement, which this submission movement attacks vehemently, following the example of its predecessor in the last century. The contemporary women's movement is labelled "diabolical," "dehumanizing," "destructive," "feminine rebellion" (Handford 1972; Andelin 1974; Elliot 1976; LaHaye 1980, 1981; Miles 1975). Miles is typical of these writers in linking female morality to national destiny, declaring that the loss of female talent from the home allegedly caused by feminism "is creating a multiplied moral drain that may well flush us all down the sewer" (1975, 97).

Submission advocates, far from viewing capitalism as a source of the supposed decline of the family, support it uncritically. Admittedly, Morgan (1975, 47) urges the wife "to build him [the husband] up for the day [at work]" and every evening to "neutralize [in him] the world's daily dose of poison." But the roots of this poison are never explained. Instead, detailed instructions are given for the relief of work-induced tension in husbands, particularly in terms of meeting their sexual needs.[13]

The capitalist ethos of personal success and self-interest is mirrored in a technique intended to make submission more acceptable and to make it appear entirely in the interest of women themselves. This technique consists of promises to women that submission will ensure the love and fidelity of their husbands and protection from other men, from Satan, and from worldly pressures (Andelin 1974; Basham 1974; Christenson 1970; Miles 1975). Indeed, the whole submission movement can be described as based on a "theology of success," designed to appeal particularly to women experiencing marital difficulties. Much of the movement's literature focusses explicitly on how women, through submission, can persuade men to be faithful husbands and good fathers, by taking the initiative while not seeming to do so. In this way, women can avoid any apparent or real threat to male privilege and authority. Rose, in a study of a Charismatic community's patriarchal gender relations model led on the Old Testament, provides some ethnographic evidence for this analysis. Women in this fellowship knowingly relinquished their desires for independence and equality in marriage in order to allow "their husbands to appear strong and in control" (1987, 255), and to try to ensure their husbands' love, faithfulness, and emotional growth. In return for female submission, the men also granted their wives some influence, i.e., "hidden power." Nevertheless, Rose argues that the costs for these women have included "a denial of personhood, a dampening of spirit and stultification of power and talent" (1987, 256).[14]

Counter-movements

Social movements can focus on resisting changes brought about at least in part by other movements. Such efforts constitute counter-movements. This term appears to fit the activities of Evangelicals who mobilized themselves politically in order to defend the hierarchical gender relations that they had legitimated through the submission doctrines. Conservative Christians, led by TV evangelists, and certain Mormon and Jewish groups together created the "New Christian Right" (NCR) in the United States.15 These politicized religious coalitions emerged, along with secular neo-conservatism, in 1979 and the early 1980s (Liebman 1983; Crawford 1980; Pierard 1984; Hunter 1981). Although they mobilized conservative religious groups on a range of issues including abortion, lesbian and gay rights, feminism, the Equal Rights Amendment, sex education, and "secular humanism" in the schools, the NCR leaders subsumed such matters under their general "pro-family" and "pro-morality" stance. Acting in accordance with the American tradition of civil religion,[16] they claimed that to be "pro-family" was tantamount to being pro-America (Hunter 1981; Stahl 1987). They identified a number of enemies, such as feminists, homosexuals, and "secular humanists," all of whom they viewed as destructive to the family (LaHaye 1980, 1981; Falwell 1980). Analysts of the NCR view it, in part, as a protest against the state: conservative Christians believe that the government supports their "enemies" and their enemies' philosophies (Liebman 1983; Simpson 1983; Wacker 1984).

In Canada, the New Christian Right also emerged simultaneously with the secular New Right, which is represented by such organizations as the Fraser Institute[17] and the National Citizens' Coalition, in addition to the Bennett and Vander Zalm governments in British Columbia and the Devine government in Saskatchewan (McNiven 1987; Warnock 1988; Riches 1986). As in the United States, Christian organizations in Canada such as Renaissance International and Positive Parents have formed coalitions with anti-abortion groups.[18] They define the "enemies" of the traditional family similarly to their American counterparts. They include feminism, the lesbian and gay rights movement, the pro-choice movement in abortion, and government action perceived as supporting these movements, including the Canadian Charter of Rights. For example, the Pro-Family Coalition advertised a "Canada in Crisis" rally in March 1981, calling upon "responsible Canadians to prevent the imposition on the Canadian people of a Charter of Rights that is without 'God', immoral, and threatening to our future freedoms." The ad invited people to

> come and find out why the Trudeau "Charter of Rights" is a "Charter of Injustice" and what is being done by a recently formed, broadly-based, pro-family and freedom coalition in non-sectarian, non-partisan response to this outrageous scheme to impose "this clumsy collection of Orwellian concepts" on an unsuspecting and unwilling Canadian population!

Furthermore, it asked the following rhetorical questions:

> Do you want all laws based on positive male/female differences to be forcibly eradicated? Do you want homosexual marriages and child-adoptions approved by law? Do you want tax-paid abortion clinics? Do you want five judges* appointed by the Prime Minister to decide such important issues for you (*a simple majority of the 9 member Supreme Court, appointed by the Prime Minister)? Do you want "God," the primacy of the family and the right to hold property left out of the Constitution? Do you want your rights limited by such a charter?

American speakers invited to speak at Canadian New Christian Right meetings have included Tim and Beverly LaHaye and Jerry Falwell, all of whom advocate female submission.

Some women's organizations have also emerged with a "pro-family" stance as their main concern, accompanied by strong criticism of state support for feminism and other "anti-family" policies. REAL (Realistic, Equal, Active for Life) Women was created in 1983, initially in response to a suggested removal of the tax deduction for dependent spouses so that more money could be given to public day care (Crittenden 1988). Victorious Women, a Saskatchewan-based organization that supports REAL Women, is led by a former Tory MLA (By field 1987). Both these organizations claim to be non-partisan and interdenominational and both have among their objectives the affirmation of "the family" (specifically defined as based on heterosexual marriage) and support of full-time homemaking as "a challenging, creative, and rewarding career." They also support the promotion of legislation "that upholds the Judeo-Christian values on marriage and family life" and the defence of Canada as a free-enterprise nation. A study of members of REAL Women and of Campaign Life found them to be characterized by "moral absolutism" and avid support for "male-headed" families (Cherry 1988, 31; Erwin 1988). Among the policies REAL Women and Victorious Women oppose are lesbian and gay rights, mandatory affirmative action, "easy" divorce, abortions (for *any* reason), and public and tax policies that discriminate against homemakers. Both groups have taken pro-free trade and pro-privatization positions.[19]

These platforms support my contention that such politicized Christian organizations constitute counter-movements—that is, they are engaged in resisting social changes that they believe have been brought about by other movements. Consequently, the leaders of these counter-movements attack those other movements as "the enemies." In so doing, they ignore the major impact that the economic system has on gender relations and the family in general. Most married women are employed because their husbands cannot earn enough to support the family. This inadequacy in male wages is related to the increasing inequality in income distribution—those in the lower income ranges have been receiving a smaller share of the nation's total income, while those in the higher income ranges have been increasing their share (Armstrong and Armstrong 1984, 172–78). In other words, it is not the women's movement but the structured inequality inherent in capitalist relations that has undermined the status of the male as sole wage earner. Furthermore, it is capitalism that has created the demand for the labour of women, typically in low-paying jobs in marginal sectors of the labour market (Connelly 1978; Armstrong and Armstrong 1984). Given the uncritical support that both the submission movement and its politicized version, the New Christian Right, give to capitalism, this refusal to acknowledge its effects is hardly surprising.

It should be noted, however, that the Canadian situation differs from the American one in several respects. Canada does not make the mythic connection between God and country inherent in the civil religion of the United States. Although it is true that the Canadian Pro-Family Coalition did try to mobilize public opinion in 1981 against the Charter of Rights on the grounds that it was "without God and immoral," the attempt was rather unsuccessful. Furthermore, the dominant mainstream denominations in Canada have shown little sympathy for a prominent source of moral conservatism in the United States, the religious entrepreneurship of TV evangelists such as Pat Robertson and Jerry Falwell. Finally, Catholics make up a larger proportion of the population in Canada than in the United States, so conservative Protestants are very much a minority here (Westhues 1978).

Trying to gauge the degree of effectiveness of both the submission movement and the New Christian Right is beyond the scope of this essay. Certainly, it seems that a revitalized conservative religiosity has provided further support for the secular neoconservatism that has developed in North America in recent years. Stahl (1987) is probably right in his suggestion that the strength of the NCR lies in its success in placing morality in the public sphere—a realm that liberals have rendered amoral. The NCR has thus been able to set the political agenda and it is *its* questions that tend to take centre stage in public debate. In so far as conservative Christians are able to affect the content of public debate, they may be able to block or at least slow the implementation of progressive social policies. It is possible, for example, to speculate that the strong opposition of REAL Women and other Christian groups to publicly subsidized daycare centres did influence the 1988 federal decision to use the tax system to support private child care instead of devoting the entire amount of new funding to daycare centres as originally proposed.

Nevertheless, evidence shows that the *leaders* of the pro-family movement in Canada may be more in favour of neoconservative policies, such as those advocated by the Reform Party, than are the rank and file. On the basis of a 1986–87 survey, Erwin (1993) has provided evidence that pro-family members do not support either the cutbacks in social services or the neoconservative fiscal position advocated by the movements' leaders. Furthermore, Erwin has been able to make comparisons between pro-family adherents and the Canadian public by including questions taken from national surveys in her questionnaire. She comments, "On some indications they [the pro-family supporters] appear to be equally or even more liberal than Canadians generally.... Only when an issue identified with feminism is raised does the pro-family group digress sharply from the Canadian norm" (1993, 414).

Erwin suggests that this discrepancy between the neoconservativism of the leaders and the more liberal views of the general membership may result in the pro-family movement losing its early momentum, and in its neoconservative prospects being limited. Her comments, however, were made before the 1993 federal election. The electoral success of the Reform Party, with its strong pro-family policies, will ensure that antifeminist groups in Canada will continue to have their platforms well represented in Parliament and in the media.

Conclusions

The relationship between people's religiosity and their economic situation provides a context in which to examine a social movement—the submission movement, which began in the 1960s and whose aim is to entrench the "traditional" family defined by its hierarchical gender relations. These relations are perceived to be undermined particularly by the increasing employment of married women, which began in the 1950s and 1960s. Instead of identifying the expansion of capitalist relations as the source of this threat to male hegemony in the family, conservative Christians have identified other movements of the 1970s as the origins of their problems. With a well-developed defence of domestic ideology drawn from the submission movement, these Christians, with some support from other faiths, have mobilized themselves politically through the so-called New Christian Right. They have attacked the women's movement, the lesbian and gay rights movement, and those government actions that are considered to be influenced by the philosophies of these "permissive" movements, including "secular humanism."

This situation contains several ironies. For example, conservative Christians deplore and protest conditions that are caused primarily by the very economic system that they support. Furthermore, by following (often unwittingly) in the steps of their nineteenth-century predecessors, Evangelicals are replicating the same contradictory policies. Their strategy places most of the responsibility for morality and for the emotional and physical wellbeing of the family on women. It simultaneously reinforces male dominance and restricts female talent and energy to the home. But this social order has impoverished both the domestic and the public realms for more than two hundred years. It has allowed men to benefit from the domestic work of women without participating and has obscured both this inequity and the violence with which many men have enforced their privileged status in the home. Coping with family responsibilities and facing innumerable social and economic obstacles, women have been handicapped in their struggle to move beyond "their proper sphere," domesticity. Furthermore, constituting women as more moral than men perpetuates the double standard of morality (Eichler 1980). Yet it is men who predominate in political and professional positions, and so this double standard is hardly conducive to achieving a more moral public realm—one of the objectives of Evangelicals.

It is exactly this ethically impoverished situation that the women's movements of the nineteenth and twentieth centuries have tried to remedy. But feminists, of course, with their stress on personhood and gender justice, are the last persons that most Evangelicals would see as potential allies; therefore, biblical feminists in Evangelical churches seem destined to remain a minority. It seems equally probable that as long as Evangelicals continue to defend or to condone capitalist relations, they will remain oblivious to the subversive effects of capitalism on their cherished values and their vision of a new moral order. Their chain-of-command ideology does not reinforce only these capitalist relations. It also ensures that gender inequality, in all its forms, will continue to undermine the stability of the family—the institution that Evangelicals wish to defend at all costs.

Study Questions

1. Weber ignored the work of women when he wrote *The Protestant Ethic and the Spirit of Capitalism.* Reflect on the implications of this omission. Can you think of consequences other than those mentioned in this essay?

2. What difference did the nineteenth-century Evangelicals make to the social construction of the bourgeois family?

3. Can you think of ways in which people today still defend "the privacy of the home" and "the sanctity of marriage"? How do such ideas relate to wife assault and the abuse of children in the home?

4. In what ways does the double standard of morality operate in gender relations and what are the consequences in terms of social control?

5. The submission-of-women advocates teach that women should defer to their husbands, promising that such submissive behaviour will result in male fidelity and love. Can you see any problems with this scenario? If so, what are they?

6. Speculate on what would happen if large numbers of Evangelicals became conscious and critical of both capitalist relations and the chain-of-command model for marital and other relationships. Is this change of world view likely to occur?

Recommended Reading

Erwin, Lorna. "Neoconservatism and the Canadian Pro-Family Movement." *Canadian Review of Sociology and Anthropology* 30 (1993):401–20.

Hall, Catherine. "The Early Formation of Victorian Domestic Ideology." In *Fit Work for Women*, ed. S. Burman. London: Croom Helm, 1979.

Hamilton, Roberta. *The Liberation of Women: A Study of Patriarchy and Capitalism.* London: George Allen and Unwin, 1978.

Hartmann, Heidi. "Capitalism, Patriarchy and Job Segregation by Sex." *Signs* I (1976): 137–69.

Marsden, George, ed. *Evangelicalism and Modern America.* Grand Rapids, MI: Eerdmans, 1979.

Morgan, Marabel. *The Total Woman*, Markham, ON: Pocket Books, 1975. (You may be able to find a copy in a second-hand book store.)

Rose, Susan D. "Women Warriors: The Negotiation of Gender in a Charismatic Community." *Sociological Analysis* 48 (1987): 245–48.

Tolson, Andrew. *The Limits of Masculinity.* London: Tavistock, 1977.

Notes

1. The statistics for the mainline churches in Canada: Roman Catholic, 47 percent; United Church, 16 percent; Anglican, 10 percent; and Lutheran, 3 percent (Bibby 1987, 47).
2. In brief, "Biblical inerrancy" refers to the view that the Bible is without any inconsistency or error and was directly inspired by God. Evangelicals, however, do vary in their understanding of what "inerrancy" actually means (see Clark Pinnock, cited in Coleman 1980, 10–11).
3. Helen Andelin's *Fascinating Womanhood* comes out of the Mormon tradition and contains many Mormon ideas. It should be noted that the Mormon Church is not accepted as "Christian" by other churches. Yet Fascinating Womanhood seminars, in the author's personal experience, were warmly welcomed by many Evangelical churches in the early 1970s.
4. Hunter (1987, 77) states that over 1.3 million people have attended the seminars conducted by the Institute of Basic Youth Conflicts since 1964, when Gothard founded the organization.
5. The Charismatic movement is a renewal movement within the mainstream denominations that began in the 1950s. It emphasizes the gifts of the Holy Spirit, hence the use of the term "charismatic," from *charisma*, a Greek word meaning "gifts" (see Poloma 1982). Bibby (1987, 129) reports that about 3 percent of Canadians are currently involved in this movement.
6. For the American Puritan family, see Cott (1977); Bloch (1978); and Ulrich (1976).
7. It should be noted, however, that in typical Puritan fashion, such love was to be kept within "rational" limits (Morgan 1966).
8. The Clapham Sect was equally appalled by notions of equality promoted by the French Revolution—ideas that were enthusiastically applied to gender relations by Wollstonecraft in *The Vindication of the Rights of Women* (1792).
9. For other accounts of the process whereby the domestic ideology became institutionalized in North America, see, for the United States, Welter (1966); Cott (1977); Bloch (1978); and Sklar (1973). For Canada, see Cook and Mitchison (1976); Griffiths (1976); and Light and Prentice (1980).
10. Evidence for the continued increase in the employment of married women can be found in the 1985 statistics. In Canada, 54.7 percent of married women were in the labour force that year. The proportion varies with age. Of those 45 to 64 years old, 45.6 percent were employed, compared to 69.6 percent of those 25 to 34 years old. Single women had a participation rate of 67.7 percent, with single women of 25 to 34 years having the highest rate (85.3 percent) (Statistics Canada, *Women in the Labour Force*, 1986–87 edition, Women's Bureau, Labour Canada, 19).
11. Other Christians, however, take the view that Christ has brought about a "New Creation" in which male dominance is replaced by mutuality and gender equality (see, e.g., Mollenkott 1977b; Fiorenza 1983; Storrie 1984; Swidler 1979).

12. We need to note that Christianity has always held that "God's mode of personal existence transcends sexual distinctions" (Jewett 1980, 43), so any teaching that God is literally masculine runs counter to Christian orthodoxy, as does any association between divinity and mortal men.
13. Sexuality plays a prominent role in some submission literature. For example, Marabel Morgan's *Total Woman* and *Total Joy*, and Tim and Beverly LaHaye's *The Act of Marriage* essentially are Evangelical sex manuals, which urge women to work hard to achieve "super sex." Morgan (1975, 150–51) rather surprisingly suggests that Christian women take Marilyn Monroe and call girls as their exemplars in making themselves sexually alluring—but to their husbands only.
14. Pohli (1983) has documented the isolation and insularity of many Evangelical women through interviews with 123 of them. She has found that such women "are locked into a space that is psychologically and emotionally confining." She comments: "Like idealized Victorian women, Evangelical women are kept powerless and isolated from public life by being treated as the more spiritual sex" (544).
15. Among the Evangelical organizations that belong to this counter-movement are Christian Voice, Jerry Falwell's Moral Majority (now named Liberty Federation), Religious Roundtable, and the Coalition for the First Amendment (Hadden 1983; Guth 1983).
16. Civil religion refers to an elaborate system of practices and beliefs that contains symbolism and ritual borrowed from specific religions but is not associated with any single religious group. In the United States, civil religion originates in America's unique historic experience, in which belief in God and patriotism were made synonymous (Bellah 1967).
17. The Fraser Institute describes itself as an "independent Canadian economic and social research and education organization." One of its objectives is "the redirection of public attention to the role of competitive markets providing for the well-being of Canadians" (*Fraser Forum* 1989, 2). Its board of trustees consists of representatives of corporations such as Canadian Pacific, Imperial Oil, and MacMillan Bloedel; Peter Pocklington is a leading member of the board. Among its policies are the establishment of "organized resistance to the leftward tilt of the church and its ecumenical travelers." The institute has asserted that Christianity should be on the side of free enterprise and capitalism.
18. Among these anti-abortion groups are Campaign Life, Coalition for Life, and Right to Life. Renaissance International, one of the more active of the politicized Evangelical groups, was founded in the mid-1970s by Ken Campbell, an Ontario fundamentalist evangelist. Its purpose is to propagate "the values and philosophy of our Judeo-Christian heritage, the foundation of a free and responsible society."
19. The quotes and the platform statements cited in this section are taken from various pamphlets and other publications put out by REAL Women and Victorious Women.

References

Adams, J.E. 1972. *Christian Living in the Home.* Nutley, NJ: Presbyterian and Reformed Publishing Company.

Andelin A. 1974. *Man of Steel and Velvet.* Santa Barbara, CA: Pacific Press.

Andelin, H.B. 1963. *Fascinating Womanhood: A Guide to a Happy Marriage.* rev. ed. Santa Barbara, CA: Pacific Press.

Aries, P. 1962. *Centuries of Childhood.* New York: Vintage

Armstrong, P., and H. Armstrong. 1984. *The Double Ghetto: Canadian Women and Their Segregated Work.* rev. ed. Toronto: McClelland and Stewart.

Basham, D. 1974. "Women in Ministry." *New Wine* (October): 22–24.

Bellah, R. 1967. "Civil Religion in America." *Daedalus* 96: 1–21.

Bendroth, M. 1984. "The Search for 'Women's Role' in American Evangelicalism, 1930-1980." *Evangelicalism and Modern America*, ed. G. Marsden. Grand Rapids, MI: Eerdmans. 122–34.

Bibby, R.W. 1987. *Fragmented Gods: The Poverty and Potential of Religion in Canada.* Toronto: Irwin.

Bibby, R.W., and M.B. Brinkerhoff. 1973. "The Circulation of the Saints: A Study of People Who Join Conservative Churches." *Journal for the Scientific Study of Religion* 12: 273–83.

———. 1983. "Circulation of Saints Revisited: A Longitudinal Look at Conservative Church Growth." *Journal for the Scientific Study of Religion* 22: 253–62.

Bloch, R.H. 1978. "American Feminine Ideals in Transition: The Rise of the Moral Mother, 1785–1815." *Feminist Studies* 4, no. 2: 100–126.

Bockelman, W. 1976. *Gothard. The Man and His Ministry: An Evaluation.* Milford, MI: Quill Publications.

Braverman, H. 1974. *Labour and Monopoly Capital: The Degradation of Work in the Twentieth Century.* New York: Monthly Review Press.

Brown, M. 1983. *The Christian in an Age of Sexual Eclipse.* Wheaton, IL.: Tyndale House.

Byfield, V. 1987. "The Family: Uh-oh, Here Comes Another One." *Western Report* (November 2): 35

Carpenter, J. 1984. "The Fundamentalist Leaven and the Rise of an Evangelical United Front," In *The Evangelical Tradition in America.* ed. L. I. Sweet. Macon, GA: George Mercer University Press. 97–125

Carrigan, T., B. Connell, and J. Lee. 1987. "Hard and Heavy: Toward a New Sociology of Masculinity." *Beyond Patriarchy: Essays by Men on Pleasure, Power and Change*, ed. M. Kaufman. Toronto and New York: Oxford University Press. 139–92.

Cherry, M. 1988. "Founding Convention: Victorious Women in Canada." *Network* (Saskatchewan Action Committee, Status of Women, December/January): 29–32.

Christenson, L. 1970. *The Christian Family.* Minneapolis, MN: Bethany Fellowship.

Christianity Today. 1979. "We Poll the Pollster: An Interview with George Gallup, Jr." (December 21): 11–19.

Coleman, R.J. 1980. *Issues of Theological Conflict. Evangelicals and Liberals*, rev. ed. Grand Rapids, MI: Eerdmans.

Connelly P. 1978. *Last Hired First Fired: Women and the Canadian Work Force.* Toronto: Women's Press.

Cook, R., and W. Mitchison. 1976. *The Proper Sphere: Women's Place in Canadian Society.* Toronto: University of Toronto Press.

Cooper, D.B. 1974. *You Can Be the Wife of a Happy Husband.* Wheaton, IL: Victor.

Cott, N. F. 1977. *The Bonds of Womanhood.* New Haven and London: Yale University Press.

Crawford, A. 1980. *Thunder on the Right: The New Right and the Politics of Resentment.* New York: Pantheon Books.

Crittenden, D. 1988. "REAL Women Don't Eat Crow." *Saturday Night* 103 (May): 27–35.

Dayton, D.W. 1976. *Discovering an Evangelical Heritage.* New York: Harper and Row.

Dineen, J., and L.C. Johnston. 1981. *The Kin Trade: The Day Care Crisis in Canada.* Toronto: Copp Clark.

Easton, B. 1979. "Industrialization and Femininity: A Case Study of Nineteenth-Century New England." In *Understanding Minority-Dominant Relations*, ed. E.J. Davis. Arlington Heights, IL: AHM. 27–39.

Eichler, M. 1980. *The Double Standard: A Feminist Critique of the Social Sciences.* London: Croom Helm.

———. 1983. *Families in Canada Today.* Toronto: Gage.

Elliot, E. 1976. *Let Me Be a Woman.* Wheaton, IL: Tyndale.

Errington, J. 1988. "Pioneers and Suffragists." In *Changing Patterns: Women in Canada*, ed. S. Burt, L. Code, and L. Dorney. Toronto: McClelland and Stewart. 51–79.

Erwin, L. 1988. "What Feminists Should Know About the Pro-Family Movement in Canada: A Report on a Recent Survey of Rank-and-File Members." In *Feminist Research: Retrospect and Prospects*, ed. P. Tancred-Sherif. Montreal and Kingston: McGill–Queen's University Press. 266–78.

———. 1993. "Neoconservatism and the Canadian Pro-Family Movement." *Canadian Review of Sociology and Anthropology* 3: 401–20.

Falwell, J. 1980. *Listen America.* New York: Harper and Row.

Finch, J. 1983. *Married to the Job: Wives' Incorporation in Men's Work.* London: Allen and Unwin.

Fiorenza, E.S. 1983. *In Memory of Her: A Feminist Theological Reconstruction of Christian Origins.* New York: Crossroad.

Fitzsimmons-LeCavalier, P., and G. LeCavalier. 1980. "Social Movements and Social Change." In *Sociology*, 3d ed, ed. R. Hagedorn. Toronto: Holt, Rinehart and Winston. 557–86.

Fraser Forum. 1989. Vancouver: Fraser Institute (February): 2.

Friedan, B. 1963. *The Feminine Mystique*. New York: Norton.
Frye, R. M. 1955. "The Teachings of Classical Puritanism, on Conjugal Love." *Studies in the Renaissance* 2: 148–59.
Gilder, G. 1973. *Sexual Suicide*. New York: Pelican. Revised as *Men and Marriage* (New York: Pelican, 1986).
Gisborne, T. 1801. *Duties of the Female Sex*. London: Cadell and Davies.
Griffiths, N. 1976. *Penelope's Web: Some Perceptions in European and Canadian Society*. Toronto: Oxford University Press.
Guth, J. L.1983. "The New Christian Right." In *The New Christian Right: Mobilization and Legitimation*, ed. R. C. Liebman and R. Wuthnow. New York: Aldine. 31–45.
Hadden, J. 1983. "Televangelism and the Mobilization of a New Christian Right Family Policy." In *Families and Religion: Conflict and Change in Modern Society*, ed. W. D'Antonio and J. Aldous. Beverly Hills, CA: Sage. 247–66.
Hall, C. 1979. "The Early Formation of Victorian Domestic Ideology." In *Fit Work for Women*, ed. S. Burman. London: Croom Helm. 15–32.
Haller W., and M. Haller. 1942. "The Puritan Art of Love." *Huntington Library Quarterly* 5: 235–72.
Hamilton, R. 1978. *The Liberation of Women: A Study of Patriarchy and Capitalism*. London: Allen and Unwin.
Handford, E.R. 1972. *Me? Obey Him? The Obedient Wife and God 's Way of Happiness and Blessing in the Home*. Murfreesboro, TN: Sword of the Lord Publishers.
Hardesty, N., and L.S. Groh. 1984. "Starting from the Ground Up." *Daughters of Sarah* 10, no. 6 (November-December): 5–7.
Hartmann, H. 1976. "Capitalism, Patriarchy and Job Segregation by Sex." *Signs* I: 137–69.
———. 1981. "The Unhappy Marriage of Marxism and Feminism: Towards a More Progressive Union." In *Women and Revolution*, ed. L. Sargent. Montreal: Black Rose Books. 1–41.
Hunter, A. 1981. "In the Wings: New Right Ideology and Organization." *Radical America* 15, no. 1–2: 113–38.
Hunter, J.D. 1981. "Operationalizing Evangelicalism: A Review, Critique and Proposal." *Sociological Analysis* 42: 363–72.
———. 1983. *American Evangelicalism: Conservative Religion and the Quandary of Modernity*. New Brunswick, NJ: Rutgers University Press.
———. 1987. *Evangelicalism: The Coming Generation*. Chicago and London: University of Chicago Press.
Jewett, P.K. 1980. *The Ordination of Women*. Grand Rapids, MI: Eerdmans.
Johnston, B. 1986. *After the Honeymoon...* Burlington, ON: Welch.
LaHaye, T. 1968. *How To Be Happy Though Married.* Wheaton, IL: Tyndale House.
———. 1980. *The Battle for the Mind.* Old Tappan, NJ: Revell.
———. 1981. *The Battle for the Family*. Old Tappan, NJ: Revell.
LaHaye, T., and B. LaHaye. 1976. *The Act of Marriage*. Grand Rapids, MI: Zondervan Books.
Lasch, C. 1977. *Haven in a Heartless World.* New York: Basic Books.
Lechner, F.J. 1985. "Fundamentalism and Sociocultural Revitalization in America: A Sociological Interpretation." *Sociological Analysis* 46 (Fall): 243–59.
Liebman, R.C. 1983. "The Making of the New Christian Right." In *The New Christian Right: Mobilization and Legitimation*, eds. R. C. Liebman and R. Wuthnow. New York: Aldine. 227–38.
Light, B., and A. Prentice. 1980. *Pioneers and Gentlewomen of British North America 1713-1867.* Toronto: New Hogtown Press.
Luxton, M. 1980. *More Than a Labour of Love: Three Generations of Women's Work in the Home.* Toronto: The Women's Press.
Marty, M.E. 1984. "Fundamentalism as a Social Phenomenon." In *Evangelicalism and Modern America*, ed. G. Marsden. Grand Rapids, MI: Eerdmans. 56–68.
McNiven, C.R. 1987. "Social Policy and Some Aspects of the Neoconservative Ideology in British Columbia." In *The Canadian Welfare State: Evolution and Transition*, ed. J.S. Ismael. Edmonton: University of Alberta Press. 300–26.
Miles, J. 1975. *The Feminine Principle. A Woman's Discovery of the Key to Total Fulfillment.* Minneapolis, MN: Bethany Fellowship.

Mollenkott, V.R. 1977a. "Evangelicalism: A Feminist Perspective." *Union Seminary Quarterly Review* 32 (Winter): 95–103.

———. 1977b. *Women, Men, and the Bible*. Nashville: Abingdon.

More, H. 1799. *Strictures on the Modern System of Female Education*. London: Cadell and Davies.

Morgan, D. 1981. "Men, Masculinity, and the Process of Sociological Inquiry." In *Doing Feminist Research*, ed. H. Roberts. London: Routledge and Kegan Paul. 83–113.

Morgan, E.S. 1966. *The Puritan Family*. New York: Harper and Row.

Morgan, M. 1973. *The Total Woman*. Old Tappan, NJ: Revell; Markham, ON: Pocket Books, 1975.

———1976. *Total Joy*. New York: Berkley Medallion Books.

Pierard, R.V. 1984. "The New Religious Right in American Politics." In *Evangelicalism in Modern America*, ed. G. Marsden. Grand Rapids, MI: Eerdmans. 161–74.

Pohli, C.V. 1983. "Church Closets and Back Doors: A Feminist View of Moral Majority Women." *Feminist Studies* 9: 531–58.

Poloma, M. 1982. *The Charismatic Movement: Is There a New Pentecost?* Boston: Twayne.

Prentice, A., P. Bourne, G.C. Brandt, B. Light, W. Mitchinson, and N. Black, eds. 1988. *Canadian Women: A History*. Toronto: Harcourt Brace Jovanovich.

Riches, G. 1986. *Food Banks and the Welfare Crisis*. Ottawa: Canadian Council on Social Development.

Roberts, W., ed. 1834. *The Life and Correspondence of Mrs. Hannah More*. London: Seeley and Burnside.

Rose, S.D. 1987. "Women Warriors: The Negotiation of Gender in a Charismatic Community." *Sociological Analysis* 48: 245–58.

Rossi, A. 1974. *The Feminist Papers*. New York: Columbia University Press.

Ruether, R.R. 1973. "The Cult of True Womanhood." *Commonweal* (November): 127–32.

Ryrie, C. 1968. *The Place of Women in the Church*. 2d ed. Chicago: Moody Press.

Scanzoni, L. 1976. "The Great Chain of Being and the Chain of Command." *Reformed Journal* (October): 14–18.

———. 1984. "Biblical Feminism as a Social Movement." *Daughters of Sarah* 10, no. 6 (November-December): 18–20.

Sennett, R. 1980. *Authority*. New York: Vintage Books.

Simpson, J.H. 1983. "Moral Issues and Status Politics." In *The New Christian Right: Mobilization and Legitimation*, ed. R.C. Liebman and R. Wuthnow. New York: Aldine. 187–205.

Sklar, K.K. 1973. *Catharine Beecher: A Study in American Domesticity*. New York: Norton.

Sölle, D. 1984. *The Strength of the Weak*. Boston: Westminster.

Stahl, W. A. 1987. "The New Christian Right." *The Ecumenist* 25, no. 6 (September-October): 81–87.

Storrie, K. 1984. "New Yeast in the Dough: Jesus Transforms Authority." *Daughters of Sarah* 10, no. 1 (January–February): 6–10.

Swidler, L. 1979. *Biblical Affirmations of Women*. Philadelphia: Westminster Press.

Sydie, R. 1987. *Natural Women: Cultured Men. A Feminist Perspective on Sociological Theory*. Toronto: Methuen.

Tolson, A. 1977. *The Limits of Masculinity*. London: Tavistock.

Ulrich, L.T. 1976. "Vertuous Women Found: New England Ministerial Literature, 1668–1735." *American Quarterly* 28 (Spring): 20–40.

Wacker, G. 1984. "Searching for Normal Rockwell: Popular Evangelicalism in Contemporary America." In *The Evangelical Tradition in America*, ed. L.I. Sweet. Macon, GA: Mercer University Press.

Warnock, J.W. 1988. *Free Trade and the New Right Agenda*. Vancouver: New Star Books.

Weber, M. 1958. *The Spirit of Capitalism and the Protestant Ethic*. New York: Scribner's.

Welter, B. 1966. "The Cult of True Womanhood: 1820–1860." *American Quarterly* 18 (Summer): 151–74.

Westhues, K. 1978. "Stars and Stripes, the Maple Leaf and the Papal Coat of Arms." *Canadian Journal of Sociology* 3: 245–61.

Wilson, S.J. 1986. *Women. The Family and the Economy*. 2d ed. Toronto: McGraw-Hill Ryerson.

Wood, J.L. and M. Jackson, eds. 1982. *Social Movements: Development, Participation, and Dynamics*. Belmont. CA: Wadsworth.

CHAPTER 4

Family Problems and Problem Families

Leslie J. Miller

Learning Objectives

No society is equally accepting of all forms of family and household life. Even in tolerant times, the family is the focus of ongoing struggles to protect and support some styles of home life and child rearing, while stigmatizing others by defining them as social problems about which "something must be done." The family ideal that has predominated since the last century has been the nuclear, bourgeois patriarchal family; alternative domestic arrangements that diverge from the ideal type have been, and continue to be, discredited and controlled. The study of family problems is the study of the historical and political process whereby one community tries to impose its version of the good family upon other less-powerful communities; family forms designated as problems (for example, the "slum" family or the lesbian family) are the losers in the contest. Students are encouraged to investigate how this process works. Only by asking the question "problem for whom?" will the student be able to see why it is that relatively harmless forms of domestic life have been relentlessly attacked, while other blatant injustices, such as the abuse of women, have been perceived as unproblematic for so long.

Introduction

The idea that social problems are social constructs is no longer news, but the force of this insight continues to prod us into creatively questioning tacitly accepted realities around us. Two fields of scholarship—feminist studies and the sociology of deviance and social control—have located their critical edge precisely in the challenge they pose to taken-for-granted conceptions of how the world is and where its troubles reside. The goal of this chapter is to present a discussion of family problems that is responsive to the insights that have emerged from these fields of scholarship.

Social constructionists in the sociology of deviance define a social problem not as an objectively discoverable thing in the world, but rather as an interaction between two groups, one desiring to impose its definition of social reality on the other (Rubington and Weinberg 1981). Thus the "discovery" of a social problem—say, Quebec's declining birthrate—must be recognized as an expression of power. The labelling of some event as problematic or "deviant" becomes a deeply political act. This means that the study of social problems is the study of the process whereby one group in society sets out to *problematize* some activity—to discredit or stigmatize it—in the hope of mobilizing a campaign of intervention, formal or informal, against that activity. Stephen Pfohl has observed: "The outcome of the battle of deviance and social control is this. Winners obtain the privilege of organizing social life as they see fit. Losers are trapped within the vision of others" (1985, 3). Writing about the family, Berger and Berger remind us that the objects of deviant labels (Pfohl's "losers") may well fail to understand why their family life is supposed to be a problem about which "something must be done"—"slum" families in turn-of-the-century North American immigrant ghettos, for example, or "backward" farm families in the 1920s and 1930s, like that of Oliva Dionne, father of Ontario's famous "quints." For the Bergers, too, social problems are to be understood as social relationships. They write: "It is not enough to say that a problem has arisen; one must also ask whose problem it is. One person's taken-for-granted reality is another's problem" (1984, 8). As we shall see, this insight applies with special force to women, and feminist scholars have demonstrated persuasively that the taken-for-granted realities of family life in a patriarchal society are the urgent social problems of those victimized by that order.

In what follows, I shall argue that the family problems of this century and the last can be understood only against the backdrop of the emergent bourgeois family ideal, the patriarchal "cult of domesticity" that had the effect of sanctifying a single familial arrangement as the only proper or respectable one. This ethos or ideal, which began to develop in Northern Europe during the seventeenth century (Elias [1939] 1978), provided the standard against which all familial arrangements would come to be measured. In general, I shall be suggesting that the family problems (and the "problem families") of the nineteenth and much of the twentieth centuries, from the "slum" family to the "blended," homosexual, or communal one, are precisely those whose arrangements appear to diverge from the ideal.

In the first part of the chapter I outline the historical process that produced the modern ideal, as well as the picture of the "fit" family it implied, and review attempts to enforce the latter by regulating alternative or "unfit" forms. Though efforts to reform the "unfit" family have taken various guises over the last century and a half, the image of the "normal" family is still regularly invoked to justify the social control of a whole range of more-or-less discredited alternatives. Despite the variety of domestic arrangements that have proliferated since the Second World War, scholars in general agree with Barrett and McIntosh when they lament that the domestic ideal still captures "the family of desire and myth" (1982, 28). Indeed, the thrust of many a feminist critique of the family comes down to the demand that the labelling of such alternative arrangements as immoral, evil, or unhealthy be abandoned. But as scholars are coming to see, such core images in the culture cannot simply be argued away; they demonstrate a remarkable resilience, and their moral authority is enforced in a range of formal and informal mechanisms that make them extremely difficult to dislodge.

The second part of the chapter develops the insights of feminist scholars more directly. As I have just noted, one of the consequences of the rise of the domestic ideal was to focus attention upon families that failed to measure up. A second important consequence was the protective cloak of secrecy that enclosed modern family life. It is one of the ironies of social history that as the institution of the modern domestic family has risen to a central place in Western society around the figure of the wife/mother, whole areas within it—especially the contributions of women—have dropped from view. And as feminists have documented, the norm of privacy characteristic of the modern family obscured not only women's contributions, but also the inequalities and abuses they and their children suffered. The point I shall be emphasizing in this part is that these long-hidden aspects of family life represent forms of conduct that are now *in the process of being problematized*. Such family realities as the unrecognized and unpaid labour of housewives, the "normal" violence of routine family life, and the structural impoverishment of women are being targeted by various groups wanting to raise their visibility and thus society's recognition of them as urgent social problems. These campaigns propose to turn these practices, often seen as the "normal," scarcely noticeable features of the daily round, into occasions for intervention and social control. In this part I shall take up some of these not-yet-problematized or newly problematized aspects of family life, as well as the socio-cultural factors that have kept them beneath the threshold of attention for so long.

In the chapter's final section I note some of the contradictions and ambiguities associated with the demand for social intervention into family life. If the families that failed to measure up to the bourgeois ideal can be thought of as constituting the family problems of yesterday and today, then the inequities hidden by this same ideal are the problems of tomorrow. For feminists, the first set of problems has suffered from *too much* intervention; the second set, *too little*. Though not always consistent, feminists aim generally to shift the state's power, so that it may be used not to perpetuate the injustices of patriarchy but to redress them (Pupo 1988, 212, 219).

Problem Families Then and Now

The Rise of the "Cult of Domesticity"

For readers unfamiliar with the recent renaissance in the social history of the family, I sketch below the emergence of the ideal that has so powerfully influenced our thinking about the way our life in families goes (and ought to go) round. Social historians are agreed that over the eighteenth and nineteenth centuries in Northern Europe there arose in the burgeoning middle class not only a novel form of household organization,[1] but also a novel ethos of family life, a cult of domesticity that made the new form an object of veneration.[2] The most influential of these scholars, Philippe Ariès, describes the emergence of the modern family as "a revolution in sentiment." His ground-breaking book, *Centuries of Childhood* (1962), deals with the changes in family life from the late Middle Ages until the end of the nineteenth century and focusses mainly on France. Ariès claims that until the late 1700s the family existed as a political and public body, a lineage or "house," with little or no private character. Gradually there emerged toward the middle of the eighteenth century a recognizably modern form of family, termed "intimate" or "domestic." This newly domestic family is characterized as a little nest of natural sentiment forged as a bulwark against the impersonal public arena.[3]

In general, the vast body of data assembled by the early writers, including Ariès, documented a new anxiety over "public immorality"—rowdy public festivals and drunkenness, celebratory public torture and executions, and wandering bands of youths. It found, as well, a new sense of the vulnerability of the child, the spread of the "little school" and of discipline, and a changed conjugal relation marked by a new emphasis on the importance of sentiment, manners, and hygiene. The outcome was a clear distinction for the first time between public and private spheres of life. With the concern for the protection of the child from the rough-and-tumble of the street and a growing intimacy between spouses, the domestic family had seemingly emerged from a sea of brutality and had become an object of veneration.

The nature and progress of the "domestic revolution" is a topic of scholarly debate. For our purposes, however, it is sufficient to note that its rise parallels the rise of the modern state. And for the officials of the new state, the *premodern* family was "the problem"—an outmoded or "parasitic" institutional form whose members were thought to be making insufficient contribution to the welfare of the larger society. The result was a host of attempts to reform the family so as to organize this flotsam within the "productive" fold. From this perspective, the new ethos of domesticity appears as an ideological key to improving the "problem family" by making it both more visible and more productive of good and useful citizens (Donzelot 1979). The "parasitic" and what to do about it was a popular theme with revolutionary thinkers—notably Saint-Simon and Comte—at the end of the *ancien régime*. For some lively minds, the problem was not the family itself but the groups of individuals who dwelt on its fringes, and who, like those on the fringes of the economy, remained unharnessed to the state's goals: spinsters, for example, who usually wound up in nunneries, and hence represented a loss of reproductive power; or prostitutes, whose fertility represented a double loss to the state because they and their illegitimate offspring were considered outside the family proper, and hence beyond the reach of the state. Flamboyant proposals for highly regulated quasi families made their appearance. For example, in 1769 the French author Restif de la Bretonne proposed the "pornographe," a new institution that would exist alongside the family to catch such individuals for the state—prostitutes, spinsters, and children, all housed together in a sort of state nursery centred on modern ideas of child rearing for good citizenship (Donzelot 1979, 25).

Most of the state's reform policies were not intended to supplant or augment the family, but to improve it, and so were aimed at the family itself. Scholars like Donzelot interpret such reforms, and the ethos of domesticity itself, as stages in the state's ever-strengthening propensity to regulate family life. The baby bonus, for example, which began as a state payment to any mother willing to raise illegitimate children in her own family, is depicted as a mechanism whereby the state bought the right to scrutinize and evaluate the physical and moral hygiene of the bourgeois, and later the poor family, by measuring it against the standard of the new domestic ideal. (For a similar interpretation of mothers' allowances as an instrument of social control in early twentieth-century Canada, see Strong-Boag 1982, 173, 220 n.55.) I shall return again to the thesis of state "tyranny." Whether or not one accepts it in its entirety, however, the outcome of the emergence of the domestic ethos seems beyond dispute: the standard of bourgeois family life—at least in its idealized form—was invested with moral and legal weight, and imposed[4] upon the other strata of society.

Though the ethos of domesticity is of European origin, the force of its influence elsewhere—in the United Kingdom (Barrett and McIntosh 1982; Gittins 1986; Lewis 1986), in the United States (Demos 1970; Bremmer et al. 1970–74), and to a lesser extent in Canada (Nett 1981; Houston 1982; Strong-Boag 1982)—is well documented. In these societies, as in Europe, the increasing privilege accorded to the new ideal worked to produce a moral distinction between the "respectable" middle-class family seen to approximate the model most closely and the working-class family, which appeared to be unable to measure up. Such "deficient" families came to be defined as social problems—as threats to public order. In Europe the working-class family took the brunt of these reforms; in North America, immigrant and Native families became the favoured targets, especially when it came to the cruder forms of intervention (for example, the "apprehension" of children) from homes now deemed unfit.

Rearing the Vulnerable Child

What was it, in particular, that was deemed problematic about the "problem family"? A whole complex of new ideas about family life expressed in the new rhetoric of domesticity encompassed beliefs about the ideal "feminine" woman (passive, refined, and maternal), about the ideal conjugal relationship (intimate or compassionate), about the value of privacy as a necessary condition of the above, and about the place of the family in the larger milieu (a "haven in a heartless world"). And at its centre was the belief in the nature of childhood (innocent and vulnerable). In contrast to the premodern family, in which a large and diverse household encompassed servants, lodgers, and kin, and in which the community played a central role, the modern or domestic family is described as *child-centred*. For our purposes, child-centredness makes reference to the following two new ideas. First, in contrast to the medieval view that tended "to ignore childhood as a transitional period soon finished and of no importance" (Ariès 1962, 109-110), the early modern view regarded childhood as a distinct social category defined by innocence and vulnerability. This meant that the child and "society" must now be segregated, for the child is seen to be open to society's corrupting influences. Second, in contrast to the medieval view that assumed the child's unpliability, the early modern view regarded the child as malleable or teachable. This view is merely one aspect of a broader set of novel assumptions about the world, usually characterized as "rationality," which suggested that the world (and hence the child) is lawful, that individual action is efficacious, and hence that human beings "can affect the future by manipulating the environment and controlling themselves" (Morantz 1984, 352). While social historians usually stress the links between rationality and the rise of science, we are here interested in its effect upon the reorganization of perceptions of social reality around the concern for the child's welfare and upbringing. In this context, then, rationality produces a new outlook that sees the world for the first time as a *tutorial environment* for the child.

This modern view of the world produced an image of society as a vast potential curriculum, a set of social circles (home, street, school, and "society") that could now be assessed for the dangerous influences they represented to the innocent child. In contrast to the modern view, which decrees that the child should remain in the sanctuary of the home—and later, in the protected realm of the school under the eye of the teacher who would stand *in loco parentis*—the premodern view did not regard a child's exposure to the adult world as contamination. In this regard, it is instructive to note the opinion of one Maréchal de Caillière, who from his vantage point at the end of the *ancien régime* advocated the old view, declaring that the well-taught child must broaden her or his school learning with knowledge of "the real world" (as we would put it today)—knowledge to be found "in the Palaces, in the alcoves of ladies ... in the company of soldiers." Caillière recognized the growing popularity of the modern demand to keep the world and the child apart, but he rejected it. The world, he proclaimed, "is a great book" (quoted in Ariès 1962, 379). Views like Caillière's are the basis for Ariès's much-challenged claim that the premodern world failed to recognize childhood as an altogether different stage of life (Parr 1982, 8–9). Whatever the truth of his thesis, it is certainly the case that the modern age did indeed recognize such a separate stage, and moreover invested it with a new innocence. By the end of the nineteenth century, the child who had had the misfortune to read the "great book" of the world would be regarded as an impulsive degenerate, vagabond, or guttersnipe, whose failings would be clearly linked to the world's corruption, and not its enriching influence (Donzelot 1979, 131; Houston 1982).

The upshot of the new view of the child was a revision in expectations about parenthood, and its effect was to produce an evaluation of immigrant, Native and working-class families as quagmires of parental neglect rather than havens of care and responsibility. At the heart of the matter was the new demand that the "fit" parent carefully segregate the child from the street ("society")—that is, from the world of adults (meaning men) where bad influences were felt to lie. The child's proper sphere was to be the bourgeois home, now reformulated as a nursery of refinement and civility under the moral guardianship of the mother ("the angel of the hearth").[5] Here the mother's role was crucial: while her husband was engaged in the pursuit of a family wage, her responsibility was to clean up the home—to purge it not just of germs and dirt (see Ehrenreich and English 1979, Chapter 5), but of all traces of the crude and vulgar world at the doorstep. Maintaining the moral as well as the physical hygiene of the child's world required a constant vigilance against dangerous intrusions from the world of men and work. In the Victorian era such bad influences came in the person of the servant, from whose "dreaded promiscuity ... lewd talk and foolish remarks" the child must be protected (Ariès

1962, 379), and from the father, the "hairy brute" whose unrestrained sexuality and general lack of refinement must be carefully policed by the watchful mother. Thus much of the burden of good parenting fell to the mother, and one of her central responsibilities would be the patrolling of "the shame frontier" (Elias [1939] 1978).

Thus did the social rhetoric of domesticity map the world into separate spheres: the safe (purified) home, dominated by the child and the now infantilized mother, and the street, the unregulated realm of strangers, work, and war. The demand that these two spheres be kept apart, and that the child be kept on one side of the boundary (excepting carefully monitored excursions into "society"), is a relatively recent view of home and parenting. This approach has specific, traceable historical origins, and constitutes the most powerful criterion used by family reformers for identifying the unfit family and the negligent parent. Failure to meet this criterion, it was assumed, would produce an unruly child, a delinquent youth, and a criminal adult. The unfit family (in effect, the unfit mother) was thus labelled a social problem in its own right, but also because it was thought to spawn a host of other problems down the road. As Ehrenreich and English observe, the mother's "mission" was depicted as the moulding of the future society, and so the unfit mother would place that future in jeopardy.

I am proposing, then, that the roster of "urgent" family problems—the slum family of the late 1800s and early 1900s, the alternative family forms of recent decades (divorced and "blended," gay/lesbian, and lone-parent families), and the "problem" that spans the entire period, the employed mother—all have this in common: they are defined as inadequate tutorial environments for the child (in the specific sense outlined above). It is this judgement that will provide the rationale for state or informal intervention against them. Those families deemed to be reformable will be taught; the policing of others will be accomplished by different means, principally by denying them the status of "real" families. In the following section I take up the "problem" of such families, and the array of efforts mounted to "remedy" them.

Policing the "Unfit" Family

The "Degenerate" or "Slum" Family

Although groups of unsupervised youths are a feature of society in every era, it is important to realize that their designation as a social problem is relatively recent. Excerpts from the journals of Thomas Platter, a young man who wandered the European countryside in the 1500s living hand to mouth in the company of fellow students, reveal that such persons might be pitied or they might be despised (like Platter and his friends, who were evidently lumped with brigands and locked each night outside the city walls for the peace of mind of the good burghers), but they were not yet defined as *occasions for social intervention.* In a world viewed as ordained, such groups will be treated as if they were natural visitations, like floods and plagues; their revolts and disruptions convey neither social nor political significance.[6] As Stanley Cohen has rightly observed, "the very idea that a social problem is solvable needs an appropriate belief system" (1985, 197–98), and street youth as well as the families from which they came were not perceived as a problem in the modern sense until they were seen to be open to reform.

For the scholar of social problems, then, the concept of modernity must make reference to the watershed idea that the world (and people in it) are changeable. Early and sensational studies of "degenerate" families—here I am thinking specifically of Dugdale's study, *The Jukes: A Study in Crime, Pauperism and Heredity* (1877), which described a rural family "flawed" by rampant sloth, immorality, disease, and criminality—formulated their deviance as hereditary, and so associated treatment not with reform (for they were thought unteachable) but with efforts to control the spread of "inferior stock" (for example, by compulsory sterilization). But as I have already noted, the new view of the child includes the assumption of teachability, and so the family loses significance as a repository of bio-physical characteristics and takes on value as a learning, or tutorial, milieu.

Ehrenreich and English have remarked that the American home itself—even the middle-class home—was a topic of anxious discussion in the years of rapid immigration and industrialization between 1860 and the First World War, being portrayed as an anchor in a world of instability. Despite this, they agree that all critics reserved their greatest concern for the urban slum, where lay the greatest threat to the child, to the family, and hence to social order ("civilization") (1979, 170).

The middle-class definition of the slum family as an unfit child-rearing milieu focussed on the most visible aspect of the problem: the "idle youth" who were marginally employed as bootblacks and newsboys, or those who were neither at school nor at work and simply roamed the streets (some 55 percent of children between thirteen and sixteen years of age, according to Katz's study of Hamilton in the 1850s; see Katz, in Nett 1981, 252). Solutions to what would become "the problem of juvenile delinquency" included "surrogate institutions for the lower classes approximately analogous to middle-class family life" (Glazebrook, in Nett 1981, 252)—orphanages, training schools, and the like—programs that installed the child in a "better" home, and, later, attempts to teach the working-class mother modern methods of child rearing *in situ*. Programs of this sort began in the 1850s with the New York Children's Aid Society plan to send city children to upstate rural homes (Zelizer 1989, 381), where they were expected to grow into useful citizens. And in Canada, farm families in Ontario and the Maritimes—families that were enshrined in the ideology of the day as arcadian sanctuaries of all the old virtues—were the destination of children from the "slums" of Glasgow and other cities in Britain, where, it was assumed, poverty and moral squalor stood between the child and his or her birthright as a useful and upright citizen.

While the idea that the child must be nurtured in a protected milieu has remained fairly constant over the last century, the sense of what constitutes a threat to that innocence—and hence which styles of parenting will be designated as "unfit"—has continued to evolve. As Zelizer notes in her study of changing adoption practices since the late 1800s, the early programs of the "child savers" were directly predicated on the child's *economic* usefulness (1989, 381). This reminds us that work was not defined as a contaminant of childish innocence in the nineteenth century. But by the 1930s, parents who allowed or encouraged their children to work more than part-time were in danger of being labelled negligent, for school had become installed as "the dominant experience of growing up" (Gaffield 1982, 69).

Canadian scholars tell us that school was becoming an increasingly important net of good influence in the last half of the nineteenth century, especially for the middle-class child. But the working-class child still had to choose earning over learning (Coulter 1982, 156), and children's wages provided an important part of family income. The retention of work as a legitimate component of childhood and youth is a vestige of the premodern view of the world, and from this perspective the nineteenth century appears as a transitional period, incorporating both modern and premodern elements, for the child was depicted both as needful of protection and as economically useful. But as the fully modern image of childhood took hold, and the demand for youth labour decreased, good parenting increasingly came to imply the complete segregation of the child from the "adult" (male) world of paid labour.

It appears that the working-class family continued to be defined as "the problem" even as the conception of the problem shifted. In the earlier era, the unfit family is the one considered *incapable* of raising an economically useful child; Mas Juke, Dugdale says, was a bad father partly because he was himself "averse to steady toil." But less than half a century later, the problem family becomes the one that fails to impose *dependence* upon the child. By this point it is the "precocious" (i.e., employed) child who has become the sign of the problem family.

Zelizer's work shows clearly how the new emphasis on the dependent child worked to make the earlier array of alternative child-care solutions unacceptable: seeking a destitute child for its labour, or taking in a homeless baby for the sake of a cash bonus, equally transgressed the sentimental value of the child and rapidly became taboo. The result, Zelizer says, was a move by welfare workers to replace mercenary foster parenting of any kind with a new approach more suitable for the now "economically useless" child (1989, 382).

Other writers, Canadian and American, have stressed the institutionalized ways in which the criterion of child dependency was invoked to stigmatize and regulate working-class culture and the working-class family. In a study of "waifs and strays" in turn-of-the-century Toronto, Houston comments that "the very traits that came to single out certain youngsters as delinquent (precocity and independence of adult authority) precisely opposed the institutionalized dependency that was becoming characteristic of middle-class youth. By the end of the nineteenth century, a life-style—*a street culture*—had become the most common definition of 'juvenile delinquency' " (Houston 1982, 131).[7] And in an American study of the juvenile court system in the first two decades of this century, the author remarks that while court intervention into delinquency was formulated as benevolent rather than punitive (probation rather than confinement was stressed), the outcome for the working-class family was the same:

> The juvenile court functioned as a public arena where the dependent status of the children was verified and reinforced and where the incapabilities of lower-class immigrant parents were, in a certain sense, certified. *The juvenile court flunked parents just as the public school flunked children;* in both instances, the lower-class immigrant was the principal victim.
>
> (Schlossman, cited in Cohen 1985, 279; emphasis added)

The point at which the child is seen to overstep the boundary of innocence into the work-world of the adult is still an issue of moral and legal significance. As Zelizer concludes, the new value attached to the "useless" child has meant that "child work becomes acceptable only as part of an 'educational programme'" (1989, 382). The effect of the domestic revolution on the image of childhood is at the root of our uneasiness with the parent who "hires" the child to do household chores, for example, as well as our recent concern over the tendency of high school students to embark too wholeheartedly upon paid work. Indeed, the pressure to legitimate child work by defining it educationally—as a learning rather than an earning experience—leads some parents today to support differential pay rates for youth and adult labour. Other parents, however, deplore any legislation that would restrict the development of an entrepreneurial spirit in their children. Even this last view is not as "premodern" as it might first appear: the fact that the parent, not the child, is the one going to bat for the child's alleged interest reminds us that this view, too, is deeply predicated on the assumption of the child's innocence (unpreparedness to voice his or her own concerns).

Although the child's relation to work has played a highly visible role in the effort to regulate the "slum" or working-class family in this century, work (or failure to attend school) is only one of the many threats that were seen to endanger the vulnerable child. In general, families where the parents failed to observe the proper distinction between home life and street life, between the realm of the child and that of the (male) adult, were labelled as social problems (Miller 1990a). Any familial arrangement that embodied the old sociability—the mixing of young and old, the too-numerous children who stayed up too late and spilled off their porches into the city streets, and thus were exposed to the sights and sounds of adult talk and conduct (especially sexuality)—such a mixing of family and "world" increasingly symbolized danger to the tutorial spirit. In the homes of the poor, complained a settlement-house worker in 1900, "there is no meal hour and no bedtime, the children retiring late with the parents and eating where and when they please" (quoted in Ehrenreich and English 1979, 206). By appearing to invite too close a connection between the corrupting society and the priceless child, French Canadian, immigrant, and Native families were defined in professional and lay opinion as demoralized and unregulated. This feature, rather than their class background, their ethnicity, or their poverty per se, was the rationale that made social control campaigns against them credible.

Excursus: The Shifting Shape of Social Control

The social history of attempts to regulate family life is a complex and interesting topic in its own right, but there is space enough here only to touch on it briefly. There is good reason, however, for turning to it in the context of attempts to reshape the "slum" family along the lines dictated by bourgeois refinement. For this part of the story reveals as well as any that such attempts went forward on several fronts and in several very different guises. Through their diversity can be glimpsed their common goal: the enforcement of the ideal of bourgeois domesticity.

Prior to the rise of the modern state, the local community, including the local church, was the major agent of social control. When historians tell us that the family was embedded within the local community to a far greater extent than it is today, they mean in part that members of the community were involved in important family events—births, marriages, deaths—most of which we tend today to confine to "family and close friends." In the premodern world, the community participated in and in a sense validated these important turning points in people's lives, and so it is no surprise that the community, too, played a pivotal role in the control of family life.

Shorter's (1975) study of the modernizing family in Europe shows that gender-role violations—the husband who failed to control his wife, the man who did women's work—were the primary targets of regulation, and that collective responses to such transgressions were geared not to rectifying injustice, but to preserving the dominant social and moral order of the community. The mechanisms of social control were local and informal, and included noisy public demonstrations called "shivarees," which were designed to humiliate the transgressor into right conduct. Such intervention worked because a person's good reputation was of real material and moral consequence in a small world.

But the rise of the modern state signalled the weakening of community authority, and the social control of the family became increasingly standardized, formal, and remote. Elsewhere I have described the bifurcation of the institution of social control into two prongs: one, the shaping and enforcement of law; the other, the shaping and enforcement of manners and morality (Miller 1987). This is a gendered division of labour: as the first prong gains in prestige and is stamped as a man's domain, the second is sloughed off to woman and "her sphere." The androcentric bias of modernity tends to trivialize the second form, but both came to play a part in the regulation of the nineteenth- and twentieth-century "slum" family.

Early attempts to correct the "slum" family tended to take the form of direct and sometimes brutal programs for the physical removal of the child, as I have remarked already. But these programs had little contact with and knowledge of working-class life, and they gradually gave way to the effort to "improve" the working-class mother in her own home. Historical studies have documented the stream of school and health "visitors" who exerted subtler forms of pressure upon mothers in an effort to improve the cleanliness and order of their homes or to ensure their children's attendance at school. Unlike more heavy-handed efforts to change the working-class family, this was a women's movement. The visitors themselves were sometimes male professionals, but more often were well-to-do wives who saw the project of reforming the homes of the poor as a natural extension of their role as guardians of "manners and morals." Visitors were instructed to give advice and encouragement, but never money; their interventions were couched in the language of friendship (Ehrenreich and English 1979, 172).

Theorists have described the drift from direct repression to benevolent reform as the emergence of a characteristically modern form of domination (Foucault 1979; Lasch 1977; Ehrenreich and English 1979). The process is depicted as a joint effort in which the power of the state, as embodied in the new professionals of the twentieth century (psychologists, social workers, sociologists, and psychiatrists), forges an alliance with bourgeois mothers for the imposition of the middle-class ethos upon the working-class family. The new form of discipline is, according to this line of thinking, all the more powerful for its subtlety and benevolent rhetoric.

While some authors have noted that bourgeois women found in this alliance a springboard into positions of influence in the public sphere as leaders of reform and purity movements (for example, the Society for the Reformation of Juvenile Delinquents in the early 1800s, and the Prohibition movement of the early 1900s), they argue that the subtler powers of the moral guardians were exploited by male professionals, the better to soften up the working-class family. Even if the conspiratorial overtones in this account are rejected, it still remains the case that women's allegedly natural, feminine skills were the wedge that opened the working-class home to intervention.

The "slum" family can be seen as a kind of battleground for the whole range of social-control strategies employed since the rise of the modern state. Sometimes the target of direct attack, it became at the turn of the century the object of women's civilizing mission. By the 1920s, however, that project had come to look like amateurish and unscientific tinkering, and the "problem" of the "slum" family became in its entirety the property of the new (male) child-care professionals.

A poignant example of the "tyranny of the experts" can be found in the history of the famous Dionne quintuplets of Callander, Ontario. Elzire and Oliva Dionne had raised several other children, in rural, French-Catholic tradition, until the birth of their five daughters in 1934. Though poor and uneducated, M. Dionne had never failed to provide a family wage—the measure of a successful husband and father. But their "lifestyle" and parenting customs (calculated to rear useful rather than priceless or precious children) proved a scandal to the child-care professionals whose attention they drew.

In a study of the reconstruction of child care by professional expertise, aptly titled "Intruders in the Nursery," Strong-Boag notes the experts' dismay with the Dionnes' family environment:

> [The Dionnes] had met the requirements for exemplary parenthood according to their faith and culture: five living children, all nourished and housed without recourse to public assistance.... [But] their farmhouse, without indoor plumbing or electricity, and their time-honoured familial customs were hardly calculated to win the approval of the experts who flocked to attend Canada's greatest tourist attraction. A press largely sympathetic to the professionals helped mobilize sentiment against the seemingly backward, obstinate, greedy and irresponsible Dionne parents. (1982, 174)

The author goes on to describe the loss of traditional parental authority suffered by the Dionnes, who were defined as unfit parents soon after the birth of their five daughters. They surrendered the girls to the state, who were then taken to a hospital and raised there in an appropriately scientific environment under the supervision of Toronto psychologist Dr. William Blatz, then guru of the child-study movement.

For the Dionnes, the unique value of their very existence made them the target of an act of state intervention more brutal than was currently in vogue. For the voice of (male) professional child-care experts in general took the view that families should be kept together and that parenting practices should be improved through lessons, manuals of advice, indirect government subsidy, and visitors of various stripes, although the apprehension of children from "unfit" parents—especially Native families—has not even today been eradicated.

The tale of heavy-handed attempts to ensure the best upbringing for the quintuplets reminds us that efforts to enforce the ideal of bourgeois domesticity by influencing child-rearing practices have taken more than one form. Scholars have emphasized the shift from direct regulation to benevolent "improvement," and rightly so. More recently, however, they are coming to recognize the role of rhetoric as a form of social control. Finkelstein's (1985) analysis of nineteenth-century school reform movements shows nicely how the image of the street was exploited and manipulated by zealous reformers in order to persuade parents to confine their children to the ideal environments favoured by current theories. Such groups painted for parents a picture of street life (the workplace, streets and fields, and the informal sociability of strangers and other ethnic and class "undesirables") as a place of ignorance and crime, and played on the image of a street full of strangers and dangers in an effort to enforce the view that "an isolated domestic sphere ... an environment purged of worldly character" was the only fit milieu for children (Finkelstein 1985, 124).

Finkelstein wishes to emphasize that the manipulation of popular perception is a form of social control that is "hortatory and didactic, rather than systematic and coercive" (1985, 127). That is to say, parts of the social terrain can be discredited informally through persuasion (myth, legend, or rumour) as well as through direct attack (repressive programs and policies). Such campaigns differ in form but not in content from more concerted efforts at social control. Both are engaged in the same project—the enforcement of the domestic ideal—and hence both are deeply political.

The "Problem" of the Employed Mother

It should be clear by now that at the heart of the ethos of domesticity is the figure of the vulnerable child, together with the mother who is expected to make that child her first concern, even above herself. The increasing child-centredness of the family since the last century is reflected in the extent to which the claim of unfit parenting is invoked to justify the control of familial arrangements that differ from the bourgeois standard. A century ago some social observers were prepared to make war on the "slum" family directly and unapologetically because it appeared to them self-evidently degenerate or barbaric, and concern for the child was only one element in a more broadly based attack. Today, by contrast, the claim that a family is an unfit *child-care* environment is certainly the most important (one is almost tempted to say the only) rationale that will legitimate intervention in the family. From a social-control perspective, this means that the issue of child care increasingly becomes the *mechanism* through which the indirect regulation of "deviant" families has been carried out—the assumption being that direct intervention would be unacceptably discriminatory in a liberal or "tolerant" society. Nobody would object to working mothers, or even to lesbian ones (the argument goes)—after all, what people choose to do is their own business—unless the welfare of the child were threatened; and that is a different story. Some scholars argue, in fact, that a roster of claims about the nature and needs of the child, as set out in the cult of domesticity, is the cover for unjustified attacks upon legitimate and workable alternative familial arrangements. Read this way, the bourgeois concept of the child, and of the child-centred family, becomes the key to understanding several important "family problems" of this century.

Demographers and historians assure us that mothers have always worked in and around the household for the family economy, and often in the paid labour force as well. But the "problem" of working mothers—by which is meant the view that mothers who should be minding their children are instead out working—does not arise until the emergence of the ethos of domesticity, which decreed that the role of mother, of nurturer, should become the central mission in a woman's life. This made paid work a man's activity, permissible for women only as secondary "help" (for "luxuries" or "pin money") or in an emergency.

A number of writers have detailed the narrowing of the woman's role associated with the domestic revolution (Shorter 1975; Gittins 1986). Shorter's work reveals the array of jobs taken on by women in the premodern world—gardening, dairying, spinning and weaving, water and wood carrying, in addition to child care—and stresses that these were reduced to a single idealized core of mothering and emotional support as modernization proceeded. The twin aspects of the core role (practical care, and emotional and moral guardianship) quickly became lodged in the cultural stock of knowledge as the defining characteristics of a "womanly" nature (Dally 1982; Margolis 1984). Shortly after the domestic revolution, they were reformulated as "natural"—a clear sign of their cultural centrality—and invoked in order to rationalize the political division of social life, that is, to affirm the *rightness* of women's participation in the home, and their exclusion from the activities of the public sphere, notably "real" work, politics, and war.

The variety of attempts mounted by "experts" since the late nineteenth century to enjoin women to mother, especially by discouraging their efforts to encroach on the "proper" sphere of men, are described by Ehrenreich and English in *For Their Own Good*. They range from the threat of illness, to the promise of a new, socially useful evolutionary mission, to an attempt in the 1940s and 1950s to professionalize the "job" of mother in an effort to make its status the equal of the husband's. The perennial theme is the damage she would do if she "worked"—damage to *herself* (only a century ago women were warned that their reproductive organs would atrophy under the stress of "real" work, and that the home was the only medically safe focus for a woman's energies; see Ehrenreich and English 1979, 149), and to her *spouse* (whose emotional needs would go unfulfilled—or else he must satisfy them elsewhere). But all observers agreed that the greatest damage would be done to the *child*.

Despite the warnings of professional child care experts, the overwhelming fact is that mothers, especially those with small children, have been steadily drawn into the work force since the turn of the century. Female participation in the work force was a mere 16.1 percent in 1901 (Statistics Canada 1974, 113); by 1951 it had increased marginally to 24 percent. The biggest jump came between 1961 and 1981; in these two decades women's participation nearly doubled, from 29.5 to 51.8 percent (Armstrong and Armstrong 1988, 276). In their overview of Canadian women at work, Lupri and Mills conclude that

> the single most dramatic and pervasive trend in the status of Canadian women since World War 11 has been the increase in the proportion of married women who work for pay. The five-fold increase in the proportion of married women entering the labour force has been almost twice the increase for all women. But more important, the largest increase in labour force activity has occurred for the group viewed as least likely to work—mothers of preschool-age children. (1983, 44)

The trend described by these two researchers continues unabated: by 1984 the proportion of women in the labour force with children under three was 51.5 percent (Cooke 1986, 7–8). To be sure, professional concern has abated somewhat since its height in the fifties. Then, deprivation theories were in vogue, like Bowlby's, which argued that parental (i.e., maternal) rejection accounted for most cases of intractable juvenile delinquency (Pfohl 1985, 99). More recent reviews of the research (e.g., Etaugh 1974) fail to locate evidence of adverse effects of working mothers on their children's wellbeing. Nevertheless, the psychiatric profession continues to trace adult deviance to "the psychic scars of childhood," and such an approach routinely points to the mother behind the child (Pfohl 1985, 100). The working mother is *still* a focus of anxiety, as recent debates in connection with the push for more day-care funding show.

Histories like that of Ehrenreich and English would seem to suggest that the problematizing of the employed mother has been a fairly consistent project of the experts since industrialization. Other scholars have challenged this conclusion, however, noting that the problematic character of the working mother—the extent to which her paid work is regarded as a threat to her child—has in fact waxed and waned according to the demands of a capitalist economy. These scholars point out that "familistic" values weaken in times of labour shortage—in economic booms, especially in wartime, but also seasonally, for example, at Christmas—and then strengthen as the need for their labour declines (Armstrong and Armstrong 1988, 278). Thus it is suggested that wives, together with other low-paid, low-skilled groups in the society, make up a "reserve army" of labour, whose troops are called to the front when the need is essential and sent back into the home when that need abates. This means that the "problem" of the employed mother is an urgent one in some eras but not in others—and, more importantly, that the problem itself is an artifact of a system (the economy) *external* to the family. Not only does the "problematic" status of the working mother come and go—now you see a problem, now you don't—but its motor, so to speak, is located in the needs of capitalism, rather than the needs of the child. While all aspects of this argument are not persuasive, its thrust reminds us that the source of alleged family problems may well lie in structures beyond the family, and that the family, as a structure and as a social rhetoric, does not exist in isolation from other social institutions.

Employed Mothers: Whose Problem?

Even though recent evidence fails to support any link between the working mother and the damaged child, there is no question that the *rhetoric* surrounding the negligent employed mother continues to have a powerful effect. Some studies emphasize that the way we think about the family is really determined by larger structural factors (for example, by capitalism). These tend to depict family rhetoric as a myth or fiction foisted off on an unsuspecting and resistant population. Barrett and McIntosh, for example, refer to the ideal of the bourgeois family (including the view that mothers ought to be devoted single-mindedly to child care) as a ramshackle "house of cards," an edifice built by others and imposed upon women and children (1982, 79–80). This way of framing the issue locates the problem "out there"—in capitalism or in patriarchy—and implies that such "myths" are ones in whose maintenance women themselves have played no part.

But while it may be true that such ideologies *originate* with capitalism or with the experts, mounting evidence shows that they are reiterated and reproduced by women themselves. Recent research that focusses on the *meaning* women attach to what they do shows how they confront, and have confronted in the past, the tension between an economic reality that demands they work for pay, and a powerful rhetoric of domesticity that tells them that their place is in the home. The effect of this newer research is to shift the location of the problem from others to mothers; it shows how they make the problem their own, and struggle to bring a kind of solution to it.

The strategies women have used to resolve—that is, to live with—this tension are not new. Ayers and Lambertz, and Roberts, for example (both cited in Lewis 1986), describe the range of artful practices devised by working-class wives in turn-of-the-century Liverpool and in the north of England to manage the appearance of middle-class respectability (which called for a homebound wife), all the while bringing in a pay cheque to make ends meet. These strategies included suppressing the visibility of their own paid work—say, by taking a job in a remote neighbourhood—and normalizing other forms of paid work by conducting it within the household. Canadian studies reveal that the strategies were sometimes different, but the objective was the same: to provide the household with additional income while adhering to the bourgeois ethos. Bradbury's historical research on fragmented families in nineteenth-century Montreal suggests that the stigma attached to working mothers was so great that hard-pressed families turned to their children, rather than to the mother, for additional income (1982, 109). And when this strategy proved inadequate, working-class families chose to place their greatest drain (their youngest and least employable children) into orphanages until they became old enough to work. "Only seldom did a wife and mother work for wages," states Bradbury (109), and this usually followed on the death or serious illness of the main breadwinner, her husband. The point is not that women were ready to put their children out to work to spare themselves, but rather that of the two solutions to the problem of too little money—the child works, or the mother does—these women chose[8] the one conforming most closely with the demands of the domestic ethos (which, as we recall, did not yet stigmatize the labouring child).

Decades later—and their march into the work force notwithstanding—mothers continue to show considerable ambivalence about the appropriateness of their own paid work: they work, or plan to, and all the while insist that their proper place is at home, "at least while the children are young" (Gaskell 1988, 157). Gaskell reminds us that the unsureness she witnessed in the girls she interviewed in Vancouver is a reflection of the way Canadians as a whole react: on the one hand they endorse equal opportunities for women "overwhelmingly," but on the other they strongly believe in mother-centred patterns of child rearing (Gibbins et al., quoted in Gaskell 156).

This conflicting pair of demands, states the researcher, is the real problem girls must come to terms with. And if the solution in an earlier era was to hide the paid work one did, or to delegate it to someone defined as more acceptable by the rhetoric of domesticity, then the contemporary solution seems to be to define it as secondary work (that is, work that "helps out" the main breadwinner and provides "extras"), even though such work may well represent the largest financial contribution to the household (Brannen and Moss 1987; and see also McKee 1987). This discursive strategy allows women to work in the labour force at the same time that it allows them to define mothering as their *first* commitment (their primary or "real" work).[9]

The implications of these kinds of studies are important ones. By restoring some sense of agency to the actor (and by investigating the way actors construct their worlds as meaningful places) they restore to women an active role in their own life situations. But at the same time they make it clear that women actively collude in the reproduction of an ethos that subordinates them. The strategies documented in British and Canadian studies (also see Miller 1990b) indicate an unquestioned acceptance of the view that, whether the mother is employed or not, the care of children remains her responsibility.[10] Such strategies reiterate and reproduce the social rhetoric of domesticity (here, the ethos of mother-centred child care) in routine ways, and thus contribute substantially to its durability. In addition to material factors that enforce the domestic ideal—the gender-segregated work force and continued inadequate day-care funding (Gaskell 1988)—we must recognize the part that women's own sense-making strategies play in shoring up that ideal.

A New "Problem": The Lesbian Family

At the outset of this chapter I contended that those family forms that deviated from the domestic ideal would be labelled as problems and were likely to become targets of social-control campaigns. Perhaps the most obvious challenges to the bourgeois ideal of the nuclear, heterosexual, male-dominated family are the communal families of the 1960s and the alternative family forms of the 1970s and 1980s, including gay and lesbian families, and single women who have chosen to have and rear children without a live-in man. For those in the society who deem these arrangements a problem—a problem representing the "decline" or "decay" of the family—they are not alternative families but non-families, whose claims to "real" family status are entirely without legitimacy.

It is the opinion of some sociologists that such a hard-line commitment to a single family form has been gradually replaced over the decades since the 1950s with a genuine pluralism. Speaking about ethnic diversity, for example, Hareven contends that, until very recently, alternatives to the ideal of the private nuclear family were "misinterpreted as 'family disorganization' simply because they did not conform to the official stereotype"; now, however, diversity is "being valued as a source of strength and continuity." Even more radical alternatives, according to Hareven, are at least tolerated. if not actually valued:

> Much anxiety has [also] been expressed over the increase in the proportion of couples living together unmarried, over homosexual partners or parents, and over a whole variety of alternative family forms and life styles.... [These] have now become part of the official fiber of the society, because they are now being tolerated much more than in the past. In short, what we are witnessing is not a fragmentation of traditional family patterns, but rather, the emergence of a pluralism in family ways.
> (1989, 54–55)

Most feminists accept Hareven's construction of the issue, but reject her sunny conclusion. The official view, they would argue (especially the official Canadian view), continues to define alternatives to the ideal as deviant, and engages in direct and indirect policing of these numerous and often workable arrangements by denying them legal, economic, and social support.[11]

An examination of the state's treatment of one of these alternatives reveals a reality more complex, and more sociologically interesting, than either of the two positions taken above. I refer here to an interesting study of the five court cases specifically dealing with lesbian custody to appear in Canadian law reports prior to 1984 (Arnup 1988). This study showed that court decisions neither repressed nor tolerated lesbian families as such, but instead distinguished between "good" and "bad" lesbian families. Custody of children was awarded to those mothers who were prepared to support the ideal of (heterosexual) domesticity by maintaining a discreet public appearance and suppressing their involvement in lesbian proselytizing and political activities, but was denied to those who were deemed to be challenging the ideal by "flaunting" their lesbianism. The lifestyle of the latter, the judges argued, was found to have adverse effects on the welfare of the child.

Arnup's study has important implications for the question of the state's role in controlling at least this alternative family form. The first point concerns the form social control takes. Here we should note that the court avoids a direct attack on lesbians or lesbian mothers, preferring to use the child as the rhetorical mechanism of intervention. As in the case of employed mothers, the child becomes the crucial legitimate point of entry into the otherwise private doings of the family. The legal discrediting of the "bad" lesbian mothers takes indirect rather than direct form; that is, the court's decision is framed not as the repression of the lesbian parent per se (indeed, this argument is explicitly rejected) but in terms of a benevolent concern for the child's "best interests." This bears out Foucault's thesis about characteristically modern forms of power. Moreover, the protective stance seems only a cover for the indirect policing of "bad" lesbian families, as there is a total lack of judicial interest in assessing the negative effects of consigning a child to a family whose members are bound over, as it were, to live a lesbian social reality in private and to proclaim a heterosexual one in public.

A second point concerns the goal of the state's efforts. It is clear from Arnup's study that the state's concern is not with the existence of lesbian families per se, but with the appearances such families create, that is, with the way they orient themselves publicly with regard to the domestic standard or ideal. As Arnup observes, the determining factor in a judge's decision is not the mother's sexual orientation but rather what she "does" with it (1988, 249).[12] For our purposes, this means that the "problem" in a problem family does not lie in the domestic arrangement itself, but in the degree of public challenge it is seen to pose for the rhetoric of domesticity. Here the courts appear to be saying that what will jeopardize a child's "best interests" is not living in a lesbian family, but living in one that declares lesbian family life to be *good*. In short, it is family rhetoric, not family structure, that the state is interested in policing.

The claim that the state will repress all alternative family *forms* is thus misguided. Arnup's study suggests that the liberal state is more likely to tolerate the existence of many of these forms, so long as those involved agree to conduct themselves as reasonable facsimiles of the nuclear family (1988, 254). This strategy allows the state to preserve the appearance of tolerance while neutralizing rhetorical, public challenges to the heterosexual ideal. Researchers, for their part, must balance their focus on domestic structure with greater attention to the management of appearances, in particular to the social realities family members fashion for themselves and for public consumption.[13]

Problematizing the Hidden Injustices of "Normal" Family Life

Because of the challenges they appear to pose to the ideal of bourgeois domesticity, the problems discussed in the first part of this chapter have all been hot topics in their day. Each has had (or is currently having) its moment of glory as the putative cause of society's collapse or decline. In short, their high social visibility and their status as problems have been taken for granted by laypersons and professionals alike, who have focussed their energies on solutions.

The long view, however, reveals that social problems wax and wane, and that collective anxiety about any one may intensify or subside quite independently of any clear remedy. Scholars attuned to the historical aspect of the construction of social problems have attempted to capture it in the concept of the *career*. By inviting us to think of a problem as having a birth, a zenith, and a decline, such a formulation reminds us of the *process* of problematization, which any issue undergoes. As an issue of public concern, the problem of the "slum" family is, for the moment, in decline, the problem of homosexual families on the rise. "Working mothers" is a problem that makes a comeback whenever the subject of alternative child-care arrangements is reopened.

I turn now to categories that have only recently become visible, and whose status as social problems is far from secure. These are *in the process of being problematized* and, in contrast to the problems already discussed, are at the beginning of their careers. Perceived by many in the society as more-or-less normal—"no big deal"—they are the focus of anxious concern to others, who cry, "Look at that! Here is a problem that *must* be redressed." The two nascent social problems I consider here are domestic violence and the "feminization of poverty." Both issues are the object of determined efforts by women's groups and others, who propose to heighten their visibility in the hope of achieving a remedy. Part of the problem then, for these groups, is that issues like these are not yet seen as problem *enough*.

The invisibility of women's poverty and abuse is part of the more general invisibility of the bourgeois family itself. Social historians have shown that an important consequence of the separation of social life into private and public spheres is the shift in responsibility for social control over the family from the local community to the newly emerging state. As the public and informal policing of deviant family conduct (through customs such as the shivaree) gives over to the formal (legal) regulation of the state, family life itself is subjected to a *lower* degree of overall scrutiny. "Everywhere the shivaree helped maintain order in individual families," declares Shorter; its demise—the demise of community authority as a whole—signals an absolute decrease in control over family life. At the same time, the modern family becomes more autonomous from the community, and the desire to keep the latter at bay is enshrined as a right: the right of privacy. For the first time, what goes on in the family is regarded as "one's own business," and neighbours who intervene in one's "private" family life will no longer be seen as fulfilling a common obligation, but will be regarded as nosy busybodies whose "meddling" can now be legally curtailed. As Laslett (1973) has remarked, privacy permits variability in conduct, for better or worse; it gives some cover for our harmless eccentricities, but it also permits excesses of patriarchal authority to go unseen.

Only over the last two decades have feminist scholars come to recognize the degree to which the dynamics of family life are *terra incognita*. Intimately familiar to all, but containing experiences too private or too mundane to be made the topic of deliberate study, the black box of the household has only recently been opened (Brannen and Wilson 1987,1). The problems that have been exposed all have their root in the gendered inequities of power embedded in the patriarchally organized domestic family.

The Feminization of Poverty

The feminization of poverty—meaning that women face a higher risk of poverty than men, and comprise a growing percentage of the poor—is a "significant long-term trend" (Battle 1988, 117). Figures for 1986 showed that lone women in Canada are more likely to be poor than are lone men (38.5 percent versus 29.2 percent), and that families headed by women are more likely to be poor than are those headed by men (40 percent, versus 10 percent). There are many more women-led, single-parent families and this situation has become steadily more common: the number of poor women-led families tripled between 1961 and 1986 (Battle 1988, 2). Moreover, the overall reduction in poverty among the lone elderly in the 1980s continued to favour older men, who remain less likely to be poor than are older women (31.9 percent for men over 65, versus 46.1 percent for women; see Battle 1988, 115).

Why are women still more likely to be poor? As one might expect, the chance that *any* person will be poor is directly linked to that person's attachment to the labour force. Women who remained housewives all their adult years were disadvantaged materially by their total economic dependence on a husband whose support might suddenly disappear through divorce, desertion, or death, or who might fail to provide for them in pensions or wills.

The lot of the employed woman is not vastly different. All evidence points to the fact that while women's entry into the work force is unprecedented, the jobs for which they are hired continue to be, in overall terms, the worst: they offer the lowest pay and the fewest benefits. Feminist scholars have noted that women's paid work is a kind of extension of the jobs they do at home: cooking, tending and cleaning, paperwork of various kinds; in short, the care and feeding of the social rather than the private household. Viewed historically, the picture is not much better; as particular skills or occupations become "feminized"—the job of secretary, for example, formerly male—their wages fall and they lose prestige (Lipman-Blumen 1984, 39). In sum, ever greater numbers of women are in paid work, and a small percentage have considerable economic security, but the gendered segregation of the labour force, and the profile of women's participation in it (often marked by frequent "times out" for child rearing) means that women continue to be poorer, as workers and retirees, than men.

As policy-makers who advocate "rational" economic solutions to the problem of poor women discover, cultural assumptions about the nature of femininity play a crucial role in both the causes of women's poverty as well as the failure to problematize it (to transform it into an urgent social problem). In this connection I would argue that women's poverty is seen as an extension of the normal role of dependence, as this is laid out according to the ethos of domesticity. If dependence on a husband is seen to be women's "normal" state, then the dependence of a single mother on the state will not "stick out" as a problem. As Schur (1984) has observed, certain forms of deviance are commonsensically regarded as more appropriate for women than for men; being poor is one of these.

This assumption is compounded by the general devaluation of all the activities in the domestic sphere since the domestic revolution. The ideal of the home as a sanctuary has meant that "work" was reassigned to the public sphere, and hence mothering and child care were denied the status of "real" (i.e., paid) work. The dualism imposed by the radical separation of public and private spheres can be seen in the conviction that what women properly do in the home is the opposite of what goes on outside it. Rational arguments mounted by feminists in support of wages for housework continue to fail in the face of the resilient cultural assumption that "home" is precisely the spot where work is absent.

Employed women who work the "double day" suffer the disadvantages of the invisibility of home and housework, but the heaviest burden of poverty falls to the women who never entered the labour force at all. These women are disadvantaged by a second, but related assumption defining women as having "no head for figures." Accepted by wives and husbands alike to a considerable degree (the math phobia of female high school students is the contemporary equivalent), some wives have no knowledge or understanding of their husband's financial situation until his death.

Wills themselves are a clue to the embeddedness of cultural assumptions about women as "properly" or "naturally" dependent. In her historical study of bequests to women in turn-of-the-century Ontario, Cohen discovered that the vast majority of fathers with assets (mainly land and livestock) left only a tiny portion of those assets (an animal, some furniture) to their daughters, despite the life-long labour they contributed to the family economy (1988). These fathers stipulated, or simply assumed, that a woman's grown brothers, or her spouse, would see to her keep. And as recently as 1979, some 90 percent of Canadian married working men having survivor-benefit options in their pension plans chose *not* to take up these options for their wives (Novak 1985, 151).

Here we see some of the ways in which cultural assumptions deriving from the ethos of domesticity legitimate the impoverishment of women. The problem of women's poverty is at root the problem of the resilience of the ethos of domesticity, especially as it applies to the role of women. What releases *new* or novel support or resources? That was the question asked by McKee in a study of the flow of resources between households in times of unemployment (1987, 96–116). The most significant finding was that exchanges of resources are "infused by assumptions about who has proper responsibility for maintenance of the nuclear family," and these assumptions, not need, determine the nature of the exchange. She states:

> It would seem that the transfer of assistance between households is influenced by much more than either actual resources or actual need. The best endowed are not necessarily the natural "givers" nor are the most deprived necessarily the natural receivers.... [*Need*] *is unlikely by itself to produce entirely new or uncharacteristic patterns of assistance.*
>
> (1987, 104; emphasis added)

What does this bode for the problem of poor women? Unless the state is free of the cultural assumptions characteristic of the society around it—and there is every reason to reject this possibility—then its perception of poor women's needs, and hence of a problem to be rectified as well as the resources that can be mobilized to offset it, will continue to flow through channels carved out by the cultural assumptions of the bourgeois family. In blunt terms this means that "society" (and this includes impoverished women themselves) will continue to ascribe primary financial responsibility for the woman to "her" man. Structural changes in the labour force or in pension legislation will alleviate this situation marginally, but in the final analysis it must be dealt with in a way that challenges, not reiterates, the old cultural assumptions.

The Problem of Family Violence

Domestic violence is sometimes "woman-to-man" (Lupri 1990a), but more often women and children are men's victims. Although it has addressed the problems of definition and perception to a degree, the scholarly literature on this subject has focussed largely on the matter of cause (or predisposing factors). Several early studies (Gelles 1979; Straus et al. 1980) revealed the degree to which violent conduct between members was a routine occurrence. They documented the existence of a gap between the image of the bourgeois family as a nest of harmony and safety, and the reality of family life, which proved to be awash in the punches, slaps, bites, and kicks of "routine" as well as severe violence (shootings, knifings, burnings). Only recently, Lupri's national survey of spousal violence in Canada reported a roughly similar picture:[14] members of six out of every hundred couples admitted to having slapped their partners within the past year, and 2.5 percent of the men, as well as 6.2 percent of the women, had beaten up their spouses. In addition, one person in every two hundred couples had taken a knife or gun to his or her partner, according to individuals' own reports (1990b, 8).[15] Nor were these incidents one-time occurrences (1990b, 9–10). A recent Canadian survey indicates that 29 percent of women have experienced violence at the hands of their current or previous marital partner (Statistics Canada, 1993).

The Canadian study makes it clear that no group in the society is entirely free of violent family behaviour. Nevertheless, low income, unemployment, part-time employment, and incomplete university education, all appear to increase the chances of interspousal violence, and are all formulated by the author as stress-producing events (Lupri 1990b, 18–19).

As many texts on the family now point out, the topic of family violence was virtually ignored until the 1970s. Now so widely discussed and studied that it has become a vulgar cliché in the popular media, its high visibility would suggest that it is regarded as a more pressing social problem than, say, the impoverishment of women. Indeed, scholarly reports tend to give the impression that even if violent family *conduct* has not abated, then at least the *myth* of the harmonious family has been successfully debunked. Confronted by vast quantities of data, one would think that individuals have at last come to recognize the reality of the family for what it is: a violent place.

But this conclusion is unfounded. Though sociologists of the family warn that parental homicide is the most common killer of children, parents continue to fear the maniac in the schoolyard and the Halloween sadist (Best and Horiuchi 1985), and "streetproof" their children in defence against the largely ephemeral threat of the violent stranger. While the ChildFind organization assures us that fully 95 percent of child disappearances are at the hands of family members, we continue to fear the child stealer in the park. Although studies report that women are more likely to be attacked by people they know than by people they don't, front door peepholes (to let you know "who it is" before opening up) are still standard equipment for self-protection. And high school students, young men and women alike, continue to believe that they are most likely to be raped by a stranger, despite the efforts of the staff of organizations such as the Calgary Sexual Assault Centre to convince them that 90 percent of the time "rapes are committed by family members or dates" (Cooney 1986, B1). These beliefs and products all rest on one assumption, and it is a keystone of the ethos of bourgeois domesticity: the stranger is danger, but the familiar is safe.

What are we to make of such findings? The problem of the violent family is by no means a self-evident one for social scientists; even less is it so for ordinary members of society. The few studies that attempt to address the problem of *meaning* in violent families—how members involved in violent events interpret their own activities—suggest that violent conduct is defined in ways that reiterate, rather than debunk the dominant imagery of family harmony.

How do actors accomplish such definitions? The literature on family violence generally distinguishes between "normal" and "deviant" violent acts; Denzin, for example, differentiates violence that is "intentional, believed in, authentic, doubted neither by the person nor by the family associates," from that which is "paradoxical, spurious, accidental, pretended or playful" (1984), a scheme that emphasizes intent, as does Gil (1970), who in addition emphasizes severity. Most researchers, however, now recognize that "there is no objective behaviour which can automatically be recognized as ... abuse" (Gelles 1977) and so the distinction between normal and deviant violence is treated as a matter of communal definition.

Elsewhere I have described in detail the discursive techniques or strategies that allow family members to integrate successfully both types of violent events into the image of harmony, in a way that manages the apparent contradiction between harmonious ideal and rough reality (Miller 1990b). With respect to "normal" or routine deviance, the rhetoric of the domestic family provides terms such as "discipline" and "roughhousing," which are invoked by family members to normalize—that is, to redefine as acceptable—some potentially problematic act. Fights between siblings, for example, are reinterpreted as culturally acceptable roughhousing; wife-slapping may be normalized as an act of quasi-parental concern ("It's like when your kids do something wrong—you have to do something; you do it because you love them": National Film Board of Canada 1979). Such terms function as discursive shock troops to cushion and absorb events that threaten the rhetoric of harmony, knitting these discrepant aspects of family life into an apparently unproblematic whole.

If "normal" violence is redefined as an extension of culturally acceptable conduct ("roughhousing" and the like), what about "real" or "deviant" violence, that is, conduct clearly identified by members as transgressions of the image of harmony? How do perpetrators and victims of stabbings and brutal beatings make sense of what has occurred? I have argued (1990b) that when they are unable to stretch the rhetoric of family to cover a violent act, they may make it understandable by symbolically withdrawing family status from the perpetrator, and reassigning the event to the street and the stranger, that is, to the culturally appropriate site of danger according to the ethos of bourgeois domesticity. Thus, accounts of severe family violence are filled with comments that redefine the intimate as "strange" or "other": "This wasn't the man I married!", "I just don't recognize her when she's like that," and so forth. By discursively reassigning the violent act(or) to a sphere (the street) and a category of others (strangers/non-family) that, since the emergence of the domestic family, has been the culturally appropriate site of violence, the violent act is remade in understandable form.

It is important to remember that these strategies are not dreamed up by the perpetrators of violent acts, nor by the victims. Instead, they rely on standard cultural assumptions or scripts provided by the patriarchal rhetoric of the bourgeois domestic family. Thus, the rationalization of the wife-beater ("It's because you love them.") only makes sense in a culture that has endowed women with the weak and vulnerable nature of a dependant (thus, too, the culturally sanctioned analogy between a wife and a child, and the possibility of redefining wife-beating as the responsible intervention of a concerned parent). Like the image of the harmonious home itself, this image of women is, as we have seen, a historically specific construction, one that is a part of the larger nexus of beliefs I have referred to as "the ethos of domesticity." And the strategy of reassigning extreme violence out of the family works only because certain self-evident beliefs associating danger with strangers are ready at hand to invoke.

These considerations mean that a violent event is not merely an interaction between a victim and a perpetrator, but a more complex collaboration between these two and one or more social rhetorics on which they draw to make sense of the interaction. They reveal both the strength of our continued loyalty to the image of family harmony, as well as the creative ways we rely on commonsense knowledge to bolster it. Instead of giving the lie to the rhetoric of family harmony, strategies like the ones mentioned here end up reiterating it. The study of such practices takes us to the heart of the contradictions and enigmas surrounding family violence.

Social Control

These kinds of findings help to show why it is that family violence is so persistently regarded as a rare or a pathological phenomenon (Lupri 1990, 2), despite the evidence. For by reassigning severe or "deviant" violence to "others," we evade the recognition that our intimates can also do us harm. Our culturally structured inability to accept the deeply dialectical nature of intimate relationships (Lupri 1990b, 29) has important implications for the visibility, and hence for the social control, of family violence. Despite attempts to demonstrate "scientifically" that violence is distributed throughout the ambit of human experience, the violent person who is also an intimate is not yet a culturally credible category of deviant. We have no such trouble with the idea of a dangerous stranger, for strangers remain members of a systematically devalued category (Schur 1984). We feel we can justifiably act against the intruding axe-murderer, the pervert at the schoolyard gate, the con artist; but to act against an assailant who is also our spouse, parent, or child calls up in us deep feelings of ambivalence. Only by *externalizing* the discrepant aspect of our intimate relationships as other, strange, perverse, or not quite of us, are we able to deal unambivalently with domestic violence—to make it the object of some policy of social control. This is the legacy of the rhetoric of family harmony.

The tendency to "medicalize" family violence by attributing it to physical or mental illness worsens the problem. Quite apart from its lack of empirical support, this approach blinds us to the cultural roots of the way we understand the family and violence within it. By denying that normal (healthy) family members may *also* be violent and dangerous—without taking leave of their senses—this rationalization reaffirms the rhetoric that normal families are harmonious and violent ones aberrations.[16]

Thus the immediate problem of violent conduct and what to do about it gives way to the deeper problem: the persistence of the myth of family harmony. If not more painful, this problem is more insidious, because the long-term effect of the sense-making techniques I have described here, both lay and professional, is to shift problems out of the family onto others. It is through these kinds of mechanisms that the "invisibility" of family violence is sustained.

Conclusions

The increased attention paid to social control and its historical evolution, especially since the publication of Foucault's *Discipline and Punish* (1979), has led to a re-evaluation of the linkage between family and state. Much of this literature reflects a growing distaste with what are perceived as the ever subtler and more insidious attempts by state agencies, especially by the "psy" professionals, to "besiege" the family in the name of solving its problems. Some of these writers (e.g., Lasch 1977) note the contradiction embedded in ever stronger efforts to shore up the family by expanding the state's role in it—in short, by undermining, it still further as a source of autonomy. For these observers, the direction of state intervention is not the problem: the problem is intervention *itself*.

But the feminist scholarship of the 1970s and 1980s has revealed the difficulty in adopting a position uniformly for or against state intervention in the family. To be sure, feminist scholars have come to recognize the various ways in which the state's attempts to suppress or improve "problem" families has gone against women's own interests. As I have argued, state enforcement of the domestic family ideal has sometimes meant the direct or indirect repression of other evidently workable domestic arrangements, including those that women have worked out to make their lives easier (for example, the mother who puts herself or her child into the work force to make ends meet). Furthermore, historians have documented how a whole array of local institutions tying women in with their neighbours and kinsfolk were slowly eroded as they ran afoul of the domestic ideal, which advocated women's dependence on their husbands alone, and encouraged a relatively isolated family existence (Gittins 1986). And from the nineteenth century to the present, the gradual replacement of local forms of skill and knowledge by state-regulated professional expertise (for instance, the supplanting of midwifery by professional medicine or working-class methods of child rearing by "scientific" ones) has further depleted the authority of family members and of women in particular (Ehrenreich and English 1979; Donzelot 1979). In all of these instances, the very *solutions* that women have evolved to solve their family *problems* are themselves regarded as problems by the state. For these reasons and others, feminists stand alongside non-feminist conservative scholars in their opposition to further intervention in the family.

On the other hand, feminists have come to see that women now and in the past have welcomed, even actively sought, the intervention of state agencies into their home lives. The first family scholars to open the black box of the household shed light on the taken-for-granted worlds of childhood, marriage, mothering, and the family economy, and immediately confronted "invisible" inequities between husbands and wives (such as wife-abuse) that the state was soon pressured to recognize, then to redress. In sum, while the state has worsened—if not actually created—some family problems, it is regularly asked to remedy others.

The question is often raised of whether the state, given its subservience to the interests of capital and hence its patriarchal bias, can ever be expected to act *against* those interests by taking the side of women in the family.[17] But recent studies have begun to rethink the view that the state is a monolith implacably opposed to the interests of women. Some of these studies show how bourgeois women have used alliances with the state to their collective political advantage. Others show how working-class women sought help from state agencies in matters of child rearing, or in order to escape domestic violence, and upon becoming clients, aggressively attempted to influence agency policy, sometimes successfully (Gordon 1989). And a third group of studies, those that focus on the sense-making strategies of women living their lives in the interstices of a dominant patriarchal order (e.g., Brannen and Wilson 1987; Gaskell 1988; Smith 1987), suggest that the state cannot be adequately conceptualized as an external force controlling the lives of its passive victims.

In sum, all of these studies point to a more complex view of the relationships between family, women, and the state than was previously assumed. Instead of debating whether state intervention into family life is good or bad, family theorists have begun to reconceptualize the state as an environment within which family members are seen to be the agents of their own lives.

Study Questions

1. Make a list of the family problems you see mentioned in today's newspaper (not forgetting letters to the editor). Which interest groups are promoting the visibility of these issues? What techniques are they using to accomplish this? What obstacles stand in their way?

2. Compare your own family to the bourgeois domestic ideal. If you live in an "alternative" family, assess the social forces, if any, that pressure the members of your family to conform to the ideal. Consider both formal and informal mechanisms of social control in your answer. What strategies does your family employ to cope with these pressures?

3. Ask your grandparents to recall the urgent family problems of their day. How are they different from today's? Do they see these problems as having been "solved"? In their view, what measures must be (or have been) taken to reach a solution?

4. Assemble a list of the entire range of behaviours your own family members would classify as "family violence." Would the very same behaviours be seen in the same light if they occurred between strangers? What might account for such a difference?

Recommended Reading

Donzelot, Jacques. *The Policing of Families.* New York: Oxford University Press, 1979.

Ehrenreich, Barbara, and Dierdre English. *For Their Own Good: 150 Years of the Experts' Advice to Women.* Garden City, NY: Anchor Press/Doubleday, 1979.

Gordon, Linda. *Heroes of Their Own Lives.* New York: Viking Penguin, 1988.

Zelizer, Viviana A. *Pricing the Priceless Child: The Changing Social Value of Children.* New York: Basic Books, 1985.

Notes

1. Scholars have generally rejected the once widely held view that associated modernization with a shift from extended to nuclear households. Contemporary studies now suggest that while the premodern household was never filled with kin, it did include an assortment of *others* we would now define as strangers (lodgers, apprentices, clients, and servants). The presence of these others signifies the sociability of the premodern family and its embeddedness in the local community, and this is the point contemporary scholars wish to emphasize. For a summary of this issue, see Hareven (1989, 41–42).
2. This statement is accurate so long as it is restricted to those historians who make an important place in their theoretical approaches for commonsense belief. For a brief introduction to other schools of thought on the origins of the modern family, see Anderson (1980). In this essay I am mainly concerned with what Anderson calls the "sentiments school," whose most influential figure is Ariès.
3. Though some of Ariès's claims have been severely criticized (in particular his famous thesis that childhood was not recognized as a distinctive phase of social life in the premodern world), his overall account of the emergence of a split between public and private spheres of social life and the new tenor of sentimentality that came to characterize the latter continue to be accepted.
4. More recent sociological studies tend to reject the idea that such standards are foisted upon a passive working class. These later studies illuminate the ways actors actively construct their worlds so as to reproduce or resist dominant social orders. I return to this issue later in this essay.
5. The North American suburb of the 1950s—a thoroughly feminized world—is a vivid expression of this view.
6. For example, the historian Barbara Tuchman has noted that the uprising of English peasantry led by Wat Tyler in the late 1300s was associated with an earthquake and the "pestilens" in the popular verse of the day, which concluded that all these events "beeth tokens of grete vengaunce and wrake / that schulde falle for synnes sake" (quoted in Tuchman 1979, 378).
7. For an account of the remapping of social reality around the spheres of safe home and dangerous street, and the discrediting of the latter, see Miller (1990a).
8. I use the word *chose* advisedly in this context, for the choices open to women are both limited and channelled by the cultural context.
9. It appears that the relatively recent emergence of the concept of "quality time" performs the same function for women in the work force; that is, it manages or eases this dilemma by diminishing the significance of time spent away from young children and exaggerating the smaller portion of time spent at home,
10. In direct parallel to the rhetoric of women's secondary paid work, men define themselves as "helping out" in the work of the household.
11. For an excellent account of the difficulties lesbian parents encounter in their efforts to gain social recognition as a family, as they deal with neighbours, educators, and others, see Nelson (1992).
12. American president Bill Clinton appears to have arrived at just this sort of solution to the "problem" of homosexuals in the military: "Don't ask; don't tell."

13. Arnup's paper clearly demonstrates the greater political acceptability of some constructions or interpretations of family life over others. For a discussion of the way linguistic realities and metaphors structure our understanding of birth contracts (surrogate motherhood), see Vandelac (1988).
14. One of Lupri's most surprising findings was the high incidence and severity of woman-to-man violence. See his discussion of the problems of interpretation posed by such data (1990b, 8–9).
15. Since these acts were self-reported, it is likely that the actual incidence of spousal violence is even higher.
16. See, in this connection, Pfohl's discussion of the way in which the social-work profession defined its "problem" in the period 1930–50. He states: "Social work has identified its professional advance with the adoption of a psychoanalytic model of casework.... This perspective, rather than generating a concern with political inequities internal to the family, *focussed instead on psychic disturbances internal to its members*" (1984, 107; emphasis added). Rather than challenging the rhetoric of the safe and harmonious family, the model of social work Pfohl refers to trades off the commonsense notion that domestic problems (including violence) result when the stranger moves in to corrupt the happy home by taking over the mind of the family members. This supports the contention that abuse from intimates is understandable only when it can be reformulated as stemming from the "stranger within." Also relevant to the present discussion is Menzies's (1985) paper, which demonstrates in a variety of ways the power of the cultural imperative (my term, not his) linking violent behaviour with insanity (the stranger within) in the public mind, despite the plethora of studies tending to disprove this link.
17. For a summary of this issue, see Pupo (1988).

References

Anderson, M. 1980. *Approaches to the History of the Western Family, 1500–1914*. London: Macmillan.

Ariès, P. 1962. *Centuries of Childhood: A Social History of Family Life*. New York: Alfred A. Knopf.

Armstrong P., and H. Armstrong. 1988. "Women's Work in the Labour Force." In *Gender and Society*, ed. A.T. McLaren. Toronto: Copp Clark Pitman.

Arnup, K. 1988. "Lesbian Mothers and Child Custody." In *Gender and Society*, ed. A.T. McLaren. Toronto: Copp Clark Pitman.

Barrett, M., and M. McIntosh. 1982. *The Anti-Social Family*. London: Verso.

Battle, K. 1988. *Poverty Profile 1988: A Report by the National Council of Welfare*. Ottawa: Minister of Supply and Services.

Berger, P.L., and B. Berger. 1984. *The War Over the Family: Capturing the Middle Ground*. Garden City, NY: Anchor Press/Doubleday.

Best, J., and G.T. Horiuchi. 1985. "The Razor Blade in the Apple: The Social Construction of Urban Legends." *Social Problems* 32: 488–99.

Bradbury, B. 1982. "The Fragmented Family: Family Strategies in the Face of Death, Illness, and Poverty, Montreal, 1860–1885." In Parr, *Childhood and Family*. 109–28.

Brannen, J., and P. Moss. 1987. "Dual Earner Households: Women's Financial Contributions after the Birth of the First Child." In Brannen and Wilson, *Give and Take*. 75–95.

Brannen, J., and G. Wilson. 1987. Introduction *Give and Take in Families: Studies in Resource Distribution* by Brannen and Wilson. London: George Allen and Unwin.

Bremmer, R.H., J. Barnard, T.K. Hareven, and R.M. Mennel, eds. 1970–74. *Childhood and Youth in America*. 3 vols. Cambridge: Harvard University Press.

Cohen, M. 1988. *Women's Work, Markets and Economic Development in Nineteenth-Century Ontario*. Toronto: University of Toronto Press.

Cohen, R.D. 1985. "Childsaving and Progressivism, 1885–1915." In *American Childhood*, ed. J.M. Hawes and N.R. Hiner. Westport, CT, and London: Greenwood Press. 273–309.

Cohen, S. 1985. *Visions of Social Control*. London: Basil Blackwell.

Cooke, K., ed. 1986. *Report of the Task Force on Child Care*. Ottawa: Minister of Supply and Services.

Cooney, R. 1986. "Sexual Assault Confuses Girls." *Calgary Herald*. February 21: B1.

Coulter, R. 1982. "The Working Young of Edmonton, 1921–1931." In Parr, *Childhood and Family.* 143–59.

Dally, A. 1982. *Inventing Motherhood: The Consequences of an Ideal.* London: Burnett Books.

Demos, J. 1970. *A Little Commonwealth: Family Life in Plymouth Colony.* New York: Oxford University Press.

Denzin, N.K. 1984. "Toward a Phenomenology of Domestic, Family Violence." *American Journal of Sociology* 90, no. 3: 483–513.

Donzelot, J. 1979. *The Policing of Families.* New York: Oxford University Press.

Dugdale, R.L. 1877. *The Jukes: A Study in Crime, Pauperism and Heredity.* New York: Putnam.

Ehrenreich, B., and D. English. 1979. *For Their Own Good: 150 Years of the Experts' Advice to Women.* Garden City, NY: Anchor Press/Doubleday.

Elias, N. 1978 [1939]. *The History of Manners.* New York: Urizen Books.

Etaugh, C. 1974. "The Effects of Maternal Employment on Children: A Review of the Research." *Merrill Palmer Quarterly* 20. 71–98.

Finkelstein, B. 1985. "Casting Networks of Good Influence: The Reconstruction of Childhood in the United States, 1790–1870." In *American Childhood,* ed. J.M. Hawes and N.R. Hiner. Westport, CT, and London: Greenwood Press. 111–52.

Foucault, M. 1979. *Discipline and Punish.* New York: Vintage Books.

Gaffield, C. 1982. "Schooling, the Economy, and Rural Society in Nineteenth-Century Ontario." In Parr, *Childhood and Family.* 69–92.

Gaskell, J. 1988. "The Reproduction of Family Life: Perspectives of Male and Female Adolescents." In *Gender and Society,* ed. A.T. McLaren. Toronto: Copp Clark Pitman. 146–68.

Gelles, R.J. 1977. "Demythologizing Child Abuse." In *Family in Transition,* 2d ed. A.S. Skolnick and J.H. Skolnick. Boston and Toronto: Little, Brown. 385–94.

———. 1979. *Family Violence.* Beverly Hills, CA: Sage.

Gelles, R.J., and M. Straus. 1979. "Determinants of Aggression in the Family: Toward a Theoretical Integration." In *Contemporary Theories About the Family,* vol 1, ed. W. Barr et al. New York: The Free Press. 549–81.

Gil, D.G. 1970. *Violence Against Children: Physical Child Abuse in the United States.* Cambridge: Harvard University Press.

Gittins, D. 1986. *The Family in Question: Changing Households and Familiar Ideologies.* New York: Humanities Press.

Gordon, L. 1989. "The Politics and History of Family Violence." In *Family in Transition,* 6th ed., ed. A.S. Skolnick and J.H. Skolnick. Glenview, IL: Scott, Foresman. 68–86.

Hareven, T.K. 1989. "American Families in Transition: Historical Perspectives on Change." In *Family in Transition,* 6th ed, ed. A.S. Skolnick and J.H. Skolnick. Glenview, IL: Scott, Foresman. 39–57.

Houston, S.E. 1982. "The 'Waifs and Strays' of a Late Victorian City: Juvenile Delinquents in Toronto." In Parr, *Childhood and Family.* 129–42.

Lasch, C. 1977. *Haven in a Heartless World.* New York: Basic Books.

Laslett, B. 1973. "The Family as a Public and Private Institution: A Historical Perspective." *Journal of Marriage and the Family* 35: 480–92.

Lewis, J., ed. 1986. Introduction to *Labour and Love: Women's Experience of Home and Family 1850–1940,* by Lewis. Don Mills, ON: Oxford University Press.

Lipman-Blumen, J. 1984. *Gender Roles and Power.* Englewood Cliffs, NJ: Prentice-Hall.

Lupri, E. 1990a. "The Dialectics of Conjugal Violence." *Familiendynamik—Interdisziplinare Zeitschrift für Praxis und Forschung* 15.

———. 1990b. "Harmonie und Aggression: Über die Dialektik ehelicher Gewalt." *Kölne Zeitschrift für Soziologie und Socialosychologie.* 42, no. 3: 199. (Page references cited in the text are from the English version of this paper, which is available from the author.)

Lupri, E., and D.L. Mills. 1983. "The Changing Roles of Canadian Women in Family and Work: An Overview." In *The Changing Position of Women in Family and Society: A Cross-National Comparison,* ed. E. Lupri. Leiden: E.J. Brill. 43–77.

Margolis, M. 1984. *Mothers and Such: Views of American Women and Why They Changed.* Berkeley: University of California Press.

McKee L. 1987. "Households During Unemployment: The Resourcefulness of the Unemployed." In Brannen and Wilson, *Give and Take.* 96–116.

Menzies, R. 1986. "Psychiatry, Dangerousness and Legal Control." In *The Social Dimensions of Law*, ed. N. Boyd. Scarborough, ON: Prentice-Hall. 182–211.

Miller, L.J. 1987. "Uneasy Alliance: Women as Agents of Social Control." *Canadian Journal of Sociology* 12, no. 4: 345–61.

———. 1990a. "Safe Home, Dangerous Street: Remapping Social Reality in the Early Modern Era." In *Perspectives on Social Problems*, vol 2, eds. G. Miller and A. Holstein. Greenwich, CT: JAI Press. 45–66.

———. 1990b. "Violent Families and the Rhetoric of Harmony." *British Journal of Sociology* 41, no. 2: 261–86.

Morantz, R.M. 1984. "Making Women Modern: Middle-Class Women and Health Reform in 19th Century America." In *Women and Health in America*, ed. J.W. Leavitt. 346–58.

National Film Board of Canada. 1979. *Loved, Honoured and Bruised.*

Nelson, F. 1992. "Lesbian Motherhood." Unpublished Masters Thesis, Department of Sociology, University of Calgary, Calgary, Alberta.

Nett, E. 1981. "Canadian Families in Social-Historical Perspective." *Canadian Journal of Sociology* 6, no. 3: 239–60.

Novak, M. 1985. *Successful Aging*. Toronto: Penguin Books.

Parr, J. 1982. Introduction to *Childhood and Family in Canadian History*, by J. Parr. Toronto: McClelland and Stewart.

Pfohl, S.J. 1985. *Images of Deviance and Social Control: A Sociological History*. New York: McGraw Hill.

Pupo, N. 1988. "Preserving Patriarchy: Women, the Family, and the State." In *Reconstructing the Family: Feminist Perspectives*, ed. N. Mandell and A. Puffy. Toronto and Vancouver: Butterworths. 202–37.

Rubington, E., and M.S. Weinberg, eds. 1981. *Deviance: The Interactionist Perspective*. 4th ed. New York: Macmillan.

Schur, E. 1984. *Labeling Women Deviant: Gender, Stigma, and Social Control*. Philadelphia: Temple University Press.

Shorter, E. 1975. *The Making of the Modern Family*. New York: Basic Books.

Smith, D.E. 1987. *The Everyday World as Problematic: A Feminist Sociology*. Toronto: University of Toronto Press.

Statistics Canada, Canadian Centre for Justice Statistics. 1994. *Family Violence in Canada*. Ottawa: Minister of Industry, Science and Technology.

Statistics Canada. 1993. "The Violence Against Women Survey." *The Daily*, Nov. 18.

Statistics Canada. 1974. *Perspective Canada 1*. Ottawa: Information Canada.

Straus, M.A., R.J. Gelles, and S.K. Steinmetz. 1980. *Behind Closed Doors*. Garden City, NY: Anchor Books.

Strong-Boag, V. 1982. "Intruders in the Nursery. Childcare Professionals Reshape the Years One to Five, 1920–1940." In Parr, *Childhood and Family*. 160–78.

Tuchman, B. 1979. *A Distant Mirror: The Calamitous Fourteenth Century*. New York and Toronto: Ballantyne Books.

Vandelac, L. 1988. "Mothergate: Surrogate Mothers, Linguistics and Androcentric Engineering." In *Gender and Society*, ed. A. T. McLaren. Toronto: Copp Clark Pitman. 257–71.

Zelizer, V.A. 1989. "Pricing the Priceless Child: From Baby Farms to Black-Market Babies." In *Family in Transition,* 6th ed., ed. A.S. Skolnick and J.H. Skolnick. Glenview. IL: Scott. Foresman. 380–87.

PART II

Race, Ethnicity and Class

INTRODUCTION

Racial and ethnic inequality is a basic feature of the Canadian mosaic. "Racial" privileges, like class privileges, reach far back into the Canadian past. The colonization of the Native population, racist immigration policies directed against South Asians and Chinese, the internment of the Japanese—all attest to the racist policies and practices of the Canadian state. These policies and practices are present as well in the other institutions in this society, and continue to affect the current status of racial minorities in this country. Recent studies have exposed the myth that we have seen the end of racial inequality and that racism is a thing of the past. Instead, they show that racial minorities continue to occupy disadvantaged positions in Canadian society in spite of state policies to promote the cultural heritage and identity of various social groups, as well as educational programs to promote better understanding and tolerance. While patterns and practices of discrimination have changed over time, racial domination and racial inequality remain as permanent features.

The first two readings in this section address the issues of racism and racial inequality, and the institutional structures and arrangements that continue to sustain racial inequalities. The third reading provides an overview of the development and implementation of multiculturalism as a state policy. The last reading in this section provides a discussion of the Meech Lake Accord.

The chapter by Vic Satzewich, entitled "Social Stratification: Class and Racial Inequality," examines the dimensions, meaning, and consequences of racism and racial inequality in Canada. Satzewich reviews various theoretical explanations of racial inequality and presents a critique of psychological, cultural, and human capital approaches. Racism, he argues, is not simply articulated and significant at the level of interpersonal relations; rather, racism and racial inequality are structural aspects of both the past and the present operations of Canada as a capitalist country. They have been central to the formation and reproduction of capitalist relations of production via the regulation of labour procurement.

Despite the fact that Canada was initially viewed as a white dominion, capitalism in the country has been unable to function without the presence of non-European workers. Still, people defined as non-European have occupied a precarious position in social, political, and economic relations. Their experiences in Canada have been affected in no small degree by institutional racism. This chapter identifies various forms of institutional racism to which non-European groups have been subject, and traces the continuities and variations in its meaning. It is manifested in various forms of exclusionary practices, in the allocation of people to specific sites in production relations, and in the social and political marginalization of groups of people. In conclusion, Satzewich argues the continuing relevance of racism in this country, to the extent that there are costs and benefits in the job market associated with ethnic origin.

Of all its racial minority groups, Canada's First Nations population has faced the worst racism and racial exploitation. They live in an impoverished and subjugated position because of past colonization, in its various manifestations, as well as the current political, economic, and social oppression that they face. Their maintenance in a state of underdevelopment is manifested both economically and socially. In economic terms, they suffer poverty, unemployment, and welfare dependency; socially, they are plagued by conditions that include family breakdown and suicide. James Frideres, in his chapter entitled "From the Bottom Up: Institutional Structures and the Native People," addresses many of the issues facing the First Nations. His thesis is that these problems must be discussed in the historical context of their political, economic, and social subordination.

Frideres provides health, education, and economic data to demonstrate the conditions of inequality in which the aboriginal people live. They suffer high infant mortality, low life expectancy, and an abnormal rate of infectious diseases associated with, among other things, poor sanitation and housing. Their level of participation in education is low, and their dropout rate is high. Unemployment and welfare dependency affect their personal lives and undermine their communities. Frideres argues that these inequalities are the result of institutional structures and institutional discrimination against the Native people.

The chapter also provides a brief discussion of two other crucial issues, Native land claims and self-government. While Frideres sees developments here in a favourable light, he is less optimistic about a rapid transformation of the situation of Canada's First Nations as a whole.

One of the federal policies that has received considerable attention in recent years is the policy on multiculturalism. Victor Ujimoto, in the chapter entitled "Multiculturalism, Ethnic Identity, and Inequality," discusses some of the salient aspects of this policy since its original announcement in 1971 and its ultimate proclamation in the Canadian Multiculturalism Act of 1988.

Multiculturalism is the most visible program designed by the state to promote the cultural heritage of minorities and to "assist all members of all cultural groups to overcome cultural barriers to full participation in Canadian society." The purpose of the policy, according to Prime Minister Trudeau, was "to break down discriminatory attitudes and cultural jealousies ... [and] form the basis of a society which is based upon fair play for all." Despite this intention, there is little indication, as the previous two readings show, that racial prejudice, discrimination, and inequality have become any less evident. This is because, as many critics have noted, this policy aims to solve non-cultural problems with cultural solutions. As is evident in Trudeau's statement, the government has considered "cultural barriers," and not racism or structured inequality, to be the "barriers to full participation."

Racism and racial inequality have political and economic roots in the history and social institutions of Canada, and their solutions lie beyond the removal of "cultural barriers." With its emphasis on culture, multicultural policy is quite rightly criticized as one of depolarization of minority issues, one that deflects their political and economic demands into linguistic and cultural alleys. Ujimoto points out that much has indeed been accomplished in the form of linguistic and cultural programs. However, he argues, structural changes are required to enable all Canadians to achieve equal access to and participation in Canadian society.

In the last chapter in this section, entitled "The Meech Lake Shuffle: French and English Language Rights in Canada," by Wilfrid B. Denis, we shift from multiculturalism to bicultural, bilingual, and constitutional issues.

The Meech Lake Accord generated much interest, both positive and negative. It was defended by its promoters, especially Prime Minister Mulroney and Premier Bourassa, as a necessary step for the full integration of Quebec into Confederation. It was also presented as a necessary step before any further constitutional amendments could be considered, whether in the areas of fisheries, aboriginal, minority, and women's rights, or Senate reform. The accord was supposed to correct a defect of the 1982 patriation of the Constitution—the fact that it was never ratified by Quebec.

Although the issue of integrating Quebec into the Canadian Constitution is certainly an important one, this chapter argues that from a longer historical perspective, the Meech Lake Accord was also an attempt to deal with the very difficult problem of recognition of a dual society within a federal state. The controversy surrounding Quebec's "distinct society" status simply reflects the ongoing tension around Canada's two official languages. This problem has its roots in Canada's earliest history.

Previous efforts to resolve such tensions have never succeeded entirely. As a result, Meech Lake attempted to recognize the distinctness of Francophone society in Quebec, while at the same time trying to preserve the current status of the English language. To do so, Ottawa also had to recognize the existence, rights, and needs of the other official language minority, that of Francophones located outside Quebec.

Meech Lake came to be regarded as the "Quebec round." Its failure lead to a second round of negotiations known as the "Canada round," which culminated in the Charlottetown Agreement of August 28, 1992 and a Canada-wide referendum on October 26, 1992. The Charlottetown Agreement failed because outside Quebec it appeared to give Quebec too much, while within Quebec it was rejected because it did not give Quebec enough. The failure of these accords, Denis argues, reflects the contradictory visions of Canada.

The unequal treatment received by Francophones outside Quebec compared to Anglophones in Quebec indicates that official language issues have complex ties that go beyond language alone. Denis suggests that language legislation passed in Quebec over the past 25 years reflects a growing challenge to Anglophone dominance by the rising French-Canadian bourgeoisie of that province. In spite of the recent attention drawn to restrictions on the use of the English language in Quebec, any cursory comparison between the position of Anglophones in that province and that of Francophones outside Quebec clearly indicates that the former still benefit from rather favourable linguistic and institutional conditions, in contrast to the latter.

The unequal treatment reserved by governments for the two official language minorities, to the general detriment of the Francophone minorities, reflects differences in the class composition of these groups. Anglophones in Quebec are able to benefit from the economic and political resources that they control or influence by virtue of their importance as a significant fraction of the English Canadian bourgeoisie. The Francophone minorities, deprived of such resources, can rely only on their dwindling numbers and on their weight as an official minority within the scope of federal policies.

CHAPTER 5

Social Stratification: Class and Racial Inequality

Vic Satzewich

Learning Objectives

This chapter critically examines the dimensions, meaning, and consequences of racial inequality in Canada, and reviews various theoretical explanations used to explain racism and racial inequality. Students are encouraged to be sensitive to different theoretical perspectives and to subject them to critical analysis. They should be able to demonstrate their understanding of the dimensions and meaning of institutional racism. In addition, students are encouraged to examine how racism and racial inequality have been central to the formation and reproduction of capitalist relations of production.

Introduction

Canadians of European origin have, at best, a checkered history when it comes to dealing with groups of people defined as being ethnically or racially different from themselves. The idea that Canada is a tolerant, peaceful, and welcoming society is still drawn upon from time to time, particularly when the Canadian government wants to occupy the high ground in international politics. This image of Canada does have some basis in reality, particularly when compared to the situation in Germany, where neofascists harass, abuse, and even murder Turkish, eastern European, and Asian refugees and immigrants. Over the years, Canada has indeed become home to hundreds of thousands of refugees and immigrants from around the world. While not a myth, the image of Canada and Canadians as tolerant is not entirely accurate. The reception that various immigrant and refugee groups have received following their arrival has tended to fall somewhat short of the ideal. While racism and discrimination are arguably not as prevalent in Canada as in some other countries that come to mind, racism and discrimination do indeed constitute important parts of our social, political, and economic structures. While some of the more pernicious aspects of racist ideology and practice are now rejected by many Canadians, a sense still prevails whereby groups defined as "non-white" continue to be seen as "other" and as problem populations largely responsible for their own circumstances.

Even though most academics will acknowledge that racism and discrimination continue to be present within Canadian society, few agree as to its social significance and meaning. The first purpose of this chapter is to examine some of the theories of "race" and ethnic relations that have been used to try to explain the nature of social inequality between different groups of people. Second, this paper presents a historical discussion of the meaning of "race," and how racism was linked to the wider system of capitalism with its attendant structure of unequal class relationships. Finally, the chapter provides some contemporary evidence of the social significance of ethnic origin in the current operation of the Canadian labour market.

Racism and Capitalism

When the social sciences in North America were dominated by the structural-functional school of thought in the 1950s and 1960s, the literature on "race" and ethnic relations was dominated by sociologists constructing theories to either play down or explicitly deny the impact of racism and discrimination on the social position and experiences of groups of people. Since inequalities between groups of people were too obvious for even structural-functionalists to ignore, they tried to deflect attention away from the possibility that racism and discrimination were structural components of modern industrial societies. They also denied the possibility that the largely "white" majority was doing anything to subordinate, marginalize, or exclude groups defined as "non-white." As an alternative to explanations of social inequality that focussed on racism and discrimination, and sometimes after some very interesting mental gymnastics, sociologists tried to place the source of the "problem" on the people who were poor and who suffered the consequences of poverty, racism, and discrimination.

One strategy used by sociologists in their analysis of ethnic relations was an attempt to *a priori* explain away the possibility that racism and discrimination might be a "problem." For some analysts racism is regarded as an irrational attribute in an otherwise fair, equal, and achievement-oriented society. Racism is either an anomaly that will eventually vanish because of the universalizing and levelling tendencies associated with "post-industrialism," or an otherwise secondary feature of social, economic, and political relations. Edward Herberg, in his recent book, *Ethnic Groups in Canada: Adaptations and Transitions*, presents the former position rather succinctly when he optimistically tells the reader that

> the maintenance of Canada's existing post-industrial society, and especially its economy, requires an absolutely unrestrained integration of workers in the society and economy, based on individual merit and potential for productive contribution. This kind of essential egalitarianism is absolutely incompatible with any kind of legal or geographic

> constraints on either free movement or the rights of all ethnic peoples and communities to participate voluntarily (1989, 299–300).

The implication of his argument is clear. It suggests that racism, which involves both the delineation of group boundaries on the basis of physical or genetic criteria (such as skin colour, eye shape, head shape, or gene frequencies), as well as the development of ideas that involve evaluations of superiority or inferiority based on group differences, is a dysfunctional, irrational feature of social relations in the country (Miles 1982, 32–34; 1989). Furthermore, social practices based on racially or ethnically defined criteria that inhibit individual freedom and initiative are regarded not only as unconscionable, but also as unnecessary for present-day capitalist social and economic development. Thus, practices like job segregation or discrimination in employment that are based on race, ethnicity, or gender are seen to be remnants of a long-distant past.

Others, however, have taken a different tack. A theme running through the literature on ethnic relations is the individualization, or personalization, of the explanation of ethnic and racial inequality. As with the analysis of racism, these explanations tend to emphasize the anomalous nature of social inequality within a largely fair and equal society: there is an assumption of equality of opportunity within a framework of inequality of condition. The problem of inequality is not located in the structural operation of capitalist societies but rather tends to be located in the particular cultural or psychological characteristics of groups of people.

Many years ago, Rosen (1956, 1959), for example, suggested that ethnic groups differ with respect to their psychological make-up. He argued that groups differ in their levels of achievement motivation; their value orientations, which define and implement achievement oriented behaviour; and their educational and vocational aspirations. That is, they differ with respect to their "psychological need to excel, [the] ... initial possession of or willingness to adopt the high valuation placed upon achievement and success" (Rosen 1959, 48). He studied six groups in the United States and concluded that Jews, Greeks, and white Protestants possess a higher level of achievement motivation than do Italians, Africans, and French Canadians. These differences in achievement syndrome, he argued, help explain the greater degree of upward mobility and economic success of the former groups in relation to the latter groups.

A similar line of argument has been pursued by psychologists interested in IQ differences among ethnic groups. In Canada, Vernon (1984) has recently argued that Natives and "orientals" differed with respect to their scores on intelligence tests. These apparent psychological differences in IQ are then used by Vernon to explain why the latter achieve higher levels of formal education and occupy higher-status occupations than do Native people.

More recently, Phillipe Rushton, a psychologist from the University of Western Ontario, has suggested that the "white," "Oriental," and "Negro" "races" differ fundamentally in terms of personality and culture. These differences, according to Rushton (1987, 1988), are rooted largely in the biological make-up of the groups. He argues that, on average, "Orientals" possess larger brains and smaller genitalia than "whites" and "Negroes," and that "Negroes" possess smaller brains and larger genitalia than the other two groups. In both cases, "whites" fall between the other two groups in terms of brain size and genitalia. According to Rushton and his colleagues, these supposed genetic differences "explain" numerous personality and social differences between the groups, including what they see as a propensity to crime and poverty by "Negroes" and a propensity to lower criminality and licentiousness and "higher" culture for "Orientals" (see Rushton 1987, 1988).

Cultural explanations of inequality share a focus with psychological explanations in that the root of the problem is seen to lie either in the apparent failure of groups to assimilate into mainstream social relations (Gordon 1964), or in the existence of a "culture of poverty," which precludes the possibility of social and economic mobility for certain groups of people (Lewis 1966). Within the assimilationist school, groups are seen to be held back from economic advancement by their unwillingness to relinquish "old world" values, attitudes, and beliefs, which are incongruent with the demands of industrialized, competitive, and achievement-oriented societies.

Within the culture-of-poverty school, Oscar Lewis (1966), an anthropologist, argues that living in a state of poverty creates a certain culture, which is characterized by, among other things, a low level of social organization; a deep-rooted hostility toward representatives of the larger society; and feelings of hopelessness, dependence, and inferiority. For Lewis, living within a culture of poverty sets into motion a self-fulfilling prophecy and creates internal, cultural barriers to social mobility and economic advancement.

In the United States, cultural arguments have been applied especially often to the situation of those of African descent in northern urban "ghettos." The Moynihan report, for example, argued that, during the course of the 1960s, the American government had increasingly removed structural barriers to the advancement of Africans by implementing various pieces of anti-discrimination legislation. However, formal, legal equality would not be enough to bring about substantive equality between "black" and "white" Americans. The past treatment of Africans meant that they could not take advantage of the new opportunities afforded to them through such legislation. The root of the problem, Moynihan argued, lay in the "deterioration" of the African American family. This deterioration was initially the result of slavery, the particular patterns of Reconstruction, and the position of the African American man, who, because of poverty, discrimination, and unemployment, could not earn a wage that would be sufficient to support his family. The emasculation of these men resulted in the rise of matriarchy within the community, which was then equated by Moynihan with a "tangle of social pathology." The latter included low levels of educational achievement among "ghetto" youth, high rates of crime, and an overall sense of alienation. Thus, the lack of a stable family structure resulted in the improper socialization of these youths and created the conditions whereby Africans could not take advantage of the ever-increasing opportunities in America.

Interestingly, this view of family structure as the root of the problem of "race relations" was also incorporated into the strange mix of political discourse and popular culture that characterized the thinking of Dan Quayle, the former vice-president of the United States. Former vice-president Quayle's remarks about the "glorification" of single motherhood on the television program *Murphy Brown* was only part of a wider neoconservative discourse in the United States in the late 1980s and early 1990s about the negative impact on society of single-parent families. Coming from a very different perspective, the Hollywood movie *Boyz in the 'hood*, reinforced Quayle's ideas. While the social and political messages contained in the movie are complex, it implies, nonetheless, that young African American males need proper adult male role models in order to escape the cycle of poverty, crime, and gang violence in which many are caught. Conversely, this message suggests that female single parents are partially responsible for the many problems young children in urban American communities are experiencing.

Assimilationist and cultural arguments have also been applied to Canada's aboriginal people (Nagler 1972; Herberg 1989; but see Wien 1986, 89–90, for a critique). Nagler, for example, argues that Natives in Canada are not assimilated. The institutionalization of the reserve system in the late nineteenth and early twentieth centuries allowed Native people to retain many aspects of their traditional cultures. Coupled with a century of enforced idleness on the reserves, this created a culture of poverty inconsistent with the demands of urban living. He says that the lack of assimilation reflected in aboriginal peoples' different value structure has prevented their full participation in Canadian society. Thus, in Nagler's terms, "their basic values are at variance with the value system possessed by North American society. As such, the value of punctuality, saving, future orientation and the work ethic serve to maintain a vast separation between Indians and the rest of North American society" (1972, 134).

Within this context, some have used the presumed existence of cultural differences between groups as a basis for opposing the federal government's policy of multiculturalism. John Porter (1965) was one of the first Canadian sociologists to systematically study the link between social class and ethnicity, and he identified racism as an important variable in explaining the socio-economic differences between various ethnic groups in Canada. He was nevertheless opposed to the idea of a multicultural policy, in part, because it would permit groups to retain aspects of their cultures, which he felt would inhibit their mobility within modern, industrial societies (1986).

These explanations of inequality have been criticized on a number of grounds. First, the concept of assimilation is ill-defined. Assimilation implies that there are certain objective, widely accepted standards of behaviour that are indicative of social and structural integration (Li 1987, 215). Yet researchers rarely define which social practices are both necessary and sufficient conditions of being "assimilated." The central question that remains, then, is which behaviours indicate that a person is assimilated, and which behaviours indicate that a person is not assimilated.

Second, psychological tests of IQ tend to be culturally biased. What counts as knowledge differs from one group to another, and therefore intergroup differences in IQ probably measure the defects inherent in the measuring instruments rather than reflect actual differences in intelligence between groups (Bowles and Gintis 1977).

Third, these explanations tend to blame the victim (Ryan 1976). Ryan suggests that blaming the victim is an ideology that either intentionally or unintentionally mystifies social reality in order to justify the status quo. It is a mode of thinking in which poor people are seen to be entirely responsible for their own fate. Their personal "social maladjustment" or "social defects" structure and limit their economic opportunities. The victims of poverty are seen to be responsible for the lowliness of the positions in which they find themselves. Thus, it is a mode of thinking that individualizes the problem by attributing causal priority to factors within the victims themselves.

Fourth, these explanations confuse cause and effect in the explanation of inequality (Valentine 1968; Horan 1978). Values, attitudes, and orientations are assumed to be key causal variables in the stratification process. Still others assume that these values exist in relative isolation from the material circumstances in which poor people find themselves. This issue is especially noticeable in the Moynihan report, where the problems of the African American family are seen to be rooted in history, not in current social and economic arrangements (Rainwater and Yancey 1967).

And, finally, these arguments do not recognize the impact that racism and discrimination have on social inequality. The remainder of this chapter suggests that, contrary to popular conception, racism has had and continues to have an important meaning within Canadian society. It argues that the negative evaluations of groups of people made on the basis of socially selected physical or genetic criteria have been central to the formation of Canadian capitalism. Racism is therefore centrally linked with racial inequality.

Population and Labour-force Participation

Since the "discovery" by Europeans of what is now Canada, there has been de facto diversity, albeit existing under a set of ideological, political, cultural, and economic conditions that emphasized and gave priority to anglo-conformity. Over the years, this diversity has increased, in part because of the increasing demand for labour by Canadian employers and the inability of the traditional sources—Britain, Western Europe, and the United States—to fill this demand (Hawkins 1974).

Table 5.1 gives an indication of the changing ethnic composition of Canadian society between the 1901 and 1981 censuses. It shows that during the early years of the twentieth century, people of Asian, African, and Native ancestry accounted for 3.1 percent of the total population. Their proportion of the total population declined to 1.8 percent in 1951. Since the mid-1960s there has been a progressive increase in the size of the non-European population in the country. In 1961, the three groups made up 2.3 percent of the population; in 1971 this figure increased to 3.0 percent and by 1981, 4.8 percent. The British and French proportion of the total population has correspondingly declined from 87.7 percent in 1901 to 70.8 percent in 1981.

Table 5.2 presents data on ethnic origins collected during the 1991 Census. The question on ethnic origin was changed in the 1986 Census to allow for people to identify their "roots" rather than their paternal line of descent. The change from "line of descent" to "roots" meant that Canadians could identify more than one ethnic origin in the 1986 and 1991 censuses. As indicated in Table 5.2, 71.1 percent of the Canadian population identified a single ethnic origin while 28.9 percent identified two or more ethnic origins. Using the new census categories, 20.8 percent of the population identified themselves as having British origins only, while 22.8 percent identified themselves as having French origins only. The addition of multi-

TABLE 5.1: Ethnic and Racial Composition of Canada, 1901–1981

ETHNICITY	1901	1911	1921	1931	1941	1951	1961	1971	1981
Asian	0.4	0.6	0.7	0.7	0.6	0.5	0.7	1.4	2.2
Chinese	0.3	0.4	0.5	0.4	0.3	0.2	0.3	0.6	1.2
South Asian	—	0.1	0.1	0.1	0.1	0.1	0.2	0.6	0.8
Japanese	0.1	0.1	0.2	0.2	0.2	0.2	0.2	0.2	0.2
African	0.3	0.2	0.2	0.2	0.2	0.1	0.2	0.2	0.6
Natives	2.4	1.5	1.3	1.2	1.4	1.2	1.4	1.4	2.0
British	57.0	54.1	55.4	51.9	49.7	47.9	43.5	44.4	43.6
French	30.7	28.5	27.8	28.2	30.3	30.8	30.4	28.5	27.2
East European	0.6	2.3	3.1	5.6	5.7	5.9	7.6	6.0	4.8
West European	7.0	7.9	6.6	8.2	7.8	8.4	10.3	9.5	7.7
South European	0.2	0.7	0.9	1.0	1.1	1.2	2.6	4.5	4.7
Jewish	0.3	1.1	1.4	1.5	1.5	1.3	1.0	1.4	1.2
Other	1.1	3.1	2.6	1.5	1.7	2.7	2.3	2.7	6.0
TOTAL[a]	100.0	100.0	100.0	100.0	100.0	100.0	100.0	100.0	100.0

[a]Figures were rounded to add to 100.
Source: Edward N. Herberg, *Ethnic Groups in Canada: Adaptations and Transitions* (Scarborough, ON: Nelson, 1989), pp. 40–43. © 1989 Nelson Canada. A Division of Thomson Canada Limited.

ple response categories in the 1986 and 1991 censuses makes it difficult to compare the relative size of ethnic groups using previous census data.

Table 5.3 confirms that non-Europeans are becoming increasingly important in the Canadian economy. It gives an indication of the labour-force participation and unemployment rates of selected ethnic groups, subdivided by gender. In general, it shows that non-Europeans tend to have greater labour-force participation rates than average, and greater rates than those people who are of British origin. For males, Central and South Americans had the highest labour-force participation rate, but the five groups with the next highest rates were Indo-Pakistanis, Pacific Islanders, Africans, Japanese, and Koreans, respectively. For females, the group with the highest participation rate were Pacific Islanders, and the groups with the four next highest rates were Africans, Koreans, Chinese, and Indo-Pakistanis.

Figure 5.1 confirms previous data, showing that, with the exception of the elderly, immigrant men and women have higher rates of labour-force participation than their Canadian-born counterparts.

The contribution of immigration to economic development is also reflected in the sources of growth in the labour force. Between 1966 and 1986, the labour force grew by 5 547 000 persons, an increase of 74 percent. Of the growth in the labour force, 23 percent was due to the arrival of immigrants (Beaujot 1992, 55).

Table 5.4 shows that, for the non-European groups, a high proportion of those active in the labour force were born outside of Canada, and have migrated to the country since 1970. For males, it shows that 98.8 percent of Koreans, 97.9 percent of Pacific Islanders, 97.1 percent of Indo-Chinese, 97.0 percent of Indo-Pakistanis, 88.9 percent of Africans, and 86.6 percent of the Chinese population that was active in the labour force were born outside of Canada. For females, 98.9 percent of Koreans, 98.6 percent of Pacific Islanders, 97.6 percent of Indo-Chinese, 96.4 percent of Indo-Pakistanis, 91.5 percent of Africans, and 86.0 percent of Chinese women in the labour force were of immigrant origin. This compares with an average of 19.2 percent for all males and 18.8 percent for all females. The majority of both non-European men and women active in the labour force have migrated to Canada since 1970.

Finally, figures 5.2a and 5.2b present data on the occupational composition of the immigrant and Canadian-born components of the labour force. Figures 5.2a and 5.2b show that while the distribution of immigrant women and men in the labour

TABLE 5.2: Ethnic Origins of Canadian Population, 1991

Origins	Males	Males %	Females	Females %	Total	Total %
Single						
British	2 793 060	20.9	2 817 990	20.6	5 611 050	20.8
French	3 016 400	22.6	3 130 205	22.9	6 146 605	22.8
West Europe	686 350	5.1	669 130	4.9	1 355 480	5.0
North Europe	106 610	0.8	106 995	0.8	213 605	0.8
East Europe	473 010	3.5	473 800	3.5	946 810	3.5
South Europe	711 295	5.3	667 735	4.9	1 379 030	5.1
Other Europe	125 755	0.9	125 385	0.9	251 140	0.9
Arab	85 995	0.6	66 995	0.5	152 990	0.6
West Asian	45 450	0.3	36 200	0.3	81 650	0.3
South Asian	217 215	1.6	203 080	1.5	420 295	1.6
E. & S.E. Asian	464 440	3.5	496 780	3.6	961 220	3.6
African	14 740	0.1	11 695	0.1	26 435	0.1
Pacific Islands	3 500	0.0	3 720	0.0	7 220	0.0
L.C.S. America	43 325	0.3	42 205	0.3	85 530	0.3
Caribbean	43 625	0.3	50 765	0.4	94 390	0.3
Black	107 195	0.8	117 420	0.9	224 615	0.8
Aboriginal	230 865	1.7	239 750	1.8	470 615	1.7
Other	403 960	3.0	376 080	2.8	780 040	2.9
Total Single Orig.	9 572 790	71.7	9 635 930	70.5	19 208 720	71.1
Multiple Orig.	3 770 460	28.3	4 023 790	29.5	7 794 250	28.9
TOTAL	13 343 250	100.0	13 659 720	100.0	27 002 970	100.0

Source: Statistics Canada, *Ethnic Origins, 1991 Census of Canada*, Cat. no. 93-315 (Ottawa: Minister of Industry, Science and Technology, 1993). Reproduced by authority of the Minister of Industry, 1994.

TABLE 5.3: Labour Force Participation and Unemployment Rates of Selected Ethnic Groups, by Gender, 1981

Ethnic group	Participation rate %	Unemployment rate %
MALES		
British	77.8	5.6
French	76.2	9.7
Other European	80.9	3.9
Indo-Pakistani	85.7	4.5
Indo-Chinese	77.6	8.3
Japanese	82.4	3.1
Korean	82.2	4.9
Chinese	79.0	4.2
Pacific Islands, including Philippines	84.8	3.4
African	83.0	7.3
Native People	60.7	16.5
Central/South American	86.2	6.9
Total male labour force	78.2	6.5
FEMALES		
British	51.4	7.7
French	47.9	12.4
Other European	54.0	5.9
Indo-Pakistani	60.3	10.3
Indo-Chinese	58.9	12.3
Japanese	58.6	5.0
Korean	63.7	6.6
Chinese	61.0	5.4
Pacific Islands, including Philippines	75.3	4.3
African	65.2	9.5
Native People	36.7	17.3
Central/South American	57.9	7.1
Total female labour force	51.8	8.7

Source: Privy Council Office, *Royal Commission Report on Equality in Employment* (Ottawa: Minister of Supply and Services, 1984), p. 82. Reproduced with the permission of the Minister of Supply and Services Canada, 1994.

force reflects the wider gendered division of labour extant in Canadian society, immigrant women tend to be under-represented in professional, clerical, and sales occupations and over-represented in service, processing, and product fabricating, assembling, and repairing occupations. In the case of men, immigrants tend to be over-represented in professional, service, processing, and product fabricating

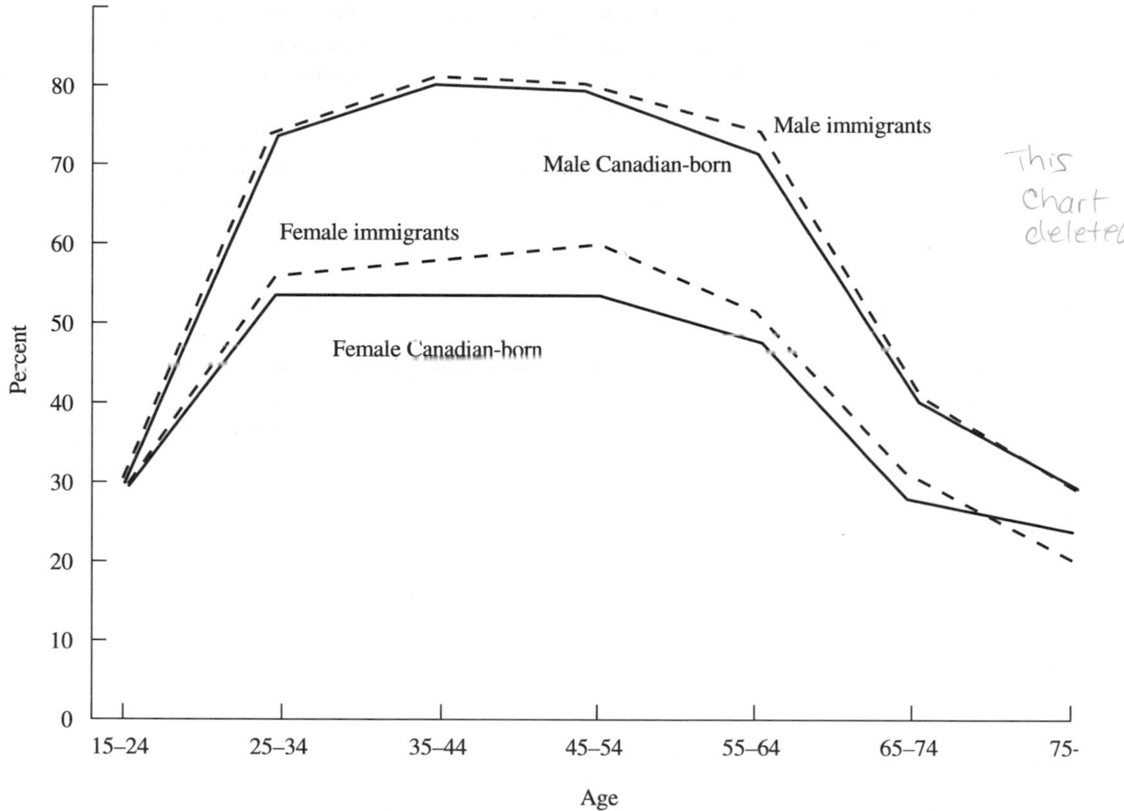

FIGURE 5.1: Proportion Working Full-time, by Age, for Immigrants and Canadian-born, 1986

Note: The proportion working full-time is the proportion of a given age–gender–group that worked full-time for 40 or more weeks in 1985.
Source: Roderic Beaujot, "The Socio-Demographic Impact of Immigration" in S. Globerman (ed.), *The Immigration Dilemma* (Ottawa: Statistics Canada, 1992), p. 56. Reproduced by authority of the Minister of Industry, 1994.

occupations and under-represented in clerical, sales, and primary occupational categories.

Institutional Racism: Canadian Dimensions

Because of the initial definition of Canada as a "white" dominion and the need to rely, at least partially, on non-European labour, people defined as non-European have historically occupied a precarious position in social, economic, and political relations. Non-Europeans have consistently been denied the same rights and privileges associated with citizenship that their counterparts have taken for granted. They have, both historically and at present, been defined as a particular type of problematic population. Their existence in Canada has been affected in no small degree by racism, particularly institutional racism.

In contrast to individual expressions of racism, institutional racism refers to sets of social practices that are institutionally based, make reference to invidious distinctions based on physical or genetic criteria, and have the effect of structuring what

TABLE 5.4: Immigrant Status of Labour Force by Ethnicity and Gender, 1981 (percent distribution)

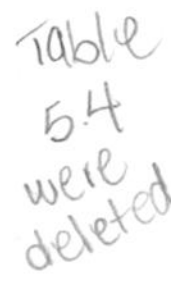

Ethnic group	% Born in Canada	% Born outside Canada	PERIOD OF IMMIGRATION Before 1970	After 1970
MALES				
British	87.3	12.7	9.8	2.9
French	97.9	2.1	1.4	0.6
Other European	58.5	41.5	35.3	6.1
Indo-Pakistani	3.0	97.0	30.2	65.9
Indo-Chinese	2.9	97.1	8.1	89.0
Japanese	75.9	24.1	12.5	11.6
Korean	1.2	98.8	23.3	75.3
Chinese	13.4	86.6	34.8	51.8
Pacific Islands	2.1	97.9	16.2	81.6
African	11.2	88.9	37.4	51.4
Native People	95.0	4.9	1.6	3.3
Central/South American	8.7	91.3	18.4	72.8
All males	80.8	19.2	13.9	5.2
FEMALES				
British	86.3	13.7	10.5	3.2
French	97.8	2.2	1.5	0.7
Other European	62.5	37.5	30.8	6.7
Indo-Pakistani	3.6	96.4	23.6	72.8
Indo-Chinese	2.4	97.6	10.2	88.3
Japanese	76.5	23.5	13.8	9.7
Korean	1.1	98.9	23.3	75.6
Chinese	14.0	86.0	31.0	55.1
Pacific Islands	1.4	98.6	25.4	73.2
African	8.5	91.5	40.0	51.4
Native People	93.9	6.1	1.6	4.4
Central/South American	5.7	94.3	21.5	72.6
All females	81.2	18.8	13.1	5.8

Source: Privy Council Office, *Royal Commission Report on Equality in Employment* (Ottawa: Minister of Supply and Services, 1984), p. 83. Reproduced with the permission of the Minister of Supply and Services Canada, 1994.

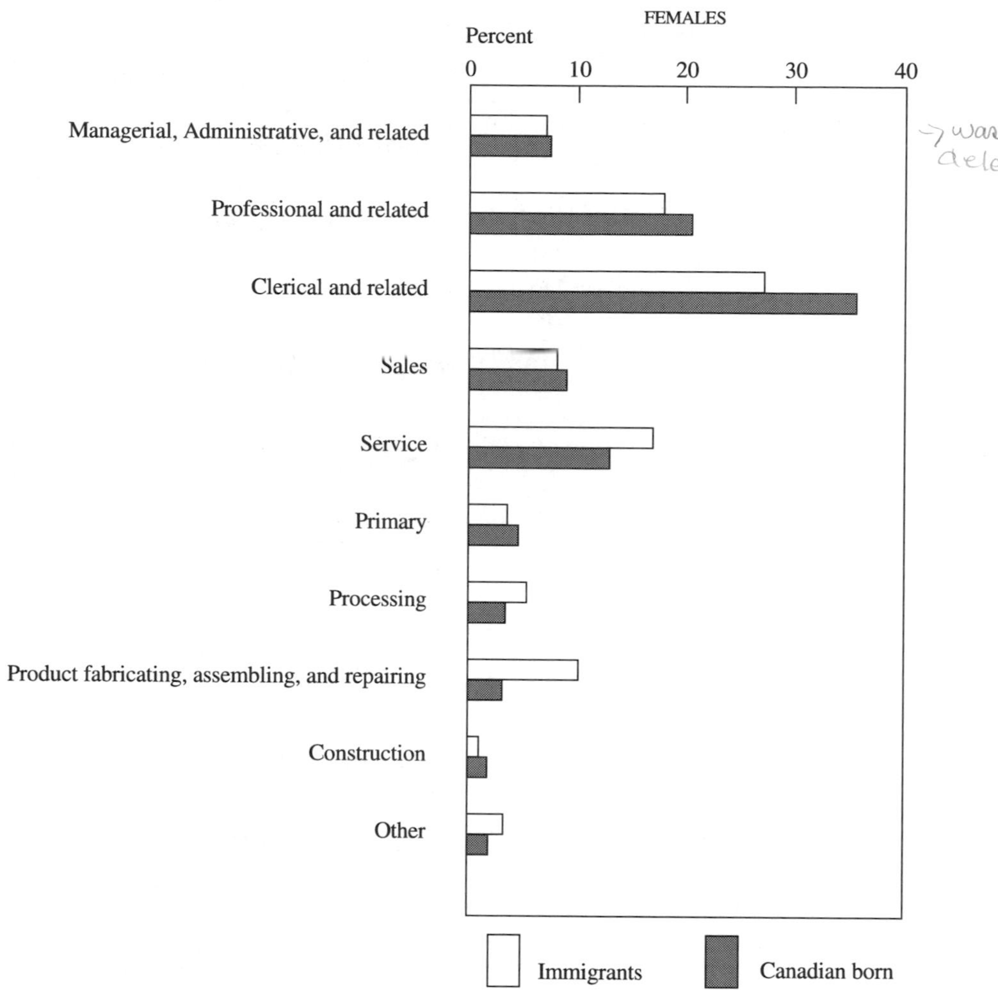

FIGURE 5.2a: Percentage Distribution by Major Occupation Groups, Sex of the Immigrant and Canadian-born Female Labour Force, Canada, 1986

Source: Roderic Beaujot, *Dimensions: Profile of the Immigration Population,* Cat. no. 93-155 (Ottawa: Statistics Canada, 1989), p. 58. Reproduced by authority of the Minister of Industry, 1994.

certain groups of people can and cannot do (Bolaria and Li 1985, 21). In Wilson's terms, "when the ideology of racial exploitation gives rise to normative prescriptions designed to prevent the subordinate racial group from equal participation in associations or procedures that are stable, organized and systematized ... institutional racism exists. Institutional racism therefore represents the structural aspects of racist ideology" (1973, 34).

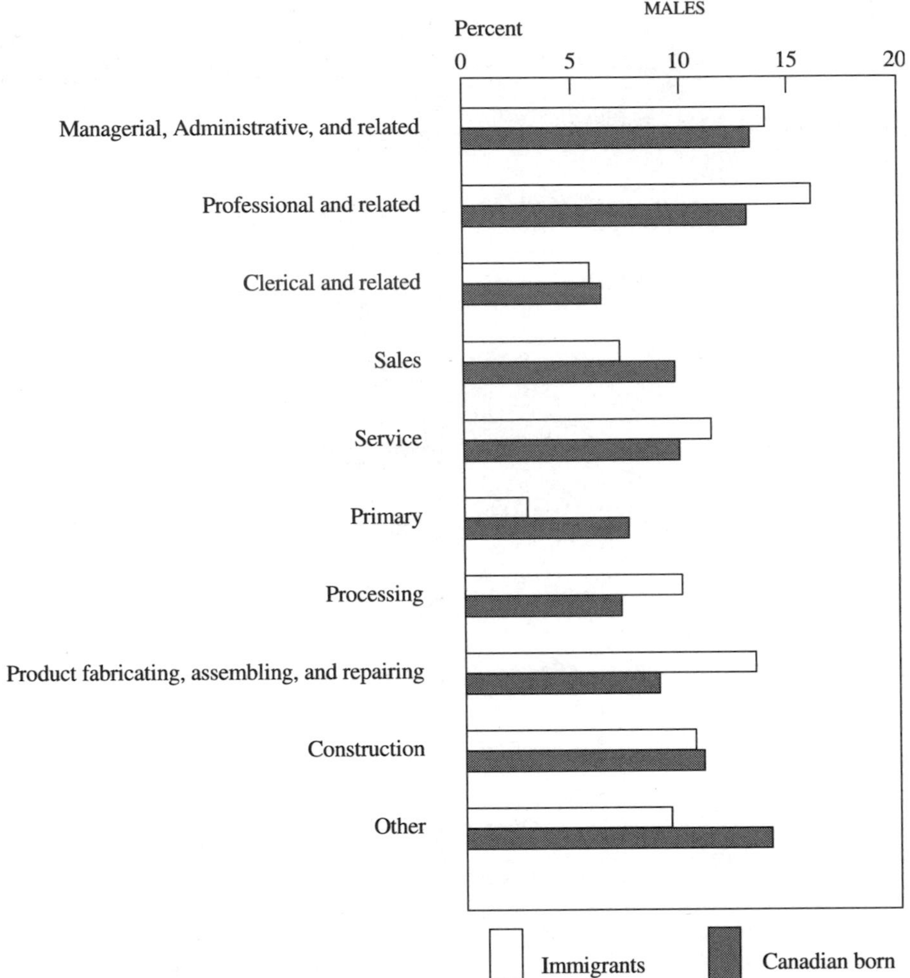

FIGURE 5.2b: Percentage Distribution by Major Occupation Groups, Sex of the Immigrant and Canadian-born Male Labour Force, Canada, 1986

Source: Roderic Beaujot, *Dimensions: Profile of the Immigration Population,* Cat. no. 93-155 (Ottawa: Statistics Canada, 1998), p. 59. Reproduced by authority of the Minister of Industry, 1994.

Institutional racism has taken on a number of dimensions and has had a range of meanings within Canadian society. But this does not mean that the expressions of institutional racism have been haphazard and without implications for the operation of Canadian capitalism. Nor does it mean that it is unrelated to other developments within Canadian society. As Bolaria and Li (1985, 1) suggest, "race problems begin as labour problems." As such, the analysis of institutional racism must be linked to the analysis of the process of capital accumulation.

Institutional racism has acted to exclude certain groups of people from entering the country. This has been especially evident in the realm of state immigration controls, which in part are a means to regulate the labour supply so that large pockets of unemployed workers do not form within the spatial boundaries of the nation-state (Petras 1980). Immigration controls have acted to regulate the size and composition of the "reserve army of labour" to ensure that employers have access to required amounts and kinds of labour power, and that this army of unemployed does not get sufficiently large to cause a legitimation problem (through excessive unemployment), which the state would then have to resolve (Nikolinakos 1975; Castles and Kosack 1973).

The Chinese were one of the first groups subject to racially motivated immigration controls. Chinese labourers began to immigrate to Canada in the 1860s, and were drawn in on a large scale in the early 1880s by Andrew Onderdonk in order to complete the construction of the Canadian Pacific Railway (CPR). Once their labour power was no longer needed for the construction of the CPR, the Canadian state imposed in 1885 a $50 head tax on Chinese labour migration. Any person of Chinese origin who intended to sell his or her labour power for a wage in this country had to pay a tax of $50 upon arrival in Canada. This initial tax did not deter Chinese migration. As a result, the head tax was increased to $100 in 1900 and $500 in 1903. In 1923, Chinese migration was essentially outlawed when the state implemented the Chinese Immigration Act. The act barred from entry to Canada all persons of Chinese descent, with the exception of merchants, diplomats, and students (Li 1979; Satzewich 1989c).

Other groups have also been subject to exclusionary racist immigration controls. South Asians were subject, by virtue of an order-in-council, to the "continuous journey" rule. Implemented in 1908, the order-in-council was directed specifically at curtailing South Asian migration to Canada. A small number of South Asians had arrived in Canada in 1905, and by 1908 a total of 5079 had entered Canada. Their entry sparked a hostile reaction on the part of government officials and the working class, which resulted in the passage of the regulation. According to this measure, immigrants who came to Canada "otherwise than by continuous journey from the countries of which they were natives or citizens, and upon through tickets purchased in that country may be refused entry" (Bolaria and Li 1985, 145). The only company that provided one continuous journey from India to Canada was the Canadian Pacific Railway steamship service, and the government issued directives that prohibited the company from selling South Asians a through ticket to Canada (Bolaria and Li 1985, 146). Other companies broke up the journey in Hawaii, so they could not carry any of these potential immigrants (Hawkins 1989, 17).

Furthermore, the South Asians who managed to enter the country before the passage of the continuous-journey regulations were "encouraged" by Canadian officials to leave because they, like the Chinese, were seen as unable to assimilate and as unwanted competition in the labour market (Ward 1978, 87; Satzewich 1989c). In 1908, the Department of the Interior attempted to organize an indentured labour scheme in which it would pay for the transportation of South Asian labourers who were resident in Canada to British Honduras. The plan never came to fruition because the department could not enlist the support of South Asian community leaders (Ward 1978, 87).

Various exclusionary mechanisms were also directed at those Chinese and other non-European workers who gained entry to Canada and remained in the country. In British Columbia, employers used Chinese workers primarily as cheap labour. They were also used to break strikes in mining or other resource-extraction industries (Ward 1978; Sampet-Mehta 1972). This resulted in an intense degree of working-class agitation directed against the Chinese. Many anti-Asian associations were formed, and much trade-union activity took the form of anti-Chinese agitation. While there were calls for the total elimination of Chinese immigration to Canada (which, as already noted, became a reality in 1923), much of the agitation was also directed at limiting the choices of employment of Chinese workers.

For instance, the Chinese were barred from working underground in coal mines they could not hold a hand-logger's licence, they could not settle on crown land, they could not take up the professions of the law or pharmacy, and in the Prairie provinces, those Chinese who managed to start up a business of their own could not hire "white" women to work for them in restaurants or laundries (Li 1979). As Bolaria and Li (1985, 27) suggest, such forms of exclusion are an effective barrier that prevents non-European workers from moving away from undesirable jobs.

Institutional racism has also been used as an allocative mechanism: a means to allocate groups of people to certain sites in production relations. Capitalist production is such that some sectors require the existence of large pools of cheap and relatively docile workers that can be drawn upon when they are needed and displaced when not needed.

During the postwar period, one of the sectors of employment that was consistently short of labour was domestic service. Employers in search of domestics faced a recurring set of recruitment and retention problems. Because of the low pay and poor working conditions, Canadian women tended, if at all possible, to avoid this type of employment. With a dwindling supply of European women resident in refugee camps in Germany, Italy, and Austria who were willing to fill these jobs for even a short period of time, Canadian officials had to turn to non-traditional sources to fill this demand. That is, Canada had to turn to groups who were otherwise barred from entry into the country by virtue of the application of racist immigration practices (Satzewich 1989b).

In 1955, Canada agreed to allow women from the Caribbean to enter the country on a contractual basis to fill positions as domestic servants for middle-class Canadians. A quota of 200 women per year was initially established, but by the mid-1960s, the annual number of entrants increased to over 1000. They were initially granted entry on a migrant-labour basis in that their stay in the country was conditional upon their remaining in domestic employment for one year after their arrival (Bolaria and Li 1985, 178).

While these women were recruited to fill a genuine demand for domestic labour, it appears that Caribbean women were allowed in because of a process of racialization. Racialization refers to the attachment of social significance to patterns of physical differences like skin colour. In this case, incorporating these women as migrant labour was more desirable than as immigrant labour to the extent that the costs of the reproduction of labour power were to be borne in the Caribbean rather than in Canada. This made female Caribbean labour relatively inexpensive from the Canadian state's point of view. But, while the state officials wanted Canada's middle class to have access to these women's labour power, they also rather consistently expressed a concern over the possibility that Caribbean women might form families, give birth to Canadian-born offspring, and thus increase the resident African population. They feared the growth of such a population because it was felt that it would be the cause of "race relations" problems and hence disrupt the comparatively peaceful process whereby capital was accumulated in the country (Satzewich 1989b). This concern was in turn rooted in racist and sexist stereotypes about the sexuality of African women, which have their origins in eighteenth- and nineteenth-century justifications of slavery (Walvin 1987). Canadian state officials tended to regard African women from the Caribbean as promiscuous.

This concern was made manifest in several ways. The women were subject to compulsory medical examination. Ian Mackenzie, in his as yet unpublished research into the recruitment of domestic workers, states:

> women arriving under the scheme were not only subjected to extensive medical tests in their home countries—including x-rays and tests for tropical diseases—but were subjected to extensive gynecological examinations (testing for syphilis) when they arrived in Canada. The governments of Jamaica and Barbados were expressly not informed of the tests. (quoted in Stasiulis 1987, 6)

Domestic servants who were of European origin were not subject to gynecological examinations.

Furthermore, in 1966, when the Canadian state was attempting to terminate the agreement by which Caribbean women came to Canada as domestic servants, the director of the Immigration Branch of the Department of Citizenship and Immigration argued that "West Indian mores are quite different from ours. Illegitimacy is pretty well accepted as a fact of life. It is not uncommon for a single girl to have children by 2, 3, or 4 different men" (quoted in Satzewich 1989b, 92).

These expressions of concern over black female sexuality were structured in turn by a concern over the growth of the resident African population in the country. Very generally, Africans were defined by state officials as troublesome, to the extent that they were said to be the cause of social and racial problems in the country. As such, they were identified as a potential "enemy within," an enemy that would disrupt the relatively smooth processes of capital accumulation and social reproduction. Their incorporation as migrant labour was an attempt to solve a labour problem without disrupting the social order within which capitalist production took place.

Institutional racism has also been involved in the civil and political marginalization of groups of people. Status Indians (those people defined as an Indian by virtue of the Indian Act) could not vote in federal elections until the early 1960s. The Chinese were barred from voting in British Columbia elections from 1875 until the late 1940s, and the Japanese were disenfranchised in 1895. In 1896, the latter two groups were barred from voting in municipal elections in the province (Ujimoto 1985, 106).

Trade unions in British Columbia during the early years of the twentieth century generally excluded non-Europeans from joining and participating (Bolaria and Li

1985, 95). At the turn of the century, Chinese children were informally discouraged from attending public schools with European children (Ward 1978, 49). During the Second World War the Canadian government believed that the population of Japanese origin would constitute a "fifth column" that would help the Axis powers organize an attack on North America. As such, all Japanese in British Columbia were rounded up and placed in camps in the interior of the province or in work camps across the country. Their property was confiscated and then sold at bargain prices to their European neighbours (Ujimoto 1985, 133). After the war, some Japanese were deported at the same time that Canadian government officials were giving serious and thoughtful consideration to a proposal put forward by farmers that German prisoners of war held in camps in Ontario be allowed to stay and settle permanently in Canada if they took farm jobs (Satzewich 1989a). This suggests quite clearly that the Japanese Canadians, as non-Europeans, were seen as a greater threat to Canada than the possible admittance of a few thousand veterans of Hitler's army.

In general, non-Europeans have historically been regarded by state officials as "racially" incapable of participation in bourgeois democratic political traditions. That is, they were regarded as incapable of taking on the responsibilities and duties of citizenship, which involved voting, getting an education, and participating in community life. The denial of the franchise and the inability to participate in mainstream union activities had the effect of further marginalizing these groups of people and of undercutting part of the political basis upon which they could resist their exploitation by capitalist employers.

Institutional racism has also contributed to the formation of social inequalities, particularly in the area of the denial of family life. Because non-Europeans have historically been defined as a problematic presence in the country, as already noted, state policies have been structured by a desire to preclude the emergence of Canadian-born generations of non-Europeans. Under the terms of the Chinese Immigration Act of 1923, even those married Chinese males who had already migrated to Canada, leaving their families in China, could not bring their wives and children with them to Canada. The law remained in force until after the Second World War (Li 1980). This prevented the formation of a second generation. It also led to a heavy reliance on ethnic associations for emotional and other support for Chinese men. In addition it "provided the conditions for certain vice industries, such as gambling and prostitution, to thrive among Chinatowns in North America, especially when the Chinese were generally denied acceptance into Canadian social life" (Bolaria and Li 1985, 95)

Similarly, female workers from the Caribbean and male Caribbean farm workers have been admitted to the country on a migrant basis, in part because the state does not want these people to form family units and create a Canadian-born African population. It fears that they cause social and racial problems.

From the above it should be clear that racism has not been a secondary, anomalous feature in an otherwise free, equal, and universalistic Canadian society. Institutional racism has had important effects on particular groups of people, and the expressions of institutional racism have had strong, although not entirely determinate, links to the process of production.

In short, institutional racism can be seen as a set of social practices stemming from an ideology of racism. Ideas of inferiority and superiority, based on socially selected physical characteristics, are thus particular ideological mechanisms that contribute to the process of social reproduction—the reproduction of labour power and the social relations of production.

Ethnic and Racial Inequality

The various forms of institutional racism described above have both direct and indirect relationships to the economy and the dynamics of the Canadian labour market. Another specific area of concern within Canadian sociology has been the study of what Abella (184) refers to as "systemic discrimination." According to Abella (1984, 10), systemic discrimination consists of

> the institutionalized systems and practices [that] result in arbitrary and extensive exclusions for persons who, by reason of their group affiliation, are systematically denied a full opportunity to demonstrate their individual abilities.

As noted above, the analysis of systemic discrimination in Canadian society was largely initiated by the late John Porter (1965). Porter, in *The Vertical Mosaic*, made extensive use of census data to argue that there was a reciprocal relationship between ethnicity and social class in Canada. For Porter, this meant that a person's ethnic background had a significant impact on where he or she ended up in the larger system of class relations and social inequality within Canada. Since people of British and northern European origins controlled many of the political and economic resources in Canada, and since they regarded themselves as superior to groups from eastern Europe, Asia, and Africa, they tended to allocate the latter to subordinate positions in the labour market. That is, for Porter, racism and discrimination played an important role in the historical operation of the labour market in Canada.

Since the publication of *The Vertical Mosaic*, numerous Canadian sociologists have sought to further test the validity of Porter's arguments (Clement 1975; Lautard and Loree 1984; Satzewich and Li 1987; Beaujot, Basavarajappa, and Verma 1988; Darroch 1979; Boyd 1992). While the methods used to test the hypothesis of continued discrimination in the labour market have become more complex since the time that Porter wrote, many of the studies provide at least partial support for the suggestion that continued systemic discrimination still affects the Canadian labour market. Indeed, the entire premise of federal employment equity legislation introduced in 1986 is that women, visible minorities, aboriginal people, and the physically challenged face systemic discrimination in the labour market, and that this discrimination needs to be corrected, in part, through state intervention (Abella 1984).

TABLE 5.5: The Wages and Salaries of Foreign-born Women and Men, 1986

	Women Wages and Salaries			Men Wages and Salaries		
	Actual (1)	**Adjusted (2)**	**Rank (3)**	**Actual (4)**	**Adjusted (5)**	**Rank (6)**
Non-visible Minority						
British	910	385	5	5827	3306	1
French	2711	1245	1	538	416	7
Dutch	–1564	–582	20	2661	321	8
German	–65	238	7	837	–326	12
Scandinavian	–432	105	9	3102	1715	3
E. European	–629	–395	17	–807	–669	13
Ukrainian	1527	507	4	1089	692	6
Jewish	3224	540	3	6979	2577	2
Croatian	–321	1001	2	–314	894	5
Greek	–2696	–154	10	–7023	–3344	21
Italian	–1780	–226	12	–1742	12	9
Portuguese	–2574	–400	18	–5113	–300	11
Other European	–12	–221	11	39	–194	10
Other	1356	259	6	2852	945	4
Visible Minority						
British	–1557	–591	21	–5346	–2842	18
W. Asian	–1800	–1928	22	–1703	–912	14
S. Asian	–862	–491	19	–1937	–1829	15
Chinese	143	237	8	–4149	–2816	17
Filipino	2935	–301	14	–4783	–5809	22
S.E. Asian	–1934	–233	13	–6745	–2877	19
African	515	–373	15	–6063	–3235	20
Other	–435	–392	16	–4177	–1879	16
Grand Mean			$15,144			$28,074

Source: Monica Boyd, "Gender, Visible Minority, and Immigrant Earnings Inequality: Reassessing an Employment Equity Premise," in V. Satzewich (ed.), *Deconstructing a Nation: Immigration, Multiculturalism and Racism in '90's Canada* (Halifax: Fernwood Press, 1992), pp. 305–306.

Table 5.5 presents data derived from the 1986 Census of Canada and analyzed by Monica Boyd (1992). This table specifically examines the wages and salaries of foreign-born men and women in Canada. In her analysis, Boyd (1992) seeks to test one of the central premises of employment equity legislation; namely that systemic discrimination operates in the Canadian labour market. Boyd examines the earnings of the foreign-born population of Canada by initially dividing this group into visible and non-visible minorities. Included in the former category are those who identify as British, West Asian, South Asian, Chinese, Filipino, Southeast Asian, African, and "other." Included in the latter are fourteen different groups of European origin. In her analysis, Boyd finds that the average income in 1985 for the total foreign-born population was $15 144 for women and $28 074 for men.

Column one for the women and column four for the men provide information on the actual average wages and salaries of the various groups. The incomes are expressed as deviations from the mean, which means, for example, that British women had an average income which was $910 above the average for all foreign-born women, and the average income of West Asian women was $1800 less than the average for all women. But, differences in the wages and salaries that groups of people earn are subject to many factors, and it is necessary to control for variations in income owing to these factors before one can get a clear indication of the impact of racism and discrimination in the labour market.

Boyd (1992) suggests the wages and salaries can vary because of age, region of residence in Canada, Census Metropolitan Area (CMA) of residence, marital status, education, occupation, and employment status (that is, whether someone worked full- or part-time). Therefore, columns two and five present the variations in income which remain after these other sources of variation in wages and salaries are statistically controlled-for in a multiple regression equation. The adjusted incomes in columns two and five, then, are the incomes of groups after controlling for the sources of variation. What Boyd's analysis provides, is an indication of what the average wages and salaries of the 23 groups would be if they all shared the same age distribution, all lived in the same region and CMA, all shared similar levels of education, were of the same marital status and occupation, and had a similar employment status.

The data indicate generally that both visible-minority men and women tend to earn lower average wages and salaries than non-visible minority men and women. In the case of women, West Asian women earned over $1900 less than the average for all women. Other groups of visible minority women earned between $233 and $591 less than average. The only exception to this pattern were Chinese women, who earned $236 above average. Conversely the highest income groups were French women, who earned over $1200 more than the average and Croatian women who earned just over $1000 more than the average. Other above-average groups of women were Jewish, Ukrainian, British, "other," German, and Scandinavian.

The pattern of differences in earnings between visible and non-visible minorities is even more apparent in the case of men. With the exception of Greek men, who earned $3344 less than average, the eight male visible-minority groups were also the eight lowest earning groups. Filipino men earned over $5800 less than average, while other groups earned between $912 (West Asian) and $3235 (African) less than average. Again, the highest earning groups were Europeans, with British men earning the highest average income, $3306 above the average for all men.

While care needs to be taken in the interpretation of this data, other studies using different measures, different sample populations, and different techniques tend to confirm these findings (see Li 1988, 1992). What they suggest, but do not necessarily prove, is that groups of people with the same qualifications, gender, experience, and occupation face discrimination in the labour market.

This discrimination can take the form of a submerged split labour market (Bonacich 1976, 1979) whereby entrenched European workers have been able to impose differential pay scales for the employment of recent immigrants and non-Europeans (see Calliste 1987; Li 1979). It can also take the form of employers' refusal to accept foreign-earned employment credentials, hence causing employer-based discrimination. This is a theme that emerged out of the hearings held by the government's task force on multiculturalism in the preparation of its report, *Equality Now!* (Special Committee on Visible Minorities 1984), and that was echoed in the royal commission report, *Equality in Employment* (1984). According to the latter, non-European immigrants have reported that "they were people with recognized qualifications and proven job skills who found, nonetheless, that they were simply not promoted or given the same opportunities as whites with similar qualifications" (Royal Commission 1984, 47). Thus, individuals with the same qualifications and experience are unequally rewarded because of the belief of some employers that such experience is less relevant to Canadian conditions, or not comparable to Canadian training. The economic savings that employers stand to gain from these practices would not be inconsiderable. Given the increasing importance of non-European labour in the labour market, these earnings differentials could become the object of increasing concern, if not hostility, on the part of the non-European factions of the working class.

Conclusions

Racism and racial inequality have been central to the formation and reproduction of capitalist relations of production in Canada. Racism is not an anomalous feature of social and economic relations that will eventually disappear of its own accord. Rather, racism is intrinsically linked with the process of capitalist production via the regulation of the labour supply, the allocation of groups of people to particular sites in production relations, and the political marginalization of groups of people, which makes them less able to resist exploitation by employers by political means.

This conception of institutional racism does not bode well for state-funded efforts to improve "race relations" (Bolaria and Li 1985, 29–31). Given a structural analysis of institutional racism, efforts to reduce racism that focus on multicultural education and increasing intercultural contacts are doomed to be of limited value and success. The assumption underlying such efforts is that racism is the result of ignorance or malevolence on the part of individuals, and that education is all that is required for amelioration. The analysis of racism that is inherent in these efforts and practices simply contributes to the further mystification of institutional racism, and hence is nothing more than an attempt to "give the appearance of change without changing the status quo" (Bolaria and Li 1985, 29).

Study Questions

1. What is the major focus of the psychological and cultural explanations of ethnic and racial inequality? What are the criticisms that have been made against these explanations of inequality?

2. What are the dimensions of institutional racism in Canada? How can they be linked to the operation of the capitalist system?

3. What evidence is there for racially based earnings inequalities in Canada? Do costs and benefits associated with ethnic origin exist in the job market? How are these inequalities rooted in the operation of the capitalist system?

4. To what extent are efforts to eliminate institutional racism likely to be successful if they focus attention on education and cross-cultural misunderstanding? Why?

Recommended Reading

Bolaria, B. Singh, and Peter Li. *Racial Oppression in Canada.* 2d ed. Toronto: Garamond Press, 1988.

Bonacich, Edna. "The Past, Present, and Future of Split Labour Market Research." In *Research in Race and Ethnic Relations,* eds. C. Marrett and C. Leggon. Greenwich, CT: JAI Press, 1979.

Lewis, Oscar. *La Vida: A Puerto Rican Family in the Culture of Poverty.* New York: Random House, 1966.

Li, Peter. *Ethnic Inequality in a Class Society.* Toronto: Wall Thompson, 1988.

Rainwater, L., and W. Yancey. *The Moynihan Report and Politics of Controversy.* Cambridge, MA: MIT Press, 1967.

Ryan, William. *Blaming the Victim.* New York: Vintage Books, 1976.

Satzewich, Vic. "Racism and Canadian Immigration Policy: The Government's View of Caribbean Migration, 1962–1966." *Canadian Ethnic Studies* 21 (1989): 1–13.

References

Abella, R.S. 1984. *Equality in Employment: A Royal Commission Report.* Ottawa: Minister of Supply and Services.

Beaujot, R. 1992. "The Socio-Demographic Impact on Immigration." In *The Immigration Dilemma*, ed. S. Globerman. Vancouver: The Fraser Institute.

Beaujot, R., K. Basavarajappa, and R. Verma. 1988. *Current Demographic Analysis: Income of Immigrants in Canada.* Ottawa: Statistics Canada.

Bolaria, S., and P. Li. 1985. *Racial Oppression in Canada.* Toronto: Garamond Press.

Bonacich, E., 1976. "Advanced Capitalism and Black–White Race Relations in the United States: A Split Labour Market Analysis." *American Sociological Review* 41: 34–51.

———. 1979. "The Past, Present and Future of Split Labor Market Research." In *Research in Race and Ethnic Relations*, ed. C. Marrett and C. Leggon. Greenwich, CT: JAI Press. 17–64.

Bowles, S., and H. Gintis. 1977. "I.Q. in the U.S. Class Structure." In *Power and Ideology in Education*, ed. J. Karabel and A. Halsey. New York: Oxford University Press. 215–31.

Boyd, M. 1992. "Gender Visible Minority and Immigrant Earnings Inequality: Reassessing an Employment Equity Premix." In *Deconstructing A Nation: Immigration, Multiculturalism and Racism in 1990s Canada*, ed. V Satzewich. Halifax: Fairwood.

Calliste, A. 1987. "Sleeping Car Porters in Canada: An Ethnically Submerged Split Labour Market." *Canadian Ethnic Studies* 19: 1–20.

Castles, S., and G. Kosack. 1973. *Immigrant Workers and Class Structure in Western Europe*. London: Oxford University Press.

Clement, W. 1975. *The Canadian Corporation Elite*. Toronto: McClelland and Stewart.

Darroch, G. 1979. "Another Look at Ethnicity, Stratification, and Social Mobility in Canada." *Canadian Journal of Sociology* 4: 1–25.

Gordon. M. 1964. *Assimilation in American Life*. New York: Oxford University Press.

Hawkins, F. 1974. "Canadian Immigration Policy and Management." *International Migration Review* 7: 141–53.

———. 1989. *Critical Years in Immigration: Canada and Australia Compared*. Montreal and Kingston: McGill–Queen's University Press.

Herberg, E. 1989. *Ethnic Groups in Canada: Adaptations and Transitions*. Scarborough, ON: Nelson.

Horan, P. 1978. "Is Status Attainment Research Atheoretical?" *American Sociological Review* 43: 534–41.

Lautard, H., and D. Loree. 1984. "Ethnic Stratification in Canada, 1931–1971". *Canadian Journal of Sociology* 9: 333–43.

Lewis, O. 1966. *La Vida: A Puerto Rican Family in the Culture of Poverty*. New York: Random House.

Li, P. 1979. "A Historical Approach to Ethnic Stratification: The Case of the Chinese in Canada." *Canadian Review of Sociology and Anthropology* 16: 320–32.

———. 1980. "Immigration Laws and Family Patterns: Some Demographic Changes Among Chinese Families in Canada, 1885–1971." *Canadian Ethnic Studies* 12: 58–73.

———. 1987. "Race and Ethnic Relations." In *An Introduction to the Social World*, ed. R. Richardson and L. Tepperman. Toronto: McGraw-Hill Ryerson. 211–35.

———. 1988. *Ethnic Inequality in a Class Society*. Toronto: Wall and Thompson.

———. 1992. "Race and Gender as Basis of Class Fractions and Their Effects on Earnings." *Canadian Review of Sociology and Anthropology*. 29: 488–510.

Mackenzie, I. 1986. "The Canadian State and Domestic Workers From the Caribbean: The Domestic Scheme." Paper. Carleton University.

Miles, R. 1982. *Racism and Migrant Labour*. London: Routledge and Kegan Paul.

——— . 1989. *Racism*. London: Tavistock.

Nagler, M. 1972. "Minority Values and Economic Achievement: The Case of the North American Indian." In *Perspectives on the North American Indian*, ed. Nagler. Toronto: McClelland and Stewart. 131–41.

Nikolinakos, M. 1975. "Notes Towards and General Theory of Migration in Late Capitalism." *Race and Class* 17: 5–18.

Petras, E. 1980. "The Role of National Boundaries in a Cross-National Labour Market." *International Journal of Urban and Regional Research* 4: 157–95.

Porter, J. 1965. *The Vertical Mosaic*. Toronto: University of Toronto Press.

———. 1986. *The Measure of Canadian Society*. Ottawa: Carleton University Press.

Rainwater, L., and W. Yancey. 1967. *The Moynihan Report and the Politics of Controversy*. Cambridge: MIT Press.

Rosen, B. 1956. "The Achievement Syndrome: A Psychocultural Dimension of Social Stratification." *American Sociological Review* 21: 203–11.

———. 1959. "Race, Ethnicity, and the Achievement Syndrome." *American Sociological Review* 24: 47–60.

Royal Commission on Equality in Employment. 1984. Report. Ottawa: Minister of Supply and Services.

Rushton, P., and A. Bogaart. 1987. "Race Differences in Sexual Behaviour: Testing an Evolutionary Hypothesis." *Journal of Research in Personality*. 21: 529–51.

———. 1988. "Race Versus Social Class Differences in Sexual Behavior: A Follow-up Test of the r/k Dimension." *Journal of Research in Personality*. 22: 259–72.

Ryan, W. 1976. *Blaming the Victim*. New York: Vintage Books.

Sampat-Mehta R. 1972. *International Barriers*. Ottawa: Harpell's Press.

Satzewich, V. 1989a. "Canadian Capitalism and Unfree Labour: The Incorporation of Polish War Veterans." *Studies in Political Economy* 26: 98–123.

———. 1989b. "Racism and Canadian Immigration Policy: The Government's View of Caribbean Migration, 1962–1966." *Canadian Ethnic Studies* 21: 77–97.

———. 1989c. "Racisms: The Reactions to Chinese Migrants in Canada at the Turn of the Century." *International Sociology* 4: 311–27.

Satzewich, V., and P. Li. 1987. "Immigrant Labour in Canada: The Cost and Benefit of Ethnic Origin in the Job Market." *Canadian Journal of Sociology* 12: 229–41.

Special Committee on Visible Minorities in Canadian Society. 1984. *Equality Now!* Ottawa: Minister of Supply and Services.

Stasiulis, D. 1987. "Rainbow Feminism: Perspectives on Minority Women in Canada." *Resources for Feminist Research* 16: 5–9.

Ujimoto, V. 1985. "The Japanese." In Bolaria and Li, *Racial Oppression*. 105–36.

Valentine, C. 1968. *Culture and Poverty*. Chicago: University of Chicago Press.

Vernon, P. 1984. "Abilities and Achievements of Ethnic Groups in Canada with Special Reference to Canadian Natives and Orientals." In *Multiculturalism in Canada*, ed. R. Samuda et al. Boston: Allyn and Bacon. 382–95.

Walvin, J. 1987. "Black Caricature: The Roots of Racism." In *"Race" in Britain*, ed. C. Husbands. London: Hutchinson. 59–72.

Ward, W.P. 1978. *White Canada Forever*. Montreal and Kingston: McGill–Queen's University Press.

Wien, F. 1986. *Rebuilding the Base of Indian Communities: The Micmac in Nova Scotia*. Montreal: Institute for Research on Public Policy.

Wilson, W. 1973. *Power, Racism, and Privilege*. London: Collier Macmillan.

CHAPTER 6

From the Bottom Up: Institutional Structures and the Native People

James S. Frideres

Learning Objectives

This chapter discusses many of the economic and social consequences for the Native people of institutional racism and racial exploitation. The data on economic and social indicators demonstrate that Canada's Native people live in the most impoverished conditions of any group in this country. These inequalities are the result of the history of colonial exploitation and of the current institutional structures and institutional discrimination against the First Nations peoples. Students are encouraged to consider and analyze the issues of economic and social inequality, land claims, and self-government in historical and contemporary contexts.

Introduction

The problems now facing the First Nations peoples are not new. The plight of Natives in Canadian society has been recognized for well over two centuries. It was clear by the seventeenth century that they were not participating fully in the economic and political structure of what was to become Canada. Their situation is the result of the historical and current distribution of power, particularly economic power, and their domination by powerful interest groups. The Native people have had interaction with Canadian society on the economic, political, and social levels that have shaped their unique position in Canada's stratified system; nevertheless, their involvement has been marginal and episodic.

As we shall discover, the state is *not* a neutral agent of the people, but is biased in favour of those with wealth—the upper social classes and the large corporations. As we analyze the bias of the system, we shall begin to see that, contrary to popular belief, the social system does not produce a society that is democratic, just, and equal in opportunity. Rather, we may find that society is an "upside-down" society, with a few benefiting at the expense of the many. Finally, we shall see how our society itself is the source of social problems (Eitzen and Zinn 1989, 21).

Many people tend to view "society" as the cause of social problems. The process of attributing a cause to such an abstraction allows the individual to deny any personal responsibility. Society does not cause anything; rather, the structure of society (the arrangement of the various institutional orders) has an impact on people's behaviour. It is this institutional order and its linkages that will be the focus of this chapter, as it attempts to unravel the causes that have placed, and continue to place, aboriginal Canadians in the lower class of society.

Minority Groups

Canada is a mosaic of various ethnic groups. However, they are not all equal in power, resources, prestige, or presumed worth. But why is one group alleged to be superior to another? The main reason is differential power—power derived from superior numbers, technology, property, or economic resources. Those holding superior power in a society establish a system of inequality by dominating less-powerful groups, and this system of inequality is then maintained and perpetuated by power (Eitzen and Zinn 1989).

Minority groups are composed of people with similar characteristics that differ significantly from the dominant group. The characteristics are visible, though not necessarily physical, because any symbol can be used to differentiate groups—for example, skin colour, hair texture, clothes, place of residence, and culture. Another common attribute that all minority groups have is that they are singled out for differential and unfair treatment compared to the treatment received by the dominant group. In the end, the discrimination may be subtle or blatant, but it is always detrimental to members of the minority group.

Over time, some ethno-cultural groups have overcome some aspects of discrimination and moved into the mainstream of society, while other groups have remained in subordinate status. Natives have not become assimilated into Canadian society. they continue to be victims of discrimination. Two factors seem particularly germane here. First, Natives can easily be identified by physical, or phenotypical, attributes, such as the colour of their skin. They find it hard, if not impossible, to escape the negative stereotypes that have been attached to those attributes. Second, the nature and duration of their contact with the dominant group has shaped the position they now occupy in Canadian society. Negative stereotypes and infrequent contacts with the dominant group have contributed to their inferior status and marginal participation in the socio-economic system.

The behaviour and characteristics of most Natives are stereotyped and systematically condemned by the dominant or majority group members of Canadian society. They typically are victims of stereotyping by the dominant groups, because these negative generalizations allow members of dominant groups to discriminate against them, which in turn keeps them in a subordinate status.

Before we proceed to an analysis of these matters, our first task will be to give an account of Canada's aboriginal population—their numbers, location, and classification into various categories. Then the chapter will provide a brief historical review of Native–European contact, and go on to discuss selected socio-economic attributes of Native people. It will conclude with an explanation of how their marginal position could have come about and then been sustained for well over two centuries.

Aboriginal Canadians

Under the Canadian Constitution of 1982, aboriginal Canadians are defined as status Indians, Inuit, and Métis. Today's official government population count suggests that there are well over one-half million status Indians, Métis, and Inuit. Native people argue that if one adds non-status Indians to the list, there are nearly two million aboriginal Canadians. Within each of these groups there are several subcategories, such as treaty and reserve Indians. Table 6.1 provides the specific details.

In the last quarter-century, the number of registered Indians has more than doubled—from 192 000 to 521 000. This dramatic increase in population has resulted from the population's extremely high annual growth rate of nearly 3 percent.[1] This rate of growth is more than double the general Canadian growth rate. Where are these First Nations people? Nearly one-quarter (22 percent) reside in Ontario. About 18 percent are in British Columbia, with 16 percent and 15 percent in Saskatchewan and Manitoba, respectively. An additional 13 percent live in Alberta, while only 10 percent are in Quebec. The remaining 7 percent reside in the Atlantic provinces and in the northern regions of Canada.

TABLE 6.1: Different Categories of Aboriginal Peoples in Canada by Population, 1991

Status Indians[a]	521 461
Treaty reserve	74%
Treaty non-reserve	4%
Non-treaty reserve	20%
Non-treaty non-reserve	2%
Métis[b]	225 000
On colony	2%
Off colony	98%
Inuit	37 000
With disc number	57%
Without disc number	43%
Global estimates for those with Native ancestry	1+ million

Notes: [a]Status Indians are sometimes referred to as registered or legal Indians. [b]This figure is based on the 1986 census.

Sources: Department of Indian Affairs and Native Development, *Indian Register, 1961–87* (Ottawa: Minister of Supply and Services, 1987); DIAND, *Basic Departmental Data - 1991* (Ottawa: Minister of Supply and Services Canada, 1992). Reproduced with the permission of the Minister of Supply and Services Canada, 1994.

Fewer than one-third (29 percent) of Natives don't live on a reserve, although there is some variation among provinces; for example, 34 percent live off the reserve in Saskatchewan, 14 percent in Quebec. Most Natives live in rural areas, although nearly as many (37 percent) live in or very near an urban centre. The remaining Natives either live in remote areas where there is no year-round road access, or live a considerable distance (more than 350 km) from an urban centre.

Natives live on more than 2250 reserves—lands set aside for Natives but held in trust for them by the federal government—across Canada. The size of these reserves varies from a few hectares in British Columbia to thousands of hectares in Alberta. These reserves are entrusted to political structures referred to as bands. Currently there are nearly six hundred bands. This, of course, means that in many cases one band will inhabit more than one reserve.

TABLE 6.2: Registered Indian Population and Lands, by Region, 1991

	Atlantic Prov.	Quebec	Ontario	Man.	Sask.	Alberta	BC	NWT	Yukon	Canada
Total Indian population, 1991	19 935	50 728	117 152	76 793	78 573	63 169	87 135	11 856	6450	511 791
% of total Indian population, 1991	3.9	9.9	22.9	15.0	15.4	12.3	17.0	2.3	1.3	100.00
% of total provincial/territorial population, 1984	0.6	0.5	0.9	4.9	5.4	1.9	2.2	17.2	16.5	1.4
% living off reserve, 1984	28.2	14.4	31.9	26.7	34.0	24.7	35.9	7.2	24.5	28.7
Number of Indian bands, 1985	33	39	126	60	68	41	196	14	17	594
% of Indian bands, 1985	5.2	6.6	21.3	10.1	11.5	6.9	33.1	2.4	2.9	100.0
Number of reserves and settlements, 1985	67	33	185	103	142	90	1610	29	25	2284
% of reserves and settlements, 1985	2.9	1.4	8.1	4.5	6.2	3.9	70.5	1.3	1.1	100.0

Sources: DIAND Program Reference Centre, *Registered Indian Population by Sex and Residence*, and *Schedule of Indian Bands, Reserves and Settlements* (Ottawa: Minister of Supply and Services, 1986). Reproduced with permission of the Minister of Supply and Services Canada 1994; A. Siggner, "The Socio-demographic Conditions of Registered Indians," *Canadian Social Trends* Cat. no. 11-008E (Winter 1986): 3. Reproduced by authority of the Minister of Industry, 1994.

What do the labels *Indian, Métis, non-status*, and *Inuit* mean, and why have they become important? First of all, the labels identify different groups of people who have different obligations, responsibilities, and privileges. The genesis of the labels is not discussed in this chapter, but their current consequences are very important. Registered Indians have been given "legal" definition and are enrolled in the register of the Department of Indian Affairs. They are subject to the provisions of one of the most pervasive pieces of federal legislation, the Indian Act, and thus are under federal jurisdiction. Non-status Indians have no such special standing. Along with status Indians, they are often referred to as Natives or the First Nations. The term *Métis*, represents a group composed of the offspring of Native/European marriages. These people are now in the process of trying to establish a clear definition of who can legitimately call themselves Métis and to acquire some aboriginal rights. Until recently they have been considered, for the most part, as Canadians without any special status; they generally come under provincial legislation. Inuit (Inuvialuit) usually reside in the Northwest Territories (in Nunavut or Denendeh) or in northern Quebec. While they are dealt with through the provisions of the federal Indian Act, they are not Indian. In addition to being partly under federal jurisdiction, they are also subject to some provincial or territorial legislation.

The development of a number of categories of aboriginal people has not been a historical accident. It is a classic example of how minor (cultural and physiological) differences are accentuated over time when it is in the interest of the dominant group. Eventually groups begin to accept their labels, the attributes associated with those labels, and the boundaries of their group. Under these conditions, the dominant group will define the various groups and treat them as either homogeneous or heterogeneous, depending upon what is in the dominant group's best interest. For this reason, you will see that the definition of who is Indian, Métis, and Inuit has changed over time. Their rights also have changed.

Extent and Origin of the Native Problem

To understand the "Native problem" fully, we must see it in historical perspective. The number of Natives in Canadian society has changed over the past three centuries. It is estimated that in the 1600s there were approximately 900 000 Natives living in North America, of whom about 250 000 were in what we now call Canada. However, by the late eighteenth century, Canadian Natives had been reduced to fewer than 200 000, and by 1867 the population stood at only approximately 102 000 (Siggner 1986). Epidemics, poor health, and European-inspired wars led to the massive reduction of the population. For the first half of the twentieth century, the Native population fluctuated between 100 000 and 125 000. Only after the Second World War did the Native population begin a pattern of continued growth (see Figure 1). Others, such as the Métis, were simply written out of history in 1940 by the dominant group; the Métis did not re-emerge as a bona tide ethnocultural group until they were recognized as a legitimate group under the Canadian Constitution of 1982.

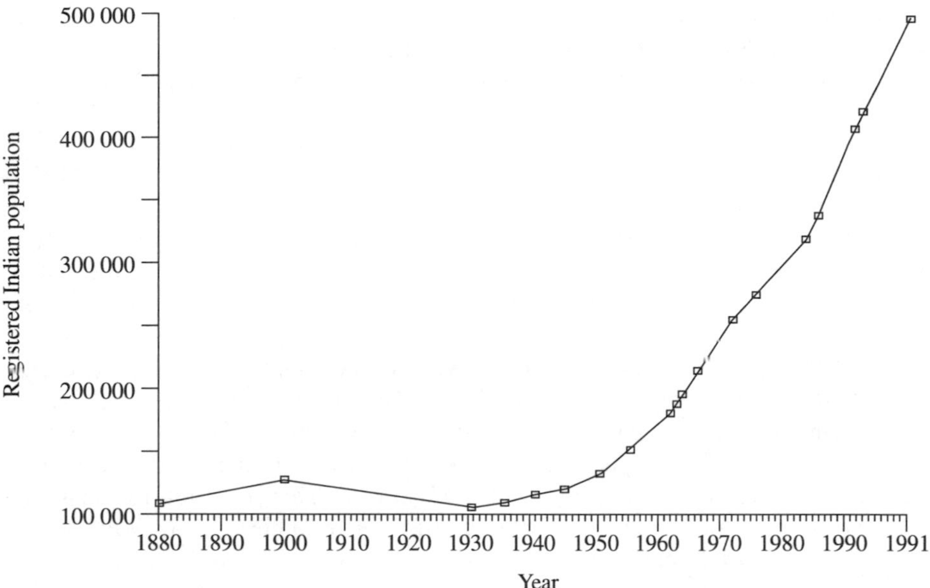

FIGURE 6.1: Population of Native People in Canada, 1881–1991

Source: DIAND, Evaluation Directorate, *Basic Developmental Data* (December) (Ottawa: Minister of Supply and Services, 1988), pp. 3–13. Reproduced with the permission of the Minister of Supply and Services, 1994.

Since the early nineteenth century, when Native–European contact became regularized and sustained, the Canadian government has continually enforced a policy of "civilizing" the Natives. Early contacts in the East were generally symbiotic, but it was not long before the pressure of European settlement changed the nature of the relationship. At first, the military was particularly interested in creating and maintaining positive relations with Native people; contractual relationships such as military alliances predominated. In the early 1800s, Natives played a prominent role in the development of Canada and were treated respectfully, since they were allies of the government and important to the Canadian economy. After the War of 1812, however, the usefulness of Natives as military allies against the Americans was minimal. By the 1830s their military role was obsolete, and they were no longer a valued group in Canadian society. As time went on, they became an obstacle to European settlers attempting to cultivate the land. As Trigger (1986) points out, from the mid-1800s Natives ceased to be a living presence in the lives of Canadians.

As a tentative solution to dealing with the First Nations, Peace and Friendship Treaties were established in the Maritime provinces from quite early on.[2] The Royal Proclamation of 1763 was one such attempt simultaneously to maintain the peace, allow settlement of the country, and pacify the Natives. Nevertheless, as more and more immigrants entered the country, greater pressure for land and settlement emerged. Immigrants began to settle in the countryside and develop an extensive agricultural economy. This influx began to put pressures on the Native people's traditional lifestyle. Their nomadic way of life was disturbed and they had to share the natural food supply with the settlers. Ecological changes began to have an effect on the flora and fauna. The Native population struggled for survival against diseases and epidemics.

Disease did more than decimate the Native population; it prepared the way for subsequent phases of European contact by breaking the First Nations' morale and by cracking their spiritual edifice. Martin (1974) points out that epidemics were events that made the Natives believe that their cultural system had lost control or influence over the supernatural realm. In short, the epidemics subverted the Native cultural system and opened the way to a corruption of the Natives' relationship with the land.

The federal government was still responsible for dealing with the Natives. By the mid-1880s, the government's responsibility shifted to that of caretaker, particularly of their land. It also passed statutes exempting Natives from taxation and sought to ban the selling of liquor to Natives as well. The protection being offered Natives was only to continue until they became "civilized." This intention to assimilate them is most explicitly stated in the Civilization of Indian Tribes Act (1857). Paternalism would dominate Native–non-Native relations for the next century. As Bartlett (1988) points out, during the Depression, federal government interference in the daily lives of Natives reached its peak.

In the middle of the nineteenth century, the federal government embarked upon a policy of "negotiating" treaties with the Native population as part of the larger strategy of "taking care" of the Natives. The Robinson Huron Treaties were quickly followed by the numbered treaties, which were still being drafted in the early twentieth century. Figure 6.2 identifies the land area encompassed in the treaties. It was the Saulteaux who first insisted on a specific treaty. Fear of violence motivated the government to respond (Morris 1880). The government had assumed, at the outset, that they could simply take over the land occupied by First Nations. Their resistance forced the government to reconsider their strategy of developing the West.

These treaties created reserves for Natives and extinguished all aboriginal land rights for the Natives making the treaty. This period in Canadian history was pivotal in the placement of aboriginals in Canadian society.

The Canadian government, having established reserves in order to allow for European settlement and agricultural development of the land, did not develop a coherent or consistent policy for dealing with the Native population. All agreed that the Natives needed to assimilate into the dominant society and that integration was inevitable. It was widely agreed that Natives would become "extinct" within a few years. As a result, the government's notion of itself as the Natives' caretaker changed and it began to consider how the process of assimilation could be facilitated. Some felt that isolation of Natives on the reserves would render them harmless and that within a few years they would either die out or lose their identity through the proselytizing efforts of various religious groups. Others felt that social and physical integration of Natives was the solution to the "Indian problem". Over time, both strategies were employed. Both had their problems. In the end, the government concluded its experiments before they showed any obvious effect. What was clear, however, was that the First Nations were no longer defined as an

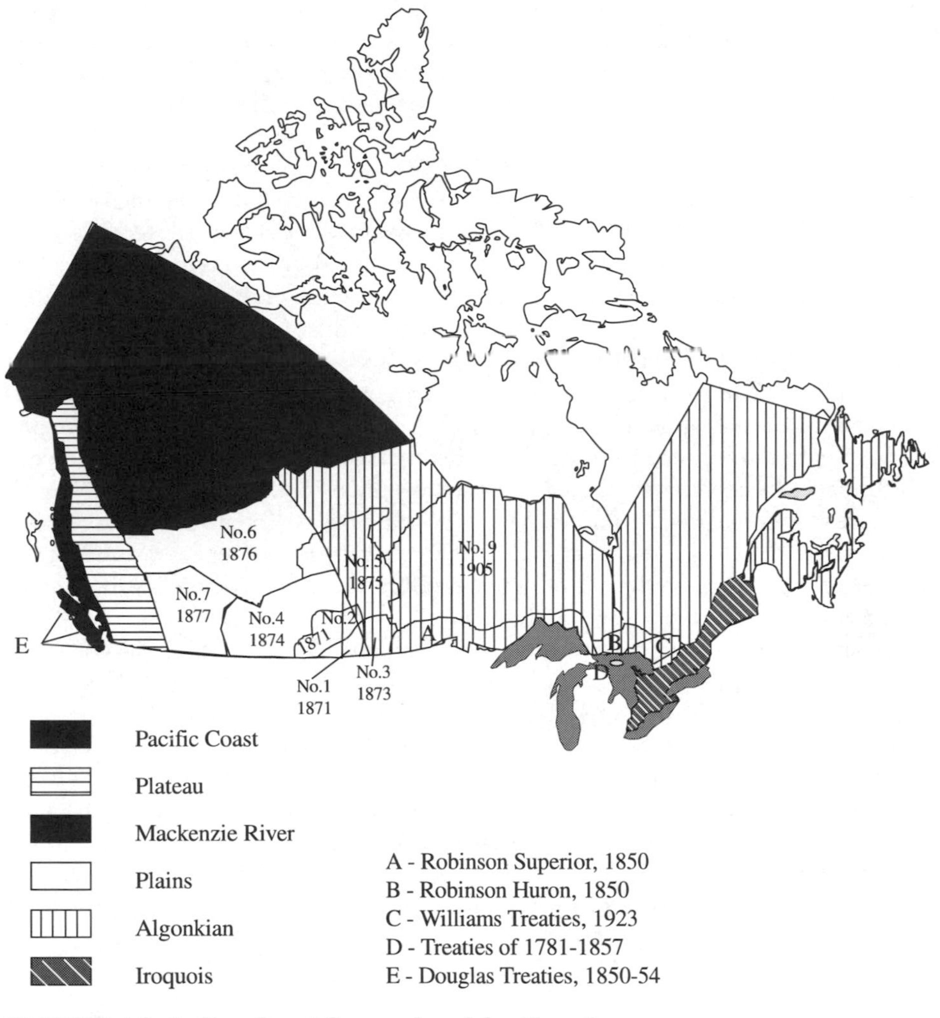

FIGURE 6.2: Indian Land Surrendered for Treaties

Source: James S. Frideres, *Native Peoples in Canada: Contemporary Conflicts* (Scarborough, ON: Prentice-Hall, 1988), p. 10.

important segment of our society. As Trelease (1960) points out, as Native people grew economically subordinate to Europeans, their confidence in their own value system was undermined and they became increasingly susceptible to Christian proselytizing. By the 1920s, they had been relegated to the periphery of our modern, industrial society.

Nevertheless, Native people still constituted a visible segment of the Canadian population, and the government continued to develop policies and programs to handle this problematic group. Early policies were piecemeal and independent; they dealt with Native issues only as they emerged. Even though the Indian Act was implemented in 1876, it was simply a compilation of previous acts and an attempt to sort out their contradictions. Nevertheless, once it was consolidated the Indian Act became (and continues to be) the most pervasive piece of federal legislation in regulating and controlling the lives of status Indians, as well as defining who is an Indian.

One hundred years after the Indian Act of 1876 was implemented, legal authority over the management and control of Indian lands and property remained with the Superintendent of Indian Affairs. The amendments of 1884 and subsequent years prohibited status Indians from engaging in certain cultural activities, such as the Potlatch and the Tamanawas. Bartlett (1988) points out that the policy of "civilization" adopted by the federal government has included, as its control thesis, cultural destruction of the First Nations.

After the Second World War, the Canadian government gave up its caretaking role and embarked upon a "democratization" role. Federal policies were implemented that produced the illusion that status Indians had decision-making powers. This process has continued to evolve, as status Indians today attempt to implement strategies for complete self-government. Nevertheless, assimilation of Natives continues to remain the pre-eminent goal of the government. As recently as 1969, the federal government developed a policy in a White Paper that declared as its aim the total assimilation of the Native population.

Because most Natives lived in rural areas until after the Second World War, their presence and contribution to the building of Canada were minimized. Repressive legislation kept them from organizing and building social movements to promote their interests, and their isolation on the reserves restricted their participation to the margins of the larger society. Their attempts to improve themselves included migration to the urban areas. As the cities expanded in the 1950s and 1960s, more jobs became available and Native migration accelerated. In 1930, nearly all Natives lived in rural areas; by 1980, well over one-third of the Native population lived in urban areas. However, they quickly found that, in a segregated society, life in an urban area did not open the door to economic opportunity or prosperity.

Social Structures

Institutional Discrimination

Until recently, Native people were without any real power. Most of the day-to-day decisions that influenced them were made by Indian Affairs officials. Any decision made by band councils was subject to approval by the Department of Indian Affairs and Northern Development (DIAND), whose officials were the major political and economic force on the reserve. Status Indian peoples were not allowed to handle their own affairs because of an administrative structure that denied them the opportunity to learn new ways of doing things while at the same time rendering the traditional culture ineffective (Thomas 1966–67).

As Wax (1971, 67) has clearly pointed out, the land that was eventually set aside for Natives was selected because it was away from the main routes of travel, not suitable for agricultural development, and lacking in visible natural resources such as mineral wealth. The result has been that most reserves have not had an adequate ecological basis for their existence as self-sufficient communities. From their inception, the reserves have required extensive subsidization; in turn, this has legitimized Indian Affairs involvement in Native communities.

The major policy trend in Canadian society since the turn of the century has been the development of the welfare state, which has resulted in the transformation of previously private relationships into public ones. The state has entered into almost all social and economic aspects of Canadian life in an attempt to increase equality by redistributing income. As Brooks (1989) points out, however, the welfare state as it exists today has been constructed without any significant reduction in the unequal distribution of income. This is particularly notable in the case of Canada's Native people. Since the turn of the century, Natives have not enhanced their economic status or relative position in the Canadian class system.

Three institutional structures illustrate how the pervasive nature of institutional discrimination has affected Native people: health, education, and economic opportunities.

Health

In 1950, the mortality rate for status Indians was 11 per 1000 population; by 1990 this had been reduced by nearly two-thirds—to 3.8 per 1000 (see Table 6.3). While this figure represents a substantial decrease, it is still twice the national rate for

TABLE 6.3: Number of Deaths and Mortality Rates for the Registered Indian Population (rate per 1000), Canada, 1955–1986

Year	Number of Deaths	Mortality Rate
1955	1578	10.5
1960	1623	8.8
1967	1932	8.4
1976	1875	7.3
1982	1709	6.0
1983	1642	5.7
1986	1671	5.3
1990	1357	3.8

Sources: **1955–1967:** Adapted from *Health and Welfare Canada Annual Reports, 1962* and *1967*; Statistics Canada, *Reference Census Canada* (Ottawa: Minister of Supply and Services, 1987); **1990:** DIAND, *Basic Departmental Data - 1992* (Ottawa: Minister of Supply and Services, 1993). Reproduced with permission of the Minister of Supply and Services, 1994.

Canadians. For specific age groups, such as those aged five to nineteen, the mortality rate of status Indians is four times the national rate. There has been a dramatic decrease in the infant mortality rate: in 1960, the rate was 82 per 1000; in 1986 it was 16.5; it has now decreased to 10.2. Nevertheless, the newer rate still represents nearly double the national standard. Life expectancy is another indicator of health. In the 1950s, status Indians could expect to live 54 years. As Table 6.4 shows, there has been a consistent increase in life expectancy for status Indian men and women. These figures, while representing great strides in life expectancy, still fall short of the general Canadian life expectancy— 78.2 years (see Table 6.4).

In the first half of the twentieth century, infectious and parasitic digestive and respiratory diseases were the main cause of death of Native people. Since then, some of these diseases have sharply declined in importance. Since the 1960s, however, injury and poisoning, circulatory system diseases, and neoplasms (malignant tumours) have become the main cause of death within status Indian communities (see Table 6.5). Information from Indian Affairs and from medical services shows that nearly 60 percent of status Indian illnesses and deaths are alcohol related. As Bienvenue (1985) points out, general living conditions and feelings of uselessness and estrangement from the larger society are considered important factors underlying the nature and circumstances of Native illness and death.

Housing is another dimension of health. Governmental assistance in providing housing is necessary because of the legal framework of the Indian Act. Until very recently the Department of Indian Affairs has administered and delivered all aspects of housing for status Indians. Therefore, First Nations people have had little to say in the design, planning, and building of their own housing.

While the status Indian population has steadily increased, the number of dwellings on reserves has fluctuated as new housing programs have been phased in and out. For example, in the period 1975 to 1977, the growth rate of housing stock was less than 2 percent. From 1980 to 1981, however, the increase was 28 percent. As a result of the increasing number of houses on reserves, the number of persons per

TABLE 6.4: Life Expectancy at One Year for the Registered Indian Population by Gender, Canada, 1961–1981

Year	Male	Female
1961	59.7	63.5
1971	60.2	66.2
1976	61.1	67.6
1981	63.2	69.6
1991	65.7	73.0

Sources: **1961–1976**: R.H. Knox, *Indian Conditions: A Survey* (Ottawa: Indian and Northern Affairs Canada, 1980), p. 15; **1976–1981**: N.H. Lithwick, Marvin Schiff, and Eric Vernon, *An Overview of Registered Indian Conditions in Canada* (Ottawa: Indian and Northern Affairs Canada, 1986), p. 38; **1991**: DIAND, *Basic Departmental Data - 1992* (Ottawa: Minister of Supply and Services, 1993). Reproduced with the permission of the Minister of Supply and Services Canada, 1994.

TABLE 6.5: Number of Deaths, and Mortality Rates by Cause Among Registered Indian Population in Canada (rate per 100 000), Selected Years

	Rate			
	1955	**1978**	**1986**	**1990**
Infectious and parasitic	74.7	14.3	N/A	4.2
Neoplasms	48.0	61.3	51.8	52.1
Endocrine, nutritional and metabolic diseases, and immunity disorders; diseases of the blood and blood-forming organs	9.3	15.0	N/A	10.7
Mental disorders	N/A	12.3	N/A	3.9
Diseases of the nervous system and sense organs	5.3	10.8	N/A	4.5
Diseases of the circulatory system	166.7	176.8	124.9	105.0
Diseases of the respiratory system	231.3	57.8	39.7	30.8
Diseases of the digestive system	69.3	30.8	25.1	16.8
Diseases of the genito-urinary system	16.0	13.1	N/A	10.6
Complications of pregnancy, childbirth, and the puerperium	6.0	0.0	N/A	0.3
Diseases of the skin and subcutaneous tissue; diseases of the musculoskeletal system and connective tissue	8.7	3.9	N/A	1.6
Congenital anomalies	24.7	16.6	N/A	10.1
Certain conditions originating in the perinatal period	99.3	22.7	N/A	5.3
Symptoms, signs, and ill-defined conditions	100.0	29.3	N/A	16.8
Injury and poisoning	122.0	276.6	161.1	107.2
Others	70.7	11.2	N/A	N/A

Sources: **1955–1960:** Health and Welfare Canada, Medical Services Branch, *Annual Report 1962*; **1978–1982:** Health and Welfare Canada, *Indian and Inuit Canada, Health Status Indicators, 1974–1983* (Ottawa: Demographics and Statistics Division, 1986); Department of National Health and Welfare, Medical Services Branch (Ottawa: Demographics and Statistics Division, 1988); DIAND, *Basic Departmental Data* (Ottawa: Minister of Supply and Services, 1993). Reproduced with permission of the Minister of Supply and Services Canada, 1994.

house has steadily decreased over the past 30 years; in the early 1960s, there were more than six persons per house, while today there are fewer than five. Although the quality of the housing has increased over time, it is still considerably lower than the general Canadian standards. A relatively high percentage of status Indian houses require major repairs, more than one-third of the units are overcrowded, and almost a third lack running water or sanitation facilities; 13 percent require complete replacement. Finally, as Bienvenue (1985) points out, Indian housing is considered to be substandard in construction materials and heating systems. The incidence of fires in homes on the reserves is over seven times the national rate. Today, nearly all bands deliver their own housing programs. Nonetheless, they still have little say in the process that determines the total band budget, of which housing is but one component.

The extent to which a people are dependent on social assistance represents a third dimension of health. In the early 1960s, about 3000 status Indian children were under government care. This represented about 3.4 percent of the children under 16 years of age. This number steadily increased until the late 1970s, when the numbers peaked at well over 6100—nearly 7 percent of status Indian children. While there has been some decrease in numbers since that time, the cost of caring for these children has escalated over the past three decades. In the early 1960s, the cost of providing child care was about $2.5 million for a per-child expenditure of $883. By the late 1970s, the cost had jumped to $35 million, and today the total expenditures have reached well in excess of $100 million, with an average per-child expenditure of nearly $25 000 (see Table 6.6).

There has also been a substantial increase in the number of adult status Indians in residential care. In the early 1970s, there were only about 300 adults in care, which represented about 3.82 per 100 000. Today, the number of adults has increased to over 1000, which represents nearly 7 per 100 000. As with child care there has been a rise in the cost of providing adult care. In the 1986–87 fiscal year, the total expenditures were nearly $14 million, representing a per-adult expenditure

TABLE 6.6: Total and Per-Child Expenditures Excluding Service Delivery for Registered On-Reserve Indian Children in Care in Canada, 1965/66–1986/87

Fiscal year	Total children in care	Total expenditures (Current $)	Total expenditures (Constant 1986 $)	Per-child expenditures (Current $)	Per-child expenditures (Constant 1986 $)
1965/66	2 889	2 464 000	7 247 058	853	2 508
1970/71	5 156	10 042 000	31 479 624	1 948	6 105
1975/76	6 078	16 076 000	36 371 041	2 645	5 984
1980/81	5 716	29 485 700	43 877 530	5 158	7 676
1985/86	4 000	50 107 900	66 529 583	12 527	16 632
1986/87	3 612	52 411 400	71 979 700	14 510	19 978
1991/92	4 586	137 943 200		30 079	23 835

Source: DIAND, Evaluation Directorate, *Basic Developmental Data* (Ottawa: Minister of Supply and Services, 1992), p. 61. Reproduced with permission of the Minister of Supply and Services Canada, 1994.

of about $14 000 per year. In 1991/92 the total expenditure was nearly $18 million with a per capita expenditure of just over $26 000. Overall, the annual average number of status Indian social assistance recipients and dependants per month is now about 51 000, which means that if the dependants of these recipients are included, the total number is well in excess of 100 000. The cost of operating such a program is nearly $400 million per year and projections suggest that the cost will continue to increase.

Education

The constitutional basis of the federal government's special relationship with Natives stems from the Constitution Act, 1867. The federal government has chosen to legislate with respect to the education of Native children. Different sections of the Indian Act empower the minister of Indian Affairs to operate schools and to enter into agreements with provincial governments, school boards, and religious or charitable organizations for the education of Native children. Under various cabinet decisions and Treasury Board authorities, the government has extended its educational and support services to include prekindergarten and postsecondary programs. At no time were Natives consulted or, until recently, allowed to participate in the formal education of their children.

Early educational services were provided by various religious organizations. After the Second World War, however, the state intervened and substituted a secular education for the missionary efforts. It was also at this time that the federal government began to develop agreements with the provinces to force Native students to be educated in provincial schools along with non-native children, to ensure their assimilation. Over the past two decades, this plan of action has changed, and band schools (schools operated and controlled by local Native people on the reserve) have become an important element in the educational system. The significance of band schools can be assessed by looking at their growth: in the early 1960s there were none at all, but by 1988 there were over 250 (see Table 6.7).

Over the past quarter-century, the number of status Indian students has steadily increased. Enrolment in 1960 was 42 000, which represented 72 percent of the population aged 4 to 18. Today there are over 96 000 students, representing 95.5 percent of school-age children. Students are also remaining in school longer. In 1960, about 4 percent of the students who had enrolled in school twelve years earlier graduated from the school system. Ten years later, this percentage had increased to 15 percent. Today the rate has increased to over one-half of the students, although this still represents about half the retention rate for non-Natives. As a result, 70 percent of the status Indian population lack a high school degree, compared to the national average of 45 percent (see Table 6.8).

This longer stay in elementary and secondary schools has led to a greater number attending postsecondary educational institutions and universities. In 1960, there were about sixty Indian students attending university and about three hundred enroled in a postsecondary program. Today there are over six thousand status Indian students enrolled in university and another 21 000 thousand attending some other postsecondary educational institution. While these figures represent significant

TABLE 6.7: Indian Enrolment in Kindergarten, Elementary, and Secondary Educational Institutions by Type, and Expenditures (on Reserve Population)

Year	Number	Expenditure (Millions $)
Federal[a]		
1981/82	22 525	N/A
1982/83	21 825	N/A
1983/84	21 893	57.8
1984/85	21 669	72.9
1985/86	19 943	62.4
1986/87	18 814	66.1
1987/88	17 322	68.5
1988/89	14 219	62.6
1991/92	6 180	64.7
Band-operated[b]		
1982/83	15 912	N/A
1983/84	16 715	48.0
1984/85	18 372	58.6
1985/86	20 968	71.3
1986/87	23 424	78.7
1987/88	26 429	99.6
1988/89	29 696	107.8
1991/92	45 665	123.4
Provincial[c]		
1982/83	38 511	148.2
1983/84	39 474	157.7
1984/85	40 080	160.3
1985/86	39 712	170.0
1986/87	40 078	180.6
1987/88	40 520	195.5
1988/89	40 925	199.9
1991/92	43 092	203.1

Notes: [a]There are 123 federal schools. [b]There are 262 band schools. Thirty percent of the schools offer at least one year of high-school education. [c]Thirty-five percent of these students are in high schools.
Sources: DIAND, "Information Sheet No. 5," *Indian and Inuit Elementary and Secondary Education* (Ottawa: Minister of Supply and Services, 1989), pp. 1-8; DIAND, *Basic Departmental Data* (Ottawa: Minister of Supply and Services, 1993), p. 43. Reproduced by permission of the Minister of Supply and Services, 1994.

increases, they still only include 5 percent of the status Indian population over 20 years of age. This compares to the nearly 30 percent of the national population who are attending postsecondary educational institutions. Just as Natives were beginning to make inroads into postsecondary educational institutions, the federal government introduced Bill C-91, ostensibly as a cost-saving procedure, which limits the fund-

TABLE 6.8: Percentage of Registered Indian Students Remaining in Grade 12 or 13 for Consecutive Years of Schooling in Canada, 1960/61–1991/92

Year	Percentage	Year	Percentage
1960/61	3.4	1975/76	15.8
1961/62	4.3	1976/77	14.3
1963/64	4.1	1977/78	17.0
1964/65	5.8	1978/79	17.2
1965/66	6.0	1979/80	18.9
1966/67	5.1	1980/81	19.6
1967/68	7.5	1981/82	20.7
1968/69	10.6	1983/84	30.5
1969/70	12.6	1984/85	30.6
1970/71	14.6	1985/86	33.9
1971/72	15.6	1988/89	41.4
1973/74	17.4	1991/92	53.6
1974/75	13.6		

Sources: **1960/61–1977/78:** Statistics Division, Program Services Branch, DIAND, September 1979; **1978/79–1985/86:** Nominal Roll, Education Branch, DIAND, September 1985; DIAND, *Basic Departmental Data* (Ottawa: Minister of Supply and Services, 1993), p. 37.

ing of Native students and makes it more difficult for them to complete their postsecondary education.

Economic Opportunities

The proportion of the on-reserve population in the labour force has increased slightly over the past two decades. As assessment of provincial variations for 1986 shows that about one-third to one-half of the population 15 years and over participated in the labour force during the previous year (see Table 6.9). Nevertheless, unemployment is chronic in Native communities, with an average of 35 percent employed at any given time. Of those 35 percent, a large percentage are underemployed or employed as seasonal or part-time workers, often in service and unskilled jobs.

Income levels are related to both education and employment. As Table 6.10 shows, average annual income for status Indians is far less than the average Canadian income. The average income for status Indians living on the reserve is even lower. Significant differences also exist between Indians and the overall Canadian population with regard to the source of income. Government transfer payments, for example, old age and disability pensions, contributed nearly 40 percent of status Indian income, compared to about 16 percent for the general population.

Another measure of economic wellbeing is the dependency ratio. This represents the ratio of the number of people who are dependent (under 15 and over 65 years of

TABLE 6.9: Distribution and Proportion of On-Reserve Population 15 Years and Over in the Labour Force by Province, 1971, 1981, 1986

	1971			1981			1986[a]		
	On-reserve population 15 years and over	In the labour force		On-reserve population 15 years and over	In the labour force		On-reserve population 15 years and over	In the labour force	
Province		No.	%		No.	%		No.	%
PEI	165	65	39.4	165	75	45.5	255	165	64.7
Nova Scotia	1 830	575	31.4	2 475	930	37.6	3 087	1 101	35.7
NB	1 710	495	28.9	2 340	785	33.5	2 969	1 363	45.9
Quebec	12 595	5 230	41.5	18 240	7 465	40.9	21 144	8 870	42.0
Ontario	18 845	6 635	35.2	25 935	11 445	44.1	28 602	14 388	50.3
Manitoba	12 110	3 555	29.3	15 415	5 465	35.4	21 706	8 757	40.3
Saskatchewan	11 400	3 285	28.8	13 595	4 785	35.2	16 077	6 030	37.5
Alberta	10 905	3 800	34.8	13 205	5 100	38.6	17 897	7 644	42.7
BC	17 820	6 670	37.4	26 800	12 835	47.9	32 601	16 348	50.1
TOTAL[b]	87 380	30 310	34.7	118 170	48 885	41.4	144 338	64 666	44.8

Notes: [a]Population data for 1986 also include Indian settlements. [b]Numbers have been rounded.
Source: DIAND, *Basic Departmental Data* (Ottawa: Minister of Supply and Services, 1988) Table 1 and 1A, pp. 92–93.

age) per 100 persons in the labour market. Status Indians have a dependency ratio of nearly 90, compared to a national rate of 50.

Two additional issues that are related to the Native people's position in Canadian society need to be discussed before a sociological interpretation can be presented: land claims and self-government. Status Indians believe that a stable land base and self-government are necessary in order to retain their identity and adapt to the forces of the dominant society.

Land Claims

A large portion of Canada is currently the subject of comprehensive and specific claims by aboriginals (see Figure 6.3). Comprehensive claims are based on aboriginal peoples' traditional use and occupancy of the land. Specific claims are based on allegations that the government did not fulfil specific obligations to the First Nations under the treaties, the Indian Act, or some other agreement (Cassidy and Dale 1988).

Comprehensive claims have arisen in Yukon, Labrador, most of British Columbia, northern Quebec, and the Northwest Territories. They include such issues as land title; specified hunting, fishing, and trapping rights; financial compensation; and other rights and benefits. Nearly three hundred specific claims have been

TABLE 6.10: Average Family Income, Aboriginals and All Canadians, 1980 and 1985 (1985 constant dollars)

Group	1980	1985
Canada Average	39 100	38 700
All Status Indians	24 600	21 800
Indians:		
on reserve	21 400	20 900
off reserve	28 200	22 900
Inuit	28 200	27 800
All Aboriginals	27 200	29 300

Source: N.J. Hagey, G. Larocque and C. McBride, *Highlights of Aboriginal Conditions, 1981–2001* (Ottawa: Minister of Supply and Services, 1989), p. 38. Reproduced with permission of the Minister of Supply and Services Canada, 1994.

submitted for negotiation, with another fifteen hundred to two thousand expected by the twenty-first century. Of these, fewer than thirty have been settled.

Why have these claims emerged, and why now? Since the time of first contact, Europeans and First Nations have entered into agreements in an effort to reconcile or accommodate their divergent interests and aspirations. These early agreements between the government and aboriginals, and the later treaties, formally recognized the existence of the aboriginals' interest in the land and implicitly recognized their political rights (Task Force 1985). In signing a treaty, Natives surrendered all title to the land covered by the treaty. By the 1930s, when sufficient land had been acquired from Natives for agricultural, residential, and industrial development, the treaty-signing process was ended.

While land claims have now become commonplace, many of these claims originated years ago. Their acknowledgement today results from legal as well as political changes that have taken place over the past century. At one time they were obstructed by legislation that made it difficult for Natives to proceed with legal challenges regarding land claims; in 1927, section 141 of the Indian Act was passed to prohibit status Indian people from raising money or retaining a lawyer in order to pursue a land claim. The federal government also took the position that it had met all of its obligations regarding land compensation for Natives, and that where land had not been "treatied out," there were no aboriginal land rights.

This position was adhered to by the federal government until 1973, when the *Calder* decision forced them to reassess their position. In that decision, the Supreme Court agreed that aboriginal land rights existed and that a process of extinguishment had to be established. As a result, the government established separate units in Indian and Northern Affairs to deal with the land claims, both comprehensive and specific. Today, the government has placed a limit of six on the number of comprehensive negotiations that may proceed at one time (Task Force 1985). Nevertheless,

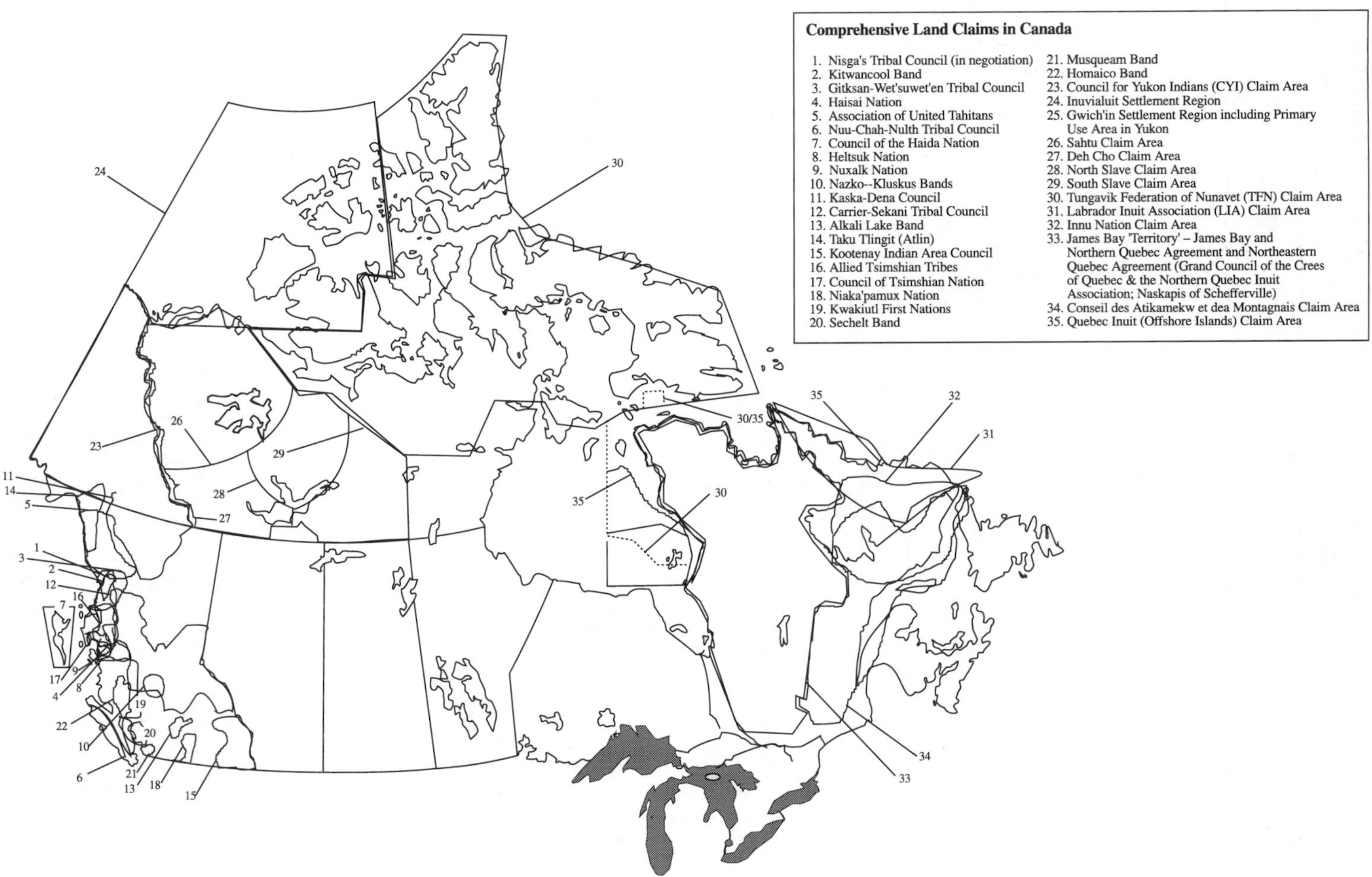

FIGURE 6.3: Comprehensive Native Claims in Canada

Source: Indian and Northern Affairs: The Task Force to Review Comprehensive Native Claims in Canada, *Living Treaties, Lasting Agreements: Report of the Task Force to Review Comprehensive Claims Policy* (Ottawa: DIAND, 1985). Reproduced with the permission of the Minister of Supply and Services Canada, 1994.

nearly twenty more have been accepted and await negotiation. Several additional claims are currently under review and may be accepted for negotiation in the future. Thus far only four comprehensive claims have been settled—the James Bay and Northern Quebec Agreement (1975), the Northeastern Quebec Agreement (1978), the Gwich'in Agreement (1992), and the agreement with the Inuvialuit of the western Arctic (1984). In 1977 the Gitksan and Wet'suwet'en's (Northwestern B.C.) land claim was accepted for negotiation by the federal government. By 1991, however, the government had rejected the claim. Currently the case is under appeal. In 1993, the Tungavik Federation of Nunavut (Eastern N.W.T.) signed an agreement with the federal government (which will come into effect in 1999) that will vest title to 350 000 square kilometres with the Inuit. Also, in 1993 the federal government, Yukon territory government, and the Council for Yukon Indians signed an Umbrella Final Agreement, which sets out the terms for final land claims settlements in Yukon. Finally, negotiations for a final agreement with the Sahtu Dene and Métis were completed in 1993. Tripartite task forces are now being established whereby the federal and provincial governments as well as First Nations negotiate settlements.

The federal government has until recently approached all settlement of claims with the aim of securing title to the land and extinguishing all claims. Native people, however, want the comprehensive claims agreements to affirm their aboriginal rights. In addition, they want the agreements to encourage economic development and help Native communities achieve self-sufficiency. They also hope that the process will enable them to establish political, social, and economic institutions that will allow their communities to become self-governing.

Although the government has agreed to negotiate land claims brought forward by Natives, it has not actively tried to resolve the differences emerging from these negotiations. As a result, it is estimated that it will take more than a century to settle those land claims currently accepted as valid. Several government reports have encouraged the federal government to change its stance and facilitate the process of negotiation; it has become clear that the status quo is unacceptable. Many argue that if settlements are achieved, Natives and non-Natives may enjoy mutual benefits and co-operation, and the economic position of Indians in Canadian society could be enhanced.

Self-Government

In their quest for economic self-sufficiency, Natives are also trying to achieve control over the management of matters that have direct impact on them. After the repatriation of the Canadian Constitution in 1982, aboriginal self-government began to emerge as a prominent issue in the constitutional debates. Natives are taking the position that self-government is an aboriginal right that predates European arrival in Canada. They believe that self-government is necessary for the achievement of the changes and goals they desire.

The issue of Native self-government has been discussed for many years. Its most recent formal discussion was at the fourth First Ministers' constitutional conference (1987). Because the provincial premiers would not endorse the policy, however, no constitutional procedures were undertaken to implement Native self-government. Instead, the federal government has embarked on a number of non-constitutional initiatives to achieve Native self-government, and has taken the position that each community should be able to tailor its form of government to its own needs and aspirations. Some of these forms are specified within the Indian Act, while others fall outside its provisions. An example of the latter is the Sechelt Indian Band Self-Government Act, 1986. The legislation under this act provides, among other things, for the transfer of full title of Sechelt lands to the band, and the management of those lands by the band, and includes a provision for the negotiation of funding agreements in the form of grants or transfer payments to be administered by the band council. The Sechelt community will be a legal entity, and will be able to enter into contracts and agreements, sell land, acquire property, and spend, invest, and borrow money.

The issue of Native self-government has produced considerable tension between Natives and non-Natives. The negotiations that the federal government is conducting do not affect treaty or other aboriginal rights, including land claims, and the government intends to continue the special relationship between Native people and the federal government. Nevertheless, Natives are concerned that these negotiated self-government agreements will give them powers that are merely those of a municipality. Most Natives see such limitations as inadequate and potentially dangerous. In addition, municipal governments are, in the end, answerable to the provinces, who have steadfastly resisted Native self-government. Finally, Natives are afraid that these municipal governments can be dealt with differentially and will thus be vulnerable to a "divide and conquer" strategy (Miller 1989).

A Sociological Perspective

Why do we find Natives occupying the lowest social status in our society? We might choose to provide an explanation based on the behaviour of individuals. Using this perspective, we would conclude that prejudicial and discriminatory behaviour by individual non-Natives has produced the condition in which Natives now find themselves. However, not all non-Natives discriminate against Natives. We now have laws designed to prevent discrimination. Few non-Native people come into sustained contact with Natives and engage in overt individual discriminatory behaviour. Why then do we still find Natives in a subjugated position?

The sociological perspective is that, over time, the structure of society has promoted unequal treatment of different peoples. Members of the dominant group have readily accepted and promoted social structures that operate in their favour. Through socialization they accept and defend the structures that reinforce their position in society. This institutional discrimination means that individuals can refrain from engaging in overt individual discrimination because the institutions of a society are organized in such a way that certain groups of people will be placed in a disadvantaged position.

We now turn to the questions of how this happened and how it continues. Our explanation focusses on institutionalized discrimination, both direct and indirect.

This refers to organizationally or community prescribed actions that have a negative impact on members of a minority group (Feagin and Feagin 1986). It is important to realize that these actions may have been established and carried out with no intent to harm members of minority groups. This does not mean, however, that members of a minority group never experience the hostility of a bigot. It simply means that a more complete explanation must take into account the structure of institutions in our society, their linkages, and the norms that support the institutions. These institutional structures create a pattern that has a cumulative impact on certain groups, and which places them in a disadvantageous position.

Until recently, overt, direct discrimination was common in many institutions within Canadian society. For example, many employers routinely refused to hire Natives. By the 1970s, however, human rights and anti-discriminatory legislation brought about a substantial decrease in direct, individual discrimination against ethnic minorities. But while evidence of overt individual discrimination has decreased, a commensurate increase in the social position of Natives has not been evidenced. Here is further confirmation that individual discrimination is not the sole explanation for the disadvantageous position in which Natives find themselves. Other factors are at work, and need to be investigated. These factors are the institutional structures and their linkages.

In the area of employment, actions such as recruitment and soliciting practices, screening practices, terms and conditions of employment, and layoff practices are all amenable to institutional discrimination. For example, Natives have not been able to move into administrative positions because of seniority or tenure practices that were established years ago, independent of ethnic considerations. Because Natives were excluded from certain jobs in the past, they have not accumulated the experience or tenure necessary to meet the criteria for advancement. Another example of institutional discrimination is evident in the recruitment practices carried out by organizations. Employment procedures usually begin by word of mouth. Since individuals already hired are usually non-Native, Natives do not fit into the existing network, and thus are excluded from even knowing about the potential pool of prospective employees. Feagin and Feagin (1986) also point out that job segregation has, until recently, been written into the rules (written or unwritten) and regulations of organizations. Non-Natives were channelled into better-paying, higher-status jobs. Once an employee was channelled into the low-paying, low-status track, it was very difficult to switch to the other.

Institutional discrimination also exists in housing. While the forms of the discrimination are different on and off the reserve, the structures and processes accomplish the same end. For example, off the reserve, real estate boards attempt to protect and maintain the homogeneity of ethnic groups in specific locations throughout a city. Realtors move on the assumption that one of the major techniques for protecting housing values is to assure the stability and compatibility of neighbourhoods. This homogeneity would be destroyed if homes in a non-Native neighbourhood were sold to Natives. Realtors argue that this would lessen the value of the surrounding homes (a cost borne by individuals) and "the loss is not only individual, but public, inasmuch as reduced values means reduced taxes" (Helper 1969, 25). Rental practices are also subject to discriminatory action on the part of realtors when Natives are involved. While blatant, overt strategies are no longer used, subtle strategies aimed at excluding Native tenants are widespread and difficult to deal with. Discrimination in the labour market also limits the quality of housing and neighbourhoods to which Native people have access. In turn, poor housing has an impact on the health of Native populations.

The mechanisms of discrimination in employment and housing, then, are interlocked. A third area, education, is also linked to employment and housing, and creates a seamless web that determines the life chances of Native people. In general terms, we can note that our elementary and secondary schools are intolerant of any educational philosophy that does not stress discipline, punctuality, submission to authority, and individual accountability (Bowles and Gintis 1976, 240). All ethnic minority groups are expected to suppress their cultural values if they differ with those of the dominant group. This ideology pervades our educational system. In addition, the creation of neighbourhood schools has led to a school system that reflects the socio-economic condition of the neighbourhood. High-income residential areas will have superior schools, while low-income areas will have schools with less-than-adequate facilities and worse-prepared teachers. This is particularly evident in schools on the reserves.

Institutional structures in other areas of our lives, for example, courts, health systems, and the political process, are interrelated with education, employment, and housing. In the end, all the institutions of society are interconnected and have an impact on every individual's life chances.

The Normative Underpinnings of Discrimination

A number of cultural and normative factors in society support the institutional discrimination that is in place. We shall provide some examples of how these work. We are all opposed to poverty and deviant behaviour. A general consensus says that poor people need help and should be provided with resources. At the same time, however, we find that Natives are poor and exist in a marginal milieu. Instead of offering sympathy or being concerned for them, we define the situation in such a way that they become responsible for their poverty, or that they deserve to be poor. In the end, this ideology allows those who are not poor to relieve themselves of responsibility. It supports their inaction when it comes to helping poor people. In the end, stereotypes are attached to visible minority groups, such as Natives, and they are then labelled as disreputable, lazy people (Ryan 1971).

There is also a strong tendency to blame social problems on individuals rather than on the social system. Most people define a social problem as behaviour that deviates from the norms and standards of society. Because people do not ordinarily examine critically the way things are done in society, they tend to question the exceptions. The normative system that is taken for granted has, for most people, an aura of sacredness about it. Traditions and customs associated with the social system are generally evaluated ethnocentrically and then defined as the "right" way. Logically, then, those who deviate from these norms are the source of trouble. The obvious question is; why do these people deviate from norms? Because most people view themselves as law abiding, they feel those who deviate do so because of some kind of personal defect or individual maladjustment.

Interpreting social problems solely within a person-blame framework has serious consequences. First, it frees the government, the economy, the system of stratification, the system of justice, and the educational system from any blame. This protection of the established order against criticism makes it more difficult to change the dominant economic, social, and political institutions (Eitzen and Zinn 1989, 12–13). The person-blame approach also enables the authorities to control deviants under the guise of being helpful. Another social control function of the person-blame approach is that it allows deviant individuals and groups to be controlled in a publicly acceptable manner. Deviants—whether they are criminals or social protesters—are incarcerated in social institutions and administered a wide variety of therapies. In the end, a person-blame approach requires the individual to change, not the structure of society that is causing the problem.

The person-blame approach finds support in a certain logical fallacy. We all have the tendency to overgeneralize. When we use one or two striking examples to illustrate a general principle, we commit the *fallacy of dramatic instance*. As Lauer (1978) points out, this tendency may be difficult to overcome because of the limited number of cases that make up an individual's personal experience. When people argue that Natives can be as successful if they would only act like "whites," they typically cite one or two Natives who make a million dollars a year or are successful in some other way. If it is objected that this is an exception to the rule, it will be claimed that if one Native can make it, they all can!

Conclusions

Native people have been exposed to overt individual discrimination as well as institutional discrimination for the past two centuries. They have been pushed into the marginal sectors of our society and have had their culture systematically devalued. The federal government has consistently advocated, under various guises, an assimilationist policy. Paramount in this policy is the belief that Native people are not qualified to govern themselves. The Indian Act historically has accepted this premise, as it continues to do today.

Being exposed to systemic discrimination for such a long period has excluded Natives from participation as full partners in Canadian society. The linkages of various institutions have formed a seamless web that has prevented Natives from benefiting from the improved quality of life that most Canadians have experienced over the past half century. Many different programs have been implemented to deal with the "Indian problem," but they have not been successful. The government's inability to alter substantially the position of Native people in Canadian society is indicative of the strength of these institutional barriers and their interconnectedness.

Recent government policies may fundamentally alter the position of Natives in society. The willingness to entertain comprehensive land claims, the introduction of self-government programs, and the transfer of some power to the band councils in areas such as education and health care suggest that changes may occur. Nevertheless, change for the Natives will be slow and small.

Study Questions

1. Can you show how various aspects of your own life are part of a larger interdependent network? How does this compare to the institutional linkages that have an impact on Native people?

2. How does history have an impact on current events?

3. This essay identifies three areas in which Native people are subject to institutional discrimination. Can you think of others? Compare the data for non-Natives to see if Native people occupy a disadvantageous position.

4. Can you think of other ways that Canadians explain away the problems facing Native people?

5. Natives have faced discrimination for a long time. As a result, they occupy a marginal position in our society. Why did they wait so long before engaging in more militant actions in an attempt to change the system?

6. How are the experiences faced by Natives similar to those of other visible ethnic groups in Canadian society?

7. Why has the federal government continued to control the lives of Native people? Why isn't Native self-government an option from the point of view of the government?

8. Why do you think Native issues are in the news today? What makes them so important that the news media cover them with regularity?

9. What are some of the dangers in taking a "system-blame" orientation in explaining why Natives occupy the lowest social status positions in Canadian society?

Recommended Reading

Asch, Michael. *Home and Native Land: Aboriginal Rights and the Canadian Constitution*. Agincourt, ON: Methuen, 1984.

Cassidy, Frank, and Norman Dale. *After Native Claims?* Victoria, BC: Morriss Printing Company, 1988.

Frideres, James S. *Native Peoples in Canada: Contemporary Conflicts*. Scarborough, ON: Prentice-Hall, 1993.

McMillan, Alan D. *Native Peoples and Cultures of Canada.* Vancouver, BC: Douglas and McIntyre, 1988.

Morrison, R. Bruce, and C. Roderick Wilson, eds. *Native Peoples: The Canadian Experience.* Toronto: McClelland and Stewart, 1986.

Ponting, J. Rick, ed. *Arduous Journey: Canadian Indians and Decolonization.* Toronto: McClelland and Stewart, 1986.

Waldrum, James B. *As Long as the Rivers Run.* Winnipeg: University of Manitoba Press. 1988.

Notes

1. In 1984, changes were made to the Indian Act, which allowed previously defined "non-Indians" to apply for the status of Indians. If the resulting increase in the status-Indian population is considered in the growth rate (annual), the figure increases to 7.66 percent (1985–86), 7.24 percent (1986–87), and 7.05 percent (1987–88).
2. Nevertheless, by the mid-1800s, the Beothuk of the Atlantic region had been annihilated.

References

Bartlett, R. 1988. *The Indian Act of Canada.* Saskatoon, SK: Native Law Centre, University of Saskatchewan.

Bienvenue, R. 1985. "Colonial Status: The Case of Canadian Indians." In *Ethnicity and Ethnic Relations in Canada*, 2d ed, ed. R. Bienvenue and J. Goldstein. Toronto: Butterworths. 199–216.

Bowles, S., and H. Gintis. 1976. *Schooling in Capitalist America.* New York: Basic Books.

Brooks, S. 1989. *Public Policy in Canada.* Toronto: McClelland and Stewart.

Canada. 1988. *Basic Departmental Data.* Ottawa: Indian and Northern Affairs Canada.

Cassidy, F., and N. Dale. 1988. *Alternative Claims? The Implications of Comprehensive Claims Settlements for Natural Resources in British Columbia.* Lantzvill, BC: Oolichan Books; Halifax, NS: Institute for Research on Public Policy.

Eitzen, S., and M.B. Zinn. 1989. *Social Problems.* 4th ed. Boston: Allyn and Bacon.

Feagin, J., and C.B. Feagin. 1986. *Discrimination American Style.* 2d ed. Malabar, FL: Kriege Publishing.

Helper, R. 1969. *Racial Policies and Practices of Real Estate Brokers.* Minneapolis: University of Minnesota Press.

Kornblum, W., and I. Julian. 1989. *Social Problems.* Englewood Cliffs, NJ: Prentice-Hall.

Lauer, R. 1978. *Social Problems and the Quality of Life.* Dubuque, IA: Wm. C. Brown.

Martin, C. 1974. "The European Impact on the Culture of a Northeastern Algonquian Tribe: An Ecological Interpretation." *William and Mary Quarterly*, 3d series, 31: 3–26.

Miller, J.R. 1989. *Skyscrapers Hide the Heavens: A History of Indian-White Relations in Canada.* Toronto: University of Toronto Press.

Morris, A. 1880. *The Treaties of Canada with the Indians of Manitoba and the Northwest Territories.* Toronto: Public Archives of Manitoba.

Ryan, W. 1971. *Blaming the Victim.* New York: Pantheon Books.

Siggner, A. 1986. "The Socio-demographic Conditions of Registered Indians." *Canadian Social Trends* (Winter): 2–9.

Task Force to Review Comprehensive Claims Policy. 1985. *Living Treaties: Lasting Agreements.* Report of the Task Force to Review Comprehensive Claims Policy. Ottawa: Department of Indian Affairs and Northern Development.

Thomas, R. 1966 67. "Powerless Politics." *New University Thought* 4: 44–53.

Trelease, A. 1960. *Indian Affairs in Colonial New York: The Seventeenth Century*. New York: Random House.

Trigger, B. 1986. "The Historians' Indian: Native Americans in Canada in Canadian Historical Writing from Charlevoix to the Present." *Canadian Historical Review* 67. 3: 315–42.

Wax, M. 1971. *Indian Americans*. Englewood Cliffs, NJ: Prentice-Hall.

CHAPTER 7

Multiculturalism, Ethnic Identity, and Inequality

K. Victor Ujimoto

Learning Objectives

This chapter focusses on some of the most significant aspects of the policy of multiculturalism, from its inception in 1971 to its proclamation in the Canadian Multiculturalism Act in 1988. The main objectives of this policy are to promote the cultural heritage of minorities and to break down discriminatory attitudes and cultural barriers to minorities' full participation in society. This policy is criticized because of its focus on "cultural barriers" to equality and its failure to recognize the historical and structural roots of racism and racial and ethnic inequality. Students are encouraged to consider the positive contributions of the policy of multiculturalism in promoting linguistic and cultural programs, and its limitations in solving problems of racism and racial inequality, which require the removal of structural and institutional barriers.

Introduction

An examination of recent immigration trends in Canada reveals that more and more immigrants are coming from Asia, Africa, and South America than from the traditional immigrant source-countries in Europe. Residents of centres such as Montreal, Toronto, and Vancouver do not have to consult government statistics to recognize the changing demographic composition of Canadian society. Along with this demographic change go cultural and social changes as well. The heterogeneous nature of Canadian society was recognized by the Canadian government in 1971 when it announced its policy on multiculturalism. How did this policy come about and what was its impact on the various ethnic groups in Canada? In this chapter we shall examine some of the salient aspects of multiculturalism as a state policy from the time of its original announcement through to its ultimate proclamation in the Canadian Multiculturalism Act in 1988.

In announcing the government policy on multiculturalism on October 8, 1971, Prime Minister Pierre Elliott Trudeau stated the following in the House of Commons:

> National unity, if it is to mean anything in the deeply personal sense, must be founded on confidence in one's own individual identity; out of this can grow respect for that of others and a willingness to share ideas, attitudes and assumptions. A vigorous policy of multiculturalism will help create this initial confidence. It can form the base of a society which is based on fair play for all.

This recognition of the diversity of Canadian society occurred after many decades of debate over the question of relations between English and French, culminating in the appointment of the Royal Commission on Bilingualism and Biculturalism. Burnet (1987, 67) has observed that ethnic independence movements were active throughout the world and Quebec was already caught up in the growing nationalism. The federal government's response was to establish the royal commission which was asked to make recommendations on "what steps should be taken to develop the Canadian Confederation on the basis of an equal partnership between the two founding races." At the same time, the terms of reference of the royal commission referred to "the contribution made by other ethnic groups to the cultural enrichment of Canada, and the measures that should be taken to safeguard that contribution."

The Royal Commission on Bilingualism and Biculturalism was "to deal with other ethnic groups only as they affected English–French relations" (Burnet 1987, 68). Although only eight ethnic groups made written submissions on the cultural contributions of their respective ethnic groups, it soon became evident that many more ethnic groups wanted to be recognized. The resulting Book 4 of the report of the commission was therefore devoted to the history, economic structure, social patterns, and the maintenance of language and culture of many other ethnic groups. The final report, which was released in March 1970, recommended that "the teaching of languages other than English and French, and cultural subjects related to them, be incorporated as options in the public elementary school programme, where there is sufficient demand for such classes." One of the many difficulties to be encountered later in taking action on this recommendation was that educational matters were within the jurisdiction of the provinces; consequently, the introduction of new curriculum material varied from province to province.

On October 8, 1971, the federal government's response to Book 4 was to accept all of the recommendations and to proclaim a policy of multiculturalism. Burnet (1987, 68) has summarized the essential aspects of the government response as follows, in a passage taken from the debate held in the House of Commons:

> First, resources permitting, the government will seek to assist all Canadian cultural groups that have demonstrated a desire and effort to continue to develop a capacity to grow and contribute to Canada, and a clear need for assistance, the small and weak groups no less than the strong and highly organized.

> Second, the government will assist members of all cultural groups to overcome cultural barriers to full participation in Canadian society.
>
> Third, the government will promote creative encounters and interchange among all Canadian cultural groups in the interests of national unity.
>
> Fourth, the government will continue to assist immigrants to acquire at least one of Canada's official languages in order to become full participants in Canadian society.

In order to implement the policy of multiculturalism, the government established six programs: programs for the federal cultural agencies—for example, the National Museum of Man, National Library, Public Archives, and National Film Board; programs for the teaching of official languages; programs for Canadian ethnic studies and ethnic histories, and the culture development program; and other multicultural grants to support the development of various cultures and languages. Initially, these programs were targeted to the "other ethnic groups" (other than Anglophones and Francophones); however, the policy of multiculturalism applies to all groups today. Individuals "drawn from forty-seven ethnocultural backgrounds" constituted the first Canadian Consultative Council on Multiculturalism, whose specific mandate was to advise the minister responsible for Multiculturalism. Since then, several other committees have emerged to establish both short-term and long-term priorities for multicultural policy and research. Short-term priorities dealt with the establishment of local community cultural centres or multicultural centres, and facilitating the arts, ethnic press, and media in a multicultural society. Long-term issues that have been addressed concern federal-provincial policy on language and cultural retention.

Since the introduction of the policy on multiculturalism in 1971, much has been accomplished at various levels. At the community level, there has been active participation in various ethnocultural activities. Multicultural centres have been established in many locations, including some communities that are quite small. At the provincial level, formal organizations have been established to co-ordinate diverse multicultural activities. The Ontario Multicultural Association/Association Multiculturelle de l'Ontario (OMAMO), the Multicultural Council of Saskatchewan, and the Affiliation of Multicultural Societies and Service Agencies (AMSSA) of British Columbia are specific examples. At the national level, the Multiculturalism Directorate of the Department of the Secretary of State has initiated several research and publication projects, such as the non-official languages study by O'Bryan, Reitz, and Kuplowska (1976) and the studies on attitudes toward multiculturalism conducted by Berry, Kalin, and Taylor (1977). Recent publications by Fleras and Elliott (1992), Hryniuk (1992), and Satzewich (1992) have made significant contributions to our understanding of multiculturalism. More recently, the inclusion of multiculturalism as an important component in developing health policies and programs has been advanced by Masi, Mensah, and McLeod (1993). These publications and others enabled members of the ethnocultural communities to examine their place in Canadian society and to strengthen their own ethnic identity.

The Concept of Multiculturalism and Ethnic Identity

Multiculturalism as a concept has been viewed in several different ways since its introduction. First, as Kallen (1982, 51) has observed, the term *multiculturalism* has been used "to refer to the 'social reality' of ethnic diversity." As a reflection of the cultural diversity of Canadian society, multiculturalism as a state policy has legitimized the values, norms, beliefs, and identity of ethnic groups. A development concomitant with cultural pluralism has been the questioning of the meaning of assimilation. In a pluralistic society, what are the dominant values to which people are expected to assimilate or acculturate? Kallen observes that "people are coming to the realization that their own personal dignity is bound up with the collective dignity of their ethnic community." In contemporary Canadian society, then, multiculturalism has served to facilitate the individual's identity as well as that of the ethnic community.

A second way in which multiculturalism has been used, as described by Kallen (1982, 51), is "to refer to the federal government policy designed to create national unity in ethnic diversity." She notes that several assumptions are rooted in this model of multiculturalism. The first assumption is that "members of all ethnocultural collectivities are both able and willing to maintain their ethnocultural distinctiveness." The second is that "levels of prejudice and discrimination between ethnic collectivities are low enough to allow mutual tolerance." The third assumption is that there is a "rough equivalence in the distribution of power among the various ethnic collectivities, so that no one population can assume dominance and control over others." Finally, the model assumes that "members of the different ethnic collectivities in society will mutually agree to limit and control the extent, spheres and nature of interaction between them." Given all of these assumptions, Kallen argues that interethnic relations would take the form of ethnic segmentation and that every citizen's identity would "become hyphenated, i.e., ethnic-national, with equal weights on both sides of the hyphen."

A third way in which multiculturalism has been used, according to Kallen (1982, 51), is "to refer to the ideology of cultural pluralism (the Canadian mosaic) underlying the federal policy." She observes that "unlike the ideal model of cultural pluralism which assumes that every individual and group desires to maintain a distinctive ethnic identity and heritage," the Canadian policy of multiculturalism recognizes the freedom of individuals to choose their own affiliations either within or outside their own ethnic collectivities. In addressing those ethnocultural groups that have the desire or possess the organizational abilities to develop their own traditional cultures, the Multiculturalism Directorate of the Secretary of State will facilitate or assist them to meet their objectives. As noted earlier, the government will also assist members of the various ethnic groups to participate fully in the social, economic, cultural, and political spheres of Canadian society. Some ethnic groups, however, must still overcome barriers before they can become fully integrated members of Canadian society. We shall now examine some of the criticisms that have been made of the policy on multiculturalism.

Multiculturalism: Myth or Reality

Since its proclamation in 1971, multiculturalism as a state policy has been examined and debated by the public and by members of the academic community. The complexities of the issues surrounding multiculturalism will become obvious when we consider some of the arguments advanced by Canadian scholars. At a conference held at the University of Alberta in 1975, Burnet (1981, 44) noted that although the use of the term *multiculturalism* was "less dangerous than the use of multiracialism," there were problems with the term. It is a very imprecise term, Burnet observed, one that is used in several different ways even among social scientists; in addition, this term "emphasizes the past." Burnet argued that the ambiguity in the word *multiculturalism* was created by "the ambiguity between culture as separateness and culture as distinctiveness." In general, Burnet recognizes the very essence of culture as "a reference to the recurrent, to tradition, to heritage," but pointed out that in the modern world even complete and living cultures undergo change. Since much of multiculturalism has to do with the retention or preservation of traditional culture, Burnet noted, we do not have a clear understanding of whether it is the collective heritage or the particular heritage of individuals that has to be maintained.

Concerning this issue, it should be noted that for some ethnic groups in Canada, such as the Japanese Canadians, there are other complications in that there are distinct intergenerational differences. Only the *issei*, or immigrant generation, was socialized in the living traditional culture of Japan. For the *nisei*, or second generation Japanese Canadians, only a small proportion of those who were born before the Second World War possessed any knowledge of the folk customs and traditions of their parents. Because of political and historical circumstances, such as their internment, there were interruptions in the educational and socialization processes of the *nisei*; this necessitated a relearning, of or reintroduction to, traditional Japanese culture at a later time, when it became fashionable to re-examine one's cultural heritage and ethnic identity.

Over the years, a number of studies have used the concepts of ethnicity and multiculturalism in a similar vein. Peter (1981, 56) notes that both of these terms have been characterized by emphasizing such concepts as "ethnic identity, emerging ethnic boundaries, ethnic boundary markers, ethnic recognition," and he takes issue with Burnet's interpretation of multiculturalism. According to Peter, Burnet holds that

> multiculturalism within a bilingual framework can work if it is interpreted as is intended—that is, as encouraging those members of ethnic groups who want to do so to maintain a proud sense of the contribution of their own group to Canadian society. Interpreted in this way, it becomes something very North American: voluntary marginal differentiation among peoples who are equal participants in the society. If it is interpreted in the second way—as enabling various peoples to transfer

> foreign cultures and languages as living wholes into a new place and time—multiculturalism is doomed.

Concerning the above quotation, what is at issue for Peter is the assumption that "there is such a thing as a Canadian society which exists more or less independently of ethnic groups and toward whose development ethnic groups are encouraged to make their various contributions." Peter argues that it is "perhaps more justifiable to claim that the interaction of various ethnic groups, including the multiethnic English and French speakers, in fact does constitute Canadian society." Peter asks: "Why is there always the assumption that ethnic groups are somehow outside the mainstream of Canadian society; that they need to make selected contributions, etc.?" He answers his own questions by noting the distribution of political power among various groups in Canadian society today. Peter (1981, 57) argues that multiculturalism presented as a liberal policy is essentially a policy of "ethnic group containment" and that ethnic groups are "steered away from any contact with political and economic powers and are neutralized in their role as providers of individual satisfaction."

The relationship between ethnicity and power has been examined by Isajiw (1978, 33), who draws our attention to the fact that social mobility and occupational competition may lead to a greater awareness of one's ascriptive characteristics, or ethnicity. This awareness may eventually transcend the private sphere and move into the much broader political environment. Before this can occur, however, there must be a restructuring of institutional arrangements within both the ethnic community and Canadian society at large, as institutional arrangements define the position of ethnic groups in the hierarchy of power relationships. Peter (1981, 59) faults Isajiw and other sociologists for not taking their analysis of ethnicity in terms of power and politics any farther. This reluctance of theirs to deal with ethnicity in terms of power and politics, Peter argues, is "proportionate to their commitment to the policies of bilingualism and multiculturalism, and ultimately to the concept of Canadian unity as proposed by the Liberal government."

He advances several good reasons why this should be so. One reason stems from the fact that Quebec was actively seeking independence, and thus the possibility of providing additional fuel to an already simmering issue was avoided at all costs. What this situation really indicated was the very fragile nature of Canadian Confederation at this time. The gravity of the situation appears to have been weighed subsequently in typical Canadian fashion by the creation of the Task Force on Canadian Unity. Peter argues that the task force "felt it necessary to deal with those factors which the B. and B. report desperately tried to avoid—the nature and distribution of political powers in Canada" and questions why "neither French Canada nor Canada's diverse ethnic groups could be pacified by the bilingual-multicultural policy."

Peter lists two main purposes that the Canadian government policy of multiculturalism within a bilingual framework was intended to serve:

1. The policy of bilingualism was at once an appeasement policy toward a revitalised Quebec and a containment policy regarding its claim to political power.

2. The policy of multiculturalism served as a device to legitimize the continued dominance of the ruling English-speaking elite and secure its position in society at a time when its position was threatened by Quebec's claim to political power on the one hand and by the economic and cultural vitality of ethnic groups on the other hand.

He argues that the very essence of the "B. and B." report was "to obscure the French Canadian challenge to political power and deflect it into linguistic and cultural directions. " The reference to the development of "the Canadian Confederation on the basis of an equal partnership" could be construed as referring to "a redistribution of political powers on the basis of equality between French and English Canadians" (Peter 1981, 60). It appears, however, that this interpretation of the term "equal partnership" was diverted to cover only the linguistic and cultural dimensions of equality. Similarly, in the matter of ethnic politics, Peter argues that multiculturalism was "mainly intended to buy off the compliance of ethnic groups and thereby legitimize and justify the B. and B. policy." This was neatly achieved by "modernizing the traditional conception of ethnicity as an element standing somewhat outside the mainstream of Canadian society, from which individuals were expected to graduate in order to become full-fledged Canadians." This expectation on the part of the dominant groups meant they never seriously considered ethnic groups as competition for power, status, and resources. As Peter has cogently argued, "bilingualism, biculturalism and multiculturalism were based on a model of ethnic acquiescence to the rule of the dominant groups, forestalling all ethnic self-assertion in the form of ethnic interest groups." Although it is beyond the scope of the present chapter, there are similarities to be observed in the political dimensions of the B. and B. Commission, the Task Force on Canadian Unity, and the deliberations on the Meech Lake Accord. While the accord took into account the "distinct society" aspects of Quebec, it did not recognize multiculturalism, aboriginal rights, the equality of all Canadians (for example, the equality of men and women), and the commitment of Canadian society to fundamental rights and freedoms.

Multiculturalism and Inequality

It has been noted above that when the Royal Commission on Bilingualism and Biculturalism was established, there was already a political movement in Quebec seeking independence. A concomitant development based on social changes that were occurring within the Native Canadian communities was the "Red Power" movement. The government at the time did not view Native Canadian issues to be as important as those of French Canada. As Burnet (1987, 67) has noted, the government did not establish a royal commission to address Native Canadian demands, but instead appointed a committee of anthropologists to report on selected Native issues. The extent to which Native Canadian issues were viewed as being peripheral to central Canadian issues was reflected in the failure to address aboriginal rights in the Meech Lake Accord. Furthermore, it is noted by Burnet that the

Hawthorn–Tremblay report dealt with only about a quarter of the Indian, Inuit, and Métis people.

The words "equal partnership" that were included in the mandate of the Bilingualism and Biculturalism Commission obviously referred to the two founding peoples. However, the extent to which the concept of equality can be generalized to other ethnic groups remains unclear. It can be argued that some ethnic groups, particularly those belonging to the visible minorities, are particularly disadvantaged. Perhaps an example will illustrate this. While it is true that the policy of multiculturalism attempts to facilitate the retention and development of one's culture and language, not all ethnic groups are capable of applying for the available government support. Some groups have many members who are well educated and possess the necessary skills and organizational abilities to take advantage of government programs, while other groups, such as the more recent refugee arrivals in Canada, are not very well equipped to do so. Furthermore, not all groups have access to the information required for applying for government support in the first place. In those instances where ethnic minorities do manage to apply for grants, these grant applications will very likely be rejected because the evaluation criteria often do not coincide with the needs of the ethnic community that made the grant application. As Peter (1981, 58) has noted, it is the classic case of a relationship in which one group defines the rules of the game to which the other group, in this case the ethnic minority, must comply.

Another inequality stems from the fact that not all ethnic groups are equally represented in Canadian society. Thus, although the government may provide financial support to some ethnic groups, that support is based essentially on the strength of the community, which in turn is based on its membership size. This implies that small ethnocultural groups will not be able to maintain their language and culture to the same extent as the larger ethnic groups. This differential ability of ethnocultural groups to maintain their language and culture will thus have an impact on the maintenance of their ethnic identity as well.

A crucial variable to examine in our analysis of the relationship between multiculturalism and inequality is the degree to which multicultural education is available in our schools. As noted previously, educational matters fall within the jurisdiction of the provincial governments and thus the development of multicultural curricula varies across the country. Through the federal government policy of multiculturalism, funds have been made available to relevant provincial departments for the teaching of languages other than English and French. However, Mazurek (1983, 27) has observed that not all ethnic groups are represented in the curriculum. Those immigrant groups that are numerous and well organized and who are able to exert some political leverage on the provincial departments of education have been the most successful in securing a place in the curriculum for their languages, courses in their history, and other subjects. At present, Ontario, Manitoba, Saskatchewan, and Alberta have taken the lead in providing multicultural education; however, all provinces have now taken some initiatives in multicultural education. Because educational matters remain a provincial responsibility, a universal curriculum is not foreseen, However, there is a considerable amount of information exchange on curricula between provinces. It must be noted in passing that while the federal government has provided support for non-official languages, Rocher

(1984, 45) has observed that no federal support has been given in establishing French education outside of Quebec. Rocher is concerned that, in Montreal, the policy of multiculturalism within a bilingual framework has already resulted in a bilingualism that is English–Greek, English–Italian, and English–German rather than the English–French bilingualism desired by the Montreal school boards.

Multiculturalism: Continuing Issues

The present debate in Canada on language, cultural pluralism, and education will continue into the future (Hryniuk 1992). The devisive issues may be further exacerbated if our political leaders do not comprehend the main principles of earlier pieces of legislation such as the Canadian Constitution of 1982, the Charter of Rights and Freedoms, the controversial Quebec language legislation in Bill 101, and the implications of the failure of the Meech Lake Accord. Many of our current problems stem from the fact that we have addressed each of the issues concerning language, cultural pluralism, and education as separate entities rather than as interrelated aspects of Canadian society. How else can one explain that the separate institutional arrangements at various government levels—federal, provincial, and municipal or county—often work to the disadvantage of one another? We have now arrived at the point in our nation building that we should think more systemically, that is, in terms of interdependencies and reciprocal relationships between various levels of government and other institutions in this society. This would help avoid duplication of programs, eliminate contradictory policies, and provide a framework for addressing, in a comprehensive manner, linguistic, cultural, educational, and constitutional issues, and contributing to national unity and nation building.

Mallea (1984, 1) informs us that in our public schools very little progress has been made in adopting a more positive stance toward other languages and cultures; rather, the public schools have gone out of their way to eradicate them. There seems to be far greater appreciation of the assimilation and conformity models than the multicultural model of Canadian society. There must be a far greater emphasis on the desirability of cross-cultural understanding and harmony as an integral aspect of the "capacity to grow and contribute to Canada," one of the key statements in the original policy on multiculturalism (Ujimoto 1982, 111). Instead, the leaders of the ethnocultural communities have taken to political action to seek better representation for their particular groups. This works only for those able to mount a political lobby and to mobilize community resources. This mobilization is often at the expense of individual interests and also risks the possible segmentation of ethnic communities.

The issues noted above require a much more careful analysis than is possible in one chapter. Only two important factors of contemporary society will be noted briefly. First, it must be recognized that the demographic composition of Canadian society has changed. Not only is our population rapidly aging, the ethnic composition of our population is rapidly changing. These two characteristics of our demography have necessitated changes in our educational curricula through the introduction of gerontology courses and transcultural nursing and medicine courses in a few of our universities. The first national conference on health care and multiculturalism was held in Toronto from March 30 to April 1, 1989. Second, we are now well into the postindustrial or the information age. We are able to communicate globally in seconds, not days, and the global society we are creating requires further break down of international, national, and regional barriers. Although these factors may appear to be outside the scope of our immediate concerns with regard to multiculturalism, the recognition and appreciation of emerging demographic transition and information technology would contribute not only to *nation* building at home, but also to a global society and a future role and position for Canada in the community of nations (Ujimoto 1992; 352).

Conclusions

In this very brief essay, we have examined some of the key aspects of the policy of multiculturalism. Academics will continue to debate the issues in the years to come as we grapple with the demographic changes in our society and the need to reflect these changes in our educational curricula, but we need more than debate. Structural changes are required in our society if we wish to develop more creative approaches to enable all Canadians to achieve equality of access and equality of participation in various Canadian institutions. With the passage of the Canadian Multiculturalism Act, Bill C-93, on July 12, 1988, we were all very optimistic. However, events since the failure of the Meech Lake Accord do not bode well for multiculturalism in Canada. There is no longer a separate House of Commons Standing Committee on Multiculturalism, an effective all-party group that dealt with multicultural policy issues. Furthermore, like many other programs and services, multiculturalism has not escaped the budget cuts limiting program funding. Regardless of these setbacks, the policy framework and foundation for multiculturalism in Canada have been firmly established to enable it to continue and to flourish, and perhaps to serve as a model for other nations.

Study Questions

1. What were some of the social and political factors taking place in Canadian society that resulted in the formation of the Royal Commission on Bilingualism and Biculturalism?

2. What aspects of the policy of multiculturalism have been criticized?

3. What aspects of multiculturalism as a state policy do you think have enhanced Canadian society?

4. Given the recent changes in the demographic composition of Canadian society, how important is the Multiculturalism Act of 1988?

5. Do you agree or disagree with Karl Peter that the policy of multiculturalism is essentially a policy of "ethnic group containment"?

6. Why do you think that the Meech Lake Accord did not recognize multiculturalism, aboriginal rights, and equality between men and women, when it was first formulated?

Recommended Reading

Fleras, Augie, and Jean Leonard Elliott. *Multiculturalism in Canada: The Challenge of Diversity*. Scarborough: Nelson Canada, 1992.

Hryniuk, Stella. *20 Years of Multiculturalism: Successes and Failures.* Winnipeg: St. John's College Press, 1992.

Kallen, Evelyn. "Multiculturalism: Ideology, Policy, and Reality." *Journal of Canadian Studies* 17, no. 1: 51–63.

Lewycky, Laverne. "Multiculturalism in the 1990s and into the 21st Century: Beyond Ideology and Utopia". In *Deconstructing a Nation: Immigration, Multiculturalism, and Racism in 90s Canada*, ed. Vic Satzewich. Halifax: Fernwood Publishing, 1992.

Multiculturalism: The First Decade. Special issue of *Journal of Canadian Studies* 17, no. 1.

Ujimoto, K.V. "Multiculturalism and the Global Information Society." In *Deconstructing a Nation: Immigration, Multiculturalism, and Racism in 90s Canada*, ed. Vic Satzewich. Halifax: Fernwood Publishing, 1992, 351–57.

References

Berry, J.W., R. Kalin, and D.M. Taylor. 1977. *Multiculturalism and Ethnic Attitudes in Canada.* Ottawa: Ministry of Supply and Services.

Burnet, J. 1981. "The Definition of Multiculturalism in a Bilingual Framework." *Multiculturalism in Canada.* Edmonton: University of Alberta. 43–57.

———. 1987. "Multiculturalism in Canada." In *Ethnic Canada: Identities and Inequalities,* ed. L. Driedger. Toronto: Copp Clark Pitman. 65–79.

Fleras, A., and J.L. Elliott. 1992. *Multiculturalism in Canada: The Challenge of Diversity.* Scarborough: Nelson Canada.

Hryniuk, S. 1992. *20 Years of Multiculturalism: Successes and Failures.* Winnipeg: St. John's College Press.

Isajiw, W.W. 1978. "Olga in Wonderland: Ethnicity in a Technological Society." In *The Canadian Ethnic Mosaic*, ed. L. Driedger. Toronto: McClelland and Stewart. 29–39.

Kallen, E. 1982. "Multiculturalism: Ideology, Policy, and Reality." *Journal of Canadian Studies* I (Spring): 51–63.

Lewycky, L. 1992. "Multiculturalism in the 1990s and into the 21st Century: Beyond Ideology and Utopia." In Satzewich, *Deconstructing a Nation.* 259–401.

Mallea, J.R. 1984. "Cultural Diversity and Canadian Education." Introduction to *Cultural Diversity and Canadian Education*, ed. J.R. Mallea and J.C. Young. Ottawa: Carleton University Press. 1.

Masi, R., L. Mensah, and K.A. McLeod, eds. 1993. *Health and Cultures: Exploring the Relationships.* vols. 1 and 2. 1983. Oakville: Mosaic Press Publishers.

Mazurek, K. 1983. "Multiculturalism and Schools: A Critical Analysis" in *Racial Minorities in Multicultural Canada*, ed. Li and Bolaria. Toronto: Garamond Press, 26–30.

O'Bryan, K.D., J.G. Reitz, and O.M. Kuplowska. 1976. *Non-official Languages: A Study in Canadian Multiculturalism*. Ottawa: Minister Responsible for Multiculturalism.

Peter, K. 1981. "The Myth of Multiculturalism and Other Political Fables." In *Ethnicity, Power and Politics in Canada*, ed. J. Dahlie and T. Fernando. Toronto: Methuen. 59–60.

Rocher, G. 1984. "The Ambiguities of a Bilingual and Multicultural Canada." In Mallea and Young, *Cultural Diversity*. 41–47.

Satzewich, V. 1992. *Deconstructing a Nation: Immigration, Multiculturalism, and Racism in 90s Canada*. Halifax: Fernwood Publishing.

Trudeau, P.F. 1975. Speech, House of Commons, October 8, 1971. Ottawa: Canadian Consultative Council on Multiculturalism.

Ujimoto, K. V. 1982. "Visible Minorities and Multiculturalism: Planned Social Change Strategies for the Next Decade." *Journal of Canadian Studies* I (Spring): 111–21.

———. 1992. "Multiculturalism and the Global Information Society." In Satzewich, *Deconstructing a Nation*. 351–57.

CHAPTER 8

The Meech Lake Shuffle: French and English Language Rights in Canada

Wilfrid B. Denis

Learning Objectives

This chapter focusses on French and English language rights in Canada in reference to reform. However, a full appreciation of the significance of both Meech Lake and the Charlottetown Accord, as well as their weaknesses, is possible only if one keeps in mind the historical context and precedents and the class differences of the linguistic groups involved.

Students are encouraged to consider these accords as simply the most recent steps in a long series of attempts to deal with the very complex issue of linguistic rights in Canada. This is an area in which class differences not only determine access to resources and possibilities for survival and development of the "official language minorities," but also bias the intervention of the federal government in favour of the strongest group, for the most part.

Introduction

Constitutions and constitutional reform are integral to Canadian history. The past 30 years are no exception as prime ministers and premiers keep proposing various formulations for a renewed federalism (Russell 1993). As part of this ongoing process, the Canadian Constitution was patriated from Britain in 1982 but with the agreement of only nine of the ten premiers. Quebec was excluded because the new constitution failed to meet certain of its preoccupations. In an attempt to resolve this unfinished matter and to integrate Quebec fully into the 1982 Constitution, the Meech Lake Accord was hammered out among the ten premiers and Prime Minister Mulroney between April and June 3, 1987. This accord proposed major changes to Canada's constitutional structure (Hogg 1988, 1).

At the very centre of the accord is the issue of Canada's linguistic duality and Quebec's distinctiveness. To deal with these, it proposed to modify other jurisdictional areas as well. There is no doubt that, ostensibly, language is the primary reason for Quebec's exclusion from the 1982 Constitution and for the subsequent negotiations leading to the accord. The issue is certainly more complex than this. But since Canada's official languages are at the centre of the controversy surrounding both Quebec's place in Confederation and the recent proposals for constitutional amendments, one can get a better grasp of the origins of the proposals, their possible repercussions, and the contradictions that they embody, by placing them in the context of the ongoing tensions and struggles among the various social groups that comprise the two official language groups in Canada.

The Early Origins of Meech Lake

For many, the Meech Lake and Charlottetown Accords originated either in the 1982 patriation of the Constitution, to which Quebec was not a party, or the 1980 Quebec referendum. However, these are only the two most noteworthy events in a long series that stretches all the way back to the initial encounters of two European empires on this continent. The current importance of Canada's linguistic duality rises out of historical events and circumstances that have significantly affected Canada's development and have produced critically different effects for the official language groups, whether in Quebec or the rest of Canada. To review some of these is to place these accords in a broader historical context than simply that of the last decade. The issue, then, appears not only as one of agreeing to a series of demands made by premiers Lévesque and Bourassa of Quebec, but more importantly, as a further continuation and extension of the historical contradictions arising from Canada's linguistic duality.

Conflict and tension between French and English in Canada today originated in the wars between the French and British empires. The final military conflict was the Seven Years' War, from 1756 to 1763. Following the capitulation of Quebec City in 1759, the British colonial government and the British merchants who established themselves in the newly acquired territory attempted to deal with the French Canadian population in contradictory ways. Some sought the outright assimilation of the Canadiens by replacing all French institutions, including the Catholic religion and the French language, with their British counterparts. This option was expressed quite clearly in the Proclamation of 1763, Durham's 1839 *Report on the Affairs of British North America*, and the Act of Union of 1840. Faced with the Canadiens' opposition and their unwillingness to assimilate quietly, others favoured the acceptance of the Canadiens' religious and linguistic rights. The Quebec Act of 1774 recognized French property and civil law along with English criminal law, admitted Catholics to official positions, called for the publication of ordinances in both French and English, and implicitly recognized the use of French in the courts (Conway 1992, Russell 1993, Sheppard 1971, 15)

These movements back and forth culminated in the official recognition of French in the British North America (BNA) Act of 1867, whose section 133 allows the use of French or English in the federal Parliament and the Legislature of Quebec, and in all federal courts as well as those of Quebec, and requires the printing of laws, records, and journals of both these Houses in both languages. Section 133 of the British North America Act reversed the earlier assimilationist policies of 1763 and 1840. It is the official recognition in Canadian constitutional law of the prevailing use of French in French Canada and of the resistance and resilience of the French Canadians since 1759, in spite of several very conscious and determined efforts to make them disappear as an ethnolinguistic entity (Sheppard 1971, 55–69). Ironically, while this act granted constitutional protection to the French language and certain French-Canadian institutions in Quebec, it simultaneously extended the same protection to the English language, thereby insuring its significant role in that province's governmental, judicial, and educational institutions.

The next one hundred years witnessed few attempts to deal with language through legislation in Quebec. In 1910, the Lavergne Law required "public utility companies to place the French version alongside the English one in printed matter sent to customers"; in 1937, the Duplessis Law granted priority to French in interpreting certain laws, but the Anglophone outcry was such that the law was rescinded the following year (Braen 1987a, 37; Laporte 1983, 92). This *modus vivendi* remained largely unchanged until the late 1960s.

On the other hand, the impact of section 133 was minimal for Francophones anywhere outside Quebec, not because language was not an issue for these minorities, but because this section provided no protection for them. Language was already an issue in 1755 and thereafter, when the Acadians of Nova Scotia and Prince Edward Island were deported and their land and belongings confiscated for the benefit of British settlers. However, the Acadian struggle for cultural and linguistic survival attained a certain degree of provincial and national recognition only after 1969.

Manitoba was created in 1870, following the armed resistance of the Red River Métis. Since the majority of Métis were French Catholic, they sought constitutional protection for their religious and linguistic rights. Section 23 of the Manitoba Act was analogous to section 133 of the BNA Act, and provided the same protection for French in Manitoba as existed in Quebec. In spite of this official recognition of French, the Manitoba Legislature "adopted in 1890 an Act declaring English to be the only official language of legislation and the courts" (Braen 1987a, 28).

Political and juridical structures for the remainder of what were then the North-West Territories were officially established with the North-West Territories Act of 1875, in which no mention was made of language. In 1877, an amendment that was adopted and eventually became Article 110 of this act, allowed the use of both French and English in the courts, in the Council, and in its journals and records, and required that the Ordinances be printed in both languages. In 1892, however, in spite of opposition, a further amendment was passed to record and publish the proceedings of the Legislative Assembly in English only. Even if it never received royal assent and thus was without force, and even if it applied only to the publication of Assembly proceedings, in practice the Territorial government and subsequently those of Alberta and Saskatchewan relied on this resolution to prevent the use of French in provincial courts, legislatures, and their records from 1892 to 1988 (Denis and Li 1988). Much the same situation prevailed in the Northwest Territories and Yukon, although their courts could make use of French since they were under federal jurisdiction (Sheppard 1971, 303–304, 312).

Over the past century, education has been the major preoccupation of French minorities. Language rights in the schools were seriously affected by the BNA Act. Prior to 1867, denominational Catholic and Protestant schools had been established in Upper and Lower Canada. Section 93 of the BNA Act recognizes the rights of denominational schools already in existence when a province joins Confederation. In Quebec, language and religion coincided to a great extent, so that *de jure* religious protection produced de facto linguistic protection. But in other provinces this was less the case. Although the argument was made that linguistic rights were implicit in section 93, the Privy Council ruled in 1917 "that the separate schools were based on denominational and not linguistic differences" and that, consequently, confessional schools could not guarantee any particular language (Sheppard 1971, 68). From 1917 to 1982, language rights in education were relegated to provincial jurisdiction. In nine provinces, therefore, the education system was an English one; Francophones have had to seek educational rights and services from nine separate governments.

In the tenth province, Quebec, a dual education system has been in place since the 1850s, allowing the small number of Anglophones full access to their own education system (Laurendeau and Dunton 1968, 25–38). Except for rather brief periods, separate Protestant and Catholic education committees each reported directly to cabinet up to 1964. The committees' autonomy allowed the Protestant population to control programming, teacher training, taxation rates, and all other matters pertinent to their education needs. As a result, "an impressive English-language minority school system has been established in Quebec, through the public schools out of tax funds. It has been administered by English-speaking Protestants for English-speaking children in the province, and has thus reflected the aims and aspirations of the minority. Protestant boards even benefited from the taxes from most non-Catholic rate payers, whether they were Protestant or not" (32–33). English Catholics were served under the Catholic system; English was used as the language of instruction in their schools, and school inspectors were vigilant in ensuring a fair treatment of minorities (34).

The education systems for Francophone minorities were different. In the Maritimes, after the Acadians returned, French was generally tolerated but not officially recognized as a language of instruction, nor did it receive any specific administrative support. In some instances an Acadian school inspector might be appointed, but up to the 1960s Acadian education suffered from a lack of official recognition, legislative protection, adequate funding, programs, teacher training, and administrative support (Laurendeau and Dunton 1968, 98–114). Only in 1968 were some reforms on the horizon, especially in New Brunswick, but it will take years and countless efforts by Acadians for these to materialize.

In Ontario, anti-French and anti-Catholic sentiment led the government in 1912 to adopt Regulation 17, which reduced the use of French as a language of instruction to an insignificant amount. Although the regulation was revoked in 1927, the lack of access, quality, financing, and control over their own education by Francophones remained a major source of controversy into the 1990s.

In 1871, Manitoba had set up a dual system of education similar to that of Quebec, with separate Catholic and Protestant sections each under its own superintendent. But twenty years later anti-French and anti-Catholic sentiment pushed for one provincial school system. "Accordingly, in 1890, at the same time as the official use of the French language was abolished in the legislative assembly, the civil service, and the courts, the dual system of education was replaced by a nondenominational system under a single board of Education" (Laurendeau and Dunton 1968, 45). The ensuing controversy over the next few years produced the Laurier–Greenway compromise in 1897, which did not change the system but allowed the hiring of Roman Catholic teachers to teach Roman Catholic students. It also allowed religious instruction after regular school hours. Some predominantly Catholic schools were also qualified for government and municipal funding, although this proved to be more of a problem for English Catholic schools in Winnipeg (Comeault 1979; Staples 1974). This compromise also allowed the use of French or any other language along with English as a language of instruction. The influx of large numbers of immigrants was seen to strain the education system considerably. Consequently, the government unilaterally abolished the use of any language other than English in schools in 1916. Manitoba made few changes in this respect until the 1970s (Blay 1989).

Saskatchewan and Alberta followed much the same trends. Although French was accepted as a language of instruction on the same basis as English in the territories in the 1870s, this recognition was reduced gradually over the years as controversies flared up and died down. By 1931, English was the sole language of instruction allowed, although French could still be taught as a subject for one hour a day. The situation remained largely unchanged until 1968 in Saskatchewan (Denis and Li 1988) and Alberta (Laurendeau and Dunton 1968, 118).

In British Columbia, the lack of denominational schools did not allow French Canadians to regroup within Catholic institutions. Instead, they opted for their own private schools, a common arrangement in other provinces as well.

Apart from education, Francophone minority groups have also been very preoccupied with access to courts, legislation, and media in their language, but little movement was obtained from provincial governments on any of these prior to the 1970s. Thus, after an extensive review of Canadian language jurisdiction and law from the 1700s to the 1960s for the Bilingualism and Biculturalism Commission, Sheppard concluded:

> The BNA Act itself is totally unsatisfactory and does not even provide minimum guarantees to either the French or the English minorities in Canada. Such linguistic rights as exist ... will be found to be based on custom, practical considerations, or political expediency. When they are embodied in provincial or federal statutes, they can be abrogated at will.... There are only two jurisdictions in which there is no doubt that both languages enjoy almost equal official status: the federal and Quebec jurisdictions.... It just does not make sense that New Brunswick, 35.2 percent of whose population is French-speaking, should be unilingually English while Quebec, whose English population is only 13.26 percent

> of the total and mainly centred on the island of Montreal, is totally bilingual.
>
> (1971, 105, 313)

By the 1960s such views had come to be fairly broadly shared among Francophones and a significant number of academics and federal politicians. Even more pressing, however, was the rising tide of nationalism in Quebec, which demanded greater recognition of French even within its own borders.

Changing Times: 1960–1980

The impact of immigration, industrialization, and urbanization was already perceptible in Canada in the early 1900s. These changes gained momentum over the years and became quite pronounced during the Second World War and its aftermath.

Quebec 1960–1980

During the Second World War and in the following decade, industrialization, urbanization, and other concomitant social changes transformed Quebec society. French Canadians in Quebec were increasingly dissatisfied with being the wage-workers for non-Quebec employers who very often imposed English as the language of work and promotion. Quebec nationalism, which assumed various forms over the years, also took on a different orientation in the late 1950s and early 1960s as many Québecois felt that Quebec had to catch up to the rest of North America, but in French (Rioux 1973). To compete and develop within the Canadian and continental economy, Quebec had to modernize its political and economic infrastructures and its education system. But it also had to strengthen and protect the status of the French language if it was to retain the very core of its history and culture, which made it unique in North America.

Thus, in the early 1960s, a series of significant reforms and changes known as the "Quiet Revolution" drew from, and sustained, a growing Québécois nationalism. Apart from political, administrative, and economic reforms, the survival of the French language itself had become an issue, as increasing numbers of Québécois children and immigrants into Quebec opted for an English education. Already aware of the growing need to protect and promote its language, the Quebec government established the Office of the French Language in 1961, as well as the Parent Royal Commission on Education.

The Parent Commission's investigation of the whole education system resulted in a five-volume report, issued between 1963 and 1966. Some of its recommendations, incorporated in Bill 60 in 1964, finally led to the creation of a Department of Education with its own minister. It also led to a massive reorganization of education as a whole, including curriculum, administration, and funding. Nevertheless, even if the autonomy of the Protestant, and to a lesser extent the Anglo-Catholic, minorities was reduced somewhat, the appointment under the new act of two deputy ministers of education, one Catholic and the other Protestant, ensured that the ensuing structure respected the right to Protestant education, to independent schools and school administration, and to services in English (Laurendeau and Dunton 1968, 55–72).

On the political front, small nationalist parties had already surfaced in the 1950s including the Rassemblement pour l'Indépendance Nationale (RIN) on the left and the Rassemblement National (RN) on the right of the political spectrum. A number of events in the 1960s, including the findings of the federal Royal Commission on Bilingualism and Biculturalism, convinced many Québécois that federal institutions could not meet the needs of Quebec. In 1967, René Lévesque left the reformist Liberal Party of Jean Lesage and founded the Mouvement Souveraineté-Association (MSA), which called for the political independence of Quebec combined with some form of economic union with Canada. The increasingly popular notion of an independent Quebec led the following year to the amalgamation of the two other major pro-independence parties, the RIN and the RN, with the MSA, to become the Parti Québécois (PQ). Eight years later, on November 15, 1976, the Parti Québécois was elected to office. Its victory rested in part on the strategy of separating the election of an independence party from the decision to opt for Quebec's independence. Thus, electors could vote for the PQ without automatically voting for independence (Saywell 1977). Quebec independence was presented as a separate issue to be resolved by a referendum.

At the same time as the notion of Quebec's independence took political form in the 1960s and 1970s, the language issue also became increasingly acute. The first steps taken in 1961 were considered by many as totally ineffectual in protecting and promoting the French language. Three different political parties grappled with the issue while in office, each with its own language legislation. In 1969, the Union Nationale's Bill 63, the Act to Promote the French Language, was passed to overcome "language inequalities which maintain French in an inferior position" (Braen 1987a, 38). The ineffectiveness of this first law produced heated debate, with nationalists pushing for much more stringent legislation. The Commission of Inquiry into the Status of French and Linguistic Rights (the Gendron Commission) investigated some of these questions. Its report, tabled at the end of 1972, eventually led Premier Bourassa's Liberal government to adopt Bill 22 in 1974. This new language bill, the Official Languages Act, declared French to be the official language of Quebec for all purposes pertaining to public administration, public corporations, professions, industry, and commerce, although English versions of all documents were allowed as long as a French version existed. In education, language tests were imposed on those who wished to attend English schools (Delorme 1974).

The coming to power of the nationalist Parti Québécois in 1976 gave Francophone critics of Bill 22 the opportunity to strengthen the protection of the French language. Within a few months of taking office, the PQ produced a White Paper, *La politique québécoise de la langue française*, much of which was embodied in Bill 101, the charter of the French Language, adopted in 1977. The charter declared French to be the official language of Quebec for the courts and the legislature. It made French compulsory in the public service, and all government-related organizations, and in labour relations, commerce, and business. It restricted access to English schools to children who have one parent educated in English in Quebec.

Finally, "the Act creates a supervisory agency and attempts to implement measures to improve the quality of the French language" (Braen 1987a, 39). The charter remains the strongest legislation yet in Canada to protect and promote the French language, but it is confined to Quebec. It also provided Ottawa with its greatest impetus to act on language issues in the 1980s.

Relations between Quebec and Ottawa during the 1960s and 1970s were not always cordial. During these two decades, numerous events created great apprehension among federalists both inside and outside Quebec. Some of the more sensational events included the "Vive le Québec libre!" of France's General de Gaulle during the 1967 Expo and Centennial celebrations; the more extreme actions of small groups of "terrorists" such as the FLQ and RCMP *agents provocateurs* in the 1960s, culminating in the kidnapping of James Cross and the assassination of Quebec minister Pierre Laporte in the October Crisis of 1970; the subsequent federal War Measures Act of 1970; and the personally antagonistic and often acrimonious exchanges between Premier Lévesque and Prime Minister Trudeau (Caron et al. 1978; Lévesque 1986).

As pressure for an independent Quebec mounted, it became imperative for federalist forces to ensure that both Francophones and the French language be given more equitable treatment in federal institutions. For Prime Minister Trudeau, any call for special treatment for Quebec was a call for ghettoization, for juvenile affirmation of autonomy, to which he opposed his vision of a bilingual Canada united from coast to coast through bilingual federal institutions that could serve all Canadians in the official language of their choice. This vision, shared by many in the three major federal parties and by federalists in Quebec, had evolved out of the experiences of the 1960s.

Federal Government 1960–1980

Growing discontent among Francophones both inside and outside Quebec in the early 1960s threatened Canada's national unity and its prospects of surviving for another hundred years (Laurendeau and Dunton 1965, 21–24). Accordingly, in 1963 the federal government established the Royal Commission on Bilingualism and Biculturalism to investigate language inequality in Canada, to be chaired by André Laurendeau and Davidson Dunton. Sociological studies such as Porter's influential *The Vertical Mosaic* or Joy's *Languages in Conflict* identified major inequities detrimental to Francophones in all areas of society prior to the release of the commission's first report in 1967. The commission's many studies corroborated these findings and made numerous recommendations, some of which were implemented by federal and provincial governments over the next few years.

Thus, the federal government made some attempts to reduce inequities between the two official language groups. Radio-Canada's mandate to serve the whole of Francophone Canada was strengthened. This meant much stronger support for Radio-Canada and a greater presence in the minority communities outside Quebec. It increased its coverage in the Atlantic provinces and in British Columbia, and eventually purchased the four independent radio stations set up in the late 1940s and early 1950s by Francophones in the Prairies.

Probably the most significant change was the Official Languages Act of 1969, which "confers official and equal status to the French and English languages within the federal Government" (Braen 1987a, 34). With few exceptions, all citizens have the right to communicate with federal institutions in the official language of their choice. Judgements from federal courts and quasi-judicial bodies and all federal documents intended for the public must be in both languages. The federal civil service and federal agencies must become increasingly bilingual and provide equal opportunities for Francophones. French must become an effective language of work in those areas. "The declared intention is therefore to achieve true equality of the two official languages" (Braen 1987a, 34).

In addition, the 1969 legislation established a commissioner of Official Languages to oversee implementation of the act. The secretary of state was made specifically responsible for official language minorities. Federal funding to these groups increased over the years from around $2 million in 1970 to $26 million in 1987 (Secretary of State 1970, 1987). Although the 1987 figure may seem generous, the commissioner of Official Languages complained that, from 1969 to 1977, "budgetary allocations barely kept up with inflation" (Commissioner 1977, 20). Undoubtedly these efforts were important initially, but the more significant changes at the federal level occurred after 1980.

The Rest of Canada 1960–1980

A similar pattern arose in the rest of Canada where a few provinces introduced some changes in language legislation in the late 1960s. New Brunswick recognized both French and English as official languages with its Official Languages Act in 1969, although most of its clauses remained ineffectual until the late 1970s (Commissioner 1979, 23). Most provinces modified their education system or laws to allow the use of French as a language of instruction and to provide some support either for programs or teacher training (Chevrier 1983, 47–55). By 1930, but generally much earlier, most provinces had made English the only language of instruction in their schools (Blay 1989; Chevrier 1983; Denis and Li 1988; Laurendeau and Dunton 1968). French was reinstated as a language of instruction for one hour a day in Saskatchewan in 1967, and the following year, schools could be designated where French could be used for all subjects except compulsory English courses (Denis and Li 1988, 359). Similarly, in 1970, Manitoba allowed French as a language of instruction but it would take another decade for the establishment of classes and schools where French was the language of administration. Alberta permitted the use of French in school without making any distinction between French immersion and French as a first language. British Columbia introduced a new policy on French education in 1979, which guaranteed the establishment of a French class when requested by the parents of ten students. The success of this approach led British Columbia authorities to open a homogeneous Francophone school in Vancouver in September 1983 (Chevrier 1983, 44–55). Prince Edward Island's Bill 33 recognized the right to education in French for Francophones in 1980. The following year, Nova Scotia's Bill 65 acknowledged the right of Francophones to schools in their mother tongue "where numbers warrant." In New Brunswick, not only was the use of French in school allowed, but so was the establishment of homogeneous French schools and school boards. Ontario promised that by 1982 all Francophone children would have access to education in French, and Francophones would obtain certain management rights through guaranteed positions on existing Anglophone boards (Chevrier 1983, 44–55)

Since 1970 Ontario has offered some bilingual services in certain districts in education, social services, health and welfare, justice, and culture, even if it has always refused to become officially bilingual. By 1979, Franco-Ontarians were to have the right to a trial before a French-speaking judge or jury for criminal offences and in 1982 for civil trials (Chevrier 1983, 44–55). These services remain very uneven, and constrained by financial and administrative requirements (Chevrier 1983, 36).

Few modifications, if any, were introduced to any other area of legislation, policy, or government service to Francophones by Anglophone provinces. Impressive as the changes above may appear at first glance, most of them remain purely formal. Modifications to laws or regulations do not automatically translate into better access and better quality education in French at the local level if funding and resources are inadequate, and especially if there is no direct minority control over education. Since many decisions pertaining to French education were left to the discretionary power of ministers of Education, and since implementation schedules were absent or incomplete, Francophone parents often had to engage in endless lobbying, even resorting to court actions to force recalcitrant school boards to comply with the law (Chevrier 1983, 33–55; Denis and Li 1988, 360; see the section on "minorities" in yearly reports of the commissioner of Official Languages). Even when school boards did comply with the law, most education legislation did not respect minority rights in spite of the changes noted above (Foucher 1987). Many of the federal efforts were very slow in having any concrete beneficial effects for Francophones at the community level. Most of the modifications affected the internal operations of federal institutions, with little immediate impact on Francophone communities. Some changes, such as the extension of Radio-Canada service, brought very mixed blessings.

Language and Law: Court Challenges

In the 1980s, a number of very significant events occurred in respect to language legislation both in Quebec and in the rest of Canada. These had direct repercussions on the Meech Lake Accord. The 1969 Federal Official Languages Act, combined with the 1982 Charter of Rights, changed the setting within which minority language rights were to be recognized. But even the language provisions of the Charter of Rights were a reaction to existing legislation, particularly that of Quebec.

English in Quebec

As stated earlier, Quebec's Bill 101, adopted in 1977, made French compulsory in the legislature, the courts, in education (except for students of Anglophone origin), in public institutions and services, and on commercial signs. The justification for the act is that the Québécois remain a minority within both Canada and the North American continent; the influx of immigrants who assimilate into the English language and culture, coupled with the drastic drop in Francophone fertility, would in the long run transform them into a minority even within their own territory. Strong protection is required, not to assimilate Anglophones and deprive them of their rights, but to protect the French language.

Reaction by Quebec Anglophones to Bill 101 is well known. Over the years, public organizations such as school boards and corporations, as well as individuals, have contested clauses of Bill 101 in the courts, very often successfully. Already in 1979 a Supreme Court decision reimposed bilingualism in the Quebec legislature and courts; in July 1984, the Supreme Court broadened access to English schools in Quebec to comply with Section 23 of the Canadian Charter of Rights; lower courts made employer–employee communications in French compulsory only when these are addressed to all employees (*Miriam* case); certain language test requirements for professionals were declared to be invalid (*Forget* case); and Quebec's Superior Court also produced two contradictory rulings on commercial signs: on the one hand it ruled that Quebec had the right to prescribe the exclusive use of French on signs (*Devine* case), while on the other it held that the exclusion of languages other than French on such signs contravenes freedom of expression (*Brown et al.* case) (*Le Devoir* February 6, 1985: 9; *Le Devoir* February 7, 1985: 11; see also Deschênes 1980, 285–389). The last two decisions were appealed to the Supreme Court and eventually gave rise to the controversial Bill 178, in December 1988. As a result of these judgements, legislation in Quebec is adopted and published in both languages, and both languages may be used in the courts. Some administrative rules of Bill 101 have been eliminated or otherwise weakened, and entrance to Anglophone schools has been broadened. According to the Conseil de la langue française, the combined effect of these judgements severely reduces Quebec's ability to develop French as its major public language. Overall, these judgements transform Quebec from a province where French predominates to one where both French and English can be used, to the serious detriment of the French language (*Le Devoir* February 6, 1985: 9; *Le Devoir* February 7, 1985: 11). Thus the basic and necessary protection required to maintain French as the official language of the province is undermined.

Apart from court challenges, Anglophones used other tactics to discredit the Quebec legislation. For example, some Anglophone corporations such as Sun Life Insurance very noisily moved their head offices from Montreal to Toronto (Kierans, Brecher, and Naylor 1982). Some professionals left likewise. As well, Quebec's Anglophones had access to and made extensive use of some very crucial instruments to defend their rights and to lobby for change: their own Anglophone politicians and cabinet ministers in both Ottawa and Quebec, and their own media. In recent years more explicit lobbying organizations have appeared to promote Anglophone linguistic rights within Quebec. In particular, Alliance Quebec, founded in 1981, has played a very active role in challenging various articles of Bill 101, or of supporting individuals, organizations or companies who do so. The strong Anglophone reaction to Bill 101 belies the fact that other clauses and other laws such as sections 93 and 133 of the BNA Act as well as the Quebec Charter of Rights provide protection to this group. Also, in 1986, Quebec adopted Bill 142, which guarantees health and social services in English, although some regional health councils are accused of being slow in implementing access plans (Commissioner 1988a, 225). Even Bill 101 grants Anglophones the right of access to their own educational system and to education in their own language.

French Outside Quebec

Francophones outside Quebec have used court challenges where possible to obtain changes to provincial legislation and to services or institutions. They have used the commissioner of Official Languages to obtain better service in French from federal agencies and offices. They have also continued to establish their own institutions where possible, often against great odds. Some events revealed quite well the contradictory climate of the times. For example, when the Francophone MLA Léo Piquette of the NDP dared to use French in the Alberta legislature in 1987, the Speaker asked him to apologize publicly. His refusal to do so was seen by many, including the Speaker, as quite outrageous (*Le Devoir* 25, 27, 29, June 30, 1987). Yet this same province signed the Meech Lake Accord, a few months later, whereby it agreed "to preserve the fundamental characteristic of Canada's [linguistic dualism]" (Meech Lake Accord section 2[2]).

Francophones have lobbied extensively to obtain federal funding for their communities, organizations, and institutions. As a result, they have come to rely to a large extent on funding and support from the secretary of state, although this has not been without difficulties. Ironically, programs that were intended to assist the Francophone minority outside Quebec, by being directed at "official language minorities" have often provided great assistance to the Anglophone group in Quebec. For example, in 1976, secretary of state grants to minority communities averaged $12 000 for Anglophone projects in Quebec in contrast to $7000 for Francophone projects outside Quebec. In 1977 the figures were $16 700 and $9300, respectively (Secretary of State 1976; 1977, 37–39). Pressure from the Francophone minorities forced the secretary of state to revise some of the department's funding policies so as to be more equitable in its allocations. Unfortunately, no recent data broken down by province are available to indicate which minority is best served by these programs.

In the Official Languages in Education Program, which funds the teaching of French and English as first and second languages, the secretary of state has increased the department's annual spending from $57.5 million in 1970 to $201 million in 1986-87. Although an impressive increase at first glance, the 1986-87 figure is in fact lower than the 1970 figure in constant dollars. Part of the problem that the secretary of state faces in this regard is getting the provinces to increase their contributions in this area of education (Commissioner 1988a, 22–23).

In the first ten years of this program, Francophone minorities complained constantly that the federal funds for their education never reached their communities. Often, Anglophone school boards and provincial governments could not account at the local level for all the federal funds that they claimed to have spent on Francophone education. In some cases up to half of the funds earmarked for French minority education were lost between Ottawa and the community school. Federal funds were misused, as in "building highways for school buses" (Fédération des Francophones Hors Québec [FFHQ] 1981; 45–54). Similarly, 67.5 percent of money spent on special projects outside Quebec in the early 1970s went for French immersion for Anglophone children (FFHQ 1981, 41). For Francophone minorities, probably the most painful aspect of these programs was that Quebec collected nearly 58 percent of the $1.08 billion spent by Ottawa on these programs between 1970 and 1978 (FFHQ 1981, 20b). In some cases, Quebec's share was as high as 74 percent of the federal funds (FFHQ 1981, 37). The major reason for this was that Anglophones in Quebec already had numerous schools in place, as well as a number of school boards, so that they qualified more readily for these funds. Ironically, the outcome of these programs meant that the weaker the minority, and the more oppressed by its local and provincial authorities, the less likely it was to obtain anything from Ottawa, since it was less likely to meet federal criteria.

The numerous complaints forced Ottawa to impose stronger accountability procedures on provincial governments and to revise the manner in which funds were allocated. As a result, in the 1980s a growing share went toward French education in English speaking Canada, including immersion, rather than to Quebec, although its share remained as high as 45 to 48 percent, at least up to 1985 (Task Force 1985, 221). According to Taylor-Browne (1988, 198), "more than half of the Secretary of State's funds for bilingualism in education actually go to supporting English language educational programs in Quebec. Half of the remaining amount supports French-language education for non-Francophones outside Quebec. As a result only a tiny amount is available for minority Francophones." This view may exaggerate slightly the actual distribution, although it is difficult to know exactly how much money is spent through the various programs for each province. In 1988, Ottawa paid $60.2 million for Quebec's 111 862 Anglophone students, an average of $538 per student, compared to $68.4 million for the 151 063 Francophone students outside Quebec, or an average of $453 per student. Anglophone students outside Quebec received $57.1 million to learn French as a second language, which is nearly as much as the Francophone minority received (Vastel 1989b).

In spite of increased federal funds, dissatisfaction among Francophones remained high. By the time the relevant articles of the Charter of Rights were enacted in April 1985, parents in Nova Scotia, Prince Edward Island, Ontario, Manitoba, Saskatchewan, Alberta, and British Columbia were already considering court proceedings against their respective governments to obtain recognition of their educational rights. In spite of provincial variations in judgements and different interpretations of these articles, the educational rights of official language minorities have been recognized (Foucher 1987, 263-97). Generally, it is recognized that article 23 means that the official language minority has the right to instruction in their mother tongue, the right to autonomous, homogeneous schools, and the right to the management and control of these schools. In an important decision, *SANB et al. v. The Association of Parents for Fairness in Education et al.*, Judge Richard ruled that "immersion classes cannot be held equivalent of French language instruction for the purposes of the minority education rights guaranteed in the Charter" (Commissioner 1987, 162). Further, the 1987 decision by Judge Proudfoot in British Columbia also specified that, under article 23, Anglophone parents have no constitutional right to immersion education. For these parents, education in the second language remains a privilege (Commissioner 1987, 163).

Most judgements recognize existing provincial education legislation as being unconstitutional. In practice, Anglophone provinces often deny Francophones what they provide for Anglophones—small classes, small schools, multigrade classrooms, school boards covering a broad territory, and ultimately Francophone control of their own school boards. The Supreme Court finally rendered its first ruling regarding the rights included in Article 23 in the *Mahé* case from Alberta on March 15, 1990. The court recognized that this article confers the rights of management and control of their educational establishments, which includes the right to their own autonomous school boards, to official language minorities, where numbers warrant. Where numbers don't warrant full control, a sliding scale of control should be applied to allow for some control, depending on the size of the minority population. The court did not specify what the numbers should be for each level of the sliding scale (*Mahé* 1990).

Although crucial, court challenges to education laws have not been the only area of activity. New Brunswick's Bill 88, passed in 1981, should eventually result in a bilingual civil service and greater equality between the two linguistic groups (Chevrier 1983, 39). Implementation of the legislation is not as rapid as the Acadians would like, however.

In Ontario, minor amendments to existing legislation have been introduced over the years, including Bill 08 in 1986, which is to increase government services in French in certain regions of the province (Braen 1987a, 42; Chevrier 1983, 39; *Le Devoir* November 24, 1986: 1). But the most significant administrative and legislative change of the last decade is Bill 109, adopted in 1988, which created in Ottawa Carleton a Francophone school board with a thousand teachers, eighteen thousand students, and an operating budget of $100 million. This board was split into two separate boards in 1993, one Catholic and one public (Paquette-Legault 1994). Public Francophone school boards have also been established in Toronto and Prescott–Russell (Secretary of State 1988, 221). The Ottawa–Carleton board had been recommended by a provincial commission in 1976 and had, at that time, support from "the English boards, the local press, and French and English community leaders" (Commissioner 1979, 32). One hates to consider how long it would have taken the province to act if there had been strong local opposition.

The NDP government has increased the number of Francophone service regions under Bill 08 from 22 to 23, created two francophone colleges, one for northern Ontario and one in the south, which are to open in September 1995. They also established a Royal Commission on Education under the joint chairs of Monique Bégin and Gerald Caplan (Dansereau, 1994). However the lack of substantial improvements in the recognition of French linguistic rights or the provision of services has lead some disillusioned Francophones to file a formal complain of cultural genocide against the Ontario Government before the United Nations' Commission on Human Rights in Geneva in the summer of 1994.

The situation in Manitoba was different. The *Forest* case, initiated in 1976, finally obtained a Supreme Court ruling in 1979 that re-established official bilingualism as set out in Article 23 of the Manitoba Act of 1870 (Deschênes 1980, 391–430). An attempt by the Francophone community to exchange the translation of all laws for a partial translation of laws along with some provincial services in French failed, so that Manitoba was given until 1990 to translate all its laws (Braen 1987b, 84–92). Since 1982, following the *Bilodeau* case, most Manitoba laws have been enacted in both languages (Braen 1987b, 88).

Other provinces are not affected by section 133 of the BNA Act, nor have they legislated recently on language, except for New Brunswick and the special cases of Alberta and Saskatchewan (Braen 1987b).

In spite of the Official Languages Act, the commissioner of Official Languages, and increased funding through the secretary of state, language loss among Francophones continued to increase during the 1970s (Commissioner 1984, 176–77). This is not surprising, since there were few real changes in the provincial institutional and legislative structures. The impact of the federal language policies of the last twenty years has begun to manifest itself in the figures of the 1991 census. In virtually all provinces, there is a slight increase in the number of persons of French or English mother tongue who speak both languages, since the 1981 census. Such trends should become more pronounced in the censuses of 1996 and 2001 as students from French immersion and the new minority schools reach adulthood, as long as enrolments do not decrease. In the meantime, bilingualism remains very much the responsibility of the Francophone communities in English Canada, and, to a lesser extent, of the Anglophone group in Quebec. Excluding New Brunswick and Quebec, persons of French mother tongue who speak both languages range from 85 percent in Newfoundland to 91.6 percent in Nova Scotia, whereas bilingual Anglophones range from 2.8 percent in Newfoundland to a high of 7.5 percent in Ontario. In all cases there has been an increase of about 1 percent in the decade 1981–1991. In New Brunswick, Francophones are 62.5 percent bilingual with an increase of 2 percent over 1981 compared to only 12 percent for Anglophones in spite of an increase of 3 percent. Similarly in Quebec the proportion of bilingual Francophones has increased by 2 percent to reach 31 percent whereas the greatest increase in all of Canada has been among Quebec's Anglophone population, now 58.5 percent bilingual with a 5 percent increase over 1981 (Statistiques Canada 1985, Table 6; 1991, Table 3; percentages for 1991 are calculated on single responses only). As Lieberson (1970, 13) argues, ability to speak the dominant group's language becomes a risk factor, since it becomes the first step in language shift. Except for Quebec, the onus to speak the other group's language falls almost entirely on the Francophone minority, since so few of the dominant group can converse in the minority language. In Quebec, Bill 101 requires Anglophones to become increasingly bilingual in many occupations; however, they are also guaranteed access to education, the legislature, the judiciary, and to health and social services in English. So even with Bill 101, many Quebec Anglophones can go through life in Quebec without learning or using French. Such is not the case for most Francophone minorities. According to Vastel (1989b [my translation]) "the only right that Francophones enjoy all across the country is the right to be sent to jail in one's mother tongue."

The total effect of the last twenty years of struggle and change is not immediately visible in statistics on language loss. The inertia and subordination arising from generations of oppression and denial of rights is very difficult to overcome, and it will probably take another decade before significant changes in the Francophone groups are reflected in census data and before we know whether federal bilingualism policies have in fact strengthened the Francophone minorities or hastened their demise.

The Context of Meech Lake

The 1976 election of the PQ focussed federalist fears even more sharply on the threat of Quebec independence. As promised during its election campaign, the new PQ government eventually organized a referendum on the question of Quebec independence on May 20, 1980. Quebec legislation required that those favouring one side or the other regroup under an umbrella organization for either the "yes" or the "no" vote. Each side could spend up to $2 122 257 during the campaign. Officially, those opposing Quebec independence spent $2 060 455. It is claimed, however, that Ottawa injected an additional $17.5 million into the "no" campaign (*Le Devoir* December 14, 1987: 1). In the referendum, 60 percent of voters opted to stay in Canada, and 40 percent chose independence for Quebec. The Francophone vote, however, was split near the 50 percent mark, thus leaving many Québécois even more disillusioned about federal interference in Quebec affairs and about the place of Quebec and of Francophones within a primarily English Canada (Lévesque 1986, 401–20). Ironically, in spite of the referendum results, the PQ won the next provincial elections on April 13, 1981, raising doubts about a political system that allows a population to reject its political independence and yet retain an independence party in government.

The federal government referendum campaign led by the ruling Liberals had repeatedly assured the Québécois that a "no" vote was not a vote for the status quo; changes would be made in Ottawa and in the rest of Canada to respect their legitimate rights and aspirations. With the Quebec referendum behind them, the federal government pressed even more strongly for patriation of the Constitution. Debate over patriation, an amending formula, and protection of citizens' rights in a Canadian charter had already occupied much of the political stage in the late 1970s (FFHQ 1981, 12–14; Russell 1993, 107–126). In these debates, language issues remained at the forefront of the political agenda. Trudeau expected that action in these areas could satisfy Quebec and fulfil his referendum promises.

The provincial premiers had failed to reach unanimity on constitutional matters in previous constitutional talks in 1927, 1931, 1935–36, 1950, 1961, 1964, 1971, 1975–76, and 1978–79 (Palmer 1988, 39). Well aware of this, Trudeau favoured unilateral federal action, if necessary, until he was blocked by a Supreme Court ruling that constitutional change required a "substantial degree of provincial consent" (Hogg 1988, 45). Constitutional talks on November 5, 1981, seemed headed toward the usual stalemate. However, a late-night agreement worked out on a kitchen counter by representatives of Saskatchewan, Ontario, and Ottawa rallied all the premiers from English Canada. But it did not accommodate Quebec's position sufficiently. Premier Lévesque subsequently left the constitutional talks with the result that Quebec was never included as a formal signatory to the 1982 Constitutional amendment.

The ensuing Charter of Rights enshrined elements of the Official Languages Act of 1969 in the Constitution. Section 16 recognizes French and English as the official languages for Canada and New Brunswick, with equal status, rights, and privileges. This applies to the debate and publication of statutes, records, and journals of debate for Parliament and the Legislature of New Brunswick, to all institutions and courts, and to all services provided to the public from any head or central office of the federal or New Brunswick governments. As well, the Charter retains the previous provisions on language contained in Section 133 of the BNA Act and Section 23 of the Manitoba Act (Statutes of Canada [SC] 1982, s16–s21).

Although education is a matter of provincial jurisdiction under the 1867 Constitution, the Charter establishes the rights of linguistic minorities and sets obligations for provinces to provide them with adequate educational opportunities (SC 1982, s23). In an attempt to weaken Quebec's Language Charter (Bill 101), the Canadian Charter extends the same educational rights granted the linguistic minority to members of the majority who obtained their education in the language of the minority or whose children are presently so receiving their education. This applies across provincial boundaries. In other words, in Quebec, Anglophones with English as a first language, others who have obtained their education in English anywhere in Canada, or the siblings of those presently enrolled in English schools are entitled to education in English. The converse is applicable to French outside Quebec. Section 23 does recognize that, where numbers warrant, minority education is to be made available in "minority language educational facilities provided out of public funds" (SC 1982, s23[3b]). As well, Article 24 allows recourse to tribunals to obtain remedial action in case of denial or infringement of rights.

As indicated earlier, the Charter opened new possibilities for official language minorities, especially through judicial challenges to provincial legislation. Ottawa also introduced other changes. Amendments to the Criminal Code in June 1978 guarantee that, after provincial proclamation, an accused will have the right to a trial by judge or jury in his or her language anywhere in Canada (Commissioner 1978, 30). By 1987, implementation of these amendments, as Part XIV(I) of the Criminal Code, permitted such trials in French in Saskatchewan, Nova Scotia, Prince Edward Island (Commissioner 1987, 156–61) and Alberta (*Le Devoir* September 11, 1987: 4). Of course, such trials have been possible in English in Quebec since 1867 under section 133 of the BNA Act.

The secretary of state also increased the funding to minority groups, to $26 million annually by 1987. In reality, this amounted to an average allocation per project of only $28 000 (Secretary of State 1987, 25). Since some of these projects include national organizations, the amount is far from outlandish. As well, federal support has been provided for education to assist official language minorities and promote official languages through the Official Languages in Education Program. By the late 1980s, Ottawa distributed about $225 million annually to the provinces through this program, although there is little agreement on how well the funds have been used.

One final area of federal activity of great significance is the Court Challenges Program, which had been utilized hardly at all prior to 1982. The program provides financial support for those eligible who seek court rulings to clarify official language rights under the Charter, Sections 93 or 133 of the BNA Act, or Article 23 of the Manitoba Act (Secretary of State 1983, 38-39), or for those who seek recognition and promotion of official language rights in Canada through the courts (Canadian Council on Social Development [CCSD] 1986–87, 34). In 1982-83, funding was provided for two cases. The following year, this had already increased to five cases before the courts and five others in preparation. In 1985, the secretary of state entered a five-year agreement to have the fund administered independently by the Canadian Council on Social Development. Over the years, the number of requests has increased, from 22 in 1985, to 32 in 1986, and 35 in 1987, although not all requests get funding, and the same case may submit a number of requests as it proceeds through the various levels of the judiciary. Between 1985 and 1989, the CCSD approved $1.2 million for court challenges pertaining to linguistic matters. This program has allowed minorities to defend their rights more effectively through the courts than was ever possible in the past. It has had a major impact on provincial activities and legislation, both in Quebec and in the rest of Canada, as most of the court challenges to provincial legislation have been funded in part by this program.

From the time of the negotiations for patriation in 1981–82 until now, Quebec has still been affected by changes at the federal level, even if it has not been included in the new Canadian Constitution. Federal money has been used to successfully challenge Quebec legislation in the courts and force modifications. These funds have also been used to provide services to the Anglophone group. Even though Quebec had not signed the Canadian Charter of Rights, it found itself bound to it by the Supreme Court. On the other hand, even though the Supreme Court ruled that Quebec did not in fact have veto power over constitutional change, it became increasingly clear to the other provinces that it would be very difficult to obtain any further modifications to the Constitution, whether in questions of jurisdiction, such as fisheries or federal spending, or of structure, such as an elected Senate or provincial selection of judges, without Quebec's participation.

Two changes in government opened a new opportunity for federalists to resolve the "Quebec question" once and for all within the framework of Canadian federalism. They were the election in Quebec of the federalist Liberals under Bourassa, and the replacement in Ottawa of Trudeau's Liberals by the decentralizing Conservatives under the "mediator" Mulroney

The "Distinct Society" Clause for Quebec

The Quebec Liberal Party adopted its constitutional position in a document entitled *Maîtriser l'avenir*, in February 1985. From this, the government of Quebec outlined five conditions that had to be met for the province to be reintegrated into Canada's constitutional fold. These were:

i) recognition of Quebec as a distinct society and the principal homeland of French-speaking Canadians in a preamble to the new constitution;
ii) either a general veto over constitutional amendment, or full compensation where the province exercises its right to "opt out" of an amendment, combined with a veto over changes to national institutions or the creation of new provinces;
iii) participation in the appointment of the three Supreme Court of Canada justices from Quebec;
iv) entrenchment of a right for Quebec to determine jointly with the federal government the number of immigrants to Quebec each year and the selection of those immigrants; and
v) limitation of Parliament's spending power (Murray 1988).

The first condition was a watered-down version of the concept of "nation" that was used in the 1960s and had constantly irritated former prime minister Trudeau, who always felt that any "special status" for Quebec was a sure way to lead to its independence. This condition recognizes that Quebec is the only region in North America where French is the predominant language and where a sufficiently large portion of the population is of French origin, thereby giving its provincial government a particular responsibility in safeguarding and promoting that society's language, culture, and unique institutions.

The second condition was intended to give Quebec protection against constitutional changes that might jeopardize its distinct character. There was also a guarantee that if Quebec decided not to join a program or accept an amendment so as to protect its uniqueness, it would receive financial compensation comparable to the benefits obtained by the other provinces. Family allowance is a case in point, where Quebec developed its own program independently of the federal one.

The third condition would have enshrined in the Constitution the tradition of having three Supreme Court judges from Quebec. It would also ensure that Quebec would select the candidates for appointment. This is particularly important given that the Supreme Court is the final arbiter of federal-provincial disagreements. Thus, it is essential for Quebec that some Supreme Court judges understand the needs and preoccupations of Quebec, and bring more than a federal point of view to bear on matters touching Quebec. Also, "Quebec has been concerned that at least three judges [be] competent to hear cases based on Quebec's distinctive civil code" (Thomson 1988, 96).

Quebec already participates to a certain extent in the selection of immigrants into Quebec under an arrangement called the Cullen–Couture Agreement. Quebec wanted this role to be recognized and amplified in the Constitution. Quebec would have received a number of immigrants equal to its proportion of the Canadian population, and would have had control over the integration programs. This would have ensured an appropriate number of immigrants, who would then be integrated into the Francophone community (Thomson 1988, 96).

The final condition intended to limit Ottawa's ability to spend in areas of provincial jurisdiction, and was seen as necessary given the tendency over the preceding twenty years for Ottawa to fund directly all sorts of programs and projects without consideration for provincial priorities or jurisdiction.

The last four conditions can be seen as more specific aspects of the first condition. To maintain and promote its distinctiveness, Quebec must have control or protection in these specific areas.

The discussion and events around Meech Lake and the subsequent Charlottetown Agreement are already history. The Meech Lake Accord itself, in the typical manner of political compromise where everyone is supposed to win something, gave Quebec what it wanted, only by giving most of the same to all the provinces. Thus, Article 2(1)(a) recognized the dual nature of French and English Canada—the former concentrated in Quebec, the latter in the rest of Canada, but each with its minority of the other official language group—as being the fundamental characteristic of Canada. Furthermore, 2(1)(b) recognized "that Quebec constitutes within Canada a distinct society." The Parliament and provincial legislatures had the obligation to "preserve" this fundamental characteristic while respecting existing language rights, whereas Quebec had the obligation to "preserve and promote" its distinct society.

All provinces were to obtain the right to submit names of persons, acceptable to the Privy Council, for the Senate. Quebec could request Ottawa to negotiate an agreement regarding the province's role in the area of immigration—but so could any other province. At least three Supreme Court judges were to be named from lists provided by the government of Quebec, although the other provinces could also submit names for the other six positions. All provinces obtained the right to withdraw from national programs in areas of provincial jurisdiction, with compensation from Ottawa. Finally, the veto that Quebec sought so as to protect its "distinct society" was granted not only to Quebec but to all provinces. In effect, the nine premiers and the prime minister were caught in the age-old problem of saying, "Yes, Quebec is a different and unique province, but on the other hand it is still a province." Formally, the agreement recognized Quebec's distinctiveness, while in reality most of the powers or protections that Quebec wanted were also granted to the other provinces, thereby diluting Quebec's distinctiveness.

Quebec was the first province to adopt the Meech Lake accord after its final drafting in June 1987. Saskatchewan followed in September, and Alberta in December 1987. In June 1988, the federal Parliament passed the accord in second reading. Five other provinces eventually ratified the agreement as well. New Brunswick and Manitoba were the last two to hold out. Complete ratification was to be concluded by June 1990. The longer the process dragged out, the more various groups reconsidered their initial support of the accord. On December 19, 1988, Premier Filmon withdrew Manitoba's resolution to ratify the accord. By the summer of 1989, British Columbia Premier Vander Zalm was suggesting that it might be appropriate to have a parallel agreement on some of the issues raised by the wording. Alberta still wanted an elected Senate at all costs, and the newly elected premier Clyde Wells of Newfoundland warned of the possibility of rescinding his province's support. The Western NDP withdrew their support, as did some members of other political parties. Newfoundland eventually did withdraw from the accord, while New Brunswick adopted it just days before the constitutional deadline for its ratification. It expired on June 23, 1990, with the failure of the legislatures of Manitoba and Newfoundland to pass it.

Much of the reason for this hesitation stemmed from events succeeding June 1987. It is true that, even at the outset, the accord was judged by many to be incomplete. In particular, those who wanted an elected Senate or the provincial appointment of federal judges, those advocating aboriginal rights, women's rights, a labour bill of rights, or stronger protection for multiculturalism remained very critical of the accord (Gibbins 1988). But the most serious criticism of the accord was the lack of definition of its central term "distinct society." Without a proper definition, it was not clear what elements compose Quebec's distinct society, whether the bilingualism of the BNA Act's Section 133 or the French society of Bill 101, nor was it clear what measures were to be used to "preserve and promote" this society (Dion 1987). Similarly it was not certain what the other provincial governments were to do to "preserve" Canada's dualism, particularly in regard to their Francophone minorities. This weakness of the agreement was demonstrated precisely on the issue that the accord was supposed to resolve—namely language.

Meech Lake also failed because inexperienced leaders were struggling with a new process. The era of executive federalism, wherein first ministers behind closed doors determine the constitutional structure of Canada, was over. Many first ministers and their advisors "did not sense the difficulty in combining the traditional practice of executive federalism with the new requirement in the constitutional process for ratification in provincial legislatures" (Russell 1993, 135). Matters were to become even more complicated in the next round of constitutional reform.

Meech Lake came to be regarded as the "Quebec round," since in this accord Quebec had tried to answer the perpetual question, what does Quebec want? When Meech failed, the Quebec government's position was to wait for a counter-offer from the rest of Canada. It was quite obvious to political leaders and many others across Canada that the constitutional deadlock could be broken only by an agreement that would satisfy Quebec's needs but that would also meet some needs of the other provinces, so as to not appear to cater to Quebec. To further complicate matters, it was also obvious that subsequent constitutional changes would have to include input and participation of ordinary citizens if it was to succeed. Adoption of such changes by legislatures was no longer adequate to give them legitimacy.

These constraints eventually materialized into a second round of negotiations known as the Canada round, which culminated in the Charlottetown Agreement of August 28, 1992, and a Canada-wide referendum on October 26, 1992. Between the death of Meech Lake on June 22, 1990, and this referendum, the constitutional process became increasingly complex and confusing. Aboriginal land rights and self-government was thrust onto the agenda with the Oka crisis in the summer of 1990. The rise of the Reform Party in Western Canada added Senate reform to the discussion, while the creation of the Bloc Québécois, an independent federal party in Quebec, ensured that Quebec's needs would not be ignored (Dion 1993, Johnston 1993, Russell 1993). In Quebec, constitutional alternatives for Quebec were considered through two bodies carrying out public consultations, one under the ruling Liberal party (the Allaire Committee) and the other as a joint committee of the National Assembly (the Bélanger-Campeau Commission). The federal government followed suit with five initiatives: a parliamentary committee on the amending process (Beaudoin-Edwards); a citizens' forum under Keith Spicer; a set of highly tentative proposals for constitutional reform under the title "Shaping Canada's Future Together" in September 1991; a parliamentary committee under Castonguay-Dobbie (and later Beaudoin-Dobbie) to carry out provincial consultations; and a series of meetings with first ministers between the end of June 1992 and the Charlottetown Agreement (Russell 1993, 190–227).

Out of this very complex process emerged a complicated package that offered less than Meech Lake to Quebec but that included proposals for an enlarged House of Commons where Quebec would be guaranteed 25 percent of the seats, a smaller reformed Senate, a more restrictive amending formula, and some clarification but little real changes on federal–provincial division of powers. In spite of the much more open process, Canadians rejected this second agreement by a vote of 54.4 percent (Dion 1993, Johnston 1993).

On the one hand it is easy to point to the fact that the constitutional negotiations were not tied to the referendum process, so the electorate was ill-prepared to make a judgement on the agreement. Also, by trying to do too much in one shot, the agreement was almost doomed from the start. But ultimately the Charlottetown Agreement failed because outside Quebec it appeared to give Quebec too much, while within Quebec it was rejected because it did not give Quebec enough (Russell 1993, 226). The failure of this latest round reflects again the contradictory visions of Canada. For Canadians outside Quebec, generally, Canada consists of individual citizens with equal rights grouped in provinces with symmetrical powers. For most Québécois, Canada consists of provinces where one has unique characteristics of language, culture, and history and a need for an asymmetrical division of powers to protect its distinctiveness (Russell 1993, 229).

Meech Lake and Minority Rights

The issue of Quebec's "distinct society" drew national attention in December 1988, when the Supreme Court of Canada ruled that the law mandating French-only business signs in Quebec contravened the Quebec and Canadian charters of rights. The Supreme Court, therefore, recognized that Anglophones had the right to bilingual signs in their places of business, contrary to Bill 101. It added, however, that given the "recognized need to protect the French language" in North America, Quebec could use Article 1 of the Canadian Charter—the "notwithstanding clause"—to impose collective rights over individual rights (Commissioner 1988a, 227). The Quebec government used the door opened to it by the Supreme Court in passing Bill 178, which uses the "notwithstanding clause" to exclude the bill from the Charter of Rights and to impose French-only signs on businesses in Quebec, while permitting bilingual signs only inside places of business.

It is doubtful that Bourassa's solution, French signs outside and bilingual signs inside, is the best way of preserving the French language in Quebec while respecting Anglophone rights. Nevertheless, the defiance and overt refusal to comply with the spirit of Bill 101, which in some cases became overt provocation against Francophones by some English businesses, did force the Quebec government to take a very firm line on the issue. The legislation raised a national furor and led to the resignation of three Anglophone ministers from Bourassa's cabinet (*Le Devoir* December 21, 1988: 1). There were many denunciations of the Quebec government by Anglophones both inside and outside Quebec who saw Bill 178 as an attack on the basic freedoms of Anglophones in Quebec.

Placed in its wider context of constitutional guarantees to this group and their institutional completeness within Quebec, however, Bill 178 should be considered an "irritant" rather than the " negation of fundamental vested rights" (Braen 1987a, 39). In spite of this furor, the earlier comment from the commissioner of Official Languages (1978, 31) that "there is no gainsaying the fact Quebec's Anglophones are much better off than their Francophone counterparts in other provinces," still seems most accurate.

A number of other events in 1988 had a direct impact on other language issues in the country. In February, the Supreme Court finally ruled on a case that had begun in 1980 when one Father Mercure was issued a unilingual English speeding ticket in Saskatchewan. The plaintiff argued that Article 110 of the North-West Territories Act guaranteed him the right to a trial in French. After eight years, the Supreme Court confirmed that parliamentary, judicial, and legislative bilingualism still applied to Saskatchewan, but it also recognized "that provincial legislators have the authority to amend such language requirements unilaterally, and indeed even to abrogate the language rights that flow from them" (Commissioner 1988a, 39; Beaudoin 1988).This decision applied to Alberta as well.

Also in February, the Court of Queen's Bench ruled that Saskatchewan's Education Act was unconstitutional, since it did not provide for Francophone control of their schools, as guaranteed under Section 23 of the Charter. Under the existing legislation, Anglophone school boards administer and control all Francophone schools. In Alberta, a similar case was sent to the Supreme Court; a strange alliance formed around this case, with Quebec and Saskatchewan supporting Alberta in arguing against minority Francophone education rights.

In reaction to the Supreme Court judgment, Saskatchewan passed Bill 02 in April 1988 and Alberta passed Bill 60 in July. Both acts recognize English as the only official language of the province, but include certain provisions for French. For example, in Saskatchewan, French may be used in the legislature, but all statutes, regulations, or ordinances are to be published in English, except for those that may be published in English and French at the discretion of the Lieutenant-Governor in Council. Similarly, French can be used before some provincial courts. All existing statutes, regulations, and ordinances passed in English only are validated retroactively. "In short, the two statutes comply with the letter of the Supreme Court decision, but hardly with its spirit" (Commissioner 1988a, 40). After nearly one hundred years, Francophones from these two provinces finally had their claims to linguistic rights vindicated by the highest tribunal in the land, only to have these rights abrogated almost immediately. There was no outcry from Anglophones, and, ironically, even Quebec's Premier Bourassa refused to support the Francophone minorities in an attempt to save Meech Lake.

There was some minor consolation for Saskatchewan Francophones when the secretary of state signed a framework agreement with their province to enhance their educational opportunities and their control over their schools, and to provide for the translation of certain laws. The agreement is seen by many as a model of financing for Francophone minorities, as it allows for greater co-ordination of efforts by the federal and provincial governments in consultation with the minority concerned. Nevertheless, a few months later, Francophones were having second thoughts about the agreement, as the Saskatchewan government's commitment to translate certain laws bogged down in the "Giga text scandal" (*Star-Phoenix* [Saskatoon] May 31, 1989: A9; June 2, 1989: 3), and its commitment to provide higher-education opportunities for Francophones resulted in a $15 million *multilingual* institute at the University of Regina (*Le Devoir* December 27, 1988: 2). Efforts to grant Francophones control of their schools was proceeding at a snail's pace.

Federal action was not limited to Saskatchewan. The secretary of state signed a comprehensive agreement with New Brunswick and lesser agreements with Ontario, Prince Edward Island, and Yukon to promote official languages and develop the official language minority in these jurisdictions (Secretary of State 1988, 202). As well, pressure from the commissioner of Official Languages, through the department's annual reports and other means and from minority groups, led to more federal intervention on language issues through a new Official Languages Act, passed in July 1988. In the words of the prime minister, Bill C-72 was to give the courts "legislative guidance to interpret the official languages provisions of the Charter." Bill C-72 confirmed the previous languages act, provided more explicit directives for its implementation, gave more authority to the Commissioner's Office in overseeing the act and to the Treasury Board in policy development and monitoring. The act provided "a legislative framework setting out the powers and co-ordinating role of the Secretary of State in promoting the official languages and providing support to official language minority communities" (Commissioner 1988b, 7). Only actual implementation of this legislation over time will determine its positive effects, if any, for official language minorities. In the meantime, these minorities face rather different realities as they try to consolidate their positions, without the Meech Lake Amendments.

Meech Lake as Class Compromise

Much in the federal language policies, since the 1970s at least, is based on the recognition of two official language minorities in Canada: Anglophones in Quebec and Francophones outside Quebec. This is quite obvious also in the recent unsuccessful constitutional accords. This tenet rests on the false assumption of symmetry among Canada's official language minority groups. It also reflects the tendency of jurors and drafters of legislation to conceptualize rights in the abstract, without considering the sociological reality in which rights are exercised. Very little sociological information is required to demonstrate that symmetrical abstract rights for Quebec's Anglophones and for Francophones outside Quebec result in inequality of treatment by governments and asymmetrical outcomes unfavourable to the latter.

These two minorities have vastly different institutional structures. Quebec Anglophones have had their own school boards and schools for over a century. In 1989, there were seven Anglophone CEGEPS to provide pre-university technical and professional training, and two bilingual ones, out of a total of forty-seven (Vastel

1989a). Three Anglophone universities, of which McGill is one of the most prestigious in Canada, carried 28.2 percent of university enrollments, but granted 31.2 percent of MA degrees and 38.6 percent of PhDs in Quebec in 1989 (Vastel 1989a). Some seventy-nine health establishments are required to provide services in English (Vastel 1989a); these include senior citizens' homes, centres for the developmentally and physically challenged, and centres of rehabilitation for socially maladjusted youth and juvenile delinquents (Schachter 1982, 179–210). There were three English-speaking dailies (28.1 percent of Montreal's circulation), eighteen weeklies, eleven radio stations (36 percent of the audience), and three television stations, with thirty other TV stations, including all the American networks on cable. Some 46 percent of moviegoers view movies in English and 32 percent of rented video cassettes are English (Vastel 1989a). There are Anglophone museums, libraries, theatre, and a variety of community organizations including YMCAS and YWCAS (Schachter 1982, 235–96). Many of these Anglophone institutions have been solidly established for years: McGill University and Montreal General Hospital were founded in 1821, Bishop's University in 1853, and the Royal Victoria Hospital in 1894 (Schachter 1982, 166, 210).

It is true that legislative and administrative changes have had an impact on these institutions. Meeting the requirements of Bill 101 does require some adaptation for public institutions and professionals. But for the institutions themselves, "the overall result of the language legislation has not seriously damaged the ease with which English-speaking citizens can be served in their mother tongue on the Island of Montreal" (Schachter 1982, 189). If we add to these institutions the churches, some municipal governments, and the private-sector institutions including commerce, finance, industry, and services owned by Anglophones and providing service in English, the Anglophone "minority" in Quebec is seen by some as "one of the best served in the world" (Vastel 1989a), especially in contrast to the Francophone minorities outside Quebec.

The degree of institutional completeness of Francophone minorities varies in each province (Breton 1964, 1984; Théberge 1987, 34). In Ontario, the first Francophone school board required its own specific legislation before it could be instituted, while the Nova Scotia law remains inoperative, since its judges ruled against Article 23 of the Charter. Implementation of the *Mahé* judgement has varied enormously across the country. In Manitoba, a 1990 Court of Appeal decision was also sent to the Supreme Court in December 1992 with a decision favouring the Francophone parents in March 1993. On May 17, 1993, legislation was introduced to establish the required school boards (Acker 1993). Elections were held in January 1994, which will allow the transfer of twenty schools to Francophone governance in July. In June 1992, Saskatchewan adopted Bill 39, but the regulations are still pending, so no elections have been held and no school is yet under Francophone governance. Alberta also adopted legislation, in the summer of 1993, and three Francophone school boards were elected on March 3, 1994. British Columbia and Newfoundland are still dragging their feet. Ontario's situation is unchanged with three Francophone school boards only and a dysfunctional proportional representation on Anglophone school boards elsewhere. The Northwest Territories has promised a Francophone board for its one school by June 1995, whereas Yukon has granted control for a number of years but has failed to provide adequate facilities.

Prince Edward Island has operated a province-wide Francophone school board since 1989.

Outside of Quebec there were two Francophone universities in 1986 and five affiliated colleges, but the number of bilingual universities had actually decreased—there were only two in 1986, while in 1978 there had been three (Théberge 1987, 35). Of the four homogeneous Francophone community colleges in Canada, three are in New Brunswick, whereas six of the nine bilingual colleges are in Ontario (36). Every year the annual report of the commissioner of Official Languages acknowledges the frailty of Francophone media outside Quebec. In 1989, Ontario and New Brunswick each had a French daily; there were about twenty weeklies whose financial problems perpetually placed them on the brink of collapse; and there was Radio-Canada's television and radio. While the latter reach almost every major Francophone community, this creates its own problems, especially since Radio-Canada has to compete primarily in the Montreal market. Because Radio-Canada is overly Montreal-centred, Francophones outside Quebec, and probably even within the outlying regions of Quebec, find identification with and participation in it very difficult. French TV has existed in Ontario since 1987. "Apart from this, it is a cultural desert" (Vastel 1989b).

Health, social, and community services have changed very little since the FFHQ (1977, 1978) demonstrated years ago the virtual non-existence of amenities provided in French outside Quebec. Ontario and New Brunswick introduced some changes to their legislation, but implementation at the local level is far from adequate and is usually limited to regions "where numbers warrant." No other province has any such policy, except for Newfoundland's toll-free telephone line to a Francophone hospital in Moncton, New Brunswick (Vastel 1989b). That constitutes that province's complete health service in French. Federal services in outlying regions are more readily available in both official languages than a few years ago, but the Annual Reports of the commissioner of Official Languages indicate there is still much to be done to provide services in French and to make French an effective language of work in federal institutions.

The asymmetry of the institutional structures of official language minorities reflects the differences in economic and political power of the two groups. Quebec Anglophones include a very strong component of the Canadian bourgeoisie, who have developed in Quebec since 1759 and who have accumulated the resources to establish their own private institutions as well as the political clout to guarantee their public support where necessary (Brym 1985; Clement 1975; Niosi 1978, 1985; Sales 1979). Their political strength manifests itself in the number of cabinet posts occupied in both Quebec and Ottawa, regardless of the party in power, with the exception of the PQ in Quebec.

In contrast, the Francophone minorities outside Quebec have consisted essentially of dispossessed Acadian farmers, fishing families, Métis freight-transporters, and hunters, immigrant peasants, and poor Québécois without access to arable land in their home province (Wade 1967). For the most part, except for a few professionals and clergy, this group consisted of independent commodity producers. With urbanization and industrialization, many of these, like their counterparts of other ethnic origins, were proletarianized and drawn into cities where their institutional structures were particularly weak. The few who made it as capitalists have not been numerous enough to have any impact, nor have they sought to play a leadership role on behalf of the minority community. Francophones outside Quebec have lacked the resources to develop a comparable institutional framework; they lacked the political power of a strong bourgeoisie to obtain legislative and constitutional protection for their language rights, or continued state support when they did manage to establish them.

Without legislative recognition and protection, it is almost impossible for a minority to develop any kind of institutional completeness. The Charter of Rights is supposed to provide some protection, but by limiting the right to minority institutions to populations "where numbers warrant," the Charter includes a permanent "notwithstanding clause" for Anglophone legislators, jurors, and administrators, who can easily find that the number of Francophones in a given region is never sufficient to merit any institutional structures or services in their language.

The artificial symmetry underlying federal language policies of the last twenty years, including Meech Lake, gives the appearance of formal equality to two "official language minorities." By failing to take into account the constitutional, historical, and social inequalities of these two groups, federal policy and programs produce tremendously unequal results. Thus, Ottawa spends over $60 million a year on Anglophone education in Quebec through an education system that has existed for over a century and stretches from day care and preschool to Ph.D-granting universities, while Francophones in eight provinces wait for over a decade for court decisions to obtain some control over their elementary and secondary schools. So-called symmetry of treatment produces only asymmetry of outcome, to the disadvantage of the most disadvantaged.

By the end of 1989 and the first half of 1990, Anglophone backlash against the French language threatened the limited legislative protection available to Francophones. Reactionary Anglophones and much of the Anglophone media continued to present Quebec's Bill 178 as the most blatant discriminatory and prejudiced action of any government in Canada's history, thus overlooking the treatment of Francophone and other minorities over the years. This reaction was compounded further by the coming into effect of Ontario's Bill 08 on November 19, 1989. This legislation requires the twenty-two regions or municipalities where Francophones constitute 10 percent of the population or number 5000 or more to offer bilingual services. Hitherto ignored groups such as the Association for the Protection of English in Canada (APEC) attracted much media attention by getting nearly 50 municipalities or cities to pass "English only" resolutions that declare them to be unilingual English (Adams 1990). The racism and intolerance of this approach became manifest when APEC spread its efforts to other regions of Canada. Some rural municipalities and small towns in Manitoba and Saskatchewan also declared themselves to be unilingual English even though there were hardly any Francophones living in these communities, no requests had been made for services in French, and no provincial legislation existed or was even being contemplated to create or require bilingual municipal services. The defence that such actions were attacks on the federal deficit rather than on the French failed to overcome accusations of bigotry and Francophobia.

Such resolutions, passed in cities such as Thunder Bay, Orillia, Niagara Falls, and Sault Ste Marie, were identified as the "Saute Ste Marie Syndrome" (Bonin

1990). That nearly as many communities or cities passed "bilingualism resolutions" or refused to pass the "English only" resolutions hardly received any media attention. Even in "far-away British Columbia," resolutions supporting Canadian linguistic duality were adopted by Vancouver, Victoria, Nanaimo, and Kelowna (Hébert 1990). Yet these received little coverage, as did denunciations of APEC by Alliance Quebec and other organizations (*Le Devoir* March 16, 1990: 2; Tison 1990).

The climate of intolerance was further abetted by numerous other incidents, such as TV coverage of Brockville residents wiping their feet on a Quebec flag, a televised comment by Jack Andrews of APEC that "English Canada needs French as much as they need AIDS," and the loud jeering of a stanza of "O Canada" sung in French at the opening of a Blue Jay game in Toronto.

At about the same time, the RCMP commissioner recognized that, under laws protecting religious freedom, Sikh officers could wear a turban instead of the regulation hat while on duty. This decision brought widespread denunciations all across the country. In western Canada, racist buttons and calendars directed against visible minorities attracted much attention while justice departments and human rights commissions tried to determine whether or not they were infringements of human rights legislation. The climate of intolerance reached alarming proportions.

It is doubtful that federal constitutional initiatives in the spirit of Meech Lake will have much impact on such intolerance or on the Francophone minority's imbalance of power. Any real changes will become obvious in a few years from now, and only then will we know whether or not APEC and like organizations have had any lasting impact, or whether the events of 1989 and 1990 were the "death gasp of the reactionary Anglophone right-wing elements" (Bonin 1990).

Conclusions

Whether the institutional context of a language is favourable or detrimental to its survival determines if it will flourish or die. But the institutional context depends on the political and economic resources that particular groups control, as well as on the underlying structure of society. In a capitalist society, distribution of economic resources depends first on class. And class has a significant impact on linguistic groups, since different social groups rarely have equivalent class composition. Language policy and legislation are therefore not the outcome of tension and struggle between ethnic groups, but rather of struggle between ethnic groups with different class compositions and subsequent inequality of political and economic power and resources.

In Canada, there is no necessary correlation between class and language (Li 1988). However, insofar as members of a linguistic group are concentrated in one social class, or a social class consists primarily of members of such a group, class has a direct bearing on language issues and on relations between linguistic groups. The long history of language policies and legislation in Canada reflects the changing structure and composition of its social classes. The Anglophone bourgeoisie, that dominated in Quebec from 1760 to the 1960s, was able to ensure the place of

English in Quebec. The same bourgeoisie in the rest of Canada engaged in an active policy of Anglo-dominance. Without a comparable Francophone bourgeoisie outside Quebec, Francophone minorities were left with few economic or political resources. As long as they remained isolated in small enclosed communities and engaged in small family enterprises, these Francophones could retain their language and culture for a few generations. But industrialization and urbanization forced them out of parochial environments into mass society where the dominant language is omnipresent not only at work but also in consumption, media, and educational spheres, and their own language is deprived of legitimacy and constitutional protection.

The rise of a French-Canadian bourgeoisie in Quebec since the 1960s threatens the Quebec fraction of the Anglo-Canadian bourgeoisie. Protection of this fraction requires increasing federal intervention, which is nevertheless constrained by section 133 of the BNA Act. Ottawa can intervene in the language issue in Quebec only under the guise of official bilingualism, a policy that does open the door to federal financial support to Francophone minorities. However, given that the key sectors necessary to develop any minimum of institutional completeness for these minorities are under provincial jurisdiction and thus escape federal control, Anglophone provinces benefit from federal funds to the detriment of their Francophone minorities and yet can thumb their noses at Ottawa regarding minority rights.

The Meech Lake/Charlottetown fiasco may seal permanently the fate of the Francophone minorities, with the exception of that in New Brunswick. The reactions of Alberta and Saskatchewan to the *Mercure* decision of the Supreme Court, immediately after ratifying the accord, clearly indicate their interpretation of their responsibilities for "preserving" their Francophone minorities. It is difficult to imagine how they will feel bound to observe more faithfully similar responsibilities contained in any future constitutional accord. Similarly, the silence of the other provinces in the face of Bill 02 and Bill 60 reveals a broad consensus in this respect. The only hope left for these minorities rests in an enlightened Supreme Court that will take Sections 23 and 24 of the Charter seriously and force recalcitrant provinces to respect minority rights that are now part of Canada's Constitution. However, if the provincial appointment of Supreme Court judges ever materializes, these minorities may face in the Court the same provincial perspective on minority rights that prevails in the legislatures. This may be the death blow.

Study Questions

1. What difference emerges on the language issues surrounding Meech Lake if the historical context taken is the narrow one of a decade, rather than the broad view of centuries?

2. What are the most salient contradictions between the Francophone and Anglophone groups in Canada that appear within the Meech Lake Accord?

3. What are the possible outcomes of official language issues in Canada, and which one seems most likely in the next twenty years?

4. Can you expand on the argument that official language issues in Canada reflect class differences between the Francophone and Anglophone groups?

5. How can the class contradictions between the French and English groups in Canada, and their differential impact on language, be extended to aboriginal groups and the "Third Force" non-Anglophone and non-Francophone ethnic groups?

6. In the light of the failure of the Meech Lake and Charlottetown Accords to resolve the basic contradiction between Quebec's "distinct society" status and its status as one among ten provinces, what alternatives might you suggest?

Recommended Reading

Bastarache, Michel. *Language Rights in Canada.* Montreal: Les éditions Yvon Blais, 1987.

Conway, John. *Debts to Pay.* Toronto: James Lorimer, 1992.

Gibbins, Roger. *Meech Lake and Canada: Perspectives From the West.* Edmonton: Academic Printing, 1988.

Milner, Henry, and Sheilagh Milner. *The Decolonization of Quebec.* Toronto: McClelland and Stewart, 1973.

Russell, Peter. *Constitutional Odyssey.* Toronto: University of Toronto Press, 1993.

Sheppard, Claude-Armand. *The Law of Languages: Studies of the Royal Commission on Bilingualism and Biculturalism.* vol. 10. Ottawa: Information Canada, 1971.

References

Adams, R. 1990. "La Crise linguistique en Ontario." *Le Devoir* February 24: A9

Bastarache, M., ed. 1987. *Language Rights in Canada.* Montreal: Editions Yvon Blais.

Beaudoin, G. 1988. "The Matter of Mercure." Commissioner of Official Languages 1988b, 19–20.

Blay, J. 1989. "Les Droits linguistiques au Manitoba: un accident ou une volonté politique?" *Ecriture et politique.* Acts of the Seventh Conference of the CEFCO. Edmonton: University of Alberta (Faculté Saint Jean). 185–201.

Bonin, D. 1990. "Le Syndrome Sault Ste Marie." *Le Devoir* February 28: 7.

Braen, A. 1987a. "Language Rights." *Language Rights.* In Bastarache 3–63.

———. 1987b. "Bilingualism and Legislation." *Language Rights.* In Bastarache 68–117.

Breton, R. 1964. "Institutional Completeness of Ethnic Communities and the Personal Relations of Immigrants." *American Journal of Sociology* 70, no. 2 (September): 193–205.

———. 1984. "Les institutions et les réseaux d'organisation des communautés ethnoculturelles." Presented to the Conference on the Status of Research on Francophone Communities outside Quebec, Ottawa.

Brym, R, ed. 1985. *The Structure of the Canadian Capitalist Class.* Toronto: Garamond Press.

Caldwell, G., and E. Waddell. 1982. *Les Anglophones du Québec: de majoritaires à minoritaires.* Quebec: Institut Québécois de recherche sur la culture.

Canadian Council on Social Development (CCSD). 1987-88. *Court Challenges Program: Annual Report.* Ottawa: CCSD.

Caron, N., et al. 1978. *La police secrète au Québec.* Montreal: Editions Québec-Amérique.

Chevrier, R. 1983. *Le français au Canada: situation à l'extérieur du Québec*. Quebec: Conseil de la langue française.

Clement, W. 1975. *The Canadian Corporate Elite*. Toronto: McClelland and Stewart.

Comeault, G.-L. 1979. "La question des écoles du Manitoba—un nouvel éclairage." *Revue d'histoire de l'Amérique française* 33 (June): 3–23.

Commissioner of Official Languages. 1971–1988a. *Annual Report*. Ottawa: Supply and Services.

———. 1988b. *Language and Society*. 23 (Ottawa: Supply and Services, Summer).

Dansereau, Suzanne. "Éducation: la commission Bégin-Caplan est résolue à répondre au besoin d'auto-gestion des Franco-Ontariens". *La Presse* [Montréal] 23 décembre 1993.

Delorme, L. 1974. *Bill 22; le Waterloo de Bou Bou*. Laval: Éditions de Duvernay.

Denis, W., and P. Li. 1988. "The Politics of Language Loss: A Francophone Case from Western Canada." *Journal of Education Policy* 3, no. 4: 351–70.

Deschênes, J. 1980. *Ainsi parlèrent les tribunaux...; Conflits linguistiques au Canada*. Montreal: Wilson et Lafleur.

Dion, L. 1987 "Le Quebec, une Société distincte." *Le Devoir* May 21: 11.

Dion, S. 1993. "The Quebec Challenge to Canadian Unity." *Political Science and Politics* 26, no. 1 (March): 38–43.

Fédération des Francophones Hors Québec (FFHQ). 1977. *Les héritiers de Lord Durham*. Ottawa: FFHQ.

———1978. *Deux poids, deux mesures*. Ottawa: FFHQ.

———. 1981. *A la recherche du milliard*. Ottawa: FFHQ.

Foucher, P. 1987. "Language Rights and Education." In *Bastarache* 259–311.

Gibbins, R. 1988. *Meech Lake and Canada: Perspectives from the West*. Edmonton: Academic Printing.

Hébert, C. 1990. "La menace d'un Sault-Sainte-Marie n'existe pas en Colombie Britannique." *Le Devoir* March 5: 14.

Hogg, P. 1988. *Meech Lake Constitutional Accord Annotated*. Calgary: Carswell.

Johnston, R. 1993. "An Inverted Logroll: The Charlottetown Accord and Referendum." *Political Science and Politics* 26, no. 1 (March): 43–48.

Kierans, E., l. Brecher, and T. Naylor. 1982. "L'affaire de la Sun Life." In Caldwell and Waddell, *Les Anglophones*. 248–63.

Laporte, P.E. 1983. "Language Planning and the Status of French in Quebec." In *Two Nations, Many Cultures*, ed. J.E. Elliott. Scarborough, ON: Prentice-Hall. 91–109.

Laurendeau, A., and D. Dunton. 1965. *A Preliminary Report of the Royal Commission on Bilingualism and Biculturalism*. Ottawa: Queen's Printer.

Lévesque, R. 1986. *Attendez que je me rappelle*. Montreal: Éditions Québec-Amérique.

Li, P. 1988. *Ethnic Inequality in a Class Society*. Toronto: Wall and Thompson.

Lieberson, S. 1970. *Language and Ethnic Relations in Canada*. New York: John Wiley and Sons.

Mahé, J.C., A. Martel, and P. Dubé et al. V. *Alberta*, Supreme Court of Canada, March 15, 1990.

Milner, H, and S. Milner. 1973. *The Decolonization of Quebec*. Toronto: McClelland and Stewart.

Murray, L. 1988. "The Process of Constitutional Change in Canada." *Choices* (Halifax: Institute for Research on Public Policy), (February).

Niosi, J. 1978. *The Economy of Canada: Who Controls It?* Montreal: Black Rose Books.

———. 1985. *Canadian Multinationals*. Toronto: Between the Lines.

Palmer, H. 1988. "The Flaws of the Meech Lake Accord: An Alberta Perspective." In Gibbins, *Meech Lake*. 37–44.

Paquette-Legault, Diane. 1994. "Écoles françaises: le divorce est consommé". *Le Droit* [Ottawa-Hull] 30 juin 1994.

Rioux, M. 1973. "The Development of Ideologies in Quebec." In *Communities and Culture in French Canada*, ed. G. Gold and M.A. Tremblay. Toronto: Holt, Rinehart and Winston.

Russell, P. 1993. *Constitutional Odyssey*. Toronto: University of Toronto Press.

Sales, A. 1979. *La bourgeoisie industrielle au Québec*. Montreal: Presses de l'Université de Montréal.

Saywell, J. 1977. *The Rise of the Parti Québécois 1967–76*. Toronto: University of Toronto Press.

Schachter, S., 1982. *Working Papers on English Language Institutions in Quebec*. Montreal: Alliance Quebec.

Secretary of State. 1969–1988. *Annual Reports*. Ottawa: Supply and Services.

Sheppard, C.-A. 1971. *The Law of Languages: Studies of the Royal Commission on Bilingualism and Biculturalism*. Vol 10. Ottawa: Information Canada.

Staples, J. 1974. "Consociationalism at the Provincial Level: The Erosion of Dualism in Manitoba 1870–1890." In *Consociational Democracy: Political Accommodation in Segmented Societies*, ed. K. McRae. Toronto: McClelland and Stewart.

Star Phoenix. 1989. "Gigatext Scandal" [Saskatoon] 31 May 1989 A9, 2 June: 3.

Statistiques Canada. 1985. *La situation linguistique au Canada (Language in Canada)* (Cat. 99-935). Ottawa: Minister of Supply and Services.

Statistics Canada. 1991. *Knowledge of Language* (Cat 93-318). Ottawa: Minister of Supply and Services.

Statutes of Canada. Constitution Act. 1982 (79)c. 11 Schedule B. "Canadian Charter of Rights and Freedoms."

Task Force on Program Review (Erik Nielsen, chair). 1985. *Service to the Public: Education and Research*. Ottawa: Supply and Services.

Taylor-Browne, K. 1988. "The Francophone Minority." In Gibbons, *Meech Lake*. 185–200.

Théberge R. 1987. "Scandale nationale: même là où le nombre le justifie." Acts of the conference of the Commission nationale des parents francophones, Montreal, November 13-15. 23–39.

Thomson, D. "Quebec and Meech Lake." In Gibbins, *Meech Lake*. 91–98.

Tison, M. 1990. "Alliance Québec se dit outrée par la lutte que mène l'APEC contre les Canadiens français." *Le Devoir* March 22: 10.

Vastel, M. 1989a. "La minorité anglophone du Québec est une des mieux servies au monde." *Le Devoir* January 25: 1.

———. 1989b. "Les services aux francophones sont négociés au compte-gouttes." *Le Devoir* January 26: 1.

Wade, M. 1967. *The French Canadians 1760-1945*. vol. 1. London: Macmillan.

PART III

Health and Illness

INTRODUCTION

A number of issues and contradictions regarding health, illness, and the health care system are currently being debated in Canada. The perceived rapid rise of health care costs has contributed to the critical examination of the organization and structure of health care delivery. The relationship of population characteristics to health is being questioned in the light of evidence that different socio-economic groups are unequal in their health status. Meanwhile, we have also come to associate inadequate working conditions and environmental degradation with injury and illness.

Broader demographic issues also make their impact on health and health care. The "demographic transition"—commonly spoken of as the aging of Canada's population—is expected to have vast implications. Some of them are already visible in changing Canadian patterns of morbidity and mortality.

Faced with this range of pressing issues, Canadians have come to re-examine the general principles on which their health insurance program was founded. The chapters in this section examine this question and the others outlined here.

In Chapter 9, Herbert C. Northcott discusses a number of contemporary health issues, which include changes in mortality and morbidity patterns and their effect on health services, differential health status and differential utilization of services by socio-economic status, the trend toward "medicalization," and gender inequality in the health sector. Northcott first examines the historical and contemporary patterns of morbidity and mortality both for Canada and for selected other countries. There are considerable variations in these patterns, partly attributable to demographic and epidemiologic transitions.

While Canadians enjoy a health status that is, overall, one of the highest in the world, life expectancy, health, illness, and disability are not equally distributed throughout the population. The evidence presented here indicates that substantial disparities in life expectancies and mortality rates persist across income, gender, and racial lines. Data also show differential utilization of health care services by different socio-economic groups. Proposals that have been advanced for the improvement of Canada's health care system include the elimination of fee-for-service, ceasing to insure selected services, reintroduction of premiums and/or user fees, health promotion and illness prevention, reprivatization, home care as opposed to institutional care, and changes in lifestyles and consumption patterns.

The questions of overall health care costs and the financing of health care services tend to dominate the discussion. Issues include the level of funding on the one hand and overutilization or unnecessary demand (abuse) by the consumers on the other. Northcott argues that, if they are implemented, cost reduction proposals such as user fees are likely to adversely affect the sick and the poor, and further increase the disparity of health status between high and low socio-economic groups. Regarding the elimination of unnecessary demand, Northcott notes that the "need" for health care services depends in part on both professional and lay definitions of health and illness. He argues that the patterns of and responses to definitions of health, illness, and illness behaviour partly reflect the social and cultural contexts in which people live. He illustrates this with a discussion of the "medicalization" of what was previously defined as non-medical. Stress, for example, which in the past was perceived as a "normal" consequence of modern society, has now come to be defined as a medical problem. Feminists argue that birth control, pregnancy, abortion, and aging have been medicalized as a result of the male-biased, male-dominated medical system that denies women control over their bodies and lives. They have called for the elimination of gender inequality in the health sector, and its restructuring so that women may come to play a more central role in the health care system.

Karen R. Grant, in the next chapter, entitled "Health Care in an Aging Society: Issues, Controversies, and Challenges for the Future," discusses the relationship between demographic and epidemiologic transition and the demand on health services, with particular focus on the aged population.

The demographic profile of Canadian society is rapidly changing. It is projected that, by the year 2031, the elderly will constitute 20 percent of the Canadian population. Of these, about 45 percent will fall into the category of "old"—seventy-five years of age or older. Another demographic factor worth noting is that more than half of the elderly are women.

The elderly population is by no means homogeneous. It is diversified and stratified by socio-economic status, gender, and ethnicity. Regardless of this diversification and stratification, all elderly people face some common health problems. Advancing age is accompanied by a normal decline in physical and mental ability, and by increasing difficulty in functioning in society. This raises the issue of how well the health sector and other institutions will respond to the health and other needs of the aged population.

Grant provides a review of the demographic characteristics of the Canadian population and the socio-economic characteristics of the aged. She also gives an overview of the development of Canada's health insurance system and the five principles on which it was initiated: accessibility, comprehensiveness, universality, portability, and public administration. It is evident that medicare has not met all its objectives. For example, different groups experience differential access to and utilization of services. Urban–rural inequalities in Canada are reflected in the regional maldistribution of services.

The morbidity patterns of the aged are different from those of the rest of the population. Epidemiological evidence indicates a much greater likelihood of chronic conditions and various functional limitations in the later stages of life. While health seems to diminish with age, there is much variability among the aged in incidence and type of sickness by income, gender, and other social variables.

As would be expected, the elderly have been found to make disproportionate use of acute- and chronic-care hospital beds and long-term facilities. All health facilities and services are expensive. Because of aged patients' presence in these facilities, the aged population is being blamed for escalating health costs and the related fiscal crisis. Grant argues, however, that, rather than blaming the elderly for the fiscal crisis, we should look at the demands for services generated by the providers of care (specifically, medical doctors), and at existing treatment orientations, patterns of medical practice, and, generally, at the organization of the health care system. The increasing "medicalization" of conditions and their treatment, the extensive use of pharmaceuticals, and the trend to hospital-based care and technological-intensive treatment need to be scrutinized. Likewise, modern medicine's curative rather than preventative orientation, and its individualistic and reductionist diagnoses and intervention, all require careful analysis in any reasoned discussion of the current contradictions of the health care system, and its reform and transformation.

Michael Clow and Lawrence Felt, in the chapter entitled "Industrial Development and Environmental Integrity: Contradiction or Co-existence," focus on the magnitude and seriousness of damage to the ecosystem and discuss the framework for the evaluation of competing assessments of this damage.

Evidence presented in this chapter shows that extensive environmental degradation exists even now. Deadly pollutants in the waterways, ozone thinning, air pollution, and damage to forests, are all too apparent. The human cost of environmental degradation is substantive and increasing in the form of illness and deaths arising from extensive and prolonged exposure to various pollutants. The rise of global corporations and the increased scale of economic integration have meant the globalization of environmental degradation.

Clow and Felt argue that the twin themes of insatiable human needs and never-ending economic growth, which have simultaneously driven and justified economic activity in the past, are no longer sustainable. The reality of ecological constraints requires us to shape future activities in ways that prevent further environmental damage. The protection of the ecosystem, Clow and Felt argue, will require fundamental changes in human cultural values, human ethical standards, and the organization of human society.

In the last essay in this section, entitled "Mental Disorders as a Social Problem," James Stolzman discusses a number of issues involved in the definition, diagnosis, and treatment of mental disorders. He also examines the rationale and implications of divergent perspectives brought to the study of mental disorders by sociologists, psychologists, and psychiatrists.

Stolzman points out that mental disorder is difficult to define. This is largely because there is no one property shared by all types of mental disorders, nor is there any single trait that distinguishes the mentally disturbed from the mentally sound. He outlines the generally accepted criteria that aid in the identification of mental disorders, but later returns to the problem of the subjectivity of such judgements.

Sociological analysis of mental disorder puts the focus on factors in the social environment that affect the patterning of psychological distress. The biomedical conception of madness as a disease, he argues, is a socially constructed interpretation whose hegemony may be attributable more to its consonance with certain cultural beliefs than to its scientific utility. Stolzman discusses the social and historical circumstances that fostered the "medical model," and suggests that the acceptance of the view of madness as a disease has been aided by the progressive encroachment of medicine into more and more areas of modern life—the "medicalization" of life. Psychiatric diagnoses, he points out, are social judgements subject to bias. Rosenhan's study of "normal" people who sought and gained admission to mental hospitals illustrates the contextual nature of psychiatric assessments.

Many social scientists, as well as foes of psychiatry, have criticized the medical model. It is contended that the medical terminology and the myth of value-free science disguise the social control function of modern psychiatry. Similarly, as Stolzman points out, the aura and trappings of medicine that surround mental illness designations may hide their intimate connection with prevailing societal values. Psychiatric assessments are not independent of political, social, and cultural contexts. A notable demonstration of this thesis was the debate within the American Psychiatric Association that led to its vote to remove homosexuality from its official list of mental illnesses, following challenges by gay rights activists.

The medical model's exclusive concentration on the individual ignores the role of social factors in the origin of mental disorder. Stolzman presents a remarkable psychiatric case study to demonstrate how, contrary to appearances, the source of psychological distress may reside in the family environment of the people identified as mental patients. Other features of the social environment are known to contribute to differential rates of mental disorders among the population—for example, unemployment, social class, gender, and marital status.

Stolzman points out that the relevance of social factors in analyzing mental disorders has been seriously underestimated by both the mental health community and the public at large. He argues that social factors are thoroughly involved in both the assessment and the causation of mental disorders. Our cultural assumptions that equate mental health with normality, conformity, and adjustment serve to conceal disturbances that stem from collectivities and social relationships. It is perhaps our persistent fear of madness that accounts for much of the public appeal of the medical model.

CHAPTER 9

Health Status and Health Care in Canada: Contemporary Issues

Herbert C. Northcott

Learning Objectives

This chapter examines the historical and contemporary patterns of morbidity and mortality in Canada. Other issues discussed include the distribution of health, illness, disability, and death in Canadian society; the differential utilization of and access to health services by different groups; and the cost and funding of health services. Students are encouraged to consider the contradictions between the stated goals of universality, equality, and accessibility, and the empirical reality of differential health status and differential utilization and accessibility of services. Students are also encouraged to consider the issues involved in the cost and funding of health care services in this country.

Introduction

Life expectancy has risen dramatically in Canada in the twentieth century. Canadians are less likely to die at an early age and more likely to die at an advanced age. They are less likely to die from infectious disease and more likely to die from degenerative pathologies such as heart disease and cancer. Nevertheless, the risk of illness and death is not equally distributed throughout the Canadian population. Furthermore, while Canada's medicare system has done much to remove barriers to equal access to health care, certain recent proposals, if implemented, would reintroduce inequities in our health care system.

This chapter examines contemporary issues and contradictions regarding health and health care in Canada. In particular, the discussion will focus on the social origins of health, illness, and illness behaviour. First to be examined will be historical and contemporary patterns of health, illness, disability, and death. The focus will then shift to a discussion of Canada's health care delivery system and to an examination of social definitions and responses to illness. The chapter will conclude with a discussion of the relationship between stress, coping, and health, and with an examination of gender differentials in health and health care with a particular focus on women

Health Status in Canada

The Transition

It has been said that each society has its own way of dying. It is well known that the developed nations today have patterns of morbidity (sickness) and mortality (death) that differ from those of less developed countries. Table I shows considerable variation from one nation to another in infant mortality and life expectancy. (As you can see from Table 9.1, Canada currently ranks very high as a "healthy" country.) Further, we know that, historically, the Europeans brought their patterns of sickness and death with them to the New World with disastrous consequences for the Native

TABLE 9.1: Infant Mortality, Life Expectancy, Population Growth, and Percentage of the Population 65 Years of Age and Older, for Selected Countries, 1993

Region or country	Infant deaths per 1000 live births	Life expectancy at birth (Years)	Population doubling time in years (at current rate)	Percentage of population aged 65+
Japan	4	79	217	13
Sweden	6	78	210	18
Canada	7	77	87	12
Australia	7	77	91	11
United Kingdom	10	76	267	16
United States	9	75	92	13
Europe	10	75	382	14
Former USSR	28	70	123	9
China	53	70	60	6
Mexico	38	70	30	4
Brazil	63	67	46	5
India	91	59	34	4
Africa	94	54	24	3
WORLD	70	65	42	6

Source: Compiled from Population Reference Bureau, *1993 World Population Data Sheet* (Washington, DC: Population Reference Bureau Inc., 1993).

populations that previously had their own patterns of morbidity and mortality (Young 1987). On the other hand, Dubos (1959, 244) notes that the Europeans contracted syphilis in the New World and took it back to Europe, where it spread with great virulence. Finally, increases in Canadian life expectancy and changes in causes of death show that Canada's contemporary profile of morbidity and mortality is quite different from that of earlier times.

These variations in patterns of morbidity and mortality from society to society and from time to time have been described as the *epidemiologic transition* and are part of a larger social transformation known as the *demographic transition*. The demographic transition describes the typical evolution of a society's birth and death rates. In the past, birth and death rates tended to be high. Various causes of infant mortality, child mortality, maternal mortality, and so on, raged their devastation, and life expectancy generally remained low. The least-developed nations today still exhibit these patterns. When a country begins to develop economically, public sanitation and modern medicine are introduced, poverty is reduced, standards of living improve, and death rates begin to fall. The birth rate tends to stay relatively high for a time and the population begins to grow rapidly in size—to "explode"—as more and more people survive infancy and childhood. Finally, the demographic transition is completed as birth rates decline and stabilize at relatively low levels.

The shift from high to low birth rates slows population growth and puts an end to the population "explosion," but at the same time it causes the population to age—that is, it results in a dramatic increase in the percentage of the population that is elderly. Table 9.1 shows that the more-developed countries such as Japan, Sweden, and Canada have low rates of population growth (as measured by the estimated number of years required for the country's population to double in size) and also have relatively high percentages of their populations aged 65 years and older. In other words, one "crisis" is replaced by another. Several decades ago, attention was focussed on the population explosion (see, for example, Paul Ehrlich's *The Population Bomb,* 1968) and it was feared that overcrowding would put excessive pressure on global resources and result in widespread famine, disease, and warfare. Currently, attention is shifting to the aging of the population and concern is expressed that increasingly large elderly populations will excessively tax the ability or willingness of future societies to provide pensions, health care, and so on.

The demographic transition is closely tied to changes in death rates, in other words, population health status. Of course, every person has exactly the same probability of dying, given that each life ends in death. What has changed is the timing and cause of death for individuals. These changes are known as the epidemiologic transition (Omran 1971; Olshansky and Ault 1986). Historically, at the beginning of the epidemiologic transition, the infectious and parasitic diseases exacted a heavy toll, especially on infants, children, and women in their reproductive years. Influenza, cholera, smallpox, pneumonia, tuberculosis, and other diseases, were major killers at that time. Developments in public health and medical technology, and rising standards of living, brought these diseases increasingly under control, and life expectancy rose dramatically. Instead of dying early in life, more and more people now survive to old age. Instead of dying of infectious diseases, people typically die now as a result of degenerative problems such as heart disease, cancer, or stroke. Table 9.2 shows that the leading causes of death in

TABLE 9.2: Leading Causes of Death in Canada in 1991

	PERCENTAGE OF ALL DEATHS	
Cause of Death	**Females**	**Males**
Circulatory Disease	41.0	37.1
• Ischemic Heart Disease (Heart Attack)	21.6	23.2
• Cerebrovascular Disease (Stroke)	9.1	5.7
Cancer	27.0	28.1
• Breast Cancer	5.2	N/A
• Lung, Trachea, and Bronchus Cancer	5.1	9.2
Respiratory Disease	8.0	9.1
Accidents, Homicide, and Suicide	4.5	8.7
Other	19.6	16.9
TOTALS[a]	100.1	99.9

Note: [a]Totals do not add to 100.0 because of rounding.
Source: Calculated from Statistics Canada, *Mortality - Summary List of Causes 1991*, Cat. no. 84-209 (Ottawa: Minister of Supply and Services, 1993), Table 2. Reproduced by authority of the Minister of Industry, 1994.

Canada for both males and females—accounting for two-thirds of all deaths—are circulatory disease (particularly heart disease) and cancer (particularly breast cancer in females, and lung cancer).

Health Status and the Social Distribution of Health

While Canadians now enjoy a life expectancy longer than at any other time in the country's history, nevertheless, health, illness, disability, and death rates are not equally distributed throughout the population. Tables 9.3 and 9.4 show that life expectancy and infant mortality, for example, depend in part on whether one is male or female, rich or poor, Native or non-Native. Similarly, various studies of the health of Canadians show this pattern of unequal health status. Selected studies are reviewed below, followed by some observations on the social origins of health and illness.

Canadian Sickness Survey, 1950–1951

Canada's first national health survey (Department of National Health and Welfare and Dominion Bureau of Statistics 1960; see also Kohn 1967) of some 10 000 households found that, on an average day, 86 percent of the population felt healthy,

TABLE 9.3: Life Expectancy by Income, Race, and Sex

	LIFE EXPECTANCY (IN YEARS FROM BIRTH)	
	Female	**Male**
All Canadians, 1990[a]	80.6	74.0
Urban Canadians by income quintiles, 1986[b]		
1. Highest	80.9	76.1
2.	80.8	75.3
3.	80.7	74.4
4.	80.4	73.5
5. Lowest	79.1	70.4
All incomes, urban 1986	80.4	73.8
Registered Indians, 1990[c]	74	67

Sources: **a)** Statistics Canada, *Report on the Demographic Situation in Canada 1992: Current Demographic Analysis*, Cat. no. 91-209E (Ottawa: Minister of Industry, Science and Technology, 1992), p. 60; **b)** R. Wilkins, O. Adams and A. Brancker, "Changes in Mortality by Income in Urban Canada from 1971 to 1986," *Health Reports*, Cat. no. 82-003S, No. 1 (Ottawa: Minister of Industry, Science and Technology, 1990), pp. 137-174. (For Canada's 25 census metropolitan areas. Each census tract within the CMA was ranked according to the percentage of the population below the low-income cut-off, and the census tracts were grouped so that each group contained about one-fifth of the total non-institutional population of the CMA); **c)** Department of Indian Affairs and Northern Development, *Basic Departmental Data - 1992* (Ottawa: Minister of Supply and Services, 1992), p. 23. Reproduced with the permission of the Minister of Supply and Services Canada, 1994.

and 20 percent had reported no illnesses in the previous year. Generally, females, the elderly, and the poor were most likely to be ill (Kohn 1967, 13–14, 122, 344–57). Health care utilization (for example, going to a doctor, being admitted to a hospital) was higher for women and for the elderly, although, despite the high rate of illness among the poor, the lowest-income groups were least likely to make use of health care services while the highest income group enjoyed both the best health and the highest rate of health service utilization.

Nutrition Canada National Survey, 1970–1972

This study of a representative sample of 19 000 Canadians assessed nutritional status, and found iron deficiency in a large proportion of men and women, protein deficit common during pregnancy, calcium and vitamin D shortages in the diets of many young people, vitamin C deficiency for Natives, and especially Inuit, and a large proportion of overweight adults (Nutrition Canada 1973).

TABLE 9.4: Infant Mortality by Income, Race, and Sex

	INFANT MORTALITY (per 1000 live births)
All Canadians, 1990[a]	6.8
Urban Canadians by income quintiles, 1986[b]	
1. Highest	5.8
2.	5.7
3.	7.7
4.	8.0
5. Lowest	10.5
All incomes, urban 1986	7.5
Registered Indians, 1990[c]	10.0

Sources: **a)** Statistics Canada, "Deaths 1990," *Health Reports*, Cat. no. 82-003S, Suppl. No. 15, Vol. 4, No. 1 (Ottawa: Minister of Industry, Science and Technology, 1992), Table 7. Reproduced by authority of the Minister of Industry, 1994. **b)** See Table 9.3, note b; **c)** See Table 9.3, note c, page 27. Reproduced by authority of the Minister of Industry, 1994.

Canada Health Survey, 1978–1979

This nationwide survey, whose initial sample consisted of some 12 000 households, found that almost one-half of the Canadian population reported that they were currently not suffering from any health problem such as arthritis, hypertension, hearing disorders, influenza, or diabetes, one-quarter reported one problem, and the remaining one-quarter reported more than one health problem (Canada Health Survey 1981). Generally, health problems were more often reported by persons with lower incomes and lower levels of education, and were more often reported by women than men, and by older persons. Psychological distress was most often reported by women, teenagers, the elderly, the widowed, divorced, and separated, persons with lower incomes and little education, and persons in poor physical health. About three out of every four Canadians had visited a doctor in the previous twelve months; females, the elderly, and persons with higher incomes (despite fewer health problems) were most likely to have seen a doctor. About one-half of Canadians had visited a dentist in the previous twelve months, and again, females were more likely to have sought dental services. Persons with lower education and lower incomes were more likely to report that they did not have time to seek medical help for a health problem. About one-half of the population had taken a drug during the previous two days; some two-thirds of these drugs were prescription medicines, while about one-third were over-the-counter non-prescription medications. Women and the elderly were more likely to be taking medicine.

Canada Fitness Survey, 1981

This study and survey examined the activity patterns and fitness of a national sample of over 21 000 Canadians. It was found (Canada Fitness Survey 1982) that males were more likely to engage in sports, while females were more likely to engage in exercise activities. Those most likely to engage in sports were young and of higher socio-economic status. Males showed better cardiovascular fitness and muscular endurance, while females showed greater physical flexibility. Both activity and fitness tended to decline with advancing age. A follow-up survey of 4000 persons who had participated in the 1981 study was conducted in 1988 (Stephens and Craig 1990).

Canadian Health and Disability Survey, 1983–1984

This was the first national study focussing on long-term (six months or more) functionally limiting disabilities (with respect to seeing, hearing, speaking, moving about, and mental capability, for example). It was done as a supplement to the ongoing monthly Labour Force Survey. Over 126 000 people were screened, yielding about 16 000 persons with some form of disability—almost 13 percent; the latter were then interviewed in some depth about their limiting conditions (Statistics Canada and Department of the Secretary of State, 1986). Two-thirds of disability problems limited physical mobility. The study found that the likelihood of being disabled increases with age and is higher for females and for persons not currently married or with less education and low income. (More accurately, it should be pointed out, persons with disabilities are more likely to miss out on education and are less likely to be in the labour force and therefore are more likely to be poor.)

Health Promotion Survey, 1985 and 1990

The 1985 study was the "first national survey to focus on health orientation and behaviour rather than health status ... to explore the health knowledge, attitudes, beliefs, and behaviour of adult Canadians—to find out what Canadians think, feel, and know about their health, and how these things relate to what they do" (Health and Welfare Canada 1987, 5). Over 11 000 persons were interviewed, with the aim of better understanding how to "promote health." It was found that low-income Canadians and those with less education are more likely to rate their health as poor. People with low incomes "encounter more barriers to health than do upper income Canadians—they are much more likely to be unemployed and poorly educated, and their friends are more likely to smoke and less likely to exercise regularly. They are much more likely to be exposed to sidestream smoke in their workplace, and less likely to have received health information in the workplace" (35–37).

The 1990 study provided an update of the previous 1985 survey and also examined additional topics including sexual health, environmental practices, and workplace stresses (Health and Welfare Canada 1993, 4). Over 13 000 people were interviewed. The 1990 study found that the poor have the lowest health status, are more likely to suffer long-term activity limitations resulting from health problems, have a higher average number of days away from work due to sickness, injury, or disability, have worse dental health, and are less likely to have programs at work to improve their health. Poor women are less likely to have had a Pap smear in the preceding three years or a mammogram (264–65).

General Social Survey, 1985 and 1991

The General Social Survey is conducted annually; it investigates various social issues and trends (Statistics Canada 1987). The first (1985) survey examined health and lifestyle topics and interviewed over 11 000 Canadians. One interesting finding was that low-income Canadians now were more likely to see a physician than were higher-income Canadians, a reversal of the pattern observed during the 1950–51 Canadian Sickness Survey. It was also found that those most likely to report being unhappy were the elderly, widowed, separated, or divorced, and the unemployed. Finally, it was observed that those persons who both smoke and drink heavily were more likely to report health problems. The 1991 survey of almost 12 000 Canadians once again focussed on health issues.

Health and Activity Limitation Survey, 1986–1987 and 1991–1992

These surveys followed the 1986 and 1991 censuses. In each census a "disability" question was asked of 20 percent of the population. Following each census, Canadians with and without disabilities living in the community and persons with disabilities residing in health-related institutions were surveyed to create a profile of disability in Canada. The studies showed that disability increases with age and that many people with disabilities are unable to work because of their disability, suffering limited incomes as a consequence. In 1986 there were an estimated 3.3 million persons of all ages with disabilities in Canada. The 1991 survey estimated that 2.3 million people of working age (15–64) had disabilities. (See Statistics Canada 1990 and 1993 and related reports.)

National Alcohol and Other Drugs Survey, 1989

In 1989, over 11 000 Canadians aged 15 and over were asked about their use of alcohol and other drugs including illicit, prescription, and over-the-counter drugs (Health and Welfare Canada 1990). It was found that young adult males are more likely to drink alcohol, use cannabis (marijuana or hashish), and use cocaine or crack. Women are more likely to use prescription narcotics, sleeping pills, and tranquillizers.

National Population Health Survey

This survey is to begin in 1994 and be conducted every second year thereafter (Catlin and Will 1992). Its purpose is to assess the distribution of health in the population including "the economic, social, demographic, occupational and environmental correlates of health" (314).

These various surveys are important in that they document the *social distribution* of health, illness, and disability in the Canadian population. While sickness and disability can lead to unemployment or poverty, it is also true that poverty has negative implications for health. Further, not only have the poor been at greater risk for health problems, but until recently, they were *less* likely to see a doctor because of the costs of taking time off work, the costs of paying for care (before medicare), and so on. Poverty, however, is not the only social variable of note. The surveys frequently find differences in health status and health care utilization for the various age groups, and for males and females. Not all of these differences can be explained physiologically. Accordingly, we turn our attention to the socio-cultural origins of health, illness, disability, and death.

The Social Origins of Health and Illness

In the early 1920s in Canada, a male had a life expectancy of about 59 years, while a female could expect to live almost two years longer. By the early 1980s, a male's life expectancy had risen to almost 72 years, while the gap between males and females had increased to over 7 years (Nagnur 1986, 70–73). These increases in life expectancy reflect improvements in public sanitation, standards of living, and medical technology. The increasing gap in life expectancy between men and women reflected, in part, reductions in mortality relative to child bearing and females' generally healthier lifestyles and environments. Women, for example, have been (in the past, at least) less likely to smoke and drink, and less likely to work at dangerous jobs. Nevertheless, the gender differential in life expectancy appears to have peaked. In the years 1975 to 1977, female life expectancy exceeded that of males by 7.3 years. In 1980 to 1982, this figure had decreased to 7.1 and by 1984 to 1986 it had declined further to 6.8 years (Statistics Canada 1988b, 12). In 1990, the difference was 6.6 years (Statistics Canada 1992, 13). While both male and female life expectancies continue to increase, male life expectancy is beginning to catch up, perhaps in part because male and female lifestyles and environments are more similar than in the past. Women are more likely to work outside the home, to work in traditionally "male" occupations, and to indulge in "vices" more often opted for in the past by males alone—for example, alcohol, tobacco, and sexual freedom. It is noteworthy that death rates from lung cancer are currently rising rapidly for women at a time when they have levelled off for men (National Cancer Institute of Canada 1992, 45 and 47).

These trends in male and female life expectancy highlight the role of socio-cultural lifestyles and societal environments in the causes and timing of death. Indeed, the government of Canada has argued that these two factors—lifestyle and environment—are significant sources of "premature" death in Canada (Lalonde 1974). Examples of "premature" death include motor-vehicle traffic accidents (MVTAs), suicide, and lung cancer (brought on by smoking or occupational hazards, for example). Litven (1985) lists lung cancer, suicide, and MVTAs as the second, fourth, and eighth leading causes of death for males between 25 and 75 years of age. For females, these causes ranked fourth, seventh, and eleventh. Wigle, Mao, Semenciw, McCann, and Davis (1990) (see also McCann 1988) studied potential years of life lost (PYLL) for various causes of death (that is, the difference between life expectancy and actual age at death) and found that car accidents, suicide, and lung cancer ranked second, third, and fourth as the leading causes of PYLL for males under age. For females, these same causes of PYLL ranked third, sixth, and fifth. Nagnur (1986) reported that the major causes of death for children aged 1 to 4 were accidents, poisonings and violence. Similarly, these causes accounted for two-thirds of the deaths of males and one-half the deaths of females aged 5 to 14, and four-fifths of the deaths of males and two-thirds of the deaths of females 15 to 24 years of age. Even for the 25 to 44 age group, accidents, poisonings, and violence accounted for over one-half of male deaths and a third of female deaths. In the 45 to 64 age group, cardiovascular disease and cancer, followed by accidents, poisonings, and violence, are the leading causes of death.

Many of these "premature" deaths are preventable. Alcohol, for example, plays a major role in accidental and violent deaths. Smoking plays a major role in lung cancer etiology. Similarly, lifestyle variables including smoking, alcohol consumption, diet, and so on, play a role in the early onset of cardiovascular disease. Occupational exposure to hazards such as silica dust, coal dust, grain dust, sawdust, and to fibres such as asbestos, or to chemicals, pesticides, radiation, and so on has been linked to various cancers and respiratory diseases (Reasons, Ross, and Paterson 1981). Modern technology has brought many blessings—and also exposure to chemicals in the air we breathe, the water we drink, and the food we eat. We do not yet fully understand the implications of these environmental pollutants, although we know something about the disastrous effects of mercury poisoning on people, for example (Fleetwood 1979), or of DDT and acid rain on the environment.

Today, our mortal enemies include alcohol, tobacco, drugs, lack of exercise, stress, inadequate diet, being overweight, failure to use seat belts, and "careless" sex—lifestyle variables that have been the focus of such studies as the Canada Health Survey, 1978–79, and the Health Promotion Surveys of 1985 and 1990. Our mortal enemies today also include environmental variables such as industrial and motor-vehicle pollutants and design problems, including unsafe working environments, dangerous highways, and so on. Never before have we lived in a healthier context or been so healthy as a people. Never before has society collectively, and individuals personally, had more knowledge and opportunity to control many of the causes of sickness and premature death. And yet people continue to die prematurely.

Of course, it is easy to say that individuals should choose healthy lifestyles and environments. It is easy to blame the individual who chooses to smoke or who drinks too much or who goes to work in the oil fields or in the mines. However, the individual is not solely to blame. It is necessary that more attention be paid to the social origins of these individual decisions. It is our society as a whole that is dependent on polluting fossil fuels, our agriculture that is dependent on pesticides and fertilizers, and our culture and media advertising that endorse the consumption of alcohol. The decision to develop the nuclear energy industry or to market consumer goods whose manufacture or use contaminates the environment is a collective responsibility. Similarly, unemployment, poverty, and despair have their social origins and their health costs. In summary, it is possible for Canadians to have healthier, longer lives if responsible decisions are made both individually and collectively. (For an argument along these lines of thought, see Epp 1986.)

Health Care in Canada

It was noted above that in the past poorer Canadians, despite worse health, made less use of the health care system than did wealthier Canadians. Recently, the poor, who still have the worst health, have been making more use of the health care system than the wealthier (and healthier) classes. What has made the difference is medicare, which has removed many of the economic barriers limiting access to care. The 1957 federal Hospital Insurance and Diagnostic Services Act and the 1966 federal Medical Care Act provided hospital and medical (for physician's services, for example) insurance for all Canadians. Canada's medicare system is based on several principles: (1) that of universality and accessibility—all Canadians are covered by medicare and therefore all enjoy access to available services; (2) comprehensiveness—a wide range of services are insured; (3) portability—coverage is transferable from province to province; and (4) public administration on a non-profit basis (for a fuller discussion, see Northcott 1988).

Although Canadians tend to be very proud of their health care system, medicare does have its problems—most of which are linked to the issue of funding. It is very difficult to define an adequate level of funding. Medical professionals who want more facilities, more technology, higher salaries, and so on, argue that the system is underfunded (Evans 1987). Government, constrained by huge budget deficits and reluctant to raise taxes—which are already high—argues for restraint. Patients, caught in the middle, want better care and shorter waiting lists on the one hand, but fear increased taxes on the other.

The issue of funding led to the battle over extra-billing in the early 1980s and to discussions of privatization. In response to alleged underfunding, many physicians had begun to charge more for services than the negotiated fee schedule allowed. The extra cost was borne directly by the patient. These charges most disadvantaged the poor, sick, and elderly, who most needed medical care but could least afford its costs. In other words, it was argued, the practice of extra-billing violated the principle of universal and equitable access to care. Accordingly, the 1984 Canada Health Act banned extra-billing (Northcott 1988).

Tensions remain. Some argue that the problem of funding can be resolved by reprivatizing the health care system, that is, by reducing government involvement and returning health care to the marketplace. For example, hospitals might be owned or operated by private corporations on a for-profit basis, as many nursing homes are today. (Indeed, fears were expressed during the 1988 Free Trade debate that medicare would be judged a "subsidy," be "put up for sale," and taken over by American corporations.) Alternatively, others argue that the problem of funding can be resolved by increasing government controls—for example, putting physicians on salary rather than paying them on a fee-for-service basis (as has been done in 1994 in Ontario for specialists in teaching hospitals), or restricting the number of physicians who may practice in a given area.

Pressures on funding will tend to increase well into the twenty-first century because of the aging of the population resulting from the demographic and epidemiologic transitions. As the percentage of the population that is elderly increases from the 11.6 percent recorded in the 1991 census to over 20 percent by 2030 (McDaniel 1986, 106; Denton, Feaver, and Spencer 1986), the demand for medical, pharmaceutical, hospital, and nursing-home care will increase, as will the demand for support for persons cared for at home. While most agree that the "crisis" will be manageable (see for example Denton, Feaver, and Spencer 1986; Denton and Spencer 1983; McDaniel 1986: 115–118; Evans 1987), nevertheless, demographic trends suggest that the funding debate will be with us for some time.

A variety of proposals designed to reduce costs have been put forth. Many of those who believe that the fee-for-service payment mechanism motivates service providers to increase usage of the health care system beyond what is necessary favour putting all health care professionals on salary—as nurses are, for example. Others, fearing that any movement toward civil-service medicine will result in an inadequate level or quality of services, argue that health care should be returned to the free enterprise marketplace, where factors such as the entrepreneurial spirit, competition, and supply and demand will create cost efficiencies. A more moderate version of this argument suggests that some, but not all, health care services be no longer insured and be returned to the private marketplace. Critics of this reprivatization fear that a movement back to free enterprise medicine will result in a two-tier system of health care—one private-sector tier for those who can afford to pay for services and another tier for those who cannot. Still others argue that the solution to underfunding is simply to generate more revenue through increased taxation or through the reintroduction of, or increase in, health care premiums and user fees. And there are some who suggest that those who indulge in unhealthy lifestyles should have to pay for their health care; in a sense, the so-called sin taxes on alcohol and tobacco already accomplish this goal.

Finally, some argue that it is the nature of the health care system itself that is problematic. There are critics who point out that the emphasis on cure, even in the face of terminal illness, and the reliance on expensive high-technology medicine are not always practical. Concepts such as triage (selection of those persons who can most benefit from treatment), health care "rationing," and euthanasia (allowing certain persons to die without attempting to prolong their lives) are still controversial; nevertheless, there is increasing resistance to the idea that life should be prolonged at any cost. Notions such as the right to die, palliative care (emphasis on minimizing the symptoms of the terminally ill without attempting a cure), and dying at home (substituting home care and "hospital in the home" for expensive institutional care), all express the growing resistance to an impersonal, high-technology death in an expensive, cure-oriented institution. Along these lines, it is argued that home care is less expensive than, and often superior to, institutional care. Furthermore, it is argued that our health care system is really an "illness care system" dominated and exploited by a medical-industrial complex consisting of organized professional interest groups and large multinational corporations that manufacture and distribute pharmaceuticals, medical equipment, and so on. Critics of the illness care system suggest that there needs to be far more emphasis placed on the promotion of health and the prevention of illness. Increasingly, we are being told that adequate jobs and incomes, for example, are as important to health as clean water or adequate nutrition. In other words, health promotion and illness prevention recognize that social conditions have an important influence on our individual and collective health.

The Social Construction of Health, Illness, and Disability

In the debate over funding, one often hears allegations that the health care system is overutilized—that users request and receive care that they do not "need." As this implies, there is a tendency to blame over utilization on the consumer of health services. However, there is another side to overutilization. As Evans (1984, 85–88) points out, the health care system itself plays an important role in the generation of demand for services. There is some truth to the old aphorism that a hospital bed built is a hospital bed filled. In other words, doctors generally have both the motivation and the opportunity to admit patients to the hospital, and also determine to a considerable degree patterns of referral, repeat visits, laboratory work, drug prescriptions, and so on. Not all of this represents a simple direct response to patient "need." In short, under a fee-for-service system of remuneration, the doctor has some incentive to maximize the use of services.

Actually, both overutilization and underutilization may be problematic. Consider the following examples. A person with a common cold visits the doctor (overutilization). A person with a common cold who fears that his or her symptoms may indicate a more serious problem visits the doctor (overutilization? Are unfounded fears legitimately "treated" by the health care system?). A person who says that his or her cough is "only a cold" refuses to visit the doctor (underutilization? others have reason to suspect that the persistent cough and the fact that the person is a smoker indicate a more serious problem). Turning to the physician, we might find a doctor who has a patient return for an unnecessary follow-up visit, perhaps to advise the patient that laboratory tests indicated no problem: the doctor can bill for an office visit but not for a phone call, which would have been sufficient (overutilization). A doctor spares no effort to extend the life of a terminally ill patient (overutilization?). A doctor finds nothing wrong with a patient, and suspecting that the person is hypochondriacal, sends him or her away (underutilization—the patient is indeed sick but has been misdiagnosed). In short, both the lay person and the health care professional are responsible at different times and in different ways for both overutilization and underutilization.

The problem is that medical "need" is not always obvious or always defined objectively. To a considerable degree, health, illness, and disability are socially and culturally defined. Further, socio-cultural definitions dictate the "appropriate" response to and the "appropriate" behaviour for a person who has been defined as healthy, ill, or disabled. A person who is defined as sick, whether sick or not, is supposed to seek medical care and may receive sympathy and release from normal role obligations. A person who is defined as healthy, whether healthy or not, is not entitled to medical care, sympathy, or reduced role expectations.

To complicate matters, laypersons and professionals often have different definitions of health and illness. For example, a layperson who perceives herself or himself to be sick may be labelled by the physician as healthy and therefore a hypochondriac. Alternatively, a person who perceives himself or herself to be healthy might be labelled, for example, hypertensive by the doctor and be prescribed medication. Not feeling ill, the patient might refuse to take the medicine. This suggests that these different lay and professional views of sickness and health not only influence service utilization but also influence compliance, that is, they determine whether or not the patient follows the physician's advice.

In summary, many of the problems treated by our modern health care system originate not only in biological problems but also in our contemporary way of life. This is referred to as *sociogenesis*. Further, the very definitions of health, illness, disability, and even death constitute social constructions and result from the social interaction of patient, significant others, and health care professionals.

Stress and Health

Stress is one contemporary issue that illustrates the interplay of biological, psychological, and sociological factors. Our society has a tendency to "medicalize" various problems, that is, to define and respond to problems in medical terms rather than in, for example, social or moral terms. Alcoholism, drug addiction, compulsive gambling, family violence, menopause, pregnancy, aging, and stress have been to a degree medicalized. Does a person doing routine automated assembly-line work and experiencing boredom, fatigue, anxiety, irritability, and depression—symptoms of stress, or more accurately, psychological distress—have a medical problem? Is the problem comparable in some way to back strain or a damaged lung? Is the distressed worker eligible for worker's compensation? Should he or she be?

Psychophysiological distress, like morbidity generally, is unevenly distributed throughout the population. Stress has social origins, largely in occupational and social roles (Mirowsky and Ross 1989). Some of these roles (for instance, assembly-line work, housework) may be more problematic than other roles (see, for example, Kornhauser 1965; Gove 1984; Karasek and Theorell 1990). Further, access to resources that may facilitate coping with role strains (a supportive family or a high income, for example) is also unevenly distributed throughout the population so that the poor and socially isolated are among those most vulnerable to the stresses of life. Just as health status and access to health care have their social origins, so do psychophysiological distress and access to coping resources have social determinants. Further, just as the definition of health and illness is a social construction, so also is the definition of stress. And just as health and illness are to a degree a subjective phenomenon, so too is stress.

Everybody seems to have stress these days—indeed, one might argue that there is an epidemic of stress. Students studying for examinations or enrolled in professional and graduate schools, kids playing on pee-wee hockey teams, business executives and factory workers, physicians and homemakers, teachers and nurses, police officers and social workers—all are stressed. All run the risk of "burnout."

Frequently, symptoms of distress are taken to the health care system. Frequently, the health care system defines and treats these distresses as medical problems, thereby increasing the use and cost of the health care system and increasing the health care system's control over our lives. Not everyone sees these developments positively (see, for example, Illich 1976).

Stress is a thorny issue. We expect daily fatigue, but at some point fatigue can become excessive. We expect frustrations and we have our normal fears, but at some point depression and anxiety become problematic. We expect life's irritations, but at some point unhappiness and anger inhibit our normal functioning. Where, and how, will the lines be drawn? Given that a medical diagnosis gives a person access to the benefits of the sick role and allows one to escape one's usual role demands, how will "slackers" be separated from the "legitimately" distressed? This last question is especially perplexing, in part, because the stress process is inherently subjective. What one person finds stressful, another person does not. The transactional model of stress (Lazarus and Folkman 1984) argues that distress as an outcome depends on the presence and nature of the stressor, the subjective appraisal of the stressor, the availability of coping resources, the subjective assessment of coping resources, and the coping strategies used—whether designed to solve the problem or manage the emotion generated by the problem. In short, stress is an important socio-cultural and socio-psychological phenomenon that has important implications for contemporary definitions of health, illness, and disability. Stress also has important implications for death, given that distress can lead ultimately to behaviours or pathologies that threaten life.

Women and Health

As discussed previously, the gap between the life expectancies of men and women in Canada has increased during this century to about seven years. This gap reflects a combination of physiological factors, lifestyle variables, and the environmental contexts in which men and women play out their respective roles. Women, once disadvantaged by their reproductive functions, now enjoy a substantial advantage over men in life expectancy. One of the great ironies, however, is that while women currently live longer, they are nevertheless sick more often (suggesting the facetious conclusion that being sick is good for your health). According to the surveys discussed previously, women are more likely to report illness, disability, and psychological distress and are more likely to utilize health care services (see Gee and Kimball 1987, 29–33; Cockerham 1982, 31–32; D'Arcy and Schmitz 1987; Trypuc 1988, 155).

There are a number of possible explanations for gender differentials in patterns of morbidity (D'Arcy and Schmitz 1987; Gee and Kimball 1987, 34–40; Trypuc 1988, 159–162; Verbrugge 1985; 1989). These patterns may reflect real differences in male–female health or may reflect apparent, though not always real, differences resulting from socio-cultural definitions of health and illness—definitions that may vary for men and women. If women are in reality sick more often than men, their excess morbidity may originate physiologically or socially. The physiological explanation would suggest that women, even after taking into account reproductive functions including pregnancy, are physiologically more vulnerable to illnesses generally, or at least to the more minor illnesses and distresses. In contrast, the social explanation focusses on the different roles that men and women play, and consequently, on the differential exposure of males and females to stresses and other role-related sources of illness and distress. For example, it is commonly argued that women's roles may be simultaneously more demanding and less rewarding than men's roles, leading to greater female psychophysiological symptomatology.

The above arguments accept that gender differences in morbidity are real, whether their origins are physical or social. But it is also possible that gender differences in morbidity are more artificial than real, that they are socially constructed and reflect gender-specific social definitions and behaviours. Gender socialization processes may encourage females to be more expressive and males to be less expressive, and may encourage women, but not men, to seek help. Consequently, women may pay more attention to their physical and psychological symptoms, may report complaints—especially minor ones—more often, and may be more willing to take the sick role and seek medical attention. (Note that this implies either that males tend to be "underutilizers" of the health care system or that females tend to be "overutilizers," or both.) A second argument suggests that women have more opportunity than men to take the sick role. This explanation will be less and less plausible as women increasingly enter the labour force. A third argument suggests that doctors, most of whom are men, diagnose men and women differently, imputing more (minor) problems to women generally, prescribing drugs more often for female patients, and admitting them to the hospital more frequently. Finally, women may have more interest in health, may make a greater effort to learn about health and illness issues, and may tend to take the lead in monitoring and protecting their own and their families' health. There is some evidence that women's excess morbidity largely involves minor and sometimes less-obvious complaints (Verbrugge 1985, 157–63), which gives some credence to the argument that social definitions are at least partly responsible for gender differences in illness behaviour.

While women report medical problems more often than men and more often take the sick role and seek out medical assistance, nevertheless, there are those who argue that matters of female health have been overly medicalized, reflecting and fostering women's disadvantage in a male-dominated medical system and society. Further, women's own definitions of their health needs have received little attention (Walters 1992). Reflecting this line of argument is the 1977 book *Seizing Our Bodies: The Politics of Women's Health*, by Claudia Dreifus, whose chapter titles include "The Birth Controllers," "The Theft of Childbirth," "The Politics of Breast Cancer," "The Epidemic in Unnecessary Hysterectomy," "What Doctors Won't Tell You about Menopause," "What Medical Students Learn about Women," and "Vaginal Politics." Medicalization will be discussed here with reference to birth control, pregnancy, abortion, childbirth, menopause, aging, and "emotional" problems. Finally there will be a brief examination of the role of women as health care workers and the implications of their increasingly central role in the social construction of women's health.

The term *medicalization* refers to the process whereby an aspect of life previously defined as non-medical (for example, as "normal" or as a moral issue) comes to be redefined as a medical issue appropriate for medical intervention. This redefinition may result when health care professions expand their spheres of influence and control or when laypersons come to expect and demand that health care professions solve an increasingly wide range of "problems" (Kaufert and Gilbert 1987; Illich 1976).

Societies are often, some would say always, organized such that men have more privilege and advantage than women. That is, inequality between the sexes has been, and continues to be, widespread. In many past and present societies women have been socialized to believe that their role in life is to satisfy men sexually and to bear and raise children. Feminists argue that these role definitions benefit men at the expense of women and suggest that if women are to be "liberated' they must take control of their own sexuality and fertility (Pollock 1988). Medicalization must therefore be resisted and fought because it tends to give control of contraception, abortion, pregnancy, and childbirth to male-dominated and male-serving health care professions. Demedicalizing contraception might be accomplished by making birth control pills, for example, available at the pharmacy without a doctor's prescription. Further, while sterilization and abortion are medical procedures, nevertheless, they can be demedicalized by making them available solely on the strength of the woman's decision and by offering them in woman-centred and woman-controlled facilities. Pregnancy can be demedicalized by treating it less as an illness and more as a natural process. However, the emergence of the new reproductive technologies such as *in vitro* fertilization (fertilization of a woman's egg outside of her body) and surrogate motherhood (implantation of a woman's fertilized egg in another woman's womb, or artificial insemination of a woman who provides both egg and uterus) may further erode the control of women over their reproductive processes. One extreme scenario suggests that two classes of women might emerge in the future: a breeder class that rents its uteruses and sells its babies, and a consumer class that purchases reproductive services (Eichler 1983, 227). Eichler (1988, 305) notes that, while the new reproductive technologies have helped those who want children and in the past might not have been able to have any, children, and therefore parenthood, have become commodities that can be bought and sold. Besides being commodified, says Eichler, pregnancy has become *judicialized*, that is, increasingly a subject for legal definition and intervention. Finally, the new technologies have made reproduction even more medicalized. All of these developments, Eichler suggests, mean that a woman's control over her own reproductive processes has been diminished.

Another natural process that has been medicalized is menopause, or more generally, the process of female aging. The physical signs of female aging have become medical problems to be treated with wrinkle creams, face lifts, liposuction (surgical removal of fat), and estrogen replacement therapy. Menopause, associated with decreases in estrogen production by the ovaries, has been defined as a "deficiency disease" to be treated by the physician (Kaufert and Gilbert 1987; McCrea 1983). Feminists argue that menopause and aging should be demedicalized, that is, accepted as normal, thereby freeing women from both stigmatizing definitions and demeaning dependency on the medical professions.

Medicalization is also evident in the health care institution's response to women's emotional complaints. On the one hand, for example, women are more likely to seek help from physicians for emotional problems and are more likely than men to be prescribed tranquillizers and other mood-altering drugs (Pollock 1988, 174; D'Arcy and Schmitz 1987). On the other hand, there is a tendency to dismiss women's emotional complaints as trivial. Little is gained either way. The stresses and strains of women's contemporary lives, as manifest in emotional symptomatology, ought to be accorded legitimacy, addressed directly, and not buried through either trivialization or tranquillization.

In centuries past, women played a greater role in health care definition and treatment. This role was increasingly eroded by the emergence of modern medicine, dominated by men. As women play increasingly important roles in contemporary medicine, not only as (subordinate) nurses but also as physicians, and not only as technical assistants but also as independent practitioners, it should follow that women's concerns will receive a more balanced treatment. Pollock (1988, 172) argues that "woman-centred and woman-controlled health care" is needed to counterbalance the biases against women inherent in the male-dominated medical system. As the proportion of women in medical school and in the medical profession increases, as nurses and rehabilitation therapists expand their roles and gain increasing autonomy and responsibility, as independent nurse practitioners and midwives gain acceptance, it will follow that the established health care system will increasingly reflect women's points of view.

Conclusions

Patterns of health and illness vary from society to society and from time to time. As societies "modernize," death rates and, later, birth rates tend to decline (a process known as the demographic transition), resulting in a slowing of population growth and an increase in the average age of the population. The decline in death rates that precipitates the demographic transition typically involves a shift from the occurrence of death at a younger age as a result of acute infectious diseases to death at an older age as a result of chronic degenerative diseases (the epidemiologic transition). Given that patterns of morbidity and mortality reflect the socio-historical context, it can be argued that health, illness, disability, and death have social as well as physiological origins. Our contemporary causes of death, and surveys of the Canadian population, show that standards of living (including poverty) and lifestyles (including diet, exercise, smoking, and drinking) predict health status and health service utilization. In other words, health has social determinants and is unevenly distributed throughout the Canadian population. Generally speaking, the poor, Natives, those who smoke or drink, elderly persons, and women are more likely to report health problems, and (except for women and the elderly) to die "prematurely."

While Canada's medicare system has not eliminated all social inequities in health status, it has, nevertheless, eliminated most barriers to access to health care services. Despite the popularity of medicare, however, the program has its problems. It is widely seen to be underfunded. The question of underfunding may become more acute as an increasing proportion of the population reaches old age. Suggestions for the improvement of Canada's health care system that are being discussed include elimination of fee-for-service, ceasing to insure selected services, health care "rationing," reintroduction of premiums or user fees, reprivatization, home care as opposed to institutional care, health promotion and illness prevention, and a shift in emphasis for the terminally ill from cure to palliation.

It is sometimes argued that part of the solution to the problem of underfunding is the elimination of unnecessary demand. However, the "need" for health care services depends in part on both professional and lay definitions of health and illness. Stress is a case in point. In the past, stress might have been perceived as a normal and legitimate consequence of a demanding job or life. Today there is a tendency among laypersons and health care workers alike to define stress as a medical problem. Such changes in definition are called "medicalization." Some critics argue that far too many inherently non-medical phenomena have been redefined in medical terms and thereby brought under the control of the medical system. Feminists argue that issues such as birth control, pregnancy, abortion, childbirth, menopause, aging, and emotional health have been medicalized to the extent that women have lost control over their bodies and lives, and are increasingly subjected to a medical system that is male-dominated and male-biased. Accordingly, feminists call for the establishment of a woman-centred and woman-controlled health care system. As women come to play a more central role in health care, definitions of health and illness will indeed change to reflect the female experience. This responsiveness of health and illness definitions and behaviours to evolving social structures and perspectives reflects the central theme of this chapter—that patterns and definitions of health, illness, and illness behaviour reflect the social and cultural contexts in which we live.

Study Questions

1. What is the demographic transition? What is the epidemiologic transition? What is the relation between these two processes? How do these two transitions relate to the phenomenon of population aging?

2. To what extent are health, illness, disability, and "premature" death equitably distributed though out the Canadian population? What are the social origins of health, illness, disability, and variable death rates?

3. How is illness "socially constructed"? Is "stress" a legitimate medical issue? Defend your point of view.

4. What is "medicalization"? Discuss the feminist point of view regarding the medicalization of women's issues.

Recommended Reading

Bolaria, B. Singh, and H.D. Dickinson, eds. *Sociology of Health Care in Canada*. 2d ed. Toronto: Harcourt Brace Jovanovich, 1993.

Coburn, David, Carl D'Arcy, George M. Torrance, and Peter K. New, eds. *Health and Canadian Society: Sociological Perspectives*. 2d ed. Markham, ON: Fitzhenry and Whiteside, 1987.

Epp, Jake. *Achieving Health for All: A Framework for Health Promotion*. Ottawa: Minister of Supply and Services, 1986.

Lazarus, R., and S. Folkman. *Stress, Appraisal and Coping*. New York: Springer, 1984.

Mirowsky, J., and C.E. Ross. *Social Causes of Psychological Distress*. New York: Aldine de Gruyter, 1989.

References

Canada Fitness Survey. 1982. *Canada's Fitness: Preliminary Findings of the 1981 Survey*. Ottawa: Fitness Canada.

Canada Health Survey, Health and Welfare Canada and Statistics Canada. 1981. *The Health of Canadians: Report of Canada Health Survey*. Ottawa: Minister of Supply and Services.

Catlin, G., and P. Will. 1992. "The National Population Health Survey: Highlights of Initial Developments." *Health Reports* 4: 313–19 (Statistics Canada, cat. 82-003).

Cockerham, W.C. 1982. *Medical Sociology*. 2d ed. Englewood Cliffs, NJ: Prentice-Hall.

D'Arcy, C., and J.A. Schmitz. 1987. "Sex Differences in the Utilization of Health Services for Psychiatric Problems in Saskatchewan." In *Health and Canadian Society: Sociological Perspectives*, 2d ed., ed. D. Coburn et al. Markham, ON: Fitzhenry and Whiteside. 185–98.

Denton, F.T., and B.G. Spencer. 1983. "Population Aging and Future Health Costs in Canada." *Canadian Public Policy* 9: 155–63.

Denton, F.T., C.H. Feaver, and B.G. Spencer. 1986. "Prospective Aging of the Population and its Implications for the Labour Force and Government Expenditures." *Canadian Journal on Aging* 5: 75–98.

Department of National Health and Welfare and Dominion Bureau of Statistics. 1960. *Illness and Health Care in Canada, Canadian Sickness Survey 1950–51*. Ottawa: Queen's Printer.

Dreifus, C. 1977. *Seizing Our Bodies: The Politics of Women's Health*. New York: Vintage.

Dubos, R. 1959. *Mirage of Health*. New York: Harper.

Ehrlich, P.R. 1968. *The Population Bomb*. New York: Ballantine.

Eichler, M. 1983. *Families in Canada Today*. Toronto: Gage (2d ed., 1988).

Epp, J. 1986. *Achieving Health for All: A Framework for Health Promotion*. Ottawa: Minister of Supply and Services.

Evans, R.G. 1984. *Strained Mercy: The Economics of Canadian Health Care*. Toronto: Butterworths.

———. 1987. "Hang Together, or Hang Separately: The Viability of a Universal Health Care System in an Aging Society." *Canadian Public Policy* 13: 165–80.

Fleetwood, B. 1979. "The Tribe that Caught Cat Dancing." In *Culture, Curers, and Contagion*, ed. N. Klein. Novato, CA: Chandler and Sharp.

Gee, E.M., and M.M. Kimball. 1987. *Women and Aging*. Toronto: Butterworths.

Gove, W.R. 1984. "Gender Differences in Mental and Physical Illness: The Effects of Fixed Roles and Nurturant Roles." *Social Science and Medicine* 19: 77–91.

Hay, D.A. "Mortality and Health Status Trends in Canada." In *Sociology of Health Care in Canada*, ed. B.S. Bolaria and H.D. Dickinson. Toronto: Harcourt Brace Jovanovich. 18–37.

Health and Welfare Canada. 1987. *The Active Health Report: Perspectives on Canada's Health Promotion Survey, 1985*. Ottawa: Minister of Supply and Services.

———. 1990. *National Alcohol and Other Drugs Survey: Highlights Report.* H39-175/1990E. Ottawa: Ministry of Supply and Services Canada.

———. 1993. *Canada's Health Promotion Survey 1990: Technical Report.* Ed. T. Stephens and D. Fowler Graham. (cat. H39-263/2-1990E). Ottawa: Minister of Supply and Services Canada.

Illich, 1. 1976. *Limits to Medicine*. Harmondsworth, England: Penguin.

Karasek, R., and T. Theorell. 1990. *Healthy Work: Stress, Productivity, and the Reconstruction of Working Life.* New York: Basic Books.

Kaufert, P. A. and P. Gilbert. 1987. "Medicalization and the Menopause." In *Health and Canadian Society: Sociological Perspectives,* 2d ed., ed. D. Coburn et al. Markham, ON: Fitzhenry and Whiteside. 172–84

Kohn, R. 1967. *The Health of the Canadian People*. Ottawa: Queen's Printer.

Kornhauser, A. 1965. *Mental Health of the Industrial Worker.* New York: John Wiley and Sons.

Lalonde, M. 1974. *A New Perspective on the Health of Canadians.* Ottawa: Health and Welfare Canada.

Lazarus, R., and S. Folkman. 1984. *Stress, Appraisal, and Coping.* New York: Springer.

Litven, W. 1985. "Leading Causes of Death, Canada, 1983." *Chronic Diseases in Canada* 6: 35–37.

McCann, C. 1988. "Potential Years of Life Lost, Canada, 1982 to 1986." *Chronic Diseases in Canada* 9: 98–100.

McCrea, F.B. 1983. "The Politics of Menopause: The 'Discovery' of a Deficiency Disease." *Social Problems* 31: 111–23.

McDaniel, S. 1986. *Canada's Aging Population*. Toronto: Butterworths.

Mirowsky, J., and C.E. Ross. 1989. *Social Causes of Psychological Distress.* New York: Aldine de Gruyter.

Nagnur, D. 1986. *Longevity and Historical Life Tables, 1921–1981*. Ottawa: Minister of Supply and Services.

National Cancer Institute of Canada. 1992. *Canadian Cancer Statistics 1992.* Toronto.

Northcott, H.C. 1988. "Health Care Resources and Extra-Billing: Financing, Allocation, and Utilization." In *Sociology of Health Care in Canada,* ed. B.S. Bolaria and H.D. Dickinson. Toronto: Harcourt Brace Jovanovich. 38–50.

Nutrition Canada. 1973. *Nutrition: A National Priority*. Ottawa: Information Canada.

Olshansky, S.J., and B.A. Ault. 1986. "The Fourth Stage of the Epidemiologic Transition: The Age of Delayed Degenerative Diseases." *Milbank Memorial Fund Quarterly* 64: 355–91.

Omran, A.R. 1971. "The Epidemiologic Transition: A Theory of the Epidemiology of Population Change." *Milbank Memorial Fund Quarterly* 49: 509–38.

Pollock, S. 1988. "Feminism and Reproduction." In *Sociology of Health Care in Canada,* ed. B.S. Bolaria and H.D. Dickinson. Toronto: Harcourt Brace Jovanovich. 167–82.

Reasons, C.E., L.L. Ross, and C. Paterson. 1981. *Assault on the Worker: Occupational Health and Safety in Canada*. Toronto: Butterworths.

Statistics Canada. 1987. General Social Survey Analysis Series. *Health and Social Support 1985.* Ottawa: Minister of Supply and Services Canada.

———. 1988a. *Health Reports*. Ottawa: Minister of Supply and Services.

———. 1988b. *Causes of Death 1986*. Ottawa: Minister of Supply and Services.

———. 1990. *Highlights: Disabled Persons in Canada, The Health and Activity Limitation Survey.* (cat. 82-602). Ottawa: Minister of Regional Industrial Expansion.

———. 1992. *Report on the Demographic Situation in Canada, 1992: Current Demographic Analysis.* (cat. 91-209E). Ottawa: Minister of Industry, Science, and Technology.

———. 1993. *Adults With Disabilities: Their Employment and Education Characteristics, 1991 Health and Activity Limitation Survey.* (cat. 82-554). Ottawa: Minister of Industry, Science, and Technology.

Statistics Canada and Department of the Secretary of State of Canada. 1986. *Report of the Canadian Health and Disability Survey 1983–84*. Ottawa: Minister of Supply and Services.

Stephens, T., and C.L. Craig. 1990. *The Well-Being of Canadians: Highlights of the 1988 Campbell's Survey*. Ottawa: Canada Fitness and Lifestyle Research Institute.

Trypuc, J.M. 1988. "Women's Health." In *Sociology of Health Care in Canada*, ed. B.S. Bolaria and H.D. Dickinson. Toronto: Harcourt Brace Jovanovich. 154–66.

Verbrugge, L.M. 1985. "Gender and Health: An Update on Hypotheses and Evidence." *Journal of Health and Social Behavior* 26: 156–82.

———. 1989. "The Twain Meet: Empirical Explanations of Sex Differences in Health and Mortality." *Journal of Health and Social Behavior* 30:282–304.

Walters, V. 1992. "Women's Views of Their Main Health Problems." *Canadian Journal of Public Health* 83:371–74.

Wigle, D.T., Y. Mao, R. Semenciw, C. McCann, and J.W. Davies. 1990. "Premature Deaths in Canada: Impact, Trends, and Opportunities for Prevention." *Canadian Journal of Public Health* 81: 376–81.

Young, T.K. 1987. "The Health of Indians in Northwestern Ontario." In *Health and Canadian Society: Sociological Perspectives,* 2d ed., ed. D. Coburn et al. Markham, ON: Fitzhenry and Whiteside. 109–26.

CHAPTER 10

Health Care in an Aging Society: Issues, Controversies, and Challenges for the Future

Karen R. Grant

Learning Objectives

This chapter examines a number of issues and controversies related to health care and aging in Canadian society and explores the relationship between the demographic and epidemiologic transitions and the demand on health services by the aged population. Students are encouraged to become aware of the trends in population aging and to identify the factors responsible for the greying of Canadian society. Upon reading this chapter, students should also be able to describe the patterns of health, disease, and health care utilization among elders and in comparison with other age groups; assess the arguments concerning elders' use of health services; and assess the adequacy of the current structure of health care in meeting the needs of Canada's growing elderly population.

Introduction

> I am not mad, only old. I make this statement to give me courage.... I am in a concentration camp for the old, a place where people dump their parents or relatives exactly as though it were an ash can.... I have to hang on to every scrap of information I have to keep my sanity, and it is for that purpose that I am keeping a journal. Then if I forget things later, I can always go back and read them here.
>
> I call it *The Book of the Dead*. By the time I finish it I shall be dead. I want to be ready, to have gathered everything together and sorted it out, as if I were preparing for a great final journey. I intend to make myself whole here in this Hell. It is the thing that is set before me to do. So, in a way, this path inward and back into the past is like a map, a map of my

> world. If I can draw it accurately, I shall know where I am. (Sarton 1973, 3–4)

So begins the journal of 76-year-old Caro Spencer who, following a heart attack, finds herself sent off by her family to a home for the aged. Through this journal we learn of the despair and degradation, the loneliness and helplessness of an elderly woman whose experience is increasingly more common in our contemporary society.

Although there has been a progressive aging of the Canadian population over the past century, it is only in the last few decades that this phenomenon has attracted much attention from academics and the popular press. A voluminous research literature has been amassed, and it is now commonplace to see headlines decrying the problems of a growing elderly population. We hear of old people "inappropriately" occupying acute-care beds as they await transfer to long-term institutions, a practice that contributes to long queues for people in need of acute care in Canadian hospitals. We hear of elders making extensive use of health care and social services, thus placing undue economic (and other) burdens on our welfare-state institutions. Expressed in terms of "old age dependency ratio"[1] the impression that is left is one of elders not making a "real" contribution to society, but instead exacting a burden on the rest of society. We hear of drug dependency and various iatrogenic consequences (that is, conditions caused by medical treatment itself) experienced by elders because of the numerous prescription medications they receive. And so on.

To a considerable degree, aging has become a social problem (Macintyre 1977), or what C. Wright Mills called a *public issue* (1959). For Mills, understanding any phenomenon using a "sociological imagination" involves the ability to transcend a problem's personal, individual qualities, so that it can be seen within the larger social and historical milieux. In this way, *private troubles* (such as of growing old) are no longer private matters at all, but rather *public issues* that involve the entire array of social institutions and values of a society.

This chapter is devoted to a consideration of the very public and social nature of population aging, and the response of the health care system to a changing demographic profile within this country. Throughout, the objective is to reinforce the belief that population aging highlights many of the contradictions and conflicts with the health care system and within society at large. Consequently, it is argued that to see aging in reductionist terms, as the private troubles of discrete individuals, is misguided and problematic. This chapter examines several issues and controversies related to health care and aging in Canadian society, and asks whether the much-feared "crisis" in health care is real. More directly, the discussion asks whether the elderly have become a scapegoat for the failures of Canadian medicine and medicare.

In the first section of the essay, a demographic profile of Canada's aging population is offered. This is followed by a brief look at Canada's medicare program, a description of the health of Canada's elderly population, and a discussion of some of the relevant empirical work done by sociologists and gerontologists on the health care utilization patterns of elders. This latter discussion is intended to address the question of whether the elderly, as a group, make disproportionately greater use of the health care system than other age groups. Finally, a glimpse at the elderly's use of prescription drugs is given, to highlight the problems and challenges associated with population aging in contemporary Canadian medicine and society. The discussion closes with a consideration of how Canada will deal with its aging population as it moves into the twenty-first century.

A Demographic Profile of Canada's Elderly

In recent years, a good deal has been written about the aging of the Canadian population. Various demographers and gerontologists have described what amounts to a "seniors boom" (Stone and Fletcher 1986), which is having a profound effect on the cultural and economic institutions of Canadian society. Canada's population is in a state of transition.[2] It is not too much of an exaggeration to say that Canada has been "greying".

Just a century ago, Canada's population pyramid[3] was heavily weighted toward the younger ages, with elders constituting only a relatively small fraction of the total population. More recently, however, the pyramid's shape has changed, such that younger people are fewer in number, and there is an increase in older age groups, most notably persons in their middle years ("baby boomers"). As shown in Table 10.1, the number of seniors in Canada has increased steadily over the last century. Whereas in 1891 elders accounted for 4.5 percent of the total Canadian population, at the present, more than 11 percent of the population is 65 years or older (Statistics

TABLE 10.1: Number and Percentage of Population Aged 65 and Older, Canada, 1891–1986

Year	Number of persons aged 65+	Percentage of population
1891	218 790	4.5
1901	271 201	5.0
1911	335 315	4.7
1921	420 244	4.8
1931	576 076	5.6
1941	767 815	6.7
1951	1 086 237	7.8
1961	1 391 154	7.6
1971	1 744 405	8.1
1981	2 360 975	9.7
1986	2 697 580	10.7
1991	3 169 975	11.61

Sources: N.L. Chappell, L.A. Strain, and A.A. Blandford, *Aging and Health Care: A Social Perspective* (Toronto: Holt, Rinehart and Winston, 1986) p. 19; Statistics Canada, *Age, Sex and Marital Status*, Cat. no. 93-310-1991 (Ottawa: Minister of Supply and Services, 1992), Table 1, p. 6. Reproduced with permission of the Minister of Supply and Services Canada, 1994.

Canada 1992). Based on current projections, it is estimated that the elderly will constitute approximately 20 percent of the total Canadian population by the year 2031 (Statistics Canada 1986, 1987).

A similar characterization can be made of other industrialized nations, such as the United States, where more than 11 percent of the population was 65 or older in 1981 (Institute for Philosophy and Public Policy 1988; Brody, Brock, and Williams 1987; Dorney 1983; Stone and Fletcher 1988). Some European countries have somewhat larger populations; for example, in 1981, approximately 15 percent of Britons and 16.5 percent of Swedes were 65 or older (McDaniel 1986). By contrast, countries in the developing world do not have large numbers of elders. To be sure, the differences in the demographic make-up of any society are tied very much to social and economic conditions; in the developing world, conditions are not always conducive to a long life.

What has just been described is something demographers call *population* or *demographic aging*. Demographic aging refers to the progressive aging of a population (as opposed to the aging of individuals). There are several reasons underlying the phenomenon of demographic aging in Canada and other industrialized nations (McDaniel 1986; Stone and Fletcher 1986). First of all, improvements in health care (a subject to which we will return later in this chapter) have led to significant declines in mortality over the past century, and this has contributed to the aging of Canada's population. It is important to note, however, that reduced mortality and increased longevity owe more to improvement in sanitation, personal hygiene, and living standards than to specific medical measures, per se (McKeown 1979; McKinlay et al. 1983). This is not to suggest that doctors have made no contribution—only that public health measures have had a more significant impact on declines in mortality.

This having been said, the effects of improved health care on population aging really are limited, since it is the young who have benefited most from health care and not the old (McDaniel 1986). Medicine has been most effective in dealing with acute conditions, which are more likely to affect younger members of society. In the past century, prophylactic measures have been developed to control or eliminate most infectious diseases. The same is not true for chronic conditions, which more readily affect older members of the population. Though some medical measures allow for the extension of human life, McDaniel (1986) suggests there is a ceiling to the biological life span, and medicine has not appreciably altered this. McKinlay et al. (1983) also indicate that where medical measures have lengthened life, this has often produced more years of disabled life, a very high cost indeed.

The second major factor contributing to population aging is immigration. Canada's relatively open immigration policy has brought a steady influx of mostly young immigrants from various parts of the world over the past century. In the first half of the 1900s, the wave of immigration was from Eastern and Western European countries. More recently, a substantial proportion of the immigrants coming to Canada are natives of Southeast Asia, the Indian subcontinent, and Latin America. The early twentieth-century immigrants to Canada are now among the elderly, while the more recent immigrants "contribute to the relative youthfulness of the country and ... stave off [the] aging of the population" (McDaniel, 1986, 6).

The third, and most important, factor responsible for population aging is the decline in fertility. While the effects of declining fertility are obvious in terms of family size and composition (the average number of children per family is now less than two), the effects on population aging are not as readily apparent. Yet the reduced fertility of Canadians in the past century has meant that while the absolute number of elders in the population may not have increased, the fact that younger age groups are smaller automatically increases the proportional size of the elderly segment of the population. Gee (cited in McDaniel 1986, 6) puts this rather succinctly: "Population aging is an unplanned byproduct of planned parenthood."

With the aging of Canada's population has come the realization that not all individuals have an equal likelihood to survive to advanced age. There is considerable variation in the distribution of the elderly population within Canada. As Table 10.2 shows, proportionally, the greatest numbers of elders are found in Prince Edward Island, Saskatchewan, and Manitoba, while in the Northwest and Yukon territories elders make up only a small fraction of the total population. The reasons for these differences are social and economic.

If we look at the age composition of the elderly population, here too, we find important variation. Evidence from Statistics Canada indicates that a substantial number of Canada's elderly can be classified as "old" (75 years or older). The growth rates of the aged and of the oldest old have continued to increase over the past century, as is revealed in the data presented in Table 10.3. Demographers project that the rate of population growth for all elders will decline somewhat at the start of the next century, but this will be followed by an increase in the proportion of elders around 2030.

TABLE 10.2: Percentage of Elderly by Province and Territory, Canada, 1991

Province/Territory (Rank order: high–low)	Number of persons aged 65+	Percentage of population
Saskatchewan	139 925	14.15
Manitoba	146 605	13.43
Prince Edward Island	17 080	13.16
British Columbia	422 010	12.86
Nova Scotia	113 405	12.60
New Brunswick	88 140	12.18
Ontario	1 183 475	11.74
Quebec	770 920	11.18
Newfoundland	55 160	9.70
Alberta	230 550	9.06
Yukon	1 100	3.96
Northwest Territories	1 605	2.78
Canada	3 169 975	11.61

Source: Statistics Canada, *Age, Sex and Marital Status*, Cat. no. 93-310-191 (Ottawa: Minister of Supply and Services, 1992), Table 1-13, pp. 6–18. Reproduced with permission of the Minister of Supply and Services Canada, 1994.

TABLE 10.3: Population Growth Rates and Sex Ratios at Age 65 and 85, Canada, 1920–2030

	Average Annual Population Growth Rate				Men per 100 Women	
Time period[a]	**Total**	**65+**	**75+**	**85+**	**65+**	**85+**
1920–30	1.79	3.72	3.18	1.76	104.9	81.2
1930–40	1.15	3.36	4.24	4.32	108.9	81.6
1940–50	2.05	4.12	3.99	5.33	104.1	77.5
1950–60	3.03	2.92	4.44	4.25	95.2	77.0
1960–70	1.95	2.49	3.54	6.96	82.0	67.2
1970–80	1.26	3.49	3.08	4.57	75.0	50.5
1980–90	1.13	3.49	4.58	3.94	73.2	39.9
1990–2000	1.20	2.36	3.84	5.76	75.2	40.0
2000–2010	0.90	1.56	1.81	3.51	76.3	40.8
2010–2020	0.82	2.94	1.34	1.03	77.7	43.0
2020–2030	0.70	2.51	3.57	1.70	78.3	43.9

Note: [a]Figures after 1980 are based on projections.
Source: L.O. Stone and S. Fletcher, "Demographic Variations in North America," *North American Elders* (Contribution to the Study of Aging, No. 8) ed. E. Rathbone-McCuan and Betty Havens (Westport, CT: Greenwood Press, 1988), p. 13.

One of the more interesting sources of variation among Canada's elderly has to do with gender. Put rather succinctly, aging is a women's issue (Dulude 1978; Nett 1982; Estes, Gerard, and Clarke 1984; Reinharz 1986; Russell 1987; McDaniel 1986), since women are disproportionately represented among the elderly. The gender imbalance became most apparent after the 1950s (see Table 10.3). The imbalance of the sexes owes much to the greater longevity of females and the higher rates of mortality among males, topics to be considered shortly.

The importance of gender differences in longevity is seen in terms of the sex ratio. In Canada, for every 100 women aged 65 or older, there are only approximately 75 men in the same age range. The ratio becomes even more lopsided among those older than 85: only about 40 men for every 100 women. The consequences of this imbalance are profound in terms of health and social policy, as well as at a more personal level. For example, widowhood is "an expectable life event" for most women, particularly elderly women (Martin Matthews 1987) and it has been estimated that most women who marry can expect to live ten years as widows. The adverse effects of widowhood have been well documented (see, for example, Znaniecka Lopata 1987). Beyond this, the survival of large numbers of elderly women who may or may not have sources of support (because of the loss of spouse or peers) means that community and other institutional supports need to be found for this segment of the elderly population.

Another variable that is often considered when describing the elderly is their socio-economic situation. It is commonplace to hear of elders barely eking out a living on their pension monies. For many elders in Canada, the loss of financial security is a part of growing old. It has been estimated that most elders can expect their incomes to drop by about half at retirement. While the economic lot of most elders has improved substantially as a result of government and private pension plans instituted in the post-Second World War era, there remains a risk of poverty for large numbers of elderly persons, particularly women. Dulude has noted that "to be old and female is the best combination to ensure being poor in Canada ... to be old and a widow is an even better one" (1978, 38).

According to the National Council of Welfare (1984), in 1982 the median annual income of families with an aged head was $16 927, a figure almost 60 percent of the median income for all families. For single elders, the median income in 1982 was a mere $7458, two-thirds of the median income of all single individuals, and no more than 39 percent of the median income of persons aged 35 to 44. In 1982, for a single elderly woman, the median income was $6512, as compared to $7189 for a single elderly man (National Council of Welfare 1984). Overall, women continue to face a much higher risk of poverty, particularly unattached or elderly women—a phenomenon that has become known as the "feminization of poverty." (National Council of Welfare, 1990). This discrepancy substantiates Dulude's comment that aging has become a women's issue.

Elders' primary sources of income include Old Age Security, the Guaranteed Income Supplement, and the Canada (or Quebec) Pension Plans. In addition to these programs, various provinces have created programs and tax subsidies for elders. Together, all public programs account for about half of elders' incomes (National Council of Welfare 1984). For many elders, the public monies they receive are augmented by private pensions funded through payroll deductions. As noted by the National Council of Welfare (1984, 68), however, "the failings of private pension plans are glaring: most working Canadians are not covered by them (especially lower-wage earners and workers in the private sector) and the minority who do belong typically receive meager pensions that are not adequately protected against inflation." And, it should be added, most private plans do not assist women, since relatively few of today's elderly women were employed outside the home; consequently, they stand a much greater chance of finding themselves in poverty in their "golden years."

The economic situation described above is, of course, not the lot of everyone. There are affluent persons among Canada's elderly. At the same time, the idea of old age being some kind of Shangri-La should be dispensed with. For a substantial number of elders, old age brings financial insecurity along with various other trials.

Demographic differences such as those noted above are among the most salient of the variables that influence health and wellbeing, the primary focus of this chapter. There are other sources of variability among Canadian elders, as well, including urban or rural residence, educational level, marital status, living arrangements, and so on (see Chappell, Strain, and Blandford 1986; Novak 1988). It is important to note how heterogeneous the elderly are as a group. Indeed, the demographic make-up of elders often parallels the demographic make-up of the rest of society, and we would do well to acknowledge the differences among them.

Typically, we tend to lump all persons with a particular attribute together, and to make assumptions based upon various stereotypes. We do this for elders just as we do for other identifiable social groups. While stereotypes can tell us something about their attributes, more often than not, half-truths and outright lies are mixed into the stereotypes we develop. When these stereotypes misinform, they have the potential to cause divisions and conflicts between people. In their most vile form, stereotypes of elders lead to a form of bigotry described by Robert Butler as *ageism* (1969, 1980). Ageism is a form of prejudice against the aged that "reflects a deep seated uneasiness on the part of the young and middle-aged—a revulsion to and distaste of growing old, disease, disability; and fear of powerlessness, 'uselessness,' and death" (Butler 1969, 243). Based on many unfounded myths,[4] ageism often has the result that the elderly feel stigmatized and devalued, and this may exacerbate the difficult conditions that may be associated with growing old (Dorney 1983). As we shall almost surely all grow old some day, it is time to rid ourselves of these misconceptions. It is also time to enhance our understanding of the aging process and its implications for society and its institutions. Perhaps one of the institutions most affected by population aging is the health care system, and it is this to which we now turn.

A Brief Look at Canada's Health Care Program

In recent years, Canada's health care system has come under increasing scrutiny and criticism. Seldom a day goes by without a headline in one newspaper or another claiming that the health care system is in a state of crisis. Long queues for surgery and specialist care, bed closures, shortages of nurses and doctors, and striking health care workers are now commonplace. Yet despite these concerns, Canada's health care system and its medicare program are viewed around the world as exemplary (Hatcher 1981). Indeed, few Canadians today can imagine a time when medicare did not exist.

Comprehensive, universal government-funded health insurance, or medicare, is approximately twenty years old. Though the first hospital insurance plans were introduced in 1947 in Saskatchewan and in 1957 throughout Canada, it was not until 1972 that all Canadians had coverage for medical and hospital services through the Hospital Insurance and Diagnostic Services Act and the Medical Care Act. In recent years, these two pieces of legislation have been superseded by the Canada Health Act of 1984.

The early federal government initiatives in health care came largely as a result of the 1964 Hall Royal Commission on Health Services, although the impetus underlying the program had its base in the government's post-Second World War reconstruction plan (which also included federal initiatives in pensions). Guided by the knowledge that many Canadians did not have access to quality medical care, Justice Hall recommended that the provincial and federal governments introduce a program that would remove the economic barriers that prevented many Canadians from receiving necessary medical care (Torrance 1981). Funding for the program came through taxation, and initially the government agreed to share the costs of health care on a fifty-fifty basis with the provinces, provided that each provincial plan met five requirements:

1. accessibility (reasonable access should be guaranteed to all Canadians);
2. comprehensiveness (all necessary medical services should be guaranteed, without dollar limit, and should be available solely on the basis of medical need);
3. universality (all Canadians should be eligible for coverage on uniform terms and conditions);
4. portability (benefits should be transferable from province to province); and
5. administration by a public, non-profit agency or commission.

Beginning in 1977, as a result of the implementation of the Established Programs Financing Act (EPF), the formula for the sharing of costs was changed. In part, this change was introduced by the federal government as a cost-saving mechanism. Following the introduction of medicare, the governments of Canada (particularly the federal government) found the costs of this program difficult to bear. By the mid-1970s, approximately 7 to 7.5 percent of the GNP was being allocated to health care. In order to put a ceiling on this, the federal government introduced EPF, which tied federal contributions to the size of the population. Rather than providing dollar-for-dollar funding, the federal government provided each province with a block of funds (transfer payments), to be used by the provinces in support of health services and education. It has been estimated that the changes brought by EPF have reduced federal contributions to medicare from 50 percent to approximately 38 percent (Barber 1989).

Given the increasing costs of health care and the changing disease profile (mostly chronic) and demographic profile (increasingly older) of the country, many critics and policy-makers alike have expressed concern that Canada's medicare program is a "sacred trust" under attack. Efforts by the federal government to privatize Crown corporations raise the spectre that medicare may some day be privatized as well, returning Canada to a system not unlike that of the United States. Signs of this appeared to some observers in the 1988 federal election campaign, which saw free trade endorsed through the election of a second consecutive Conservative majority government. There is still genuine concern that the integrity of medicare may be challenged by the government's fiscal and free trade policies.

Although progressive in its intent to promote universal access to health services, Canada's medicare program is what Waitzkin (1983) calls a reformist rather than revolutionary reform.[5] Medicare simply changed the way that people paid for health services, rather than reorganizing the way services were provided. As noted by Swartz:

> State hospital and medical insurance effected no change in the nature of the health care system. Its control remained firmly in private hands, held by physicians and the drug and medical supply corporations. What health insurance amounted to was an unlimited subsidy to these fractions of the bourgeoisie in the form of a guarantee by the state of payment for any services and goods physicians mandate (1987, 581).

Medicare left intact a private, fee-for-service type of medical practice, and ensured public payment (Evans 1984; Swartz 1987). This is not an unimportant point, as many of the problems that elders have with the health care system can be traced to the nature of medical practice in this country.

Even the most ardent supporter of medicare would readily acknowledge that the system is not fail-safe. Indeed, many problems remain in Canada's health care system. Services, facilities, and personnel continue to be maldistributed among urban, rural, and remote areas of the country. Physicians and hospitals are primarily found in urban centres, as are research and teaching facilities. Even within cities, not everyone has equal access to the same quality of medical care. Various groups, differentiated on the basis of age, gender, race, and socio-economic status may have different susceptibilities to disease and disability; they may also experience differential access to health services. This problem is best summarized by what Julian Tudor Hart called "the inverse care law": "the availability of good medical care tends to vary inversely with the need for it in the population served" (1971, 412; cf. Grant 1988).

A second major problem noted in recent years concerns the alleged overuse of the health system by the public. It is claimed that because most Canadians (like their American counterparts) have an almost insatiable appetite for medical services, because Canadians do not pay for health services at the time they receive them, and because they have no knowledge of the actual costs of care, they use the system inappropriately. Frequenting emergency rooms for routine care is perhaps the most common example of this misuse.

Utilization studies have shown that Canadians began to use health services more extensively following the introduction of the national program (Evans 1984). To deal with the public's alleged overuse or misuse of the system, user fees and co-payments have been implemented at various times and in different jurisdictions. In 1968, for example, the Saskatchewan government introduced a system of modest co-payments for office, hospital, and outpatient visits. Initially these user fees resulted in a reduction in days spent in hospital, but the effects were only temporary. Beck (1973, 1974) observed that co-payments had reduced use of physicians' services by the poor by approximately 18 percent, and approximately 6 to 7 percent for the entire population. In light of this evidence that co-payments resurrected economic barriers to care, the Saskatchewan government discontinued the program in 1971. More recently, the federal government banned extra-billing, a practice that was fairly widespread in many provinces in the 1970s and early 1980s, on the argument that it compromised medicare's principle of reasonable access.[6]

Though patients may not always use the health care system as efficiently as possible, some health economists have argued that the system is provider- rather than user-driven. That is, doctors determine how resources will be used—they determine who gets what, when, why, and how much. Doctors prescribe drugs, admit patients to hospitals, and determine how long patients stay in hospitals and what services they receive while in hospital. Hospital care is the most expensive component of health care (Evans 1984). According to Evans, while physicians earn only about 20 percent of every dollar spent on health, they influence how the rest of that dollar is spent. In light of this, reforms to individuals' utilization "habits" would be seen best in terms of physician, rather than patient, behaviour.

While medical care is a crucial component of the health delivery system, the needs of many Canadians and of elders, in particular, cannot be met by medical services alone. In short, more medical care does not lead to better health. The realization that the formal system of health care must be augmented by informal and community-based care has come only in recent years; still, by and large, programs like these have not received the kind of funding characteristic of medicare, or they have been add-ons with varying services, eligibility requirements, user fees, and so forth (Schwenger 1987). Furthermore, while federal legislation more or less guarantees that all Canadians shall have access to medical services, no such guarantees exist with respect to community services. The decentralized nature of health and social programs for the elderly makes assurances of equal access problematic (Chappell, Strain, and Blandford 1986; Chappell 1987, 1988; Statistics Canada 1986).

The final problem is the cost crisis in Canada's medicare program. The cost crisis is twofold: first, more money is spent on health care today than ever before (as noted previously), and, second, according to constant hue and cry, the system is underfunded. These seemingly contradictory claims highlight one of the major challenges to medicare in the modern era. How to effect a desirable solution to the cost crisis remains a matter of considerable debate.

This look at Canada's health care system has been extremely cursory, and the issues are indeed very complex. Yet we have touched on several important points that have a bearing on how health care is delivered and how the system responds to the demands made by consumers and providers. These, and various related issues, will be elaborated and applied to elders in particular later on. First, however, a look at the health of Canada's elderly is required.

A Health Profile of Canada's Elderly

As Canadian society has aged, much attention has focussed on the health consequences of this demographic shift. Inasmuch as declining health has been associated with aging (Longino and Soldo 1987), questions have been asked repeatedly about the association between sickness and the aging process. Recent evidence suggests that the health and life expectancy of elders may be improving, and at a quicker pace than is true for other age groups (Guralnik and Kaplan 1989; Brody 1989). A fundamental question, then, is, how well do the health and medical care systems deal with an increasingly aged population? Before answering this question, we shall present a profile of the physical health[7] of elders today.

Health can be assessed in a number of ways, the most common of which use life expectancy, mortality, and morbidity statistics. In the past century, dramatic increases in life expectancy have been achieved in Canada and other industrialized countries. As noted in Table 10.4, a male born in 1986 could expect to live almost 73 years, while a female could expect to live to the ripe old age of 80. In the period between 1931 and 1986, the net gains in expected years of life for males and females

TABLE 10.4: Life Expectancy by Sex, at Birth, Age 60, and Age 80, Canada, Selected Years, 1931–1986

Year	At birth		At age 60		At age 80	
	Male	Female	Male	Female	Male	Female
1931	60.00	62.10	16.29	17.15	5.16	5.92
1941	62.96	66.30	16.06	17.62	5.54	6.03
1951	66.33	70.83	16.49	18.64	5.84	6.38
1956	67.61	72.92	16.54	19.34	5.89	6.75
1961	68.35	74.17	16.73	19.90	6.14	6.90
1966	68.75	75.18	16.81	20.58	6.36	7.26
1971	69.34	76.36	16.95	21.39	6.41	7.88
1976	70.19	77.48	17.23	21.96	N/A	N/A
1981	71.88	78.98	17.96	22.85	N/A	N/A
1986	73.04	79.73	18.41	23.17	N/A	N/A
Gains:						
1931–76	10.1	15.38	0.94	4.81	N/A	N/A
1931–86	13.04	17.63	2.12	6.02	N/A	N/A

Sources: Statistics Canada, *Canada Year Book 1994*, Cat. No. 11-402E (Ottawa: Minister of Industry, Science and Technology, 1994), Table 4.1, p. 148; M.C. Urquhart and K.A.H. Buckley (eds.), *Historical Statistics of Canada*, 2nd edition, Cat. no. 11-516E (Ottawa: Minister of Supply and Services, 1983), B59-74. Reproduced with permission of the Minister of Supply and Services Canada, 1994.

were, respectively, 13.04 and 17.63 years. Table 10.4 also shows the increases in life expectancy at age 60 and age 80. What is obvious from these data is that longevity has increased for both genders, although for women the increases have been more substantial.

Table 10.5 documents the leading causes of death for all Canadians and for those aged 65 and older. It is apparent that elders have higher death rates for these causes than the population as a whole. This is not unexpected, in view of the fact that the leading causes of death (with the exception of accidents, suicides, and murders) are chronic conditions, which are much more likely to appear with advanced age.

The gender differences in causes of death are noteworthy. With the exception of circulatory diseases, male deaths are higher for all the leading causes than females. It has been suggested by health researchers that the discrepancy in mortality experience between males and females owes much to how we live. For example, differences in socialization and social role behaviour, risk-taking behaviour (tobacco and alcohol consumption, lack of physical fitness, disregard of preventive health behaviours, and so on), stress, and coping abilities (for example, the Type A or "coronary-prone" behaviour pattern) are all thought to contribute to the differential mortality experience of males and females (cf. Grant 1989, for a review of the literature on gender differences in health). Biological factors may also operate here (Waldron 1976), though sociologists have long argued that social factors are more important.

TABLE 10.5: Leading Causes of Death in Canada in 1991

Causes of Death	Percentage of All Deaths: All Ages Males	All Ages Females	65 and Over Males	65 and Over Females
Circulatory Diseases	37.1	41.0	42.6	46.9
Cancer	28.1	27.0	28.1	22.7
Respiratory Diseases	9.1	8.0	11.8	8.9
Accidents/Suicides/Homicides	8.7	4.5	2.5	2.5
All Other Causes	17.5	19.5	15.0	2.5
ALL CAUSES	100.0	100.0	100.0	100.0

Source: Calculated from Statistics Canada, *Mortality - Summary List of Causes 1991*, Cat. no. 84-209 (Ottawa: Minister of Supply and Services, 1993), Table 4, pp. 12–15. Reproduced by authority of the Minister of Industry, 1994.

Although it would be incorrect to assume that all elders are sick, epidemiological evidence indicates a much greater likelihood that chronic conditions and various forms of functional limitation occur in the later stages of the life cycle. Data from the Canada Health Survey indicate a significantly higher prevalence of chronic health problems among elders than among younger persons (Grant 1989). Acute illnesses are less common among elders than other age groups; however, they may be more debilitating for older persons (Verbrugge 1985).

While the mortality data clearly favour women, the same is not true of measures of morbidity. Put succinctly, the research evidence suggests that "women get sicker, but men die quicker" (Grant 1989). Women report a greater prevalence of most chronic health problems at all ages and in the 65-years-and-older age bracket (Statistics Canada, 1981, 151).[8] American data based on self-reports and physical examinations show a similar pattern (Verbrugge 1985, 1986; Wingard 1984).

Verbrugge has pointed to the fact that there is no necessary correspondence between cause of death and illness experience (cf. Statistics Canada 1986; Chappell, Strain, and Blandford 1986). For example, in the U.S. Health Interview Survey, it was found that older women report a high rate of coronary and other circulatory symptoms, yet (older) men are more likely to die of heart disease. It is possible that women's experience with various chronic conditions may be less severe and less lethal than men's. Some of the chronic conditions afflicting elderly women, such as arthritis, may be the source of diminished functioning, but they are unlikely to be the primary cause of death (Verbrugge 1985). According to Statistics Canada (1986), the leading causes of illness among elders are (in order) arthritis and rheumatism, hypertension, heart disease, respiratory ailments, and diabetes. (These conditions and their ordering do not exactly correspond to the leading causes of death reported earlier in this chapter.)

Based on data from the Canada Health Survey (1981), physical functioning declines with age. This study found that less than 10 percent of persons under 65 had any limitations on their usual activities, while almost 40 percent of those aged 65 and older were limited in their activity to some degree. Furthermore, approximately the same proportion of males and females experienced partial or total activity limitation at all ages, as well as in the older age brackets. Women reported more "disability days," however—time taken off from their usual activities as a result of poor health. This latter finding was true of all ages, elders included (Statistics Canada 1981, 121, 125).

Table 10.6 provides data on total disability days in 1985, by gender and age. Overall, 14 percent of Canadians aged 15 and over reported at least one disability day during the two-week period prior to the survey. It is also evident that reported disability days increase considerably after age 64, increasing to 17 percent among those 65–74, and 24 percent among those aged 75 years and over. A higher proportion of females report disability in all age groups. The largest difference is in the age group 75 and over — 28 percent for females and only 18 percent for males.

The foregoing brief discussion of health status, points to a number of important facts. Being old and being sick are *not* synonymous. While some elders may experience impairment with advancing years, this is not the lot of everyone. Health seems to diminish with age, although there is much variability in degree of and susceptibility to poorer health. We have noted gender differences; there are also important differences by age, income, and other social variables. Let us now consider how elders use health care and how well their needs are being met by the formal system of care.

Health Care and Aging in Canada

"The elderly who receive medical care receive more of it than the young" (Barer et al. 1987, 858). This statement cogently summarizes the nature of health services utilization by elders. It suggests that elders with heightened medical needs may be

TABLE 10.6: Proportion of Population 15 Years of Age and Over by Disability-Days, by Age Group and Sex, Canada, 1985

	Both Sexes	Male	Female
All Age Groups	14	11	17
15–64	13	10	15
65–74	17	14	19
75 years and over	24	18	28

Note: Figures in this table combine bed-days and major activity-loss days to arrive at total disability-days.
Source: Calculated from Statistics Canada, *Health and Social Support, 1985*, Cat. no. 11-612, No. 1 (Ottawa: Minister of Supply and Services, 1987), Table 39, p. 134. Reproduced by authority of the Minister of Industry, 1994.

intensive users of medical care, but that elders as a group cannot be said to use the health care system disproportionately. Consider the following data.

According to an examination by Roos, Shapiro, and Roos of Manitoba health statistics (1984), persons 65 years and older (9 percent of the total population in 1977) consumed 43 percent of all acute hospital days. In 1978, these researchers found that elders consumed 36 percent of all short-stay hospital days. They went on to suggest that hospital use increases with age. For example, persons 85 years of age or older consume ten times more hospital days than those under 60, and those 70 to 85 years of age use three times as many hospital days as those under 60 (cf. Shapiro and Roos 1986; Shapiro and Tate 1985). In other words, a small segment of the elderly population, that is, those 85 years of age or older, accounts for a large proportion of utilization of the system.

Looking at the overall Canadian statistics, persons 65 and older had the highest rate of hospital separations in acute-care facilities and the highest number of days spent in hospital per separated case in 1981–82 to 1984–85 (Statistics Canada 1988, 3–23; 1990, 3–23). As well, the average length of stay increased with age in a linear fashion. Similar patterns are observed for hospitalizations involving surgery. The data also show that the rate of operated hospital cases increased with age, as did the number of hospital days per operated case. More recent data, 1986–87 to 1990–91, as reported in Table 10.7, basically support the conclusion that people 65 and older have the highest rate of hospital separations and the highest number of days spent in hospital. As well, the average length of stay increased with age, again in an almost linear fashion. Noticeably, the largest increase in average length of stay is for the age group 65 and over. Chappell, Strain, and Blandford (1986) indicate that hospitalization is more common in Canada than in the United States (cf. Garnick and Short 1985), and this is true with respect to the young and old alike.

It has been estimated (based on 1981 census data) that 7.5 percent of persons aged 65 and older and 35.6 percent of persons aged 85 and older reside in long-term care institutions (residential treatment centres, nursing homes, personal care homes, etc.) (Forbes, Jackson, and Kraus 1987). Studies suggest that there has been a steady increase in long-term institutionalization over the past several decades, particularly for the old.

These data simply confirm the observations that elders are more commonly hospitalized than other age groups, and that there is an institutional focus to medical care in this country. Chappell (1988) suggests that the very name *medi*care underscores the emphasis of Canada's health care system. It should not escape notice that relatively few elders are institutionalized. But this type of care is quite labour- and technology-intensive, owing to the nature of the chronic diseases and functional impairments that elders in such institutions suffer. Hospital care, whether for frail elders or others, is expensive, consuming approximately half of every health dollar in Canada (Chappell, Strain, and Blandford 1986; Evans 1984).

Whether elders are served best by acute-care or long-term care facilities is a separate issue. Sociologists have long decried the adverse consequences of institutional life, which include fostering "learned helplessness, "institutionalism," and so on. (cf. Goffman 1961; Gubrium 1975). Numerous critics have suggested that there are plenty of people in Canadian hospitals who don't belong there and that Canadians are kept in hospitals too long (Evans 1984). Can a system that stresses reactive,

TABLE 10.7: Separations and Days, Rates per 100 000 Population and Average Days per Separation and Selected Age Groups, 1986–87 to 1990–91

	15–24	25–34	35–44	45–54	55–64	65+
1986–87						
Separations No.						
Males	79 647	90 961	89 431	98 678	150 573	275 749
Females	230 985	400 622	166 245	112 094	125 303	279 774
Days in Hospital No.						
Males	576 915	673 913	720 132	969 143	1 733 713	4 703 211
Females	1 142 698	2 116 069	1 181 418	1 006 540	1 463 906	5 822 287
Average Days in Hospital						
Males	7.2	7.4	8.1	9.8	11.5	17.1
Females	4.9	5.3	7.1	9.0	11.7	20.8
Separations per 100 000						
Males	3 791	4 035	4 872	7 709	13 374	24 047
Females	11 311	17 546	9 057	8 796	10 409	17 666
Days per 100 000						
Males	27 459	29 983	39 227	75 714	153 985	410 152
Females	55 954	92 676	64 361	78 981	121 607	367 638
1987–88						
Separations No.						
Males	74 363	89 039	88 685	97 765	149 390	283 180
Females	216 401	396 524	164 771	110 389	124 054	285 070
Days in Hospital No.						
Males	526 442	664 718	719 285	903 582	1 701 156	4 832 825
Females	1 054 804	2 038 776	1 134 674	981 310	1 461 581	5 966 344
Average Days in Hospital						
Males	7.1	7.5	8.1	9.2	11.4	17.1
Females	4.9	5.1	6.9	8.9	11.8	20.9
Separations per 100 000						
Males	3 604	3 882	4 683	7 505	13 149	23 950
Females	10 847	17 095	8 675	8 490	10 286	17 400
Days per 100 000						
Males	25 513	28 980	37 979	69 362	149 736	408 730
Females	52 872	87 897	59 739	75 474	121 192	364 179
1988–89						
Separations No.						
Males	69 968	86 435	87 645	96 531	145 678	285 266
Females	206 108	397 236	163 558	107 178	119 253	286 307
Days in Hospital No.						
Males	498 563	642 757	720 125	887 867	1 624 024	4 766 210
Females	998 868	2 035 957	1 127 142	946 609	1 384 852	5 963 579

Continued

TABLE 10.7: Separations and Days, Rates per 100 000 Population and Average Days per Separation and Selected Age Groups, 1986–87 to 1990–91 — Continued

	15–24	25–34	35–44	45–54	55–64	65+
Average Days in Hospital						
Males	7.1	7.4	8.2	9.2	11.1	16.7
Females	4.8	5.1	6.9	8.8	11.6	20.8
Separations per 100 000						
Males	3 463	3 715	4 488	7 218	12 721	23 469
Females	10 593	16 903	8 323	8 016	9 876	16 949
Days per 100 000						
Males	24 679	27 624	36 875	66 393	141 811	392 119
Females	51 337	86 633	57 355	70 801	114 688	353 042
1989–90						
Separations No.						
Males	64 964	84 028	86 842	94 653	141 129	286 174
Females	200 102	404 039	161 681	103 904	113 465	287 249
Days in Hospital No.						
Males	459 182	636 128	681 694	883 177	1 584 512	4 747 804
Females	961 293	1 991 147	1 067 669	921 060	1 292 843	6 013 013
Average Days in Hospital						
Males	7.1	7.6	7.8	9.3	11.2	16.6
Females	4.8	4.9	6.6	8.9	11.4	20.9
Separations per 100 000						
Males	3 278	3 573	4 302	6 861	12 277	22 881
Females	10 513	17 039	7 933	7 529	9 412	16 490
Days per 100 000						
Males	23 169	27 049	33 772	64 022	137 844	379 612
Females	50 504	83 969	52 386	66 743	107 245	345 179
1990–91						
Separations No.						
Males	63 048	83 899	90 068	95 854	141 309	296 771
Females	195 662	407 792	167 517	106 543	113 241	296 846
Days in Hospital No.						
Males	452 335	618 118	740 044	883 013	1 543 237	4 866 665
Females	912 066	1 925 329	1 101 765	990 023	1 272 137	6 063 165
Average Days in Hospital						
Males	7.2	7.4	8.2	9.2	10.9	16.4
Females	4.7	4.7	6.6	9.3	11.2	20.4
Separations per 100 000						
Males	3 217	3 539	4 316	6 725	12 243	23 081
Females	10 429	17 115	7 927	7 469	9 386	16 533

Continued

TABLE 10.7: Separations and Days, Rates per 100 000 Population and Average Days per Separation and Selected Age Groups, 1986–87 to 1990–91 — Continued

	15–24	25–34	35–44	45–54	55–64	65+
Days per 100 000						
Males	23 081	26 077	35 463	61 948	133 706	378 492
Females	48 615	80 808	52 137	69 412	105 440	337 687

Sources: Statistics Canada, *Health Reports: Surgical Procedures and Treatments 1986–87*, Cat. no. 82-003S Suppl. no. 2, Vol. 2, No. 1 (Ottawa: Minister of Supply and Services Canada, 1990), Table 1, pp. 2–9; Statistics Canada, *Health Reports: Surgical Procedures and Treatments, 1987–88*, Cat. no. 82-003S, Suppl. no. 2, Vol. 2, No. 2 (Ottawa: Minister of Supply and Services, 1990, Table 1, pp. 2–9; Statistics Canada, *Health Reports: Surgical Procedures and Treatments, 1988–89*, Cat. no. 82-003S, Suppl. no. 2, Vol. 3, No. 1 (Ottawa: Minister of Supply and Services, 1991), Table 1, pp. 2–9; Statistics Canada, *Health Reports: Surgical Procedures and Treatments, 1989–90*, Cat. no. 82-003S, Suppl. no. 2, Vol. 4, No. 1, (Ottawa: Minister of Industry, Science and Technology, 1992), Table 1, pp. 2–9; Statistics Canada, *Surgical Procedures and Treatments, 1990–91*, Cat. no. 82-217 (Ottawa: Minister of Industry, Science and Technology, 1993), Table 1, pp. 2–9. Reproduced by authority of the Minister of Industry, 1994.

acute care adequately deal with individuals who suffer from chronic conditions, which require a more holistic, social, and health (as opposed to medical) focus?

Recently, attention has been focussed on elderly persons whose discharge from hospital is delayed, and who consequently block acute-care beds in general hospitals (Marshall 1987). It is routinely argued that "geriatric bed-blockers" are difficult to place in long-term care facilities, and that family members are reluctant to provide supportive services to frail elders about to be discharged. On closer inspection, however, Marshall suggests that the reimbursement system in Canada's medicare program promotes delayed discharges because it does not consider the level or severity of care. Hospitals are reimbursed for acute-care beds even if occupied by chronic-care patients. In a general hospital, a patient awaiting discharge is a relatively "cheap" patient, but in a long-term care facility, that same patient (who might require several hours of intensive nursing care) is an "expensive" patient. It requires no advanced degree in economics or managerial science to figure out why frail elders are occupying acute-care beds!

The reluctance of families to take their frail elderly relatives home probably has much to do with the negative connotations of nursing homes that have been cultivated over the past few decades. Forbes, Jackson, and Kraus (1987), among others, have suggested that the manner in which Canada's medicare program evolved may also help explain why an institutional focus remains and why families prefer hospital to nursing-home care. Hospital services, they point out, were insured first, only later to be followed by medical services and some community/home services.

What about other types of health services use? National data on ambulatory care are not readily available, but Manitoba data are instructive here. Roos, Shapiro, and Roos (1984) report that elders make more visits to physicians per annum than those in younger age groups, but not significantly more. In 1974–75, persons aged 65 years and older made, on average, 5.2 visits, while persons 45 to 64 made 4.3 visits and persons aged 25 to 44 made 3.5 visits. In any given year, about one-fifth of the population (elders included) never sees a physician (Roos, Shapiro, and Roos 1984).

It is difficult to make broad generalizations about ambulatory care, because the available statistics are limited, and generally do not distinguish patient-initiated from physician-initiated visits. Roos, Shapiro, and Roos (1984), McKinlay (1972), and Grant (1984) suggest that utilization is influenced by numerous factors, including the attributes of patients and physicians, and the settings in which medicine is practised. Keeping this in mind, Roos, Shapiro, and Roos note that "although the elderly initiate most ambulatory physician visits, the physician largely determines whether an individual will be admitted to a hospital" (1984, 35). Charges, then, that elders make disproportionate use of the health system should be tempered by some understanding of the reasons for various types of utilization, and the source of the decisions. Roos, Shapiro, and Roos suggest that "a preoccupation with the influence that increasing numbers of elderly will have on the health care system should not mask the potentially even greater impact that the increasing physician supply in North America is likely to have on health expenditures during the next decade" (35).

This latter point is significant because, in many ways, it hints that the elderly have become the scapegoats for the funding crisis in medicare today. The prospect of population aging sends chills down the spines of health ministers! Branch, Sager, and Meyers (1987) describe long-term care policy in the United States as being "mired in trench warfare" and population aging as a "demographic time bomb." Elders' omnipresence in long-term facilities, and their occupying an increasing number of beds in acute-care hospitals make them easy targets. More reasoned scrutiny of Canadian medicine and medicare would suggest that population aging is not so much the problem. How health and illness (of young and old alike) are currently dealt with by doctors and hospitals creates much of the crisis in health care. It is beyond the scope of this chapter to provide a detailed account of the failures of Canadian medicine and medicare, but a few examples that intimately touch the lives of many elders should suffice to illustrate the basic argument.

The use of pharmaceuticals in medical practice today is extensive. One American study estimated that in the United States elders use 25 percent of all prescription drugs (Basen 1977). More recently, German and Burton (1989) have reported that 75.2 percent of elders in the United States who visit physicians are issued at least one prescription, if not more. Cooperstock's research in Canada indicates that the likelihood of receiving prescription medications increases with age and that elderly women receive a disproportionate number of prescriptions each year, many of which are mood-altering or psychotropic medications (1971). Harding's Saskatchewan study (1986) found that although the elderly constitute only 16 percent of the population, they received 43 percent of all central-nervous-system drug prescriptions, and fully 19 percent of persons 60 years and older had at least one prescription (the most common drug being Valium or Diazepam).

Though typically viewed as a blessing, drugs or "magic bullets" can be a curse as well, particularly for elderly persons. According to Hoppel (1985), adverse drug reactions are more common among elders than other age groups, and may be a factor contributing to mental impairment and behavioural imbalances that precipitate hospitalization. Many elders take multiple prescriptions, and often combine the use of prescription and over-the-counter medications or alcohol (Pascarelli 1974). Such practices can lead to interactions that effectively neutralize the beneficial effects of some drugs, or, worse yet, can create adverse drug reactions that may lead to a number of deleterious health consequences or even drug dependency (Harding 1986).

Drug surveillance programs have been instituted in a number of cities, to aid elders and educate them about their use of medications. As important as these programs are, they are like "all the King's horses and all the King's men [who] couldn't put Humpty together again." There is no effort to stop the problem at its source (which is doctors' prescribing behaviour), revealing an undercurrent of "victim-blaming" in these programs as well. Moreover, these programs do not address the question of why drugs have become so pervasive in medical practice.

Some research on the doctor–patient relationship suggests that the brevity of their encounter may be a factor (Grant 1984). The average medical encounter lasts only between six and ten minutes (Balint and Norell 1973), and Keeler et al. found that the duration of medical encounters declined with the age of the patient (1982). The problem of ageism, mentioned earlier, may also lead to inappropriate prescribing (Butler 1969, 1980; Carson 1977; Rodin and Langer 1980) or differential treatment of elders as compared with younger patients (Linn and Linn 1982). Although attitudes toward aging and the aged have changed, long-held stereotypes and avoidance behaviours on the part of younger physicians remain problematic (cf. Haug and Ory 1987; Spence et al. 1968; Karasu et al. 1979; Cyrus-Lutz and Gaitz 1972; Ford and Sbordone 1980; Hickey et al. 1976; Ray et al. 1985).

The prescription pad is often used by doctors to terminate the encounter. Anecdotal information from medical practitioners suggests that some prescribe drugs because they think that patients want drugs (Grant 1984). The pharmaceutical companies, which aggressively market their products to doctors, cannot be ignored as a powerful influence on physicians' prescribing behaviour. It is estimated that approximately 20 percent of each company's manufacturing costs are spent on advertising of one sort or another ($209 million in total in Canada in 1983), and approximately 45 percent of all promotional activities involve sales representatives. This works out to costs in the neighbourhood of $5000 per physician per year (Lexchin 1988).

The widespread use of drugs in the doctor–patient relationship may also reflect the degree to which the medicalization of the human condition has taken hold in North American society (Zola 1986). Sandelowski offers this account:

> The presence of the prescription pad validates the physician's right and obligation to treat an ever-growing number of human concerns, and it also signifies that only he can give "health" to another person because only he can legally prescribe drugs.... Life itself is viewed as an illness requiring the skilful intervention of a physician.... It is the physician who has become the final arbiter as to when and how human beings will become well.... The physician has been instrumental in causing a "sickening" dependence upon drugs, especially among women (1981, 236).

Old age has been medicalized (Arluke and Peterson 1981), and women's bodies have similarly been a prime target of medicalization (Reissman 1983). Being old and female is a double whammy (Sontag 1972; Posner 1977; Chappell and Havens 1980; Dulude 1978). With a biomedical definition of a problem, it is not long before the technology of medicine will find an application!

Do the "magic bullets" work? Or do they simply exacerbate existing health and social problems for elders? Do they create new iatrogenic (physician- or treatment-induced) problems? What role do pharmaceuticals play in promoting, rather than preventing, disease and disabling conditions? What proportion of cases seen by physicians or admitted to hospitals are in some measure the by-product of therapeutic processes? These are questions for which there are no hard and fast answers, but they underscore some of the controversies and contradictions of modern medical practice, and suggest the need for reforms to the system so that the health needs of patients young and old, can be more readily accommodated.

Conclusions

At the outset of this essay, it was noted that aging is best viewed as a public issue rather than a private trouble. Routinely, the social nature of aging and the consequences of the aging process are forgotten or ignored. The experience of growing old is seen to be either a trial or just another stage of life. Either way, growing old in this society is viewed largely in individualistic terms.

In this chapter, we have considered some aspects of the health care system's response to the aging of Canadian society. It would seem that the medical profession and the institutions and policies making up Canada's health care system have a way to go before a correspondence evolves between patient needs and service provision.

The medical profession's treatment (some would say, mistreatment) of elders suggests that urgent reform is needed in the health delivery system. Medicine has a traditionally narrow scope and understanding of disease etiology. Consequently, diagnoses and interventions tend to be carried out at a highly reductionistic and individualistic (rather than social) level. Therapeutic practice is heavily weighted toward hospital-based, technology-intensive medical care. And pharmaceuticals are often given to elders. These drugs may simply mask symptoms, without addressing the underlying cause of disease among the elders.

Indeed, many of the problems of elders are not amenable to traditional forms of medical treatment. Studies of community care reveal that medical solutions are not necessarily indicated for problems that are social in origin (Chappell, Strain, and Blandford 1986). In other words, health and social services are increasingly needed where medicine has been used in the past.

The changing epidemiological picture—from infectious to chronic diseases—demands a preventive, rather than reactive, approach to care. While there is some optimism that medicine is integrating a more preventive focus into medical training and into its practice, this development has yet to be seen in the forms of treatment used.

Although this chapter has touched on only a few issues, the conclusion that seems inevitable is that the current structure of health care in Canada is not yet fully prepared to meet the health needs of its elderly population. Barer et al. suggest that a "sham" policy debate is presently underway (1987). They note that policy discussions have focussed primarily on the growing numbers of elders, their increasing levels of morbidity, and the utilization of health resources that accompanies this morbidity. These discussions are used to garner additional resources for the system. Upon closer scrutiny, however, the *real* problem is seen to be the manner in which resources are allocated (or, more likely, misallocated) within the system, and that "hordes" of old people are about to descend upon us, or that they will be sicker and thus use more health services.[9] Barer et al. put it this way: "There is clearly a vested interest on the part of system providers to couch the debate in terms that will imply the need for increased funds for existing services, or to portray the solutions as health care rather than social support, tax or other system initiatives" (1987, 860).

It is indisputable that something must be done, because our aging society has already offered the health delivery system challenges to which it has not always been able to respond well. Throwing more money at the system is not necessarily a solution; at best, it would provide only momentary relief. Redirecting funds to make non-institutional, community-based services more readily available should be seriously evaluated, and where efficacious, these services should be integrated into a more socially oriented health care system. We would also do well to insist upon reforms that challenge some fundamental beliefs and values that we have about health care, about the role of the profession of medicine within the health delivery system, and about aging. To do otherwise is to become a part of the problem, rather than the solution.

Study Questions

1. What are the experiences of other countries (or the ten provinces) with respect to population aging and the health system's response to this demographic shift? What, if anything, can we learn from international policies concerning the aged and health care?

2. Are the health needs of elders being met by the current structure of health care in Canada? If not, why not?

3. Suppose that you were in an advisory position in the Department of National Health and Welfare (or the provincial ministry). What policy recommendations would you make to ameliorate some of the problems noted with respect to aging and health care?

4. What are the reasons for the institutional focus of health care in Canada? What non-institutional alternatives are there, and how can these be integrated into the health delivery system?

Recommended Reading

Chappell, N.L., L.A. Strain, and A.A. Blandford. *Aging and Health Care: A Social Perspective*. Toronto: Holt, Rinehart and Winston, 1986.

Marshall, V.W., ed. *Aging in Canada: Social Perspectives*. 2d ed. Toronto: Fitzhenry and Whiteside, 1987.

McPherson, B., *Aging as a Social Process: An Introduction to Individual and Population Aging*. 2d ed. Toronto: Butterworths, 1990.

Novak, M. *Aging and Society: A Canadian Perspective*. 2d ed. Toronto: Nelson, 1993.

Notes

1. The age-dependency ratio is the ratio of persons 65 years and older to those in the labour force.
2. According to the United Nations, a population is considered "aged" when persons 65 years and older constitute more than 7 percent of the population (McDaniel 1986). On the basis of this index, Canada is considered an aged nation.
3. A population pyramid is a graphical depiction of the population of any country. It shows the age and gender structure of a population, with two sets of bar graphs laid back to back.
4. Some of the common myths about aging: (1) that elders are unhappy, lonely, and live in isolation; (2) that elders are, by definition, sick; (3) that elders are traumatized by retirement and the loss of economic, social, and familial roles; (4) that elders' interest in sexual activity declines with their age—indeed, elders are sexless; (5) that elders are set in their ways; (6) that elders are doomed to senility. These are just a few (Chappell, Strain, and Blandford 1986).
5. According to Waitzkin, reformist reforms provide small material improvements while leaving intact overall political and economic structures; in other words, reformist reforms help preserve the system. By contrast, non-reformist (revolutionary) reforms achieve long-term changes in the structure of power and finance; they do not merely modify material conditions. Revolutionary reforms expose and highlight structural inequities (Waitzkin 1983).
6. Extra-billing was banned in the Canada Health Act of 1984. It became illegal to charge patients fees over and above those negotiated between provincial medical societies and the governments. The federal government stipulated that any provinces permitting doctors to extra-bill would lose federal money for health care, equivalent to the amount that doctors extra-billed their patients. The issue of extra-billing became extremely intense in 1986 in Ontario, where the practice was widespread. The provincial government introduced legislation banning extra-billing, which led physicians to strike, claiming that the government had intruded in their relations with patients to a degree that threatened their autonomy. Amid public criticism, and in the realization that this was a battle that could not be won, the physicians returned to work after a three-week walkout.
7. The mental health of elders is not considered in this discussion.
8. A word of caution is needed with respect to the Canada Health Survey data, and other studies involving self-reported information. There is the possibility that morbidity data based solely on self-reports may be unreliable, particularly if this type of data is not validated through, for example, some objective form of measurement. In addition, many studies (including the Canada Health Survey) use one person in a household to report on the health of the entire unit, and commonly this is the woman of the house. Research tells us that when one reports on oneself there is greater accuracy than when one reports on others. Consequently, it is possible that proxy reports may either inflate or deflate (depending on who the reporter is) estimates on measures of sickness and wellbeing. These methodological considerations should be kept in mind when examining the data presented in Table 10.6.
9. The linkage between morbidity and utilization is a somewhat tenuous one at best. Medical sociologists have struggled with the fact that people who need medical care do not always avail

themselves of it, even when economic and other barriers have been removed (e.g., Becker 1974). By the same token. many people frequent doctors and hospitals with dubious complaints.

References

Arluke, A., and J. Peterson. 1981. "Accidental Medicalization of Old Age and its Social Control Implication." In *Dimensions: Aging, Culture and Health*, ed. C.L. Fry. New York: Praeger. 271–84.

Balint, E., and J.S. Norell. 1973. *Six Minutes for the Patient: Interactions in General Practice Consultation*. London: Tavistock.

Barber, J. 1989. "Sick to Death." *Maclean's*, February 13: 32–35.

Barer, M.L., R.G. Evans, C. Hertzman, and J. Lomas. 1987. "Aging and Health Care Utilization: New Evidence on Old Fallacies." *Social Science and Medicine* 24: 851–62.

Basen, M.A. 1977. "Elderly and Drugs: Problem Overview and Program Strategy." *Public Health Reports* 92: 43–48.

Beck, R.G. 1973. "Economic Class and Access to Physician Services Under Public Medical Care Insurance." *International Journal of Health Services* 3: 341–55.

———. 1974. "The Effects of Co-payments on the Poor." *Journal of Human Resources* 9: 129–42.

Becker, M.H., ed. 1974. *The Health Relief Model and Personal Health Behavior.* Thorofare, NJ: Charles B. Slack.

Branch, L.G., A. Sager, and A.R. Meyers. 1987. "Long-Term Care in the United States: A Study in Trench Warfare." In *Health in Aging: Sociological Issues and Policy Directions*, ed. R.A. Ward and S.S. Tobin. New York: Springer. 215–32.

Brody, J.A. 1989. "Toward Quantifying the Health of the Elderly." *American Journal of Public Health* 79: 685–86.

Brody, J.A., D.B. Brook, and T.F. Williams. 1987. "Trends in the Health of the Elderly Population." *Annual Review of Public Health* 8: 211–34.

Butler, R.N. 1969. "Ageism: Another Form of Bigotry." *The Gerontologist* 9: 243–46.

———. 1980. "Ageism: A Foreword." *Journal of Social Issues* 36: 8–11.

Carson, R.A. 1977. "Stereotyping, Segregating and Stigmatizing the Old." In *Social Issues in Health Care*, ed. D.J. Self. Norfolk, VA: Teagle and Little. 52–63.

Centre on Aging. 1985. *The Provincial Fact Book on Aging: Manitoba: Fiction, Fact, and the Future.* Prepared for the Fourth Manitoba Conference on Aging, Winnipeg, MA, May.

Chappell, N.L. 1987. "The Interface Among Three Systems of Care: Self, Informal and Formal." In *Health in Aging: Sociological Issues and Policy Directions*, ed. R.A. Ward and S.S. Tobin. New York: Springer. 159–79.

———. 1988. "Long-Term Care in Canada." In *North American Elders: United States and Canadian Perspectives*, ed. E. Rathbone-McCuan and B. Havens. New York: Greenwood Press. 73–88.

Chappell, N.L., and B. Havens. 1980. "Old and Female: Testing the Double Jeopardy Hypothesis." *Sociological Quarterly* 21: 157–71.

Chappell, N.L., L.A. Strain, and A.A. Blandford. 1986. *Aging and Health Care: A Social Perspective.* Toronto: Holt, Rinehart and Winston.

Cooperstock, R. 1971. "Sex Differences in the Use of Mood-Modifying Drugs: An Exploratory Model." *Journal of Health and Social Behavior* 12: 238.

Cyrus-Lutz, C., and C.M. Gaitz. 1972. "Psychiatrists' Attitudes Toward the Aged and Aging." *The Gerontologist* 12: 163–67.

Dorney, R.P. 1983. "Old Age and Long-Term Care in the U.S.A." Critical essay. Boston University.

Dulude, L. 1978. *Women and Aging: A Report on the Rest of their Lives.* Ottawa: Canadian Advisory on the Status of Women.

Estes, C.L., L.E. Gerard, and A. Clarke. 1984. "Women and the Economics of Aging." *International Journal of Health Services* 14: 55–68.

Evans, R.G. 1984. *Strained Mercy: The Economics of Canadian Health Care.* Toronto: Butterworths.

Forbes, W.F., J.A. Jackson, and A.S. Kraus. 1987. *Institutionalization of the Elderly in Canada.* Toronto: Butterworths.

Ford, C.V., and R.J. Sbordone. 1980. "Attitudes of Psychiatrists Toward Elderly Patients." *American Journal of Psychiatry* 137: 571–75.

Garnick, D.W., and T. Short. 1985. *Utilization of Hospital Inpatient Services by Elderly Americans*. Hospital Studies Program, Hospital Cost Utilization Project Research Note 6. Washington, DC: U.S. Department of Health and Human Services.

German, P.S., and L.C. Burton. 1989. "Medication and the Elderly: Issues of Prescription and Use." *Journal of Aging and Health* 1: 4–34.

Goffman, E. 1961. *Asylums*. New York: Anchor Books.

Grant, K.R. 1984. "Critical Essay: Clinical Decision-Making as Social Triage: The Influence of Non-Biomedical Factors on Physician Behavior." Manuscript.

———. 1988. "The Inverse Care Law in Canada: Differential Access Under Universal Free Health Insurance." In *Sociology of Health Care in Canada*, ed. B.S. Bolaria and H.D. Dickinson. Toronto: Harcourt Brace Jovanovich. 118–34.

———. 1989. "Gender, Lifestyle, and Health: An Examination of the Canada Health Survey." Dissertation. Boston University.

Gubrium, J. 1975. *Living and Dying in Murray Manor*. New York: St. Martin's Press.

Guralnik, J.M., and G.A. Kaplan. 1989. "Predictors of Healthy Aging: Prospective Evidence from the Alameda County Study." *American Journal of Public Health* 79: 703–708.

Harding, J. 1986. "Mood-Modifiers and Elderly Women in Canada: Medicalization of Poverty." In *Adverse Effects: Women and the Pharmaceutical Industry*, ed. K. McDonnell. Toronto: Women's Press. 51–86.

Hatcher, G.H. 1981. *Universal Free Health Care in Canada.* 1947–1977. Washington, DC: US Department and Human Services.

Haug, M.R., and M.G. Ory. 1987. "Issues in Elderly Patient-Provider Interactions." *Research on Aging* 9:3–44.

Hickey, R., W. Rakowski, D.F. Hultsch, and B.J. Fatula. 1976. "Attitudes Toward Aging as a Function of In-Service Training and Practitioner Age." *Journal of Gerontology* 31: 681–86.

Hoppel, C.L. 1985. "The Uses and Misuses of Pharmacology." In *The Physical and Mental Health of Aged Women*, ed. M.R. Haug, A.B. Ford, and M. Sheafor. New York: Springer. 207–16.

Institute for Philosophy and Public Policy. 1988. "The Graying of America." *Report of the Institute for Philosophy and Public Policy* 8: 1–5.

Karasu, T.B., S.P. Stein, and E.S. Charles. 1979. "Age Factors in Patient-Therapist Relationship." *Journal of Nervous and Mental Disease* 167: 100–104.

Keeler, E.B., D.H. Solomon, J.C. Beck, R.C. Mendenhall, and R.L. Kane. 1982. "Effect of Patient Age on Duration of Medical Encounters." *Medical Care* 20: 1101–1108.

Lexchin, J. 1988. "Profits First: The Pharmaceutical Industry in Canada." In *Sociology of Health Care in Canada*, ed. B.S. Bolaria and H.D. Dickinson. Toronto: Harcourt Brace Jovanovich. 497–513.

Linn, B.S., and M.W. Linn. 1982. "Patient Symptoms and Physician Prescribing Patterns in the Elderly." *Social Science and Medicine* 16: 1531–38.

Longino, C.F. Jr., and B.J. Soldo. 1987. "The Graying of America: Implications of Life Extension for Quality of Life." In *Health in Aging: Sociological Issues and Policy Directions*, ed. R.A. Ward and S.S. Tobin. New York: Springer. 58–85.

Macintyre, S. 1977. "Old Age as a Social Problem: Historical Notes on the English Experience." In *Health Care and Health Knowledge*, ed. R. Dingwall, C. Heath, M. Reid, and M. Stacey. London: Croom Helm. 41–63.

Marshall, V.M. 1987. "Older Patients in Acute-Care Hospital Setting." In *Health in Aging: Sociological Issues and Policy Directions*, ed. R.A. Ward and S.S. Tobin. New York: Springer. 194–208.

Martin Matthews, A. 1987. "Widowhood as an Expectable Life Event." In *Aging in Canada: Social Perspectives*, 2d ed. ed. V.M. Marshall. Toronto: Fitzhenry and Whiteside. 343–66

McDaniel, S.A. 1986. *Canada's Aging Population*. Toronto: Butterworths.

McKeown, T. 1979. *The Role of Medicine: Dream, Mirage, or Nemesis?* Oxford: Basil Blackwell.

McKinlay, J.B. 1972. "Some Approaches and Problems in the Study of the Use of Services: An Overview." *Journal of Health and Social Behavior* 13: 115.

McKinlay, J.B., S.M. McKinlay, S.E. Jennings, and K.R. Grant. 1983. "Mortality, Morbidity, and the Inverse Care Law." In *Cities and Sickness: Health Care in Urban America*, ed. A.L. Greer and S. Greer. Beverly Hills, CA: Sage. 99–138.

Mills, C.W. 1959. *The Sociological Imagination*. New York: Oxford University Press.

National Council of Welfare 1990. (Summer) *Women and Poverty Revisited.* Ottawa: Supply and Services Canada.

National Council of Welfare. 1984. *Sixty-Five and Older: A Report of the National Council of Welfare on the Incomes of the Aged.* Ottawa: Minister of Supply and Services.

Nett, E.M., ed. 1982. "Women as Elders." *Resources for Feminist Research* 11 (Special issue).

Novak, M. 1988. *Aging and Society: A Canadian Perspective*. Toronto: Nelson.

Pascarelli, E.F. 1974. "Drug Dependence: An Age-Old Problem Compounded by Old Age." *Geriatrics* 29: 109–15.

Posner, J. 1977. "Old and Female: The Double Whammy." *Essence* 2: 41–48.

Ray, D.C., M.A. Raciti, and C.V. Ford. 1985. "Ageism in Psychiatrists: Associations with Gender, Certification, and Theoretical Orientation." *The Gerontologist* 25: 496–500.

Reinharz, S. 1986. "Friends or Foes: Gerontological and Feminist Theory." *Women's Studies International Forum* 9: 503–14.

Reissman, C.K. 1983. "Women and Medicalization: A New Perspective." *Social Policy* 14: 3–18.

Rodin, J., and E. Langer. 1980. "Aging Labels: The Decline of Control and the Fall of Self-Esteem." *Journal of Social Issues* 36: 12–29.

Roos, N.P., E. Shapiro, and L.L. Roos. 1984. "Aging and the Demand for Health Services." *The Gerontologist* 24: 31–36.

Russell, C. 1987. "Ageing as a Feminist Issue." *Women's Studies International Forum* 10: 125–32.

Sandelowski, M. 1981. *Women, Health, and Choice*. Englewood Cliffs, NJ: Prentice-Hall.

Sarton, M. 1973. *As We Are Now*. New York: W.W. Norton.

Schwenger, C.W. 1987. "Formal Health Care for the Elderly in Canada." In *Aging in Canada: Social Perspectives*, 2d ed., ed. V.M. Marshall. Toronto: Fitzhenry and Whiteside. 505–19.

Shapiro, E., and N.P. Roos. 1986. "High Users of Hospital Days." *Canadian Journal on Aging* 5: 165–74.

Shapiro, E., and R.B. Tate. 1985. "Predictors of Long-Term Care Facility Use among the Elderly." *Canadian Journal an Aging* 4: 11–19.

Sontag, S. 1972. "The Double Standard of Aging." *Saturday Review* 55: 29–38.

Spence, D.L., E.M. Feigenbaum, F. Fitzgerald, and J. Roth. 1968. "Medical Student Attitudes Toward the Geriatric Patient." *Journal of the American Geriatrics Society* 16: 976–83.

Statistics Canada. 1981. *The Health of Canadians: Report of the Canada Health Survey*. Ottawa: Ministry of Supply and Services.

———. 1986. Age, Sex, and Marital Status (Cat. 93-101-1986). Ottawa: Minister of Supply and Services. Table 1–13.

———. 1987. *Fact Book on Aging*. Ottawa: Minister of Supply and Services.

———. 1987. *Health and Social Support, 1985.* (Cat. 11-612). no. 1. Ottawa: Minister of Supply and Services.

———. 1988. *Canada Year Book 1988.* Ottawa: Minister of Supply and Services.

———. 1990. *Canada Year Book 1990.* Ottawa: Minister of Supply and Services.

Stone, L.O. and S. Fletcher. 1986. *The Seniors Boom: Dramatic Increases in Longevity and Prospects for Better Health.* Ottawa: Minister of Supply and Services.

———. 1988. "Demographic Variations in North America." In *North American Elders: United States and Canadian Perspectives*, ed. E. Rathbone-McCuan and B. Havens. New York: Greenwood Press. 9–36.

Swartz, D. 1987. "Conflict and Accommodation in Canadian Health Policy." In *Health and Canadian Society,*, 2d ed., ed. D. Coburn, C. D'Arcy, G.M. Torrance, and P. New. Toronto: Fitzhenry and Whiteside. 568–89.

Torrance, G.M. 1981. "Socio-Historical Overview: The Development of the Canadian Health System." In *Health and Canadian Society*, ed. D. Coburn, C. D'Arcy, P. New, and G.M. Torrance. Toronto: Fitzhenry and Whiteside. 9–28.

Tudor Hart, J. 1971. "The Inverse Care Law." *The Lancet* 1: 405–12.

Urquhart, M.C., and K.A.H. Buckley. 1983. *Historical Statistics of Canada.* 2d ed. Ottawa: Statistics Canada.

Verbrugge, L.M. 1985. "An Epidemiological Profile of Older Women." In *The Physical and Mental Health of Aged Women*, ed. M.R. Haug and A.B. Ford. New York: Springer. 41–64.

———. 1986. "From Sneezes to Adieux: Stages of Health for American Men and Women." *Social Science and Medicine* 22: 1195–1212.

Waitzkin, H. 1983. *The Second Sickness: Contradictions of Capitalist Health Care*. New York: Free Press.

Waldron, I. 1976. "Why Do Women Live Longer Than Men?" *Social Science and Medicine* 10: 349–62.

Wingard, D.L. 1984. "The Sex Differential in Morbidity, Mortality and Lifestyle." *Annual Review of Public Health* 5: 433–58.

Znaniecka Lopata, H., ed. 1987. *North America*. Vol. 2 of *Widows*. Durham: Duke University Press.

Zola, I.K. 1986. "Medicine as an Institution of Social Control." In *Sociology of Health and Illness: Critical Perspectives*, 2d ed., ed. P. Conrad and R. Kern. New York: St. Martin's Press. 379–90.

CHAPTER 11

Industrial Development and Environmental Integrity: Contradiction or Co-existence

Michael Clow and Lawrence Felt

Learning Objectives

This chapter focusses on the magnitude and seriousness of damage to the ecosystem and discusses the framework for the evaluation of competing assessments of this damage. It is argued that the twin themes of insatiable human needs and never-ending economic growth, which have simultaneously driven and justified economic activity in the past, are no longer sustainable. The reality of ecological constraints requires that we shape future human activities in ways to prevent further environmental damage. Students are encouraged to consider the contradictions between unbridled growth and our survival, and the fundamental changes that might be required of our cultural values, ethical standards, and the ways human societies are organized to protect the ecosystem.

Introduction

Increasingly persuasive evidence shows that humans may well be on the way to making the earth unfit for their continued existence (Mungall and McLaren 1991). Despite unparalleled industrial expansion, the most palpable lesson of the late twentieth century is that humans are but *one* among *many* living species that must co-exist within the natural boundaries of a complex life-support system composed of air, water, and a thin layer of soil (Wagner 1974). The combination of this life-support system and the complexes of living organisms living in some degree of interdependence is termed an *ecosystem*.

The failure to properly consider this ecosystem has led to a scale and rate of environmental damage unprecedented in human history (Gould 1993). Does this mean that continued pursuit of industrial development and our survival are incompatible? If fundamental changes are required in the ways human societies are organized, what are they? Are new cultural values and ethical standards needed? We shall attempt to answer these questions by focussing on four issues: 1) the magnitude of environmental damage; 2) various assessments concerning its seriousness and ease of repair; 3) strategies for evaluating competing assessments; and 4) some implications should we need to redirect human activity to avoid unimpeded industrial expansion and economic growth.

The Extent of Environmental Damage

For most of our fifty-odd thousand years on this planet, humans have shaped and reshaped their physical environment to meet real or perceived needs. Earliest humans set forest fires to clear land, built weirs to harvest fish, and diverted waterways for irrigation. While most, if not all, such actions inflicted damage upon the environment, effects tended to be localized because of the relatively small numbers of humans living in dispersed settlements, the primitive technology utilized, and the frequent presence of cultural values emphasizing interdependence between humans and their environment.

In the past 200 years, and most importantly during the past 60 years, the situation has changed dramatically. The harnessing of science and technology in the name of industrial development has brought hitherto unimaginable material prosperity to a minority of the world's population. Increasingly, however, we have come to recognize the horrendous price being exacted in environmental and human terms for this prosperity. Deadly pollutants in our waterways, the thinning of the ozone layer, cities choked with smog, the ravaging of non-renewable resources to fuel an apparently insatiable demand, the plundering of other living creatures without regard to consequences—these are all increasingly characteristic of human life on earth (Allen 1994). The rise of global corporations and the drastically increased scale of economic integration has meant that no place or creature remains immune to environmental damage[1] or plunder. Indeed, some informed commentators, such as Dr. David Suzuki, have warned that humans have perhaps ten years to save the earth from becoming unfit for themselves and their offspring.

The magnitude of degradation is truly staggering. Consider the thin layer of atmosphere that surrounds earth. It consists of oxygen, a protective layer of ozone, as well as major concentrations of carbon dioxide and water vapour. The atmosphere plays a critical role in sustaining life by promoting photosynthesis and maintaining temperature so that water remains liquid. Natural changes have occurred within the atmosphere over the centuries, but, nonetheless, this delicate life-maintaining balance has managed to remain within limits that allow life to thrive.[2] That humans pollute the air they breathe is certainly not news. Intensive burning to clear or replenish agricultural land, smelting operations to create metals, and the use of hydrocarbon-based materials (wood, coal, and petrochemicals) all emit potentially damaging by-products into the air. Incidents of localized air pollution go back at least to the very first cities (World Meteorological Association 1989).

Increasingly, however, the damage is global as population increases dramatically and industrialized activities penetrate to more-remote regions. Clearly the atmosphere is not a limitless ocean of gas into which we can endlessly spew our refuse. Changes in the abundance of carbon indicates some of the deleterious change. A by-product of combustion and a critical component in the gas carbon dioxide, carbon is appearing in the atmosphere in excessive amounts, contributing to the greenhouse effect of increased global warming.[3] In the last ninety years, amounts of carbon as well as carbon dioxide have risen to levels above 300 parts per million volume. Such amounts are unprecedented in scientific data going back 100 000 years.

These increases have largely resulted from cutting down forests, which absorb carbon dioxide and release oxygen; tilling lands, and burning fossil (hydrocarbon-based) fuels. Other harmful by-products have also resulted from these activities, including acid rain, airborne toxic chemicals, and artificially produced chlorofluorocarbons (CFCs).

Damage to our water and land has been equally dramatic. Vast as the earth's oceans appear, their use as a dump for sewage and toxins has now come to have

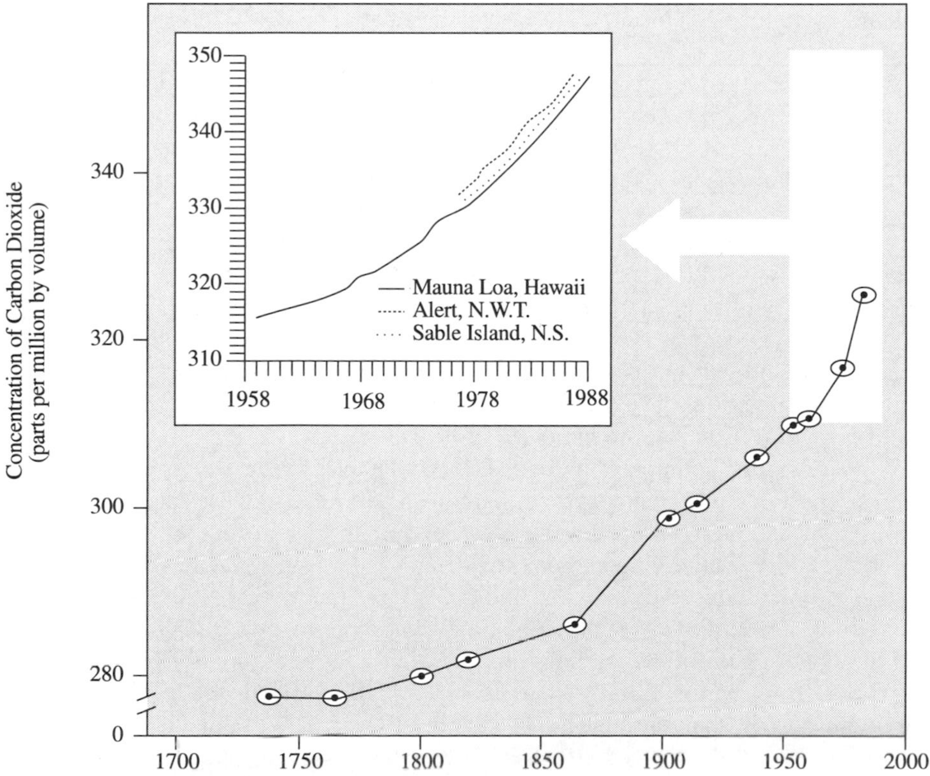

FIGURE 11.1: Concentration of Carbon Dioxide

Source: Atmospheric Environment Service Canada, Canadian Baseline Program.

significant effects. As a result, their capacity to neutralize toxins as well as produce living organisms—from the smallest phytoplankton necessary for photosynthesis to larger animals harvested for human consumption—is diminishing. A tragic example of the latter are the Beluga whales of the lower St. Lawrence estuary. Once abundant, these animals are now ailing—both individually and as a species—as a result of chemical toxins escaping from plants far upriver. Recently, they were added to Canada's list of endangered species.

Fresh water fares no better. Many, if not most, of the largest lakes and rivers suffer from various forms of damage. In many parts of the world, supplies of unpolluted fresh water are becoming increasingly scarce (Keating 1986). In some instances, fresh water is present but is too polluted for human consumption. In other situations, overuse has lowered the water table with resulting drought. Even supplies of water deep in the earth, termed aquifers, are becoming contaminated. Nor is this a phenomenon only of western industrial, urban societies. Even in remote northern Thailand, water is becoming a scarce commodity. Water supplies there have decreased by 50 percent in the last 30 years (*Globe and Mail*, February 15, 1994; A11). The flow of the Ping River, the major river in northern Thailand, has decreased by over 40 percent as a result of forestry activities. Forest cover is necessary for retaining rainfall and releasing it slowly throughout the year. Foreign demand for lumber has meant that nearly half of the Thai forests have been chopped down in the past 30 years.

As indicated above, terrestrial damage has also accelerated substantially. In the last 10 000 years, approximately one-third of the earth's forests have been removed, most during the past 80 years. As you read this, large portions of the tropical rain forests of South America and Southeast Asia are being removed to promote highly mechanized, large-scale farming or livestock grazing. Given the shallowness and generally low nutrient levels associated with rain-forest soil, subsequent agricultural use is typically of fairly short duration and the possibility of rain-forest regeneration negligible. If current rates of deforestation continue, much of the Amazonian rain forests will be gone by the year 2000. The conflict between preservation and cutting of forests is occurring throughout the world. In Canada, pitched confrontations have recently occurred in British Columbia over the removal of old-growth forests that are hundreds of years old.

Why are forests so important? Forests might be termed the "lungs of the world" because the trees and plants take in carbon dioxide and release oxygen through photosynthesis. Forests are the world's greatest engine for storing the sun's energy, which they do by converting carbon dioxide and water into living tissue. In a single day, a lone deciduous tree can pump and transpire as much as 20 000 litres of water, converting carbon dioxide at the same time. By doing this, trees play an important role in regulating the global carbon-dioxide balance. In addition, trees filter various pollutants from the air. Finally, dense forests, particularly in the tropics, play an important part in maintaining global genetic diversity. Without the dense forest mantle, much of the animal life we know cannot survive and would not have evolved (Mungall and Mclaren 1991, 171).

Our damage to the earth's environment is not just physical. Some creatures are depleted inadvertently as habitat is destroyed, while others feel the effects of individual pursuit. Humans, the ultimate predators, secure much of their food through various forms of hunting. Increasingly, we have turned to the oceans as our last hunting frontier. Despite their vastness, the effects of human predation are abundantly clear there as well. The populations, and hence the harvests, of many marine animals, particularly fish, have begun to decline. In eastern Canada, two recent scientific assessments (International Committee on Northwest Atlantic Fisheries [ICNAF] 1992; Alverson 1991) indicate that stocks of northern codfish (*Gadus atlantica*) have plummeted to their lowest levels in history, necessitating a complete fishery closure and displacing over 30 thousand fishers and plant workers. So low is the spawning biomass (number of fish of spawning age) that some doubt whether recovery is even possible. Similar stories can be told of other times and places. So efficient have modern, technologically sophisticated fishing boats become that fish no longer have any sanctuary (McGoodwin 1990).

Human health has not escaped the effects of environmental degradation. Whether through the air we breathe, the water we drink, the food we eat or the job at which we work, the human cost of environmental damage is substantial and increasing. Be it Minimata disease from ingesting mercury-contaminated fish or radiation contamination from drinking milk produced by cows downwind of airborne radio-ac-

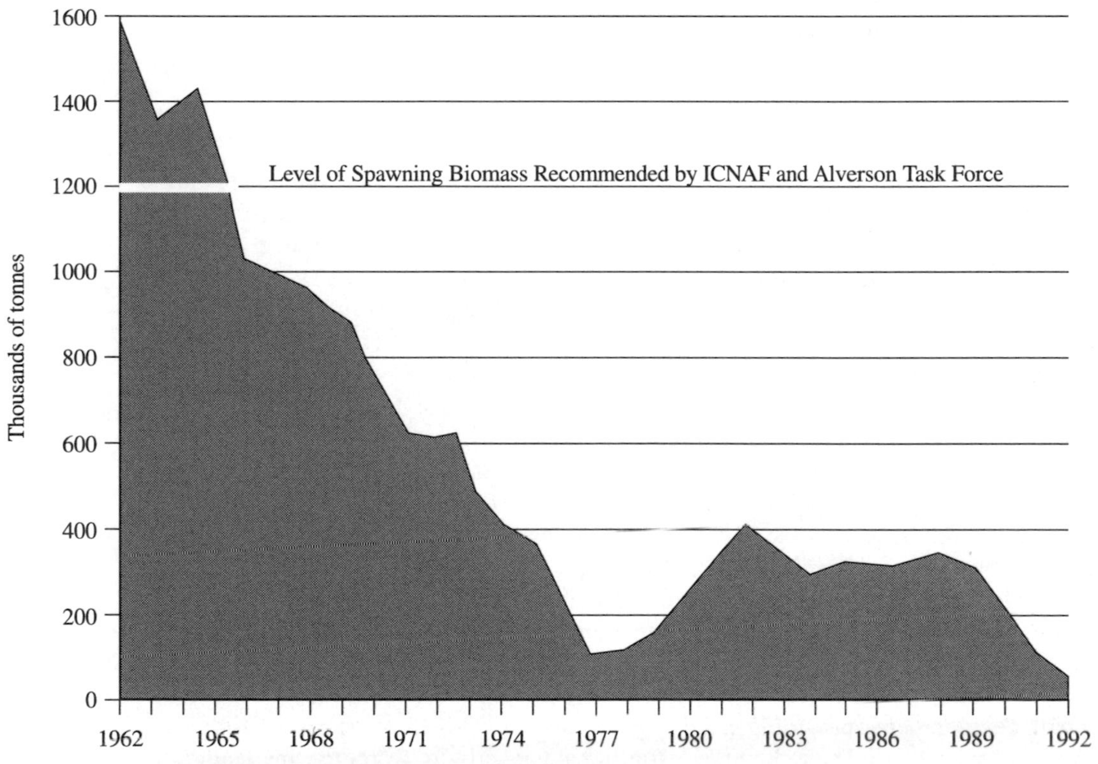

FIGURE 11.2: Northern Cod Spawning Biomass, 1962–1992
Age 7 and Over

Source: Fisheries and Oceans Canada.

tive pollution, illness and death represent and increasingly serious problem. For large numbers of workers, the effects of various pollutants routinely produced in the workplace is more direct (Bolaria 1991). Asbestos, coal, and uranium, as well as hundreds of chemicals, are known to cause serious, often life-threatening illnesses with new linkages occurring continuously as the period of exposure increases. In light of such a litany of damage to humans and the environment, one is well advised to consider the future course of industrial development.

Is Global Industrialization Sustainable?

This question is largely rhetorical since little persuasive evidence doesn't suggest that we *must* change current economic activities to reduce, if not eliminate, environmental damage. The more germane questions are what amount of reduction is required and how might it be accomplished? Three alternative perspectives attempt to answer these questions. They vary considerably in their assessment of the seriousness of environmental damage and the social reorganization necessary to deal with it. The three are popularly known as the classical liberal, limits to growth, and environmental management perspectives.

Classical Liberal Perspective

The classical liberal view minimizes the seriousness of environmental damage and suggests that technological "fixes" are possible to remedy the worst manifestations of damage. In this view, the natural environment is both passive and forgiving; it provides a cornucopia of resources for human advancement[4] (Evernden 1985; 1992). This perspective provided the ideological justification for early industrialization in the nineteenth century, though it is still very much in vogue. It considers damage to habitat, atmosphere, oceans, and soil to be localized and therefore of no general concern to human society at large. Nature is an external storehouse of resources, natural forces, and "lower" living organisms to be channelled and reshaped through science and technology for humankind's continuous and unlimited economic growth and development. The pursuit of economic growth is equated with moral progress, and elements of the environment are considered but cheap factors of production or repositories of waste products.

Within this perspective, modernization and development are central concepts of social change both in the developed West and in the developing world. Modern industrial societies represent the apex of human potential and offer the highest quality of life for its citizens. As such they represent the culmination of human social development, providing a beacon for less-developed societies to follow. Modern societies are marked by the institutional capacity to overcome any technological or organizational limitations to economic expansion and increasing affluence. Educational institutions, the division of labour in society, and the very organization of firms, government policy, city planning, and indeed all our societal arrangements, are seen as the means to material progress.

Although best known for his biting criticism of the contradictions within capitalist economic development, Karl Marx shared much of this classical liberal view insofar as the environment and environmental damage was concerned. He was in wholehearted agreement with capitalist thinkers on the central importance of human progress. Marx openly identified both increasing abundance and power to appropriate the natural environment as the natural goal of humanity and the key to continuing general human improvement (Marx 1973, 409).

Marx viewed the process of capitalist industrialization as a special breakthrough in the history of human development because it created unprecedented expansion of the productive capacity of people and transformed our relationship with the natural world. The great civilizing influence of capital was its capacity to end material scarcity and to make abundance possible. Marx predicted that, following the socialist revolution and the elimination of class conflict, the resulting society would be able to speed up technological innovation and economic expansion for the benefit of all.

Limits to Growth Perspective

The classical liberal view of human dominance and its general optimism about the future has been severely challenged in recent years. The most radical challenge has been labelled the limits to growth perspective after the famous study at the Massachusetts Institute of Technology that gave currency to its basic premise (Meadows et al. 1972). This perspective argues the existence of clear ecological limits to the scale and kind of economic activity in which humans can engage. The argument is predicated on an analysis of the consequences of human activity on the earth's biosphere.

To understand the complex relationship between human activity (particular industrial activity) and the natural environment, we must move beyond the isolated, necessarily fragmented understanding embodied in the theories of physics, chemistry, biology, and geology. We must aim, instead, for a more holistic understanding of life based on a complex network of living plant and animal communities, called *habitats* and on the non-living cycles of the air, water, and land, which connect and sustain them. Together, earth's habitats and its ocean, air, and soil cycles constitute the *biosphere* (Chant 1970; Commoner 1971, 11–14).

Our dependence on the biosphere for economic activity is twofold. First, materials, energy sources, and life processes produced and reproduced by the biosphere are what humans appropriate as renewable resources. Second, we rely on the biosphere to absorb our wastes by recycling biodegradable wastes back into the elements of the biosphere, and by harmlessly and invisibly disposing of non-biodegradable materials, including highly toxic by-products created in our factories. As the scale and complexity of economic activity increases, the greater the demand on the biosphere.

Central to the limits to growth perspective is the idea that the biosphere as a whole produces the plants, animals, water, and air that we term "renewable resources." The plants and animals of each community, or habitat, can survive only because the habitats are connected and supported by the air, water, and soil cycles of the earth. This interdependence is critical. While we may talk as if we depend on the recovery of a particular fishery resource such as northern cod or for a certain amount of rainfall to ensure bountiful wheat harvests, our dependency is more complex. We do not depend solely on a particular piece of the biosphere; we depend on the operation of the whole system.

Environmental problems are human disruptions of the natural operation of the biosphere (Raskin and Bernow 1991, 87; Benton 1989, 74). As such they potentially imperil the very basis of human life, let alone economic activity. Renewable resources can be renewed only if the habitats of the planet operate; only if the ocean, atmosphere, and other physical and chemical cycles operate; and only if the wastes of our production don't poison its habitats. The limits to growth perspective argues that, because we need to maintain the integrity of the biosphere to sustain life, there must be limits both to the capacity of the biosphere to provide renewable resources for human use, as well as to the kind and volume of wastes that the biosphere can absorb without impairing its capacity to reproduce renewable resources and handle new waste.

Partisans of this approach argue that commitments to merely *minimize* the environmental impact of particular new development projects, or even of economic expansion in general, will be insufficient to prevent us from moving beyond the biosphere's capacity. Thus minimizing the negative effects of new ore smelters, making new nuclear generation plants safer, controlling urban expansion into the countryside, and preserving a small amount of special habitat to maintain biodiversity will be insufficient to deflect humankind from the path of ecological exhaustion. Inevitably, ecological constraints will limit the size of the economy as well as the kinds of technologies that we can utilize.

Proponents of the limits to growth view have long been aware that their position directly challenges the environment–society relationship on which the classical liberal view of progress and human betterment is based. In magazines such as *The Ecologist*, the liberal view has been criticized and ultimately dismissed as naively optimistic and dangerous for the future of the earth. In the same breath, advocates have dismissed most Marxian-based critiques of contemporary society, since, as we have seen, that orientation shares many of the core assumptions of the classical liberal view.

The Environmental Management Perspective

By the late 1960s it had become clear that developed societies were running out of clean air and water, trees, ores, fish, and virtually every natural resource (Marchak 1983; Marchak et al. 1987). Denial was no longer possible. If economic growth was to continue, it was necessary to take action to curb the most damaging excesses of environmental destruction (Woodrow 1977). The result was the emergence of a new conventional wisdom, one that recognized pollution and the exhaustion of renewable resources. It embraced the view that ecological problems result largely from human disruption of the biosphere. It rejected, however, what was perceived as the extremism of the limits to growth conclusion. In this new view, a technological solution exists for every ecological constraint if caution and prudence are employed.

The resulting new orthodoxy has come to be known as *sustainable development*. Coined in the popular Brundtland Report, *Our Common Future* (WECD 1987), it articulates a middle path between the traditional liberal view and the limits to growth positions, in which environmental management can be practised to ensure sustainable development. Sustainable development is a process of economic growth in which industrial expansion can occur without jeopardizing the opportunities of future generations. Such a path can preserve, not degrade, the ecological basis of economic activity without the pessimism and radical reorganization required of the limits to growth view.

The Brundtland Report assumed that reckless exploitation of renewable resources and dirty technology are primarily responsible for the disruption of the biosphere. Significantly, the report argues against the existence of a necessarily absolute constraint on economic growth per se (WCED 1987, 8). Instead, better management of the world's environment will produce more renewable resources from the land and the sea. Technological innovation will improve efficiency in the use and reuse of energy and materials, and will also reduce pollution. Confidently assuming the absence of any present or future resource shortages or pollution buildups, the report claimed that infinite economic expansion was possible and desirable if only business and governments co-operated to take the necessary measures to sustain development.

The attraction of such an environmental management perspective is obvious. It does not fundamentally challenge current societal practices nor the ideological foundation of classical liberalism upon which they rest. Material progress remains both the goal and the driving force of social development. Environmental problems are uninformed by-products of economic expansion subject to technical fixes.

Environmental management has come to fit very nicely within contemporary environmental rhetoric. Brundtland refrains from laying the blame for environmental problems at the feet of any particular actors, instead seeing environmental damage as a common problem for which we all share blame. This politically correct report did not even inflame divisions over the proper roles and responsibilities of government and private enterprise. Both free-market enthusiasts and those who wished for greater government intervention could each devise hypothetical schemes for business–government partnerships to achieve sustainable growth. Since environmental damage was a common problem, individual efforts could also assume importance. Thus, the movement for responsible environmental behaviour took off, with everyone from kindergarten students to senior citizens being cajoled to practise the three "Rs" of reduce, reuse, and recycle.

Evaluating Competing Perspectives

The question now arises as to which perspective has the greatest weight of evidence behind it. The serious contenders are clearly the environmental management and limits to growth perspectives. Documented evidence of environmental damage is so extensive that to deny the problem, as is done in the classical view, would be ridiculous. Therefore, we will direct our evaluation to these two perspectives.

Both views agree that environmental problems arise from the disruption of biospheric processes and that an intact biosphere is necessary for continued large-scale economic activity. Both agree that we have erroneously presumed our economic activity would not undermine the biosphere's ability to produce renewable resources and process waste. Both also concur that the contemporary scale and variety of economic activities simultaneously create greater dependence on the biosphere as well as greater capacity to interfere, intentionally and unintentionally, in the natural processes operating within it. In our opinion, the debate between them can be reduced to one point of fundamental disagreement: whether or not technical innovation and resource management can prevent ecological exhaustion and ultimately reduce, perhaps even eliminate, the biosphere's capacity to support human life (Clow 1990).

Through the use of Figure 11.3, we believe it is possible to assess the adequacy of each perspective. As indicated in our earlier discussion, both perspectives share a great deal in their understanding of the relationship between human economic activity and the environment. It is therefore possible to determine the kinds of efforts required to sustain increasing economic activity over some reasonable period of time. It appears that six critical sets of activities must be undertaken in a properly balanced combination if sustained growth is to be achieved.

These six are as follows:

1. Somehow get more materials and energy from the biosphere, such as from the sun or geothermal sources beneath the earth's crust, without increasing the disruption of the biosphere.
2. Somehow get more useful work from a given flow of energy and similarly waste less materials in the production process.
3. Somehow produce more durable products that therefore need to be replaced less often and make them easier to reuse, rebuild, and recycle.
4. Somehow produce products with less waste, no more waste than can be recycled or returned safely to the biosphere, and with wastes that are easier to reuse or recycle.
5. Somehow reuse more waste energy, recycle more industrial waste, and recycle thrown away or junked products without increasing energy and material use in the process.
6. Somehow dispose of wastes in the biosphere in forms, locations, and quantities that can be returned to the natural flow of such materials and energy without further disruption of the habitats and cycles of the biosphere.

The magnitude of such challenges to maintain sustainable growth without continuing environmental damage is seldom appreciated. Technological innovations increase efficiencies in the use of energy and materials in industrial processes, the production of more durable products with less waste, and the more efficient recycling of what reduced waste remains. Similarly, they stimulate both natural habitats and artificial ocean, forest, and field "agricultures" to produce more of the plants and animals we want without increasing the disruption of natural and humanly created "agricultural" habitats. Such technological innovation would have to be

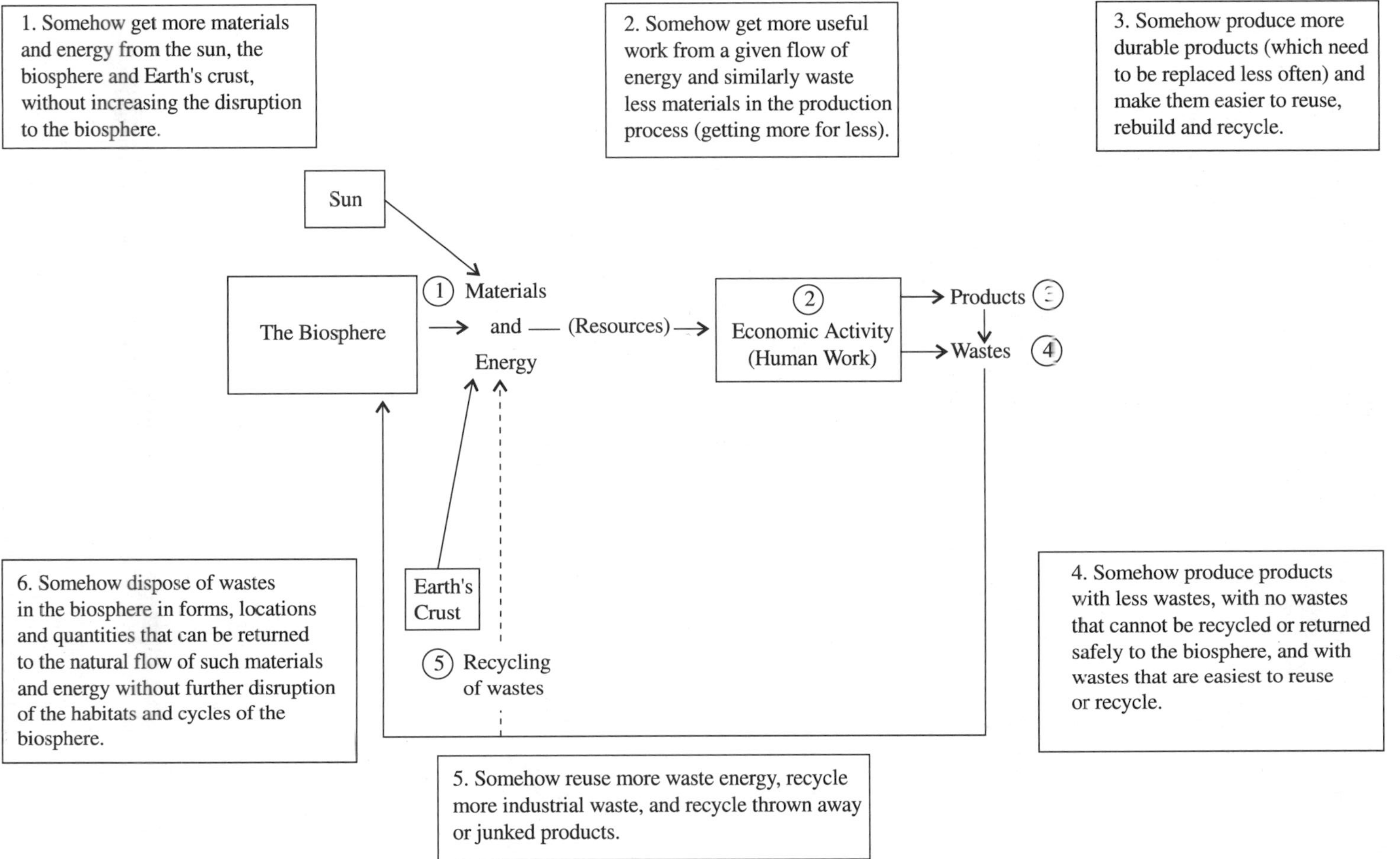

FIGURE 11.3: The Economy–Nature Relationship and the Requirements for Sustaining Economic Growth

NOTE: In order to sustain economic growth indefinitely all these measures must be continually and indefinitely refined and improved.

ongoing, synchronized, and co-ordinated to keep the ecological demands of a growing economy within the envelope of the biosphere's capacity to sustain. Big leaps forward in one area, energy production for example, would be of no help if matching gains were not made in other areas of technological innovation. For sustainable growth, this range of improvements would have to continue on an indefinite basis. Otherwise, one quickly runs into limitations on production arising from the inability of the earth to supply the ever-rising ecological demand of an expanding economy.

In light of such a presentation, it is difficult to believe that technological innovation and wise resource management will be able to indefinitely sustain economic growth while containing environmental degradation. Technological innovation and resource management are not magical, yet an act of magic seems necessary. Ever more amounts of product must be conjured up from the same amount of materials; ever more effort from the same amount of energy; ever more renewable resources from the earth; ever less waste from industrial processes; and wastes ever more integrated into the natural flows of energy and materials in the biosphere. Technology merely taps into natural processes and directs them for human ends. Technological manipulations of natural processes are doubly constrained—first by the efficiency of our processes and devices and secondly by the characteristics of the natural processes with which we are interfering.

Tasks 2 to 5 in Figure 11.3 represent efforts to "get more from less": increased efficiencies in the use and reuse of materials and energy, and reduction in the volume and toxicity of wastes in all areas of production. But, the efficiency of our devices and processes are not indefinitely improvable. The efficiency of all our devices and processes is restricted, in the last analysis, by the laws of thermodynamics (Georgescu-Roegen 1980). These scientific principles establish a limit as to how much of a flow of energy can be tapped and turned into useful effort for human purposes. Similarly, there are limits to the efficiency of our use of materials. At some point, all technologies exhaust their possibilities for improvement. In practice our machines, devices, and industrial practices seldom approach anything like their theoretical limits of efficiency because of the exponentially increasing cost of developing and utilizing what are only marginally more-efficient improvements.

The exponential increase in our production over the past two centuries has relied on the intensified exploitation of known natural forces augmented by the rapid discovery of new ones. As is all too well known, the process has also led to the exponential increase in ecological disruption. For individuals inclined to trust that new technologies will emerge based on mysteries of nature not yet uncovered, it is important to remember that for every new force of nature discovered, there will be an ecological consequence to harnessing it for human production. The 1950s belief that nuclear fission would provide clean, unlimited new electrical energy comes uncomfortably to mind.

Tasks 1 and 6 focus on constraints arising from the characteristics of the biosphere with which our ecological demand interferes. Task 1 concerns the provision of an expanding supply of renewable and non-renewable resources, while Task 6 concerns the effects of pollution.

Unfortunately, wise management of resources cannot induce the biosphere to produce more and more renewable resources. Economic activities of society are essentially parasitic upon the natural processes of the biosphere. Plants and animals consumed by the economy, and all the materials and energy in the air, water, and soil cycles appropriated by economic activity, are pulled out of their role in the normal operation of the biosphere. As in any parasitic relationship, too much appropriation from the host interferes with its ability to reproduce. With regard to non-renewable resources from the earth's crust, the extraction of materials often destroys overlying habitats and, as in example of mining, can contribute massive pollution to the biosphere. In short, it seems hopelessly naive to expect an endlessly growing supply of either renewable or non-renewable resources will come without a corresponding increase in environmental damage.

It is also impossible to guarantee that wastes from our economic activities will become increasingly compatible in volume, location, and composition with the natural flows of energy and materials to which they are added. It would appear to be a task of exponentially increasing difficulty to more and more closely match biodegradable wastes with natural biospheric flows and cycles. More difficult still, considering that wastes produced by many modern industries—notably nuclear power, petrochemicals, and mining—are simply incompatible with the health of living things. In some cases it may be possible to utilize hazardous technologies on a small scale by operating effective closed-cycle production systems, by recycling, and by destroying toxic waste in combination. There appears, however, to be no way to operate such hazardous processes in a way that would allow an ever-greater scale of use.

Despite the current popularity of sustainable development as a solution to our current ecological woes, the above review suggests that it would be difficult, if not impossible, to achieve. Technical measures to reduce the ecological demand of production on the biosphere—such as pollution controls; improved energy efficiency; extensive recycling of resources; the production of more durable, long-lasting products; and the aggressive restoration of renewable resources—can reduce the degradation of the biosphere to some degree. Production may even be increased for a time with fixed volumes of materials, energy, and waste disposal capacity. Ultimately, however, ecological constraints will indeed limit the scale of economic activity and the constitution of productive forces, in spite of our best efforts to innovate. The underlying assumption that material progress can be a permanent feature of human society is manifestly in error.

Implications of Limited Growth for Industrial Society

The twin themes of insatiable human need and never-ending economic growth, which have simultaneously driven and justified economic activity in the industrial world for over 200 years, are no longer sustainable in industrialized countries let alone exportable to less-industrialized ones. The reality of ecological constraints requires that we understand the environmental consequences of human activity and shape future activities in ways to prevent environmental damage. A strategy for this is clearest for so-called renewable resources but can be generalized to other areas as well.

Renewable resource industries are distinct from other areas of economic activity because in them we directly depend on the exploitation of the productive power of the biosphere. We harvest natural habitats and expect them to regrow more of the plants and animals we want. We extract energy and materials from the non-living cycles of the biosphere and expect them to be renewed as well. We also set up artificial, human-constructed habitats of agriculture, silviculture, and aquaculture within the biosphere and expect it to support them.

In harvesting natural habitats we are extracting wild plants and animals from communities of interdependent species (see insert on Georgian Bay fishing). If one wishes to harvest over an indefinite period of time, that is, practise sustainability, resource practices must not damage the whole habitat and, simultaneously, must not over-harvest the particular species pursued. To discern levels of what is usually termed a "sustainable yield" requires a substantive knowledge of the particular ecosystem. Similarly, extraction of renewable materials and energy from their natural cycles in the air, water, or earth's crust must not upset the physical cycles of the biosphere. As we have already seen in countless places, where natural flows of energy are diverted from their normal cycles on a large scale, for example by damming large watersheds, broad and deleterious effects on dependent habitats result.

In farming, silviculture, and aquaculture we do not actually grow the crops or animals; rather, we *appropriate* the bio-physical processes of the biosphere to grow them for us (Kelly and Sandersen 1990). We create habitats for plant and animal species we desire, with little regard to consequences for the larger ecosystem. Salmon aquaculture is a good example. As a result of massive salmon farming, new diseases have been introduced to wild fish by means of escaped individuals; specific bays and fjords become polluted with excess artificial food pellets, which sink to the bottom and decay; and the genetic integrity of many stocks becomes threatened as domesticated fish escape to interbreed with wild fish. The more intensive the pursuit of such activities, the greater the damage to natural ecosystems. The process can be stated as a validated proposition: The more intensive the production process, the greater the input required per unit of production (fertilizer etc.), the less stable the farmed or artificial habitat becomes, and finally the greater is the destruction to local, possibly even remote, ecosystems. It is increasingly being recognized by biologists, ecologists, silviculturalists, and other related professionals that stable, sustainable farming of the land and sea can only emerge by limiting the intensity of production and building more-diverse, better-balanced habitats (Jacobs 1993).

In manufacturing and service industries the dependence on resource inputs from the biosphere is often less visible. Unlike food products, the pulp and paper and extractive industries, the aircraft manufacturing industry, and the banking and computer industries are seen as relatively free from ecological constraints. Of course any reflection will reveal this is not so. Aluminum manufacturing for aircraft production is one of the largest users of energy. Banking, hospitals, and other service industries require large volumes of energy inputs, paper products, and water—all coming from the biosphere. Even computer components require large amounts of energy in the manufacture of silicon chips. They also emit radiation into the biosphere as they hum on a desk top or on someone's lap.

The ecological damage created by manufacturing and service industries, with the obvious exceptions of chemical, steel, and other heavy manufacturing, is not as obviously linked to the natural environment as resource industries. The damage usually undermines the biosphere in ways that do not directly undermine the ability of the offending industry to continue operating. Damage is more general, affecting human health and the biosphere's capacity to support other human activities. For example, acid rain produced by burning coal does not damage the supply of coal or the immediate capability of a plant to burn it. The damage is done to human lungs, plants, solid, and buildings. It is agriculture and forestry that are undermined, not manufacturing. Acid rain will only indirectly affect the ability to burn coal by eventually reducing the ability of green plants to produce free molecular oxygen.

It goes without saying that non-renewable resources must be conserved rather than recklessly pursued. As much as possible, alternative, renewable products—either natural or artificially produced—must be found as well. Where toxic waste products remain (the nuclear power industry is a good example), their effects upon the biosphere must also be considered and contained.

Above all, what is required is an integrative procedure that traces the full chain of environmental dependencies of each stage of any production process. By tracing these direct and indirect effects on the environment, it is possible to determine the scale and character of an industry's ecological costs. Such an analysis requires some knowledge of the physical, chemical and biological character of the production process and its consequences.

Service sector activities need not be treated differently from goods production in our argument. While they may consume less energy and materials and produce only information, medical assistance, amusement, or intangible products, they also involve the conversion of material and energy into wastes.

To examine the entire economy, one must add up the entire ecological demand of all economic activities. In fixing the sustainable scale of any specific activity, the competition of different industries for the same limited carrying capacity must be factored into the assessment. Proponents of managed or sustainable development would set the scale of economic activity at the level of maximum sustainable yield. In other words, economic activity could expand to some level of maximal sustainable ecological demand. This is very risky. Our ability to accurately predict maximum levels of resource extraction and waste absorption is dubious, as Canadians have recently learned with the collapse of the East Coast fisheries.

Conclusions

Spiralling environmental degradation challenges our existing understanding of how society operates, the nature of human wants, and the likely path of future development. Most social analysis inadequately addresses the ecological consequences of human activity. As well, unbridled growth is assumed both desirable and possible. Yet ecological consequences are critical and unconstrained growth unlikely. All is not lost! If we can change society before we undermine the ecological basis for a reasonable standard of living, it may be possible to maintain much of the economic achievement of the past 200 years and share these material benefits with others. The more we hesitate to move toward an ecologically sustainable economy, the less will be the planet's productive capacity when we finally do.[5]

We have a reasonably good picture of the biophysical constraints within which we will have to operate during the next century. The implications for present and future society are quite clear. They include three imperatives:

Reduce the scale of economic activity. We must not only innovate to use fewer resources and produce less waste, we must also limit the scale of economic activity to what can be supported by the environment.

Refrain from economic activities whose technological basis cannot be safely tolerated and supported by the biosphere. Many old and new technologies that we would once have hailed as the progressive fruit of industrial progress must be seen as overutilized. Some are likely to be simply unsustainable. This may very well involve a shedding of nuclear power as well as much of the petrochemical and automobile industry, and an increased wariness of bio-engineering. Technological innovation must be redirected from increasing productive forces to reducing total ecological demand.

Restore the earth's habitats and physical cycles in order to strengthen the biosphere's damaged productive capacity.

These will not be accomplished easily. Industrial societies are highly complex social entities. While there is increasing awareness of the scale of environmental damage and the need for fundamental change (Tindall 1993), economic transformations will be difficult. Powerful economic and political interests will likely balk when the magnitude of required change is more fully understood (Clow 1992). So too may many individuals and groups in the more-developed societies as they face the day-to-day consequences of such change. Yet fundamental change is essential. The human being is an animal that has moved out of ecological balance with its environment. It is imperative that we recognize this humbling lesson and reorganize human life to redress the imbalance. Implementation represents the foremost challenge for twenty-first-century society.

Study Questions

1. Environmental damage used to be considered a local problem. Why is this view inadequate?

2. It has been argued that, if present trends continue, the world will become polluted to the point where modern industrial societies cannot be sustained. What solutions would you propose to avert such a situation?

3. According to the chapter, why does the "limits to growth" perspective seem a more accurate reflection of the future than one stressing managed, sustainable development?

4. If the limits to growth perspective is an accurate prediction of the future, what specific changes would you expect to see in your own community?

Recommended Reading

Daly, H.E., and J. Cobb. *For the Common Good: Redirecting the Economy Towards Community, the Environment, and a Sustainable Future.* Boston: Beacon Press, 1989.

Gould, S. *The Flamingo's Smile.* New York: W.W. Norton, 1985.

Keating, M. *To the Last Drop: Canada and the World's Water Crisis.* Toronto: Macmillan, 1986.

Evernden, N. *The Social Creation of Nature.* Baltimore: Johns Hopkins University Press, 1992.

Jacobs, M. *The Green Economy. Environment, Sustainable Development, and the Politics of the Future.* Vancouver: University of British Columbia Press, 1993.

Owens, S. *Energy, Urban Form, and Planning.* London: Pion Press, 1986.

Wilson, E., ed. *Biodiversity.* Washington, DC: National Academy Press, 1988.

Notes

1. For a very good overview of the pervasiveness of ecological damage see Mungall and McLaren (1991). This volume is the result of a project by the Royal Society of Canada to assemble disciplinary specialists to summarize and document environmental damage and explore the implications for the planet. Written for a wide audience, it represents one of the best summaries on global damage and its implication for human life.
2. It is true that climates and relative proportions of ingredients in the atmosphere have changed slightly. For example, mean surface temperatures of the whole planet have remained within a range of only seven degrees celsius, including the ice ages. See *Proceedings, World Conference on the Changing Atmosphere: Implications for Global Security* (1989).
3. Within the atmosphere are small amounts of a number of gases, popularly called "greenhouse gases" because they alter the flow of heat and energy through the atmosphere much as the glass shell of a greenhouse does. Such gases include nitrous oxide, methane, and carbon dioxide. In historical concentrations, they play a critical role in the earth's capacity to retain heat and energy. Unfortunately, human population growth and accelerated industrial activity at a global level are increasing the concentrations of these gases at alarming rates. The effect is that greater heat is trapped near the earth's surface along with higher levels of water vapour (clouds). Massive climatic changes can result from the melting of polar ice caps (and therefore increased sea levels) to the creation of expanded desert areas from what used to be agricultural lands.
4. For a very thorough philosophical and historical analysis of how post-Enlightenment society has "socially created" a sense of nature as an object external to us whose purpose is to benefit humankind, see Evernden (1985 and 1992). It is particularly important to note that the sense of nature that informs contemporary society has been socially constructed out of specific historical circumstances and should not be considered as part of any inherent human characteristic.
5. It is essential to understand that the unbridled pursuit of growth to satisfy allegedly insatiable human needs be understood as a social construction and not the reflection of some inevitable, fixed genetic characteristic of the species. Human behaviour and organization appear too diverse to be explained by the narrow dictates of genetic determination. Had we dominating, universal instincts, such as insatiable material needs, we would likely be trapped by them in a few fixed habitats, in a particular ecological niche, and with a singular social organization set by our genetic programming, like all other animals.

References

Allen, J. 1994. *Environment 94/95.* Guilford, CT: Dushkin Publishing Group.

Alverson, L. 1991. *The Status of Stocks of Gadus Atlantica in NAFO Areas 2J, 3K, L.* St. John's: Northwest Atlantic Fisheries Centre.

Bolaria, B.S. 1991. "Environment, Work, and Illness." In *Social Issues and Contradictions in Canadian Society.* Toronto: Harcourt, Brace Jovanovich. 222–246.

Boreham, G., and R. Leftwich. 1971. *Economic Thinking in a Canadian Context.* Toronto: Rinehart and Winston of Canada.

Chant, D.A. 1972. *Pollution Probe.* Toronto: New Press.

Clow, M. 1990. "Sustainable Development Won't be Enough." *Policy Options/Options Politiques* 11, no. 9: 6–9.

———. 1992. "Ecological Exhaustion and the Crisis of Global Capitalism." *Our Generation* 23, no. 1: 1–25.

Commoner, B. 1971. *The Closing Circle: Nature, Man, and Technology.* New York: Bantam Books.

Daly, H.E., and J. Cobb. 1989. *For the Common Good: Redirecting the Economy Towards Community, the Environment, and a Sustainable Future.* Boston: Beacon Press.

Evernden, N. 1992. *The Social Creation of Nature.* Baltimore: Johns Hopkins University Press.

———. 1985. *The Natural Alien.* Toronto: University of Toronto Press.

Georgescu-Roegen, N. 1980. "The Entropy Law and the Economic Problem." In *Economics, Ecology, Ethics: Essays Towards a Steady-State Economy,* ed. H. Daly. New York: Anchor Books. 49–60.

Gould, S. 1993. *Eight Little Piggies: Reflections in Natural History.* New York: W.W. Norton.

International Committee on Northwest Atlantic Fisheries (ICNAF). 1992. *Report on the Status of Gadus Atlantica in the Northwestern Atlantic.* Halifax: International Committee on Northwest Atlantic Fisheries.

Jacobs, M. 1993. *The Green Economy: Environment, Sustainable Development, and the Politics of the Future.* Vancouver: University of British Columbia Press.

Keating, M. 1986. *To the Last Drop: Canada and the World's Water Crisis.* Toronto: Macmillan.

Kelly, M., and K. Sandersen. 1990. "Sea Changes, Sustainability, and Strategies." *Alternatives, 17, no. 1: 30–36.*

Marchak, P. 1983. Green Gold: The Forest Industry in British Columbia. Vancouver: UBC Press.

Marchak, P., N. Guppy, and J. Macmillan. 1987. *Uncommon Property: The Fishing and Fish Processing Industries in British Columbia.* Vancouver: UBC Press.

Marx, K. 1973. *Grundrisse: Foundation of the Critique of Political Economy.* Trans. Martin Nicholas. New York: Vintage Books.

McGoodwin, J. 1990. *Crisis in the World's Fisheries.* Stanford: Stanford University Press.

Mungall, C., and D. McLaren. 1991. *Planet Under Stress: The Challenge of Global Change.* Toronto: Oxford University Press.

Proceedings, World Conference on the Changing Atmosphere: Implications for Global Security. 1989. Brussels: World Meteorological Association.

Tindall, D. 1993. "The New Class Theorists: Participation in the BC Environmental Movement." Paper given at the Annual Meeting of the Canadian Sociology and Anthropology Association. Ottawa. June 1993.

World Commission on Environment and Development (WECD). 1987. *Our Common Future.* Report of the Brundtland Commission. Oxford: Oxford University Press.

Wagner, R. 1974. *Environment and Man.* 2d ed. New York: W.W. Norton and Co.

Woodrow, R.B. 1977. "The Development and Implementation of Pollution Control Programs in Canada 1966–1974." Unpublished doctoral dissertation. Guelph: University of Guelph.

CHAPTER 12

Mental Disorders as a Social Problem

James Stolzman

Learning Objectives

This chapter examines issues involved in the definition, diagnosis, and treatment of mental disorders; as well, it discusses the rationale and implications of divergent perspectives brought to the study of mental disorders by sociologists, psychologists, and psychiatrists. After reading and reflecting on this chapter, students should be able to grasp what it means to analyze mental disorders sociologically, appreciate the limitations of viewing the source of psychological distress as residing only in the minds or bodies of individuals, and cite specific social factors that sociologists believe are significant in the etiology and patterning of mental disorders. Students should also be able to identify some of the extra-scientific reasons that may account for the popularity of the medical conception of madness, and explain and assess the argument that psychiatrists in our society act as agents of social control.

Introduction

The subject of this chapter, mental disorder, poses many perplexing issues for the student of social problems. For one thing, there is considerable disagreement among mental health professionals about the nature of mental disorders and how they should be treated. To further complicate matters, the sociologist approaches this topic from a very different angle from that of the psychologist or the psychiatrist. Whereas sociologists conceptualize mental disorders as a form of deviant behaviour, most psychiatrists conceive of them as medical illnesses. Much of this chapter will be devoted to examining the rationales and implications of these divergent perspectives.

The use of the term mental *disorder* instead of the more familiar mental *illness* in the title and throughout this chapter is deliberate. For reasons that I hope to make plain in the pages that follow, I consider mental illness a loaded concept whose adoption implies some questionable prejudgements about the nature of psychological abnormality. Mental disorder, by contrast, is a neutral concept that avoids these connotations, without necessarily denying their validity.

Whatever we call it, mental disorder does not lend itself to precise definition. This is largely because there is no one property shared by all types of mental disorder, nor is there any single trait that distinguishes the mentally disturbed from the mentally sound. How then do "experts" recognize cases of mental disorder when they encounter them? Despite the absence of any one distinguishing feature, trained professionals attribute mental disorders to subjects who have a number of properties in common. Rosenhan and Seligman's delineation of the closely related concept of psychological abnormality singles out seven criteria that are considered fairly reliable indicators of mental disorder:

1. **Suffering.** The experience of a mental disorder usually involves subjectively felt pain or misery.
2. **Maladaptiveness.** When a person is mentally disordered some of the person's behaviours may interfere with his or her individual wellbeing or the welfare of society.
3. **Irrationality and incomprehensibility.** A mentally disordered person will often tend to engage in behaviour or express thoughts that seem to have no rational meaning.
4. **Unpredictability and loss of control.** When someone suffers from a mental disorder his or her behaviour may appear to others as erratic, inconsistent, and beyond self-monitoring.
5. **Vividness and unconventionality.** A mentally disordered person may display "weird" behaviour that causes him or her to stand out from others in a noticeable way.
6. **Observer discomfort.** Mental disorder may be indicated where a person's behaviour causes those around him or her to feel upset, embarrassed, or otherwise uncomfortable.
7. **Violation of moral and ideal standards.** A person's mental disturbance may manifest itself in behaviour that is not merely socially unconventional, but contravenes moral standards that are believed to characterize all "right-thinking," "right-acting people" (Rosenhan and Seligman 1984, 5–10).

I trust the reader may now appreciate that arriving at judgements about a person's sanity is not always a simple or straightforward task. For example, there are good grounds for asserting that a person's mental condition is a matter of degree, not kind. Efforts to divide the population neatly into the sane and the insane are thus bound to distort a complex reality wherein even the most severely disturbed persons exhibit complete sanity in some areas of their lives and ostensibly normal individuals occasionally manifest the sort of psychological distress or self-defeating patterns of behaviour we usually associate with the mad. Nevertheless, in attempting to ascertain the degree of a person's impairment, the psychiatrist or psychologist will utilize guidelines similar to those mentioned above. The presence of one of these traits is normally not sufficient justification to diagnose a person as mentally disordered. However, the more of these elements that are present, and the more enduring and visible each of them is, the greater the likelihood that the person's troubles may warrant designation as a mental disorder.

It is no secret that mental-health professionals have traditionally been sceptical of the sociological study of mental disorder. To their way of thinking, sociologists who explore this field of inquiry are entering foreign territory, where their theories, centring on the social environment, are misplaced and misleading. This low opinion of sociological analysis is consonant with certain common beliefs in our culture about the nature of mental disorder. Most people in our society simply take it for granted that mental disorder represents an affliction of an individual's mind or body. That is, if someone is judged to be "crazy," there is an almost automatic assumption that the source of the disturbance is internal—that it resides in the malfunctioning of his or her cognitive, emotional, or physiological processes. It would, of course, be foolish to reject this assumption totally. Where a mental disorder exists, something almost certainly *has* gone wrong with the person's mind or body. But this does not mean that factors external to the individual are thereby irrelevant to understanding many aspects of what the mentally disordered person experiences. Sociologists contend that the social world affects matters pertaining to people's mental state in myriad ways. How others (including those who treat it) react to psychiatric disturbance, for instance, is profoundly shaped by ideas and attitudes that have been learned as part of being socialized in a particular culture. Moreover, biological and psychological analysis is virtually useless for answering certain kinds of questions about mental disorder—those that concern the *social patterning* of disorders.

Epidemiologists have compiled masses of data on how various disorders are distributed in the population. Such research has repeatedly documented that the standardized rate of incidence for any given disorder is subject to considerable variation when it is broken down by categories of people—defined, for example, by age, geographical region, marital status, religion, ethnicity, gender, occupation, educational attainment, and so on. To cite a specific finding, we know that the much-publicized eating disorder, anorexia nervosa, overwhelmingly afflicts females between the ages of 15 and 25 from middle-class backgrounds. To explain this particular social profile, knowledge of what ails the individual anorexics who comprise this pattern is of little help. What we require to throw light on issues of this sort is sociological analysis.

Sociological analysis calls for an examination of how people's behaviour is affected by their membership in groups and society as a whole. In the case of anorexia, a sociological approach would lead us to inquire about the social experiences associated with being young, female, and middle class in our society. What sorts of social expectations or constraints go with these statuses? Are there certain contradictory cultural messages that impinge upon people in these social positions? Are the social bonds linking persons in these groups to other members of society supportive or alienating? In short, the sociologist argues that the task of explaining why any way of thinking, acting, or feeling is more (or less) prevalent among some sectors of society than others cannot be accomplished by studying the individuals who make up these patterns. As Durkheim's classic study of suicide forcefully demonstrated almost a century ago ([1897] 1951), a psychological or biological theory of suicide might well permit one to explain why specific individuals elect to take their own lives, but cannot account for social facts such as why Protestants have much higher rates of suicide than Catholics, or why single persons are more prone to be suicidal than people who are married. In order to understand such patterns of behaviour, we need to focus on how the collectivities to which people belong are structured or organized. The same logic Durkheim employed to explain rates of suicide applies to the sociological study of mental disorder.

To concentrate on social factors is not to dispute that biological or psychological factors figure prominently in the understanding of mental disorder. It merely implies that these other approaches do not exhaust analysis of this subject. In this chapter I hope to demonstrate that the relevance of social factors in analyzing mental disorder has been seriously underestimated by both the mental health community and the public at large. I shall argue that social factors are thoroughly involved in both the assessment and causation of mental disorder.

The Medical Model of Madness as a Social Construction

All known human societies recognize odd behaviour in terms that closely correspond with our everyday notions of mental "illness." Both throughout human history and across human cultures, people have devised concepts for identifying and thinking about behaviour that strikes them as bizarre or inexplicable (Eaton 1986, 1–2). In other words, societies typically evolve beliefs that help their members explain and cope with conduct that they regard as strange. How and what people have thought about mental disorder is thus a social construction that varies from culture to culture and from one historical era to another. The modern biomedical interpretation of madness as a disease is one such social construction that tries to make sense of bizarre behaviour. Acceptance of this conception of madness is so widespread in our society that it is hard for us to think of it as just another perspective—for once any viewpoint becomes established, people begin to regard that way of seeing things as "natural" rather than social in origin. A discussion of the social and historical circumstances that fostered the so-called medical model is therefore instructive in reminding us that viewing the mad as "sick" is an outlook that we have acquired from our culture. But first it is necessary to offer a few observations about premodern conceptions of mental disorder.

As Cockerham (1989, 4–24) points out, ideas and attitudes about mental disorder in pre-industrial European society underwent a series of alternating cycles. Periods of tolerance, in which efforts were made at understanding madness as a condition resulting from natural causes, would be eclipsed by others whose outlook attributed it to supernatural forces. In the latter phases of this cycle the mad were thought to be possessed by demons or other evil spirits. Consistent with this belief, those defined as mad were subjected to social ostracism, humiliation, and persecution. Some communities drove them out, making them homeless vagabonds; others burned them at the stake or hanged them for their alleged "sins." Where treatment of the mad was attempted, the preferred methods were clearly punitive, not rehabilitative. Some of the more telling procedures inflicted upon the mad included cauterizing their skin, drilling holes in their skulls, dunking them in ice-cold water, and spinning them in a chair at dizzying speeds.

It is against the backdrop of medieval European society and its theological interpretation of madness that we can trace the origin and development of the medical perspective on mental disorder. As Conrad and Schneider (1980) have noted, the ascendancy of physicians as the proper authorities to treat madness has its roots in the European lunatic asylums of the seventeenth and eighteenth centuries. These first madhouses were not originally medical institutions, but by the nineteenth century most of their directors were physicians. These forerunners of the psychiatric profession were both inclined and ideally situated to annex treatment of the mentally disordered to medicine's traditional jurisdiction. In hindsight, what was most remarkable about their success in this venture is the fact that it was accomplished with a modicum of scientific knowledge about the causes of insanity. What is more, there was nothing particularly "medical" about the therapies these physicians prescribed for asylum residents. Medicine's success in extending its authority into this area is far more attributable to these physicians' endeavours as humanitarians than as healers. Along with a number of progressive laypersons, a group of doctors spearheaded a movement to reform the oppressive conditions that characterized the early madhouses. Humane, or "moral," treatment of the insane was both preached and practised.

Physicians assumed this same moral leadership in the building and administering of insane asylums in nineteenth-century North America. Again, their efforts in improving the lot of the mad enabled these medical men gradually to establish a monopoly over the definition and treatment of mental disorder. Conrad and Schneider point out that this dominance was achieved well *before* the existence of any scientific evidence that some types of madness have organic components, and prior to the advent of effective treatments for mental disorder that were distinctively "medical." Indeed, it was not until the turn of the century that general paresis, perhaps the most prevalent mental disorder of that era, was found to be caused by a germ associated with syphilis. A few years later, medical researchers developed a chemical compound that proved to be highly effective in treating the dreaded disorder. This breakthrough earned credibility for the biomedical conception of madness and rekindled expectations that all psychological disturbances would someday be shown to have physical etiologies. In addition to germ research, later medical researchers have investigated the genetic transmission of mental disorders as well as the links between psychiatric symptoms and biochemical processes in the human brain.

The question we need to consider is this: To what extent has all this research into the physical causes of madness fulfilled the initial promise of the medical model? In my view, the short answer to this question is that, overall, the results must be judged as disappointing. This is not to deny that some important advances have been made. Research on schizophrenia, for example, strongly indicates the presence of both genetic and neurological factors in the etiology of this group of disorders. In one sense such findings are undoubtedly significant. When evaluated against the high hopes and ambitious goals inspired by medicine's initial discoveries in this area, however, their significance diminishes. Champions of the medical approach sought no less than to formulate a conclusive explanation of the causes of mental disorder. Over the course of this century, enormous amounts of money and scientific energy have been expended toward this end, yet it is arguable whether psychiatry today is appreciably closer to this objective. Current and future medical research will likely continue to generate relevant knowledge about the physiological aspects of mental disorder. But at this juncture, the perennial proclamation that such research will ultimately yield a definitive explanation of mental "illness" amounts to an article of faith.

Such considerations have in no way deterred the biomedical perspective from shaping the conceptual framework and organization of the mental-health enterprise in modern society. To the contrary, the medical model increasingly determines how we think about and treat severe psychological distress. Those who direct and staff the major agencies dealing with the mentally disordered are typically psychiatrists or other medically trained professionals. Not surprisingly, their basic ideas and vocabulary concerning the causes, course, and treatment of mental disorder are derived from medical idioms. The central tenet of this approach has been summarized by Grusky and Pollner (1981, 24). They state that

> aberrant patterns of affect, thought, and behavior are best viewed as "symptoms" produced by an underlying pathological condition. The medical model asserts that disease is caused by physiobiological factors that may involve genetic, metabolic, biochemical, or other organic pathology. Mental illness is like any other illness and is unique only in that the symptoms are not fevers and aches, but unusual patterns of behavior.

But why has this model become so influential and accepted if, as I earlier claimed, its pedigree as science is dubious and it has been only moderately useful as a theoretical tool? I shall indulge in some speculation on this issue in the final section of this chapter. For now, I shall briefly discuss three "extra-scientific" factors that I believe have played a part in consolidating support for the medical model of madness.

To begin with, once a plausible perspective about anything manages to attain a certain degree of credibility it no longer requires complete or continual confirmation either to win or to maintain adherents. Once that threshold has been crossed, partial or occasional supporting evidence will suffice to sustain the established point of view. Regardless of its limitations, the medical perspective on madness has obviously proved to be "true enough" to gain and retain the confidence of most members of society. As previously acknowledged, medical research has succeeded in tracing certain mental abnormalities to physiological, biochemical, and genetic causes. Furthermore, these discoveries commonly receive wide and favourable publicity, which serves to enhance the model's reputation among both mental-health workers and the general public.

A second reason for the popularity of the medical model has been the perceived effectiveness of its therapeutic measures. In line with its assumption that madness is reducible to organic causes, psychiatrists have increasingly treated mental disorders with medically grounded procedures such as psychosurgery, electroshock therapy, and psychopharmacology. To be sure, there are documented cases of failure and abuse associated with all of these therapies (Valenstein 1986). On the other hand, each of them also has its success stories. This is perhaps especially true of drug therapy. Plenty of data attest to the positive benefits of psychotropic medication in the treatment and control of mental disorders. The use of tranquillizing and antidepressant drugs has permitted many previously debilitated patients to lead relatively normal lives. Critics of the medical orientation point out that medications relieve only the symptoms of mental disorder; they do not eliminate its underlying causes. This is correct. The control of unruly, withdrawn, or bizarre behaviour by means of drugs or other medical interventions should not be mistaken as a "cure" for mental illness. Be that as it may, the fact that these therapies tend to make many patients feel better and act more "normal" is tantamount, in most people's eyes, to a massive testimonial to the whole medical approach to madness. Indeed, it is hard to imagine anything that could be more persuasive in selling the medical model to the public than the real-life scenario whereby doctors prescribe pills to their sick patients who, after ingesting them, generally get better.

Finally, acceptance of the view of madness as disease has probably been facilitated by a more encompassing trend that Illich (1976) referred to as the "medicalization of life." This phrase is used to denote the steady growth in the prestige, dominance, and jurisdiction of the medical profession in contemporary society. Medicine's earlier triumphs in treating and preventing a host of communicable diseases that had plagued humankind for centuries greatly elevated its professional status in this century. Another feature of this is that medical solutions are increasingly being sought for problematic areas of life that traditionally had little or no connection to medicine. This trend has been most evident with respect to various behaviour problems that sociologists usually classify as deviance. Peter Conrad describes some of the parameters and implications of this shift:

> With these developments has come a change of the conception of deviance; much deviance that was badness (i.e., sinful or criminal) is now sickness. While some forms of deviant behavior are more completely medicalized than others (e.g., mental illness), recent work has pointed to a considerable variety of deviance that has been treated with medical jurisdiction: alcoholism, drug addiction, hyperactive children, suicide, obesity, crime, violence, child abuse, learning problems, amongst others. Concomitant with medicalization has been a change in imputed responsibility for deviance. With badness the deviant was considered responsible for the behavior, with sickness he or she is not, or at least responsibility is diminished. The social response to deviance is "therapeutic" rather than punitive (1981, 109–10).

Some issues arising out of this trend will be taken up later in this essay. At this point I am merely suggesting that receptivity to the notion that madness is best conceived as illness has been aided by the progressive encroachment of medical practice into more and more of the troublesome areas of modern life.

A Social Perspective on Modern Psychiatry

Many social scientists and foes of psychiatry contend that the medical model paints a false picture of mental disorder. They also claim that it camouflages the manner by which psychiatrists function as agents of social control (Ingleby 1981). Before echoing these contentions, I think it best to note some salutary features of the medical approach to madness.

One virtue of the medical model is its grounding in well-established biological sciences. Although this may have encouraged a narrow focus on only the physical aspects of mental disorder, it would be equally narrow to ignore the benefits of this approach. The fact that physical therapies can often provide relief to persons suffering from mental disorders would seem to indicate that the biological bases of psychological distress are very worthy of continued investigation. Mention should also be made of the instrumental role played by the medical profession in promoting positive attitudes toward the insane. Whatever serious misgivings there may be with the conceptualization of mental disorders as illnesses, there is no gainsaying that medicalization has helped reduce the awful burden of shame that accompanies psychological disturbance.

While I will grant that many mental disorders have physiological components, I still believe that the maverick psychiatrist Thomas Szasz was on to something crucially important when he proclaimed that what psychiatrists usually term mental "illnesses" are more aptly characterized as "problems in living." Szasz (1961) observed that whereas the symptoms of physical disease are objective and independent of cultural norms, the same cannot be said for psychiatric symptoms, which tend to have subjective elements and are invariably dependent on socio-cultural standards that specify what sorts of behaviour are deemed to be "normal" or appropriate in a given social setting. To reiterate, assessment of mental disorder is a social construction inevitably based on human judgements about people in particular social situations. The inherently subjective and social character of such evaluations can be seen by scrutinizing the criteria that mental health professionals employ to identify mental disorders, enumerated at the beginning of this chapter. Applying these diagnostic guidelines is surely a far more hazardous undertaking than is the evaluation of physical ailments. There are no objective measures such as body temperature or blood pressure to gauge the degree to which a patient's behaviour is "irrational," "unpredictable," or "maladaptive." Formulating intelligent judgements about such matters is feasible, but the process, by its very nature, is highly subjective. Likewise, several of these criteria obviously refer not only to the individual patient but also to how others define and react to his or her behaviour. One cannot decide that another person's conduct is "unconventional," "violates moral standards," or "creates discomfort in others" by inspecting the condition of the patient's mind or body. Such deductions hinge on knowledge of the patient's social relationships and the behaviours expected by those with whom he or she interacts. It is an axiom of social science that the same behaviour regarded as offensive or abnormal in one cultural context may be considered normal and acceptable in another milieu.

Proponents of the medical model have generally been oblivious to these social contingencies. Their training in science and medicine has not sensitized them to such concerns. From the psychiatrist's vantage point, judgements about whether persons under their care are healthy or sick are relatively technical decisions that, as in the diagnosis of physical illness, are thought to be largely unaffected by factors external to the patient. Recent studies have called this assumption into question (Scheff 1975). This research suggests that the evidence for mental disorder is highly transient and its interpretation is susceptible to bias arising from a variety of social sources. A famous experiment by David Rosenhan (1973) dramatically highlighted how psychiatric diagnoses are influenced by the social context in which the behaviour of those diagnosed is observed. The study involved eight persons with no history of mental disorder who attempted to gain admission to different mental hospitals by alleging to the psychiatrists on duty that they had heard a voice. All eight of these "pseudo patients" were admitted. Once in the hospital they were under instructions to feign no more symptoms, to give truthful answers to questions, to co-operate with the wishes of the staff, and to behave as they normally behaved. In spite of this display of "sane" behaviour, seven of the eight were diagnosed as schizophrenic and all were eventually discharged (after an average stay of nineteen days) with the diagnosis of "schizophrenia in remission." One of the more startling findings of this study was that none of the eight was detected as an imposter by the psychiatrists or other hospital personnel, yet several of the regular patients suspected them of being journalists or professors who were "faking it" in order to do a study of the hospital!

It will likely come as no surprise to learn that the publication of this study drew the wrath of the medical profession. Irate psychiatrists attacked the methodology and ethics of Rosenhan's experiment. Some of their criticisms were, in fact, well taken, but the virulent tone and language of the critics suggests that their real objections were about something more fundamental. Quite understandably, these psychiatrists felt that the study was an indictment of both their competence and their professionalism. To them, Rosenhan seemed almost to be saying that psychiatrists are malicious quacks who lack the intelligence to distinguish between the sane and the insane. This would, of course, be a very serious condemnation and Rosenhan subsequently went to great lengths to reassure members of the mental-health professions that he was neither impugning their expertise nor accusing them of personal callousness (1981, 320).

Unfortunately, the controversy and misunderstanding stirred up by this wild reaction to the study deflected attention from Rosenhan's main finding. Rosenhan concluded that the inability of the hospital staff to detect the pseudo patients testifies to the powerful effects of contextual factors on psychiatric assessment. He conjectured that if this same ruse had been attempted outside of the hospital setting, it probably would not have taken very long for most of these same staff personnel to realize that the patients were phonies. The psychiatrists and other staff were not taken in by Rosenhan's charade because they were stupid, gullible, or poorly trained. Rather, "the fact that most patients in hospitals who hallucinate *are* schizophrenics created a compelling context for these pseudopatients to be considered schizophrenics" (Rosenhan and Seligman 1984, 181). Given the circumstances contrived by Rosenhan—strangers voluntarily presenting themselves to the admissions desk of a mental hospital and claiming that they have been hearing voices—it might actually have been a more amazing result if the staff *had* correctly diagnosed the pseudo patients as normal and refused to hospitalize them. To reiterate, what makes such an outcome hard to imagine is not psychiatrists' ineptitude at evaluating patients. This second scenario is rather far-fetched because, in Rosenhan's words, "the context of the symptoms mattered more in the diagnosis than did the symptoms themselves" (Rosenhan and Seligman 1984, 181).

Rosenhan's study also demonstrated that the labels accompanying psychiatric diagnosis are themselves a source of bias governing how mental patients' behaviour is interpreted by those around them. Labels act as perceptual filters admitting some kinds of information and interpretations, colouring other kinds, and screening out certain kinds altogether. Thus, all of the pseudo patients reported that their statements and behaviour in the hospital wards, while perfectly normal on the face of it, were seldom taken at face value. Instead, they found that the staff construed their actions and utterances in terms of its definition of them as schizophrenics. Alternative explanations that did not jibe with the diagnosis were simply not entertained.

Rosenhan's case for the contextual nature of psychiatric diagnosis has been favourably received by social scientists and "humanistic" therapists. Among mainstream psychiatrists, however, its message has seemingly fallen on deaf ears. Some have conceded that studies such as Rosenhan's pose interesting "philosophical" issues that sometimes intrude upon the practice of psychiatry. This concession easily translates into a dismissal of such concerns as incidental to the scientific thrust of medicine. Like other sciences, psychiatry aspires to be "value free." Accordingly, its practitioners take their mandate to be that of adequately describing and explaining human behaviour. Issuing value judgements about how patients behave is regarded as contrary to the psychiatrist's role as a scientist. In fact, this neutral posture is said to be a safeguard against improperly evaluating behaviour on moral or ideological grounds. Deciding whether a patient is sick or well is thought to be a purely clinical judgement. As such, it supposedly does not matter whether the physician or society approves or disapproves of how the patient acts, thinks, or feels.

This, I submit, is a specious argument. That is, it seems plausible upon first impression, but after closer examination it turns out to be fallacious. Szasz's (1961) dissection of what is actually entailed in assessing so-called delusional thought may help illustrate that clinical judgements are often not so "pure".

> Szasz says that a man's belief that he is Napoleon or is being persecuted by the Communists cannot be explained by a defect or disease of the nervous system. Statements such as these are considered to be mental symptoms only if the observer (the audience) believes that the patient is not Napoleon or is not being persecuted by the Communists. Thus the statement that X is a symptom of a mental disorder includes a social judgment. The observer must match the person's ideas and beliefs to those held by the observer and the rest of society. In other words, *a person's behaviour is judged by how well his or her actions "fit" a concept of normality held by a social audience* (Cockerham 1989, 91; emphasis added).

The clinical characterization of certain types of aberrant behaviour as symptomatic of "illness" does not prevent bias or value judgements from entering psychiatry, it merely disguises them with medical terminology. Any mental health professional operates with implicit standards of "normality" or "adjustment" that serve as benchmarks against which patients' behaviour is evaluated. These standards are bound to reflect society's or the psychiatrist's ideas about what constitutes "normal" behaviour.

If one grants the preceding point, then the charge that psychiatrists function as agents of social control is not so outrageous as one might initially think. This allegation probably conjures up an image of Soviet psychiatrists whose aid has been enlisted by the rulers of that society to have outspoken political dissidents defined as insane and incarcerated in mental institutions. Psychiatrists in our society have rarely been guilty of anything quite so blatant as this. Some radicals have sought to portray North American psychiatrists as henchmen of the establishment. This is unjustified hyperbole. For most psychiatrists a sense of professional ethics, sincere belief in the necessary objectivity of science, and a genuine concern for the welfare of their patients have all militated against knowingly becoming tools of the powers that be. A much more subtle analysis is therefore required to understand how it happens that psychiatrists and other mental-health professionals commonly participate in what amounts to policing deviant behaviour and endorsing the dominant values of society. Much of the behaviour displayed by those who come to be identified and treated as mentally ill is not simply odd, it is sometimes also disturbing, disruptive, and repugnant to those around them. Because we call these people "mentally ill" instead of mad or possessed, because medications rather than strait-jackets are the accepted means of stabilizing their behaviour, and because the authorities who will decide their fate are medical experts rather than political stooges does not alter the fact that psychiatrists are deeply implicated in the business of controlling human behaviour. Even if one believes that psychiatry's use of this power has generally been benign, the potential for abuse is ever-present. Edwin Schur (1980, 30) observes that

> because psychiatric diagnosis is inherently evaluative and hence in a way necessarily arbitrary, application of the mental illness designation is, if unchecked, almost infinitely expandable. Therefore, despite the undoubted benefits that voluntary psychotherapy may confer, and notwithstanding the good intentions of most therapists, compulsory impositions of psychiatric "help" represent a significant mode of social control. Particularly when the state becomes implicated in its public uses, psychiatry may become a latent tool for controlling any or all individuals and groups deemed to threaten or undermine the (political as well as social or cultural) status quo.

Similarly, the aura and trappings of medicine that surround mental illness designations may hide their intimate connection with prevailing societal values. What the psychiatrist calls psychopathology is not simply a biological or even psychological entity that exists independently of a given social system. On the contrary, standards for defining what is pathological are derived from society's moral code. The profoundly social and political character of psychiatric assessment was perhaps never more visible than in the challenges by gay rights activists to the American Psychiatric Association's designation of homosexuality as an illness (Bayer 1986).

In 1973, after years of rancorous debate, members of the association voted to delete homosexuality from its official list of mental illnesses. Both the definition of homosexuality as an illness as well as the subsequent decision to modify its status reveal the influence of changing social mores on standards of psychiatric assessment. The largely uncontested designation of homosexuality as an illness both reflected and reinforced society's countenance of heterosexuality. By the same token, its reclassification reflects and reinforces the recent liberalization of society's attitudes regarding sexual orientation. In either event, the crucial determinant of whether the psychiatrist defines the homosexual as "sick" depends far more on how such persons are viewed by other members of their society than on the actual condition of their minds or bodies

Social Factors in the Etiology of Mental Disorder

Any perspective is both a way of seeing as well as a way of *not* seeing. The medical model of madness is no exception to this rule. Adoption of the model directs one's attention toward some features of mental disorders and away from other features. This selectiveness cannot be faulted if, empirically, the aspects of the phenomena it neglects are relatively unimportant in comparison with the aspects the model highlights. We have seen that the medical interpretation of madness is highly attuned to the malfunctioning of the individual's body. It also sensitizes us, though to a lesser degree, to disturbances in the individual's mind or personality. But what this exclusive focus on the individual systematically shields from view is the possibility that a person's social affiliations may be a determinant of his or her psychological distress. If social factors have a hand in causing mental disorder, the medical model's selectivity is a liability rather than an asset. Social science research suggests that a host of social factors, ranging from value orientations to the level of unemployment, contribute to the incidence of mental disorders (see Mirowsky and Ross 1989). However, I believe this deficiency of the medical model is most glaringly illustrated by its omission of family dynamics in the etiology of mental disorder.

Family Dynamics

Psychiatrists have long been aware of a link between unsatisfactory family experiences and psychological distress. Many of them have discovered that some of their patient's "illnesses" can be effectively treated only by involving other family members. Still, conventional psychiatry's appreciation of the fact that family relations may affect mental health and its treatment stops well short of according causal status to this factor. To elaborate, psychiatrists are by no means averse to the proposition that the everyday relations between individuals and their families are often fertile soil for mental illness. Indeed, practical experience makes the psychiatrist acutely aware that the family is the principal domain wherein people's emotional troubles find expression. This is not equivalent to saying that families may engender mental illness in their members. It is rather a recognition that the stresses and strains of family life make the family an arena where mental disorders will commonly be manifested.[1] But the question at issue is whether or not it is valid to claim that family relationships can be a cause of mental disorder. I wish to argue that there are many situations where such a claim is warranted. To cite one such instance, I shall introduce an actual psychiatric case study.

The story of "Bobby and his parents" was recorded by the unorthodox American psychiatrist M. Scott Peck in his book *People of the Lie*. Peck encountered a 15-year-old boy named Bobby when he worked on the inpatient service of a mental hospital during his first year of psychiatric training. Bobby had been admitted to the hospital from the emergency room a day before Peck first interviewed him. He had been diagnosed as depressed by the admitting psychiatrist. A note written by the latter on Bobby's medical chart contained the following information. Eight months earlier Bobby's older brother committed suicide by shooting himself in the head with a .22 calibre rifle. Though once an above-average student, Bobby was currently failing all of his high school courses. Over the past few months, but particularly since Christmas, Bobby had become increasingly aloof and withdrawn. His parents seemed concerned about this, but found that their efforts to speak with Bobby went nowhere. Bobby did not have a history of antisocial behaviour, until he recently stole a car and, having never driven before, crashed it. This incident led to his apprehension by the police, who charged him with a criminal offence. Because Bobby was legally a juvenile, he was released into his parents' custody. They were advised to obtain an immediate psychiatric evaluation of their son.

Everything about the boy's demeanour in their initial meeting signalled to Peck that Bobby was severely depressed. Many of Peck's preliminary questions were aimed at discovering the patient's feelings about the events that had preceded his hospitalization, but Bobby's responses indicated virtually no emotional self-awareness. Many of his answers and gestures during the interview did, however, convey an attitude of self-blame. For example, when asked about how he got along with his parents, Bobby replied that they were good to him, but that he was sometimes mean to them. He cited his recent theft of the car as a case in point. During a subsequent lull in the interview, Bobby was especially uncommunicative. In an effort to invigorate the conversation and lighten Bobby's mood, Peck decided to ask him about his Christmas. Peck's account of the ensuing dialogue is reproduced here.

Peck: What did you get for Christmas?
Bobby: Nothing much.
Peck: Your parents must have given you something. What did they give you?
Bobby: A gun.
Peck: A gun?
Bobby: Yes.
Peck: What kind of gun? [Peck asked this question slowly.]
Bobby: A twenty-two.
Peck: A twenty-two pistol?
Bobby: No, a twenty-two rifle.
[There was a long moment of silence. Peck felt as if he had lost his bearings. He wanted to stop the interview. He wanted

to go home. Finally he pushed himself to say what had to be said.]

Peck: I understand that it was with a twenty-two rifle that your brother killed himself.
Bobby: Yes.
Peck: Was that what you asked for, for Christmas?
Bobby: No.
Peck: What did you ask for?
Bobby: A tennis racquet.
Peck: But you got the gun instead?
Bobby: Yes.
Peck: How did you feel, getting the same kind of gun your brother had?
Bobby: It wasn't the same kind of gun.
[Peck began to feel better. Maybe he was just confused.]
Peck: I'm sorry, . . . I thought they were the same kind of gun.
Bobby: It wasn't the same kind of gun. It was the gun.
Peck: The gun?
Bobby: Yes.
Peck: You mean it was your brother's gun?
[Peck wanted to go home very badly now.]
Bobby: Yes.
Peck: You mean your parents gave you your brother's gun for Christmas, the one he shot himself with?
Bobby: Yes.
Peck: How did it make you feel getting your brother's gun for Christmas?
Bobby: I don't know.
[Peck almost regretted the question. How could he know? How could he answer such a thing?]
Peck: No, I don't expect you could know (1983, 51–52).

The next day Peck met with Bobby's parents. He describes the couple as respectable, church-going members of the stable blue-collar class—"quiet, orderly, solid." Early in the interview Peck established that there was no history of mental disorder or suicide in either of their families. As the discussion unfolded, Peck formed the strong impression that neither of Bobby's parents had much understanding of the terrible fate that had befallen their two sons. Their responses to Peck's questions about a variety of subjects relating to Bobby's case were consistently hostile and defensive. They reacted to Peck's queries about their Christmas gift to Bobby with a barrage of angry, self-serving rationalizations. Peck was dismayed to learn that neither parent had given much thought to how the gift of his brother's suicide weapon appeared to Bobby. The brutal implications of this act were diplomatically spelled out for them by Peck. He states that while Bobby's parents seemed to accept his analysis, they showed no signs of remorse or guilt.[2]

This case study is extremely instructive for our present purposes. Peck himself addresses one of its key lessons. He states that whenever a child is brought for psychiatric treatment, it is advisable to refer to her or him as the "identified patient." The reason for this phraseology is that one must be sceptical of the supposition that the child is "ill." According to Peck,

> more often than not, as we proceed with the evaluation of the problem, we discover that the source of the problem lies not in the child but rather in his or her parents, family, school, or society. Put most simply, we usually find that the child is not as sick as its parents. Although the parents have identified the child as the one requiring correction, it is usually they, the identifiers, who are themselves most in need of correction. They are the ones who should be the patients (1983, 59).

It does not follow from such redefinitions of the situation, however, that nothing is wrong with the "identified patient." As in Bobby's case, he or she is likely suffering real psychological distress that will require professional assistance to be alleviated. In fact, it is generally a fairly safe bet that where a person has been reared in a disturbed family like Bobby's, his or her character and personality will not emerge from the experience unscathed. To take this point a step farther, one may find that although the identified patient is truly a victim of his or her family circumstances, he or she may both invite and contribute to the victimization process. The child belonging to a troubled family is extremely vulnerable to becoming an accomplice as well as a victim. This complicity obviously adds to the massive emotional confusion typically instilled by such families. The expression of this ambivalence and inner turmoil may well take the form of psychiatric symptoms. These symptoms are a natural and understandable response to the child's untenable family situation. Regardless of whether the designated patient is complicitous or not, Peck is quite right that the source of the distress resides in the particular family environment.

Bobby's case history is a telling commentary on another feature of the conventional psychiatric perspective that Peck does not discuss. You will recall his assertion that in families like Bobby's it is the parents rather than their children who should be diagnosed and treated as "mentally ill." Who would now want to dispute this opinion? Peck's graphic account and astute analysis of where the madness lay in Bobby's family is very persuasive. But, on the surface of things, the essential facts of this case were far from being transparent. The insanity in this family was very well veiled. From all appearances it was Bobby, not his parents, who needed psychiatric attention. If this case had been referred to a more orthodox psychiatrist, chances are that the madness of Bobby's parents would have gone undetected. This is neither because other psychiatrists are less qualified than Peck, nor because Bobby's parents happened to be clever actors who were adept at creating the impression of being "normal." In the final analysis, what shields people like Bobby's mother and father from being identified as psychologically disturbed by both psychiatrists and laypersons is our culturally ingrained assumptions about the nature of mental disorder. These assumptions lead us to equate mental health with normality, conformity, and adjustment to the status quo. Consequently, people like Bobby's parents do not need to put on an "act" in order to pass as sane. Though disturbed, they appear to others as normal. As long as there is nothing particularly bizarre about their outward demeanour, such people may do any number of crazy things with little risk of ever being defined as mentally ill.

The common assumption that madness is an entity lodged in the individual also serves to conceal the kind of insanity that Peck disclosed in Bobby's family. The individualistic bias of our ideas about madness encourage us to believe that a disorder is located in specific persons. This inclines us to suspect that "it" more likely dwells in the identified patient than in his or her significant others. However, there is good reason to believe that like a lot of so-called normal behaviour, insane behaviour is often a collaborative effort that arises out of interactions between individuals. Support for this contention can be gained from research by R.D. Laing and others who have observed the interaction and communication patterns of families in which one of the members has been clinically diagnosed as "mentally ill" (Laing and Esterson 1971; Henry 1963). Consonant with Peck's thesis, these studies often reveal that the ostensibly normal family members are actually more disturbed than the identified patient. But this is not the point these researchers wish to emphasize. What Laing et al. have argued is that the source of the disorder may be the harmful ways the family members routinely interact and communicate with each other—that is, their social relationships. Put another way, the disturbance may not be so much a property of any given person so much as a feature of the collectivities to which he or she belongs. This sociological formulation clearly goes against the conception of madness to which most of us are accustomed. Yet it is precisely this conception that makes families like Bobby's appear "normal." If one assumes that the locus of mental illness is within the individual, one will be predisposed to attribute the problems in such families to the member who happens to exhibit psychiatric symptoms.

Bobby's case was indisputably an extraordinary one. While there are conflicts and stresses within all families, the severity of the disturbances within most of them pale in comparison with Bobby's. But what was said earlier about the difference between "normal" and "abnormal" individuals being a matter of degree rather than kind also applies to families. I believe the impulse to regard the mentally disordered as "freaks" who are very different from ordinary folk arises out of the terrifying threat that madness poses to ordinary folk. Probably for much the same reason, it may be comforting to imagine that mental disorders are the by-product of a few dysfunctional families that are qualitatively different from the "typical family" that affords its children a positive environment. The proposition that disturbed and "normal" families resemble one another is of course an uncongenial notion. Yet a recent review of the social science literature on this issue points in the direction of this melancholy conclusion (Skolniek 1983, 92–94). In spite of what we might wish to believe, it seems that the "dysfunctional family" may not be so atypical and the typical family does not always function so well.

I have argued that family dynamics are highly consequential for people's psychological wellbeing. But families are by no means the only feature of the social environment that is known to affect the level of mental health. Social scientists have identified a number of other factors that contribute to differential rates of mental disorders. I shall briefly discuss just four of these factors—unemployment, social class, gender, and marital status.

Unemployment

Commonsense would, of course, lead one to suspect the existence of a strong relationship between unemployment and severe psychological distress. However, it was not until the publication of Harvey Brenner's *Mental Illness and the Economy* (1973) that this suspicion was subjected to rigorous empirical inquiry. Examining trend data from New York State, Brenner corroborated that fluctuations in the level of unemployment were the single most important predictor of changing rates of admission to mental hospitals. What is more, he discovered that this relationship has remained relatively stable for over 120 years. Brenner (1976) later utilized U.S. employment statistics for the period 1914 to 1970 in order to devise a formula that would enable researchers to estimate the impact of unemployment on various indices of mental and physical health. According to Brenner's calculations, a 1 percent rise in unemployment (if sustained for five years) would be expected to cause the number of first admissions to mental hospitals to increase by 3.3 percent and the suicide rate to go up by 4.1 percent.[3]

It should perhaps be noted that sociologists make no claim that unemployment, family dynamics, or other social facts show an impact on the mental health of individuals in a direct or uniform manner. As with biological or psychological factors, their influence is normally mediated by other variables. The most commonly cited intervening variable between social circumstances and psychopathology is *stress*. The sociological formulation thus asserts that social situations tend to generate varying degrees of stress that, in turn, eventuate in higher or lower rates of mental disorder. The sociologist is merely saying that insofar as stress is associated with psychiatric impairment, the social environment needs to be acknowledged as an important locus of stressors in its own right, as well as a mediator of stresses emanating from both social and non-social sources.

Social Class

Bearing the above formulation in mind, let us consider the connection between social class and mental disorders. Numerous studies in a variety of settings have repeatedly disclosed that the highest overall rates of mental disorder are found among members of society's lowest socio-economic strata (Dohrenwend 1975; Stolzman 1988). The generalization does not apply, however, to all types of disorders. Whereas lower-class persons are overrepresented in the distribution of schizophrenia and personality disorders, what psychiatrists classify as mood and anxiety disorders tend to be more common among the middle and upper classes. I believe sociological analysis can help elucidate these patterns.

Some observers have argued that the relationship between social class and mental disorders is merely a by-product of the fact that mental-illness statistics are often based on numbers of "treated cases"—that is, persons who are currently obtaining or have previously received professional treatment for their problems. This can create a false picture because, for a host of reasons, lower-class people are more apt than middle- and upper-class persons with similar disturbances to end up in the type of treatment settings (for example, public psychiatric facilities) that supply the data epidemiologists use to compile rates of mental disorders. This is a valid point. Statistics based on treated cases exaggerate the degree of class differences in the actual prevalence of psychopathology. On the other hand, there is evidence to indicate that these differences are not wholly a methodological artifact. Several researchers have addressed this issue by conducting their own psychiatric assessments of the general population (e.g., Srole et al. 1962). While their studies confirm that the number of untreated cases in the population is far higher than commonly supposed, they still find an inverse correlation between social class and mental disorders.

Among sociologists there are essentially two schools of thought as to why the incidence of psychiatric disorders is so high in the lower class. One school argues that the conditions of lower-class life routinely expose its members to inordinate amounts of stress (see Kessler 1979). To be lower-class frequently means to live in substandard or crowded housing; to work at an unsatisfying, low-wage, hazardous job; to operate under constant financial insecurity; and to reside in a community that affords little social support. The stressfulness of lower-class existence is compounded by the disrepute that attends low social status in our society. The individualistic ethos pervading North American culture decrees that anyone with talent, intelligence, and ambition can achieve occupational success. By this definition, those who fail to succeed—that is, members of the lower class—have nobody to blame but themselves (Lerner 1986). Lower-class persons are bombarded with cultural messages reminding them that, in society's eyes, they are "losers." In short, low social status is a constant affront to a person's dignity and selfhood.

The other school of thought argues that the greater vulnerability of lower-class people to psychological disturbance is only marginally attributable to the amount of stress they endure. A long-neglected finding of Langner and Michael's 1963 research was that, at any given level of stress, those of lower social standing are more prone to psychiatric disorder than those of higher social status. Recent interpretations of this finding conjecture that lower-class people are generally less adept than middle-class persons in coping with the pressures of modern life. The hypothesis is that lower-class people possess fewer and less adequate resources for dealing with environmental stress. The lower-class person is far more susceptible to having his or her life governed by events and forces outside his or her control. The reasons for this are not hard to fathom. By definition, the lower-class individual is more economically deprived and politically powerless than his or her middle-class counterpart. Consequently, he or she is usually poorly equipped to deal effectively with stressful life experiences as an individual. Melvin Kohn has proposed that the lower class is relatively disadvantaged in coping with stress in another crucial respect. He found that lower-class families tend to transmit a conception of reality that commonly instills in its members fatalism and a weak sense of personal efficacy. According to Kohn,

> the lower a man's social class position, the more likely he is to value conformity to external authority and to believe that such conformity is all that his own capacities and the exigencies of the world allow; in particular the lower a man's social class position, the more likely is his orienta-

> tional system to be marked by a rigid, conservative view of man and his social institutions, fearfulness and distrust, and a fatalistic belief that one is at the mercy of forces and people beyond one's control, often beyond one's understanding (1972, 300).

Kohn believes, and I concur, that this viewpoint should be used to supplement, not contradict, the interpretation that the lower class is exposed to greater stress than the more-privileged members of society.

Although it was not his intention, Kohn's perspective throws light on the aforementioned finding that mood and anxiety disorders are most commonly found in the middle and upper classes. In contrast to lower-class families where parents value obedience and conformity in their children, middle-class parents emphasize the development of self-direction and what Kohn calls "attitudinal conformity." Lower-class parents simply want their children to "do as they're told." The children's motives or feelings about what is expected of them do not really matter to the parents as long as their conduct is compliant. This is different from the middle-class family, where displaying "correct" behaviour is less important to the parents than the internalization of proper values and attitudes in the children. As Arnold Green (1946) pointed out over 40 years ago, the middle-class socialization pattern involves "personality absorption." Unlike the lower-class child whose parents do not seek dominion over his or her motives and feelings, the inner state of the middle-class child is very much the object of his or her parents' attention. The premium on attitudinal conformity introduces a whole range of tensions to social interaction in middle-class families that is largely absent in lower-class family relationships. Rose Coser (1982) illustrates this difference by observing that when a lower-class mother implores her young child to get out of her way while she is cleaning the kitchen, the message is straightforward and does not imply anything—one way or the other—about how the mother feels about the child. The very same incident in a middle-class family would probably take on quite different emotional significance. Mother's command to the child is apt to be fraught with ambiguity and may lead the child to wonder whether rejection or a diminution of mother's affection is being communicated (Coser 1982, 510). So, while the inculcation of middle-class values may promote conceptions of reality that reduce one's risk of becoming psychotic or schizophrenic, this mode of socialization may actually increase the chances that one will eventually suffer from an anxiety or mood disorder.

Gender

The rise of the women's movement in recent decades has sparked considerable interest in male-female differences in psychological distress and the effects of marital status on the mental health of men and women.

In general, there appears to be no significant difference between the sexes in overall rates of mental disorder. This generalization also holds true for schizophrenia, the most common primary diagnosis of both male and female admissions to mental hospitals. There are thus no statistical grounds for asserting that one sex is mentally healthier than the other. However, data on the prevalence of both treated and untreated cases reveal some interesting and consistent gender differences in the rates of certain categories of mental disorder. In his review of studies on this issue, Dohrenwend (1975) reports that rates of mood and anxiety disorders are consistently higher for women, whereas rates of personality disorders are consistently higher for men. It is also well documented that substance use and substance-abuse disorders are considerably more common among males.

It is probable that biological differences between males and females supply part of the explanation for this pattern. But socio-cultural factors are perhaps equally or even more operative in causing men and women to gravitate toward dissimilar types of psychiatric disturbances. Many observers contend that this divergent pattern is a logical outgrowth of the rigid channelling of males and females into society's traditional gender roles. Gender-based differences in "abnormal" as well as "normal" behaviour are said to be the result of socialization into socially prescribed roles for men and women. By this process, girls are taught to be passive and attuned to the needs of others, while boys are taught to be aggressive and independent. Although these traditional roles may confer certain psychological advantages to each sex (for example, unselfishness in females, confidence in males) they simultaneously carry their own characteristic psychological hazards. Thus, the traditional female role seemingly lends itself to affective disorders, especially depression, in certain fundamental respects. Depression has been described by Seligman (1975) as "learned helplessness." Other clinicians have understood this disorder as anger directed inward against the self (Eichenbaum and Orbach 1982). In either event, its connection to traits associated with the stereotypical female role is fairly apparent. Likewise, men's susceptibility to personality disorders and substance abuse, both of which frequently entail displays of violent or antisocial behaviour, may be linked to constrictions imposed by the traditional male role and its narrow standards of masculinity.

The liabilities accompanying these roles are compounded when men and women enter the world of work. This is particularly true for women who—faced with the decision of whether to be a homemaker, pursue a career, or somehow combine the two—may encounter a "double-bind" (a no-win) situation. To become a homemaker is to assume an occupational role that many women experience as frustrating, isolating, and socially devalued. Establishing a career outside the home invites another set of stresses. Gainfully employed women commonly encounter prejudice, discrimination, or sexual harassment in their jobs. Nor is it unusual for career women who manage to achieve a measure of occupational success to report feeling guilty about not adequately fulfilling the traditional maternal role. Under these circumstances, combining a regular job with being a homemaker may mean partaking of the worst of both worlds. For men, the social environment and cultural expectations tend to be much more accommodating. The perennial tension between job and family responsibilities that so exasperates women is far less likely to be experienced by men as a conflict. The primacy of the "breadwinner" role for males is culturally sanctioned.

Women's predicament is exacerbated by the existence of a double standard in how mental health is evaluated in our society. Research by Broverman and her colleagues (1970) demonstrated that the standards psychologists and other mental-health professionals employ contain a definite male bias. That is to say, both expert and popular conceptions of what constitutes "normality" tend to favour so-called masculine traits over feminine attributes. Again, this double standard places women in a "damned if you do, damned if you don't" position. If feminine traits are adopted, the woman tacitly accepts what amounts to second-class citizenship; if masculine traits are adopted, her behaviour is more apt to be defined as deviant. In general, this double standard no doubt adds to the stress women confront in attempting to comply with society's role expectations. But in certain respects it may also alleviate stress. Because females as a category are perceived as less "normal" than males, they enjoy a greater latitude of tolerance with respect to how society reacts to unusual behaviour on their part. Put another way, the double standard means that males are more likely than females to be defined as requiring psychiatric attention when they engage in abnormal behaviour. As Cockerham states, "When both men and women perform acts indicative of mental disorder, men are more likely to be perceived as mentally ill because symptoms of distress and disorganization are considered to be more usual among females" (1989, 176).

So we see that society's traditional sex-role differentiation may itself be a source of stresses that lead men and women to manifest quite different sorts of psychiatric symptoms. Indirect support for this proposition may be derived from Weich's (1968) telling observation that there are marked differences in the clinical symptoms of male and female schizophrenics. His "sex role exchange" hypothesis is summarized by Gallagher as follows: "Male schizophrenics adopt a feminine pattern of passivity, withdrawal, and submissiveness. Female schizophrenics, on the other hand, adopt masculine patterns of aggression and hyperactivity" (1980, 202) . Gallagher speculates that "it is as if schizophrenia forces the person into behaviour appropriate to the opposite sex" (1980, 202). I would go even farther and submit that it is as if people must "go crazy" in order to give full expression to personality traits that society deems inappropriate to one's gender.

Marital Status

Time and again, empirical research has documented that married people generally have better mental health than unmarried people. As I have already argued at some length, families and spouses can be, and often are instigators of psychological distress. Conversely, where marital relationships are stable and mutually supportive they can help cushion or mitigate the effects of psychosocial stress. For example, Brown and Harris's (1978) study of depression among British women discovered that the main factor differentiating females who became seriously depressed from those who did not was the quality of the women's relationship with their mates. The females in their sample who suffered severe bouts of depression were drawn disproportionately from those women who lacked intimate and supportive involvement with their spouses. Presumably, the absence of such emotional support fosters social and psychological isolation, thereby increasing these women's susceptibility to depression.

It must be noted, however, that marriage has rather uneven effects on the mental health of men and women. Although hospital admission rates for married women are lower than for single women, the degree of protection marriage affords women is relatively minor when compared to its positive effects on men. Being married seems to substantially enhance men's mental health while offering only slight advantage to females. This is once again sociologically understandable. Marriage is probably comparatively less satisfying for women than for men under the present social arrangements because for women, being married typically means having less control over their lives as well as having a dependency on the careers of their husbands. Moreover, as Gove (1972) has observed, for many women marriage is the sole or chief source of satisfaction in their lives. If this role proves wanting, women are left without an acceptable alternative to bolster their self-esteem. Married men, by contrast, usually occupy two major statuses from which they may derive meaning—head of the household and holder of a job. If one of these roles does not yield sufficient gratification, the male still has the other to fall back on as a central life interest that promotes his mental health. If this line of analysis is valid, one would predict that the recent trend of larger numbers of women entering the labour force will have beneficial consequences for their level of mental health, particularly if employment opportunities for women change in the direction of greater equality. By the same token, these changes in the job market may translate into higher aggregate rates of mental disorder for men.

Conclusions

Looking at mental disorders sociologically seems to complicate matters and to carry unsettling implications. Since this has been a recurrent theme in the chapter, it is perhaps fitting to conclude the discussion by offering some final observations on this point.

The medical conception of madness and its chief exponents, the psychiatric profession, have been challenged and criticized throughout this chapter. I hope the arguments presented will strike readers as reasoned, balanced, and constructive. However, I am afraid that arguing *for* a social perspective on mental disorders often means arguing *against* the conventional psychiatric viewpoint. The clash is virtually unavoidable because the ideas that comprise the medical model are not a bundle of untested and untried notions that are of little consequence beyond the boundaries of the psychiatric community. The point is, these ideas inform the mental-health care system of our society. Thus a rather thin line runs between critical sociological analysis of this area and "psychiatry bashing." Sociological critiques of the medicalization of madness that convey the impression that the predominance of the medical approach is a result of the political machinations of self-interested psychiatrists border on vilification. Paradoxically, this explanation is itself quite unsociological. To be sure, the emergence, consolidation, and ascendancy of the medical interpretation did not occur spontaneously or randomly. Its dominance today is largely a result of efforts taken by certain people at various times in particular places to promote it. Many, probably most, of its champions have been psychiatrists. It is also reasonable to surmise that the prospect of increased revenue, power, and prestige supplied a good portion of the motivation for this promotional activity. Like any other occupational group, psychiatry has its shadowy side, but it is by no means the only side. As I earlier acknowledged, psychiatry's defence of the medical model was also born of intellectual conviction and compassion for the mentally tormented.

To comprehend adequately how psychiatry's view of madness attained its present hegemony, I believe it is necessary to look beyond the motives and activities of its proponents. More specifically, if we want to explain why these ideas gained acceptance in the wider society, we must consider the nature of their appeal to this audience. Clearly, something about the biomedical perspective on mental disorder struck a responsive chord in ordinary citizens. I wish to argue that its mass appeal cannot be understood apart from the deep-seated fear and loathing of mental disorder that persists in our society. The prospect of madness remains one of the supreme terrors of human existence. The most conspicuous expression of these attitudes is the nearly indelible social stigma that attaches to persons defined as "mentally ill." They are reflected in our humour. The myriad jokes, cartoons, television sitcoms, etc., that allude to "craziness" and "crazy" people both play on and give vent to our anxiety about insanity. Our apprehension and scorn are attested to by the absence of telethons or similar fund-raising campaigns for disorders such as schizophrenia. Official, public attitudes toward the mentally "ill" are today probably more favourable and less intolerant than in previous eras. But I believe these more positive attitudes are but a gloss on a substratum of essentially medieval notions that still equate madness with wickedness.

Set in this context it is perhaps easier to appreciate why the medical model of madness has proven attractive to lay persons. Although it was unintended, the model in effect tells people what they want to hear. Given the public's latent fears about madness, psychiatry's message that insanity represents an illness rather than a depravity has been a more-or-less reassuring one. The diagnosis that what ails the madman lies in his genes or the neurotransmitters of his brain, while not exactly good news, is more agreeable than the suspicion he is possessed by demons. The conception of madness as disease has other attractions as well. Foremost among these may be that, in the public's mind, calling something an illness removes it from the realm of personal or social responsibility. In our society, "being sick" carries the connotation that no one is to blame for the illness; "it" simply visits some people and bypasses others for reasons that are putatively unrelated to human agency or social conditions. Never mind that this connotation is a mistaken one and rejected by many physicians; people act on the basis of what they believe to be true. Of course what we define as true is often coloured by wishful thinking. In light of our almost unspeakable fears about madness and its "real" causes, I believe we are easily seduced by the suggestion that mental disorder has nothing to do with our experiences, our families, or our society. Is it possible that the medical conception of madness is itself medicinal? If so, this may signal a fruitful point of departure for sociological analysis of the interplay between psychiatric thought and the social imagery of mental disorder.

Study Questions

1. What does it mean to analyze mental disorders "sociologically"?

2. Does a social perspective on madness necessarily imply that mental disorder is only in the eye of the beholder? Why or why not?

3. Why would Conrad and Schneider argue that the predominance of the medical conception of madness has been more of a political than a scientific achievement?

4. Why did the author suggest that it might have been a more remarkable result of Rosenhan's study if the hospital staff had recognized that the pseudo patients were imposters?

5. Explain why sociologists tend to reject the proposition that the source of psychological distress always lies within the mind or body of an individual.

6. To what extent do you believe that social class, gender, and other types of bias enter into psychiatric diagnosis? Is such a bias unavoidable or do you think it is possible to devise standards of mental health that are relatively value free?

7. The author speculates that there may be a relationship between the public's fear and loathing of madness and the appeal of the medical interpretation. How would you design a test of this hypothesis?

Recommended Reading

Conrad, Peter, and Joseph Schneider. *Deviance and Medicalization: From Badness to Sickness*. St. Louis: Mosby, 1980.

Henry, Jules. *Culture Against Man*. New York: Random House, 1963.

Ingleby, David, ed. *Critical Psychiatry: The Politics of Mental Health*. Harmondsworth: Penguin Books, 1981.

Kohn, Melvin. "Social Class and Schizophrenia: A Critical Review and a Reformulation," In *The Sociology of Mental Illness: Basic Studies*, ed. O. Grusky and M. Pollner. New York: Holt Rinehart and Winston, 1981. 127–43.

Rosenhan, David. "On Being Sane in Insane Places," *Science* 179 (1973): 250–58.

Scheff, Thomas J. *Being Mentally Ill: A Sociological Theory*. 2d ed. New York: Aldine, 1984.

Valenstein, Elliot. *Great and Desperate Cures: The Rise and Decline of Psychosurgery and Other Radical Treatments for Mental Illness*. New York: Basic Books, 1986.

Notes

1. The theoretical import of the family is not dissimilar to that accorded the physical climate. Psychiatrists will affirm that dreary, dismal weather conditions have a negative impact on people's mental state and may even contribute to mood disorders and depression. Still, no psychiatrist would claim that weather was the cause of these disorders; it is rather regarded as an extraneous factor that may affect their prevalence in a community. I have no quarrel with this formulation as it applies to the weather. Neither, of course, would I doubt the proposition that the quality of family life in a society will influence, for better or worse, its overall rate of mental disorders. I do argue, however, that family relationships, unlike the weather, may be a causal factor in some mental disorders.
2. After some protestations, the parents acquiesced in Peck's recommendation that Bobby temporarily reside with a favourite aunt in a city some distance from his home town. At last report, according to Peck, Bobby was undergoing a successful psychotherapy.
3. Aggregate data studies such as Brenner's do not imply that the individuals who become unemployed are the same persons as those who become mentally disordered or commit suicide. It is probable that only some of the additional mental illness or suicide cases occur among those who are themselves unemployed. Many, if not more, of these cases will likely be persons somewhat less directly affected by layoffs. The spouses of the unemployed and those workers whose jobs are rendered insecure by economic downturns represent two obvious groups of people whose susceptibility to psychological distress is heightened when unemployment is on the increase

References

Bayer, R. 1986. *Homosexuality and American Psychiatry: The Politics of Diagnosis*. Princeton: Princeton University Press.

Brenner, M.H. 1973. *Mental Illness and the Economy*. Cambridge: Harvard University Press.

———. 1976. *Estimating the Social Costs of National Economic Policy*. Washington, DC: U.S. Government Printing Office.

Broverman, I., D. Broverman, F. Clarkson, P. Rosenkrantz, and S. Vogel. 1970. "Sex Role Stereotypes and Clinical Judgments of Mental Health." *Journal of Consulting and Clinical Psychology* 34: 1–7.

Brown, G., and T. Harris. 1978. *Social Origins of Depression*. New York: Free Press.

Cockerham, W. 1989. *Sociology of Mental Disorder*. 2d ed. Englewood Cliffs, NJ: Prentice-Hall.

Conrad, P. 1981. "On the Medicalization of Deviance and Social Control." In *Critical Psychiatry: The Politics of Mental Health*, ed. D. Ingleby. Harmondsworth, England: Penguin Books.

Conrad, P., and J. Schneider. 1980. *Deviance and Medicalization: From Badness to Sickness*. St. Louis: Mosby.

Coser, R. 1982. "Authority and Structural Ambivalence in the Middle-Class Family," In *Sociological Theory*, 5th ed., ed. L. Coser and B. Rosenberg. New York: Macmillan. 508–18.

Dohrenwend, B. 1975. "Sociocultural and Social-psychological Factors in the Genesis of Mental Disorders." *Journal of Health and Social Behaviour* 16: 365–92.

Durkheim, E. 1951 [1897]. *Suicide: A Study in Sociology*. New York: Free Press.

Eaton, W. 1986. *The Sociology of Mental Disorders*. 2d ed. New York: Praeger.

Eichenbaum, L., and S. Orbach. 1982. *Understanding Women*. New York: Basic Books.

Gallagher, B. 1980. *The Sociology of Mental Illness*. Englewood Cliffs, NJ: Prentice-Hall.

Gove, W. 1972. "Sex Roles, Marital Roles, and Mental Illness." *Social Forces* 51: 34–44.

Green, A. 1946. "The Middle Class Male Child and Neurosis." *American Sociological Review* 11: 31–41.

Grusky, O., and M. Pollner, eds. 1981. *The Sociology of Mental Illness: Basic Studies*. New York: Holt, Rinehart and Winston.

Henry, J. 1963. *Culture Against Man*. New York: Random House.

Illich, I. 1976. *Limits to Medicine: Medical Nemesis, the Expropriation of Health.* Toronto: McClelland and Stewart.

Ingleby, D., ed. 1981. *Critical Psychiatry: The Politics of Mental Health.* Harmondsworth, England: Penguin Books.

Kessler, R. 1979. "Stress, Social Status, and Psychological Distress." *Journal of Health and Social Behaviour* 20: 259–72.

Kohn, M. 1972. "Class, Family, and Schizophrenia." *Social Forces* 50: 295–304.

Laing, R.D., and A. Esterson. 1971. *Sanity, Madness, and the Family: Families of Schizophrenics.* 2d ed. New York: Basic Books.

Langner, T., and S. Michael. 1963. *Life Stress and Mental Health.* London: Free Press of Glencoe.

Lerner, M. 1986. *Surplus Powerlessness.* Oakland, CA: Institute for Labor and Mental Health.

Mirowsky J., and C. Ross. 1989. *Social Causes of Psychological Distress.* New York: Aldine de Gruyter.

Peck, M.S. 1983. *People of the Lie: The Hope for Healing Human Evil.* New York: Simon and Schuster.

Rosenhan, D. 1973. "On Being Sane in Insane Places." *Science* 179: 250–58.

———. 1981. "The Contextual Nature of Psychiatric Diagnosis," In Grusky and Pollner, *Sociology of Mental Illness.* 319–29.

Rosenhan, D., and M. Seligman. 1984. *Abnormal Psychology.* New York: Norton.

Scheff, T., ed. 1975. *Labeling Madness.* Englewood Cliffs, NJ: Prentice-Hall.

Schur, E. 1980. *The Politics of Deviance: Stigma Contests and the Uses of Power.* Englewood Cliffs, NJ: Prentice-Hall.

Seligman, M. 1975. *Helplessness.* San Francisco: W.H. Freeman.

Skolnick, A. 1983. *The Intimate Environment: Exploring Marriage and the Family.* 3d ed. Boston: Little, Brown.

Srole, L., T. Langner, S. Michael, M. Opler, and T. Rennie. 1962. *Mental Health in the Metropolis.* New York: McGraw-Hill.

Stolzman, J. 1988. "The Distribution and Treatment of Mental Disorders by Social Class," In *Sociology of Health Care in Canada*, ed. B.S. Bolaria and H. Dickinson. Toronto: Harcourt Brace Jovanovich. 261–77.

Szasz, T. 1961. *The Myth of Mental Illness.* New York: Harper and Row. (Rev. ed., 1974.)

Valenstein, E. 1986. *Great and Desperate Cures: The Rise and Decline of Psychosurgery and Other Radical Treatments for Mental Illness.* New York: Basic Books.

Welch, M. 1968. "Behavioral Differences Between Groups of Acutely Psychotic (Schizophrenic) Males and Females." *Psychiatric Quarterly* 42: 103–13.

PART IV

State, Capital, and Labour

INTRODUCTION

Material production requires labour power. For a capitalist economy to function, its labour force has to be produced, maintained, and renewed. In the process of consuming labour power, the capitalist is able to realize a gain in value beyond the wages paid to the labourer. The value beyond that required to purchase the labour is known as *surplus value*.

The amount of the wage paid to labour—what it costs the capitalist to buy labour power—is influenced by many factors, and may range from what is needed for mere subsistence to a level sufficient to maintain a traditional standard of living. The size of the industrial "reserve army of labour," the unemployed or irregularly employed who compete with workers for their jobs, contributes to the variations in wage level. Capitalists seek every means to reduce labour costs and to increase the output of their workers so they can realize an even larger surplus. There is an inherent conflict of interest over surplus value between the capitalists and the workers; surplus value and wages are inversely related.

Capitalist relations of production are characterized by the existence of a specific set of class relations, and by the transformation of labour into a commodity, and the appropriation of surplus value by the capitalist class. It may be noted that under other social forms—slavery and feudalism—a ruling class also appropriated a surplus from the working population. Yet, in a capitalist society, the way in which a surplus is appropriated takes a special form: the capitalists exercise direct control over all the processes of labour and production through their ownership of the means of production. To be sure, the organization of work and the control of the production is primarily a product of the outcome of the historical struggle between labour and capital. Labour has had some victories, but the production process under capitalism remains characterized by the primacy of management control. The institutionalization of this control varies with the nature of the production process. In the case of low-cost labour, management's control rests primarily on the powerlessness of the workers.

The state plays a crucial role in structuring capital–labour relations and capital accumulation. The capitalist system of production and exploitation is secured by the capitalist state, which has a monopoly over the legitimate use of force; this coercive force is embodied in law and legal institutions. Collective bargaining procedures, the enforcement of labour laws, "back to work" legislation, and setting minimum wage levels are all examples of state intervention and institutionalization of capital labour relations. In sum, the extraction of surplus from workers in the process of production is an act of power by the capitalist class exercised through the capitalist state.

In capitalist countries a number of contradictions arise out of the economic and social relations of production and conflicting class interests. The state plays an important role in structuring, or "mediating," labour capital and property relations. The issues that are the outcome of these contradictions are discussed in this section.

Harley D. Dickinson, in the chapter entitled "Work and Unemployment as Social Issues," argues that unemployment is best understood as a social issue rather than a personal problem. Further, he argues that an adequate understanding of unemployment requires that it be analyzed in relation to the nature and organization of employment. Dickinson divides his chapter into five main sections. In the first section, he states that unemployment becomes a major social issue only in the context of societies where the capitalist mode of production is dominant and the majority of people are dependent on wages and other forms of employment income for their livelihood. In the second section he outlines a theory of the capitalist labour process, where he argues that the changing nature of both employment and unemployment is a consequence of capitalist employers attempting to increase worker productivity and decrease the costs of production in order to maximize profitability. More specifically, the extension of the occupational division of labour and the development of productivity-enhancing and labour-saving technology contribute to contradictory tendencies: an increased demand for wage labour of some categories of workers and a decreased demand for the labour of others. These tendencies result in different experiences of employment and unemployment for different categories of workers.

In the next section, Dickinson examines some of the ways in which this has had an effect on workers in the goods-producing sector of the economy. The major trends that he describes strongly suggest that attempts by employers to increase workers' productivity and reduce the costs of production have resulted in decreased wages and incomes, declining union membership, and increased frequency and duration of unemployment for certain categories of workers—women, younger workers, and older workers. Then he looks at the same processes in the services-producing sector of the economy, where similar forms of productivity-enhancement and cost reduction affect different categories of workers. Finally, he discusses the growth and trends in self-employment.

In conclusion, he states that the experience of intermittent unemployment is likely to be increasingly common for a growing number of workers. The problem of unemployment, he argues, requires a political solution.

Even when some segments of the labour force face high levels of unemployment, Canada continues to import foreign workers to supplement the labour pool and meet the demand for labour in some sectors of the economy. Immigrant labour has always been crucial for Canadian development and capital accumulation. As capitalism has become increasingly global in character, the internationalization of capital has been accompanied by the internationalization of labour. Global disparities allow the advanced capitalist countries, including Canada, to have access to the international labour pool. The flow of this labour to the labour-importing countries is regulated by the state through immigration laws.

In his chapter on the international migration of workers to Canada, Vic Satzewich argues that these migratory flows are structured by a dialectic of economic, political, and ideological relations. These relations, he notes, are by no means complementary or consistent. Immigration levels and the ethnic composition of immigrant groups are continuously being shaped by contradictory forces.

Satzewich identifies three sets of issues associated with international migration to Canada. These are contradictions between migration as an aspect of capital accumulation and migration as an aspect of nation-state formation; political and ideological constraints faced by the state in using immigration to solve demographic and fiscal problems associated with the declining fertility and aging of its population; and the question of whether migration contributes to economic development in labour-exporting countries or whether it is a new form of post-colonial exploitation.

Satzewich argues that immigration and migration controls are the outcome of a contradiction between the process of capital accumulation and the process of nation-state formation. This is demonstrated by the data on overall immigration to this country and restrictive and exclusionary policies with respect to certain categories of immigrants. Canada has sought out not simply inexpensive labour, but labour that could also become part of the Canadian "imagined community." Some workers may be desirable from an accumulation standpoint, but may not be considered as good potential citizens because of racial or other characteristics.

Satzewich observes that future socio-economic problems associated with population aging and declining fertility could be resolved by increasing the level of immigration to Canada. However, racism and the continued salience of race ("white man's country") in the definition of Canada as a nation-state may preclude the use of immigrant labour from non-traditional source countries to resolve Canada's social and economic problems.

Social and economic contradictions are being managed partly through immigration regulations. Through restrictions on entry, the Canadian state has been successful in converting what otherwise might have been permanent settlers into lower-cost migrant contract labour. Immigration laws allow foreign labour to be admitted without granting the workers the legal status of regular immigrants. Since the introduction of the Employment Authorization Program in 1973, thousands of workers, ranging from professionals to unskilled labourers, have been admitted as temporary workers. A case in point is the seasonal agricultural workers' program, by which Caribbean workers are admitted to work on farms without being granted landed immigrant status and subsequent citizenship rights. The evidence presented in this chapter also indicates that, contrary to the claims of the Canadian government, the earnings by Caribbean workers mostly have a "consumption effect," rather than producing modernization and economic development in the Caribbean. The admission of these workers under contractual arrangements allows the exploitation of their labour by employers in Canada, without any threat to the Canadian "imagined community."

In the last essay in this section, William K. Carroll and Rennie Warburton analyze the changing relationships among capital, labour, and the state since the Second World War. They delineate two phases: a long period of capital accumulation, followed in the mid-1970s by a global economic crisis.

The era of postwar prosperity enabled capital and labour to reach agreement within an institutional framework of "class compromise." Labour and capital continued to oppose each other over matters of wages, benefits, and working conditions, but their conflict was mediated by the Keynesian welfare state. The material basis for this compromise was provided by Fordism, which enabled capitalists to maintain relatively high profits even as they granted wage increases to their employees. Under the system of free collective bargaining, labour's agenda was narrowed to strictly economic issues.

Even during this prosperous era, the permeability of Canada's economy to continentalist pressures and the fragmentation of its labour movement limited both the state's ability to implement Keynesian policies and labour's effectiveness and independence.

The golden age of Fordism came to an end in the 1970s as capitalists responded to the downturn in profit rates by expanding mass production to countries with lower production costs. The resulting structures of global accumulation have strengthened the power of capital. In the advanced capitalist countries, the emerging post-Fordist regime is one of *hegemonic despotism*. It is "hegemonic" in the sense that, as in the heyday of Fordism, the interests of capital and labour continue to be mediated and co-ordinated by the state. But where labour used to be granted concessions based on the expansion of productivity and profits, it now makes concessions in the international competition for investment. Capital's enhanced structural power thus makes its rule more despotic, even if the formal structures of collective bargaining and representative democracy remain intact.

The shift toward hegemonic despotism has been particularly marked in Canada. Compared to other leading capitalist countries, the Canadian state has become especially involved in the movement from consent to coercion in its legislation affecting labour.

Another element in the movement away from Fordist class compromise is the general trend in the advanced capitalist countries toward a new structure of production relations that polarizes the working class into a relatively secure and protected minority and a fragmented, relatively unprotected majority of "non-established" workers. Various corporate strategies are being used to restructure the workplace and wage relations in the direction of greater managerial control, higher productivity, and a disorganized, compliant work force. Different restructuring strategies are applied to the primary labour market, typically consisting of well-established, unionized male workers, and the more vulnerable secondary labour market.

A final feature of the changed capital-labour relation is unique to Canada. It has to do with the Canada–U.S. Free Trade Agreement, described as a means of importing the Reagan revolution "via the back door," and the North American Free Trade Agreement. These agreements have been hastening the movement away from the Keynesian welfare state and toward the type of hegemonic despotism practised in the United States, where it is already most advanced.

There are several possible courses for labour to take to meet the challenges of globalized capitalism. The least likely to succeed is an attempt to return to the previous system of class compromise. A less-defensive strategy for labour would be to expand its horizons in two respects: to take innovative action and to establish new alliances with other democratic movements.

In conclusion, Carroll and Warburton explore four aspects of these strategies: the struggle for real control of production by workers; the strengthening of international labour solidarity; the creation of alliances with organizations such as consumers and community-based economic development groups; and alliances with the "new social movements"—particularly feminism, ecology, and the peace movement—which have been gaining ground while unions have seen their traditional strongholds eroded by the deepening crisis of Fordism.

CHAPTER 13

Work and Unemployment as Social Issues

Harley D. Dickinson

Learning Objectives

After reading this chapter, students will be aware of the major linkages between the nature and organization of work and unemployment in capitalist societies, and the way in which the extension of the division of labour is related to the expansion of both employment and unemployment. The student will also be able to discuss some of the reasons for the development of productivity-enhancing and labour-saving technologies and some consequences of this for unemployment patterns. Students will recognize that the likelihood, duration, and consequences of unemployment are differentially experienced by men and women and by members of different age, ethnic, and other groups in Canada. The chapter should also enable students to consider unemployment as a structural problem with political solutions as well as a personal problem with individual solutions.

Introduction

Unemployment rates on average have been rising steadily for several decades. It is commonplace to hear these rates reported on a regular basis—unemployment is accepted as an inevitable characteristic of life in modern societies. The question as to why this should be so, however, is infrequently asked, and even less frequently answered. In this chapter I examine unemployment as a social issue. Following C. Wright Mills (1959), I argue that unemployment is most appropriately understood as a social issue—and not as a personal problem. Unemployment is largely a consequence of contradictions in the nature and organization of employment, or the characteristics of work processes, in modern capitalist societies. Unemployment cannot adequately be understood in terms of the personal characteristics of unemployed individuals.

If we accept the proposition that unemployment, considered as a social issue cannot be understood in isolation from employment, then we also must accept the proposition that the causes and conditions of unemployment are no more homogeneous than are the terms and conditions of work. That is, the terms and conditions of employment, as well as the duration and extent of unemployment, vary over time by industry and occupation, and by different categories of workers. Thus, the reporting of official unemployment rates, which include everybody in the labour force, obscures substantial and significant differences among various categories of workers, in various industries, at various times. In this chapter some of these differences are examined in the context of a labour process theory that provides a framework for understanding some of the causes and consequences of changing conditions of employment and unemployment.

The chapter is divided into four sections. The first provides a general overview of the rise to dominance of the capitalist mode of production. I argue that the specific nature of capitalist class relations creates the circumstances within which unemployment emerges as a major social issue. The second section consists of a brief outline of labour process theory, with a view to showing how the pursuit of employer interests results in unemployment. The third section examines some of the ways in which the transformation of work results in changes to both the structure of the economy and the nature of employment and unemployment. Other consequences of the pursuit of employer interests, such as the growth in part-time work and the reduction in average incomes, especially among certain segments of the population, are also discussed in this section. In the fourth section I conclude that the solution to unemployment is to be found in the political realm and demands the reorganization of the social relations of work.

The Capitalist Mode of Production and Wage Labour

Dependence on employment income for survival results in unemployment being both a personal problem and a social issue. A central feature of modern capitalist societies is that many people do not have access to alternative sources of livelihood. This state of affairs is relatively recent; the creation of the modern wage-earning class characteristic of all modern capitalist societies is a process that is still going on.

Many, if not most, socially necessary goods and services in capitalist societies are produced for exchange (sale) on various commodity markets by people working for wages or salaries. The incomes derived from those wages and salaries are then used to purchase goods and service in the marketplace. In order for the capitalist system of production to expand, people must be freed from any social relationships, duties, obligations, commitments, or alternative sources of earning a living, so that they are available, willing, and able to serve as part of the wage-earning class. Much modern social policy is directed toward achieving this end. Under these circumstances, wage earners are extremely dependent upon employers for jobs.

Although it is beyond the scope of this chapter to examine the making of the modern working class in Canada, a growing body of literature exists on this topic. According to Pentland (1981) and others (Kealey 1979, 1980; Palmer 1979, 1980), the later decades of the nineteenth century saw the rise to dominance of industrial capitalism in Canada. This corresponded to the formation and transformation of an increasing proportion of the population into members of the wage-earning class, or the modern working class. In 1991 there was a total of 12.34 million workers in Canada. Excluding all those who were self-employed or unpaid family workers, we are left with about 9.87 million paid employees, or about 80 percent of all workers in Canada in 1991 whose primary source of income was wages or salaries (Statistics Canada 1992, Table 2). This represents on increase of 2.9 million workers since 1976 and the continuation of a long-term trend of growth in the absolute size of the labour force. In recent years the proportion of the labour force that received its primary income from paid employment has decreased: from 85.6 percent in 1988 to about 80 percent in 1991. Much of the growth in the labour force in recent decades is accounted for by expansion of self-employment. Between 1975 and 1986 the self-employment/population ratio has risen by more than 25 percent, whereas the paid worker/population ratio has increased by less than 2 percent (Statistics Canada 1988, 25). Selected aspects of the growth in self-employment are presented below.

The growth in the labour force and the concomitant process of integration into the working class occurs unevenly. Thus, different categories of people, at different times, are differentially integrated into or excluded from participation in the wage relation. More concretely, this means that different categories of people, such as women, the young, the elderly, and members of ethnic minorities perform different types of jobs under different working conditions, for different levels of pay and with different consequences. One consequence, of course, is a different probability and duration of unemployment.

Labour Process Theory and Unemployment

All societies must solve the problems of producing and distributing wealth. At a more concrete level, this is manifested as the problem of production and distribution of the goods and services required for a socially acceptable standard of living. The different ways of solving these problems give rise to different types of societies and different types of individuals. Capitalist societies are those in which the capitalist mode of production and circulation is dominant. This is not to say that no other modes of production and circulation exist in those societies, but rather that the noncapitalist modes are less significant in terms of the quantity of economic activity accounted for, or the proportion of the population involved.

As mentioned above, one of the identifying features of capitalism is its specific class composition and the nature of its class relations. The necessary classes for capitalism to exist are, of course, the capitalist class and the working class. This does not mean that other classes do not exist within societies where the capitalist mode of production is dominant. Rather. it means that those other classes are not necessary for capitalism, considered as a mode of production, to exist. The capitalist class and the working class exist only in relation to each other. That is, the capitalist class consists of those members of society who own and control the means of production, and who employ others. The working class consists of those members of society who do not own any means of production and who sell their labour power—their mental and physical capacity to do work—for wages or salaries to those who own the means of production. The means of production consist of those things that are necessary for production to take place. This includes plant equipment, machinery, raw materials and everything else, exclusive of labour power, that is needed for the production of goods and services.

The relationship between employers and employees consists of mutual, but unequal, dependence: Capitalist employers are dependent on an adequate supply of people who are available, willing, and able to perform the tasks and functions required by the nature and organization of existing labour processes. Members of the working class are dependent on capitalist employers for wage work that will provide them and their dependants with the income needed to purchase goods and services. Within the context of this mutual dependence, the working class is economically, socially, and politically subordinate to the capitalist class. Members of the capitalist class—employers, that is—use their dominant position to secure their own interests and objectives.

At the abstract level, the primary objective of capitalist production is expanded accumulation. At a more concrete level of analysis this objective assumes the form of attempts to maximize profitability. As indicated above, capitalist employers attempt to increase profits by securing control over the labour process in order to increase worker productivity and decrease the costs of production. Those capitalists who are successful in lowering their costs of production below those of their competitors generally lower the selling price of their goods or services and, thereby, secure a larger share of the market. One of the contradictions of capitalism is the tendency for free-market competition of this type to lead to market monopolies. Monopolies are notorious for providing consumers with overpriced, low-quality goods and services, unless they are highly regulated. A second consequence of competition-driven attempts to reduce production costs and increase productivity is the transformation of the terms and conditions of work of employees. I will limit discussion to the second point.

Historically the reduction of costs of production has been achieved in absolute or relative terms. *Absolute* reductions in the costs of production are achieved through reductions in real wages. This can be done in at least two ways. First, wage and salary rates can be reduced per time period. Second, workers can be employed for fewer hours. In Canada, and throughout the capitalist world in recent years, both techniques have been tried. The first may result in lower real earnings for individuals, although individual workers may counter this potential by working more hours or working at multiple jobs. The number of multiple job holders, for example, increased from 202 000 in 1976 to 598 000 in 1991 (Statistics Canada 1992). This suggests that workers are reacting to unemployment or lower wages by working more. The increased rate of part-time work, however, suggests that employers may be attempting to lower their costs and increase their profits by employing workers for fewer hours. Absolute reduction of the costs of production can work, however, only if worker productivity remains at the same or higher levels. This is often achieved by increasing surveillance of workers by an expanded managerial and supervisory labour force.

Relative reductions in the costs of production are achieved by increasing worker productivity so that the cost per unit produced decreases at a rate faster than the costs of production increase. Historically this has been achieved in two ways. The first is the extension of the occupational division of labour and the replacement of high-wage workers with low-wage workers. Thus, the extension of the capitalist division of labour not only reduces the costs of production in absolute terms, it also contributes to decreased costs of production in relative terms, because it results in increased worker productivity. The second way relative reductions in production costs are achieved is through the development and application of productivity-enhancing and labour-saving technologies in the workplace.

These two employer strategies are characterized by certain contradictory consequences. The extension of the occupational division of labour, for example, is generally recognized as contributing to increased worker productivity and reduced costs of production. It also requires expansion of the pool of people who are available, willing, and able to perform employer-defined work tasks. The application of productivity-enhancing and labour-saving technologies, on the other hand, results in a reduction in employment, or an increase in unemployment, at least to the extent that new technology enables fewer workers to produce more in less time. These processes are examined in more detail below.

The Capitalist Division of Labour and Work

The development and extension of the capitalist division of labour results in the need for increased numbers of wage labours. This is because the master principle underlying the development and extension of the capitalist division of labour consists of breaking down any given labour process into its constituent tasks and then assigning each of those separate tasks, or some small combination of those tasks, to individual workers and occupational groups. When Adam Smith described this capitalist process of "dividing labour" in order to show how it results in increased productivity, he chose as his example pin manufacturing.

Smith (1965) showed how pin manufacturing, which in precapitalist societies was undertaken by a single craftsperson performing all the required functions himself or herself, with perhaps a small number of assistants, came to be a labour process characterized by eighteen distinct operations and categories of workers under the capitalist mode of production. Smith argued that the increased productivity that resulted from dividing labour in this way was the result of three "circumstances": first, productivity rises because of the increased facility and speed of operation that results from the repetition of tasks; second, it rises because of the time saved when workers specialize, rather than moving from one type of task to another; and, third, worker productivity increases because of the invention of machinery that enables one worker to do the work of many (that is, because of the development of productivity-enhancing and labour-saving technology and its application in the form of machinery). In fact, only the first two reasons for increased productivity can properly be seen to result from the extension of the occupational division of labour described. I will return to this point.

The development of the capitalist division of labour has consequences other than increased productivity. The division of a work process into its constituent tasks and the assignment of each one to an individual worker has the result of reducing the skill levels required. Reduced skill requirements in turn result in lower wages. Deskilled workers often are less able to find alternative employment because the skills they possess are often industry- or even firm-specific. This results in a fewer opportunities for these workers, which in turn results in a deterioration of their bargaining position compared to that of the employer. That is, it is generally easier for employers to recruit relatively unskilled labour than it is for unskilled labour to find alternative employment. Thus, the extension of the capitalist division of labour facilitates reductions in the costs of production in both absolute and relative terms. The reduction of the costs of production in absolute terms, through the extension of the capitalist division of labour, has been referred to as the Babbage Principle (Braverman 1974). The Babbage Principle refers to an observation made by Charles Babbage in 1832. He observed that the list of advantages of the division of labour noted by Adam Smith was incomplete because it failed to include the recognition that subdividing a labour process into its component tasks, each requiring different degrees of skill and strength, enabled employers to employ workers with the minimum skills required to perform the fragmented tasks and, accordingly, to pay them lower wages.

Not surprisingly, workers have resisted the tendency toward the deskilling of work and the devaluation of wages associated with the capitalist extension of the occupational division of labour. Historically this has been one of the major forms of class struggle in capitalist societies. The results of these struggles have been uneven over time; they have varied by country, industry, and occupation. That is, different occupations have been more or less opposed, and more or less successful in their opposition, to various employer attempts to deskill work, disempower workers, and devalue labour power (Dickinson 1991).

Those occupational groups that have been relatively unsuccessful in their resistance to employer initiatives of this type are often faced with relatively poor working conditions, low pay, and high job insecurity. This often translates into more-frequent and longer periods of unemployment. Those individual workers and occupational groups that have been more successful in resisting these employer initiatives are able to transform their relative position of strength vis-à-vis the employer into better working conditions, often with higher pay and greater job security. Among other things, this translates into less-frequent and shorter periods of unemployment.

Productivity-Enhancing and Labour-Saving Technology

Capitalist employers, under the perpetual pressure of intercapitalist competition and worker resistance, must find ways other than the division of labour to increase worker productivity and reduce the costs of production. The development of new scientific and technical knowledge and its application to the workplace in the form of productivity-enhancing and labour-saving machinery is the other major mechanism for increasing profits. The term *labour-saving* is, in certain respects, misleading. It suggests that new technology has the consequence of making work easier—a common misunderstanding. Of course, in some circumstances, and to a certain degree, this is a correct interpretation. More importantly, however, labour-saving technology is labour-saving from the point of view of the employer, not the employee. From the employer's point of view, technology is labour-saving if and when it enables one worker to produce more in a given time period than he or she could without the technology. This is the third circumstance that Adam Smith claimed led the extension of the division of labour to result in increased productivity. Although the development and implementation of new technology in the form of machinery is related to the development of new divisions of labour, more often than not, technological innovations are developed to replace those well-paid occupations that have been able successfully to resist the breakdown of their skills through organizational and political means. And although it is often claimed that new technology, especially new automatic technology, will enable people to be freed from the dirty, dangerous, and dull jobs of modern industry, usually it is those types of jobs that are not replaced with new technology. This is at least partly because the dirty, dangerous, and dull jobs are the least well paid and can be filled with unskilled domestic, immigrant, or migrant labour, especially during periods of high unemployment.

The Changing Nature of Employment and Unemployment

In aggregate, decisions taken by individual employers in order to increase productivity, reduce costs, and maximize profits contribute to changes in the structural characteristics of the economy. If we look at the Canadian economy in the post-Second World War period we find some interesting developments. We see, for example, a relative and, in recent years, a real decline in the goods-producing sector of the economy and an increase in the services-producing and self-employment sectors of the economy,[1] at least in terms of employment patterns.

As Table 13.1 shows, between 1951 and 1992 the services-producing sector of the economy grew from about 2.5 million workers to about 9.8 million. During the same period the labour force in the goods-producing sector increased from 2.8 million workers to about 3.9 million. Following the major restructuring of capital that culminated in the recession of the early 1980s and 1990s, employment in the goods-producing sector decreased in real terms. Thus, by 1992 there were about 24 100 fewer workers employed in the production of goods than there had been in 1981. On the other hand, the services-producing sector employed over 1.89 million more workers in 1992 than it had in 1981 (Statistics Canada 1993). If we examine these developments in more detail we see some interesting trends.

After the recession of the early 1980s, many jobs in the goods-producing sector of the economy were permanently lost to relocation and labour-saving technology in the form of mechanized and automated production processes. Picot and Wannell (1987, 90), reporting the findings of a survey conducted in January 1986, found that of the one million workers who lost full-time jobs and who were not recalled during the 1981 to 1984 period, the largest proportion—36 percent—cited plant closure or relocation as the cause. Plant closure and relocation are most often caused by

TABLE 13.1: Labour Force by Sector, Canada, Selected Years, 1951–1992

	Labour Force (000s)					Percent Distribution				
	1951	1961	1971	1981	1992	1951	1961	1971	1981	1992
Total Labour Force	5286	6472	8627	12 005	13 797	100	100	100	100	100
Goods Producing	2806	2861	3276	4063	3856	53.1	44.2	38	33.8	27.9
Service Producing	2480	3611	5351	7942	9834	46.9	55.8	62	66.2	71.3

Note: Percentages may not sum to 100 percent because of rounding and also because every year a certain proportion of the labour force is unclassified. This category refers to individuals who have never been employed or who have not been employed for the preceding five years. In 1992, 106 000 persons were unclassified.
Sources: W.G. Picot, "The Changing Industrial Mix of Employment, 1951–1985," *Canadian Social Trends* (Spring 1987): 11; Statistics Canada, *Labour Force Annual Averages, 1981–1988*, Cat. no. 71-529 (Ottawa: Minister of Supply and Services, 1989); Statistics Canada, *Labour Force Annual Averages, 1992*, Cat. no. 71-220. (Ottawa: Minister of Supply and Services, 1993).

bankruptcy, technologically based changes to production processes (mechanization or automation), or by the export of capital to low-wage areas. The jobs that were permanently lost during the 1981 to 1984 time period were concentrated in construction and mining, and parts of the manufacturing sector. This finding lends support to the contention that changes to the occupational division of labour and the development of new technology are an underlying cause of the permanent job loss experienced in the goods-producing sector of the economy since the early 1980s.

Although Picot and Wannell (1987, 90) show that it was younger workers (aged twenty to thirty-four years) and workers with less than three years of tenure in their jobs who had the highest incidence of permanent job loss, it was older workers who, following unemployment, had the greatest difficulty finding new jobs. Those workers, aged 55 years and over who were permanently laid off, for example, experienced job searches that were longer than average, and had a higher rate of unemployment at the time the survey was conducted. Those who did find jobs took above-average pay cuts. The unemployment rate for all those surveyed, regardless of age, was 25 percent. This was more than twice the rate for the labour force as a whole (1987, 91). For older workers, the unemployment rate was higher yet. Picot and Wannell (1987, 150, Table 13) show that, similarly, of all those workers who were laid off from manufacturing jobs between 1981 and 1984 but who found new manufacturing jobs, the average weekly wage, not accounting for inflation, had decreased by more than 7 percent. Again, for older workers the average cut in wages was even higher.

As Picot and Wannell have shown, older workers are less likely than younger workers to be laid off permanently, but once laid off they are less likely to find new jobs. This is what one would expect, especially in the goods-producing sector of the economy, which historically has been relatively highly unionized, relatively highly paid, and male dominated. Unionization traditionally has been one way in which workers have organized to pursue their interests in securing higher incomes, better working conditions and benefits, and increased job security. The lower rate of permanent layoff among older workers is possibly a reflection of the relative success of unions in achieving increased job security for their members in the form of collective agreements that contain seniority clauses. In general terms, the relative success of unions in protecting the interests of their members against employer attempts to deskill work and reduce wages has led employers and their political allies to claim that union insistence on seniority rights and wage protection results in rigidities that reduce the capacity of firms to respond to changing market conditions and competition. Employer attacks on unions on the economic level, in the form of organizational and technological change, have been accompanied at the political level by changes in labour legislation that effectively limit union rights and powers. These economic and political initiatives have been accompanied at the ideological level by claims that economic prosperity, if not survival, depends upon increased "flexibility" and "adaptability" on the part of workers. Together these terms can be understood, at least in part, as being a code for reduced capacity to resist effectively employer initiatives aimed at increasing worker productivity and reducing the costs of production.

In order to facilitate flexibility among the unionized work force, many older male workers, especially those covered by collective agreements with seniority clauses and receiving relatively high wages, have been offered the choice of taking early retirement or permanent layoff, or being fired. This has resulted in a dramatic decrease in the labour-force participation rate of men between the ages of 54 and 65 years. Table 13.2 shows that while in 1975 the participation rate of men between those ages was about 76 percent, in 1992 their participation rate was down to 56 percent. This means that in 1992, 44 percent of men aged 55 to 64 years of age were not in the labour force.

This continues a trend commented on by Lindsay (1987). Lindsay shows that between 1975 and 1985, the major reason for men in this age group not to participate in the labour force was early retirement: "the number of men aged 55-64 who were no longer in the labour force, after retiring from their last job, increased almost 200%, from 33,000 to 98,000" (1987, 13). During the same period, the increase in the total male population in that age group was only 23 percent. Combining those who chose early retirement with those who were unable to find work after having been permanently laid off or fired from their last job accounts for 40 percent of the increase in unemployment for men in this age group between 1975 and 1985. As Lindsay points out, most of the rest of the increase is accounted for by those who had been out of the labour force for the last five years or who had never been in the labour force (1987, 14). Many, if not most of those who had not been in the labour force within the last five years, of course, were men who had already taken an early retirement option or else who previously had been fired or laid off and were unable to find new work.

In addition to this trend toward permanent withdrawal from the labour force by categories of people who have traditionally had high participation rates, we see a

TABLE 13.2: Labour Force Status of Men Aged 55–64, Canada, Selected Years

	1975	1985 (000s)	1988	1992
Employed	682	708	703	644
Not employed:				
Unemployed	28	65	47	70
Not in labour force				
• lost, or laid off from, last job	14	48		—
• retired	33	98	—	—
• not in labour force in previous five years or never worked	64	110	—	—
• other reasons	74	72	—	—
Total not employed	213	393	372	437
Total population 55–64	896	1101	1127	1151
Percentage employed	76.1	64.3	62.4	56.0

Sources: Colin Lindsay, "The Decline in Employment Among Men Aged 55–64: 1975–1985," *Canadian Social Trends* (Spring 1987):14; Statistics Canada, *Labour Force Annual Averages, 1981–1988*, Cat. no. 71-529 (Ottawa: Ministry of Supply and Services, 1989); Statistics Canada, *Labour Force Annual Averages, 1992*, Cat. no. 71-220 (Ottawa: Minister of Supply and Services, 1993).

trend toward increases in the incidence and rate of long-term unemployment. In 1985, for example, those who were unemployed for a year or more made up 10 percent of the total number of unemployed. In 1980 the figure had been 4 percent. The pattern is similar for those unemployed from six to twelve months. In 1985 these people accounted for 17 percent of the unemployed, compared to 13 percent in 1980 (Parliament 1987, 17).

The experience of long-term unemployment, like permanent withdrawal from the labour force, is not evenly distributed among all workers. Older male workers, that is, those over 45 years of age and especially those between the ages of 55 and 64, bear the brunt of the increase in long-term unemployment. In 1985, 46 percent of unemployed men 55 years and older, and just about 40 percent of those aged 45 to 55 years old, were unemployed for six months or more. In addition, in 1985, 21 percent of unemployed men aged 55 years and older, and 20 percent of those between 45 and 54 years, had been unemployed for more than a year (Parliament 1987, 17).

For many of the older, unionized male workers who stayed in the labour force and who remained employed, flexibility and adaptability to organizational and technological change was made more appealing by pay increases. Myles, Picot, and Wannell (1988, 89), for example, show that between 1981 and 1986 there was an upward shift in the wage distribution among workers over the age of 35 years. This upward shift in the wage distribution was greatest for males 50 years and older (see

Table 13.3). Thus, increasingly throughout the 1980s we saw fewer older male workers actually working, but those that were employed were making more money on average.

The situation is the opposite with regard to younger workers. Those between the ages of 15 and 34 years of age experienced a downward shift in wage distributions over the same period, with the youngest workers experiencing the most dramatic decline. It is not unexpected that reduced hourly wages and earnings for younger workers correspond to significant declines in the percentage of unionized workers in the younger age groups between 1981 and 1986. In the manufacturing sector, the percentage of unionized jobs held by younger workers dropped to 28 percent in 1986 from 35 percent in 1981. In resource-based industries the drop was from 52 percent to 30 percent, in construction the drop was from 26 to 15 percent, and in social services it was from 49 to 40 percent (Myles, Picot, and Wannell 1988, 126).

A closer look at patterns within the manufacturing sector reveals some other trends. Table 13.4 shows that the restructuring of capital, which culminated in the recession of the early 1980s, resulted in a decline of about 200 000 workers in the total full-time male manufacturing labour force between 1981 and 1983. Although the number of male full-time workers in manufacturing fluctuated throughout the rest of the 1980s, since the beginning of the current decade numbers have dropped quite markedly, so that in 1992 there were about 72 000 fewer full-time male workers in the manufacturing sector than there had been in 1983, the worst year of the recession.

Full-time employment of female workers in manufacturing shows similar patterns. For female full-time workers in the manufacturing sector, 1982 was the worst year. Despite gains since then, the number of females in full-time manufacturing jobs in 1992 was 15 000 fewer than it had been in 1982.

If we look at the part-time labour force in manufacturing, we see that for both males and females it increased in size between 1981 and 1992, with some fluctuation. Combined with the slight shift in the gender composition and the age composition of the manufacturing labour force, this increase in the use of part-time workers

TABLE 13.3: Percentage Change in Relative Mean Wage, by Age Group and Region, 1981–1986

	Atlantic Provinces	Quebec	Ontario	Manitoba, Saskatchewan	Alberta	British Columbia
16–24 years	–13.7	–12.1	–19.2	–14.4	–23.4	–15.9
25–34 years	–8.5	–4.6	–6.9	–4.5	–3.9	–7.8
35–49 years	5.4	3.7	4.5	0.9	6.5	4.7
50–64 years	6.3	–1.0	10.0	8.7	7.6	6.4

Source: J. Mills, G. Picot, and T. Wannell, "The Changing Wage Distribution of Jobs, 1981–1986," *The Labour Force, October 1988*, Cat. no. 71-001 (Ottawa: Statistics Canada, 1988), p. 111. Reproduced by authority of the Minister of Industry, 1994.

TABLE 13.4: Estimates of Manufacturing Labour Force, Annual Averages, Canada, 1981–1992 (000s)

	Manufacturing labour force			Employment									Unemployment					
				Total			Full-time			Part-time			Total			Unemployment rate		
	Total	Male	Female	Total	Male	Female	Total	Male	Female	Total	Male	Female	Total	Male	Female	Total	Male	Female
1981	2305	1663	642	2124	1552	571	2052	1523	529	72	29	42	181	110	71	7.9	6.6	11.0
1982	2225	1603	622	1928	1404	523	1856	1377	479	72	28	44	298	199	99	13.4	12.4	15.9
1983	2159	1536	622	1879	1347	532	1807	1319	488	72	28	44	280	189	91	13.0	12.3	14.6
1984	2195	1557	638	1954	1403	551	1886	1374	512	68	29	39	241	154	87	11.0	9.9	13.6
1985	2180	1554	626	1960	1416	544	1887	1387	500	73	29	44	220	138	82	10.1	8.9	13.1
1986	2180	1537	643	1989	1417	572	1917	1390	526	72	27	45	192	120	72	8.8	7.8	11.1
1987	2202	1552	650	2018	1442	576	1946	1411	535	72	31	42	184	111	74	8.4	7.1	11.3
1988	2271	1603	669	2104	1504	600	2026	1472	554	78	32	46	168	99	68	7.4	6.2	10.2
1989	2294	1536	674	2141	1525	609	2043	1483	559	84	34	49	170	103	65	7.6	7.2	8.1
1990	2198	1547	651	2001	1425	576	1932	1396	535	69	29	40	197	122	75	9.0	7.9	11.5
1991	2122	1497	625	1865	1331	534	1793	1302	491	72	29	43	257	166	92	12.1	11.1	14.6
1992	2046	1448	598	1788	1276	512	1710	1247	464	78	30	48	258	172	86	12.6	11.9	14.4

Sources: Statistics Canada, *Labour Force Annual Averages, 1981–1988*, Cat. no. 71-529 (Ottawa: Minister of Supply and Services, 1989), Table 10; Statistics Canada, *The Labour Force, 1989*, Vol. 45, Nos. 1-12 (Ottawa: Ministry of Supply and Services, 1990); Statistics Canada, *Labour Force Annual Averages, 1990, 1991, 1992* (Ottawa: Minister of Supply and Services, 1993).

seems to support the conclusion that less-expensive workers are being employed to replace more-expensive, older, unionized workers. Although many of the postrecession workers are doing the "same" jobs as the prerecession workers, they are doing them for less money, and under conditions of decreased job security. That is, postrecession workers are more "flexible" and "adaptable" than prerecession workers.

The major trends in the goods-producing sector described above strongly suggest that various employer attempts to increase worker productivity and reduce the cost of production have resulted in decreased wages, decreased union membership, and increased frequency and duration of unemployment for certain categories of workers. Although the growth in the services-producing sector of the economy is characterized by similar processes of productivity enhancement and cost reduction, different categories of workers are affected.

The Growth of the Services-Producing Sector

The growth of employment in the services-producing sector of the economy is largely the result of the creation of new industries, or the greatly expanded scope of operation of already existing industries that are providing new services in new ways to new consumers. The creation of new industries or the expansion of already existing industries, of course, requires a pool of people who are available, willing, and able to perform the new employer-defined work tasks. To a large extent, the creation and expansion of the services-producing sector has relied upon the recruitment of youth working part-time and women aged 25 and older to the labour force (Statistics Canada 1992, A-2).

As one would expect, the labour-force participation rate for separated and divorced women, especially between the ages of 25 and 44, is quite high. One effect of the liberalization of divorce law in 1968 was an increased divorce rate. The crude divorce rate per 100 000 persons in Canada in 1966 was 51.2, this increased to 54.8 in 1968, to 139.8 in 1970, to over 200 in 1974, and it continued a steady rise until 1982 when it peaked at 285.9. Although since then there has been a decline in the crude divorce rate, the total number of separated and divorced women who are employed has continued to rise throughout the 1980s and into the early 1990s.

If we turn our attention to labour-force participation of married women we see that it has been rising steadily throughout most of this century, and particularly since the Second World War. Between 1921 and 1941, for example, the labour-force participation rate for married women rose from 2.16 to 3.74 percent. By 1951 it had increased to 11.2 percent (Skoulas 1974, 9). It has continued to increase, with slight fluctuation, into the 1990s. In 1992 the labour-force participation rate for married women was 61 percent. It seems clear that since the Second World War in particular, conditions that make it desirable or necessary for married women to enter the waged labour force have become increasingly prevalent.

Knowledge about the factors that encourage or discourage labour-force participation among various categories of people is crucial for policy-makers concerned with economic and social planning. On the basis of his research, Skoulas (1974, 87–89) described a number of factors that affected the labour-force participation of

TABLE 13.5: Labour Force Participation Rate by Age, Sex, and Marital Status, Canada, Selected Years

	1981		1988		1992	
	Total labour force (000s)	Participation rate	Total labour force (000s)	Participation rate	Total labour force (000s)	Participation rate
MALES						
Total	7051	78.4	7422	76.6	7582	73.8
15–24 years	1648	72.3	1425	72.2	1268	67.0
25–44 years	3363	95.7	3923	94.4	4089	92.0
45 years plus	2040	63.8	2075	58.2	2225	56.4
Single	1948	71.3	2130	74.1	2156	71.0
15–24 years	1317	68.4	1204	69.5	1086	64.4
25–44 years	520	89.0	829	89.1	946	86.6
45 years plus	110	49.6	98	45.8	124	48.7
Married	4808	83.4	4909	79.5	5020	76.8
15–24 years	322	93.6	216	91.9	178	88.3
25–44 years	2687	97.2	2886	96.3	2931	94.4
45 years plus	1798	67.6	1808	61.4	1911	59.2
Separated/Divorced	246	79.5	332	77.3	362	73.1
15–24 years	7	92.7	4	83.0	—	—
25–44 years	148	93.1	196	92.1	203	90.0
45 years plus	91	63.6	133	62.4	155	58.5
Widowed	49	26.5	50	23.9	43	21.0
15–24 years	—	—	—	—	—	—
25–44 years	7	88.4	12	91.3	8	81.0
45 years plus	40	23.0	37	18.9	34	17.5
FEMALES						
Total	4849	51.7	5853	57.4	6215	58.4
15–24 years	1426	63.2	1289	66.9	1152	63.1
25–44 years	2308	65.1	3206	75.5	3469	76.7
45 years plus	1115	31.2	1358	33.7	1593	35.9
Single	1445	64.7	1601	67.9	1564	65.2
15–24 years	1009	62.5	952	65.1	874	61.1
25–44 years	336	86.3	550	84.7	590	82.8
45 years plus	99	43.1	98	40.1	100	38.7
Married	2908	50.6	3664	59.1	4005	61.0
15–24 years	396	64.9	323	73.1	268	71.0
25–44 years	1735	61.2	2353	73.5	2569	75.9
45 years plus	778	33.8	988	38.7	1167	41.7
Separated/Divorced	334	64.3	454	65.4	514	63.2
15–24 years	20	65.4	12	66.3	9	55.5
25–44 years	211	74.3	277	76.8	89	73.9
45 years plus	104	50.2	165	52.3	217	53.3

Continued

TABLE 13.5: Labour Force Participation Rate by Age, Sex, and Marital Status, Canada, Selected Years — Continued

	1981		1988		1992	
	Total labour force (000s)	**Participation rate**	**Total labour force (000s)**	**Participation rate**	**Total labour force (000s)**	**Participation rate**
Widowed	162	18.5	134	14.1	132	13.1
15–24 years	—	—	—	—	—	—
25–44 years	26	71.3	26	72.1	21	67.5
45 years plus	134	16.0	107	11.7	110	11.2

Sources: Statistics Canada, *Labour Force Annual Averages, 1981–1988*, Cat. no. 71-529 (Ottawa: Minister of Supply and Services, 1989), Table 3; Statistics Canada, *Labour Force Annual Averages, 1992*, Cat. no. 71-220 (Ottawa: Minister of Industry, Science and Technology, 1993). Reproduced by authority of the Ministry of Industry, 1994.

married women. He found that, among other things, lower family income (excluding the wife's) increased the wife's labour-force participation, as did an unemployed husband. The strength of this last relationship, he pointed out, "depends on the duration of husband's unemployment, his weekly earnings, and the 'normal' level of family income excluding wife's earnings" (1974, 87). As we have seen, lower earnings and insecure conditions of employment have been created in recent years as a result of employer initiatives facilitated by government policy. Increased labour-force participation by married women is one way families have attempted to offset the downward trend in individual wages and incomes. Increases in the number of working family members, combined with smaller families, have contributed to rising family income simultaneously with declining mean wages for individuals in certain age groups.

The growth in the services-producing sector of the economy, increased female labour-force participation, and the expansion of part-time work are all related. Lévesque (1987) examined the growth of part-time work in Canada between 1975 and 1986. Over that period, part-time employment as a proportion of full-time employment rose by 7.76 percent, from 10.6 to 18.36 percent of the labour force. By 1992, with some slight variation, it had increased to 20.2 percent (see Table 13.6). On the basis of his study, however, Lévesque (1987) found that only 20 percent of the growth in part-time employment could be explained by the changing structure of the economy—the growth of employment in the services-producing sector and the relative decline in the growth of employment in the goods-producing sector. Eighty percent of the growth in part-time employment was accounted for by changes occurring within industries. That is, all industries, whether goods-producing or services-producing, are relying more on part-time workers now than in the past.

As we have seen, the growth of part-time employment is at least partly a result of employer attempts to reduce the costs of production. The growth of part-time

TABLE 13.6: Full-time and Part-time Employment by Sex and Age, Canada, Selected Years (000s)

	Both sexes				Males			Females		
	Total	Full-time	Part-time	Part-time as proportion of full-time employment	Full-time	Part-time	Male part-time as proportion of male full-time employment	Full-time	Part-time	Female part-time as proportion of female full-time employment
1981										
Canada	11 001	9 515	1 486	.1561	6 144	413	.0672	3 372	1 074	.3185
15–24 years	2 667	2 015	652	.3235	1 118	298	.2665	897	354	.3946
25–44 years	5 318	4 828	490	.1014	3 142	42	.0133	1 686	448	.2657
45+ years	3 016	2 672	344	.1287	1 883	73	.0387	788	272	.3451
1984										
Canada	10 932	9 263	1 668	.1801	5 826	482	.0827	3 438	1 187	.3453
15–24 years	2 341	1 624	717	.4415	883	324	.3669	741	393	.5304
25–44 years	5 628	5 052	576	.1140	3 151	73	.0232	1 901	503	.2646
45+ years	2 963	2 588	375	.1449	1 792	85	.0474	796	290	.3643
1986										
Canada	11 531	9 742	1 789	.1836	6 053	514	.0849	3 689	1 274	.3453
15–24 years	2 367	1 604	762	.4750	875	343	.3920	730	419	.5739
25–44 years	6 132	5 491	640	.1165	3 362	81	.0240	2 130	559	.2624
45+ years	3 033	2 647	386	.1458	1 816	90	.0495	830	297	.3578
1988										
Canada	12 245	10 363	1 882	.1816	6 350	527	.0830	4 013	1 355	.3377
15–24 years	2 388	1 599	788	.4928	880	361	.4102	719	428	.5953
25–44 years	6 618	5 948	670	.1126	3 590	78	.0217	2 358	592	.2511
45+ years	3 239	2 815	424	.1506	1 880	88	.0468	936	335	.3579
1990										
Canada	12 572	10 640	1 932	.182	6 387	561	.088	4 253	1 371	.322
15–24	2 254	1 459	795	.545	800	365	.546	660	429	.650
25–44	6 934	6 239	695	.111	3 669	93	.025	2 570	602	.234
45+	3 383	2 942	442	.150	1 918	103	.054	1 024	339	.331
1992										
Canada	12 240	10 182	2 058	.202	6 954	618	.089	4 128	1 440	.349
15–24	1 989	1 166	823	.701	634	379	.560	533	444	.833
25–44	6 750	5 988	762	.127	3 498	122	.035	2 490	639	.257
45+	3 501	3 028	473	.156	1 923	117	.061	1 106	356	.322

Note: Full-time employment consists of persons who usually work 30 hours or more per week, plus those who usually work fewer than 30 hours but consider themselves to be employed full-time (e.g., airline pilots); part-time employment consists of all other persons who usually work fewer than 30 hours per week.

Sources: Statistics Canada, *Labour Force Annual Averages, 1981–1988*, Cat. no. 71-529 (Ottawa: Minister of Supply and Services, 1989); Statistics Canada, *Labour Force Annual Averages, 1990*; Statistics Canada, *Labour Force Annual Averages 1992*, Cat. no. 71-220 (Ottawa: Minister of Supply and Services, 1993). Reproduced by authority of the Minister of Industry, 1994.

work can be understood as a logical extension of the previously discussed Babbage Principle. The Babbage Principle recognizes that reductions in the costs of production are realized as a consequence of the capitalist division of labour because the fragmentation of work processes into their constituent tasks and their allocation to different workers or occupational groups enables employers to hire workers who possess only those skills and abilities required to perform a certain aspect of the entire work process; this reduces overall wage costs. Thus, the development and extension of the capitalist division of labour is partly an attempt by employers to ensure that they are paying for only the minimum amount of skill required to perform certain aspects of a divided labour process. Similarly, the division of the working day, week, month, or year into component parts helps employers ensure that they are paying wages to workers to perform tasks for only the minimum amount of time required for their completion. The growth of part-time work helps employers ensure that when an employee cannot be kept busy on a continuous basis performing specified tasks, he or she is let go to be recalled when, and if, enough work is available. Thus, the logic underpinning the development and extension of the capitalist division of labour is that labour processes are broken down into component tasks that are doled out to individual workers on a piecemeal or partial basis, and that working time is increasingly being partitioned into periods of employment interspersed with frequent periods of unemployment, depending on the needs of employers.

The reduction in the costs of production associated with the shift toward part-time work by employers is facilitated by government policy. Under current laws employers are not required to make compulsory contributions for part-time workers—or at least not at the full-time rate—to supplementary income plans such as health and welfare schemes, pension plans, workers' compensation, and unemployment insurance funds. As we have seen, wages and incomes have declined in recent years under the pressure of employer cost-reduction initiatives. The cost of labour to employers, however, is not restricted to wages and salaries. The contributions mentioned above represent supplementary labour costs. If we divide labour-related employer costs into the two components—wages and salaries, on the one hand, and supplementary labour costs, on the other hand—we see some interesting trends. Wong (1988) examines these two aspects of labour income in Canada for the years between 1975 and 1987.

The wages and salaries component of labour income accounts for just over 90 percent of labour income. Wong (1988, 97) shows that between 1975 and 1977, real wages and salaries grew by 5.6 percent. In 1978 they began a downward trend, which, by 1987, amounted to a 6.2 percent real decline. This decline in average labour income would have been more precipitous had it not been for a real increase of 32.7 percent in supplementary incomes from 1975 to 1987. Wong (1988, 92) points out that some components of supplementary labour income are universal and some are not. Fewer than 40 percent of all paid workers in Canada, for example, were covered by private pension plans and health and welfare benefits, which, nevertheless, accounted for about 60 percent of supplementary labour income. Canada and Quebec pension plans, unemployment insurance, and workers' compensation plans, on the other hand, are universal. One can see that employers would have an interest in employing a smaller proportion of workers for whom they had to make payments into various supplementary income plans relative to those workers for whom they did not have to make such payments. The 40 percent of workers covered by private pensions and benefits roughly corresponds to the proportion of the labour force that is unionized. From this perspective one can see that part-time workers are doubly attractive insofar as they are usually not unionized and, under current laws, even when it comes to universal labour-income plans, employers are not required to make contributions on their behalf, at least not at the same level as for full-time workers. When this is combined with the fact that part-time wage rates are generally lower than full-time rates, one would expect, all things being equal, that the trend toward increased reliance on part-time workers will continue.

It is important to point out that although most of the increase in part-time employment is voluntary—that is, the workers involved choose to work part-time for reasons of their own—the proportion of involuntary part-time workers is substantial. In 1975, 11 percent of part-time workers reported they were working part-time only because full-time employment was unavailable. This reached a high of just over 30 percent in 1984, falling to about 24 percent in 1988 and rising again to more than 32 percent in 1992.

With regard to unemployment among part-time workers, Clemenson (1987, 32) found that between 1980 and 1986 the unemployment rate for males was 14.6

TABLE 13.7: Full-time, and Voluntary and Involuntary Part-time Employment, Canada, 1975, 1980 to 1988, and 1992 (000s)

	Total employment	Full-time employment	Part-time employment		Involuntary part-time employment as a % of	
			Voluntary	Involuntary	Total employment	Part-time employment
1975	9 284	8 296	880	109	1.2	11.0
1980	10 708	9 316	1 147	245	2.3	17.6
1981	11 001	9 515	1 218	268	2.4	18.0
1982	10 618	9 090	1 149	379	3.6	24.8
1983	10 675	9 036	1 172	467	4.4	28.5
1984	10 932	9 263	1 166	502	4.6	30.1
1985	11 221	9 484	1 228	509	4.5	29.3
1986	11 531	9 742	1 283	506	4.4	28.3
1987	11 861	10 057	1 325	479	4.0	26.6
1988	12 242	10 363	1 436	446	3.6	23.6
1992	12 240	10 182	1 389	669	5.5	32.5

Note: Persons who usually work fewer than 30 hours per week, but consider themselves to be employed full-time are not included in this table. Such persons are included in estimates of full-time employment.
Sources: Ernest B. Akyeampong, "Involuntary Part-time Employment in Canada 1975–1986," *Canadian Social Trends* (Autumn 1987): 27; Statistics Canada, *Labour Force Annual Averages, 1981–1988*, Cat. no. 71-529 (Ottawa: Minister of Supply and Services, 1989), Tables 18, 19; Statistics Canada, *Labour Force Annual Averages, 1992*, Cat. no. 71-220 (Ottawa: Minister of Supply and Services, 1993).

percent, while for females it was 10.6 percent. This is the opposite of male and female experiences of unemployment in the full-time labour force, where the unemployment rate for males was 10.2 percent and for females it was 13.6 percent for the same years.

The Growth of Self-employment

As we have seen above, the nature of the Canadian economy has been changing for the past several decades. Between 1976 and 1992, for example, it has grown by 29 percent, the entire amount of which is accounted for by a 46 percent growth in the service sector (Statistics Canada 1993, A-3). The growth in the service sector over the course of this century has resulted in a dramatic alteration in the industrial structure of the Canadian economy and consequently in the types and conditions of employment available. In 1911, for example, two-thirds of employment in Canada was in the goods-producing sector of the economy, most of which involved agriculture. By 1992, less than one-third of Canadian employment was in this sector and two-thirds was in the service-producing sector (Statistics Canada 1993, A-2).

In addition to this structural shift from a predominantly goods-producing to a predominantly services-producing economy, the level of self-employment has risen. Indeed, in 1991, "the growth of self-employment and multiple job holders outpaced total employment growth" (Statistics Canada 1992, A-2). This continued a trend that began at least as early as the mid-1970s.

The number of the self-employed, both incorporated and unincorporated, has increased from 1 048 000 in 1976 to 1 842 000 in 1993; an increase of about 75 percent. The self-employed accounted for about 15.5 percent of the labour force in 1993. Most of the self-employed are men; for example, 17.1 percent of all employed men in 1986 were self-employed whereas only 8.3 percent of employed women were self-employed. Since 1975, however, self-employment among women has increased at three times the rate of men—117.6 percent compared with 39.1 percent (Statistics Canada 1988, 9).

Between 1975 and 1986, the number of self-employed who were also employers, that is who hired paid help, has been larger than among the self-employed who do not hire others—67 percent compared with 44 percent (Statistics Canada 1988, 10). In 1986, about one-half of the self-employed were also employers (Statistics Canada 1988, 5). This is significant because of the fact that in recent years "the vast majority of employment gains have been attributed to small businesses," which are generally operated by self-employed working owners (Statistics Canada 1988, 5). Current patterns of corporate and government "downsizing" support the widespread contention that it is small and medium-sized business that will generate the increased employment opportunities of the foreseeable future.

Any economic or labour-market policy that intends to deal with the problems of economic growth and unemployment by expanding self-employment and small and mid-sized business should be sensitive to the numerous forces at work contributing to the failure of many such enterprises. The number of business bankruptcies provides an indication of this; between 1978 and 1991, for example, the number of business bankruptcies increased by about 70 percent, from 5546 to 13 496 (Consumer and Corporate Affairs Canada 1978; 1991).

These figures suggest that the growth of self-employment and the number of small and mid-sized employers may not be a panacea for the problems of unemployment and slow economic growth. To the extent that these solutions reproduce the contradictions of capitalist economic practices that have been discussed above, they can at least be short-term, incomplete answers.

Conclusions

Given the changing structure of the economy and an increasingly rapid rate of organizational and technological change resulting from intensified intercapitalist competition, unemployment is likely to become a normal experience for workers. Policy-makers and planners throughout the capitalist world have been preparing us for this for some time. The culturally normal pattern of schooling, work, and retirement, we are told, is, or is soon to be, an anachronism. Workers of the future—and for many the future is now—are not to expect to pursue a lifelong career. Workers are to expect a series of jobs interspersed with periods of unemployment, during which they are to undertake to retrain themselves so as to acquire the skills required by employers. The ideology of "learning for life" is an attempt to sell this new vision of working life to people (National Advisory Panel 1984). In reality, retraining does not affect the re-employment rate for the unemployed and constitutes a significant expense (Picot and Wannell 1987). Retraining may also require individuals and their families to relocate, given that most institution-based vocational and skills-training programs are concentrated in particular areas.

Unemployment is a permanent and growing feature of societies where the capitalist mode of production is dominant. Although we have seen that the form and experience of employment and unemployment differ at various times and places for different categories of people, we can be assured that for many, if not for most, unemployment will be a part of the future. The solution to the problem of unemployment resides in the political realm, and will require a transformation of the interests underpinning economic decision making and resource mobilization and allocation.

Study Questions

1. What effect does labour-force participation of married women with children have on family size? What effect will this have on future recruitment to the labour force?

2. If unemployment results from the class interests of employers, what is the solution, if any, to the problem?

3. What is the relationship between decreasing labour incomes and unemployment?

4. What are the obstacles to the unemployed organizing to pursue their collective interests?

5. Are the employed and the unemployed political allies or adversaries? Why?

Recommended Reading

Braverman, Harry. *Labor and Monopoly Capital: The Degradation of Work in the Twentieth Century*. New York: Monthly Review Press, 1974.

Burman, Patrick. *Killing Time, Losing Ground: Experiences of Unemployment*. Toronto: Wall and Thompson, 1988.

Picot, Garnett, and Ted Wannell. "Job Loss and Labour Market Adjustment in the Canadian Economy: Findings From a Special Survey." In *The Labour Force, March 1987*. Ottawa: Statistics Canada. 85–150.

Wong, Fred. "Trends in Labour Income." In *The Labour Force, September 1988*. Ottawa: Statistics Canada. 87–116.

Notes

1. For analytical purposes the economy is often divided into two sectors: the goods-producing sector and the services-producing sector. The services-producing sector is often subdivided into commercial and non-commercial (largely government) services. Commercial services, the largest sector of the economy, are further subdivided into three parts: distributive, producer, and consumer services. Below is a list of the industries contained within each sector.

   Goods-producing sector: agriculture, manufacturing, construction, mining, oil and gas extraction, utilities, forestry, fishing

   Services-producing sector:
   1. Commercial services:
      a. Distributive services: transportation and storage, communication, wholesale and retail trade
      b. Consumer services: accommodation and food services, personal services, amusement and recreational services, other miscellaneous services
      c. Producer services: services for business management (for example, accounting, engineering, and legal and management consulting), finance, insurance, estate
   2. Non-commercial services: education, health and welfare, religious organizations, public administration (government)

   These definitions and classifications are taken from W. Garnett Picot, "The Changing Industrial Mix of Employment, 1951–1985," *Canadian Social Trends* (Statistics Canada) (Spring, 1987): 8.

References

Akyeampong, E.B.1987. "Involuntary Part-Time Employment in Canada, 1956 1986." *Canadian Social Trends* (Statistics Canada) (Autumn): 26–29.

Braverman, H. 1974. *Labor and Monopoly Capital: The Degradation of Work in the Twentieth Century*. New York: Monthly Review Press.

Clemenson, H.A. 1987. "Unemployment Rates for the Full-Time and Part-Time Labour Forces." *Canadian Social Trends* (Statistics Canada) (Autumn): 30–33.

Consumer and Corporate Affairs Canada. 1978. *Annual Statistical Summary for the 1978 Calendar Year.*

———. 1991. *Annual Statistical Summary for the 1991 Calendar Year.*

Dickinson, H.D. 1991. "The Three Ds of Vocational Training: Deskilling, Disempowerment and Devaluation." In Hitting the Books: The Politics of Educational Retrenchment, ed. T. Wotherspoon. Toronto and Saskatoon: Garamond Press and Social Research Unit, Department of Sociology. 101–18.

Kealey, G.S. 1979. "H.C. Pentland and Working Class Studies." *Canadian Journal of Political and Social Theory* (Spring/Summer).

Kealey, G. 1980. *Toronto Workers Respond to Industrial Capitalism, 1867–1892.* Toronto: University of Toronto Press.

Lévesque, J.-M. 1987. "The Growth of Part-Time Work in a Changing Industrial Environment." *The Labour Force, May 1987.* Ottawa: Statistics Canada/Supply and Services Canada. 87–107.

Lindsay, C. 1987. "The Decline in Employment among Men Aged 55–64; 1975–1985." *Canadian Social Trends* (Statistics Canada) (Spring): 12–15.

Mills, C. 1959. *The Sociological Imagination.* London: Oxford University Press.

Myles, J., G. Picot, and T. Wannell. 1988. "The Changing Wage Distribution of Jobs, 1981–1986." *The Labour Force, October 1986.* Ottawa: Statistics Canada/Supply and Services Canada. 85–138.

National Advisory Panel on Skill Development. 1984. *Learning for Life: Overcoming the Separation of Work and Learning.* Ottawa: Supply and Services Canada.

Palmer, B. 1979. *A Culture in Conflict: Skilled Workers and Industrial Capitalism in Hamilton, Ontario, 1860–1914.* Montreal and Kingston: McGill-Queen's University Press.

Palmer, B. 1980. "Working-Class Canada: Recent Historical Writing." *Queen's Quarterly*, 87.

Parliament, J.-A. 1987. "Increases in Long-Term Unemployment." *Canadian Social Trends* (Statistics Canada) (Spring): 16–19.

Pentland, H. 1981. *Labour and Capital in Canada: 1650–1860.* Toronto: James Lorimer and Company.

Picot, W.G. 1987. "The Changing Industrial Mix of Employment, 1951–1985." *Canadian Social Trends* (Statistics Canada) (Spring): 8–11.

Picot, W.G., and T. Wannell.1987. "Job Loss and Labour Market Adjustment in the Canadian Economy: Findings From a Special Survey." *The Labour Force March 1987.* Ottawa: Statistics Canada/Supply and Services Canada. 85–150.

Skoulas, N. 1974. *Determinants of the Participation Rate of Married Women in the Canadian Labour Force: An Econometric Analysis.* Ottawa: Statistics Canada/Industry, Trade and Commerce.

Smith, A. 1965. *The Wealth of Nations.* New York: Random House.

Statistics Canada. 1984a. *Women in the Work World.* Ottawa: Supply and Services Canada.

———. 1984b. *Changes in Income in Canada, 1970–1980.* Ottawa: Supply and Services Canada.

———. 1984c. *Labour Force Annual Averages, 1975–1983.* Ottawa: Supply and Services Canada.

———. 1987. *Income Distribution by Size in Canada. 1986.* Ottawa: Supply and Services Canada.

———. 1988. *Enterprising Canadians: The Self-employed in Canada.* Ottawa: Supply and Services Canada.

———. 1989a. *Labour Force Annual Averages 1981–1988.* Ottawa: Supply and Services Canada.

———. 1989b. *The Labour Force, 1989. Vol. 45, Nos. 1–12.* Ottawa: Supply and Services Canada.

———. 1990. *Women in Canada: A Statistical Report.* 2d ed. Ottawa: Minister of Supply and Services.

———. 1991. *Labour Force Annual Averages, 1990.* Ottawa: Supply and Services Canada

———. 1992. *Labour Force Annual Averages, 1991. Ottawa: Supply and Services Canada.*

———. 1993. *Labour Force Annual Averages, 1992.* Ottawa: Supply and Services Canada.

Wong, F. 1988. "Trends in Labour Income." *The Labour Force, September 1988.* Ottawa: Statistics Canada/Supply and Services Canada. 87–116.

CHAPTER 14

Capital Accumulation and State Formation: The Contradictions of International Migration

Vic Satzewich

Learning Objectives

The objective of this chapter is to highlight the contradictory forces that have influenced the direction and content of immigration policies in Canada. As such, students should understand the links between the process of migration and the capitalist mode of production. Additionally, students should be familiar with important demographic trends in the country, and the potential that immigration has to counteract such trends. Finally, students should be acquainted with issues related to the role that migration plays in the socio-economic development of developing countries.

Introduction

> It is the very qualities (real or imagined) that make certain groups particularly suitable for their role as workers that make them unsuitable for membership in the receiving society. Shared by all classes and strata in the receiving society, these integrative concerns, whether expressed in manifestly xenophobic ideologies or by way of euphemistic codes, universally impinge upon the determination of immigration policy. The conflicting interests of industrial societies—to maximize the labour supply and to protect cultural integrity—can be thought of as a dilemma to which a limited number of solutions are possible (Zolberg 1981, 15).

The spatial relocation of labour across international boundaries has been a fundamental aspect of capitalist development since the Industrial Revolution. The forms of migration have varied. They range from the forced migrations associated with indentured servitude, slavery, and contract labour to the comparatively "free" migrations of wage labour. But, despite differences in form, there is an important link between capitalism and migration (Sassen-Koob 1981).

This chapter argues that migration flows are structured by a dialectic of economic, political, and ideological relations. These relations are by no means complementary or consistent with one another; indeed, in many cases contradictions exist between the various forces that shape systems of immigration control. Three sets of issues associated with the process of international migration to Canada are identified. First, this chapter suggests, in light of Zolberg's comment above, that there is a contradiction between migration as an aspect of capital accumulation and migration as an aspect of state formation. It demonstrates that migration control in Canada results from the interaction of these two processes. Second, it suggests a political and ideological limit to the degree to which the state can use immigration to solve demographic, fiscal, and accumulation problems associated with the aging of Canada's population. Third, it examines whether migration contributes to economic development in sending countries—those countries where migrants originate—or whether it is but a new form of postcolonial exploitation.

Migration, Accumulation, and State Formation

People migrate mainly in order to sell their labour power for wages. As such, the process of migration is structured by the dynamics of the supply of and demand for labour. These dynamics are rooted in the process of *capital accumulation* and the formation and reproduction of the *reserve army of labour* (Wood 1982).

As part of the broader process of the origin and development of capitalist relations of production, the process of capital accumulation contributes to the formation of a reserve army of labour. The reserve army of labour consists of a relative surplus population of people whose labour power is not required within a particular national economy, and as such are either unemployed or irregularly employed. Such a population plays an important role in capitalist economies because these people are available for sudden increases in the demand for labour and hence ensure that employers never run short of labour. The reserve army of labour serves to keep wages low by broadening the pool of potential workers that employers can hire during upturns in the economy. Additionally, a pool of unemployed workers has the potential to take jobs away from already employed workers, hence the reserve army of labour acts as a disciplinary force over the working class.

Migration is both a cause and consequence of the process of capital accumulation (Wood 1982). Capital accumulation initially propels, or forces, certain groups of people to join the reserve army of labour and to migrate because of its associated economic dislocations. The penetration of capitalist social relations into agricultural regions of the world economy displaces workers from the production process. Marx ([1867] 1967, 640–43) refers to this as the formation of a latent reserve surplus population.

The process of capital accumulation also induces migration for those who work in industrial sectors of production already characterized by the presence of capitalist relations of production. Workers are replaced by machines through technological innovations such as the computerization of the workplace or the mechanization of jobs that were previously done by hand. With the restructuring associated with accumulation, workers are displaced from the production process. Marx refers to these people as the floating surplus population.

Capital accumulation is also a stimulus to migration in that it creates the conditions that give rise to labour demand. While, as noted above, the process of capital accumulation can throw people out of the production process, it can display a counteracting tendency to increase the demand for labour. This can occur, for example, when the amount of surplus value invested in new machinery or a new plant is sufficiently great, or when the process of investment deskills the work force and replaces relatively expensive skilled labour with relatively cheap unskilled labour (Miles 1986). Thus, to the extent that migration replenishes the reserve army of labour, migration contributes to the process of capital accumulation by increasing the supply of potential workers and by reducing pressures for wage increases when the demand for workers increases.

Thus, the process of accumulation can help explain the formation of labour pools, the broad structural pressures that force people into migrating, and the reasons states sanction and help organize the importation of foreign-born labour. But a more specific account is necessary. A singular focus on the process of accumulation cannot explain why particular groups of workers are allowed to cross the boundaries of the nation-state to sell their labour power for wages, how they are incorporated into sites in production relations, and why they end up in the jobs they do (Thomas 1985, 12). It is therefore necessary to recognize that migration is also an aspect of *nation-state formation*.

The world is today divided into nation-states. But what does the term *nation* refer to? In Anderson's terms, the nation is an "imagined community." It is *imagined* because members of even the smallest nations will never know most other members, meet them, or even hear of them, "yet in the minds of each lives the image of their communion" (Anderson 1983, 15). The nation is a community, despite the degree of exploitation or inequality that may prevail: it is regarded as a "deep, horizontal comradeship" (1983, 16). The nation-state is also limited, in the sense that it possesses certain boundaries beyond which lie other nations. It is sovereign to the extent that within it ruling groups, whether by consent or fiat, can make laws that govern "the people." Nations differ from one another in terms of the style in which they are imagined. Imagined communities are made up of assessments of "alter" and "ego" (Miles 1987)—perceptions of others set up against perceptions of self.

The nature of the imagined community constitutes an important variable in determining the permeability of the boundaries of the nation-state. This formulation raises the questions: Given a shortage of labour and the existence of a globally dispersed reserve army of labour, why are certain groups of people allowed to cross the national boundary to sell their labour power for wages, and others not? Such considerations, I suggest, are based on assessments of whether members of certain other nations can eventually become part of the community of the receiving nation as it is imagined. The criteria used to define particular nations are fundamental aspects of the process of migration control.

Thus, assessments of potential migrants are based not only on their expected capacity to expend labour power, but also on whether they can become part of the imagined community. It is these assessments over and above those associated with the capacity to labour that constitute the fundamental contradiction of immigration control. Some groups who may be good workers may not be defined as potential citizens.

This means that immigration control is subject to a set of contradictory pressures and processes. The remainder of this chapter examines how immigration controls have responded to these contradictory pressures.

Immigration Control in Canada

As a settler capitalist nation, Canada has seen migration play an important role in the initial formation of capitalist relations of production (see Pentland 1981; Denoon 1983; Ehrensaft and Armstrong 1981). In the initial absence of a class of free wage labour, migration, along with natural population growth, contributed to the formation of a pool of labour that employers could draw upon (Pentland 1959).

Since the establishment of capitalist relations of production in Canada around the middle of the nineteenth century (Pentland 1981; Palmer 1984), migration has continued to play an important role in the economic and social development of the country, especially in terms of the growth in the labour force and the reproduction of the active and reserve armies of labour. Migration to Canada has been broadly linked to the business cycle (although the correlation is not perfect): it has been structured by employers' demands for labour power to fuel the process of accumulation (Avery 1979, 37). Immigration levels were comparatively low during the 1930s, which was a period of recession. Conversely, during periods of economic expansion (1898–1916 and 1947–73) immigration levels tended to be comparatively high. The statistical dimensions of migration to Canada since Confederation are given in Table 14.1.

The contribution of net migration to labour-force growth is given in Table 14.2. The figures in this table demonstrate that during the first decade of the twentieth century, the excess of immigration over emigration contributed to 62.3 percent of the growth in the Canadian labour force. The contribution of net immigration to labour-force growth has declined since then, but is still substantial. Between 1951 and 1961, net migration contributed to 39.5 percent of the growth of the labour force.

Despite large-scale migration to the country since Confederation and the important contributions that net migration has made to the growth in the labour force, migration has not been solely a spontaneous reaction to labour demand. Since Confederation, immigration controls have also been shaped by pressures associated with the formation and maintenance of a nation state. It was expected and hoped that people who migrated to Canada would settle permanently. Permanent settlers were sought because they would contribute to the process of accumulation via the settlement of land and the expansion of the domestic market for consumer commodities. But they were also to be participants in the bourgeois democratic political process. In other words, immigrants were also to become *citizens* of a nation-state.

TABLE 14.1: Immigration to Canada, by Ten-Year Intervals, 1867–1991

Year	Number of immigrants
1867–1876	273 556
1877–1886	682 104
1887–1896	539 207
1897–1906	907 719
1907–1916	2 227 245
1917–1926	996 011
1927–1936	693 367
1937–1946	193 314
1947–1956	1 315 457
1957–1966	1 311 587
1967–1976	1 699 975
1977–1986	1 066 637
1987–1991[a]	951 039

Note: [a]Figure is for five years only.
Source: Compiled from Employment and Immigration Canada, *Immigration Statistics* (Ottawa: Minister of Supply and Services, 1991), p. 3. Reproduced with permission of the Minister of Supply and Services Canada, 1994.

Not all peoples of the world were defined as capable of becoming citizens of such a nation; accordingly, immigration control has been structured by this concern.

In spite of the anguish displayed by Canadian literati over the apparent absence of a truly Canadian identity, the history of immigration control in Canada suggests that the imagined community that constituted the Canadian nation has been defined in terms of race. Immigration restrictions suggest that the Canadian nation was conceived by its ruling groups as not only a capitalist country, but also a "white man's country." Racist immigration controls have been based on the assumption that certain groups of people, because of their "race" and "culture," are unable to participate in Canadian economic, political, and social processes.

The contradiction between migration as an aspect of capital accumulation and migration as an aspect of state formation was especially sharp in British Columbia. During the latter part of the nineteenth century, it was recognized that shortages of labour hindered the process of capitalist economic development in the province. One of the ways to promote such development was to foster the immigration of large amounts of cheap labour. But British Columbia (and Canada, more generally) was also regarded as an outpost of the British Empire. This meant that what was required in the province was not just labour, but certain types of labour: labour that would also take on the rights and duties of citizenship.

This sense of the contradictory nature of immigration was evident in the 1885 report of the Royal Commission on Chinese Immigration to Canada (xxvii). One of the commissioners rather eloquently described the nature of this contradiction in the following terms:

TABLE 14.2: Immigration and the Growth of the Labour Force

Decade	Total labour force increase		Domestic supply Component of increase		Contribution of net migration	
	Number (000s)	%	Number (000s)	%	Number (000s)	%
1901–11	910	100.0	343	37.7	567	62.3
1911–21	503	100.0	440	87.5	63	12.5
1921–31	736	100.0	694	94.3	42	5.7
1931–41	604	100.0	693	114.7	–89	–14.7[a]
1941–51	598	100.0	557	93.1	41	6.9
1951–61	1386	100.0	838	60.5	548	39.5

Note: [a]Net migration was negative during this decade. Net migration therefore contributed to a 14.7 percent decline in the labour force.
Source: M.C. Urquhart and K. Buckley, *Historical Statistics of Canada*, 2nd edition (Ottawa: Citizenship and Immigration Canada, 1983), Table 498–504. Reproduced with permission of the Minister of Supply and Services Canada, 1994.

> A government cannot look at a citizen of a free country as a mere tool in the hands of capital. The jade is much more docile than the charger, and each is useful in its place. A country is not developed merely by work. The character and habits of the workers are of importance, as well as the incidents attaching to the labour.

This same theme was echoed in the 1902 report of the Royal Commission to Investigate Chinese and Japanese Immigration (277–78):

> If the end to be sought is building up the nation, and not the exploitation of these resources, the vital interest to be secured above all others is an immigration of settlers of whom we may hope to make good Canadians, in the best sense of the word. That this object ought to be the one in view is supported by the recent public utterance of a very distinguished personage when he said: "No one who has the privilege which we have had during our tour could fail to be struck with one all-prevailing and pressing demand—the want of population. Even in the oldest of our colonies were abundant signs of this need—boundless tracts of country yet to be explored, hidden mineral wealth calling for development, vast expanses of virgin soil ready to yield profitable crops to the settler; and these can be enjoyed under conditions of healthy living, liberal laws, free institutions, in exchange for the overcrowded cities and the almost hopeless struggle for existence which, also, too often is the lot of many in the old country. I would go further and appeal to my fellow countrymen at home

> to prove the strength of the attachment of the motherland to her children by sending them only the best. By this means we may still further strengthen, or at all events pass on unimpaired, that pride of race, that unity of sentiment and purpose, that feeling of common loyalty and obligation which, knit together, alone can maintain the integrity of our Empire."

This dual theme associated with immigration control is also evident in the postwar period. Mackenzie King, in his now well-known statement in the House of Commons in 1947, suggested that while the immigration program should be structured by the interests of "the national economy," it should also select those who would be desirable "future citizens" (Rawlyk 1962, 289).

The 1952 Immigration Act concretized these criteria. Under the terms of the act, the minister of Citizenship and Immigration was given the power to limit or prohibit the entry of immigrants for any of the following reasons:

1. nationality, citizenship, ethnic group, occupation, class, or geographical area of origin;
2. peculiar customs, habits, modes of life, or methods of holding property;
3. unsuitability, having regard to the climatic, economic, social, industrial, educational, labour, health, or other conditions, or requirements existing in Canada, temporarily or otherwise;
4. probable inability to become readily assimilated or to assume the duties and responsibilities of Canadian citizenship within a reasonable time after admission. (Rawlyk, 1962, 292–93).

These twin concerns resulted in a highly skewed flow of people to the country. Very generally, people defined as "non-white," which included people from Asia, Africa, and the Caribbean, were defined as unsuitable as permanent citizens and thus restricted from entering the country. As the minister of Citizenship and Immigration noted in 1952.

> in light of experience it would be unrealistic to say that immigrants who have spent the greater part of their life in tropical countries become readily adapted to the Canadian mode of life, which to no small extent, is determined by climatic conditions. It is a matter of record that natives of such countries are more apt to break down in health than immigrants from countries where the climate is more akin to that of Canada. It is equally true that, generally speaking, persons from tropical countries or sub-tropical countries find it more difficult to succeed in the highly competitive Canadian economy (Satzewich 1988b, 225).

Table 14.3 demonstrates that, between 1950 and 1955, 94.3 percent of immigrant arrivals were from Europe and the United States, while 3.2 percent of immigrant arrivals originated in Africa and Asia. Between 1956 and 1961, 92.5 percent of immigrant arrivals were from Europe and the United States, and 3.7 percent were from Asia and Africa (see Bolaria and Li 1988, for a more detailed history of racist immigration controls in Canada).

TABLE 14.3: Distribution of Immigrants, by Source Area, 1950–1991

Area	1950–55 %	1956–61 %	1962–67 %	1968–73 %	1974–79 %	1980–85 %	1986–91 %
Africa	0.4	1.0	2.2	3.3	4.9	3.7	6.0
Asia	2.8	2.7	7.2	16.8	28.6	42.7	48.2
Europe	88.0	84.8	73.5	49.9	36.3	30.2	24.2
North and Central America (except United States)	0.7	1.0	2.8	8.4	10.4	9.1	10.9
United States	6.3	7.7	10.4	15.2	11.1	7.8	4.3
South America	0.8	1.3	1.6	3.6	6.3	4.8	5.3
Other	1.0	1.5	2.3	2.8	2.4	1.6	1.2
TOTAL[a]	100.0	100.0	100.0	100.0	100.0	100.0	100.0

Note: [a]Percentage may not sum to 100 because of rounding.
Sources: **1950–1976**: Compiled from Department of Manpower and Immigration, *Immigration Statistics;* **1977–1985:** Compiled from Employment and Immigration Canada, *Immigration Statistics, 1977–1985* (Ottawa: Minister of Supply and Services, 1986). Reproduced with permission of the Minister of Supply and Services Canada, 1994.

Since 1962, there has been a formal deracialization of immigration control in the country. Explicitly racist immigration controls became increasingly embarrassing for government officials who wanted to see Canada become a legitimate actor on the world stage. Also, there was a shift in labour-force requirements. The numbers of highly skilled workers that were in demand in Canada were unavailable in traditional "white" source countries, and Canada was forced to broaden recruitment to "non-white" countries in order to fill this demand (Hawkins 1974,146). This has resulted in an increased flow of immigrants from non-traditional source countries. Between 1962 and 1967, 9.4 percent of total immigrant arrivals originated in Africa and Asia, whereas the European and American contribution decreased to 83.9 percent. Between 1968 and 1973, 65.1 percent of all immigrant arrivals came from Europe and the United States, while 20.1 percent came from Asia and Africa. By the 1980s, the European and American contribution dropped to 28.5 percent, whereas the Asian and African contribution increased to 54.2 percent of the total flow of immigrants to the country.

Despite their firm basis in the labour market and in racism, immigration controls have also been based on medical and political criteria. Sears (1990), in his study of early-twentieth-century medical inspection in Canada, suggests that medical inspections of potential immigrants made use of a broad conception of health that encompassed the physical, mental, and moral wellbeing of the individual. Medical inspections were seen to be a crucial means by which the "interests of the nation" were to be furthered.

Similarly, Whitaker (1987) has documented the political biases that underlay the selection of postwar refugees and the granting of citizenship. In an insightful analysis of postwar immigration controls, he argues that the political selection of immigrants to the country was premised on the perceived existence of an external enemy. This enemy was defined primarily in terms of "communism." Immigration controls were structured by the desire to keep external enemies external—in other words, to prevent the formation in Canada of an enemy within. Again, the perceived existence of an enemy within was defined as a threat to the ability of Canada as a nation-state to reproduce itself.

These bases of immigration control and selection also reflected the dual nature of immigration. Even though medical selection was structured by the desire to have a healthy and productive work force that would be able to provide employers with labour power when it was required, political, racial, and medical selection were also linked to the reproduction of the nation-state as a whole. Thus, selective immigration controls have also been directed at those who have been deemed unable to participate as members of civil and political society. Simply put, sick or politically active left-leaning immigrants were seen as neither good workers nor good citizens.

What needs to be addressed more directly is the impact that racism has on present and future immigration to the country.

Aging, Immigration, and Racism

For the next several decades, Canada will be facing two demographic processes that are expected to have implications for future immigration levels. First, Canada's fertility rate is declining. The total fertility rate that is currently required for population replacement in the country is 2.1 children per woman. However, the actual total fertility rates of Canadian women have been steadily declining, and at present are below the replacement rate. It is projected that they will continue below this level in the future. The total fertility rate in Canada declined from 3.9 in 1956 to 1.7 in 1983 (Hersak and Francolini 1987, 3). If present trends continue, and net migration stands at zero, the population of Canada will begin to decline by the early twenty-first century.

The second demographic process is the aging of Canada's population. Again, if current trends continue, there will be relatively fewer people of working age to support relatively greater numbers of retired people. Table 14.4 provides projections of the relative size of three age groups (0–17, 18–64, and 65 and over) for the years 1976 through 2031. It shows that the proportion of the total population of the country 65 years and older is expected to increase from 8.7 percent to 20.2 percent in 2031.

These two demographic processes are expected to have serious social and economic consequences in Canada. It is anticipated that employers will face an accumulation crisis to the extent that sources of labour from within Canada will decline and result in upward pressures on wages. It is additionally expected that this will put more strain on the welfare state and accentuate the fiscal crisis. The tax base of the population is expected to decline, but state expenditures on the elderly are projected to increase (Myles and Boyd 1982).

One of the ways to get around the potential social and accumulation problems associated with population aging and declining fertility is to expand Canada's immigration program, especially if it is focussed on the recruitment of young workers (Foot 1986; Hersak and Francolini 1987). In allowing the entry of more immigrants, it is possible to enlarge the tax base and the pool of workers that employers in Canada can draw on.

Projections suggest that in order for migration to offset the effects of declining fertility and the aging of the population, immigrant intakes will have to expand well beyond current levels and even beyond the high levels of the 1950s. During the postwar economic boom in Canada, which peaked between 1950 and 1962, immigration levels averaged about 147 000 per year. One estimate suggests that if the total fertility rate remains at 1.7 children per woman and if emigration is 75 000 per year, by the year 2000, as many as 275 000 immigrants would have to be admitted to Canada per year in order to achieve a population growth rate of 1 percent. If the total fertility rate drops to 1.4, again assuming an emigration flow of 75 000 people, the number of immigrants required for a 1-percent rate of population growth would be 325 000 per year by the year 2000 (Romaniuc 1988, 94–95).

The central issue here is whether these immigration levels can be achieved, given the historical legacy of racism in Canada and the definition of the imagined community in terms of the "white race." The traditional source countries of America and Western Europe are drying up as pools of immigrant labour. Rising standards of living mean that Europeans are less willing to move to sell their labour power for wages. Contrary to still-popular myths, Canada is no longer defined by Europeans as the land of opportunity.

In order to achieve immigrant intake levels of over 200 000 per year, policy-makers and immigration analysts recognize that, increasingly, recourse will have to be made to non-traditional source countries: that is, Asia, Africa, the Caribbean, and Central America (Foot 1986, 16–17). The dilemma is that there continues to be hostility on the part of at least some Canadians to "non-white" immigration, and a continued imagining of the Canadian nation in terms of the "white race."

A study of Canadian attitudes toward minority ethno-cultural groups undertaken in the mid-1970s brings forth evidence that "race" is an issue in people's social acceptance or rejection of groups of people (Berry, Kalin, and Taylor 1977, 245). Attitudes toward minorities and their acceptance or rejection form a continuum based upon perception of their degree of "racial" differences. More recently, a 1989 Gallup poll indicated that 54 percent of Canadians believed that racial intolerance had increased over the past five years. This was a marked increase over the findings of a 1982 study done by Gallup, which suggested that only 42 percent of the Canadian public believed that racist intolerance was increasing. Furthermore, the same 1989 poll indicated that 27 percent of Canadians experienced some type of discrimination, and of that total, approximately one-quarter of respondents who reported that they were the victims of discrimination were the victims of racial discrimination (Gallup Poll 1989).

As the 1993 federal election campaign demonstrated, some right-wing politicians were caught in a contradiction when it came to their views on immigration. As representatives of corporate interests, they saw immigration as an essential source of labour, and, in the case of business immigrants, capital. However, some were unable to resist playing the racist card in order to win votes. They tapped into some people's anxieties about the future of Canada as a "white man's country" by problematizing what are seen as excessive levels of immigration in recent years. In that election, the Reform Party's (and others') concern over immigration was arguably a euphemism for objection to non-European immigration to Canada. To put the matter in the terms of John Oostrom, a Tory MP who sat on the House of Commons Immigration Committee in 1987, Canadians "are telling the Commons immigration committee ... that if there have to be immigrants, they should be trained immigrants from Europe." Mr. Oostrom is also reported to have defended this with the claim "that's not racism ... rather, Canadians are merely seeking people who can adjust to this climate" (*Globe and Mail* March 6, 1987).

Recent governments have displayed an ambiguous attitude toward the issue of racism. Some have argued that the 1973 Liberal government's emphasis on the "novel and distinctive features" of the recently arriving non-white immigrants, stated in its Green Paper on Immigration, provided the opportunity for Canadians to articulate, within a legitimate public forum, anti-immigrant and racist diatribes (Bolaria and Li 1988, 175). Because it was the beginning of what was to become a long recessionary period in the country, this may have been intended to prepare the way for the reintroduction of racist immigration controls.

Since that time, various governments and the Canada Employment and Immigration Commission appear to be aware of the potential of racism to hinder the process of accumulation in the future by restricting the flow of immigrants to the country. Part of their strategy seems to be focussed on efforts to convince Canadians that immigrants make "positive contributions" to the country. The 1987 *Annual Report to Parliament on Future Immigration Levels*, for example, contains an entire section on the benefits of immigration for Canada. The benefits cited range from positive effects on employment through increased domestic markets, increased consumption, and the resolution of labour-market bottlenecks, to more general notions of improved "openness" of Canadian society and improving the cultural diversity of the nation. Immigration also apparently enhances Canadian political and economic links with other regions of the world economy (Employment and Immigration Canada 1987, 28–34).

The government also appears to be in the process of establishing institutional structures to mediate the expected increase in racist hostility that will likely accompany increase of "non-white" immigrants. Within the federal government, greater political priority is being given to matters of "race relations." Before the 1988 election, the Conservative government tabled a bill that would see the elevation of Multiculturalism from the status of a directorate to the status of a full government department with representation at cabinet level. This priority is also evident in the recent formation of a "race relations" section within the Multiculturalism directorate and the passage into law of the Canadian Multiculturalism Act in July 1988. While these are laudable initiatives that may represent important gains for visible minority workers in Canada, they are motivated not so much out of a concern for the wellbeing of immigrants and their families but rather out of the potentially negative economic impact that uncontrolled racism will have on the Canadian economy.

Thus, the crucial dilemma that policy-makers face is the extent to which they are going to pander to the racist concerns of an increasingly vocal minority of Canadians. Will the economic and social contradictions associated with aging and declining fertility not be resolved because of racism?

Economic Development or Postcolonial Exploitation?

Despite attempts to convince Canadians of the benefits of immigration and Canada's apparent interest in enlarging the flow of permanent settlers to the country, the government continues to allow the entry of workers to the country on a seasonal, contractual basis—as migrant labour.

Table 14.5 provides information on the number of immigrants admitted to Canada who are destined to the labour force, and the number of employment authorizations issued to temporary workers. Employment authorizations provide non-residents of Canada the right to employment in Canada, usually in a specific job for a specific period of time. Employment authorizations are multifaceted in nature (Boyd, Taylor, and Delaney 1986) and are required for those who are only temporary additions to the labour force; foreign university students who wish to

TABLE 14.5: Immigrant and Non-immigrant Workers Admitted to Canada, 1973–1987

Year	Immigrant workers[a]	Non-immigrant workers	Non-immigrants as a % of immigrants
1973	92 228	83 912	91.0
1974	106 083	86 183	81.2
1975	81 189	96 045	118.3
1976	61 461	91 103	148.2
1977	47 625	89 120	187.1
1978	35 080	63 320	180.5
1979	47 939	94 420	197.0
1980	63 403	108 871	171.7
1981	56 978	126 583	222.2
1982	55 482	125 901	227.0
1983	37 119	130 717	352.2
1984	38 500	143 979	374.0
1985	38 453	177 165	460.7
1986	48 200	205 747	426.9
1987	76 712	231 576	301.9
1988	76 350	196 678	257.6
1989	98 227	187 989	191.4
1990	114 091	191 810	168.1
1991	131 580	202 410	153.8

Note: [a]Consists of those destined for the labour force.

Sources: **1973–1984:** Employment and Immigration Canada, *Immigration Statistics, 1984* (Ottawa: Minister of Supply and Services, 1985), pp. 53, 87; **1985:** Employment and Immigration Canada, *Immigration Statistics, 1985* (Ottawa: Minister of Supply and Services, 1986), pp. 54, 73; **1986:** Employment and Immigration Canada, *Immigration Statistics, 1986* (Ottawa: Minister of Supply and Services, 1987), pp. 66, 80; **1987 to 1991:** Canada Employment and Immigration Commission, *Immigration Statistics, 1985–91* (Ottawa: Minister of Supply and Services, 1992).

take up part-time employment while undertaking their studies in Canada, and visiting professors who come to give paid lectures or teach occasional courses at universities. Authorizations are also required for migrant farm workers (to be discussed in more detail below) and domestic servants, two categories of workers that are now permanently part of the labour force. The advantage of admitting temporary workers to fill specific kinds of jobs is that when those jobs end, the workers must leave the country.

Table 14.5 indicates that during the relatively good economic times of the mid-to late 1980s, the Canadian government admitted between three and four times more migrant than immigrant workers to the country. Since then, the ratio of migrant to immigrant workers admitted has decreased. Nevertheless, in 1990, over 200 000 employment authorizations were issued to foreign workers for employment in Canada.

One of the most significant groups of foreign workers admitted to Canada on a temporary basis are workers from the Caribbean and Mexico who work in fruit and vegetable production in southern Ontario and in the sugar beet industry in southern Manitoba and Alberta. The statistical dimensions of this migration are given in Table 14.6. While this type of migration had relatively modest beginnings in 1966, when only 264 Caribbean workers were admitted, this migration stream has grown to the point that, in 1991, over 12 000 migrant workers were admitted to Canada on a seasonal-contractual basis. The volume of the flow of this category of migrant worker has increased over the years despite downturns in the Canadian economy.

Since the end of the Second World War, Ontario farmers' organizations and representatives of a number of Caribbean governments have pressured Canadian government officials to allow importation of workers from the Caribbean on a seasonal, migrant-labour basis. The historical origins of this migration are documented elsewhere (Satzewich 1988b), but evidence suggests that Canadian officials resisted such a proposal for nearly twenty years. Between 1947 and 1965, government Officials did not allow Ontario farmers the opportunity to exploit the labour power of Caribbean workers, in part because of the belief that they would cause a "race relations" problem in this country. Canadian officials were especially concerned about the admittance of "black workers" from the Commonwealth, because "once they were here, and [because they] are members of the Commonwealth [they] would apply to remain permanently and pressurize [sic] us to that end." This is consistent with the assessment of the government's resistance to this proposal expressed in the *Financial Times* of London (England). In a 1965 article, it was suggested that

> the colour problem appears to be one of the main worries of the Ottawa government.... Since the Jamaicans are British subjects, they could make life difficult if they decided to stay in Canada once the harvest was over in the autumn. The government could expect a full scale row in the House of Commons if it were forced to explain why it has ejected a group of Her Majesty's subjects (Satzewich 1988a, 278).

The Canadian state's position on this matter reflects, in a larger sense, its historically ambiguous commitment to the Commonwealth, especially as it applies to non-European migration.

TABLE 14.6: Caribbean Seasonal Labour Arrivals in Canada, 1966–1990

Year	Seasonal agricultural worker arrivals
1966	264
1967	1 077
1968	1 258
1969	1 449
1970	1 279
1971	1 271
1972	1 531
1973	3 048
1974	5 537
1975	5 966
1976	5 455
1977	4 929
1978	4 984
1979	4 968
1980	6 001
1981	5 798
1982	5 510
1983	4 564
1984	4 502
1985	5 005
1986	5 166
1987	6 337
1988	8 539
1989	12 237
1990	12 510
1991	12 131
1992	11 115
1993	11 212

Note: [a]Figures for 1966–73 include Caribbean worker arrivals only. Figures for 1974–93 include both Caribbean and Mexican seasonal workers.

Source: "Worker Arrivals by Country and Year," Labour Market Services Branch, Human Resources Branch, Human Resources Development Canada. Reproduced with permission of the Minister of Supply and Services Canada, 1994.

Temporary migration was eventually sanctioned by government officials in 1966 because of conditions in the labour market. But it was also an attempt to stem the flow of non-European permanent settlers to the country, which had begun as a result of the deracialization of immigration control in 1962 (Satzewich 1988a).

In an effort to convince his cabinet colleagues that workers from the Caribbean should be let in on a temporary basis for the Ontario harvest, and at the same time deflect potential criticisms that such a program was simply a way that Canadian farmers could acquire "cheap labour," the minister of Citizenship and Immigration presented it as part of the government's package of development aid in the Caribbean. According to the memorandum to cabinet on the matter, submitted by the minister of Citizenship and Immigration, "the bringing in of labour from this source would fit in with the Government's general program of aid and cooperation with the West Indies" (Satzewich 1988a, 280).

If we accept for the moment what appears to have been a rather flimsy justification, to what extent has this migration contributed to the economic development of the region? Migrant labour is hypothesized to have several important effects on economic development in developing regions of the world economy. The *Daily Gleaner*, Jamaica's most influential newspaper in the 1960s, summed up rather eloquently the positive role that migrant labour could play. In addition to the direct economic benefit to be had by allowing workers to earn foreign currency, it also suggested that

> there are also indirect benefits to the West Indies on which a specific cash value cannot be placed: the value of the contact by thousands of men from the small West Indian territories with ... America and the American way of life. The workers not only see some of the bright lights of the cities and vast stretches of agricultural lands under production but they also see new techniques, methods and procedures on the farm. They also observe how the American farmer, even though he may be several financial strata above his employee—American or foreign—is still willing and able to work side by side with the humblest of labourers so as to get the task done (quoted in Segal n.d., 7).

It is difficult to measure many of the subjective changes that have occurred in the workers' world view pertaining to modernization. Therefore, what I concentrate on are the direct economic implications for development and the use to which the funds earned in Canada are put.

Evidence from a recent sample survey of Caribbean farm workers suggests that little of the funds earned by workers contributes to economic development in the region (Whyte 1984). Since the start of the migration in 1966, Caribbean workers have earned considerable amounts of money from seasonal employment in the Ontario fruit and vegetable industry. Between 1966 and 1985, it is estimated that the gross earnings of Caribbean workers were $132 325 117. There are two components of Caribbean worker earnings. The first is the workers' weekly wage, which they can spend as they see fit. Another component consists of compulsory savings—savings that workers are required to remit directly to a bank in the Caribbean. Compulsory savings constitute about 19 percent of the workers' total earnings less the contribution made to their transportation by air to Canada.

Whyte's evidence suggests that the major use to which Canadian earnings are put is the purchase of goods in Canada. The main goods that the workers Whyte studied bought in Canada were clothing for the worker's family, electronic equipment, toiletries, appliances, and food. Few farm workers purchased equipment and tools that could help them in their work in the Caribbean.

Most of the money taken home at the end of the season is expended in two ways: paying general living expenses for the family and buying or improving a family home. Investment of these earnings in land, technology, or education is rare.

The pattern of expenditure of compulsory savings is slightly different. Approximately 45 percent of the workers interviewed stated that they would save their compulsory remittances; only 4 percent reported that they would use the money to invest in education, land, or machinery; the remainder reported that they would use the savings to support their family, purchase clothes or appliances, or make home repairs (Whyte 1984, 28).

Thus it appears that much of the money earned by the workers is expended to sustain their capacity to work while in Canada (because they are responsible for their own cooking, clothing, and so on). Part of the earnings of the workers finds its way to Canadian merchants near the areas where they are employed. It appears that the funds earned through employment in Canada have had little impact on development in the Caribbean. These findings are consistent with those of other studies, which show that migrant labour remittances play a minimal role in development. Government claims that these monies promote development appear to be little more than rhetoric. In reality, the importation of Caribbean workers under contract allows Canadian employers the opportunity to exploit the labour power of Caribbean workers without threatening the imagined community of the Canadian nation, which continues to be defined, in part, in terms of the "white race."

Conclusions

Immigration has been central to the economic and social development of Canada as a nation-state. Immigrants have an important economic role to play in the process of capital accumulation. Immigrants have contributed to the initial formation of a class of free wage labour, and have subsequently contributed to the reproduction of the working class. But because Canada is a settler capitalist nation, immigration has also been a crucial aspect of state formation. This has meant that there have been conflicting and contradictory pressures placed on state officials with respect to immigration. Canada has not simply sought out immigrant labour that was inexpensive for capitalists to purchase, but labour that could also become part of the Canadian imagined community.

The continued representation of the Canadian nation in terms of the "white race" on the part of some Canadians might mean that immigration will not be used to solve the social and economic contradictions associated with the aging of the population and its declining fertility. Racism may preclude the importation of immigrant workers from non-traditional source countries. Racism continues to structure immigration control in the country to the extent that Caribbean seasonal workers are admitted to work in the Ontario fruit and vegetable harvest without being given settlement and subsequent citizenship rights.

Study Questions

1. What is the nature of the contradiction inherent in the process of migration?

2. What is the link between capital accumulation and the international migration of the reserve army of labour?

3. Do systems of migrant labour contribute to the process of development in developing countries?

4. What two demographic factors will be crucial in Canada's future? How can immigration help solve the social and economic problems associated with these demographic processes? What factors will determine whether migration will be used to solve these problems?

Recommended Reading

Anderson, B. *Imagined Communities: Reflections on the Origins and Spread of Nationalism*. London: Verso, 1983.

Castles, Steven, and G. Kosack. *Immigrant Workers and Class Structure in Western Europe*. London: Oxford University Press, 1973.

Foot, D. *Population Aging and Immigration Policy in Canada: Implications and Prescriptions*. Ottawa: Canada Employment and Immigration Commission, 1986.

Miles, Robert. "Labour Migration, Racism and Capital Accumulation in Western Europe Since 1945." *Capital and Class* 28 (1986): 49–86.

Satzewich, V. ed. *Deconstructing a Nation: Immigration, Multiculturalism, and Racism in '90s Canada*. Halifax: Fernwood, 1992.

References

Anderson, A., and J. Frideres. 1981. *Ethnicity in Canada: Theoretical Perspectives*. Toronto: Butterworths.

Anderson, B. 1983. *Imagined Communities: Reflections on the Origins and Spread of Nationalism*. London: Verso.

Avery, D. 1979. *Dangerous Foreigners: European Immigrant Workers and Labour Radicalism in Canada. 1896–1932*. Toronto: McClelland and Stewart.

Berry. J., R. Kalin, and D. Taylor. 1977. *Multiculturalism and Ethnic Attitudes in Canada*. Ottawa: Supply and Services Canada.

Bolaria, B.S., and P. Li. 1988. *Racial Oppression in Canada*. 2d ed. Toronto: Garamond Press.

Boyd, M., C. Taylor, P. Delaney. 1986. "Temporary Workers in Canada: A Multifaceted Program." *International Migration Review* 20:929–50.

Denoon, D. 1983. *Settler Capitalism*. London: Oxford University Press.

Department of Manpower and Immigration. 1974–76. *Immigration Statistics*. Ottawa: Supply and Services Canada.

Ehrensaft, P., and W. Armstrong 1981. "The Formation of Dominion Capitalism. " In *Inequality: Essays in the Political Economy of Social Welfare*, ed. A. Muscovitch and G. Drover. Toronto: University of Toronto Press. 98–155.

Employment and Immigration Canada. 1977–1978. *Immigration Statistics*. Ottawa: Supply and Services Canada.

———. 1987. *Annual Report to Parliament on Future Immigration Levels*. Ottawa: Supply and Services Canada.

Foot, D. 1986. *Population Aging and Immigration Policy in Canada: Implications and Prescriptions.* Ottawa: Canada Employment and Immigration Commission.

Gallup Poll. 1989. "Large Increase in Racial Intolerance Perceived." March 20. Toronto: Gallup Canada.

Hawkins, F. 1974. "Canadian Immigration Policy and Management." *International Migration Review* 7:141–53.

Hersak, G.A., and S. Francolini. 1987. *Immigration of Children as a Response to Demographic Concerns.* Ottawa: Supply and Services Canada.

Marx, K. 1967 [1867]. *Capital.* Vol. 1. New York: International Publishers.

Miles, R. 1986. "Labour Migration, Racism, and Capital Accumulation in Western Europe Since 1945." *Capital and Class* 28: 49–86.

———. 1987. "Recent Marxist Theories of Nationalism and the Issue of Racism." *The British Journal of Sociology* 38: 24–43.

Myles, J., and M. Boyd. 1982. "Population Aging and the Elderly." In *Social Issues: Sociological Views of Canada*, ed. D. Forcese and S. Richer. Scarborough, ON: Prentice-Hall. 258–85.

Palmer, B. 1984. "Social Formation and Class Formation in North America, 1800–1900." In *Proletarianization and Family History*, ed. D. Levine. New York: Academic Press. 229–309.

Pentland, H.C. 1959. "The Development of a Capitalist Labour Market in Canada." *Canadian Journal of Economics and Political Science* 25: 450–61.

———. 1981. *Labour and Capital in Canada, 1650–1860.* Toronto: Lorimer.

Rawlyk, G. 1962. "Canada's Immigration Policy, 1945–1962." *Dalhousie Review* 42 (Spring): 287–300.

Rex, J., and S. Tomlinson. 1979. *Colonial Immigrants in a British City.* London: Routledge and Kegan Paul.

Romaniuc, A. 1988. *Fertility in Canada: From Baby Boom to Baby Bust.* Ottawa: Statistics Canada.

Royal Commission on Chinese Immigration. 1885. *Report.* Ottawa: Queen's Printer.

Royal Commission on Chinese and Japanese Immigration. 1902. *Report.* Ottawa: Queen's Printer.

Sassen-Koob, S. 1981. "Towards a Conceptualization of Immigrant Labour." *Social Problems* 29: 65–85.

Satzewich, V. 1988a. "Modes of Incorporation and Racialization: The Canadian Case." Ph.D. thesis. University of Glasgow.

———. 1988b. "The Canadian State and the Racialization of Caribbean Migrant Farm Labour, 1947–1966." *Ethnic and Racial Studies* 11: 282–304.

Sears, A. 1990. "Immigration Controls as Social Policy: The Case of Canadian Medical Inspection." *Studies in Political Economy* 33: 91–112.

Segal, A. n.d. *Politics and Population in the Caribbean.* Rio Piedras: Institute of Caribbean Studies.

Thomas, R. 1985. *Citizenship: Gender and Work.* Berkeley: University of California Press.

Urquhart, M.C., and K. Buckley. 1983. *Historical Statistics of Canada.* 2d ed. Ottawa: Statistics Canada.

Whitaker, R. 1987. *Double Standard: The Secret History of Canadian Immigration.* Toronto: Lester and Orpen Dennys.

Whyte, A. 1984. *The Experience of New Immigrants and Seasonal Farm Workers from the Eastern Caribbean in Canada.* Toronto: Institute of Environmental Studies.

Wood, C. 1982. "Equilibrium and Historical-Structural Models of Migration." *International Migration Review* 16: 298–319.

Zolberg, A. 1981. "International Migrations in Political Perspective." In *Global Trends in Migration*, ed. M. Kritz. C.B. Keeley, and S.M. Tomasi. New York: Center for Migration Studies.

CHAPTER 15

Capital, Labour, and the State: The Future of the Labour Movement

William K. Carroll and Rennie Warburton

Learning Objectives

This chapter gives an account of the labour–capital relationship in Canada in the postwar period and the ways in which it is mediated by the state. In reading this chapter, students are expected to acquire insights into the contradictions and dynamics of capitalist development that have led employers and the state to weaken workers' rights and benefits. They should be aware of the ways in which the fragmented nature of the Canadian working class has facilitated this attack. Students should be able to analyze Fordism and class compromise as a phase in recent capitalist development, including its particular Canadian manifestations, and to account for the crisis of Fordism and the rise of hegemonic despotism. They should also be familiar with the impact of free trade on Canadian employment prospects and labour relations. Finally, students are expected to understand the challenges these developments present to Canadian workers, and the future options and possibilities facing the labour movement.

Introduction

> Unions were born out of struggles to change the status quo. Our successes extend progress beyond the workplace. Our struggles are part of a social movement for a more humane society here and for peace and justice internationally. Together, in coalitions with others committed to social justice, we are confident that progressive change is possible. We are committed to building social solidarity and a better tomorrow (Canadian Auto Workers advertisement, 1989).

To speak of the labour movement's future presumes an understanding of its past and present. The stream of events that gave rise to contemporary relations between Canadian workers, their employers, and the state can be considered in terms of four historical periods. Until about 1859 most European settlers were farmers, fishers, or self-employed artisans who produced for their own subsistence or for small, local markets. Wage-labour relations were restricted to a few sectors such as canal-building, logging, farm labouring, domestic service, and some skilled trades. By mid-century, industrialization was well under way. This gave rise to the second period, when for the first time wage-earners were a significant population. At the close of the nineteenth century, the growth of large corporations, expanded mining operations, centrally co-ordinated production, and the use of more sophisticated technology and managerial strategies comprised the third phase, the consolidation of monopoly capitalism, which lasted until the Second World War. Each of these stages was preceded by economic crisis, during which the established workplace and marketplace relationships were shaken up and steadily reconstituted on new terms (Heron and Storey 1986, 2–26). In this chapter, we discuss the fourth, post-Second World War period, and the emergence in the 1970s and 1980s of a fifth era of crisis and change.

Our theoretical position is derived from Marxism and feminism. Workers and their organizations are situated within capitalist social relations whose basic driving force is the accumulation of capital by owners of the means of production. In the system of property relations defined by the liberal state, capitalists' ownership of the means of production entitles them to the full benefits of the use of that property. Within the firms they own, capitalists thus control the labour process and its products, and they realize profits through sale of the commodities produced by their wage-earning employees. Relations between capitalist owners and workers are inherently exploitative because capitalists gain more from the use of their employees' labour than they pay the same employees as wages; indeed, if this were not the case, capitalists would have no reason to hire workers.

Class struggle describes the collective domination of capitalists over the working class, and the collective resistance of labour to that domination. Resistance has taken various forms, ranging from covert struggles in the workplace over the pace of labour, through open forms of industrial conflict, such as strikes, to political activities aimed at transforming capitalism into a democratically planned economy organized around worker-managed enterprises (Rinehart 1987, 157, 209–10). Capitalists themselves, however, are in competition with one another: each capitalist's survival depends on staying ahead of (or at least even with) the rest of the pack. It is in minimizing their costs to meet the competition that capitalists are continually compelled to attack or at least restrain the rights and welfare of workers, for example, by reducing wages, intensifying the pace of work, introducing technologies that eliminate jobs, and in the final instance firing unruly employees or relocating plants where labour is cheaper and more docile (Harvey 1985, 1–13). Struggle between capitalists' and workers' interests also occurs within the state, for example, over collective bargaining rights or day-care provisions. Liberal democracy in Canada permits legitimate capital–labour struggles, which still have to be fought for in more repressive states, including Mexico, Canada's partner in the North American Free Trade Agreement (NAFTA).

Capitalists have also benefited from women's domestic labour, which reproduces the labour power of workers while dividing the working class along gender lines. The *family-wage system*, in which the permanently employed male worker earned a wage large enough to support a dependent wife and children, was the typical form of working class household that arose from the class struggles of the nineteenth and early twentieth centuries, as unions pressed for a "living wage," a shorter working day, and an end to the super-exploitation of children and women—for a domestic life apart from the drudgery of wage labour (Curtis 1980). Although the removal of women from full-fledged participation in the labour force was not the objective of this agitation, it was one of its main effects, as the state implemented reforms that institutionalized the privileged position of men in the labour market. The result was a distinct form of women's oppression, still evident today: a "double ghetto" in which women perform unpaid domestic labour in the household and are concentrated in a limited number of low-status, gender-specific jobs in the labour force (Armstrong and Armstrong 1984). Many of these jobs involve serving or caring, similar to the work of homemakers.

A final noteworthy feature of contemporary capitalism is its susceptibility to recurrent crises. Capital accumulates in a cycle of boom and bust that influences the course of class struggle, as investment and employment levels rise and fall with the changing rate of profit. In the upswing phase, low rates of unemployment strengthen labour's hand in pressing for economic concessions and political reforms, while buoyant profits enable capital and the state to grant some of these demands in order to maintain a compliant work force or, in the case of the government in power, to retain workers' electoral support. Although New Democratic Party (NDP) provincial governments have introduced laws favouring workers' interests, in the downswing, falling profits eliminate the weaker firms and many jobs. In the resulting situation of unemployment and economic stagnation the surviving capitalists, often with the help of the state, attempt to re-establish a basis for profitable accumulation by rationalizing the process of production, exchange, distribution, and consumption, in the name of the "national interest." Labour movements are obliged to respond effectively to these rationalizing measures, which now occur transnationally, on pain of extinction.

Fordism and the Postwar Class Compromise

The changing relationships between capital, labour, and the state since the Second World War can be understood in two phases: a long, postwar wave of buoyant accumulation, followed in the mid-1970s by a global economic crisis. Unlike the open class warfare that had previously characterized labour relations, the era of postwar prosperity produced a specific social structure of accumulation, which enabled capital and labour to reach agreement within an institutional framework of "class compromise." The terms of the compromise, which emerged in Canada and in other capitalist democracies, "left the investment decision-making process in the hands of private enterprise in exchange for the adoption of economic policies to provide stable levels of employment and income for the mass of wage-earners" (Wolfe 1984, 47). Under the compromise, capital and labour continued to oppose each other directly over matters of wages and working conditions, but class conflict was *mediated* in three ways by the state. The state responded to labour's demands for trade union rights by enshrining a system of "free collective bargaining" between unions and employers. It accepted an obligation through social welfare programs to support individuals who were unable to satisfy their minimal subsistence needs through gainful employment. Finally, it adopted a Keynesian economic policy that valued full employment, high wages, progressive taxation, and social insurance as ways of buoying up aggregate demand, thus staving off the threat of economic depression.

Together, these political reforms comprised what came to be known as the "Keynesian welfare state" (KWS). Underpinning them was a particular regime of accumulation in which the method of assembly-line production pioneered by Henry Ford raised the productivity of labour to unprecedented levels. By rationalizing production in this way, Ford was able to produce a standardized product at comparatively low cost, which could be sold in a mass market that included working-class consumers. Durables such as Ford's Model T ushered in a new regime of accumulation that bears his name, as competition obliged other capitalists to adopt the same approach. Under *Fordism*, increasing levels of productivity resulting from the introduction of mass-production techniques enabled capitalists to maintain relatively high profits even as they granted wage increases to their employees, providing a material basis for the class compromise. Within each national economy in which Fordism held sway, capital and labour shared a growing economic pie, and the struggle between them was often reduced to a conflict over wage rates and benefits. Rising levels of income for both capital and labour also provided revenue for the expansive social programs of the KWS. Fordism has thus been described as a regime of accumulation effecting a correspondence between high levels of mass production and high levels of mass consumption (Houle 1983).

But Fordism was more than just a formula for capitalist expansion and class compromise; it brought fundamental changes to the working class, both on and off the job. The assembly line and the related implementation of "scientific management" schemes fragmented the labour process into many discrete tasks, thereby creating a new type of worker, the *mass worker*, dispossessed of the know-how and skills that had previously informed artisan labour, and subjected to a repetitive, monotonous labour process whose pace was controlled by capital through the speed of the assembly line (Houle 1983, 133; Rinehart 1987, 52). At the same time as it degraded the labour process and intensified worker alienation, Fordism created the *mass consumer*, participating in what Palmer (1992, 270) calls a "mass culture" organized around the privatized possession and use of televisions, cars, refrigerators, and homes, as well as commercialized popular music and takeout foods. The possessive individualism fostered by this consumerism contributed in no small way to the atmosphere of harmony that pervaded the postwar accord, as many workers became more interested in the size of their paycheques than in a broader agenda of collective struggle for social change.

During Fordism's "golden era," several prominent social scientists made confident prognoses of the boundless potential for "people's capitalism," "the affluent society," "the decomposition of class," and "the end of ideology." To be sure, the Canadian economy expanded considerably until the early 1970s, and unemployment rates remained low. Many workers prospered from inexpensive gasoline, land, and other raw materials, accompanied by high and rising real wage rates (Myles

1988, 87). The Cold War and the actual wars in Korea and Vietnam ensured that the growth of the armaments industry contributed in no small measure to the economic boom (Phillips and Watson 1984, 33; Warnock 1988, 28). But the class compromise was inherently limited by deep structural contradictions within the capitalist mode of production. By the mid-seventies they were revealing themselves clearly in lowered rates of profit, high unemployment levels, and austere forms of public policy (Strain and Grant, 1992).

Even during the "golden era," class conflict did not disappear; peace was interrupted by major disputes in the auto industry, fishery, forestry, non-ferrous mining, and smelting (Palmer 1992, 299). "Free collective bargaining" simply meant that class struggle was regulated within legislated measures in the areas of union certification, negotiation, and strike activity (Panitch and Swartz 1988, 19–22). Employers and the state "bought labour peace" with concessions that could be made without seriously eroding profits. Unions were successful during the 1950s in securing shorter hours, increased wages, paid holidays, pensions, and medical benefits.[1]

The resulting emphasis on compliance with the state's legal requirements turned union leaders' efforts away from mobilizing and organizing. Instead they were preoccupied with the development of legal knowledge and skills, which fostered a bureaucratic and "legalistic practice and consciousness in which union rights appeared as privileges bestowed by the state, rather than democratic freedoms won, and to be defended by, collective struggle" (Panitch and Swartz 1988, 26). One result was the channelling of class struggles into *business unionism*, a form of "professionalized" trade unionism in which labour's agenda was narrowed to strictly economic issues, negotiable with individual employers by an elite of paid union leaders and staff. Business unionism partially demobilized the working class, as "workers were gradually separated from the activities through which unions represented their interests" (Calvert 1987, 307). Efforts to build alliances in local communities, to struggle for social change, and to maintain and develop a working-class culture that would provide an alternative to bourgeois consumerism received less and less attention from the trade union movement.

Although Fordist class compromise became a common organizing principle among the capitalist democracies, the specific terms of the accord varied to some extent from country to country. Two significant aspects of Fordism in Canada were its *permeability* and the *fragmented* character of Canada's labour movement. In an era of unrivalled U.S. pre-eminence in the capitalist world, Canada's postwar accumulation strategy was that of mass production for mass consumption *within a continentalist framework* of resource exports, capital imports, and the branch-plant production of consumer goods (Houle 1983; Jenson 1989). The permeability of Fordism in Canada meant that Keynesian policies would be limited in impact—that the state's capacity to maintain full employment would be especially constrained by the vagaries of international markets for resources and capital. In itself, this introduced "an important element of instability into the implementation of the postwar political compromise" (Wolfe 1984, 48). Moreover, the United States-based corporations such as Ford and General Electric that led the way in consolidating Canada's Fordism brought with them a kind of "branch-plant" trade unionism: the Canadian branches of "international" (i.e., American) unions. Yet, in the "golden era," it was the American labour movement that became almost singularly committed to business unionism; for the most part, the Canadian branches of American unions followed suit (Laxer 1976). This meant not only that labour's agenda narrowed, but that communists were purged from Canadian unions under the instigation of international union headquarters and with the support of the state on both sides of the border and of the New Democratic Party's forerunner, the Co-operative Commonwealth Federation (Lembcke and Tattam 1984). Cold War anticommunism, though somewhat less pervasive in Canada than in the United States, helped cement the class compromise by eliminating many of the most capable, class-conscious leaders from the labour movement and by inculcating mass scepticism toward collective action. Not surprisingly, as the postwar boom drew to a close, much of the opposition to business unionism took the form of left-leaning Canadian nationalism, as several unions broke away from their American counterparts (Roberts and Bullen 1984, 134).

The other important specific feature of the Canadian labour movement has been its fragmentation, partly a consequence of uneven economic development within a federated state comprised of twelve regions of state jurisdiction, one of which is Quebec with its distinct national culture. As Phillips (1989, 93) has put it, "the more fragmented labour is, whether by organization, race or ethnicity, gender, skill, region or ideology, the weaker will be its political bargaining power and its ability to work for common goals." During the Second World War, the influence of the church among Quebec unions declined. The growing militancy and confrontation of the postwar era saw many sectors of Quebec society engaged in reform and modernization. The asbestos strike of 1949 brought nationalists, intellectuals, and workers together in the "opening scenes of what would later be recognized as the Quiet Revolution" (Palmer 1992, 309), while the provincial Duplessis government repressed unions, forcing them to move beyond a business-unionist approach to seek greater influence over rules of the workplace (Lipsig-Mumme 1980, 131). Revolutionary socialism was embraced by a size able minority of Quebec workers. The Quebec labour movement continues to be divided in its approach to the questions of socialism and Quebec nationalism, and therefore in its relations with the rest of Canadian labour (Lipsig-Mummé, 1991).

Perhaps the deepest divide among Canadian workers is that between the primary and secondary labour market:

> The typical worker in the primary job market is a prime-age man from the dominant ethnic or racial group, protected by a union and working for a large corporation or the public sector. A typical worker in the secondary job market is a woman, young or aged, from minority racial or ethnic groups, unprotected by unions, and working for small competitive employers or in the service or sales sectors (Phillips 1989, 90).

The most significant social determinant to one's position in these job markets is gender; indeed, the class compromise itself was literally a "gentlemen's agreement"— an accord between male capitalists and male workers in the primary labour market, which took for granted and further reinforced the family-wage system. The specific claims of working-class women—day-care, equal pay for work of equal value, maternity leave, and protection from sexual harassment—were not part of the deal. The agreement's reformist and patriarchal framework

> tended to narrow the class struggle down to the economic issue of the size of the male wage. As long as the male worker was paid a wage high enough to maintain or improve the quality of his and his family's lives, the capitalist's control over the production process went largely unchallenged (Cameron 1983, 47).

Yet a prime trend in the postwar period was the erosion of the family-wage system, as large numbers of women entered the labour force, pushed by the growing economic necessity for two household incomes and pulled by the growing opportunities for "women's work" in the burgeoning service sector. Women as a percentage of the experienced labour force increased from 22 percent in 1951 to 33.5 percent in 1971 and 40.3 percent in 1981 (Armstrong and Armstrong 1984, 27). In this period, male unionists did not distinguish themselves as progressive on gender issues. In 1971, many Quebec unionists thought that men had a prior right to jobs and that women should stay at home (Maroney 1987). But as the percentage of female union members grew from 16.6 in 1965 to 30.2 in 1980 and 39.1 in 1989 (White 1993, 56) and as a new wave of trade union feminists mobilized in women's caucuses, the drive for women's equality began to receive forceful expression in the labour movement (Roberts and Bullen 1984, 135)—just as the era of class compromise drew to a close.

The golden age of Fordism came to an end in the 1970s. Alain Lipietz (1987) has identified some of the key reasons for the onset of a period of economic crisis and heightened political conflict, which is still very much with us today. In advanced capitalist countries such as Canada, the most general feature of crisis was a socially conditioned downturn in productivity growth (Strain and Grant 1992, 81). Since "scientific management" and Fordist-style mass production seriously limited the creative input of workers, industrialists were obliged to raise labour productivity by resorting to ever more complex and expensive machines. Yet these increased capital investments eroded profit rates in the long term. The availability in the Third World of large labour forces within authoritarian states led capitalists in the 1970s to adopt "new socio-spatial strategies" to cheapen wages and to raise productivity by expanding mass production to the periphery of world capitalism. Relocation of certain industrial branches to form a "New International Division of Labour" (NIDL) did bolster corporate profits; but it did not increase worldwide demand, as relatively well-paid workers in the centre were replaced by superexploited peripheral labour. The NIDL also meant that capitalists in countries such as Canada would ultimately be caught in a profit squeeze between organized labour (keeping wages high) and foreign competitors (holding prices down). Moreover, as the economy slowed, state revenues failed to keep pace with the growing burden of social programs. Real wages fell during the 1980s while income polarization increased. The class compromise was eroded as governments allied themselves with capital and pushed labour into a defensive posture (Cox 1987).

According to Michael Burawoy (1985), the new, global structures of accumulation have strengthened the power of capital by creating a low-wage, export-processing periphery and enhancing the mobility of capital across national borders. In the advanced capitalist countries, the emerging post-Fordist regime is one of *hegemonic despotism. The regime is "hegemonic" in the sense that, as in the heyday of Fordism, the interests of capital and labour continue to be mediated and co-ordinated by the state. But where labour used to be granted* concessions based on the expansion of productivity and profits, it now *makes* concessions in the international competition for investors. Capital's enhanced structural power thus makes its rule more despotic, even if the formal structures of collective bargaining and representative democracy remain intact.

> The new despotism is the "rational" tyranny of capital mobility over the *collective* worker. The reproduction of labour power is bound anew to the production process, but, rather than via the individual, the binding occurs at the level of the firm, region or even nation-state. The fear of being fired is replaced by the fear of plant closure, transfer of operation, and plant disinvestment (Burawoy 1985, 150).

In practice, hegemonic despotism appears as a plurality of tactics that break from the Fordist class compromise. Some employers introduce "Quality of Working Life" (QWL) schemes (of which more below) in an attempt to weaken unions and to mobilize consent to increased productivity; others try to decertify unions and fire union activists. Governments—pitted against one another in the competition to attract and retain capital—grant tax concessions, relax labour legislation and welfare provisions, and foster privatization and contracting out. National (and regional) fractions of the working class are similarly obliged to outbid each other in striving to retain capital's "allegiance" (Burawoy 1985, 264).

These changes in the capital–labour relation have been evident in all advanced capitalist societies. But the shift toward hegemonic despotism can also be said to have taken a distinctly "Canadian" form. For one thing, compared to other leading capitalist countries, the Canadian state has become especially involved in what Panitch and Swartz (1988) call the movement "from consent to coercion." Beginning with the federal government's 1975–78 Anti-Inflation Program, which suspended collective bargaining rights for *all* workers, "the rules of the game established in the postwar settlement were set aside through special legislation" (1988, 34). In the ensuing decade, a raft of such "permanently exceptionalist" legislation was assembled at the provincial and federal levels of government, as the state intervened on an ad hoc basis to limit both the right to strike and the scope of collective bargaining. Along with new restrictions on workers' collective action and measures to enhance employers' access to non-union labour, permanent exceptionalism weakened the ability of workers to "take wages out of competition" (1988, 15). The increasingly coercive role of the state can be seen in increases in back-to-work legislation and in the growing number of complaints by Canadian unions to the International Labour Organization's Committee on Freedom of Association. Among the seven major capitalist countries, between 1954 and 1973 only 3 percent of such complaints came from Canada, but between 1974 and 1985 Canada accounted for one-third of the total (1988, 50–51).

Despite these encroachments on workers' collective freedoms, the formal premises of "free collective bargaining" remained intact in Canada until 1987 when the

Supreme Court of Canada rendered a landmark decision that the constitutional guarantee of freedom of association in the Canadian Charter of Rights and Freedoms "does not include, in the case of a trade union, a guarantee of the right to bargain collectively and the right to strike" (quoted in Panitch and Swartz 1988, 57). In denying any constitutional basis for trade union rights, this ruling opened the door to a much broader assault on the labour movement in both the public and private sectors.

Provinces have also been important sites in the struggle to define a new relationship between capital and labour. The most progressive labour legislation in North America was brought in by an NDP government in British Columbia. Ten years later, in 1983, a Social Credit government of that same province introduced a budget and 26 bills that have rightly been described as "a collective assault on organized workers" (Palmer 1992, 366). It provoked widespread protest that culminated in two weeks of escalating public-sector strikes. Four years later, the Social Credit government brought in the Industrial Relations Reform Act (Bill 19), which through a variety of measures shifted the balance of power dramatically in favour of employers (Carroll and Ratner 1989, 14). This provoked further protest that climaxed with a one-day general strike, followed by a labour boycott of the Industrial Relations Council, which had been established to administer the legislation. The election of an NDP government in 1991 led to the reintroduction of progressive labour legislation, but the marked decline of support for the Harcourt government could well bring about a return to a harsh climate for labour in British Columbia after the next election.

State intervention, of course, has been only one element in the movement away from Fordist class compromise. Robert Cox (1987, 281) has noted the general trend in the advanced capitalist countries toward "a new structure of production relations" that polarizes the working class into "a relatively secure and protected minority ... and a fragmented and relatively unprotected majority of nonestablished workers." This *bifurcation of labour* can be understood as a deepening of the division mentioned earlier between workers in the "primary" section and those in the "secondary" section of the labour market, who have experienced the crisis of Fordism and the restructuring of the capital–labour relation in quite different ways.

At one pole, in core industries of the primary labour market (such as automobile manufacturing) falling profits, increased international competition, and the availability of robotic and micro-electronic technologies have together led employers to implement a variety of changes in the workplace and the wage relation, under the rubric of the "Quality of Working Life" (QWL) approach. These initiatives include Japanese-style quality control circles—small groups of workers and supervisors who meet regularly to identify and solve production problems—as well as job redesign (job rotation, job enlargement, and job enrichment) (Rinehart 1984, 76–77; 1986, 508–509; Wells 1988b, 33; Robertson et al. (1992)). According to its promoters, QWL presents a humane and democratic alternative to the alienated, fragmented experience of work on the Fordist assembly line. These new industrial relations do indeed break from the logic of Fordism. There is a new emphasis on making jobs more intrinsically satisfying, on mitigating the division of manual and mental labour by consulting regularly with employees, and on shifting from an adversarial system (organized labour versus management) to a co-operative arrangement, which promises to give workers more control over their jobs and to give employers a more compliant and productive work force.

Yet as James Rinehart concludes from his case study of a QWL program at a General Motors plant in London, Ontario, "a critical question in evaluating reforms concerns which class initiates and sustains them. As long as capitalists and their agents introduce reforms, these effects will be defined, limited, and evaluated by the criteria of profit maximization and the reproduction of the relations of production" (1984, 93). In substance, QWL is the centrepiece of a new capitalist accumulation strategy in the primary labour market to meet the challenge of heightened international competition by reorganizing production and *dis*organizing labour. In many industries, the new computer-based work methods oblige employers to introduce QWL schemes as a means of securing the active consent of their employees, whose productivity is no longer dictated by the assembly line. But even where technological change is not a major factor, QWI has been introduced "to achieve greater power than ever for management—power over workers, over the way they work, and over the product of their labour" (Wells 1986, ix).

In a study of two Canadian factories, Don Wells (1986) argues that QWL can be understood as a strategy for implementing four new managerial control mechanisms. The controlled delegation of authority to a few workers encourages workers, through their participation in quality control circles, to internalize the goal of profitability and to police themselves and each other accordingly. In regularly consulting with workers and soliciting their suggestions as to how jobs can be improved and enriched, management gains greater access to workers' knowledge about production, enabling more complete management control of the labour process. By aligning work-group identities with management's profit goals, QWL undermines traditional working-class solidarity in favour of a pro-management work culture in which small work groups compete with each other and peer pressure is mobilized against fellow workers "who cannot or will not cooperate in speed-ups and the like" (1986, 21). Finally, by giving work groups (limited) responsibilities for product quality, and by enabling workers through job rotation to gain a greater sense of involvement in the making of the product, QWL promotes the workers' identification with the product of their labour (1986, 20–23, 86–87). In combination, these are mechanisms for creating a new type of "established worker," a team-player capable of participating in flexible work situations and loyal to the employing corporation. In like measure, since workers and managers co-operate in "beating the competition," "there is no room in this team ... for what management calls 'third parties' or 'go-betweens,' that is, for unions—unless they are company unions (notable for being good team players)" (Wells 1988b, 34). The tendency toward QWL in many of the workplaces of the established worker, while less confrontational than the state's shift from consent to coercion, ultimately poses a similar threat to the labour movement.[2]

Ester Reiter's (1991) study of the changing organization of work in the fast-food industry provides a good example of how the capital–labour relation is being transformed at the other pole of the dual labour market. An important part of the rapidly expanding service sector, where growing numbers of workers find employment in secondary labour markets, this industry emerged during the postwar boom, as big capital entered the restaurant business and restructured its workplace from craft-based to mass-production technologies capable of servicing a mass market. By making cheap, fast food widely available to working-class families, these changes partly socialized one area of domestic labour (selling on the market a product that was once mostly confined to the home) and at the same time offered a new work situation to working-class women and teenagers.

> People who work in these outlets generally do so because they have other obligations—either to their families or to school. The pay is so low that workers cannot support themselves on their fast food income. There are no benefits other than those legislated. Turnover is so high that, even if workers express an interest in organizing a union, by the time the certification vote takes place, the group of workers has changed (Reiter 1988, 182).

Like the traditional non-established worker, the "interchangeable worker" in the fast-food sector typically works on a part-time, temporary basis, earns a minimum wage, is not unionized, and is recruited from "marginal" social locations. In contrast to the traditional pattern, however, the interchangeable worker works not for a small firm deploying relatively simple technologies and managerial strategies, but for a large corporation in a workplace organized around computerized production methods and sophisticated management techniques that encourage employees to work hard as part of the Burger King or McDonald's "team" (1988, 181). In these latter respects, the interchangeable worker may be seen as the counterpart to the post-Fordist established worker who becomes enmeshed in QWL schemes. Positioned as they are at the secondary and primary poles of the labour market, these new forms of labour personify the results of corporate strategies to restructure the workplace and the wage relation in the direction of greater managerial control, higher productivity, and a disorganized, compliant workforce.[3]

A final aspect of change in the capital–labour relation to be considered here is unique to Canada. It has to do with the U.S.–Canada Free Trade Agreement (FTA), which took effect on January 1, 1989, and the North American Free Trade Agreement (NAFTA), which took effect on January 1, 1994. In its ideological campaign to build support for the initiative, the government of Canada posed the question of free trade as "a choice between building bridges to other lands, or looking inward and building walls around our country" (Statistics Canada 1987, 12). Yet the "bridges" spanning the forty-ninth parallel will be those that support the interests of corporate capitalists on both its sides. Such a bourgeois continentalism cannot help having profound implications for the future of the labour movement in Canada.

It is no coincidence that the major business organizations in Canada have been the strongest advocates of the FTA (Warnock 1988, 22, 114–20) and now NAFTA. Canada's capitalists have an immediate interest in gaining secure access to the vast American market; but for them the benefits of a more continental economy go much farther. Among the advanced capitalist democracies, the American working class is noteworthy for its exceptionally low level of mobilization into unions and labour-oriented parties (Brym 1986). For instance, in 1989 36.2 percent of working Canadians belonged to unions, a level not unlike those found in Western European countries but far higher than the 16.4 percent of American workers who belonged to unions in the same year (Chaisson and Rose 1990). Moreover, in Canada unionization in the public sector is quite common both in absolute terms and in comparison to the United States (Kumar, 1991). A complex set of reasons has been given for this American exceptionalism (Lipset 1977; Davis 1986), but one difference stands out: only in Canada have a social-democratic party and a relatively vibrant labour movement assisted one another for many years (Huxley et al. 1986, 131).

The weakness of the American labour movement has meant that the gains made in Canada and elsewhere through working-class mobilization in the era of the postwar class compromise (e.g., medicare and minimum-wage laws) were only partially implemented in the United States, and that the backlash of neoconservatism has been most effective there, particularly during the Reagan years (Epsing-Anderson 1985, 245).

Which returns us to the question of free trade, described by Panitch (1987, 143) as a means of importing the Reagan revolution "via the back door." As it takes effect, free trade can be expected to hasten the movement away from the Keynesian welfare state and to strengthen the tendency toward hegemonic despotism, which is already well advanced in the United States (Burawoy 1985). Advocates of the agreements point out that little in their actual wording ever mandated such a movement. Instead, the process is being determined by the competitive market relations that span the U.S.–Canada border. In a North American marketplace where capital is increasingly mobile, "factors like minimum wages, levels of unionization, unemployment rates, and unobstructive labour laws are becoming critical components of corporate investment decisions" (Lynk 1988, 28). Just as American employers in the North have long been able to use a "Southern strategy"—threatening to relocate in the low-wage Sunbelt in order to extract concessions from their employees and from Northern states—pressure to erode Canadian labour laws and social programs is coming from Canadian business. In giving Canadian corporations U.S. citizenship rights, NAFTA grants Canadian capital the same structural power to threaten "capital strikes" against work forces and governments in Canada. The effect, in Lynk's terminology, will be "forced harmonization," as states such as Texas (minimum wage: U.S. $1.40; unionization rate: 12.5 percent) compete directly for new investment capital with provinces such as Ontario (minimum wage: Can. $5.00; unionization rate: 33.7 percent) (Kumar 1988, 773).

So far, the impact of the FTA and the NAFTA have been nothing short of devastating from a working-class standpoint, particularly in Ontario, Canada's industrial heartland, where the official unemployment rate jumped from 5.0 percent to 11.3 percent between February 1988 and August 1992 (*Globe and Mail*, September 5, 1992, A1). In almost three years of free trade 65 percent of lost jobs in that province have occurred as a result of permanent plant closures (Campbell 1992, 6). Across Canada, manufacturing employment declined 26 percent between June 1989 and March 1992, resulting in job losses for over 500 000 workers. Little wonder that by mid-1992 only 4 percent of Canadians thought that the FTA was working to Canada's advantage (Watkins 1993, 126).

The Canada–U.S.–Mexico trade bloc created under the NAFTA is another mistake. It exacerbates tendencies toward de-industrialization of high-wage manufacturing sectors, opening a further "Southern strategy" for Canadian and American capitalists alike. In 1990, Mexican wages were one-tenth of those of American workers (Warnock 1992, 13). The interests of workers are not well represented in these free trade agreements and pressure is growing to force Canadian wages and labour standards down (Campbell 1992, 8).

The Future of the Labour Movement

What, then, of the future? Several possible courses for labour can be delineated, the least viable of which is a return to the status quo ante of class compromise. Advocates of this approach often envisage some sort of tripartite or corporatist arrangement— a political structure that brings organized labour and capital into "a system of representation and cooperative mutual interaction at the leadership level and mobilization and social control at the mass level" (Panitch 1979, 44). Although as recently as 1983 a "corporatist route" could still be plausibly presented among labour's options (Mahon 1983, 168–71), there are several problems with corporatism as a strategy for labour in Canada. As we have seen, the increasingly internationalized and crisis-ridden character of capitalism has led two of tripartism's would-be parties—capital and the state—to renounce the class compromise in favour of strategies that aim to improve the investment climate by attacking the collective rights of labour and lowering the value of wages. Moreover, even if capitalists and politicians were interested in re-establishing a class compromise, in Canada there are serious structural barriers to a corporatist organization of capital, labour, and state. On the one hand, the labour movement is highly fragmented: the Canadian Labour Congress (CLC), for instance, plays no role in collective bargaining and has little effective power over its affiliates. On the other hand, the federated structure of the Canadian state (in which the provinces have responsibilities for most aspects of labour relations and many social programs) limits the prospects for tripartite decision making between business, labour, and political elites at the level of the society as a whole (Panitch 1979, 80–83).

If the prospects for full-fledged corporatism seem dim, some of the more conservative elements of the labour movement still can be said to favour a strategy that "protects hard-won gains," without breaking from the style of business unionism that prevailed during the postwar class compromise. This approach, evident for instance in the mainstream of the American labour movement and the Canadian Federation of Labour, marshals labour's limited resources to defend the privileges of existing trade union members—their relatively high wages and advantageous working conditions—while accommodating itself to the new reality of international competition.

For example, Canada's textile and clothing unions, fragmented by organizational and ideological differences and hit hard as early as the 1950s by a flood of low-priced imports, responded to the crisis by entering into a coalition with textile and clothing capital. In exchange for their political support of the companies, textile unions were able to maintain historic wage patterns and to obtain new clauses in collective agreements that softened the effects of technological change. But this strategy of class collaboration is seriously flawed by its narrow, short-term perspective. In entering into a coalition with their employers, textile unions supported capital's demands rather than arriving at a definition of the situation that could have reflected their own interests. The result has been to strengthen the power of capitalists by enabling them to introduce labour-saving technologies while "continentalizing" their activities. In the 1980s, moves toward continental free trade in textiles and clothing pitted unionized Canadian workers against unorganized workers in the American South. Meanwhile, the Canadian state has been encouraging clothing companies to import certain lines from the low-wage periphery. "Faced with such competition, Canadian workers will find it difficult to benefit from industrial restructuring" (Mahon 1983, 162).

There are, as Briskin (1983b) points out, several interrelated problems with a defensive labour strategy that continues the business-unionist methods of the postwar accord. In defending the gains of established workers, this strategy does little to organize the growing numbers of non-established (or even fully "interchangeable") employees. Yet it is only by representing the majority of working class people and not simply the most advantaged stratum that the labour movement can effectively pursue collective class interests. Secondly, in accepting the narrow definition of union concerns as the bargaining of wages, benefits, and working conditions, this approach accepts that the overall organization of work and the control of its products are inalienable rights of capital. Yet in an increasingly internationalized economy, capital's power to deploy profits and new technologies on a global basis is the greatest single challenge to organized labour. Thirdly, in rejecting confrontational methods of negotiation such as walkouts and sit-down-strikes, the business-unionist approach continues a form of closed-door negotiation between union leaders and management, which all but eliminates the active participation of rank-and-file members. It thereby exacerbates one of the most serious problems facing the labour movement: "the general apathy of its membership, in spite of the numbers of militants and the newly activated groups of women in the unions" (Briskin 1983b, 264). Finally, in adopting a similarly narrow "electoralist" view of political action, this strategy limits workers' political participation to casting a ballot, as if labour's interests could be realized simply through a change in government. On all four counts, a strategy that merely adjusts the labour tactics of the postwar accord to the changing circumstances of the late twentieth century is a formula for the long-term decline of organized labour as a movement for social change.

In contrast to the defensive posture of business unionism, alternative strategies emphasize the need to expand the horizons of the labour movement in two respects. On the one hand, the very threats posed by the crisis and restructuring of capitalism can be seen as opening up new opportunities for innovative action. On the other hand, the emergence since the 1960s of new collective actors raises the possibility of new alliances between labour and other democratic movements.

The introduction of "post-Fordist" technologies and associated QWL schemes opens the possibility of collective claims to worker participation in the planning of production:

> As employers argue that new technologies and quality of working life circles and work teams will lead to increased productivity and, hence, better wages, workers will be in a position to say that, if one of the

> purposes is to improve the quality of the product by increasing the amount of control over both quantitative and qualitative aspects of production, it makes sense to allow workers to participate, directly, in the planning of production and in respect to the introduction of new technologies (Drache and Glasbeek 1988, 54–55).

Even as it poses a threat to traditional labour solidarity, the introduction of new work schemes also furnishes an opportunity for labour to make new demands for genuine workers' control at the point of production (Ross 1981). For instance, in their longitudinal study of workers at a post-Fordist automobile assembly plant in Ontario, Robertson et al. (1992; 99–101) found that workers were increasingly disillusioned with the gap between QWL philosophy and shop-floor practice. They also found that the union increasingly had to take management to task for failing to live up to its professed values of worker empowerment and co-operation.

The threat to labour posed by the internationalization of capital and the accompanying trend toward hegemonic despotism also contains an opportunity to press new claims that go substantially beyond the kinds of concessions won during the era of class compromise. In the new reality of global capitalism, to the extent that separate national sections of the global proletariat bargain individually with transnational capital, labour becomes ensnared in a losing battle where foreign workers are seen as merely competitors, and strategies for international struggle are abandoned (Ross 1981, 622). Yet a single, unified international labour movement is presently precluded by the division of the world order into different nation-states. These circumstances challenge the Canadian labour movement to develop innovative strategies for direct and indirect co-operation with other labour movements in the core and peripheral capitalist societies.

Michael Lebowitz has outlined an indirect response to this challenge. As we mentioned earlier, capital is not merely a *purchaser* of labour (looking for the lowest costs), but the owner of products of labour: it must realize surplus value by *selling* commodities to consumers. From this observation, Lebowitz concludes that labour strategies need to raise the costs to capital of pursuing a strategy of shifting investment to low-wage areas. As a means of pressuring capital to equalize wages and working conditions upward rather than downward, labour can mount boycott campaigns against corporations that resort to such super-exploitation. More importantly, labour should press for "fair trade" legislation to prevent the import of commodities from countries where wages and working conditions are substandard—or where environmentally destructive business practices prevail (Bowles 1988). Lebowitz advocates a tariff set at a level linked to the gap in the rate of exploitation, which would remove the particular advantage accruing to super-exploitation. Such a strategy, the exact opposite of the free trade approach, "not only weakens the ability of international capital to 'divide and conquer' workers immediately, but also involves an important assertion by workers of their right to control the destinies of their economies—the workers' agenda" (Lebowitz 1988, 147). By thus limiting the power of international capital to play one group of workers off against another, a basis can be laid for more direct international labour unity in the long term.

In recent years, however, critical observers of Canadian society have pointed out that increased labour solidarity is not enough; in an era of strong capital and pro-capitalist states, the future of labour rests on its capacity to build alliances with a host of collective actors whose interests converge in complex ways. By way of conclusion, it is appropriate to survey these potential partners with labour in progressive coalitions.

Given that labour is defined in the first instance as an "economic" category, the most immediate candidates for such alliances are economic actors whose interests conflict in some ways with those of capital. Two such groupings can be distinguished. Elaine Bernard (1986) has discussed a number of cases in which producers (organized labour) and consumers have united in struggling to protect existing levels of service or quality of goods. By breaking down the separation of producers and consumers and recognizing that workers are also citizens with a right to protection from such ills as environmental degradation, labour can increase its strength while building opposition to pro-capitalist policies such as deregulation, privatization, and social-service cutbacks. Such producer–consumer coalition opportunities are particularly evident in the public sector, where cutbacks and privatization simultaneously threaten the jobs of state employees and the quality of public services. Although they usually begin as defensive efforts, "the logic of these confrontations is to move beyond the preservation of what is, which is often marginal, into a positive vision of what should be" (1986, 381)—namely, more democratic ways of producing goods and delivering services.

This brings us to labour's second potential economic ally, community-based economic development (CBED). Worker co-operatives, community planning forums, credit unions, and other member-controlled economic organizations have proliferated in recent years. They function not on the basis of private ownership and global profit-maximization but on the basis of co-operative decision making for the wellbeing of local communities, and thus present democratic alternatives to capitalist economic organization (Quarter 1992). Since 1986, the CLC and other Canadian labour federations have officially supported CBED as part of a workers' agenda for the expansion of economic democracy. The former director of research for the BC Federation of Labour has argued that CBED is one way of beginning to shift wealth and power from transnational corporations to accountable and democratic institutions (Lane 1988). By mobilizing local financial resources and labour to serve community-defined needs, CBED not only creates employment, it raises basic questions about the way Canada's economy is presently shaped.

> If working people or the poor can collectively generate and save capital, create jobs, and improve their standard of living, hopefully they will be encouraged to ask questions about where money goes when it is leaked out of their communities by the banks and large multi-national corporations.... And if jobs are not being created by large corporations but by people in their own communities, why should corporations have their interests pandered to by governments? (1988, 188).

As important as it is for labour to promote the convergence of its interests with those of consumers and CBED, the future of the labour movement also rests upon its capacity to forge alliances with the "new social movements"—particularly feminism, ecology, antiracism and the peace movement—which have been gaining ground while unions have seen their traditional strongholds eroded by the deepening crisis of Fordism. Such alliances are called for at the local, national, and international levels. As Magnusson and Walker point out, these movements can help form a "world of resistances in Canada and [a] world of connections between resistances all over the globe" (1988, 68). In raising broad questions of gender justice—in personal life, in state policies, and increasingly in the work place—feminism and growing numbers of women active in the labour movement have challenged the labour movement to broaden its agenda beyond the narrow interests of predominantly male established workers (Maroney 1987). In linking the environmental crisis to unbridled capitalist industrialization, the ecology movement challenges unions to reject the capitalist view of profit-oriented economic growth as the only path toward satisfying workers' needs (Adkin 1992). Unions have also engaged in struggles against racism and for various forms of assistance to ethnic minorities (Jenson and Mahon 1993, 84). In calling for the conversion of military production to civilian production, the peace movement promotes an alternative to the wastefulness and globally destructive potential of an arms race whose chief beneficiary is corporate capital (Wells 1988a). In all three cases, the interests of the labour movement and new social movements can be seen as broadly convergent, even interdependent. For the new social movements to push beyond demands that may be accommodated within capitalism,

> they must engage in the debates for economic and institutional restructuring. That is, their struggles must intersect in the *economic* sphere, and in alliance with citizens-as-workers. At the same time, it is evident that the union movement will not become a transformative force so long as its aims and activities do not transcend the corporative [i.e., immediate] interests of its members (Adkin and Alpaugh 1988, 49).

As Watkins (1993) suggests, workers should own and control more enterprises, labour and social democratic parties should adopt more job-creating trade and development policies, and genuine alternative politics and policies should be there for all.

The NDP government in Ontario has adopted policies of restructuring advocated by international capital. Its relationship with labour has deteriorated so rapidly that the Oshawa local of the Canadian Autoworkers Union has withdrawn its support. The NDP government in British Columbia is under attack from many of its supporters for giving the forest companies (and their workers) too much in its Clayoquot Sound policy. The federal NDP has been criticized for not working with its "natural constituents", that is, its union supporters and other popular groups in the anti–free trade Action Canada Network (Jenson and Mahon 1993, 86). Relations between the labour movement and the NDP are likely to continue to be problem-ridden in the future.

Conclusions

In combination, the political claims of labour and the new social movements envisage an alternative to the hegemonic despotism that increasingly characterizes global capitalism and Canadian society. At this particular time, during the fifth phase of capitalist development in Canada, these movements face the great challenge of distinguishing between the building of durable alliances to promote democratic alternatives and the "periodic and momentary displays of popular support" that leave the capitalist order intact (Wood 1987, 199). The basic contradictions of capitalism make class politics incontrovertible; but these politics must be combined with other emancipatory struggles. Given the increasing willingness of governments to extinguish the rights of workers, such strategies can make unions the "different kinds of organizations" they must become—if they are to survive at all (Calvert 1987, 312).

Study Questions

1. How has the state's role in "mediating" the capital–labour relation changed from the postwar era of prosperity to the present period of crisis?

2. Find out which major labour union is active in your town and trace its local history through the phases discussed in this essay.

3. In what ways have the strategies pursued by labour in its struggle with capital been shaped by the changing structure of the world economy?

4. Unions are often stereotyped as organizations that exist for the selfish benefit of a privileged minority of greedy workers. Does this stereotype have a kernel of truth in the practices of business unionism, or is it a purely mythical aspect of liberal ideology?

Recommended Reading

Argue, Robert, Charlene Gannage, and David Livingstone, eds. *Working People and Hard Times*. Toronto: Garamond Press, 1987.

Armstrong, Pat. *Labour Pains: Women's Work in Crisis.* Toronto: The Women's Press, 1984.

Drache, Daniel, and Harry Glasbeek. *The Changing Workplace.* Toronto: Lorimer, 1992.

Grinspun, R., and M.A. Cameron, *The Political Economy of North American Free Trade.* Montreal and Kingston: McGill–Queen's University Press, 1993.

Heron, Craig, and Robert Storey, eds. *On the Job: Confronting Labour Process in Canada.* Montreal and Kingston: McGill–Queen's University Press, 1986.

Holmes, John, and Colin Leys, eds. *Frontyard/Backyard: The Americas in the Global Crisis.* Toronto: Between the Lines, 1987.

Jenson, J., and R. Mahon. *The Challenge of Restructuring.* Philadelphia: Temple University Press, 1993.

Warburton, Rennie, and David Coburn, eds. *Workers, Capital, and the State in British Columbia.* Vancouver: University of British Columbia Press, 1988.

Notes

1. On the other hand, although many public-sector workers were granted union recognition and bargaining rights, government employees in four provinces were denied the right to strike (Panitch and Swartz 1988. 25).
2. At the same time, however, the new managerial strategies and organization of the workplace may be creating opportunities for women workers. In her study of the introduction of quality-control circles in a plastic factory, Dorothy Smith has found that, by giving women a wider range of experience on different machines, work circles and job rotation are breaking down the old gender division between the male hierarchy of advancement and the female job ghetto. While the QWL. strategy threatens the foundations of union organization, it may also be breaking down the sexism built into the traditional job structure (Smith 1988).
3. Although space does not permit us to discuss other instances of transformation in the capital–labour relation, many other examples can be cited, in the automobile industry (Holmes 1987), in the fishery (Clement 1986), in the health care sector (Campbell 1988), in the post office (Laidlaw and Curtis 1986), and so on. The reader should consult these works for a more detailed picture of this complex social process.

References

Adkin, L.E. 1992. "Ecology and Labour: Towards a New Societal Paradigm." In *Culture and Social Change,* ed. C. Leys and M. Mendell. Montreal: Black Rose Books. 75–94.

Adkin, L.E., and C. Alpaugh. 1988. "Labour, Ecology and the Politics of Convergence." *Socialist Studies* 4: 48–73.

Armstrong, P., and H. Armstrong. 1984. *The Double Ghetto*. Rev. ed. Toronto: McClelland and Stewart.

Bernard, E. 1986. "Labour Tactics Today." In *After Bennett*, ed. W. Magnusson, R.B.J. Walker, Charles Doyle, and John DeMarco. Vancouver: New Star Books. 368–82.

Bowles, S. 1988. "Different Wavelengths." *Globe and Mail* December 3: A7.

Briskin, L. 1983a. "Women and Unions in Canada: A Statistical Overview." In *Union Sisters: Women In the Labour Movement,* ed. L. Briskin and L. Yanz. Toronto: The Women's Press. 28–43.

———. 1983b. "Women's Challenge to Organized Labour." In *Union Sisters: Women in the Labour Movement*, ed. L. Briskin and L. Yanz. Toronto: The Women's Press. 259–71.

Brym, R.J. 1986. "Incorporation versus Power Models of Working Class Radicalism With Special Reference to North America." *Canadian Journal of Sociology* 11: 227–52.

Burawoy, M. 1985. *The Politics of Production: Factory Regimes Under Capitalism and Socialism.* London: Verso.

Calvert, J. 1987. "Uncharted Waters: The Labour Movement's Dilemma in Developing a New Role Beyond the Bargaining System." In *Working People and Hard Times*, ed. R. Argue, C. Gannage and D.W. Livingstone. Toronto: Garamond Press. 307–12.

Cameron, B. 1983. "The Sexual Division of Labour and Class Struggle." *Socialist Studies* 1: 40–50.

Campbell, B. 1992. "Free Trade: Year 3," *Canadian Dimension* (January).

Campbell, M. 1988. "Management as 'Ruling': A Class Phenomenon in Nursing." *Studies in Political Economy* 27: 29–51.

Carroll, K., and R. S. Ratner. 1989. "Social Democracy, Neo-conservatism and Hegemonic Crisis in British Columbia." *Critical Sociology* 16(1): 29–53.

Chaisson, G.N., and J.B. Rose. 1990. "New Directions and Divergent Paths: The North American Labour Movements in Troubled Times." *Labour Law Journal* 41, no. 8: 591–96.

Clement, W. 1986. *The Struggle To Organize: Resistance in Canada's Fishery*. Toronto: McClelland and Stewart.

Cox, R.W. 1987. *Production, Power, and World Order*. New York: Columbia University Press.

Curtis, B. 1980. "Capital, the State, and the Origins of the Working-Class Household." In *Hidden in the Household*, ed. B.J. Fox. Toronto: The Women's Press. 101–34.

Davis, M. 1986. *Prisoners of the American Dream*. London: Verso.
Drache, D., and H. Glasbeek. 1988. "The New Fordism in Canada: Capital's Offensive, Labour's Opportunity?" *Osgoode Hall Law Journal* 25, no. 4.
Epsing-Anderson, G. 1985. "Power and Distributional Regimes." *Politics and Society* 14: 223–56.
Harvey, D. 1985. *The Urbanization of Capital*. Baltimore: Johns Hopkins University Press.
Heron, C., and R. Storey. 1986. "On the Job in Canada." In *On the Job: Confronting the Labour Process in Canada*, ed. C. Heron and R. Storey. Montreal and Kingston: McGill–Queen's University Press. 3–46.
Holmes, J. 1987. "The Crisis of Fordism and the Restructuring of the Canadian Automobile Industry." In *Frontyard/Backyard: The Americas in the Global Crisis*, ed. J. Holmes and C. Leys. Toronto: Between the Lines, 95–130.
Houle, F. 1983. "Economic Strategy and the Restructuring of the Fordist Wage-Labour Relationship in Canada." *Studies in Political Economy* 11: 127–47.
Huxley, C., D. Kettler, and J. Struthers. 1986. "Is Canada's Experience 'Especially Instructive'?" In *Unions in Transition*, ed. S.M. Lipset. San Francisco: Institute for Contemporary Studies.
Jenson, J. 1989. "'Different' But Not 'Exceptional': Canada's Permeable Fordism." Canadian Review of Sociology and Anthropology 26: 69–94.
———. 1991. "All the World's a Stage: Ideas, Spaces, and Times in Canadian Political Economy," *Studies in Political Economy* 36: 43–72.
Kumar, P. 1988. "Estimates of Unionism and Collective Bargaining Coverage in Canada." *Relations Industrielles* 43: 757–79.
Laidlaw, B., and B. Curtis. 1986. "Inside Postal Workers' Labour Process, State Policy, and Workers' Response." *Labour/Le Travail* 18: 139–62.
Lane, P. 1988. "Community-Based Economic Development: Our Trojan Horse." *Studies in Political Economy* 25: 177–91.
Laxer, R. 1976. *Canada's Unions*. Toronto: James Lorimer.
Lebowitz, M. 1988. "Trade and Class: Labour Strategies in a World of Strong Capital." *Studies in Political Economy* 27: 137–48.
Lembcke, J., and W.M. Tattam. 1984. *One Union in Wood*. Madeira Park, BC: Harbour Publishing.
Lipietz, A. 1987. *Mirages and Miracles: The Crises of Global Fordism*. London: Verso.
Lipset, S.M. 1977. "Why No Socialism in the United States?" In *Radicalism in the Contemporary Age*, ed. S. Staler and S. Sluzar. Vol. 1. Boulder, CO: Westview Press. 31–149.
Lipsig-Mumme, C. 1980. "Quebec Unions and the State: Conflict and Dependence." *Studies in Political Economy* 3: 119–46.
———. 1991. "Future Conditional: War of Position in the Quebec Labour Movement," *Studies in Political Economy* 36: 73–108.
Lynk, M. 1988. "Free Trade and the Forced Harmonization of Labour Law." *Canadian Dimension* 22, no. 5: 28–32.
Magnusson, W., and R. Walker. 1988. "De-centring and State: Political Theory and Canadian Political Economy." *Studies in Political Economy* 26: 37–71.
Mahon, R. 1983. "Canadian Labour in the Battle of the Eighties." *Studies in Political Economy* 11:149–75.
Maroney, H.J. 1987. "Feminism at Work." In *Feminism and Political Economy*, ed. J. Maroney and M. Luxton. Toronto: Methuen.
Myles, J. 1988. "Decline or Impasse? The Current State of the Welfare State." *Studies in Political Economy* 26: 73–107.
Palmer, B. 1992 [1983]. *Working-Class Experience: Rethinking the History of Canadian Labour, 1806–1991*. Toronto: McClelland and Stewart.
Panitch, L. 1979. "Corporatism in Canada." *Studies in Political Economy* 1: 43–92.
———. 1987. "Capitalist Restructuring and Labour Strategies." *Studies in Political Economy* 24: 131–49.
Panitch, L., and D. Swartz. 1988. *The Assault on Trade Union Freedoms*. Toronto: Garamond Press.
Phillips, P. 1989. "Through Different Lenses: The Political Economy of Labour." In *The New Canadian Political Economy*, ed. W. Clement and G. Williams. Montreal and Kingston: McGill–Queen's University Press. 77–98.

Phillips, P., and S. Watson. 1984. "From Mobilization to Continentalism: The Canadian Political Economy in the Post-Depression Period." In *Modern Canada, 1930–1980's*, ed. M.S. Cross and G.S. Kealey. Toronto: McClelland and Stewart.

Quarter, J. 1992. *Canada's Social Economy*. Toronto: Lorimer.

Reiter, E. 1988. "The Interchangeable Worker and Fighting Back: Identifying Some Strategic Issues." *Labour/Le Travail* 21: 173–89.

———. 1991. *Making Fast Food: From the Frying Pan Into the Fryer*. Montreal and Kingston: McGill–Queen's University Press.

Rinehart, J. 1984. "Appropriating Workers' Knowledge: Quality Control Circles at a General Motors Plant." *Studies in Political Economy* 14: 75–97.

———. 1986. "Improving the Quality of Working Life Through Job Redesign: Work Humanization or Work Rationalization?" *CRSA* 23: 507–30.

———. 1987. *The Tyranny of Work*. 2d ed. Toronto: Harcourt Brace Jovanovich.

Roberts, W., and J. Bullen. 1984. "A Heritage of Hope and Struggle: Workers, Unions, and Politics in Canada, 1930–1982." *Modern Canada, 1930–1980s*, ed. M.S. Cross and G.S. Kealey. Toronto: McClelland and Stewart. 105–40.

Robertson, D., J. Rinehart, C. Huxley, and the CAW Research Group on CAMI. 1992. "Team Concept and 'Kaizen': Japanese Production Management in a Unionized Canadian Auto Plant." *Studies in Political Economy* 39: 77–108.

Ross, George. 1981. "What Is Progressive about Unions? Reflections on Trade Unions and Economic Crisis." *Theory and Society* 10: 609–44.

Smith, D. 1988. "Women Workers and New Management Strategies." *Canadian Dimension* 22, no. 7: 24–5.

Statistics Canada. 1987. *The Canada–U.S. Trade Agreement in Brief*. Ottawa: Supply and Services Canada.

Strain, F., and H. Grant. 1992. "The Social Structure of Accumulation in Canada, 1945–1988." *Journal of Canadian Studies* 26, no. 4:75–93.

Warnock, J.W. 1988. *Free Trade and the New Right Agenda*. Vancouver: New Star Books.

Wells, D. 1986. *Soft Sell: "Quality of Working Life" Programs and the Productivity Race*. Ottawa: Canadian Centre for Policy Alternatives.

———. 1988a. "Politics and the Economic Conversion of Military Production in Canada." *Studies in Political Economy* 27: 113–36.

———. 1988b. "'Teamwork' and the New Industrial Relations." *Canadian Dimension* 22, no. 1: 33–6.

White, J. 1993. *Sisters and Solidarity: Women and Unions in Canada*. Toronto: Thompson Educational Publishing, Inc.

Wolfe, D.A. 1984. "The Rise and Demise of the Keynesian Era in Canada: Economic Policy, 1930–1982." In *Modern Canada, 1930–1980s*, ed. M.S. Cross and G.S. Kealey. Toronto: McClelland and Stewart. 46–78.

Wood, E.M. 1987. *The Retreat from Class*. London: Verso.

PART V

National and Regional Issues

INTRODUCTION

In Canada there has always been concern about American domination of our country in the economic, political, and cultural spheres. American corporate ownership of resources and production in this country is seen by some as a threat to Canadian sovereignty and cultural identity, while others see it as a boon to economic development, and a source of prosperity and high standards of living. Some of these issues were brought into sharp focus during the Free Trade Agreement (FTA) debate in the 1988 federal election. Political and economic debates about national economic development strategy, foreign investment and ownership of resources in this country, and Canadian trade and market relations with other countries cannot be divorced from the internal contradictions of regional inequality, rural–urban disparities, and similar issues. These issues and contradictions are discussed in this section.

The chapter by Harold E. Bronson, entitled "Free Trade: Political, Economic, and Social Issues and Contradictions," shows how the Canada–U.S. Free Trade Agreement (FTA) and the North American Free Trade Agreement (NAFTA) are attempts to solve the growing fundamental contradiction caused by global accumulations of surplus investment funds in a context of inadequate domestic and international buying power. It also explains how nineteenth-century ideology is being utilized to promote free trade as a remedy for the investment–consumption dilemma and for related social problems.

The FTA and now the NAFTA bring new emphasis to a number of important issues that originated as a result of the market's tendency to expand the wealth of a minority while inflicting on the majority a growing burden of poverty and insecurity. The issues identified in this chapter are environmental deterioration, the farm crisis, growing economic instability, unemployment, attacks on cultural sovereignty, curtailment of social services, greater military commitments, and the further undermining of Canadian sovereignty.

In his discussion of these issues, Bronson refers to the major arguments of the supporters and the opponents of free trade. The chapter also has an appraisal of the political, economic, and social developments that immediately followed the 1988 federal election—which appear to be generally consistent with pre-election warnings expressed by the FTA's opponents. In conclusion, Bronson presents a summary of the contending programs as alternatives to free trade and its related agenda.

The next essay turns to regional inequalities in Canada. In the first part of his chapter, Peter R. Sinclair examines the extent of Canadian regional inequality (or disparity) in both its economic and social dimensions. The basic pattern with respect to incomes is that the east is poor, while only Ontarians are significantly above average. Sinclair notes that while there has been improvement in the period 1961 to

1991 in the relative position of the poorest provinces, the progress in earned income is less than what is evident for personal incomes. Educational levels vary dramatically. The percentage of adults with less than Grade 9 education varied from a low of 9.1 percent in Alberta and British Columbia to a high of 20.8 percent in Newfoundland. All provinces have made progress in eliminating functional illiteracy and producing university graduates since 1951, but the gap between the least and the most privileged provinces has actually widened since then in their relative proportion of population with less than Grade 9 education.

Next, Sinclair looks at how social scientists in Canada have applied economic and sociological theories of underdevelopment, often borrowed from students of the Third World. The explanations are grouped into two categories: the regional deficiency approach and the systemic problems approach. In the staples perspective on deficiency theory, a region's failure to develop reflects the lack of valued resources, inappropriate state policies, or the absence of appropriate entrepreneurial actions with respect to those resources and their potential links to other economic activities. Another branch of deficiency theorists, the modernization theorists, do not accept that the Atlantic provinces have been poor primarily because of their resource endowment and location, but point, at least in part, to cultural values, especially a lack of entrepreneurship. The impact of these deficiency theories on state policy, which have been inadequate to solve regional problems, is then assessed.

Next, the theories that point to systemic problems are considered. These theories emphasize external constraints and the extraction of wealth to the benefit of external power holders. Sinclair argues that the dependency and underdevelopment perspectives that fall into this category are often oversimplified or misleading in emphasizing exchanges between territories (core and periphery) and fail to explain why Atlantic Canada, rather than some other region, should be the region to suffer most in this country. More recent attempts to examine the interconnection of different forms of production within and between regions do not escape the second problem and often rely on the assumptions that capitalism had to develop as it did in Canada and that it has certain needs that have to be met in ways that generate regional inequality.

Sinclair argues that our understanding can be improved by abandoning the quest for a single general theory of development and regional inequality. He comes out in favour of a middle-range approach that specifies a set of development paths, each of which would include one or more societies or regions, and also look for causal forces both outside and within the unit in question (external and internal factors). Finally, he points to the importance of distinguishing those factors that pertain to the origin of regional inequality from those that may later sustain it; he goes on to outline an approach to explaining the underdevelopment of the Atlantic provinces in these terms.

The next two essays in this section address issues pertaining to rural and urban areas and the disparities between them.

Alison Hayford discusses the problems that have come to be identified with urban centres. Canada has one of the most urbanized populations in the world; in 1986 nearly 60 percent of the Canadian population was concentrated in metropolitan areas. Three of Canada's cities—Toronto, Montreal, and Vancouver—contain

30 percent of the country's population; by 1986, two-thirds of Canada's population lived in the Windsor–Quebec City corridor, which constitutes only 5 percent of Canada's land area. By 1991, over three-quarters of the Canadian population lived in urban areas and Canada's three largest cities—Toronto, Montreal and Vancouver—contained nearly a third of the Canadian population.

Urbanization is the result of the development of productive forces in agriculture that promote migration from rural to urban areas and the settlement of immigrant populations in cities. In recent years, overseas immigration has contributed to the ethnic and racial diversity of cities such as Toronto and Vancouver.

Hayford discusses crime, policing, racial conflict, and problems of the social order, the urban environment, traffic, housing, and the quality of life. Many urban problems, Hayford argues, are not the product of "abnormality" or "deviance," but result from urban structures themselves, including population density, the heterogeneous and diverse nature of urban populations, and the differential power relationships within cities. Other problems—for example, those in the area of housing—are the result of contradictions between private profit and the needs of the population. These contradictions lead to high land values, unaffordable rents, and ghettoization of the poor and racial minorities in cities. Traffic congestion is the result of a combination of factors, namely, inadequate public transportation, the necessity of commuting to work, and cultural attitudes toward "independence" that express themselves in the cult of the private automobile.

Hayford argues that inequality of power and differential power relationships are the major source of urban problems. Solutions, therefore, would require structural transformation of power relations and a shift of production and development to meet human needs rather than the desire for profit.

While urban questions have been the common subject of study by sociologists, demographers, urban planners, and others, the study of rural life has received little attention for a number of years. This is partly because urbanism and the urban way of life in particular have come to be identified with social disorganization, conflict, deviance, and personal and social pathologies. Rural and farm life, on the other hand, were thought to be free of all these problems. Even today, many people continue to have an idyllic image of rural life. However, evidence presented by Bolaria, Dickinson, and Wotherspoon shows that this image is contrary to empirical reality.

The capitalization and mechanization of agriculture, along with intensive farming and the use of fertilizers, pesticides, and herbicides, all have consequences for the rural population and the communities in which it lives. They have affected the rural way of life and the rural environment. For instance, rural depopulation has led to a decline of rural communities, the loss of business, and a decline in rural services. Poverty and housing crises, so closely identified with urban centres, are also present in rural areas.

The threat to the "family farm" persists because of declining world markets for agricultural products and the cost-price squeeze. Many farmers and their family members are forced into off-farm labour to sustain the family farm.

Intensive cultivation practices and soil erosion have caused soil quality to deteriorate and agricultural land to be lost. The increasing urbanization of rural areas is also taking fertile land out of production.

Agriculture is one of the most dangerous occupations, as evidenced by a high incidence of accidents and fatalities. The increasing use of pesticides and herbicides has contributed to degradation of the rural environment and has adversely affected the health of farmers and farm workers. Farm debts and the constant threat of bankruptcies and foreclosures faced by some farmers have also contributed to stress and psychological ill health.

Evidence presented here also indicates considerable inequality in the availability and accessibility of health care and educational opportunities for the rural population.

The chapter concludes with some observations about the future of the agricultural economy and its demographic and social consequences.

CHAPTER 16

Free Trade: Political, Economic, and Social Issues and Contradictions

Harold E. Bronson

Learning Objectives

By reviewing the motivations underlying the promotion of free trade now and in the past, this chapter can help clarify the major contradictions that are intensifying as corporate marketing strategies become more international. An underlying contradiction emerges from the urgent need in each market-based country to expand its exports and to restrict its imports. An analysis of the structures and functions that produce these internationally incompatible objectives can improve our understanding of their consequences.

That analysis leads us to examine the contradiction between inadequate domestic demand, on the one hand, and, on the other, corporate insistence on further wage restraint and cutbacks in expenditures on social services and other public-sector spending. A full understanding of these conditions requires consideration of the class interests involved in these demands for restraint made by a corporate elite that simultaneously seeks government subsidies and tax concessions. Familiarity with the character, intensity, and direction of the class struggle will provide a basis for an appraisal of alternative policies.

Introduction

Most of the discussion on the Canada–U.S. Free Trade Agreement (FTA) and the North American Free Trade Agreement (NAFTA) has followed the unscientific, propaganda approach that prevails in parliamentary and legislative "debates." The arguments reflect the image-making deceptiveness that characterizes business advertising. These tactics were utilized by both sides of the free trade argument, and were especially conspicuous as Canadian political parties developed their 1988 and 1993 election campaigns. In both of these, free trade became a major issue.

Assuming the objective of maximizing human welfare, a scientific approach would weigh the contending arguments with the greatest possible accuracy and impartiality. Following that procedure, the first step would be a definition of human welfare maximization in the context of policies related to trade. This would involve social, cultural, political, and economic factors, together with related issues and contradictions.

There is probably a general consensus that human welfare maximization includes freedom from exploitation. That rules out trading tactics that involve exploitation and its supporting political mechanisms.

The FTA and NAFTA both advocate unrestricted movement of both consumer and producer goods and of money. It is therefore necessary to consider the assumption that exploitation may exist in the free flow of investment to areas where competition among masses of unemployed workers reduces wages toward subsistence levels while providing large profits to investors.

Free trade supporters defend these inequities as necessary preliminaries to the development of the productive apparatus needed for general prosperity. Opponents point out that this investment process results in severe exploitation, including job discrimination, racism, regressive taxation, reduction of social services, and economic imperialism. The debate should therefore examine these factors and their relationship to such issues as the deteriorating environment, the crisis in Canadian agriculture, and the defense of a nation's progressive cultural developments.

We should also consider how the FTA has already affected the Canadian economy, including the extent of its involvement in debt growth, speculative investment, and related class contradictions. Such concerns lead to the question of the effect on democracy if free trade expands through NAFTA and beyond.

The effect of that expansion on democracy has been indicated by references to Adam Smith's eighteenth-century warning that free market competitors regularly stop competing and conspire to fix prices. As the free trade drive reduces national powers, conspiring cartels are attaining much greater ability to control global prices and employment (Bronson 1993). That erosion of national autonomy is now widely acknowledged. As summarized by columnist Jeffrey Simpson (1993A-16), there is "a feeling of helplessness among ordinary citizens at the loss of control over their lives.... These are among the political consequences of a combination of the shackled world of government and the unshackled corporate world of the global economy." As analyzed by Janet Lowe (1992), these political consequences stem from the unshackled economic power of 25 "meganational" corporations.

Genuine democracy implies guaranteed, continuous exercise of control by a majority. Thus, there emerges a paramount political issue—divided, manipulated nations and their citizens' need to achieve control. To do this, we must consider the objectives and methods of the dominant minority.

A Hidden Agenda?

Before the election of the Progressive Conservative (PC) government to Ottawa in 1984, there had seemed to be agreement among the three main parties that bilateral free trade with the United States was undesirable. While accepting global arrangements such as the General Agreement on Tariffs and Trade (GATT), Brian Mulroney had stated that "free trade is a threat to Canadian sovereignty." Michael Wilson had declared that such a deal "would only serve to further diminish our capacity to compete internationally" (Pro-Canada 1988, 2). Reversal of these opinions after the PCs took power requires explanation, but no convincing answers have been provided by that party.

As shown in the 1988 Canadian election campaign, one influence on the government was the unprecedented dedication of the corporate and financial community to the FTA. That pressure, together with the fact that Mulroney had previously served as a manager of an American-owned branch plant in Quebec, may provide an explanation for his policy reversal.

Both sides of the debate have agreed that free trade should be seen as a component of a wider, international pattern. Opponents fear that it is just the beginning of international corporate domination that would destroy unions and social programs by using the threat and the actuality of moving production to the most "competitive" areas.

Supporters of free trade argue that great benefits can be had with the elimination of protectionism. They warn that failure to proceed would have dire consequences. In the words of economist John Crispo, "There is no future for an isolated Canada. It is essential to participate in NAFTA and what is to follow" (1992B-2). Another summary of those views has concluded that, outside of NAFTA, Canada "would fail to adjust or compete" in global trading and that "alternatives to NAFTA do not exist." (Cook 1992B-2).

The Clinton administration conveyed that message when it sought congressional approval for NAFTA in November 1993. By promising various forms of protection to concerned lobbyists, the government obtained approval. Clinton's negotiators and lobbyists also won most of their anti-subsidy and anti-dumping demands in the 117-nation GATT agreement reached in December 1993.

The adverse consequences for smaller economies were obvious enough to arouse concern even among prominent supporters of free trade, one of whom concluded that the "U.S.-inspired text on dumping" was "a gigantic loss" for Canada and the rest of the world (Cook 1993B-2). Opponents of free trade found even stronger justification for their warnings that the realities of the NAFTA and GATT agreements reflected the hidden agenda of American-dominated multinational corporations (MNCs).

The Historical Background

The argument that a free market maximizes efficiency and human welfare emerged from Britain's business environment as it developed during the late eighteenth and early nineteenth centuries. Within a growing and relatively secure empire, entrepreneurs sought the freedom to make profits in both domestic and international markets with less supervision and regulation by government. This objective helped inspire the concept of an unregulated market as a natural, efficient means of allocating resources.

Applying that concept to international markets, David Ricardo developed the "comparative advantage" hypothesis in support of free trade. His calculations were based on the trade of cloth and wine between England and Portugal ([1817] 1963, 71–72).

The model assumed that England might require the annual labour of 120 men to produce a quantity of wine, while only 80 men in Portugal could produce the same amount. England might have a similar "absolute disadvantage" in cloth production, needing 100 men to produce what Portugal could make with 90. Yet this would give England a "comparative advantage" in cloth, leaving Portugal with the advantage in wine. Thus from a purely mathematical viewpoint, both countries would be better off if each concentrated on producing its comparatively advantageous product, while acquiring the other's through trade.

The model was based on the assumption of a perfectly competitive international economy, where prices would be based on costs, and no seller or buyer could be handling quantities large enough to permit monopolistic price-fixing. Apparently disregarding the unrealistic nature of these assumptions, the pro-NAFTA debaters still seem to accept this nineteenth-century model. One of them, however, also conceded that leading MNCs achieve monopolistic advantages, and that larger countries are dominant (Kenen 1985; 159, 520–21, 534).

In a leading critique of the Ricardian model, Harry Magdoff has referred to the historical record of England and Portugal. This shows that between them "the comparative advantage that mattered was not rooted in soil or labour productivity, but in the superiority of British seapower, and in Portugal's inability to hold on to its overseas empire without the protection of the British navy." In a series of treaties concluding in 1703, Britain imposed the Ricardian trading concept on Portugal, forcing it to end protectionism against British cloth, and to concentrate on wine production.

Magdoff provided data showing that, in every year between 1703 and 1760, Portugal suffered a deficit with England in the wine and cloth exchange. The difference had to be made up in gold from Portugal's colony in Brazil. He concluded that this was a major factor in the emergence of Britain as a world banker and imperial power (1971, 1–17). Magdoff went on to show that this system adversely affected other colonial areas. He quoted the noted economic historian, Carlo Cipolla, regarding the fact that silks and calicoes from India were causing difficulties for the English textile industry.

> It was fortunate for England that no Indian Ricardo arose to convince the English people that ... it would be advantageous for them to turn into shepherds and to import from India all the textiles that were needed. Instead, England passed a series of acts designed to prevent importation of Indian textiles (1971, 12).

The continuation of such imperial objectives in profit-motivated free trade is not discussed by FTA supporters. When obliged to face the issue, they tend to repeat the argument used in the earlier centuries—that there is no acceptable alternative.

Current Ricardian Interpretations

Current business support in Canada for free trade is a reversal of nineteenth-century experience. When American protectionism and expansionism led to the termination of the 1854 Reciprocity Treaty with Canada, business supported John A. Macdonald in his "National Policy" of protective tariffs. J.W. Warnock (1988, 82) noted that the main purpose of this move was "to stimulate industrial development and employment." A Liberal attempt to re-introduce reciprocity in 1911 was a major cause of their election defeat that year.

The present remnants of business opposition to free trade arise in sectors suffering severely from American competition. Canadian book publisher Mel Hurtig has written that he expects expanded American ownership and control, including, "harmonization of standards," which would mean that "at best, we will be a country in name only" (1989, 2). His data show that while U.S. net direct investment in Canada has declined, the book value of American ownership has risen sharply as a result of the use of some profits made here for takeovers and expansion. Thus, he concluded, we are a nation "financing its own demise."

Nevertheless, most corporate leaders in Canada and elsewhere support extension of global free trade. The Associated Press (AP) (16 February 1993) reported that a coalition of more than a thousand companies had been lobbying for passage of NAFTA. Their main objective was to influence Congress and public opinion against environmental and labour groups opposing the agreement. The companies were expecting that it would create "tens of billions of dollars in trade and investment opportunities," assuming lower costs and greater competitive capability.

That investment factor—the facilitation of cross-border capital movement—is rarely discussed by free trade supporters. Yet easier transfer of money and of production and service facilities is probably free trade's most significant gift to big business: the NAFTA essentially shifts economic and political influence from national governments to the MNCs.

The European Economic Community (EEC) has also been used as an example of free trade advantages. But by early 1993, conditions there had deteriorated to the extent that unprecedented mass protests were occurring against rising unemployment, which averaged about 11 percent for 1992 (Reuters, 3 April 1993). Critics observed further disadvantages for Canada. Unlike European countries, one of its trading "partners" has an economy that is ten times larger. And the major language in Canada is the same as that in the United States, whose media and entertainment industries already predominate.[1]

The Economic Debate

While failing to provide recent or current examples of mutual benefit from the application of Ricardo's hypothesis, its defenders usually assume that academic economists almost unanimously endorsed it. That assumption was seriously undermined in 1988 when a seventeen-point critique was circulated across Canada, signed by "Canadian Economists Who Oppose the Mulroney Trade and Investment Agreement Between Canada and the United States" (Phillips et al. 1988).

These criticisms included warnings that the FTA was no guarantee of access to the American market; nor did it provide a neutral, binding dispute-settling mechanism, nor protection for Canadian culture and sovereignty. The possibilities for economic expansion and lower prices were "at best marginal" and possibly "non-existent or negative." Furthermore, the FTA has "no provisions to ease the major economic and labour force adjustments" that it would necessitate.

U.S. resistance to any benefits to Canada that might flow from the FTA was also anticipated by Harvard economist Robert Reich. He noted that the United States faces a growing trade deficit, and concluded that "there's no way Congress is going to give away any kind of authority to proscribe what it considers to be unfair trade" (1987).

Further concern was expressed by Bruce Wilkinson of the Economics Department of the University of Alberta, with his reminder that the FTA "involves the liberalization of capital flows between the two countries" while also reducing Canada's right "to impose some performance requirements on U.S. firms in Canada and on third country firms if the results would adversely affect U.S. exports to Canada." These and other aspects of economic integration led him to warn, "Our next knocking at the door might be for political affiliation" (Finn, Cameron, and Calvert 1988, 29). That issue has been further emphasized by the editor-in-chief of the *Financial Times*, John Macfarlane. Free trade, he wrote in an editorial, "forces us to ask not why we value our sovereignty, but how much" (1988).

In any event, P.D. Gigantes has been confirmed in his forecast that with the FTA, "it will be much costlier for future Canadian parliaments to launch new programs of government intervention" (1988, 68–69). Those who argue that North American integration is inevitable and even desirable seem to neglect the major contradiction to that scenario that emerges as each country tries to improve its trade balance at the expense of others—and as the United States exercises its predominant strength.

Determination to exercise that power is strengthened by adverse economic and political pressures. As emphasized in a review by Quebec publisher Jean Pare, with reference to FTA disputes, "Americans cheat. They bully.... Push each dispute to the limit.... Pork, beef, fish, lumber, steel, automobiles, beer, magnesium, trucking—you name it" (1992S-2).

Consequently, as the process of transborder trade and investment develops, critical questions emerge. In a global system, where will the ultimate control lie? And why are many small developing countries becoming indebted to the point of breakdown and outright rebellion against external domination? Can the United Nations be expected to maintain stability under such conditions?

As the economies of Third World countries have become more specialized in accordance with Ricardian trade rules as laid down by the International Monetary Fund and the World Bank, their few export items have generally declined in price and total value, while their import costs have risen. The debt-imposed fiscal policies in the "advanced" countries cause additional stress. For example, Canada's projected 10 percent cut in international aid through 1993–95, following multi-billion dollar reductions in the 1980s, has been criticized by Oxfam-Canada as a threat to long-term development programs (Brownstone 1993A-18).

Such measures can only accelerate the trend identified by the Inter-American Development Board (1987). Its report shows that during the first half of the 1980s, Latin America exported twice the volume of products sent out during the 1970s, while 1980–85 export earnings declined by an average of 5 percent annually.

For all the developing countries, trade and investment deficits have continued into the 1990s. Through 1985–91, these countries paid the International Monetary

Fund U.S. $32.8 billion "which was $6.1 billion more than they received from the IMF's sister organizations, the World Bank and other multilateral institutions" (Stackhouse 1992B-9).

This continued deterioration of the Third World's financial position has led to an increasing possibility of national debt repudiations. As taxpayers in the "advanced" countries face their own debt crises, they are less likely to provide the relief requested by international borrowers and lenders. Thus, the whole global free trade concept reveals its inherent contradictions.

Free Trade and Social Programs

As debt and taxation problems worsen, the corporate community increasingly emphasizes social service cutbacks as a solution. FTA negotiator Simon Reisman dismissed concerns over social programs in Canada, with his initial assurance that "there is no reference to them in the agreement" (1988). He avoided consideration that, for example, the FTA allows American private-profit enterprise access to hospital management, nursing homes, blood donor clinics, and most other social services.

He was thus failing to deal with questions raised by more rigorous analysis, such as the independent study by retired judge Marjorie Bowker. She noted that although the FTA makes no direct reference to social programs, it contains "indirect hazards" (1988, 36). Programs such as our health and medicare systems, unemployment insurance, the Canada Pension, and workers' compensation could all be challenged by the United States as "unfair subsidies."[2]

Bowker's concerns soon materialized after the 1988 election. The Business Journal on National Issues (27 December 1988), representing 150 large corporations, called for cuts in federal contributions to unemployment insurance—a policy that was later implemented in the April 1989 budget. That should not have been surprising, because during the FTA negotiations the U.S. side had insisted that such programs are unfair subsidies.

A similar lack of a safeguards for social programs was found by Canadian Union of Public Employees analyst Matt Sanger (1992 p. 30) in Chapters 11 and 12 of the 4300-page NAFTA agreement. He saw "no mechanism to ensure ... minimum standards." That omission would allow "harmonization of Canadian programs with inferior social programs in the U.S. and Mexico."

Such "harmonization" of social programs below current Canadian standards seems certain to continue as U.S. and Canadian trade deficit and debt problems worsen. Consumer advocate Ralph Nader has warned that under corporate pressure, the tendency will be toward "uniformity down" rather than at constant or higher levels (CBC, 15 November 1988).

Free Trade and Employment Prospects

The effect of economic crises on American interpretation of trade agreements was indicated with the inclusion of section 409 of the FTA. This section allows the president to retaliate if U.S. firms are seen to be injured by Canadian subsidies.

Critics also point out that American implementing legislation states that the FTA is subject to U.S. trade laws and to future definitions of what constitutes a subsidy. This is a major indication that free trade dispute-settlement mechanisms will not be favourable to Canada.

Experience seems to confirm that prospect. By the end of 1992, after four years under the FTA, Canadian Labour Congress president Bob White denounced the deal as the major cause of the loss of almost 350 000 jobs in Canadian resource-based and manufacturing industries (White 1992, 36). He called on Canadians to reject an extension into NAFTA, which, he said, would "lead to even stronger pressures to lower Canadian labour and social standards."

Nevertheless, a U.S. tribunal—the International Trade Commission—concluded that fears of Canadian and American job losses in free trade with Mexico were unjustified. As a judge of unfair trade complaints by U.S. industries, the ITC admitted that some industries, including the auto industry, would be losers. But the total effect of NAFTA, according to the ITC, would be a net increase in American and Canadian employment (Saunders 1993).

Yet even where job gains might be achieved, competitive pressures would tend to make them non-union, part-time, and low paying. That was practically admitted by a business journal when it emphasized that "wages and inflation are the main enemies" that could cause Canada to "fall behind" in the "global economic revolution" (Harris 1988–89, 357).

As part of that revolution, the FTA has already indicated how existing wage levels are "enemies." A major example is the garment industry, where 90 percent of the workers are women. Noting that 80 000 jobs had already been lost there under the FTA as companies shifted to lower wage areas, Denise Nadeau (1992) of the women's National Action Committee predicted that NAFTA would be a further threat, especially to immigrants and visible minorities.

Such shifting by corporations in search of lower wages had been anticipated earlier in a study by Autofacts of Pennsylvania. Reporting on that study, Devid Climenhaga (1989) had noted that Mexican wage rates are about 10 percent of U.S. rates. That would be a "powerful incentive" to shift auto parts production.

Elaborating on his report of job losses since the FTA, Bob White emphasized that the sectors with the biggest losses were those most exposed to direct competition with the United States. That competition included "arbitrary harassment" of Canadian exports by the U.S. trade authorities—a practice unchanged by the FTA. NAFTA would "significantly compound" the dominant objective of that harassment: to move jobs south toward lower wages.

In its FTA advertising, the Canadian government had used job creation as a major selling point. Its primary reference was a forecast by the Economic Council of Canada (ECC), which anticipated a net gain of 251 300 jobs over ten years, of which 75 000 would be attributable to reduced trade barriers. Reviewing these estimates, Peter Bakvis concluded that "one has only to change slightly the ECC model's basic assumptions to throw these projections completely askew." Since the FTA itself abolished many of the favourable inputs, a negative effect on job creation seemed to emerge as a reasonable estimate (Bakvis 1987, 74).

The ECC alloted most of its new jobs to the service sector,[3] implying that they would be mainly non-union, low paying, and part-time. Earlier support for that outlook had appeared at a post-election conference, where Richard Freeman of Harvard's National Bureau of Economic Research predicted that firms would be "bargaining over labour conditions" as a result of the FTA (1988).

Nevertheless, it is logical that in some sectors free trade would be one of the factors inspiring an inflow of investment to Canada. Discussing that aspect, an Action Canada review of NAFTA provisions (1992) concluded that the agreement would strengthen the trend of foreign takeovers that had been developing under the FTA.

The review noted that over 93 percent of foreign investment in Canada since 1986 had been for takeovers of Canadian businesses, involving nearly 5000 companies. Articles 1106 and 1107 of NAFTA were seen as facilitating that process by ruling out any restriction "regarding trade balance, domestic content, and technology transfer activities of foreign investors ... in effect, no more negotiated agreements like the Auto Pact." In general, the NAFTA extension of free trade would allow foreign corporations "to use economic might to restructure social life in accordance with the competitive values and principles of an unregulated and profit-motivated economy."

The emphasis on takeovers rather than on investment in new industries reflects the results of excess capacity prevalent in most sectors of Canadian private enterprise. Between 60 and 90 percent of new businesses fail in their first year (*The Globe and Mail*, 5 September 1988). American branches usually have cost advantages through economies of scale and peripheral advertising. Thus any employment gains from new foreign investment must be weighed against losses caused by closures, new excess capacity, and transfer of plants to lower-wage locations, as in Mexico.

Within Mexico, free trade attention centres on the *maquiladora* area along the northern border with the United States, where foreign-owned firms operate with special trade privileges that will be retained under NAFTA (Hossie, 1993A-6). This will mean that serious violations of environment, health, and labour standards in the area will continue. The Canadian Labour Congress has also advised that for every new job in the *maquiladora* area, five are lost in other parts of Mexico (Brock 1993).

Free Trade and Agriculture

The proponents of the FTA and NAFTA argued that they would provide exemption from American laws against Canadian exports of livestock and grains, together with processed products. At the same time, supporters offered assurances that Canada's farm marketing boards would not be threatened.

Some farm organizations, including the Wheat Pools and the National Farmers' Union (NFU), warned that the United States would eventually undermine those assurances. That concern was supported by Judge Bowker (1988, 50–55), with special reference to article 701 of the agreement. It emphasizes as a primary objective eventually eliminating "all agricultural subsidies which distort world trade." Bowker noted concerns that Canada would be flooded with American grain and meat products, and that the Wheat Board would face extinction. She added that there are no guarantees against those events.

The problem of farm subsidies came to the fore in December 1988, when the GATT meeting in Montreal failed to reach agreement on that subject. The United States, apparently assuming that it would be able to undersell most of its competitors under Ricardian free trade conditions, had been campaigning strongly for elimination of grain export subsidies. Other countries, especially in Europe, have depended on subsidies to preserve their farms. Conditions evident in some developing nations convinced them that a free-market phasing out of their farm operations would undermine their economies and leave them vulnerable in the event of world food shortages.

The problem was summarized by NFU president Art Macklin with reference to the impending extension of destructive farm competition under NAFTA. "If you don't have the power to restrict lower-priced imports from coming into your country," he said, "then you can't ensure you're going to be able to keep your best agricultural land in production, or to ensure you can produce a variety of foods" (Pugh 1993, 2). The problem intensified after Canada endorsed NAFTA in June 1993. The United States increased its wheat export subsidies by 10 percent as a means of undermining Canadian wheat sales to Mexico.

The erosion of Canadian farm supply management anticipated by Macklin and by Judge Bowker had already begun under the FTA with the elimination of oats from Wheat Board jurisdiction in 1989. By early 1993, the NFU was resisting U.S. pressure to have barley removed as well. The union was certain that existing Canadian premiums for malting barley would soon disappear after that loss of board control.

Further undermining of Canadian farm prospects occurred in December 1993 when the newly elected Liberal majority government in Ottawa accepted NAFTA, almost unchanged, and also failed during GATT negotiations to protect Canada's supply management in the production and distribution of dairy and poultry products. As a substitute, the government offered tariff protection that would be phased out over several years. Farmers who had been protected by supply management saw the change as a process that would accelerate the international movement of rural workers into urban unemployment and social distress.

There had been some hopes for increased sale of Canadian farm output to the United States. Preliminary doubts included an observation by the president of the Canadian Meat Council that his industry could only benefit from the FTA if "our dollar stays at a 25% to 30% discount" (Warnock 1988, 200). FTA resistance to Canadian meat began in May 1989 with a 3.5-cent-per-pound duty on fresh, chilled, and frozen pork. Canada appealed, and the United States challenged the appeal.

Such challenges to United States imports of Canadian farm products continued, arousing strong protests from Canadian Trade Minister, Roy MacLaren. Regarding Canadian grain, lumber, pork and steel, he complained that the United States had ignored trade-panel findings favouring Canada in order to protect the interests of American producers (*The Globe and Mail*, 25 May, 1994, A-1).

In resistance to Canadian wheat exports, the United States was joined by Mexico and Brazil. After a tour of those countries, United States Agriculture Secretary Mike Espy accused Canada of secretly subsidizing its wheat sales abroad. He indicated that such subsidies could be offset by countervailing duties and by an American "export enhancement program" (*Saskatoon Star Phoenix*, 20 May 1994, A-1).

Among the continuing examples of that procedure was a United States announcement of subsidies to sales of pasta-making durum wheat to Canada's biggest customer, Algeria. A *Saskatoon Star Phoenix* editorial (16 August, 1994) concluded that Canadians should not be surprised "at the American insistence that the world should do as they say, not as they do, in international trade".

Free trade policies had already adversely affected farmers in other ways, including a 24 percent increase in grain freight rates, a reduction in the initial price of wheat, and abolition of tax rebates on gasoline and diesel fuel (CP, 29 April 1989). Thus facts were undermining the faith and hopes that free trade would reverse the decline in Canadian family farms (Arsenault, 1992).

Free Trade and Natural Resources

Similar developments are evident in the area of natural resources. For example, pro-FTA people denied that Canada's water supplies would be endangered. They contended that the FTA only recognized existing Canadian obligations under GATT, which deals with trade in water "as a beverage." Contradicting that view, a group of trade experts, including Mel Clark, a former deputy chief of the Canadian GATT delegation, reported that water is clearly specified in heading 22.01 of a tariff schedule attached to the FTA. It was further noted that the FTA could override Canadian attempts to control water exports.[4]

Regarding resource exports such as lumber, uranium, steel, and potash, supporters have argued that free trade agreements are needed to avoid American protectionism. Opponents have anticipated countervailing actions, based on allegedly unfair Canadian subsidies, wherever the exporters were competing in an over-supplied American market.

That prediction has been generally confirmed since the FTA came into force. A typical example was the potash industry, in which Canada has been repeatedly accused of "dumping." A 1993 report brings to light "a string of American civil suits" since 1987 against "virtually all Canadian potash producers" (Martin 1993).

Where the United States needs Canadian resources, as in oil and natural gas, subsidies were allowed in the FTA, and article 608.2 of NAFTA extends that concession. NAFTA also has clauses requiring that Canadian subsidies or grants must also be given to foreign MNCs. In pricing, the FTA's article 904(b) shows that Americans must not have to pay more than Canadians (Bowker 1988, 44, p. C12).

Free Trade and Cultural Industries

In the cultural sector, the free traders argued that these industries are excluded under article 2005.1 of the FTA. Former Toronto Board of Education trustee David Clandfield (1988, 54) has pointed out, however, that, in article 1607.4, cultural corporations that Americans take over can be bought back at "fair, open market value," which means that "we have just as much power to check cultural sellouts to American interests as we had when Gulf and Western bought Prentice Hall." He also pointed out that TV cable companies in Canada will no longer be able to alter American broadcasts, for example, by replacing their commercials with ours (article 2006). And according to article 2007, it will no longer be necessary for magazines or newspapers to be typeset and printed in Canada to obtain tax deductions for advertising costs.

Clandfield saw that the FTA would have a "ratchet effect" on Canadian cultural industries, forcing them to lose their identity step by step and integrate with the United States. He referred to article 2005.2 as the clause that "will stand as a ratchet against any Canadian move to protect a cultural industry ... that could conceivably imply lost income to any party south of the border." Included would be any attempt to apply Canadian content requirements, as in school texts, videos, television, and magazines (Bronson 1991, 60–61).

As in other sectors, the global expansion of free trade through NAFTA and beyond indicates further erosion of Canadian culture. Analyzing that process, a director of the BC Teachers Federation warned that "NAFTA turns over to an international commission powers over education that are not even granted to the federal government in Canada's constitution" (Kuehn 1993). Such continuing curbs on the ability of governments to pursue national objectives support an OXFAM Canada conclusion that the free trade agenda constitutes "the latest form of colonization" (O'Neill 1992, p. 9).

Free Trade and the Environment

As in other sectors, the free trade approach to environmental issues is founded mainly on faith in the protective intentions of the governments involved. The general agreement has been that most political leaders are adequately concerned about the environment. Faith is expressed, too, in the sensitivity of the provinces, which have the primary responsibility for resources.

These people who believe that environmental protection is not being seriously neglected may have felt justified when in April 1989 the federal budget for the environment was increased by 9 percent. But environmentalist Julia Langer (1989) has pointed out that there has been a 93 percent reduction in research funding for energy conservation since 1984. Meanwhile, she added, Ottawa provides large sums for environmentally harmful new energy projects.

Such problems were consistent with a warning to Canadians by Ralph Nader. The real threats from the FTA, he said, would arise not so much from the pact's wording as from the power wielded through it by the multinational corporations. They would use the threat of job reductions to force a reduction in our environmental standards (CP, 5 November 1988).

Similar warnings were given later by Patricia Hume, a representative of the Mexican Network Against NAFTA (Barclay 1993, 23–24). She reported that "the greatest pressures on the environment in Mexico were by MNCs, "which contaminate the water, the air, the soil, and destroy the forests." That process would get worse under NAFTA, she said, because that deal "has no social or environmental limits" and it "will turn more power over to multinational corporations, which have no respect for international boundaries." That disrespect had already become evident in Mexico's northern-border *maquiladora* free trade zone, where foreign-owned firms inflicted "serious industrial pollution" that would worsen under NAFTA as they would insist on still more freedom from clean-up costs (Hossie 1993, p. A-6).

A general survey and condemnation of NAFTA's potential destruction and pollution costs was made in 1993 by a coalition of 80 Canadian environmental groups. They saw the agreement as an expansion of the corporate growth agenda, "which is accelerating our planet's demise" (Rusk 1993).

Free Trade and Militarism

Military integration is an obvious priority for the United States in its drive for North American integration. This is shown by the specific exemption of Canadian military spending from FTA retaliation (article 2003). As the American role of global policing continued even after the election of President Clinton, militarism was encouraged in several ways.

The American antideficit budget for the 1994 fiscal year avoided cuts in major weapons systems. The partners in NATO were urged to support American-dominated intervention, as in Iraq, Somalia, and Yugoslavia. There was no apparent resistance to the growing freedom of the highly profitable trade in weapons, which by its nature encourages armed conflicts.

In general, this approach conforms to the United States' strategic interests, and, as analyzed by Marion Frank (1992) of the Canadian Peace Alliance, Canada will become more tightly linked to that strategy as free trade develops through the FTA and NAFTA. Thus, she predicts, "our ability to develop our own strategies will disappear."

Such linkage was indicated when Ottawa's pre-election spring budget in April 1993 anticipated that the projected $12.7 billion allocation for "defence" in 1994–95 would be maintained (though adjusted for inflation) until 1997–98.

In general, the Mulroney government's military strategies and military spending were thus showing consistency with an economic fact stressed by G.D.H. Cole when the first signs of the Second World War appeared in Europe. Sales of new weapons, he observed, are unique in that increased sales "set up a fresh demand from other countries for something newer and deadlier still" (1933, 714).The corporate agenda must give special priority to free trade expansion of this super-profitable industry in which more supply creates more demand.

Some Reform Proposals

Throughout the arguments of the free trade supporters, there has been a persistent warning that failure to move into improved export markets can lead only to isolation and economic depression. They appeal to the general concern in most countries that extra demand provided by sales to foreign buyers is the only way to avoid higher unemployment, lower domestic currency values, and greater inflation.

Discussing their "consistent strategy of restructuring the world economy," Joyce Kolko stressed that this must be analyzed as a class struggle, that capital accumulation "is still the essence of the system," and that we must "focus primarily on the contradictions that develop" (1988, 10, 12–13). Recognizing that the formation of a world market is a new feature, she concluded that most of the world's people will remain victims of the system until they "act to take power" (1988, 350).

Evidently, those who would address these issues effectively while avoiding the corporate free trade agenda must develop a scientifically valid and credible alternative. Referring to an alternative that advocates some additional state use of central banking to deal with the trade deficit issue, Korner et al. (1986, 166) detected a weakness in the program's "implicit appeal to the enlightened self-interest of creditors to renounce short-term competitive advantage for the sake of stable long-term world economic development."

Similarly questionable confidence in enlightened business self-interest appeared in pre-election anti–free trade statements by Liberal Party leader Jean Chrétien and National Party leader Mel Hurtig. Chrétien (1992) centred on the presumed need "to help Canadian workers and industry adjust to new trade arrangements." Hurtig denied that he was contradictory in proclaiming that his party was pro-business and pro-competition as well as pro-people (Manz 1993, 22).

Alternatives proposed by New Democratic Party (NDP) analysts[5] included more government financial controls, more equitable taxation, and defense of social programs. Campaigning in 1993, federal NDP leader Audrey McLaughlin endorsed co-operation among government, business, and labour—an arrangement known as tripartism. Neither that federal program nor the performance of three NDP provincial governments produced realistic answers to the debt crises.

The PC party, while relying on the international market, still accepted some government intervention, primarily in support of corporate ventures. Far from conceding errors in their expected benefits from the FTA, PC election campaigners endorsed expansion to the NAFTA and beyond. The trade minister, Michael Wilson, argued that the NAFTA would improve Mexico's environment and living standards, while building Canada's exports (Fagan 1992). Those positions were generally accepted by the Reform Party, which advocated even greater emphasis on drastic deficit reduction.

None of these parties has addressed the fundamental issue—the growing contradiction between the accumulation of excessive wealth by a few, and the growing poverty of the majority. That issue, however, has been addressed constructively by scientific analysis.

Addressing the Main Issues

Based on a long record of accurate analysis, Sweezy and Magdoff have calculated that, in the United States, with full employment and elimination of competitive waste, there could be "at least 50% more" in total wealth produced (1989). They have identified "the domination of the profit motive and the market" as the underlying cause of waste, unused capacity, and debt. Those conditions result in "many companies sitting around on bags of cash they cannot find profitable use for" (1989, 78). Coping with such contradictions requires a definition of workable alternatives and effective democratic procedures. As a beginning, it is evident that each country must work toward a full-employment economy with assurance that the wealth made available through production or trade is equitably distributed without a debt buildup. This will usually require more self-reliance, with less dependency on foreign, corporate-dominated markets and investment.

Resources should be shifted from areas of excess capacity and wasteful duplication to production that serves the genuine present and future needs of society. In Canada, these would include improvements in education, health care, reforestation, pollution control, and soil conservation, as well as the provision of adequate food, clothing, and shelter for everyone.

These improvements could be achieved by utilizing the economy's idle and wasted capacity. This capacity exists in Canada on a comparable scale to that which Sweezy and Magdoff found in the United States (Bronson 1986, 4). However, budget surpluses and a reduction of the accumulated federal debt can be achieved immediately, as shown in precise calculations by John Fryer, leader of the National Union of Provincial Government Employees, and supplemented by John Warnock (Bronson 1993).

They found that planned progress toward full employment could have provided enough revenue increases and cost reductions to improve Ottawa's 1988–89 financial position by $43.8 billion. The additional potential revenues included restoration of corporate taxation to 1984 levels, collection of delinquent taxes, and new levies on mergers, capital gains, and high incomes. Potential expenditure cuts were mainly foreseen in lower interest rates and reductions in unemployment insurance and military spending. Similar gains over the next four years would have reduced the total federal debt by at least $10 billion annually. Instead, it grew to exceed $450 billion.

To ensure such changes take place, genuine economic and political democracy is needed. This would include liberating the media from corporate control to ensure that the electorate can have access to accurate information, rather than being overwhelmed by corporate-controlled campaigns such as the two-year, $56-million pro-FTA offensive that helped to elect Mulroney in 1988 (Fillmore 1989).[6] Antiquated voting methods could be replaced by computerized systems that would reduce costs and permit greater frequency of election. This would also facilitate use of the "Four Rs" of democracy: Recall, Referendums, Rotation of leaders, and Restricted remuneration for both political and economic administrators.[7]

No party in Canada is yet committed to such a program. A party attempting it would need to unify and mobilize massive public support, not only to ensure being elected to govern, but also to deal with the business sector's inevitable intense resistance. Workers would need to develop what Michael Lebowitz has described as "planned co-operation," recognizing that economic struggle alone is "a losing battle" because that is where business has the upper hand (1988, 137–48).

The potential effectiveness of such co-operation was indicated in the 1988 Canadian election. The "Pro-Canada Network", later named "Action Canada," organized 37 exploited groups[8] to finance the anti-FTA pamphlet, "What's the Big Deal?" Its distribution through twenty dailies and three rural papers had a major impact, forcing the corporations into massive advertising, which was apparently the only thing that could save the government at that point.

Nevertheless, the Pro-Canada effort helped consolidate on-going opposition to free trade and its consequences, and helped opposition plan alternative policies. Participating coalitions concerned with establishing a system completely independent of corporate control emerged with a commitment to set up a national congress to plan for that objective.

One anti–free trade group, Citizens Concerned About Free Trade, sought a coalition between the Liberals and the NDP before the election (Orchard 1993). Other anti–free trade groups saw that as unrealistic, reflecting early criticism of CCAFT as being "overly centred" around the personality of its leader, David Orchard (Gonick and Silver 1989). Then, in 1992, the anti–free trade National Party was formed, led by publisher Mel Hurtig. While effectively criticizing free trade, it also emphasized that it would be "pro business and pro competition as well as being pro people" (Hurtig 1992, 45). It thus failed to deal with the inherent hostility to organized labour among small businesses.

Recognizing that the NDP was weakening, Action Canada groups tended to endorse the strategy expressed by the Council of Canadians chairperson, Maude Barlow (1992, p. 3) that "we must work to elect a Liberal minority government with the NDP holding the balance". Also required was a policy of supporting only the anti–free trade candidates within the Liberal party.

That party's promise to renegotiate NAFTA helped it win 46 percent of the vote and 60 percent of the seats. The NDP and the National Party together won about 7 percent of the vote, and the NDP obtained 3 percent of the seats. Other issues were prominent in the election, including unemployment and the deficit, so only a referendum could have accurately measured public opinion on free trade.

Also, some form of proportional representation would have been needed to prevent the Liberals from obtaining the majority that enabled them to break their NAFTA renegotiation promise. That result put new pressure on Action Canada groups and organized labour to publicize the connections between free trade and other major problems, involving the broader global agenda, which includes intensified exploitation of workers everywhere.

Conclusions

We have seen how early nineteenth-century ideology, combined with the class interests of international corporate leaders, resulted in their aggressive campaign in support of the Canada–U.S. Free Trade Agreement. But soon after the agreement was signed, it became evident that many of the concerns expressed by the FTA's opponents were justified. Adverse effects are evident in all major areas of policy; they are to be seen in the rates of unemployment and inflation, the fate of social programs, the crisis in agriculture, the impairment of resources and the environment, and the threat of militarism. Expectations of even greater adverse effects of the extension of free trade through NAFTA and beyond are therefore even more credible.

With a continuing buildup of debt and the polarization of wealth, the oppressed in all countries will be driven to learn effective methods for defending and improving their rights and freedoms. They will need to terminate global domination by billionaire dynasties that represent the ultimate negation of democracy.

So far, there have been few effective challenges to this concentration of power, which is becoming even more formidable as MNCs use increased freedom in international investment for takeovers and for access to resources. Thus, it must be recognized that economic and political democracy cannot be achieved fully without ownership or control of the means of production.

The record shows that the global corporate agenda is based on obsolete, self-indulgent ideas that reveal a fundamental contradiction. That contradiction lies in the inability of the distributive systems to provide purchasing power for present and potential output, without unsustainable growth in the debt and competitive pressure for the further reduction of wages and the degradation of working conditions. In their response, the world's peoples must establish systems that can apply expanding knowledge to develop full-employment economies. These must include mutually beneficial trade that is not based on deficits, and that is dedicated to the maximization of present and future human welfare everywhere.

Study Questions

1. Including the latest data, estimate the net effects of the 1989 Canada–U.S. Free Trade Agreement (FTA) as they are perceived within the major areas of social, economic, and political concern in Canada.

2. With reference to the current arguments concerning free trade, appraise current conditions to determine whether they support or negate the Ricardian hope for mutual benefit, or the Magdoff warning that such arrangements constitute an imperial–colonial relationship.

3. Consider the validity of the argument that oppressed people must "act to take power" if they are to avoid adverse social consequences as a result of the development of a world market. Identify the main barriers to the attainment of that people's power.

4. Since full and productive employment of resources could add significantly to real wealth output in Canada and elsewhere, try to determine the factors that lead to demands for "belt-tightening" and social service cutbacks. Use this analysis to identify the remedial measures needed to ensure full-employment output and to achieve its national and international distribution without reliance on incessant debt growth.

Recommended Reading

Cohen, Marjorie. *Free Trade and the Future of Women's Work*. Ottawa: Garamond Press and Canadian Centre for Policy Alternatives, 1987.

Finn, Ed, Duncan Cameron, and John Calvert, eds. *The Facts on Free Trade.* Toronto: James Lorimer, 1988.

Gonick, Cy, and Jim Silver, eds. "Fighting Free Trade." *Canadian Dimension* (April/May, 1989).

Steger, D.R. *A Concise Guide to the Canada–U.S. Free Trade Agreement.* Toronto: Carswell, 1988.

Warnock, John. *Free Trade and the New Right Agenda.* Vancouver: New Star Books. 1988.

Notes

1. A study by Stairs and Winham (1985, 86–87) shows that "the economic, cultural, familial and other linkages between Canada and the United States are so numerous, developed and complex ... that the relationship is truly unique in the international system."
2. This was a reference to articles 1906 and 1907 of the FTA, which provide for a "working group" on the use of subsidies.
3. The EC's list of service sectors includes transportation-communication, storage and utilities, insurance, investment, health, education, accommodation, food services, public administration, wholesale and retail trade, recreation, accounting, consulting, and computer services.
4. Heading 22.01 of an FTA tariff schedule defines waters as "including natural or artificial mineral waters and aerated waters, not containing added sugar or other sweetening nor flavored; ice and snow" (External Affairs 1988).
5. For further discussion of social democracy see Warnock (1988), Chapters 19 to 22; and Bronson (1986), Chapters 11 and 12.
6. Fillmore also reported that the leading spenders supporting the 1986–88 pro-FTA media campaign were the federal government, with $6.42 million, and the Canadian Alliance for Trade and Job Opportunities, representing 150 corporate members, with $6 million.
7. Warnock has referred to Switzerland as a case where referendums and recalls are used to increase popular control (1988, 310). See also Bronson (1986, 296–300).
8. The supporting groups were made up of eleven provincial coalitions, together with groups representing Native people, labour, teachers, environmentalists, cultural organizations, farmers, seniors, nurses, and anti-poverty associations.

References

Action Canada. 1992. "NAFTA on Trial." Pamphlet. Ottawa.

Arsenault, K. 1992. "NAFTA Threatens Loss of More Family Farms." Action Canada Dossier (December):22–23.

Bakvis, P. 1987. "The Creation of 350,000 New Jobs Can Be Said to Be Based on Highly Speculative Assumption." In *If You Love This Country*, ed. L. La Pierre. Toronto: McClelland and Stewart. 73–77.

Barclay, J. 1993. "Making the Environmental Links." *Briarpatch* (May): 23–24.

Barlow, M. 1992. "Election '93." *Canadian Perspectives* (Winter 1992): 3.

Bowker, M. 1988. *On Guard for Thee.* Hull: Voyageur Publishing.

Brock, G. 1993. "Free Trade Draining Jobs From Canada, Mexico: Unionists". *Star Phoenix*, March 3: B4.

Bronson, H.E. 1986. *The Profit Parasites.* Peterborough: Beat Raven.

———. 1991. "Education and the Free Trade Agreement." In *Hitting the Books,* ed. Terry Wotherspoon. Toronto: Garamond Press. 60–61.

———. 1993. "Economic Concentration and Corporate Power." In *Contemporary Sociology*, ed. P. Li and B. Bolaria. Toronto: Copp Clark Pitman.

Brownstone, Meyer. "Redirect Aid." *Globe and Mail*, April 26, 1993: A18.

Chrétien, J. 1992. "A Deal That Leaves Canada a Sitting Duck." *Globe and Mail*, September 21, A17.

Clandfield, D. 1988. "The Free Trade Ratchet." *Our Schools Our Selves* (October): 54.

Climenhaga, D. 1989. "Mexico Alluring to Auto Parts Firms, Study Concludes." *Globe and Mail*, February 16, B9.

Cole, G.D.H. 1933. *The Intelligent Man's View of Europe Today*. London: Gollancz.

Cook, P. 1992. "A Much-Needed NAFTA." *Globe and Mail*, February 26, B2.

———. 1993. "U.S. Gets to Dump on Canada." *Globe and Mail*, December 15, B2.

Crispo, J. 1992. "Forget the Critics: Free Trade Works." *Globe and Mail*, February 26, B2.

Drohan, M. 1988. "Liberal Agenda Would Delay New Arrangements on Trade." *Financial Post*, September 5, 8.

External Affairs. 1988. *The Canada–U.S. Free Trade Agreement*. Ottawa: Supply and Services Canada.

Fagan, D. 1992. "Ottawa Facing Challenge on NAFTA." *Globe and Mail*, July 24, A1.

Fillmore, N. 9189. "The Big Oink." *This Magazine*, March/April, 5–7.

Finn, E., D. Cameron, and J. Calvert, eds. 1988. *The Facts on Free Trade*. Toronto: James Lorimer.

Frank, M. 1992. "NAFTA Promotes U.S. Strategic Interests." *Action Canada Dossier* (December): 34.

Freeman, R. 1988. "Union May Scare Off U.S. Investment: Harvard." *Globe and Mail*, December 1, B9.

Fryer, J. 1989. "Labour Head Details Deficit Reduction Plan." Canadian Press, March 10.

Gigantes, P.D. 1988. *Is the Free Trade Deal Really for You?* Toronto: Stoddard.

Gonick, C., and J. Silvers, 1989. "Fighting Free Trade." *Canadian Dimension* (April/May): 6–14.

Harris, C. 1988–89. "Report on the Nation" (Winter 1988–89) *Financial Post*: 6–8.

Hurtig, M. 1989. "The Sale Continues." *Canadian Forum* (April), 5–6.

———. 1992. *A New and Better Canada*. Toronto: Stoddard.

Hossie, L. 1993. "NAFTA Will Fuel Mexican Woes." *Globe and Mail*, March 12, A6.

Inter-American Development Bank. 1987. "Report." Washington, DC.

Kenen, P.B. 1985. *The International Economy*. Englewood Cliffs, NJ: Prentice-Hall.

Kolko, J. 1988. *Restructuring the World Economy*. New York: Pantheon.

Korner, P., G. Mass, T. Siebold, and K. Tetzlaff. 1986. *The IMF and the Debt Crisis*. London: Zed Books.

Kuehn, L. 1993. "Tri-national Educators Conference Condemns NAFTA." *Canadian Dimension* (March/April): 19.

Langer, J. 1989. "Budget Good, Bad: Environment Group." Calgary: Canadian Press, May 1.

Lebowitz, M. 1988. "Trade and Class Labour Strategies in a World of Strong Capital." *Studies in Political Economy* (Autumn): 137–48.

Lowe, J. 1992. *The Secret Empire*. Homewood, IL: Irwin.

Macfarlane, J. 1988. "Free Trade Forces to Put a Price Tag on Sovereignty." Editorial. *Financial Times*, November 7.

Magdoff, H. 1971. "Economic Myths and Imperialism." *Monthly Review* (December): 1–7.

Manz, G. 1993. "Mel Hurtig." *Briarpatch* (April): 22.

Martin, P. 1993. "Potash Industry Fixed Prices: U.S." Editorial. *Star Phoenix*, April 7, C12.

Nadeau, D. 1992. "NAFTA Threatens Working Women." *Action Canada Dossier* (December): 35.

O'Neill, B. 1992. "Free Trade: The Latest Form of Colonization." *Action Canada Dossier* (December): 9.

Orchard, D. 1993. *The Fight for Canada*. Toronto: Stoddard.

Pare, J. "Americans Aren't Fair Traders." *Financial Post*, August 17, S2.

Phillips, P., M. Seccareccia, and M. Watkins. 1988. Statement. May 31.

Pro-Canada Network. 1988. "What's the Big Deal?" Pamphlet. Ottawa.

Pugh, T. 1993. "NAFTA Deal Destroys Supply Management." *Union Farmer*, April 2.

Reich, R. 1987. "Canada Is Not for Sale." Pamphlet. Toronto.

Reisman, S. 1988. "Let's Get It Straight." *Globe and Mail*, October 4, A7.

Ricardo, D. 1963 [1817]. *The Principle of Political Economy and Taxation*. Homewood, IL: Irwin.

Rusk, J. 1993. "Dump NAFTA, Coalition Demands." *Globe and Mail*, May 6, A5.

Sanger, M. 1992. "A Tool to Dismantle the Public Sector." *Action Canada Dossier* (December): 30.

Saunders, J. 1993. "NAFTA Benefits Workers, Study Says." *Globe and Mail*, February 4, B2.

Simpson, J. 1993. "Shackled Governments in an Unshackled Corporate World." *Globe and Mail*, January 22, A16.

Stackhouse, J. 1992. "Crushing Debt Overwhelms Third World." *Globe and Mail*, August 17, B9.

Stairs, D., and G.R. Winham. 1985. *The Politics of Canada's Economic Relations With the U.S.* Toronto: University of Toronto Press.

Sweezy, P., and H. Magdoff. 1989. "Lessons of the 1988 Elections." *Monthly Review* (February): 1–9.

Warnock, J. 1988. *Free Trade and the New Right Agenda.* Vancouver: New Star.

White, R. 1992. "Free Trade Means Job Losses." *Action Canada Dossier* (December): 36.

Wilkinson, B.W. 1988. "Economic Integration." In Finn, Cameron, and Calvert, *The Facts.* 29–33.

CHAPTER 17

Underdevelopment and Regional Inequality

Peter R. Sinclair

Learning Objectives

This chapter examines the social and economic patterns of regional inequality in Canada and presents a critical review of various theoretical frameworks used to explain underdevelopment and regional disparities. Students are encouraged to consider economic, health, and educational disparities and to become familiar with the extent to which these inequalities continue to affect people in different regions. By evaluating the theoretical perspectives in a careful, reasoned manner, students should obtain a better understanding of their strengths and weaknesses. Additionally, after reading this chapter, students should have a better appreciation of regionally or provincially based social protests, regional alienation, and separatist movements.

Introduction

Why do people in some parts of the country live better than those in other parts? What explains the regional distribution of poverty? Although these are old questions for sociologists, economists, geographers, and historians, I shall argue that we still need new answers. The first part of the chapter examines the scale of Canadian regional inequality in both its economic and social dimensions. Then I look at how social scientists in Canada have applied economic and sociological theories of underdevelopment, often borrowed from analyses of the Third World. I assess the adequacy of these theories to explain Canadian regional problems and point to several critical deficiencies—principally, the failure to explain the fundamental question of the spatial distribution of inequality. Finally, I shall make some suggestions concerning the most promising path toward a better explanation.[1]

The Problem of Regional Inequality

Why did the development of Canadian capitalism take the particular uneven form that it did, with centralization in Montreal and Toronto but relatively slow growth in the Atlantic provinces and western Canada? Why has the situation endured for so long? Why can't the disadvantaged regions catch up faster? These are the regional inequality questions that have to be explained—but first a comment on the concept itself.

I consider regional inequality to be synonymous with regional disparity, but follow Matthews (1983, 16–18) in reserving the term regionalism for people's perceptions of regional identity. This chapter is only concerned with regional inequality or disparity, which I take to mean the unequal spatial distribution of goods and services. This is not a matter of explaining socially neutral differences; the differences I discuss make some regions inferior in key aspects of life when compared with other regions. Although Matthews (1983, 19–21) prefers to examine differences without implying a value preference, I believe that neutrality is impossible, since the very selection of some differences as worthy of analysis must be based on an implicit frame of evaluation that gives priority to some topics over others.

Another preliminary problem is the definition of regional boundaries. A case can certainly be made for using people's own perceptions of region as the basis for the construction of boundaries (Matthews 1983), but in the absence of a massive research program to collect new data in such a framework, it is unlikely that we could proceed very far with our analysis. Moreover, no definitive popular consensus exists as to the exact regional boundaries. Instead, I shall follow the convention of adopting our provincial political structure as the basis for presenting information and will occasionally use aggregate provincial data to refer to the Atlantic region or the Prairies.[2]

Some Dimensions of Regional Inequality

Economic Inequality

Material conditions are central to how people experience their lives. For most people, their ability to sustain or expand their consumption of goods and services is a perennial concern. This makes economic inequalities important, both sociologically and politically, and also explains why we pay so much attention to various economic indicators of inequality among regions or provinces.

Table 17.1 portrays a familiar story, because the script has changed only in detail in recent decades. The basic pattern with respect to personal income is that the East is poor, while only Ontarians are significantly above average. More positively, we should note the improvement in the period 1961–91 in the relative position of the poorest provinces; yet, if we examine earned income, the progress is less than what we observed for personal income. This implies that part of the advance towards equality in personal incomes has depended on welfare-state transfer payments rather than on the development of regional productive capacity. Figure 17.1 shows that most of the improvement up to 1981 in Atlantic Canada was due to transfer payments (there was little change in the relative share of earned incomes). Earned income did make a much greater contribution in the next decade.

TABLE 17.1: Per Capita Earned and Personal Income, by Province, 1961–1990

	Per capita earned income as % of Canadian mean			Total per capita income as % of Canadian mean		
	1961	1976	1991	1961	1976	1991
Newfoundland	56.0	58.8	67.5	54.5	67.9	76.2
PEI	52.6	61.9	68.4	55.0	70.6	75.7
Nova Scotia	68.8	68.9	81.6	72.8	76.7	83.3
New Brunswick	62.8	68.2	76.1	63.6	74.4	80.0
Quebec	90.3	92.5	92.3	84.4	94.2	94.2
Ontario	120.9	113.0	113.0	110.8	110.1	110.2
Manitoba	93.4	89.3	82.6	88.3	89.6	86.5
Saskatchewan	68.4	95.0	73.9	66.4	94.8	81.7
Alberta	101.6	103.5	104.2	93.6	101.2	101.4
British Columbia	113.4	109.0	104.3	107.5	109.0	104.4

Sources: **1947–1986:** Statistics Canada, *National Income and Expenditure Accounts*, Cat. no. 13-201 (Ottawa: Minister of Supply and Services, 1987); **1981–1991:** Statistics Canada, *Provincial Economic Accounts*, Cat. no. 13-213 (Ottawa: Minister of Supply and Services, 1992). Reproduced by authority of the Minister of Industry, 1994.

Regional disparity grows if we consider gross domestic product (GDP), which includes the value of goods and services generated within a given territory (Table 17.2). Alberta has the highest GDP per capita, which reflects the value of its resources; Albertans fare less well, however, on the per capita *income* measure. GDP in Newfoundland and PEI is only about half what it is in Ontario and Alberta. Relatively low per capita income and GDP would usually indicate high rates of unemployment and a small labour force. For the Eastern provinces, this expectation is confirmed for 1992, but, strikingly, Manitoba and Saskatchewan have average rates of labour-force participation and average or below-average unemployment (Table 2).

Education and Health

The economic dimensions of inequality provide the outline of an extensive problem—one that extends into the realm of inequities in health and education. Table 17.3 provides information on the distribution of physicians across provinces in 1987. Once again, the Atlantic provinces, with the exception of Nova Scotia, fared poorly along with Saskatchewan and Alberta, but Quebecers were best served in that they had the lowest number of people per physician. Per capita health expenditures for all provinces, however, hover more closely around the Canadian mean.

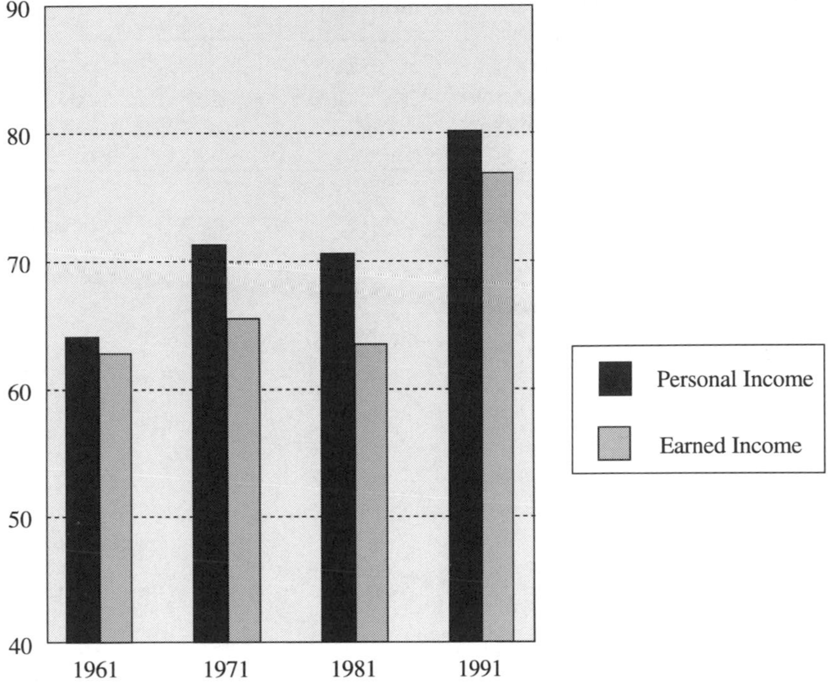

FIGURE 17.1: Personal and Earned Income Per Capita Atlantic Provinces, 1961–1991 (Canadian Mean = 100)

Sources: **1947–1986:** Statistics Canada, *National Income and Expenditure Accounts,* Cat. no. 13-201 (Ottawa: Minister of Supply and Services, 1987); **1981–1991:** Statistics Canada, *Provincial Economic Accounts,* Cat. no. 13-213 (Ottawa: Minister of Supply and Services, 1992). Reproduced by authority of the Minister of Industry, 1994.

Turning to schooling, we find that the achievement levels of the Canadian people vary more dramatically by province (see Tables 17.4 and 17.5). These differences are important because the educational level of the people of a region indicates the extent to which they are capable of participating fully in an industrialized society, in which many occupations require technical knowledge and literacy. It is often assumed that functional illiteracy is widespread among people with less than a Grade 9 level of education. Even as recently as 1991, about one in seven Canadian adults failed to meet this criterion—the percentage of adults with less than Grade 9 education varied from a low of 9.1 percent in Alberta and British Columbia to a high of 20.8 percent in Newfoundland. East of Ontario, only Nova Scotia was below the Canadian average. Although the improvement everywhere has been tremendous since 1951, the provinces that were characterized by a high percentage of people with less than Grade 9 education in 1951 were worse off relative to the other provinces by 1991. In this sense, inequalities have increased.

The percentage of people with university degrees has increased in all provinces, with Alberta and Ontario the most successful by 1991. The provinces that were

TABLE 17.2: Selected Provincial Economic Data

	GDP per capita 1992 (dollars)	GDP as % of Canadian mean	Labour force participation rate, 1992	Unemployment rate, 1992
Canada	24 968		65.5	11.3
Newfoundland	16 222	65.0	53.6	20.2
PEI	16 291	65.2	65.8	17.7
Nova Scotia	19 865	79.6	59.9	13.1
New Brunswick	19 073	76.4	59.0	12.8
Quebec	22 858	91.5	62.5	12.8
Ontario	27 273	109.2	67.3	10.8
Manitoba	21 655	86.7	66.0	9.6
Saskatchewan	19 973	80.0	66.6	8.2
Alberta	28 776	115.3	71.9	9.5
British Columbia	26 253	105.1	66.3	10.4

Source: *Canadian Economic Observer*, May 1993. Reproduced by authority of the Minister of Industry, 1994.

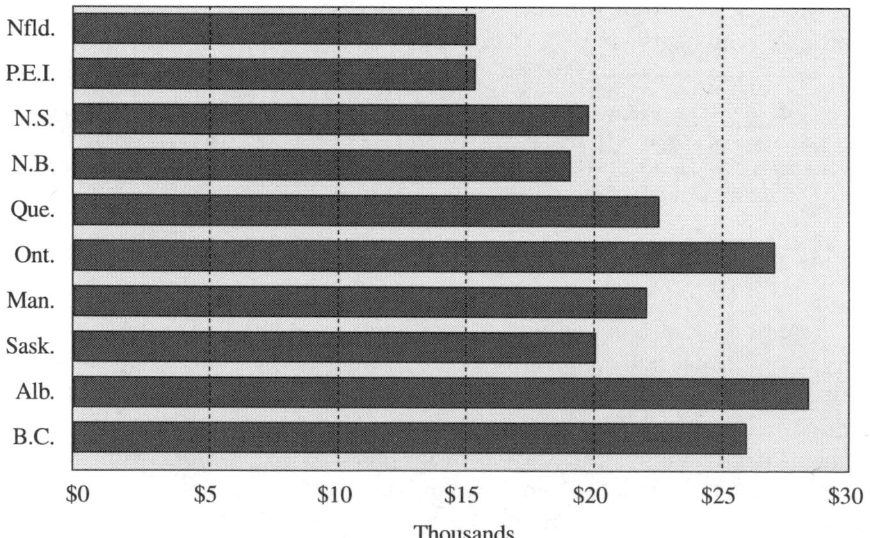

FIGURE 17.2: Gross Domestic Product, Per Capita Provinces, 1992

Source: *Canadian Economic Observer*, May 1993. Reproduced by authority of the Minister of Industry, 1994.

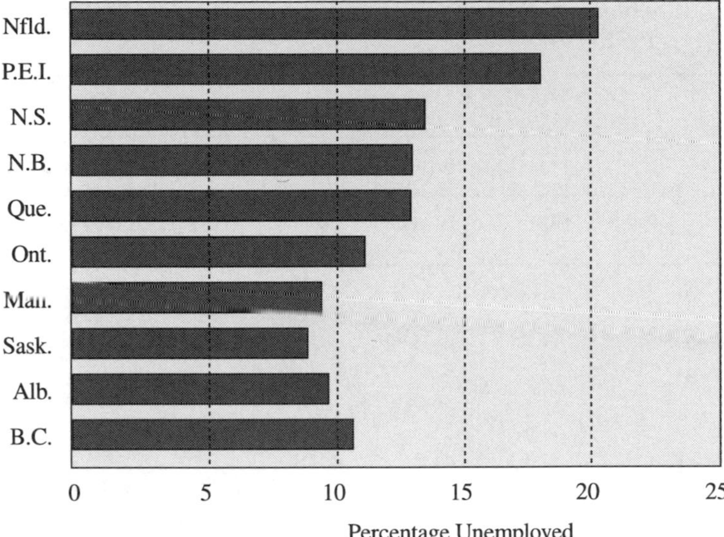

FIGURE 17.3: Unemployment Rates Provinces, 1992

Source: *Canadian Economic Observer*, May 1993. Reproduced by authority of the Minister of Industry, 1994.

TABLE 17.3: Heath Costs and Distribution of Doctors

	Per capita health expenses, 1985 (dollars)	Health expenses as % of Canadian mean, 1985	People per doctor, 1987
Canada	$1580		467
Newfoundland	1305	82.6	530
PEI	1296	82.0	690
Nova Scotia	1447	91.6	461
New Brunswick	1373	86.9	736
Quebec	1516	95.9	433
Ontario	1612	102.0	450
Manitoba	1628	103.0	486
Saskatchewan	1537	97.3	595
Alberta	1730	109.5	520
British Columbia	1629	103.1	461

Source: Statistics Canada, *Canada Year Book 1990* (Ottawa: Minister of Industry, Science and Technology, 1991), Table 3.25 and 3.34. Reproduced by authority of the Minister of Industry, 1994.

TABLE 17.4: Schooling in Canada, Population 15 Years and Older (percentages), 1951–1991

	EDUCATION LEVELS					
	Less than Grade 9			University graduates		
	1951	1971	1991	1951	1971	1991
CANADA	51.9	32.3	14.3	1.9	4.8	11.4
Newfoundland	68.7	44.4	20.8	0.5	2.1	6.6
Prince Edward Island	53.1	36.9	15.7	0.8	3.2	8.5
Nova Scotia	48.6	31.5	13.6	1.3	4.1	10.4
New Brunswick	60.3	41.2	20.1	0.9	3.4	8.4
Quebec	61.2	40.9	20.6	1.9	4.6	10.3
Ontario	46.9	28.2	11.9	2.6	5.3	13.0
Manitoba	51.2	32.1	15.2	1.3	4.6	10.2
Saskatchewan	55.7	35.6	16.3	1.0	3.5	8.6
Alberta	45.9	23.8	9.1	1.3	5.5	11.9
British Columbia	39.1	22.8	9.1	2.2	5.0	11.2

Source: Statistics Canada, *Educational Attainment and School Attendance*, Cat. no. 93-328 (Ottawa: Minister of Industry, Science and Technology, 1993), Table 1. Reproduced by authority of the Minister of Industry, 1994.

below average in 1951 improved their positions both absolutely and relatively over this time period, suggesting more successful efforts at the level of higher education than in the secondary schools. What is most encouraging about the educational situation is that differences are relatively minor in the 18–24 age group. By 1991, the percentage of young adults with less than Grade 9 was low (Quebec, at 6 percent, was the worst) and one-third or more in most provinces had achieved some form of postsecondary education (Statistics Canada 1993, Table 1).

The historically weak position of the Atlantic provinces in the area of education is not, apparently, a matter of lack of government concern or effort. Newfoundland, for example, with the worst record in Canada, actually spent more than all other provinces in 1989, when we look at expenditures on education as a percentage of total personal income or in terms of dollars per member of the labour force (Statistics Canada 1992, 234–35). Nova Scotia and New Brunswick were also above the national averages. What may be happening is that the best-educated people leave in disproportionately large numbers for work opportunities in Ontario and elsewhere. In most years since 1956, Newfoundland and the other Atlantic provinces have been net losers in interprovincial migration (House, White, and Ripley 1989, 9–11), and these migrants tend to be younger and better educated than those who stay put. Another possibility, one that I believe applies to Newfoundland, is

TABLE 17.5: Levels of Schooling by Province, As a Percentage of the Canadian Average for Persons 15 and Over, 1951–1991

	Less than Grade 9			University graduates		
	1951	**1971**	**1991**	**1951**	**1971**	**1991**
Newfoundland	132.4	137.5	145.5	26.3	43.8	57.9
Prince Edward Island	102.3	114.2	109.8	42.1	66.7	74.6
Nova Scotia	93.6	97.3	95.1	68.4	85.4	91.2
New Brunswick	116.2	127.6	140.6	47.4	70.8	73.7
Quebec	117.9	126.6	144.1	100.0	95.8	90.4
Ontario	90.4	87.3	83.2	136.8	110.4	114.0
Manitoba	98.7	99.4	106.3	68.4	95.8	89.5
Saskatchewan	107.3	110.2	114.0	52.6	72.9	75.4
Alberta	88.4	73.7	63.6	68.4	114.6	104.4
British Columbia	75.3	70.6	63.6	115.8	104.2	98.2

Source: Statistics Canada, *Educational Attainment and School Attendance*, Cat. no. 93-328 (Ottawa: Minister of Industry, Science and Technology, 1993), Table 1. Reproduced by authority of the Minister of Industry, 1994.

that funds may be used inefficiently—for example, to support the denominational school system.

Explanations

We have seen that economic and social inequality continues to characterize Canadian provinces and regions. How then can we account for it? I cannot enter into a full review of all the positions that have been brought forward to explain regional inequalities. Instead, I shall limit the discussion to examples from the two main types of explanation that have been most prominent, either in academic writing or implicitly in state policy. These two models, derived by combining two of Wien's (1988) three categories, may be labelled the *regional deficiency* approach and the *systemic problems* approach. In considering them, I shall pay special attention to their relevance for Atlantic Canada, which is clearly the most disadvantaged area in Canada on most criteria.

Regional Deficiencies

What I am calling the regional deficiency approach is more correctly a group of theories that have in common the identification of some deficiency within a devel-

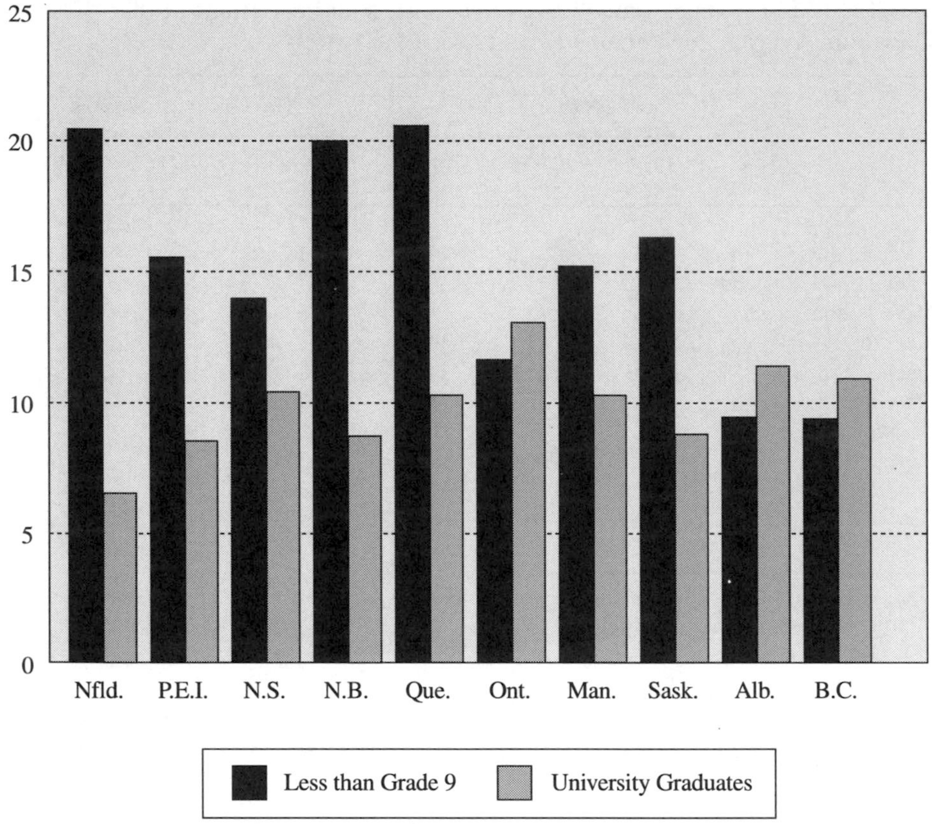

FIGURE 17.4: Educational Levels, 1991
Persons 15 and Over (Percentages)

Source: *Educational Attainment and School Attendance*, Cat. no. 93-328 (Ottawa: Minister of Industry, Science and Technology, 1993), Table 1. Reproduced by authority of the Minister of Industry, 1994.

oping or poor region that would explain its condition. It includes *staples theory* as well as more orthodox economic and geographical interpretations.

One type of deficiency is essentially environmental, in that development or its absence is considered to follow from the way that natural resources are utilized. The Canadian staples school, stemming from the seminal work of Harold Innis, identifies the key to regional development as the presence of a valued staple resource. When this staple is extracted, it should stimulate other economic activity in the region. The failure of a region to develop must reflect either the lack of valued resources, or state policies inappropriate for promoting development, or the absence of appropriate entrepreneurial actions with respect to those resources and their potential linkages to other economic activities. Thus, geographical and economic factors mix with the cultural values that are thought to promote or discourage economic activity.

The staples approach to Atlantic Canada is most fully illustrated in Saunders's (1984) economic history. Of particular interest is his account of the failure of the Maritime provinces to sustain economic growth at a rate similar to central Canada after the initial flurry of investment following Confederation. Saunders argues that the region's geography forced industry into a more dispersed, smaller-scale pattern than elsewhere in Canada. Many plants (textiles, boots and shoes, light iron and steel) closed because of central Canadian competition: central Canadian industries were nearer to the largest markets, were larger in scale, could acquire cheaper raw materials and power, and had access to better or cheaper transportation facilities. The population of the Maritimes was too small and scattered to attract the new industries of the early twentieth century, which was based on mass production of consumer goods, and the region was more distant from the emerging markets in western Canada (Saunders 1984, 84–85).

A second type of regional deficiency is primarily cultural. Atlantic Canadians are said to be poor because they lack entrepreneurship; they are not oriented to investment in productive industry and the accumulation of capital. Some commentators do not accept that the Atlantic provinces have been poor primarily because of their resource endowment and location, but point, at least in part, to cultural values. For example, George's (1970) economic analysis fails to identify any significant cost disadvantage that could explain retarded economic development in the region, and concludes that the answer must lie in the low level of entrepreneurship of the people. Acheson (1972) refers to lack of self-confidence among businessmen, and Alexander (1974, 18) alludes to the "weakness in entrepreneurship" in Newfoundland.[4] These are references to the culture of the business elite, but others point more widely to mass culture. Clark's (1978) study of rural New Brunswick puts particular emphasis on a cultural syndrome of low ambition, low achievement, and migration as the explanation for persistent poverty.

Such references to cultural deficiencies are really Canadian versions of *modernization theory*, which focussed, in the 1950s and 1960s, on the difference between the developed industrial societies and the "backward," newly formed Third World nations. A developed society was characterized as having a complex institutional structure with an industrial economic base and a modern set of values that stressed individual acquisition and achievement. What held the Third World back, supposedly, was a set of traditional and inappropriate cultures that lacked a suitable stimulus to work, save, and invest. The solution, then, was education in the value system of modernity and the transfer of the institutions and technologies of industrial capitalism.

Although there have been many program changes and much debate about appropriate strategies, deficiency theories have been influential in state policy for the past thirty years. This is perhaps primarily because they focus on internal problems and point to answers or development strategies that do not require a radical reconstruction of the social order. It may be thought that inappropriate values can be corrected eventually by appropriate education, which implies a policy of more public investment in schooling and even the transfer of funds from the central government to the provinces in order to achieve this objective. Educational levels still lag behind in Atlantic Canada, and the appropriateness of the type of education received has now come into question (see, e.g., the wide-ranging recommendations of the Newfoundland Royal Commission on Employment and Unemployment [1986]).

In so far as underdevelopment is thought to be related to dispersal of the population in small scattered communities, the political answer has been to promote growth through the encouragement of migration to "growth poles," as in the federal–provincial program of the 1960s, which sought to relocate the people of Newfoundland's outports. Unfortunately, the growth centres failed to grow and the resettlement program itself has often been criticized (see, e.g., Matthews 1983, 118–36). Where the problem is identified as poor location relative to investment and market centres, the answer has been to pour state funds into various regional development programs that provide incentives to corporate investors to establish plants in the disadvantaged regions. Equalization payments from the federal government allow the poorer provincial governments to maintain their services and programs. Indeed, about half the revenue of the governments of PEI and Newfoundland comes from Ottawa. And federal transfer payments also make up a relatively large share of the incomes of individuals in the Atlantic region. Although incomes and employment might have been less without such help, the results are still discouraging and suggest that the problem is more fundamental.

Paradoxically, the involvement of the state in the programs described, as well as the system of transfer payments to individuals, have both been criticized by neoclassical economists such as Courchene (1986) for creating another deficiency that holds down economic growth. The problem is market failure. It is argued that the state artificially supplements living standards when it introduces minimum wage laws and makes transfer payments that discourage people from accepting low-paying jobs or from migrating to other areas. The welfare-state system prevents the market from equalizing investment and labour opportunities across the country. Apart from moral objections, the key point to be made against the market failure position is that the poor regions were poor before the state intervention that they criticize. The market did not bring about adjustments; it created socially distressed regions that could not be ignored by the state (see also Sager 1987, 135).

Systemic Problems: Dependency and Underdevelopment

In the 1970s and 1980s, many sociologists grew dissatisfied with the various theories and reforms outlined above. Instead, a more radical group of theories emerged that point to fundamental, systemic problems in the structure of Canadian society, and even of the international system of which it is part, as explanations for regional inequality. Two main lines of influence may be identified in this new political economy of regionalism, one stemming from the Canadian staples theory and another from the Latin American dependency theory.

Depending on how it is developed the staples theory can have radical implications. In so far as the development of a staples economy requires external markets, a region's economic growth depends fundamentally on external demand over which it has no control. It may also be critically influenced by external state policies. Thus, having acknowledged the importance of geographical and environmental factors, several authors have complained that the federal government did not maintain a transportation policy that would have permitted more profitable production in the Maritimes. Early in the twentieth century, preferential rates for the Maritimes were abolished in response to pressure from central Canadian interests (Acheson 1977; Forbes 1977). Underdevelopment persisted because of the power of external Canadian business to influence state policy. If the remedy is thought to lie in getting a fairer deal in Confederation, there are no systemic or radical implications, but Clow (1984) points to the nature of Canadian federalism, in which most influence lies in the central regions, as a structural feature of Canadian society that systematically impeded development of the Maritimes. More recently, Brodie (1990) has emphasized that the federal government's economic development policies, dating back to the late nineteenth century, have contributed to spatial inequality in a cumulative fashion as new policies are piled on top of the lingering effects of older ones. In such ways, the staples theory can influence more radical approaches.

The second major source of influence appeared in the theories of underdevelopment in Third World countries. Modernization theory was subjected to a devastating assault with the rise of *dependency theory*, particularly by scholars whose focus was on Latin America. Rather than accept the conclusion that the causes of underdevelopment were cultural and internal, the "dependentistas" looked at underdevelopment as a function of the way that the Third World was linked to the First World. Third World countries were kept poor because more powerful, metropolitan countries extracted their economic surplus, while similar relationships existed within these societies whose own metropolitan core exploited the peripheries. The closer the ties, the worse the exploitation and underdevelopment. Societies were underdeveloped because they were dependent. This is a simplification of A.G. Frank's (1967) famous metaphor of the *metropolis-satellite chain*. The only hope for Third World development was to break the chain and escape from capitalist bondage.

Frank and his followers operated at a high level of generality and conveniently ignored that capitalist development (in the sense of economic growth) did occur in many peripheral regions. Recognizing that some economic development did take place in Latin America, Cardoso (1972; 1973) introduced the influential concept of *associated dependent development*. Third World economies were said to be dependent upon their links with more powerful economies that conditioned what was possible for them. Yet they could grow in ways directed by the inflow of foreign investment through multinational corporations. As Evans (1979, 32) put it in his study of Brazil, dependent development "implies both the accumulation of capital and some degree of independence on the periphery."

Dependency Theory in Canada

Sociological theories that were developed to analyze Third World underdevelopment have been imported, as it were, to cope with the problem of regional inequality in Canada. Davis (1971), referring to Canada as a whole, and Archibald (1971), looking only at Atlantic Canada, applied the metropolis-satellite model. Like Frank, they failed to deal adequately with social relations within the regions, and, in Archibald's case, information on the industrial development of the Maritimes that runs counter to the theory was ignored (post-1880 locally financed industrialization).

Probably the most influential Canadian dependency theorist has been Wallace Clement. Clement (1978) approaches regional inequality as a problem in class relations and capitalist underdevelopment. He begins his analysis with a summary of dependency theory, which he finds a useful guide to the Canadian situation. He emphasizes, however, that areas do not exploit other areas; rather, the capitalist class, resident primarily in the "golden triangle" of central Canada, undertakes this exploitation. Clement then presents information on the regional distribution of the economic elite as an illustration of the unevenness of economic development. In dependency terms, he sees this unevenness as a result of the extraction of surplus from the underdeveloped region (1978, 99). As Sager (1987, 120) points out, this critical assertion is not documented. Clement would have to show that the industrialization of eastern and western Canada had been prevented or arrested by the actions of central Canadian capitalists. Without specification and demonstration of the mechanism of underdevelopment, we are left with but unexplained indicators of regional inequality.

Another prominent exponent expressed strong support for Cardoso, whose "theories seem particularly relevant to an analysis of regionalism in Canadian society because they depict the Canadian situation so accurately" (Matthews 1983, 74). Matthews went on to describe the "hinterland" regions as "most assuredly *dependent developed* in that their economic growth is highly constrained and determined by decisions made outside the regions in the economic centres of this and other countries" (1983, 74). The problem, however, is the absence of the detailed analysis needed to demonstrate how a region can be developing and dependent at the same time and where the source of growth may lie. What would have happened to the poor regions in the absence of external capital and the decisions of the federal state? Would they really have become independent, autonomous regions on a par with central Canada, as this theory implies? Are the characteristics of the region itself really irrelevant?

Postdependency

Dependency theory has been heavily attacked in the general development literature. Although dependency theory was created by writers who thought they were applying Marxist principles to Third World problems, the theory received much of its most trenchant criticism from within Marxism (especially Laclau 1971; Warren 1973; 1980; Booth 1975). In summary, what emerged in the 1970s was a renewed emphasis on capitalism as a *mode of production*,[5] one that dominated but did not eliminate precapitalist modes of production in developing or dependent regions. Rather than emphasize the unequal terms of trade between centre and periphery, postdependency theory acknowledged the development of capitalism and the class relations at the structural core of capitalism as the underlying sources of underdevelopment in general. Relations within regions and not simply between regions were treated as important.

I shall now summarize the main Canadian writing in the neo-Marxist tradition. In 1978, Clement had already stressed class relations in his regional study, but he did so within the context of dependency theory. In the same volume, Cuneo (1978) approached regional inequality from a more orthodox Marxist position, with no reference to the debates in the development literature. Differences in the socio-economic characteristics of Canada's regions and population flows between regions were explained as regional dimensions of the class composition and inherent dynamic tendencies of Canadian capitalism. In effect, some regions were poor because capitalism had not become concentrated in them. That concentration and centralization of capital is part of the dynamic of capitalism is not in dispute, but why should it have occurred primarily in central Canada? Cuneo (1978, 138) is one of the few radical scholars to attempt an answer. He believes that the concentration follows from geographical proximity to centres of American capitalism, but it is hard to accept that location alone is the driving force behind investment decisions. Something must have made southern Ontario and Quebec appear more profitable for capital than other places, but we are not offered any suggestions.

Veltmeyer (1979; 1980), working on Atlantic Canada, also criticized dependency theory for its focus on exchange relations between regions rather than on the more fundamental social relations of production. He proposed that Atlantic Canada was underdeveloped because Canadian capital, concentrated historically in central Canada, required and created a source of cheap labour that might be called upon when necessary—Marx's concept of the industrial reserve army. Yet, as Bickerton (1982, 193–94) has pointed out, Veltmeyer's thesis ignores internal factors that contributed to the relative decline of Maritime industry and the continued poverty of the region's primary producers. Nor is it clear, once again, why core and periphery are located as they are (Sager 1987, 128). Why the Atlantic provinces should be the home of the industrial reserve army remains mysterious. Furthermore, the form of explanation is an untestable "Marxist functionalism"—poor people exist in Atlantic Canada because they have to in order to maintain Canadian capitalism. But Canadian capitalism does not *have* to be maintained on the backs of these people.

In the 1970s, Marxists began to discuss the articulation of modes of production in quite sophisticated ways.[6] In Canada, students of particular regions and regional industries searched for explanations of inequality within a similar framework. Both Sacouman (1977) and Veltmeyer (1979) followed this approach implicitly in portraying subsistence and independent commodity production as part of the dynamic of capitalism, which creates cheap, surplus labour. Sacouman (1979) referred to primary producers in both the Prairies and the Maritimes as engaged in a domestic mode of production (involving some combination of subsistence and commodity production) that was maintained to the advantage of capitalism and that took different forms in different regions. It was a short step from this point to his attempt to synthesize explicitly the dependency and modes of production approaches: "the central argument is that uneven underdevelopment in the rural Maritimes has occurred largely through partial/blocked transformation of the domestic mode of production. Semiproletarianization of household members of the producer unit has helped give them less than subsistence for their labour" (Sacouman 1980, 234). Semiproletarianization refers to farmers and fishers who legally own property and work it with household labour, but whose income is "more and more directly determined by capitalist dominance" (1980, 237). Although this analysis does advance our knowledge of the organization of production in the Atlantic provinces, it suffers from a reliance on functional explanation for the structures of regional inequality—i.e., inequality exists because capitalism needs it.

The problems with neo-Marxist theories of regional inequality, and of Atlantic Canada's situation in particular, are indicative of the malaise in the development literature on which they draw so heavily. It appears as if the structures of underdevelopment never change and are basically the same everywhere. That is, every case, at whatever period, in whatever location is explained with reference to the same general model. It is noteworthy, for example, that Frank (1967) can produce no policy to cope with the situation other than to appeal for a general socialist revolution. To do anything else would demand attention to particular circumstances. Thus, I agree with Mouzelis (1988, 28) that underdevelopment and dependency theories are too general to explain the widely different trajectories through which various Third World societies have moved.[7] The general models do not clearly spell out the causal mechanisms that lead to one pattern rather than another. Furthermore, the historical evidence is often missing or at variance with claims of theorists, as Eric Sager (1987) has recently shown with respect to most Marxist discussions about eastern Canada.

The Way Forward?

I think that our understanding can be improved by abandoning the quest for a single general theory of development and regional inequality. Mouzelis is on the right track when he advocates a middle-range approach that would specify a set of development paths, each of which would include one or more societies or regions. We also need to look for causal forces both outside and within the unit in question. What can provide some unity in the analyses is the need in every case to search for the way that interests are formed around lines of conflict—principally, class, gender, and ethnicity—and to establish how people have followed their interests in relation to the actions of others and the potential or limits of their natural environment.

So for the Atlantic provinces we should expect to uncover a combination of external and internal factors, given that no simple general theory exists to adequately explain development or underdevelopment. In the fisheries of northwest Newfoundland, I have shown how simplistic, unilinear, structural theories cannot account for the process of change that has actually taken place as real people respond to their environments and the actions of others. A similar general perspective is found in the work of Norman Long (1984; Long and van der Ploug 1988; Long and Roberts 1984), who advocates a type of analysis that will uncover "processes in which ordinary people—peasants, workers, entrepreneurs, bureaucrats, and others—actively engage in shaping the outcomes of processes of development" (Long 1984, 169). Long would have us look at the interplay of local and external forces, the latter always filtered through local or internal regional structures (1984, 171). In particular, the interaction of different sectors of production may be captured in the concept of

> a "regionalized system of production" that is made up of a system of linkages that develop over time between a dominant sector and its eco-

> nomic and social hinterland.... This system ... is continuously being re-molded by the struggles that go on between particular individuals and social groups, and it is also affected by the ways in which powerful outside forces impinge upon it (Long 1984, 175–56).

This having been said, it may be helpful to distinguish more clearly two separate though related issues that have been confounded to the detriment of explanations of Canadian regional inequality. The question of the *origin* of disparity may require a different explanation from that of its *persistence* once established. Most Canadian sociologists appear to have ignored the first question or mistakenly assumed that it was adequately answered by pointing to laws or tendencies of capitalism. Yet the explanation of existing conditions is unsatisfying unless one can show both the historical processes that brought them about and also specify the mechanisms that now appear to sustain them.

Let us consider the Maritime provinces. Why did they slip into the status of an underdeveloped region suffering from various disparities in comparison with other parts of Canada, a process that was becoming apparent toward the end of the nineteenth century?[8] Location is surely not irrelevant, but it is not the whole answer, either. Sager (1987, 125–57) reminds us that no compelling evidence exists that the concentration of capital in central Canada caused its relative absence in the Maritimes. Too little is known about net capital flows to be certain about the relationship. As to the Canadian capitalists who invested in the Maritimes after Confederation, there is no reason to believe that they behaved any differently than did indigenous regional capitalists. Frost (1982) has shown, for example, that the Bank of Nova Scotia did not oppose industrial investments in the region, but after the depression of 1882 to 1884 the bank's investments were increasingly focussed outside the region, and even outside the country, in areas that the managers felt would provide greater profits. In this way, Maritime capitalists drained "enormous sums of money" from the region, although there was still no local shortage.

Although industrialization did take place in the Maritimes, McKay (1983; 1986) points out that such development occurred in industrial enclaves and failed to supply a broadly based economic stimulus, at least partly because it exported profits to metropolitan centres. The mining and shipbuilding industries imported technologically advanced production goods. This limited the stimulus for local spin-off industries. At the same time, mercantile control of the agricultural, lumber, and fishing economies maintained precapitalist, low-productivity forms of production based on the household. As Sager (1987, 136) suggests, "relatively slow capitalist development was deeply rooted in the mutually sustaining interaction of sectors, and in the relationships between capitalist and pre-capitalist modes of production."[9]

Once established in a particular location, metropolitan capital pursues profits and attracts further investment in such a way as to make it more difficult for peripheral areas to achieve capitalist development. Clow's discussion of the importance of state policy with respect to the Maritimes is relevant here as one critical factor. Clow sees the trajectory of capitalist development in the Marxist model as a tendency that should not be considered necessary or inevitable (1984, 123). This is sensible. What actually happens in a particular context depends partly on political relations. Thus, Clow directs attention to the importance of state policy and political forces at work during and after Confederation, but his is more an exhortation to investigate than a definitive statement.

As to labour reserves, it is not so much that capitalism in central Canada needs or needed a reserve in Atlantic Canada. Rather, corporate capitalism could benefit from earlier historical patterns that left so many Atlantic Canadians economically stranded, determined to survive independently as long as possible, yet susceptible, finally, to the lure of wages in the capitalist labour market. That is, many small producers worked in capitalist enterprises for part of the year in order to supplement their farms or fisheries or support other family members who laboured in this way (as Sacouman and others point out). This pattern continues to this day. The labour power of such people is usually unskilled and cheap, easily replaceable and discardable, from the perspective of corporate or state employers.

Conclusions

We need to be aware that metropolitan structures have not simply been imposed upon a passive population; that is the important message in Brym and Sacouman's (1979) early work on rural social movements. Students of the region know that people get by through complex household economic strategies, involving various state programs as well as formal and informal economic activities, and occasional collective actions. If most residents simply would leave, as some neoclassical economists wish, regional disparities might disappear, though at great social cost. Disparities remain in part because people with low incomes and inferior educational qualifications find ways to evade the pressures to relocate. As House (1986) implies, we should not assume, as do so many neo-Marxists, that these are backward people, bad judges of what is best for them. Atlantic Canadians may be better off staying at home despite the economic problems than to follow the signs to Toronto. We need to understand them better and learn how to counteract regional inequality without depopulating the poor regions.

Study Questions

1. Why do you think inequality persists in the educational levels of people in the various regions of Canada?

2. How can you measure economic inequality among regions? What factors do you think best explain your findings?

3. "Atlantic Canada is poor because it is dependent." Discuss the meaning of this statement and consider its validity.

4. Imagine you are in charge of regional development policy. What would you propose and why?

Recommended Reading

Brodie, Janine. *The Political Economy of Canadian Regionalism.* Toronto: Harcourt, Brace, Jovanovich, 1990.

Brym, Robert J., ed. *Regionalism in Canada.* Toronto: Irwin, 1986.

Brym, Robert J., and R. James Sacouman, eds. *Underdevelopment and Social Movements in Atlantic Canada.* Toronto: New Hogtown Press, 1979.

Burrill, Gary, and Ian McKay, eds. *People, Resources, and Power: Critical Perspectives on Underdevelopment and Primary Industries in the Atlantic Region.* Fredericton: Acadiensis Press, 1987.

Coffey, William J., and Mario Polèse, eds. *Still Living Together: Recent Trends and Future Directions in Canadian Regional Development.* Montreal: Institute for Research on Public Policy, 1987.

Matthews, Ralph. *The Creation of Regional Dependency.* Toronto: University of Toronto Press, 1983.

Newfoundland and Labrador. *Building on Our Strengths.* Report of the Royal Commission on Employment and Unemployment, 1986.

Notes

1. I am grateful to Doug House for commenting on the text and for directing me to several sources of data that strengthen the argument, particularly on migration.
2. I agree with Gidengil (1989) that provinces are heterogeneous in many respects, but the range of available data on smaller units (like the subprovincial regions that she adopts) is too limited in time and subject for my purpose.
3. Earned income here includes wages, salaries and benefits; net farm income; and net income from unincorporated business. The latter category includes most self-employed persons, but it also includes rental income, which makes the use of the term earned income slightly inaccurate.
4. Alexander (1977) also refers to the fragmentation of the upper class in Newfoundland as a significant factor in its relative underdevelopment.
5. *Mode of production* has become a widespread term, with different nuances according to the author. Most use it to refer to the combination of the material/technical *forces* of production and the social relations in which people are engaged as participants in a system of production and distribution.
6. For an early review of the debate over the articulation of modes of production see Foster-Carter (1978).
7. I have made the same point with reference to theories that predict either the disappearance or the timeless survival of domestic commodity production (Sinclair 1985).
8. From this time, economic development took place more slowly than in central Canada and particular industries collapsed, but overall it is a mistake to refer to the region as suffering from deindustrialization.
9. Broadly similar arguments can be made for Newfoundland, where the key to underdevelopment lay in the extraction of capital from the fishing industry, which was dominated by merchant capital. See especially Antler (1979), Ommer (1985), and Sinclair (1987).

References

Acheson, T.W. 1972. "The National Policy and the Industrialization of the Maritimes, 1880–1910." *Acadiensis* 1: 3–28.

———. 1977. "The Maritimes and 'Empire Canada'." In *Canada and the Burden of Unity*, ed. D.J. Bercuson. Toronto: Macmillan. 87–114.

Alexander, D. 1974. "Development and Dependence in Newfoundland." *Acadiensis* 4: 3–31.

———. 1977. *The Decay of Trade*. St. John's, NF: Institute of Social and Economic Research.

———. 1983. *Atlantic Canada and Confederation: Essays in Canadian Political Economy*. Toronto: University of Toronto.

Antler, S. 1979. "The Capitalist Underdevelopment of Nineteenth-Century Newfoundland." In *Underdevelopment and Social Movement in Atlantic Canada*, ed. R.J. Brym and R.J. Sacouman. Toronto: New Hogtown Press. 179–202.

Archibald, B. 1971. "Atlantic Regional Underdevelopment and Socialism." In *Essays on the Left*, ed. L. LaPierre. Toronto: McClelland and Stewart. 103—20.

Bickerton, J. 1982. Underdevelopment and Social Movements in Atlantic Canada." *Studies in Political Economy* 9: 191–202.

Booth, D. 1975. "André Gunder Frank: An Introduction and Appreciation." In *Beyond the Sociology of Development*, by I. Oxall, T. Barrett, and D. Booth. London: Routledge. 50–85.

Brodie, J. 1990. *The Political Economy of Canadian Regionalism*. Toronto: Harcourt, Brace, Jovanovich.

Brym, R., ed. 1986. *Regionalism in Canada*. Toronto: Irwin.

Brym, R.J., and R.J. Sacouman, eds. 1979. *Underdevelopment and Social Movements in Atlantic Canada*. Toronto: New Hogtown Press.

Cardoso, F. 1972. "Dependency and Development in Latin America." *New Left Review* 74. 14: 83–95.

———. 1973. "Associated-Dependent Development: Theoretical and Practical Implications." In *Authoritarian Brazil*, ed. A. Stepan. New Haven: Yale University Press.

Clark, S.D. 1978. *The New Urban Poor*. Toronto: McGraw-Hill.

Clement, W. 1978. "A Political Economy of Regionalism in Canada." In *Modernization and the Canadian State*, ed. D. Glenday, H. Guindon, and A. Turowetz. Toronto: Macmillan. 89–110.

Clow. M. 1984. "Politics and Uneven Capitalist Development." *Studies in Political Economy* 14: 117–40.

Courchene, T. 1986. "Avenues of Adjustment: The Transfer System and Regional Disparities." In *The Canadian Economy: A Regional Perspective*, ed. R. Savoie. Toronto: Methuen.

Cuneo, C.J. 1978. "A Class Perspective on Regionalism." In *Modernization and the Canadian State*, ed. D. Glenday, H. Guindon, and A. Turowetz. Toronto: Macmillan. 132–56.

Davis, A. K. 1971. "Canadian Society and History as Hinterland Versus Metropolis." In *Canadian Society: Pluralism, Change, and Content*, ed. R.J. Osenberg. Scarborough: Prentice-Hall. 6–32.

Evans, P. 1979. *Dependent Development: The Alliance of Multinational, State, and Local Capital in Brazil*. Princeton: Princeton University Press.

Forbes, E. 1977. "Misguided Symmetry: the Destruction of Regional Transportation Policy for the Maritimes." In *Canada and the Burden of Unity*, ed. D.J. Bercuson. Toronto: Macmillan

Foster-Carter, A. 1978. "The Modes of Production Controversy." *New Left Review* 107: 47–77.

Frank, A.G. 1967. *Capitalism and Underdevelopment in Latin America*. New York: Monthly Review Press.

Frost, J.D. 1982. "The 'Nationalization' of the Bank of Nova Scotia." *Acadiensis* 12: 3–38.

George, R.E. 1970. *A Leader and a Laggard: Manufacturing Industry in Nova Scotia, Quebec, and Ontario*. Toronto: University of Toronto Press.

Gidengil, E. 1989. "Diversity Within Unity: On Analysing Regional Dependency." *Studies in Political Economy* 29: 91–122.

House, J.D. 1986. "The Mouse that Roars: New Directions in Canadian Political Economy. The Case of Newfoundland." In Brym, *Regionalism*. 161–96.

House, J.D., M. White, and P. Ripley. 1989. *Going Away ... And Coming Back: Economic Life and Migration in Small Canadian Communities*. Report no. 2. St. John's, NF: Institute of Social and Economic Research.

Laclau, E. 1971. "Feudalism and Capitalism in Latin America." *New Left Review* 67: 19–38.

Long, N. "Creating Space for Change: A Perspective on the Sociology of Development." *Sociologia Ruralis* 24: 168–73.

Long, N., and B. Roberts. 1984. *Miners, Peasants, and Entrepreneurs: Regional Development in the Central Highlands of Peru*. Cambridge: Cambridge University Press.

Long, N., and J.D. van der Plong. 1988. "New Challenges in the Sociology of Rural Development." *Sociologia Ruralis* 28: 30–41.

Matthews, R. 1983. *The Creation of Regional Dependency*. Toronto: University of Toronto Press.

McKay, I. 1983. "Industry, Work, and Community in the Cumberland Coal Fields, 1848–1927." Ph.D. thesis. Dalhousie University.

———. 1986. "The Realm of Uncertainty: The Experience of Work in the Cumberland Coalfields, 1870–1930." *Acadiensis* 16: 3–57.

Mouzelis, N. 1988. "Sociology of Development: Reflections on the Present Crisis." *Sociology* 22: 23–44.

Newfoundland and Labrador. 1986. *Building on Our Strengths*. Report of the Royal Commission on Employment and Unemployment.

Ommer, R. 1985. "What's Wrong with Canadian Fish?" *Journal of Canadian Studies* 20: 122–42.

Phillips, P. 1982. *Regional Disparities*. Toronto: Lorimer.

Sacouman, R.J. 1977. "Underdevelopment and the Structural Origins of Antigonish Movement Cooperatives in Eastern Nova Scotia." *Acadiensis* 7: 66–85.

———. 1979. "The Differing Origins, Organization, and Impact of Maritime and Prairie Co-operatives in Eastern Nova Scotia." *Canadian Journal of Sociology* 4: 199–221.

———. 1980. "Semi-proletarianization and Rural Underdevelopment in the Maritimes." *Canadian Review of Sociology and Anthropology*. 17: 232–45.

Sager, E.W. 1987. "Dependency, Underdevelopment and the Economic History of the Atlantic Provinces." *Acadiensis* 17: 117–37.

Saunders, S.A. 1984 [1939]. *The Economic History of the Maritime Provinces*. Ed. T.W. Acheson. Fredericton, NB: Acadiensis Press.

Sinclair, P.R. 1985. *From Traps to Draggers: Domestic Production in Northwest Newfoundland*. St. John's, NF: Institute of Social and Economic Research.

———. 1987. *State Intervention and the Newfoundland Fisheries*. Aldershot, NF: Gower Avebury.

Statistics Canada. 1992. *Education in Canada: A Statistical Review for 1990–1991. (Cat. 81–229.) Ottawa: Supply and Services Canada.*

———. 1993. Educational Attainment and School Attendance. (Cat. 93-328.) Ottawa: Supply and Services Canada.

Veltmeyer, H.1979. "The Capitalist Underdevelopment of Atlantic Canada." In Brym and Sacouman, *Underdevelopment*. 17–35.

———. 1980. "A Central Issue in Dependency Theory." *Canadian Review of Sociology and Anthropology* 17: 198–213.

Warren, B. 1973. "Imperialism and Capitalist Industrialization." *New Left Review* 81: 3–45.

———. 1980. *Imperialism: Pioneer of Capitalism*. London: New Left Books.

Wien, F. 1988. "Canada's Regions." In *Understanding Canadian Society*, ed. J. Curtis and L. Tepperman. Toronto: McGraw-Hill Ryerson.

CHAPTER 18

Urbanization: Issues and Problems

Alison Hayford

Learning Objectives

A central objective of this chapter is to provide students with concepts they can use in understanding urban society and the important issues that arise out of urbanization, urbanism, and the specific conditions of city life. Students need to be aware of the problems that exist in cities in their own and other societies; students also need to have analytical tools that enable them to understand the roots of these problems and how society might work toward solutions for them. The chapter provides students with a basic familiarity with methods of analyzing urbanism and urban problems, and with information on some of the specific issues that arise in Canadian cities and the Canadian urban system.

Introduction

Canadians like to think that we have avoided the kinds of problems that exist in U.S. cities, but we're still concerned about the quality of urban life (Central Mortgage and Housing [CMHC], 1979). While many of our concerns, such as unemployment and nuclear catastrophe, are national or even global in scope, rightly or wrongly we associate certain other issues with cities. We see such problems as crime, housing shortages, and racial conflict as a part of *urbanism*—the concentration of population in large, dense settlements, and the social patterns that emerge in such settlements. Sometimes we see cities as actually causing problems, sometimes we see problems as being worse in cities than elsewhere; in either case, we identify such problems as urban.

We regard cities with mixed feelings, as places where social and economic opportunities are matched by disorder and danger to life and safety, and where the environment itself can threaten our wellbeing. Frequently we blame urban problems on the simple fact of numbers: there are too many people in cities, people live too close together, people are strangers. Perhaps these things are factors in creating some of the social problems we associate with urbanism, but they don't explain all of the problems of cities or differences among cities. It's important to realize that cities reflect the structures and values of the societies that create and sustain them. To understand why cities have problems, we have to understand their social organization and the inequalities that characterize it.

Canadian Urbanism

Most Canadians live in cities. Nearly a third of the population lives in or near our three largest cities alone, while over three-quarters of Canadians live in urban areas. This means that most Canadians live in environments that mix social classes, races, and cultures. It means that most of us live among strangers, in places that use formal regulation to achieve order—from traffic lights and noxious weed ordinances to laws governing public morality. Yet while cities are a central fact of life for Canadians, we see them as creating problems.

An unexpected kind of problem—the most basic problem, perhaps, for scholars and policy-makers—is to define what a city is. We may know instinctively, but social scientists and politicians find it more difficult to develop meaningful definitions. How big is a city in area and population? Who governs cities? Is a low-density suburban area whose residents work in a city part of that city, or is it a separate social and political unit? Where dozens of cities have grown together, is there one city, or many?

In Canada, municipal governments are created by the provinces, which have in turn had to create legal definitions of cities (Tindal and Tindal 1979, 1–18). These definitions are important because, for example, they may determine to which federal and provincial funds a municipality has access—funds for creating and maintaining municipal services and for other important functions that are often arranged through local governments, such as subsidized housing. Different provinces have different definitions that rarely compare well. To deal with this lack of comparability, Statistics Canada has developed concepts that identify populations as urban regardless of whether the places they live in are legally defined as cities.

One concept is the *urban area*, an area with 1000 or more people and a density of 400 or more people per square kilometre (Statistics Canada 1992b). In some parts of the world, agricultural regions might fit such a definition, but urbanism reflects the characteristics of specific societies, and in sparsely populated Canada this definition of "urban" makes sense. Another important concept developed by Statistics Canada is that of the Census Metropolitan Area, or CMA, which is the main labour market of an urban core with a population of at least 100 000 (Statistics Canada 1992b). A CMA includes suburbs and other bedroom communities, and can include rural areas if at least 50 percent of the employed labour force living there works in the urban core. The CMA concept reflects the fact that cities involve more than co-occupancy of a given region—they also involve economic and social interactions that are spatially concentrated and non-agricultural.

Cities are formed in social systems that allow the geographic concentration of wealth and people (Harvey 1976, 195–284). The economies, political systems, and social organization of urban societies all support this concentration. In the past, even in urban societies most people lived in rural areas and were involved primarily in agriculture; it was only with the Industrial Revolution two hundred years ago that the massive urbanization of human populations began. Much of what rural people produce in urban societies goes to support the cities—sometimes through the market and sometimes through taxation or other forms of expropriation—and rural people have usually been subjected to centralized urban-based political power, even if it is mediated through local lords or religious leaders.

Canada, though its relatively small population occupies a huge territory, has one of the most urbanized populations in the world. Canada became predominantly urban (with more than half its population in urban centres) by the 1930s (Burke 1987b, 14). The rate of urbanization has varied greatly among provinces, however; a majority of people in British Columbia and Ontario lived in cities by 1911, while Prince Edward Island was still predominantly rural in 1986 (Burke 1987b, 14). In 1951, the first year the concept of the CMA was used, there were 15 CMAs in Canada, containing about 42 percent of Canada's population. In 1991, there were 25 CMAs, the same number as 1986 (Statistics Canada 1992a), which together contained about 61 percent of the country's population (Statistics Canada 1992b); fourteen of these were in Ontario and Quebec. Over three-quarters of Canada's population in 1991 was urban (Statistics Canada 1992b). Canada's three largest cities—Toronto, Montreal, and Vancouver—contain nearly a third of Canada's population; in 1986, two-thirds of Canada's people lived in the Windsor–Quebec City corridor alone, which includes just 5 percent of Canada's land area (Burke 1987b, 14–15).

Canada's cities, and in particular Canada's larger cities, have long been the destinations of migrants and immigrants. Only about a quarter of people moving within Canada move from urban to rural areas. Most people move from cities to other cities, often from smaller to larger centres. Of the people moving from rural areas, most end up in cities rather than smaller centres—70 percent of rural migrants by the end of the 1970s (Burke 1987b, 14–15). Immigrants from other countries are also attracted primarily to Canada's larger centres. Of all immigrants to Canada between 1981 and 1991 66 percent went to the three largest cities. This pattern was even more pronounced for Asian immigrants, 73 percent of whom went to Toronto, Vancouver, and Montreal (Badets 1993, 10). In 1991, immigrants made up 38 percent of Toronto's population and 30 percent of Vancouver's (Badets 1993, 9).

The processes of urban concentration in Canada have varied over time. Sometimes the largest centres have attracted the greatest growth, sometimes middle-sized cities and suburban or bedroom communities have been the focus of growth (Statistics Canada 1987b). The general trend, however, has been for most Canadians—those born here as well as immigrants—to live in or near the larger urban centres.

Issues of Urbanism

Urbanization does not result in social homogeneity; divisions go up between cities and countryside, as well as within cities. When we talk about urban problems, we most often refer to those that arise from internal divisions. We have become so thoroughly urbanized that few people even know of conflicts between city and countryside. Only occasionally do rural–urban issues come to public consciousness—as when farm communities are disrupted by the demands of urban-based banks, for example, or when provincial legislatures dominated by rural representatives impose particular forms of government on unwilling cities.

Often we define urban problems as those that seem to rise out of urbanism itself. Violence, crime, racial and cultural conflict, housing shortages, and other forms of social dislocation are all associated with the dense, mixed populations of large urban centres. Although such problems also exist in rural areas, we still perceive them to be worse in cities. But if we want to explain all the problems of cities, we must add to these demographic factors an understanding of cities' social organization, which invariably reflects that of the whole society.

Some social theorists argue that urban societies are inherently unequal (Badcock 1984; Childe 1950; Castells 1979, 9–19; Harvey 1976) since the social processes that allow the geographic concentration of people also involve the social concentration of wealth and power. These economic and political inequalities are matched by divisions of age and gender. which seem so natural that we rarely see them as issues. They are, nonetheless, important aspects of city life that have the potential to create problems. The specific forms urban divisions take may vary, but social inequality remains a characteristic of urban society.

Defining Urban Problems

The definition of social problems often depends on the extent to which they are recognized. Homelessness, for example, is not a new phenomenon, but only since the beginning of the 1980s have we come to see it as an important social issue. It wasn't even included in a 1970 survey of urban issues (CMHC 1979). Before the 1970s, urban environmental issues received little attention; people who were concerned about them were often regarded as crackpots, yet the problems themselves were certainly there. The urban problems we recognize are important and need serious consideration, but they often have roots in other, less-visible issues. Any discussion of urban problems must deal both with those issues we recognize and those we do not. We shall begin with a discussion of the problems we recognize.

Problems We Recognize

Crime

Perhaps the one problem that almost everyone would name if asked to make a list of urban problems is crime (CMHC 1979; Hartnagel 1978; Kennedy and Krahn 1983; Merry 1981; Sacco 1981). While we fear such things as pollution and isolation, we tend to fear our fellow humans even more—especially if they are young, male, and from racial or cultural minorities (Merry 1981, 4–10). Forty percent of urban Canadians in a 1981 survey indicated that they felt unsafe in their own neighbourhoods at night (Johnson 1988, 24). We rarely fear hackers breaking into electronic banking systems and taking money from our accounts; unless the sums are large, we may not even be aware that it has happened. Instead, we fear being assaulted by strangers or having our houses broken into. When we talk about urban crime, we usually mean physical attacks by strangers.

To some extent our association of cities and crime is warranted. While there is no simple correlation between city size and violent crime rates, overall the larger cities tend to have higher rates. In 1987, the violent crime rate was highest in the largest cities (250 000 or more people)—933 per 100 000 population; cities with 10 000 to 50 000 people had a rate of 769 per 100 000 (Johnson 1988, 29). Some large cities, however, have violent crime rates lower than those in smaller centres; Calgary, for example, whose population of 647 300 is undergoing the kind of growth and social dislocation that is often supposed to give rise to crime, had a violent crime rate of 571 per 100 000 in 1987, while small, relatively homogeneous Charlottetown, with a population of 15 800, had a rate of 892 (Statistics Canada 1988, 3-1, 3–11). These differences may reflect variations in reporting; in a small centre like Charlottetown, people may be more prone to report crime than they are in larger and more impersonal cities, where many people may perceive police as unfriendly and unco-operative. There are still anomalies, however; Calgary has the lowest violent crime rate of any of the larger cities, but Edmonton, similar to Calgary in many ways, has one of the highest (Johnson 1988, 28).

If we look at overall crime statistics, the picture is even less clear. The largest cities had an overall crime rate of 11 597 per 100 000 people in 1987 (Statistics Canada 1988, 3-1), but smaller cities had a higher rate, with cities of 50 000 to 249 000 people having overall crime rates ranging from 12 660 to 14 924 (Statistics Canada 1988, 3-3). Even the 25 000 to 49 000 group had higher overall crime rates than the largest cities: 12 926 (Statistics Canada 1988, 3-7).

Part of the difference arises from property crimes, which have higher rates in smaller cities of 50 000 to 249 000 people than in the largest cities (Statistics Canada 1988, 3-1 to 3-3). All three of the smaller-sized groups of cities also have higher rates of other crimes, which range from infractions of municipal by-laws to federal drug statutes (Statistics Canada 1988, 3-1 to 3-62). But even the smallest centres included in the crime statistics, those with populations of 100 to 2499, had violent crime rates of 784 per 100 000 in 1987, and overall crime rates of 12 691—higher than the Canadian municipal average of 12 305 and higher than the largest cities (Statistics Canada 1988, 3-1 to 3-62).

Whatever factors contribute to crime, such typically urban conditions as mixed populations, social dislocation, and the presence of strangers can provide only partial explanations. Crime statistics show that the intense, emotionally fraught relationships of family and friendship can be as dangerous as city streets (Merry 1981, 6–7). For women in particular, the family home can be more dangerous than public places. In general, the people most likely to fear street crime—women and the elderly—are the least likely to be its victims; it is young males who both commit crime and fall victim to it (Johnson 1988, 27; Kennedy and Krahn 1983, 12). Such distorted perceptions might arise in part from media coverage of crime news, which can exaggerate the dangers of crime (Graber 1980); they also arise from social structures that condone and even encourage violence in some situations.

Racial Conflict

Images of urban problems are often linked with images of racial conflict. A number of factors combine to make us associate racial issues with urbanism. Immigrant and migrant groups, many of whom are now of non-European origin (White 1986, 16), are concentrated in cities; Canada's Native population has also been undergoing rural-to-urban migration, with more than a third of status Indians now living in cities (Clatworthy and Hull 1983, 4–5; Frideres 1983, 187). Migrant groups may be more likely than the rest of the population to be poor, to have cultural values that differ from dominant ones, and to have visible social and environmental difficulties (Parrish 1986; Winn 1988).

At all levels of government, Canada has multicultural policies whose aim is to provide some kind of recognition to minority groups (Kallen 1988). What this means in practice, however, is unresolved. Governments may be happy to provide funding for ethnic dance groups and once-a-year multicultural festivals, but they may be less happy about having minority groups in city hall. Visible minorities are underrepresented in official organs of government; whether this is the result of differences in education and culture or of discrimination is a much-debated issue. In any case, visible minority groups, increasingly, see having a voice in managing the community as an important social issue.

The different cultural values and practices of some minority groups may also be seen as threatening to social order, especially when the groups form coherent communities. This is one reason we associate racial problems with the large, spatially concentrated minority populations of cities. Urban life can cause problems for those migrants who have not been prepared for it (Clatworthy and Hull 1983, 67–70; Frideres 1983, 199; Parrish 1986). Furthermore, resistance to assimilation can create social conflicts, which are increasingly focussed in cities.

Urban minority populations can be relatively large and sometimes, as in the case of Native people, highly mobile (Clatworthy and Hull 1983, 47–50; Frideres 1983, 195–96). Both these factors make it less likely that informal community structures will be adequate to deal with community difficulties (Frideres 1983, 197–207). In addition, changing political beliefs make it less likely than in earlier eras that minority groups will accept assimilation as the primary solution to social and economic difficulties (Elliott 1979, 1–6). Thus, one aspect of contemporary Canadian urban life is the need for government-funded social support structures to meet the cultural needs and demands of particular groups. Medical and social services are one area where cultural issues can arise. To help avoid problems, hospitals and courts in many Canadian cities now provide cultural training for staff, and translation services for those people dealing with these institutions. Special programs now help Native people deal with the justice system. The particular problems that minority people face in the justice system have been recognized as important issues. In most of the larger cities, various cultural and ethnic groups sponsor education programs for their children, including, in some cases, schools receiving public funding. These structures can be problematic, however, since they may cause resentment among groups that do not have such special programs. Conflict also arises within groups using social services, because community groups sometimes have internal divisions (Nagata 1979; Parrish 1986) and because control of these services may represent control over significant resources.

Urban environments

We see urban environments in two somewhat conflicting ways: as the product of natural forces, and as human creations that we can control and through which we can affect social behaviour. In Canadian cities, these conflicting attitudes toward the urban environment have had important effects. We often assume that the natural forces of the marketplace will result in a livable urban environment and that government intervention should therefore be minimal, and be regulatory rather than direct (Weaver 1984). When these forces fail to create livable urban environments, we often have few resources with which to respond.

Through the 1960s, concepts of urban issues in both Canada and the United States reflected assumptions about the impact of city environments on the social and moral characters of their residents (Jacobs 1961; Rutherford 1984, 437–38; Weaver 1977, 31). It was often assumed that crowded housing and congested streets could lead to the breakdown of social order. The establishment of housing codes, zoning ordinances, and great parks in the larger cities reflected the desire of urban reformers to control the quality of urban life and create better citizens; the spatial segregation of functions was supposed to protect families from exposure to the amoral world of industry and commerce. We still live with the consequences of these values, in cities whose commercial districts are dead outside of business hours and whose residential neighbourhoods offer few opportunities for employment and little convenience in the management of everyday life.

While today we rarely assume that simplistic causes and effects relate the physical environment to behaviour, we still assume some kind of relationship. We talk about design as a solution to some of the social problems of cities (Jacobs 1961, 143–221), especially crime (City of Regina 1983); we have fresh air funds to send poor children to the purity of the countryside; there is still strong resistance to allowing mixed-use land development.

In recent years, concerns about urban environments have changed (Miller and Newman 1988). Scandals raised about the damage to health that results from mismanagement of the environment have made ordinary citizens aware that they are at risk. One of these followed the burning of a warehouse in which PCBs were stored in a residential area in Quebec, contaminating hundreds of houses and forcing the evacuation of hundreds of people for several weeks. A public that has come to perceive such dangers as important has often come into conflict with private industry and public agencies who deny or minimize them.

Environmental problems also arise because urban areas concentrate the production of waste; city air may contain up to 25 times the contaminants found in rural areas (Spirn 1984, 42). A large city can produce hundreds of tonnes a day of carbon monoxide, smoke, toxic chemicals, and everyday household garbage. At the beginning of the 1980s, Toronto alone was producing 274 600 tonnes of solid and liquid waste a year, including organic sludges, oils and greases, and heavy metals (Ontario Waste Management Corporation 1982, 7). Pollutants that aggravate health problems or cause permanent damage to children, such as lead, may be highly concentrated in urban environments. For example, in one Toronto neighbourhood in 1984, 20 percent of the children tested were found to have toxic levels of lead, even though the lead problem had been identified more than ten years earlier and steps had supposedly been taken to correct it (Saskatchewan Council for International Development 1987). The management of waste has become a major problem for municipalities and for senior governments. In the mid-1980s, Ontario had eleven thousand industrial plants dumping wastes into municipal sewage systems, many of which in turn dumped these wastes into water systems that are sources of drinking water downstream (Keating 1986). At the same time, a quarter of Ontario's municipal sewage treatment plants were breaking three of the province's antipollution guidelines, while 64 percent failed to meet guidelines for phosphorus levels (Keating 1986).

Some industries may resist pollution controls as too expensive, even threatening to close down if governments require pollution control. Local communities may become militant about specific pollution issues in spite of the threat of economic loss, but they may not have the political power to effect change. In Canada, it is often provincial and federal governments that must deal with pollution, and the perception that politicians and civil servants at these levels have of problems may be quite different from that of local people who are directly affected. Politicians may be reluctant to impose antipollution regulations, and even when they do, there may not be enough resources to enforce controls effectively. By the end of 1988, some one thousand cases were before the courts under Ontario's strict pollution control laws, but only 50 people were investigating and preparing these cases, and waits of up to eighteen months between the time of an offence and the laying of charges were common (*Leader Post* [Regina] April 17, 1989).

Pollution, like crime, is not just a city problem. Rural and small-town people have problems with water quality that are often worse than those of people in cities, as well as problems with garbage and air pollution. In cities, however, the scale and concentration of these problems is much greater. The built environment of cities can also aggravate pollution problems, since they tend to be more humid, hot, and cloudy than surrounding rural areas, and this can worsen the effects of pollutants (Spirn 1984, 44). Because many of these problems arise from the way we organize our cities, however, it will be difficult to control pollution without making fundamental changes to the physical, economic, and political structures of cities.

Traffic, Pollution, and Quality of Life

One major problem that complicates dealing with urban air pollution is the multitude of unidentifiable sources. Almost the whole population helps create the 50 percent of urban air pollution caused by motor vehicle exhaust in our automobile-dependent cities (Goodall 1992; Spirn 1984, 44). By 1989 there were 16.7 million registered vehicles in Canada, an increase of 26 percent over 1979, and 77 percent of these were passenger cars (Goodall, 22). While Canadian cities are somewhat less decentralized than U.S. cities (Goldberg and Mercer 1986, 151–53), they nonetheless have undergone similar processes of suburbanization and spatial segregation. The low-density city has effects that go beyond those of air pollution. It means that most Canadians have to spend much of their lives journeying to work, school, and the places where they shop, seek medical care, and undertake the other activities of everyday life. Because of low population density, few neighbourhoods hold enough people to support economical alternatives to the private car.

That 80 percent of travel in Canadian cities is by private automobile (CMHC 1987b, 29) reflects both necessity and cultural attitudes. In 1980, only about one-third of Canadians surveyed lived within about three kilometres or less of work, and less than half of the people surveyed felt that public transportation was a real option (Statistics Canada 1982). The average commuting time in Canadian cities was 19 minutes in 1980, but it was 29 minutes for people using public transportation and only 11 minutes for those using private automobiles (Statistics Canada 1982); the extra time is a strong incentive to use private cars. In 1980, 90 percent of people with a choice used private cars rather than public transportation for commuting, a figure that was only slightly lower in the larger cities such as Toronto that have well-developed public transit systems (Statistics Canada 1982).

Where public transit is unavailable or slow and inadequate, individuals have little choice but to use private vehicles for commuting and errands. Yet where large numbers of people commute, public transit can also result in high levels of pollution; the only real solution to the problems of pollution and congestion is to lessen the need to travel. In most cities, however, affordable housing is available primarily in neighbourhoods and suburbs that are distant from places of employment; where inner-city neighbourhoods are improved through gentrification, housing often becomes too expensive for most wage-earners. Although decreasing the need for travel within cities may be the only real solution to the traffic and pollution problems that arise from reliance on motor vehicles, the high cost of physically restructuring our cities puts this kind of solution largely out of reach.

Housing

While much of the poor-quality housing in Canada is rural, we have come to think of housing problems as urban. One reason is that the urban working people who form the bulk of the Canadian population have begun to find it more difficult to buy housing. In the late 1970s and early 1980s, the term "urban housing crisis" meant the squeeze caused by rising interest rates and higher prices, which made it difficult for middle- and working-class people to buy houses or keep up mortgage payments. Younger families who had purchased housing under such government programs as Assisted Home Ownership Program (Rose 1980, 163–79) were particularly affected; when their subsidies ended, many families found that their incomes were not high enough to maintain their mortgage payments, and a number of families lost their houses.

A second reason for our current perception of a housing crisis is the visibility of homeless people in cities. While we do not know how many people are homeless in Canada, we know that demand for space in hostels and other shelters is high. In Toronto alone, between five thousand and fifteen thousand people seek space in shelters or sleep on the street every night, while perhaps a hundred thousand people are at some risk of becoming homeless (O'Connor 1987; Fine 1989b). It is estimated that, in Edmonton, three thousand people now live in temporary accommodations of various sorts, including caves along the river banks (*Leader Post*, August 10, 1987). Across Canada there are as many as a quarter of a million homeless people (McLaughlin 1987, 5).

Homelessness is by no means a new phenomenon, Until recently, however, the homeless were seen as deviants who had no real claim to the sympathy or even the interest of the majority of the population (Dear and Wolch 1987, 30–31). Homelessness was considered a problem chiefly to the extent that rootless populations threatened social order. Attitudes have changed in the past few years. Children are now appearing in shelters for the homeless. As we have begun to see the homeless as victims rather than as deviants, we see them as more deserving of help. It is now common to argue that the primary cause of homelessness is a lack of affordable housing, rather than the personal failures of the homeless (McLaughlin 1987; Halpern 1989, 25–26).

Whatever the levels of real homelessness, a lack of affordable housing is a problem in Canadian cities (CMHC 1987b, 23–25), especially Toronto, where in 1990 the average price of a new house was more than $459 509 (CMHC 1990, 33). Scarcity is also a problem. In 1990, rental vacancy rates in Vancouver and in Toronto and some other Ontario cities were under 1 percent (CMHC 1990, 34). This means that employed young adults in Toronto may be unable to afford housing and still must live with their parents at an age when they would normally expect to be independent (Fine 1989a).

Many of the homeless, however, are people who might have difficulty coping even if a good stock of affordable housing were available. Twenty percent of Canadian shelter users are current or former psychiatric patients, and one-third have problems with alcohol abuse (McLaughlin 1987, 5). Studies in the United States also show that large numbers of the homeless are people with mental disabilities or problems with substance abuse (Dear and Wolch 1987, 175–79; Halpern 1989, 26–27; Kolata 1989). Simply increasing the quantity of housing would not solve the problems these people face.

The Problems of Normality

Even social practices that seem normal to us can create social problems, and this is as true of life in cities as of any other area of social practice. Thus solutions to urban problems can create problems of their own, as can be seen, for example, in the phenomenon of NIMBY, or "Not in my Back Yard." Canadians want solutions to problems of waste management, housing, and other conditions of urban life, but they also want to insulate their own neighbourhoods and their own lives from these problems. People want good, human housing for the poor, the mentally disabled, and others—but not next door. People want well-managed systems for the disposal of wastes—but not down the street. People want to clean up air pollution—but not if it means they can't drive their own cars.

We still hold to the "ideal" of the private city in which different functions are spatially segregated, in which neighbourhoods are as homogeneous as possible, and in which the poor and the miserable are segregated. What Dear and Wolch call "landscapes of despair" are acceptable only at the other end of town.

One of the most important aspects of urbanism is that many urban problems are not the product of abnormality or deviance, but result instead from aspects of life that we take for granted as natural and even healthy. Urban populations are divided by ethnicity and culture, age and gender. These divisions can create differing needs and interests, which can result in social and spatial conflicts (Andrew and Milroy 1988). There are many examples of these conflicts in everyday life. The need for adults to travel to and from work on city streets can conflict with the needs of children for safe outdoor space to play in. The concentration of retail outlets in strip developments and malls means that people who can't drive have no independent access to shops and that parents can't send children to the store on errands. These issues may seem trivial, but they affect the patterns of our daily lives by imposing such needs as private cars, shopping trips, and the constant supervision of children, which might not otherwise exist and which can be a source of stress, vulnerability, and conflict. Some of these problems of normality are outlined here.

Family

Family structures are both natural and problematic in city life. The average household now needs at least two incomes to maintain a reasonable standard of living; over 60 percent of husband–wife families relied on the incomes of both spouses in 1986 (*Globe and Mail* May 13, 1989: D2). A little over 12 percent of families were living below the poverty line in 1986 (National Council of Welfare 1988, 7), while over 50 percent of the heads of poor households were in the labour force (National Council of Welfare 1988, 55). Individuals have little control over the costs of the necessities of life—housing, food, transportation, clothing—and many poor and low-income families spend over 50 percent of their incomes on food and shelter alone (Burke 1987a, 21).

The multiple-income family is socially necessary, but our cities are not set up for it. Residential neighbourhoods where shopping must be done at malls accessible only by car, and where places of employment are distant and are also accessible mainly by car, may work well for families where one adult does nothing but manage the household while another has paid employment. They do not work well where there is only one adult or where adults must combine household management with paid employment, perhaps having to travel in one direction to work, another for errands, and yet another to take care of family-maintenance tasks such as visits to schools.

The changing nature of the family has also led to more and smaller households, which has increased demand for housing (CMHC 1987b, 11; Fine 1989b). The existing private housing market and government programs have not met these expanded needs, particularly those of lower- and lower-middle-income groups. In some cases, government responses to housing problems have made them worse (CMHC 1987b, 49). For example, zoning regulations that restrict neighbourhoods to households composed of related people can keep housing costs higher for individuals by making it difficult for groups of unrelated individuals to share a home (Fine 1989b).

Social Order and Community

In general, we take everyday life for granted, and see its problems as personal rather than social. It is when social relationships involve a threat to social order that we see problems. Drug use, for example, is often tolerated as long as it seems largely restricted to marginal and deviant populations. When drug use extends to the middle class, however, it is seen to threaten social stability; when it arises even in smaller communities that are supposed to be free of urban problems, it becomes a crisis (Mayer 1989).

The issue of social order in cities has been a traditional concern of social theory. The classic formulations of the Chicago School dealt with the question of whether a breakdown of order is inherent in cities (Park 1967). Social researchers of the Chicago School argued that cities developed through natural ecological processes that sorted out the various parts of the population, thus minimizing the stress that is assumed to arise when different groups come into contact (Saunders 1981, 48–79). According to this perspective, while urbanism does break down the kind of order that might characterize traditional rural communities, cities develop their own, more formal, means of social regulation, which replace the more organic order of smaller communities (Wirth 1957). These theories have provided justification for many typical planning and development practices in North American cities, such as the development of specialized neighbourhoods and the use of zoning regulations. This legacy also helped shape community studies that showed that urban dwellers have a capacity to create social order, an idea earlier urban reformers did not share (Suttles 1968).

The Chicago School's concepts of urbanism emphasized orderly ecological processes and minimized concepts of social and political conflict. Urban theories of the 1970s and 1980s have tended to stress not order or the breakdown of order, but the idea of cities as contested terrain in which various groups have different claims upon resources such as space (Castells 1979; Harvey 1976; Saunders 1981). These theories tend to be more concerned with justice, social control, and the inequalities of the marketplace than with order (Badcock 1984; Dear and Wolch 1987; Harvey 1976; Saunders 1981, 219–48); they reveal urban contradictions and conflict in a way that the earlier theories did not. For example, Chicago School theorists argued that minority groups had the ability to create orderly communities, but they did not deal with the threat that such organized minority communities can represent to existing political and social power structures. Thus theorists in this tradition have not been able to explain why it has so often been the well-developed ethnic and working-class neighbourhoods, not the worst neighbourhoods, that are targets of urban renewal. An explanation for this comes only when we recognize that well-organized neighbourhoods represent not only community-based social order but threats to city hall (Caro 1974; Lorimer 1970).

Property and Conflict

Canadian cities are based on private property; about two-thirds of Canada's housing units are privately owned (McLaughlin 1987). Most commercial and industrial land is also privately owned. While private property may be subject to some degree of government control, such control is limited. With the rise of the shopping mall, even the kind of space that was once public—street space— has become private property—mall space—whose owners can restrict access and impose control through the use of private police forces that are often poorly trained and unrestricted.

Although private property is rarely seen as an urban problem, it can be a major source of social conflict. Public control over the quality of housing is difficult to enforce, and property rights may exceed individual political rights. Homeless people have no right to occupy vacant housing, and if they do occupy and improve it, they have no claim on it if the legal owner decides to take it back. In general, Canadian governments support the rights and interests of private property owners; in some cities, property owners still have more voting rights than people who have no property. Both public and personal conflicts can arise over the use of property, especially if the decisions of owners conflict with the needs of the larger community. When communities develop to the point where they can act in their own interests, they may come into conflict with property owners and the governments that support them.

The private housing market has had an important impact on the social structure of Canadian cities. The processes of sorting and segregation of populations may not be natural and ecological, as suggested by the Chicago School, but they do exist. Canadian cities are divided economically, with different socio-economic groups occupying different areas (Goldberg and Mercer 1986, 154–61; McGahan 1986, 154–72); sometimes geographical mobility is so limited that certain neighbourhoods function as ghettos (Clatworthy and Hull 1983, 57–59). Socio-economic status is also associated with other social factors, such as age, gender, and race, and cities are divided along these lines as well. Such factors of socio-economic status as life expectancy, employment, and educational attainment in cities also are expressed spatially through, among other things, the forces of the private housing market.

The housing market creates geographic divisions within cities because groups differ greatly in their ability to pay for housing. The poor are restricted in their choices, and often can find housing only in limited areas, where it is affordable though often of poor quality. Low-income people can rarely buy housing—they must rely on rental housing and private landlords. While every province has some regulations against discrimination, single mothers, visible minorities and other groups still encounter overt and covert restrictions on the housing to which they have access. Social housing may overcome some of these spatial divisions; while the big public housing projects of the major cities testify to earlier ghettoizing of the poor (McMillan 1987), by the 1980s infill projects that scatter social housing through various neighbourhoods had become more accepted. Social housing is limited, however. Of the units built between 1965 and 1986, 52 percent were intended for the elderly; most of the rest was for families, with virtually none for unattached individuals (McLaughlin 1987, 3).

Finding Solutions

As governments and city dwellers know all too well, there are no easy solutions to urban problems. We have invested billions of dollars in the construction of low-density cities that make it almost impossible to find alternatives to the private automobile; we have over 40 years of housing policies that encourage people to speculate in real estate and the housing market and thus undermine the stability of neighbourhoods; we have a political commitment to the rights of property owners that makes it difficult for governments to intervene on behalf of the social good. In addition, there is no general agreement that any of these problems are in fact problems.

Solutions to urban problems must ultimately be social rather than individual because the problems themselves so often result from structural factors in our society rather than from individual failings. It is also true, however, that urban problems cannot disappear without the active participation of city dwellers in identifying and implementing solutions.

Conclusions

Urban problems are real; they are more than just a matter of cultural perception or social definition. How we respond to problems, however, is very much a matter of perception and definition—we tolerate many inconveniences and even conflicts if they arise from conditions that we see as normal. Our definitions of both normality and problems have a profound impact on responses to urbanism. When we define "normal" life as taking place in communities in which social interactions are predictable and stable, then city life, with its anonymity and unpredictability, seems abnormal. Yet we can also define normality as a high level of centralized services and economies of scale, which makes cities the measure of normality. Our attitudes toward cities, their benefits, and their problems are ambivalent.

Cities in Canada, like cities everywhere, reflect the social structures and practices of the society to which they belong. Canada contains a great deal of social diversity and inequality. Men and women fill different social roles and have different social needs, as do adults and children. The population varies greatly by race and ethnic background; values and social structures also reflect regional differences. Canadians are divided as well by the kinds of work they do and by their economic and social power. Needs differ because of the different social roles and cultural practices that characterize the population and the ability of individuals and groups to meet their needs differs with their social power.

Because different groups have different degrees of decision-making power, Canada's cities do not always reflect the diversity of their populations. Usually, a relatively small number of people have the power to make the decisions that affect cities, while other people find themselves coping with problems that they do not have the power to resolve. The major decisions that shape cities tend to reflect the values and needs of the most powerful members of the community, such as large businesses and property owners, while minority groups, children, small businesses, and other less-powerful members of society find that there are few means of meeting their particular needs.

This inequality of power is a major source of urban problems; our cities reflect this in both their physical environments and their social structures. Traditional urban theories tended to see differences in power as natural rather than as problematic, defining the social processes of city life in ecological terms. While these theories contain important insights, particularly in their argument that urban communities have the capacity to create social order, they tend to downplay the importance of social inequality and conflict and the extent to which urban development reflects the decisions of powerful groups.

The large, dense, varied populations that characterize Canadian cities do create problems. Not all people in these cities have the same needs or can benefit equally from given conditions, and population size can be a problem. The wastes produced by millions of people occupying a relatively small area are not easy to handle; getting tens of thousands of people to and from work, school, and leisure activities is difficult; providing adequate housing and social institutions for populations whose family structures, values, and languages vary is more of a problem than providing these things to small, stable, homogeneous populations. Population alone, however, does not create problems. What matters is how we organize our daily lives.

In one sense, urban problems are insoluble: there is no perfect means of creating livable cities. We shall be much closer to solutions, however, if we recognize and respect the capacity of urban communities to create social order, if we move away from economic definitions of efficiency in which property has more rights than people, and if we recognize that while the interests of various groups can differ—even conflict—we must try to manage the urban community to meet those differing needs rather than to deny them. Solutions to urban problems depend on our recognition that problems are real and on our willingness to give people the power and means to find solutions.

Study Questions

1. What is a city?

2. Do cities cause social problems for their residents?

3. What particular urban problems are of most concern to Canadians? Have these changed over time? If so, how and why? What urban problems that you consider important are not discussed in this essay?

4. What kinds of social divisions exist in urban populations? How do these affect the day-to-day lives of urban residents? How do they affect the government and planning of cities?

5. In what ways do cities reflect the social organization and cultural values of the societies that create them?

Recommended Reading

Andrew, Caroline, and Beth Moore Milroy, eds. *Life Spaces: Gender, Household, and Employment*. Vancouver: University of British Columbia Press, 1988.

Dear, Michael J., and Jennifer R. Wolch. *Landscapes of Despair*. Princeton: Princeton University Press, 1987.

Goldberg, Michael A., and John Mercer. *The Myth of the North American City: Continentalism Challenged.* Vancouver: University of British Columbia Press, 1986.

Harvey, David. *Social Justice and the City.* London: Edward Arnold, 1983.

References

Andrew, C., and B.M. Milroy, eds 1988. *Life Space: Gender, Household, and Employment.* Vancouver: University of British Columbia Press.

Badcock, B. 1984. *Unfairly Secured Cities.* Oxford: Basil Blackwell.

Badets, J. 1993. "Canada's Immigrants: Recent Trends." *Canadian Social Trends* 29 (Summer): 8–11.

Burke, M.A. 1987a. "Average Expenditure of Urban Canadians." *Canadian Social Trends* (Summer): 20–21.

———. 1987b. "Urban Canada". *Canadian Social Trends* (Winter).

Caro, R. 1974. *The Power Broker: Robert Moses and The Fall of New York.* New York: Knopf.

Castells, M . 1979. *The Urban Question: A Marxist Approach.* Cambridge: MIT Press.

Central Mortgage and Housing Corporation (CMHC). 1979. *Public Priorities in Urban Canada: A Survey of Community Concerns.* Ottawa: CMHC.

———. 1987a. *Canadian Housing Statistics 1987.* Ottawa: CMHC.

———. 1987b. *Human Settlements in Canada: Trends and Policies, 1981–1986.* Prepared by Rostum. Ottawa: CMHC.

Childe, V.G. 1950. "The Urban Revolution" *Town Planning Review* 21.1 (April): 3–17.

City of Regina Planning Department. 1983. *Designing Crime out of Downtown.* Regina: City of Regina.

Clatworthy, S.J., and J. Hull. 1983. *Native Economic Conditions in Regina and Saskatoon.* Winnipeg: Institute of Urban Studies, University of Winnipeg.

Curtis, J., E. Gable, N. Guppy, and S. Gilbert, eds. 1988. *Social Inequality in Canada: Patterns, Problems, Policies.* Scarborough, ON: Prentice-Hall.

Dear, M.J., and J. Wolch. 1987. *Landscapes of Despair: From Deinstitutionalization to Homelessness.* Princeton: Princeton University Press.

Elliott, J.L. 1979. *Two Nations, Many Cultures: Ethnic Groups in Canada.* Scarborough, ON: Prentice-Hall.

Fine, S. 1989a. "Empty Nest? It's Crowded for Parents in Toronto," *Globe and Mail*, June 8, Al,2.

———. 1989b. "Fractured Families are Forced to Live 'Underground'." *Globe and Mail*, February 4, D2.

French, C. 1989. "Housing: a Slippery Treadmill." *Globe and Mail*, January 28, D5.

Frideres, J.S. 1983. *Native People in Canada: Contemporary Conflicts.* 2d ed. Scarborough, ON: Prentice-Hall.

Gingrich, P. 1984. "Decline of the Family Wage." *Perception* 7.5 (May/August): 15–17.

Goldberg, M.A., and J. Mercer. 1986. *The Myth of the North American City: Continentalism Challenged.* Vancouver: University of British Columbia Press.

Goodall, A. 1992. "Motor Vehicles and Air Pollution." *Canadian Social Trends* 24 (Spring): 21–26.

Gordon, M., and B. Free. 1985. *Alberta's Clean Air Act.* Edmonton: Environmental Council of Alberta.

Graber, D.A. 1980. *Crime News and the Public.* New York: Praeger.

Halpern, S. 1989. "The Rise of the Homeless." *New York Review of Books*, February 16, 24–27.

Hartnagel, T.F. 1978. "The Perception and Fear of Crime: Implications for Neighbourhood Cohesion, Social Activity and Community Affect." *Edmonton Area Series Report No. 5* (February).

Harvey, D. 1976. *Social Justice and The City.* London: Edwin Arnold.

Jacobs, J. 1961. *The Death and Life of the Great American Cities.* New York: Vintage Books.

Johnson, H. 1987. "Homicide in Canada." *Canadian Social Trends* (Winter): 2–6.

———. 1988. "Violent Crime" *Canadian Social Trends* (Summer): 24–29.

Kallen, E. 1988. "Multiculturalism as Ideology, Policy, and Reality." In Curtis et al., *Social Inequality.* 235–47.

Keating, M. 1986. "97 Ontario Firms Violate Guidelines for Water Pollution." *Globe and Mail*, December 24, A9.

Kennedy, L.W., and H. Krahn. 1983. "Rural-Urban Origins and Fear of Crime: the Case for 'Rural Baggage.'" *Edmonton Area Series Report No 28* (July).

Kolata, G. 1989. "Twins of the Street: Homelessness and Addiction" *New York Times*, May 22, A1,10.

Lorimer, J. 1970. *The Real World of City Politics.* Toronto: James Lewis and Samuel.

Mayer, J. 1989. "Spreading Plague: Seaford, Del., Shows How Crack Can Savage Small-Town America" *The Wall Street Journal*, May 4, A1,10.

McGahan, P. 1986. *Urban Sociology in Canada.* Toronto: Butterworths.

McLaughlin, M. 1987. *Homelessness in Canada: The Report of the National Inquiry.* Ottawa: Canadian Council on Social Development.

McLemore, R., C. Aass, and P. Reilhofer. 1975. *The Changing Canadian Inner City.* Ottawa: Ministry of State for Urban Affairs.

McMillan, S. 1987. "Forty Years of Social Housing in Toronto." *Canadian Social Trends* (Winter).

Merry, S. Engle. 1981. *Urban Danger: Life in a Neighbourhood of Strangers.* Philadelphia: Temple University Press.

Miller, D., and K. Newman. 1988. "How Much Do Canadians Care? Lots!" *Globe and Mail*, April 23, D4.

Nagata, J.A. 1979. "One Vine, Many Branches: Internal Differentiation in Canadian Ethnic Groups." In Elliott, *Two Nations*. 173–81.

National Council of Welfare. 1988. *Poverty Profile 1988.* Ottawa: Supply and Services Canada.

O'Connor, K. 1987. "Massive Home-Building Program Said Solution to Housing Crisis" *Leader-Post* (Regina), June 5, A3.

Ontario Waste Management Corporation. 1982. *Waste Quantities Study.* August. Don Mills, ON: Proctor and Redfern Group.

Park, R. 1967. *The City.* Chicago: University of Chicago Press.

Parrish, C. 1986. "Between Two Worlds." In White, *Inside Canada*. 26–28.

Rose, A. 1980. *Canadian Housing Policies, 1935–1980.* Toronto: Butterworths.

Rutherford, P. 1984. "Tomorrow's Metropolis: The Urban Reform Movement in Canada, 1880–1920." In Stelter and Artibise, *the Canadian City.* 435–55.

Sacco, V.F. 1981. "Perceptions of Crime and Anomic Adaptations." *Edmonton Area Series Report No. 34* (October).

Saskatchewan Council for International Development. 1987. *Our Land, Our Cities, Our Future.* Regina, SK.

Saunders, P. 1981. *Social Theory and the Urban Question.* London: Hutchinson.

Spirn, A.W. 1984. *The Granite Garden: Urban Nature and Human Design.* New York: Basic Books.

Statistics Canada. 1982. *Travel to Work, 1976–1980.* Ottawa: Minister of Supply and Services.

———. 1987a. *Census Canada 1986 Reference Dictionary.* Ottawa: Supply and Services Canada.

———. 1987b. *Urban Growth in Canada.* Ottawa: Supply and Services Canada.

———. 1988. *Canadian Crime Statistics 1987.* Ottawa: Canadian Centre for Justice Studies.

———. 1992a. *Census Geography: A Historical Comparison.* Ottawa: Supply and Services Canada.

———. 1992b. *Urban Areas: Population and Dwelling Counts.* Ottawa: Supply and Services Canada.

———. 1992c. *Profile of Census Metropolitan Areas and Census Agglomerations*, Part A. Ottawa: Supply and Services Canada.

Stelter, G.A., and A.F.J. Artibise. 1984. *The Canadian City: Essays in Urban and Social History.* Ottawa: Carleton University Press.

Suttles, G.D. 1968. *The Social Order of the Slum.* Chicago: University of Chicago Press.

Tindal, C.R., and S.N. Tindal. 1979. *Local Government in Canada.* Toronto: McGraw-Hill Ryerson.

Weaver, J. . 1954. "'Tomorrow's Metropolis' Revisited: A Critical Assessment of Urban Reform in Canada, 1890–1920." In Stelter and Artibise, *The Canadian City.* 456–77.

———. 1977. *Shaping the Canadian City: Essays on Urban Politics and Policy, 1890–1920.* Toronto: Institute of Public Administration of Canada Monograph No. 1.

White, C.A. 1986. *Inside Canada and the World.* (Toronto: Maclean Hunter) 52, no. 4.

Winn, C.1988. "The Socio-Economic Attainment of Visible Minorities: Facts and Policy Implications." In Curtis et al., eds. *Social Inequality.* Scarborough: Prentice-Hall. 195–213.

Wirth, L. 1957. "Urbanism as a Way of Life" *American Journal of Sociology* 44 (July 1938). Reprinted in *Cities and Society*, ed. P.K. Hatt and A.J. Reiss. New York: The Free Press, 1957.

World Commission on Environment and Development. 1987. *Our Common Future.* London: Oxford University Press.

CHAPTER 19

Rural Issues and Problems

B. Singh Bolaria, Harley D. Dickinson, and Terry Wotherspoon

Learning Objectives

This chapter discusses the consequences for the rural environment, and for rural communities and the people who live in them, of the capitalization and mechanization of agriculture, intensive farming, and the use of fertilizers, pesticides, and herbicides. These developments have affected the rural way of life: rural communities and services are in decline and the family farm is threatened. They have brought soil erosion and degradation of the rural environment, and adverse health effects to farmers and farm workers from the use of hazardous chemicals. Farm debts, market uncertainties, and the threat of bankruptcies and foreclosures contribute to stress and psychological ill health of the rural population, which, in addition, has comparatively poor access to health services and educational opportunities. Students are encouraged to consider the contradictions that arise from the impact of the capitalization and mechanization of agriculture on the rural way of life, the family farm, and the rural environment.

Introduction

While urban issues and problems have been the subject of study by sociologists, demographers, urban planners, and others, the study of rural life has received relatively little attention for a number of years. This is partly because urbanism and the urban way of life came to be identified with social disorganization, conflict, deviance, and personal and social pathologies. Rural and farm life, on the other hand, were seen as free of all these issues and problems. Even today, many people continue to have an idyllic image of rural life. Reality, however, is contrary to this image.

Capitalism and mechanization, along with intensive farming and the use of fertilizers, pesticides, and herbicides, have all contributed to increased production and efficiency in agriculture. This structural transformation of agricultural production has concomitant consequences for the rural population, rural communities, and the rural way of life. Rural depopulation and declining rural communities and rural services have come to be recognized as problems in Canada. There is considerable inequality in the availability of and accessibility to medical care and educational opportunities for rural residents. Additionally, increasing competition in world agriculture commodity markets and the cost–price squeeze pose threats to the very survival of the "family farm." Many farmers and their family members are forced into off-farm labour to avoid foreclosures and bankruptcies.

Then there are the contradictions between agricultural productivity and environmental responsibility. While the use of chemicals has substantially increased agricultural productivity, it has also led to the degradation of the rural environment. This poses a threat to the health status of the farmers and farm workers, and when some of these chemicals end up in the food chain, they threaten the health of the whole population.

Structural transformation of agricultural production has produced a number of social and economic contradictions. These contradictions and other recent issues and problems are discussed in this chapter.

Contradictions in Canadian Agriculture

Although Canada's land mass is approximately 2.28 billion acres, only about 5 percent is suitable for agricultural purposes. The value of agricultural production accounted for about 2 percent of Gross Domestic Product (GDP) in 1992, and the food processing industry contributed a further 1.8 percent (Statistics Canada 1994, 2). Despite the small proportion of GDP accounted for by agriculture, international trade in agricultural commodities remains an important source of income for Canada. In 1992, for example, the value of farm export was $12.1 billion (Statistics Canada 1994, 3). It is difficult to talk about agriculture in general terms, however, because it is not a homogeneous industry. This complex and varied industry involves the production, processing, and sale of various beverages and foods, including fruits and vegetables, poultry, eggs, dairy products, beef cattle, pigs, cash crops such as lentils and soy beans, wheat, and other grains. The type of agriculture dominant in any given region, depends, of course, on soil and climatic conditions. In addition, and more importantly for present purposes, various social, economic, and political factors also influence the nature and organization of agriculture. One often-noted feature that seems to be characteristic of all types of agricultural production is the trend toward a decreasing number of increasingly large farms, or *production units* (see Figure 1). The precipitous decline in the number of farms and the associated disruption in farm and rural ways of life is increasingly referred to as a crisis.

The "cost–price squeeze" is the most common explanation for this crisis. The cost–price squeeze refers to a situation where the cost of producing a commodity exceeds the price received for its sale. Although we cannot examine in detail the reasons for the existence of the cost–price squeeze here, existing research indicates that it is related to the ways in which agricultural policy has created a structured dependence of farmers on banks and other financial institutions, various agricultural input industries (farm machinery, fertilizers, etc.), and food processing and retailing industries (Fowke 1978a, 1978b; Winson 1988).

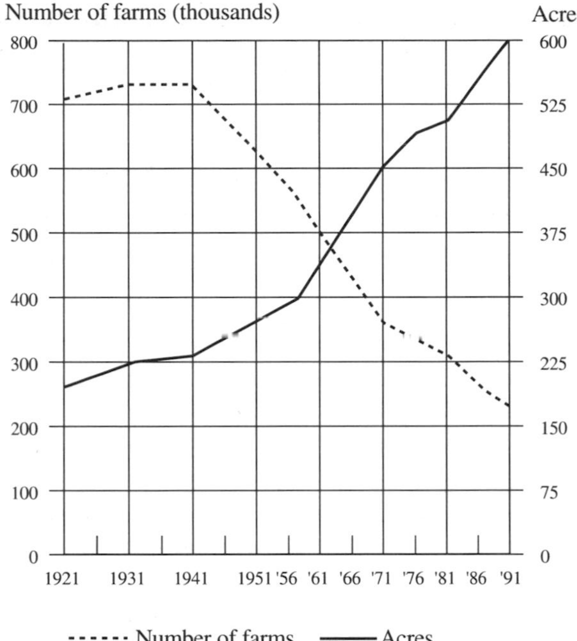

FIGURE 19.1: Number and Size (Acreage) of Farms, 1921–1991
Number of farms (thousands)

Sources: Statistics Canada, *Farming Facts*, Cat. no. C521-522-1987E (Ottawa: Minister of Supply and Services, 1988), p. 3; Statistics Canada, *Farming Facts 1992*, Cat. no. 21-522E (Ottawa: Minister of Supply and Services, 1993), p. 4. Reproduced by authority of the Minister of Industry, 1994.

Whatever the explanation for the existence of the cost–price squeeze and the farm crisis, the decrease in the total number of farms in Canada corresponds to an increase in the size of the average farm, which in turn tends to be related to a shift from labour-intensive to capital-intensive forms of production. Capital-intensive production generally corresponds to the use of more and bigger machinery, as well as various forms of chemical inputs, such as fertilizers, insecticides, herbicides, and other pesticides intended to increase productivity. Another significant factor contributing to increased productivity in many branches of agriculture is developments in plant and animal genetic research. An Agriculture Canada report (1989, 10) notes that between 1961 and 1984 overall agricultural productivity almost doubled as a result of these changes.

Table 1 shows total capital value of farms in Canada for selected years between 1971 and 1991. As we can see, during that time period there were dramatic increases in the total capital value of farms. Between 1981 and 1986, however, the total capital value declined. Most of the decline in farm capital value in the 1980s is accounted for by decreasing land values. By 1991, land values had begun to increase and the total capital slightly surpassed 1981 levels. Between 1971 and

TABLE 19.1: Total Capital Value of Farms, Canada, Selected Years, 1971–1991

	1971	1976	1981	1986	1991
			(millions of dollars)		
Total capital value	24 066	57 055	130 304	109 676	131 210
Value of land and buildings	16 936	43 556	103 275	80 088	96 742
Value of machinery and equipment	3 909	9 034	17 444	20 766	23 292
Value of livestock and poultry	3 221	4 465	9 585	8 822	11 176

Source: Statistics Canada, *Agricultural Profile of Canada, Part 2,* Cat. no. 93-351 (Ottawa: Minister of Supply and Services, 1992), Table 19. Reproduced by authority of the Minister of Industry, 1994.

1991, the reported area fertilized increased from about 17.1 million to 58.5 million acres, of which 53.3 million acres were treated with commercial fertilizers and 5.3 million acres treated with manure in 1991; the reported area sprayed for insects and disease increased from 2.3 to 6.9 million acres, a decline from 11.3 million acres reported in 1986; and the reported area sprayed for weeds and brush increased from about 21.2 to 53.4 million acres, a drop of 3.3 million acres from the amount sprayed in 1986 (Statistics Canada 1992, Tables 13.1 and 13.2). This suggests that the quantity and value of these chemical inputs also rose steadily. Thus, the decline in total capital value of farms is not indicative of declining use of machinery or other inputs such as chemical fertilizers and pesticides.

The development of capital intensive farming has resulted in dramatic declines in the number and proportion of people who make their living directly from agriculture. In 1931, the farm population was about 31.7 percent of the total Canadian population. By 1991 the farm population had declined to about only 3.2 percent of the total population. It is interesting to note that although the number of farmers is decreasing, the number of women farmers is increasing. In 1991 one quarter of Canadian farm operators were female (Statistics Canada 1992).

Table 19.2 shows rural and urban populations of Canada by number of persons and as a proportion of total population between 1871 and 1991. The rural population in Table 19.2 includes both rural farm dwellers and non-farm dwellers. Both the number and proportion of farm dwellers has decreased over time, while rural non-farm dwellers have increased slowly and steadily in terms of numbers, but decreased substantially as a proportion of the total population. Of the approximately 6 390 000 persons living in rural areas in 1991, for example, only 807 325 resided on farms (Statistics Canada, 1993, 4).

The number of urban dwellers has increased in terms of numbers and proportion of the total population. One of the consequences of this increase in the size of the urban population has been an expansion in the proportion of the land dedicated to

TABLE 19.2: Rural and Urban Populations of Canada by Number (000s) and Percentage, 1871–1991

Census year	CANADA		RURAL		URBAN	
	Number	Percentage	Number	Percentage	Number	Percentage
1871	3 689.9	100	2 966.9	80.4	722.3	19.6
1881	4 324.8	100	3 215.3	74.3	1 109.5	25.7
1891	4 833.2	100	3 296.1	68.2	1 537.1	31.8
1901	5 371.3	100	3 357.1	62.5	2 014.2	37.5
1911	7 106.6	100	3 933.7	54.6	3 272.9	45.4
1921	8 787.9	100	4 435.8	50.5	4 352.1	49.5
1931	10 376.8	100	4 804.7	46.3	5 572.1	53.7
1941	11 506.7	100	5 254.2	45.7	6 252.4	54.3
1951	14 009.4	100	5 381.2	38.4	8 628.3	61.6
1961	18 238.3	100	5 537.5	30.4	12 700.4	69.6
1971	21 568.3	100	5 157.5	23.9	16 410.8	76.1
1981	24 343.2	100	5 907.3	24.3	18 435.9	75.7
1991	27 296.8	100	6 389.9	23.4	20 906.9	76.6

Sources: Statistics Canada, *Census of Canada 1981: Urban Growth in Canada*, Cat. no. 99-942 (Ottawa: Minister of Supply and Services, 1984); Statistics Canada, *Profile of Urban and Rural areas - Part A, Canada, Provinces, and Territories*, Cat. no. 93-339 (Ottawa: Minister of Supply and Services, 1993), Table 1. Reproduced by authority of the Minister of Industry, 1994.

urban use. Approximately 100 000 hectares, or 1000 square kilometres, of rural land was converted to urban use between 1976 and 1981. In some areas prime farmland is being lost to urban expansion: "In Ontario the loss represented four percent of all prime farmland" (Environment Canada 1986, 10). In order simply to maintain current levels of agricultural production, agricultural producers will have to be more productive. In most cases this will be achieved by increasing the use of the productivity-enhancing capital inputs already mentioned. Increased agricultural productivity and reduced costs per unit of food, as we shall see below, have a number of costs. These costs are borne by farmers, farm workers and their families, rural residents in general in the form of their declining quality of life, and ultimately by us all in the form of environmental degradation and pollution.

Farm Debt and the Crisis in Agriculture

At the end of 1992, farm debt in Canada was $23.8 billion, 4 percent more than farmers owed five years earlier (Statistics Canada 1994, 4). Much of this debt was incurred by farmers attempting to buy more land in order to become more efficient. The purchase of farm machinery and of sufficient quantities of farmland to enable the machinery to be economically used, in addition to the purchase of related inputs such as chemical fertilizers and pesticides, has resulted in a crushing debt load.

Many farmers, particularly those who entered the industry since the 1970s, have seen their survival threatened by debt, especially during periods of declining prices and land values. The report of the House of Commons Standing Committee on Agriculture (1988) noted in 1985 that despite the high debt load, two-thirds of Canadian farmers were financially secure; one-third, however, were "experiencing rising levels of financial stress in spite of massive government assistance. Close to one-half of this latter group carried 56% of the .. total debt" (cited in National Farmers' Union 1989, 3)

One obvious consequence of the high levels of debt is the inability of farmers to remain profitable. This in turn contributes to bankruptcy and foreclosures. A survey of the three Prairie provinces by the National Farmers' Union (NFU) (1989, 4) estimated that "over the past 10 years ... thousands of farm families have been dispossessed." The NFU report dramatizes the situation in the following terms: "The process of farm depopulation has been silently undermining rural communities similar[ly] to the manner in which a cancer can slowly and silently but certainly break down the human system." The process of rural depopulation, according to the National Farmers' Union (1989, 8), is amplified by the increase in corporate ownership of foreclosed farm lands; revenues generated by these farming operations are more likely to be channelled out of local economies and communities which threatens these communities' future viability.

The National Farmers' Union (1989, 6) also estimates that, in the Prairie region, 1.5 million acres of farmland "may be under direct title to financial creditors." This is estimated to range from just under I percent in Alberta, through 1.77 percent in Saskatchewan, to about 2.34 percent in Manitoba. The National Farmers' Union report also suggests three reasons why these figures may actually underrepresent the extent of the transfer in ownership. A number of foreclosures are still in process or imminent, previously foreclosed lands have already been resold by the financial institution; and local municipal administrators who were interviewed claimed that, in some cases, creditors have permitted title to remain in the hands of the farmer even though the farmer's real status has become that of tenant (1989, 7). This seems to suggest that agriculture in the Prairie region may be characterized by the transformation of independent into dependent commodity producers in a manner similar to other regions and other branches of agriculture and primary food production (Winson 1988; Clement 1984).

Developments like those described above may or may not be a first step toward the proletarianization of farmers, that is, the transformation of farmers into wage employees of corporate-owned capitalist farms (Ghorayshi 1987). What is clear is that structural changes in agriculture are affecting patterns of farm work and farm family life not only for farm owner-operators and their families, as we have seen above, but also for non-owner, agricultural wage labourers.

Agriculture and the Environment

Prevailing cultivation practices, the use of new, high-yield breeds of plants, and increased use of various productivity-enhancing mechanical and chemical inputs in agriculture are all contributing to soil deterioration. This deterioration is seen in the form of the loss of organic matter in the soil, its reduced nutrient content, and its acidification, salinization, and erosion. Research shows a reduction of organic material from Prairie soils of about 40 percent since the land was first cultivated (Environment Canada 1986, 4). The reduction is related to a number of factors, including prevailing cultivation practices and the increased nutrient requirements of some new, high-yield breeds of plants. Lower levels of organic matter in the soil necessitate increased use of chemical fertilizers, particularly nitrogenous fertilizers, in order to maintain and increase productivity levels. In 1960, "crops obtained more of their nutrients from the native soil than from chemical fertilizers. By 1980, however, the situation had been reversed in all provinces except Saskatchewan and Alberta" (Environment Canada 1986, 4).

If, as these findings imply, soil nutrient levels are declining and given that new, high-yield breeds of plants require more nutrients from the soil, one might expect that Canadian agriculture will become increasingly reliant on chemical fertilizers. Some research shows that chemical fertilizers themselves contribute to soil deterioration in the form of increased acidification, which limits the productive capacity of the soil (Environment Canada 1986, 4). As much as 60 percent of the increase in soil acidity in eastern Canada in recent years has been attributed to the use of nitrogenous fertilizers (Environment Canada 1986, 5). This results in the contradictory situation wherein the use of chemical fertilizers intended to increase soil productivity contributes to soil degradation and a reduced productive capacity.

In addition to these sources of soil deterioration, prevailing cultivation practices, especially limited crop rotation and wide row planting, contribute to soil erosion. Environment Canada (1986, 5) reports that the annual value of soil loss through erosion in Canada is $1.2 billion. To offset this loss and the potential decline in soil productivity associated with the erosion of topsoil, once again farmers increase their use of fertilizer. Intensive irrigation also is thought to contribute to soil deterioration in the form of salinization. Eitzen and Zinn (1989, 94), drawing on a 1980 report by the U.S. State Department and the Council on Environmental Quality, reports that continued deterioration of agricultural soils is to be expected throughout the rest of the century: "Each year, the area of cropland and grassland becoming barren wasteland is equal in size to the state of Maine."

Thus, farmers find themselves in the contradictory situation of trying to increase agricultural output in the face both of the cost–price squeeze and environmental deterioration in ways that are themselves potentially destructive of the environment and its capacity to sustain life. This contradiction is commented on in part by an Environment Canada (1986, 5) report, which states that "economic pressures can force farmers to increase production at the expense of the long-term sustainability of the agricultural ecosystem."

The long-term sustainability of the environment is not the only concern. Prevailing farming practices have immediate health and safety consequences, not only for farmers and farm workers but for the population as a whole. The introduction of agricultural chemicals, additives used in the food processing industries, and other industrial and military toxins into the food chain and water supply have reached crisis proportions (Harding 1988). The presence of pesticides such as Temik (used to control potato bugs) in drinking water is associated with higher numbers of miscarriages and increased rates of stomach cancer (cited in Freudenberg 1989, 114). Other pesticides end up in our bodies through the food we eat. Fruits, vegetables, and meat and dairy products contain residues of toxic chemicals, as illustrated by concerns about the use of Alar as a ripening agent on apples—associated with cancer and nerve damage in children. Several chemicals are known to damage livers, kidneys, and the immune and nervous systems, or are associated with cancers, sterility, and other ill effects (Chase et al. 1973; Epstein 1979; Freudenberg 1989, 114; Kahn 1976; Milvey and Wharton, 1980).

Agriculture and Farm Health and Safety

In addition to the health and safety concerns mentioned above, increased use of productivity-enhancing technologies in agriculture results in the intensification of agricultural work processes. The intensification of farm work, especially in association with the use of machinery, has contributed to agriculture's being ranked second or third, behind mining and construction, in terms of the likelihood of being killed on the job. Although legislation has improved the safety of many other forms of work, the situation in agriculture has been getting worse, with the rates of farm-work related injuries and deaths both increasing (Sandborn 1986).

Farm-related accidents undoubtedly leave many rural residents to some degree disabled. The *Report of the Canadian Health and Disability Survey, 1983–1984* (Statistics Canada 1986b) indicated that a greater percentage of the rural population than of the urban population reported some disability. In this survey, respondents were categorized as "disabled" if they reported that over a period of at least six months they had "troubles performing any one of 17 activities of daily living (e.g., walking up and down a flight of stairs), or if they experienced a limitation in the kind or amount of activity they could perform at home, work, or school because of a long-term physical condition or health problem, or if they had a mental handicap" (Statistics Canada 1986b,10). The reported disability status in rural and special areas was 15 percent, compared to 11.9 percent in urban areas—that is, in towns of 15 000 or more population. Although these differential percentages, reflect, in part, the fact that the average age of rural residents is higher than that of urban residents, the observed differences are characteristic of all age groups. This suggests that the percentage of disabled rural residents is in fact higher than the percentage of disabled urban residents (Statistics Canada 1986b).

The higher rate of reported disability in rural areas may be related to the fact that farming is such a hazardous occupation. It may also be related to the relative lack of service and facilities, such as special housing, elevators, and ramps, that enable urban dwellers to perform the tasks of daily living. More people living in rural areas may be considered disabled because of the lack of services and facilities that are more readily available to urban dwellers. We shall return to the issue of availability of and accessibility to rural services.

Stress is another increasingly common consequence of the nature and contradictions of contemporary farming practice. High interest rates, increasing input costs, and decreasing commodity prices contribute to making agriculture an extremely stressful occupation. Added to these are the uncertainty of both weather and government subsidies and support. This stress spills over into all aspects of farm life, because most farms remain family operations, which to a greater or lesser extent rely on paid or unpaid family labour. It affects relations between husbands and wives, and between parents and children. The stress associated with farming and rural life is often manifested in psychological problems, alcohol and drug abuse, family violence, and a range of psychosomatic and physiological health problems (Gordon 1988).

In some cases, the stress of farm life is exacerbated by the need for off-farm employment in order to keep the farm going. Since the Second World War a growing proportion of the total income of farm families has been derived from off-farm employment. The proportion of farm operators in Canada who reported "some days of off-farm work" has increased. In 1990, 37 percent of all Canadian farmers reported off-farm work. This included 108 760 male farmers and 36 245 female farmers. Of those, 58 percent of the males, and 49 percent of the females (62 885 and 17 775 persons respectively), reported 190 or more days off-farm work in the past year (Statistics Canada 1992, 33).

Numerous studies indicate that farmers, farm workers, and their families have a high incidence of work-related accidents and fatalities and experience poor health status, which is reflected in such indicators as life expectancy and mortality (Rust 1990; Coye 1985; Sakala 1987; Campbell 1986; Canadian Centre for Occupational Health and Safety 1986; Cliff 1981; Dosman 1985). A number of factors contribute to this ill health: farm machinery, chemicals, intensification of farm work, ramshackle housing, low wages, non-existent sanitation facilities, and long hours of arduous labour.

Many of the accidents, fatalities, and health hazards in agriculture are associated with farm machinery. About half of all farm injuries are machinery related (Simpson 1984). Tractors are most frequently involved in farm injuries and, along with grain augers and power takeoffs, account for many severe and disabling injuries, involving crush and compound fractures and amputations (Simpson 1984). The intensification of farm work in association with farm machinery has increased the likelihood of being killed on the job (Sandborn 1986; Ministry of Agriculture 1985). One area that has received considerable attention is noise-induced hearing loss and speech-hearing difficulty with continuous and prolonged exposure to noise (Dennis 1969; Pierce et al. 1985; Alberta Agriculture 1982). While improved mufflers and soundproof cabs alleviate noise hazards to some extent in tractors, much self-propelled farm equipment lacks adequately sound-insulated cabs.

Farm machinery and farm work pose other hazards to farmers and farm workers. Farm accidents claim somewhere between 150 to 200 lives in Canada every year (Robertson 1984). A report of 23 farm fatalities in Alberta revealed that about 65 percent involved machinery, 91 percent of the victims were males, and the majority of these were over the age of 45 years. All of these accidents occurred during work, and the majority of the victims were working alone. Most of the victims died as a result of loss of blood or suffocation after the accidents. Many factors account for these fatalities. As the report states: "Most of the farm deaths involve the victim doing something they already knew was unsafe but due to fatigue, haste, stress, age and poor attitude they did it anyway" (Alberta Agriculture 1983). There are numerous non-fatal farm accidents that lead to severe and permanent injuries and, in some cases, amputation. As discussed later in this article, farm accidents also involve children, leading to deaths or serious injuries every year (Alberta Agriculture 1983; Ontario Ministry of Agriculture 1985).

In any discussion of the health risks in agricultural production, the chemical industry occupies a central place. There has been a tremendous increase in the use of chemicals in agriculture (Bird and Rapport 1986). While these chemicals control pests such as insects and weeds, they also pose environmental hazards. As Bird and Rapport (1986, 174) state: "Some of these pesticides are known to be highly persistent, mobile and bio-accumulative and have already been associated with adverse ecological or human health effects." The human cost of the use of agricultural chemicals has been severe. It is estimated that each year they are responsible for the deaths of 10 000 and the acute poisoning of 400 000 people in the Third World (Rogers et al. 1988, 284). These health hazards are not confined to the Third World. Agricultural workers in Canada and the United States face extensive chemical exposure and associated health risks (Matsqui, Abbotsford Community Services 1982; Stringini 1982; Stubbs et al. 1984; Barthel 1981). A study of 488 farmers in Alberta indicated that 10 percent of them had suffered symptoms of pesticide poisoning during the survey year (Hussain 1983). The study also reported that within the previous five years, 26 percent of the sample had experienced some poisoning and 3 percent reported chronic health problems related to pesticides. The 10-percent-a-year pesticide-poisoning amounts to a very large number of farmers at risk (Hussain 1983; Moore 1984). It amounts to approximately 5000 farmers in Alberta (Hussain 1983) and over 7000 in Saskatchewan (Moore 1984).

Direct exposure to chemicals has quite serious health consequences for farm workers. Since the use of many chemicals in agricultural production is relatively new, the long-term consequences are only just beginning to appear. The link between pesticides and cancer has received the most attention (Burmeister 1985; Gallagher et al. 1985; Harding 1988; Barthel 1981; Mills et al. 1984). Other long-term ailments associated with chemicals include birth defects, neurological disorders, reproductive disorders, and sterility (Chase et al. 1973; Epstein 1979; Freudenberg 1989; Kahn 1976; Milvey and Wharton 1980; Bull 1982).

The deplorable working conditions of both the domestic transient farm labourers and the migrant imported workers are well documented (Sanderson 1974; Labonte 1980, 1982; Sandborn 1983, 1986; Canada Department of Manpower and Immigration 1973; Report of the Special Committee on Visible Minorities in Canadian Society 1984; Sharma 1983; Kelly 1983; B.C. Human Rights Commission 1983). Workers and their families are often exposed to harmful substances on farms. There is inadequate or non-existent enforcement of the Health Act Regulations, in addition to physical danger, occupational diseases, pesticides, and a high risk of injury. Also, farm workers are not fully or adequately protected by minimum-wage legislation, working-hour limits, or overtime wages (Report of the Special Committee on Visible Minorities in Canadian Society 1984). Both the living and working conditions of farm labour contribute to their ill health. A federal task force report in 1973 on seasonal migrant farm workers uncovered instances of "child labour, sick, pregnant, and otherwise unfit adults working in the fields; and of entire families working with only the head of the family being paid" (Sanderson 1974, 405). The task force was "shocked, alarmed, and sickened" at the working conditions, wage levels, malnutrition, nonexistent health facilities, and people living in "indescribable squalor" (Canada, Department of Manpower and Immigration 1973, 17; Sanderson 1974).

The working and living conditions of farm workers in British Columbia are similar to those faced by minority workers in Ontario. They receive low wages; face exploitation as a result of the labour contracting system, long hours of work, no overtime pay or benefits, unhealthy working conditions, lack of toilet or drinking water facilities on many farms, and crowded and dangerous shacks. As well, they are exposed to chemicals and pesticides in the field (Sharma 1983; Canadian Farmworkers' Union 1980; Labonte 1980, 1982–83; Kelly 1983).

The entire family works and "lives" in the fields. Because of poor sanitation and hygiene facilities and poor water supply, farm workers have a very high incidence of infectious diseases and diseases linked to fecal contamination (Arbab and Weidner 1986). Lack of proper toilet facilities may affect the female workers more seriously than other farm labour. For instance, among women, high rates of urinary infections are often associated with prolonged retention of urine (Jasso and Mazorra 1984). The need for toilet facilities was highlighted in evidence presented to a tribunal investigating such facilities for field workers. In her statement, a worker indicated that "whenever there is a ditch or woods nearby, we go there. When this does not exist, we just have to wait. Or otherwise a group of us get together and stand around the person and cover him or her up" (Jasso and Mazorra 1984, 90).

Because of the lack of day-care facilities for the children of mothers who are forced to work to support their families, several incidents of drowning have been reported (Sharma 1982; Sharma 1983). The coroner's jury, which, in August 1980, investigated the death of a child who rolled off a bunk and drowned in the water bucket, recommended that immediate steps be taken to establish standards for farm labour housing. The irony is that even the existing standards established in 1946 are not being enforced (B.C. Human Rights Commission 1983).

Since young children are an important source of farm labour, they are subject to occupational injury and health risks. Some U.S. estimates indicate that children 15 years of age or younger suffer 14 to 24 percent of all fatal injuries on farms (Field and Purschwitz 1987). It is also estimated that persons 19 years of age and younger are involved annually in 300 injury deaths (Rivara 1985), and that this group also accounts for 29 percent of fatal injuries involving tractors (Karlson and Noren 1979). Other studies also report that, primarily due to their involvement with farm machinery, minors suffer from many severe work-related injuries (Cogbill et al. 1985; Salmi et al. 1989; Swanson et al. 1987). A study of children of migrant agricultural workers in Wisconsin concluded: "Our analysis of preventive medical care, morbidity, and mortality among children of migrant workers supports the view that this group is at substantially greater risk of health problems and early mortality than the general population" (Slesinger, Christenson, and Cautley 1986, 72). A more recent study of minors involved in farm work, covering the period 1986–89 in Washington State, concluded that "farm work is dangerous for young children" (Heyer et al. 1992, 557).

A few incidents that occurred in British Columbia (Canada) and Washington State (United States) during the past few years illustrate the continuous health risks and mortality faced by children:

1. In 1988, Binh Thanh Hoang, 9, is left alone in a parked car on a Matsqui, B.C., farm, where his mother is picking raspberries. He is killed when the car rolls down an embankment.
2. In September of that year, Joel Campos, 14, is cutting vines in a hops field in Moxee, Washington. He falls asleep in a furrow and is crushed to death by a truck.
3. Dina Pedro, 7, drowns in an uncovered and unfenced tank of pesticide on a Saanich, B.C., farm.
4. A child under 10 is killed crossing a road to work in a Washington State asparagus field.
5. Gurjit Pejatta, 8, his brother, Sumin, 9, and Boota Bassi, 10, all drown in a pond in Aldergrove, B.C., in 1980. The parents are picking berries at a nearby farm. A few miles further up the Fraser Valley, an infant, Sukhdeep Madhar, rolls off a cot in a farm-worker cabin and drowns in a bucket of water. (MacQueen, 1990, p. B1).

It is evident from the above discussion that numerous factors contribute to rural environmental degradation and adverse health effects for farmers, farm workers, and their families. Ironically, while the producers and workers are indispensable for the production of fruit, vegetables, and other food commodities that are essential for a nation's health and nutrition, they themselves suffer from a vast range of work-related health risks. This portrayal of the rural environment and way of life is quite contrary to the idyllic image of rural Canada still held by many people.

Rural Poverty, Living Conditions, and Services

Rural life in Canada encompasses wide extremes of wealth and living standards. Given the disparity of rural settings and socio-economic conditions, it is not useful to think in terms of a "typical" rural lifestyle. In 1992, for example, 32 percent of Canada's 1.7 million rural households had incomes of under \$25 000, while 25 percent had incomes of \$55 000 and over (Statistics Canada 1994a, 84–85). These income distributions are not surprising given that the population officially defined as rural ranges from small communities of luxury properties near major metropolitan areas to substantial corporate farming operations, small family farms, and isolated pockets of poverty.

As previously indicated, rural Canada is in the midst of a major transformation as cities and urban fringes expand outward into surrounding areas, and farms and farm communities disappear. What this trend means is that individuals and families in more isolated rural settings frequently are faced with a continuous struggle for both their own daily sustenance and the survival of their communities. Rural areas that are dependent on primary industries such as farming, fishing, mining, and logging are highly susceptible to seasonal employment patterns and volatile market fluctuations, which can jeopardize the economic survival of a community or region. Under such conditions, individuals are often forced or motivated to leave the area, usually for cities or larger centres that provide employment and educational and social opportunities. Those who leave are predominantly the young people who are skilled, educated, and active in community and social affairs. This process is part of the vicious cycle, most evident in Atlantic Canada, the West, and northern regions, in which the loss of active community members entails both a transfer of investment in education, job training, and human services from rural to urban areas, and the depletion of a base of human and economic resources that are necessary to revive depressed areas (Adams et al. 1971, 64–65). At the same time, however, there is a parallel process of redevelopment and redefinition of communities in rural areas as people struggle to develop effective strategies to meet the challenges and changing profile of rural life.

Poverty, for example, is generally regarded as an urban issue. While rural people tend to have lower incomes than those in urban areas (1991 census data reveal a median family income level of just under $40 000 for rural families compared to a national level of nearly $45 000), rural areas, compared to cities, experience relatively fewer incidences of poverty and have lower proportions of low-income families (Statistics Canada 1994b, 16). Using data for 1990, the National Council of Welfare (1992, 40) estimates that 9.1 percent of rural families, and 22.8 percent of individuals living in rural areas had incomes below the poverty line, compared to figures of 14.6 percent for families and 36.7 percent for individuals living in Canada's largest cities. Nonetheless, the application of a higher low-income cut-off rate for urban areas because of the differences in costs of living can sometimes obscure the depth and experience of poverty in rural areas. While 10.7 percent of total income for urban residents in 1991 was provided through government transfer payments such as welfare and unemployment insurance, for instance, the corresponding figure was 14.2 percent for rural residents (Statistics Canada 1994b, 14).

One of the major consequences of the transfer of population and resources from rural areas is the intensified development of "pockets of poverty." An American study has defined these as areas characterized by high rates of unemployment and social assistance, low educational levels, and high proportions of minority populations including African-Americans, Hispanics, Native people, and female-headed families, people who frequently have been the targets of discrimination (Weinberg 1987). These characteristics are also found in many regions across Canada, represented especially in the conditions prevalent on many status Indian reserve lands, with about 95 percent of the on-reserve Native population located in rural areas. Analysis of 1986 census data revealed that nearly one-half (47.2 percent) of Native families living on-reserve were classified below the poverty line (Oberle 1993, 5).

Rural residents in Canada often have few opportunities for employment and social mobility, and are further limited by lack of community services and alternatives. In the face of rising housing costs, for example, the rural poor have little access to subsidized housing or other adequate accommodation arrangements (Canadian Council on Social Development 1981, 76). There continue to be strong disparities in housing conditions between rural and urban areas. While one in fourteen homes occupied in 1991 by urban Canadians required major repairs in order to meet basic accommodation standards, the figure for rural areas was just over one in eight; 80 percent of homes occupied by rural people had central oil, gas, or electrical heating compared to 95 percent for the total population; and 1.1 percent of households in rural areas, compared to an overall national rate of 0.5 percent, lived in dwellings without bath facilities (Statistics Canada 1993, 28, 84). Housing and living conditions tend to be most severe for minority groups that experience a combination of discrimination and social dislocation. On Canada's Native reserves, just under 10 percent of dwellings lacked an adequate water supply and 20 percent did not have adequate sewage disposal as recently as 1992 (Indian and Northern Affairs Canada 1992, 63). Reports of substandard housing, inadequate levels of employment and wages, and extreme impoverishment are also common for other groups such as West Indian and Asian agricultural workers in British Columbia and Ontario (Bolaria and Li 1988).

Poverty and related social problems are often exacerbated in rural areas because of isolation and the diffusion of resources. Poverty and the consequences of social disarray in rural areas remain mostly hidden phenomena, which do not receive the same degree of attention as they do in urban areas where supportive organizations, facilities and programs such as food banks, and community aid groups are concentrated.

The stagnation and decline of the rural population, which is related to the nature and organization of agriculture, undermines the ability of those who remain to finance and staff the infrastructures and services required by the community. Many rural towns and villages have disappeared. Although the proportion of the total Canadian population living in rural areas as non-farmers has stabilized at about 20 percent over the past ten years, their earlier decline in numbers was accompanied by decreasing political influence. As they continue to lose political influence they are likely to become increasingly disempowered in the pursuit of their interests. This may undermine their ability to secure the passage of legislation and the implementation of policies to facilitate their continued survival.

Rural Health Care

The well-known inability of rural communities to recruit and retain physicians is related to their lack of cultural and social amenities as well as to the lack of adequate hospital facilities. These, in turn, derive from the inability of a declining rural population—or their declining economic base—to support services and amenities. The decline of the small rural hospital may be a case in point. A recent survey of 500 people who live in the small towns and rural areas served by three Saskatchewan hospitals found that over 92 percent reported that the existence of a hospital was an important factor when people were deciding whether or not to live in a small rural community after retirement. About 64 percent of those surveyed reported that people would move out of their community if the local hospital were closed. (Dickinson and Andre 1989). Despite these sentiments, in recent years governments have facilitated the closure of small rural hospitals and the expansion of larger urban hospitals.

The province of British Columbia has attempted to remedy the maldistribution of physicians by withholding medicare billing numbers from newly graduated physicians unless they agreed to set up practice in underserviced rural areas. Another strategy used to solve the doctor shortage in rural areas has been to allow foreign trained doctors into the country on the condition that they practise in rural areas. These doctors are mostly on temporary employment visas. It is recognized that in the foreseeable future the needs of underserviced areas will continue to be met by foreign physicians working on visas (Bolaria 1992). Practices such as these, although better than nothing, are little more than band-aid solutions. They do little to solve the problems of maldistribution of health care and medical services. This may be a reflection of the decreasing political significance of rural dwellers. If this is the case, the legitimacy of the claim that all Canadians are equal is fundamentally threatened.

Rural Education

The image of schooling in rural settings has a strong appeal for many. As with common notions of rural life in general, the sense of relative independence and challenge, community cohesiveness, closeness to the natural environment, and a view that "small is better" are cited frequently by educators as major advantages of rural schooling (see, e.g., Haughey and Murphy 1983). Despite these idyllic images, however, there are pronounced disparities between rural and urban school systems in educational attainment, organization, and activities. In particular, rural schools are beset by recurrent problems associated with instability, insecurity, and lack of resources.

Overall, urban populations have higher levels of educational attainment than do rural ones. The 1991 census revealed that 18.2 percent of Canada's rural population, compared to 12.6 percent of the urban population, had less than Grade 9 education, while the proportion of the urban population that had at least some university education (23.0 percent) was substantially higher than the corresponding figure for rural areas (13.2 percent) (derived from Statistics Canada 1994b, 10). These trends are not surprising given an aging rural population and the relative concentration in cities of jobs and services that require educational credentials, and of institutions that offer postsecondary education. Research findings indicate little significant difference between rural and urban students in intelligence, school achievement, and basic skill development when factors such as gender, age, and parental occupation and income are taken into account (Debertin, Clouser, and Huie 1986; Ryan, Sackney, and Birnie 1981). Nonetheless, rural residence, combined with lower socio-economic status levels, is associated with both lower educational aspirations and lower levels of attainment for rural youth in comparison to urban youth (Anisef et al. 1984, 103–104; Porter, Porter, and Blishen 1982, 67–69).

Rural students face several critical barriers in education. Two major problems experienced by rural schools throughout North America, especially in smaller and isolated centres, are restricted program offerings and less-qualified teachers (Debertin, Clouser, and Huie 1986). In Saskatchewan, for example, Ryan, Sackney, and Birnie (1981) observed in the early 1980s that high schools that had fewer than 150 students (nearly all these schools were rural) offered an average of 33 credit courses, while high schools with over 900 students (all urban) offered on average

110 credits. Because of the need to concentrate resources and to ensure that students are provided with the necessary prerequisites for postsecondary studies, the smaller schools are most likely to offer academic courses in a few core areas. As rural residents often complain, however, such courses are oriented to urban life and to those students who will be leaving the rural setting, despite the fact that most rural students do not require advanced academic credentials for their expected life activities (Saskatchewan Education 1981, 32). In the context of these conditions, it is perhaps not surprising that rural students are reported to be more likely than urban students to leave school before high school graduation and, among those who do leave, to leave earlier. According to data from a recent national survey, for instance, 42 percent of those who left school in rural areas, left school prior to the completion of Grade 10, compared to 29 percent of those in urban areas. (Government of Canada 1993, 22).

Problems in curriculum and school programs are experienced most intensely by students in isolated settings or economically depressed areas, where there appears to be little relevance in the education system, and therefore little opportunity for advancement. The most pronounced problems associated with education in rural areas are evident in, though not restricted to, the experiences of aboriginal peoples (Satzewich and Wotherspoon 1993, 144–45). In 1986, among the adult population not attending school full-time, about 37 percent of Canada's aboriginal people and 45 percent of on-reserve, status Indians (of whom 95 percent live in rural areas) had less than Grade 9 education, compared to fewer than 17 percent of the non-aboriginal population (Larocque and Gauvin 1989). However, problems related to isolation and rural schooling are not confined to Canada's aboriginal people. Nagy, Drost, and Banfield (1985), for example, report that in a survey of Grade 6 students in Newfoundland, rural conditions adversely affected school achievement when combined with isolation and poor socio-economic conditions. In more general terns, poverty and disadvantage are associated with an increased likelihood that individuals will experience such problems as inadequate housing, discrimination, malnutrition, and health concerns, all of which restrict opportunities for educational and occupational success (Gilbert and Orok 1993, 4).

The combined effects of poor facilities, inadequate resources, a limited tax base, isolation, insecure socio-economic conditions, and poorly prepared teachers often mean that basic survival prevails over careful planning in educational programs. Sackney (1983) observes that the consequence of sustained crisis conditions in many rural school districts, along with intensified local competition over the fear of having to close a local school, are conservatism, efficiency measures, and loss of innovative staff. While the consolidation of small rural schools, districts, and tax bases—a trend that began in the 1940s—has meant that rural school districts tend to have larger, more stable programs and facilities than in the past, problems of rural population loss and increasing educational centralization still threaten the closure of many rural schools. This threat is likely to continue, especially with a renewed reliance on local funds for school expenditures. The proportion of total education expenditures in Canada that originated at the municipal level has increased steadily from 15.2 percent in 1982–83 to an estimated 20.3 percent in 1993-94 (Statistics Canada 1987; 1993). As ability to raise funds locally becomes more crucial to the maintenance of school operations, schools in smaller and poorer rural districts are likely to face further setbacks in their struggle to provide adequate staff and programs. Ultimately, they face a threat to their survival through a mutually reinforcing series of contradictions. Diminishing resources force rural schools to neglect local concerns so that they can offer programs that cater to students who must leave the area in order to continue with their studies and find work for which they are qualified. At the same time, however, rural students are often discouraged from continuing their studies because of either a lack of curricular relevance or the high costs of leaving home to pursue advanced education.

Rural Crime

Contrary to common media images and policy orientations that emphasize crime in cities, crime is not a uniquely urban problem. Criminal Code offence rates are generally lower for rural areas than for urban areas, particularly for property crimes. Nonetheless, overall official rates of offences are often higher in rural areas and small cities than in Canada's largest cities, with reported figures for 1987 of 12 691 offences per 100 000 people in areas with populations of 100 to 2499, compared to 11 597 crimes per 100 000 people in cities with populations of at least 250 000 (Statistics Canada 1988). The one category of offences for which rates are predominantly higher in rural areas and smaller centres is violations of provincial statutes, most frequently for Liquor Act offences.

Within these general trends exist strong regional variations in reported crime rates. While overall crime rates and property crime rates are generally higher in city areas, in some provinces, such as Newfoundland and Alberta, rates of violent crimes are higher in smaller centres and rural areas. A closer examination reveals even more prominent variations in crime rates. Data from 1988 reveal that many rural and isolated communities have significantly higher crime rates than the national averages of 920 violent crimes and 6606 property crimes per 100 000 people. Tracadie, New Brunswick, for example, has a violent crime rate of 2708 and property crime rate of 6958; Fort Qu'Appelle, Saskatchewan, has a violent crime rate of 2579 and a property crime rate of 11 474; and Lac La Biche, Alberta, has a rate of 4538 violent crimes and 15 077 property crimes per 100 000 (Statistics Canada 1988). Such figures are an indication of a national tendency for crime rates to rise from east to west and south to north across Canada, or in other words, to be highest in areas that have higher proportions of isolated populations.

It is important to recognize that these figures are based on official crime statistics, which must be interpreted with caution. Studies of victimization, such as the Canadian Urban Victimization Survey conducted in 1982, report that over half of all crimes involving victims are not reported to police. Nearly two-thirds of incidents of assault go unreported, as do over 70 percent of incidents of personal theft (Griffiths and Verdun-Jones 1989, 82–88). Unfortunately, few comparative studies have been undertaken to examine victimization in rural areas. However, there is some indication that large proportions of rural crimes also are not officially reported to police. Researchers such as Lee (1982) observe that rural residents, especially on farms, have a higher general fear of crime than do urban residents; this is consistent with accounts that elderly farm populations report a higher incidence of victimization among friends and relatives than city residents. Kennedy and Krahn (1986) report the effects of "rural baggage" in which city residents with rural backgrounds, especially among older populations, feel less safe than those with urban backgrounds. In other words, while rural crime rates generally are lower than urban crime rates, there are variations in the extent and perception of crime in rural areas. Factors like social and geographic isolation increase both the real and potential negative consequences of rural crime.

One factor that accounts for variable crime rates, and in particular the tendency of rural areas to have lower property crime rates than cities, is what some criminologists call "environmental opportunities" (Engstad 1980). Property offence rates can be expected to be higher in areas that have a concentration of facilities such as businesses, hotels, and shopping centres, which serve as targets of theft and other crimes. In other words, rural property crime rates may be lower than urban rates not necessarily because of any inherent differences between urban and rural ways of life, but rather because there are relatively fewer opportunities for crime to take place in rural settings. Moreover, since populations and facilities are often spread across a wide area in agricultural and isolated rural areas, police surveillance becomes more difficult with the consequence that actions or offences that may be detected and recorded as crimes in cities are not reported in rural areas. At the same time, however, there is evidence to suggest that police in rural areas follow through on charges more systematically than their counterparts in cities. Boydell (1985) reports that rural areas have a much higher proportion than do urban areas of eases proceeding to court charges and convictions following arrest. This result is consistent with research findings that indicate that, with respect to sentencing and other procedures, criminal justice system operations in rural areas tend to be more arbitrary and discriminatory, especially toward Native people, than in urban areas (Hagan 1977).

As Hagan's research reveals, the phenomenon of rural crime is most problematic for Canada's aboriginal population. Native people are overrepresented throughout the criminal justice system. On reserves and in northern communities, police activities tend to be concerned with social rather than legal matters, resulting in some of the extremely high reported crime rates illustrated above (Griffiths and Verdun-Jones 1989, 554; Satzewich and Wotherspoon 1993, 201–03). Moreover, as represented in the high rural rates of provincial statutory infractions, aboriginal people tend to be arrested and incarcerated for less-serious offences, such as motor vehicle infractions, defaulting on fines, and most significantly alcohol-related offences (Verdun-Jones and Muirhead 1982, 267–74). The incidence and processing of rural crime, especially as reflected in relatively high rates of alcohol-related and violent crimes, indicate the strong degree of social disorganization and the poor living conditions that characterize rural life in many regions, especially for dispossessed segments of the population (Hartnagel 1987, 91).

A less-commonly recognized, but nonetheless important, dimension of rural crime is corporate crime. Like street crime and other violations of the law, illegal practices engaged in by businesses in the conduct of their operations tend to be viewed as urban phenomena. However, especially as the scale of farming and agribusiness increases and industrial firms expand their operations beyond urbanized areas, both the direct and indirect impact of corporate crimes on rural areas is growing. Violations of environmental, labour, and combines legislation, irregularities in the banking and financial sector, and farming and business practices that contribute to environmental pollution and other health and safety risks (see, e.g., McMullen 1992; Snider 1993) compound the problems that characterize rural life.

Conclusions

Although the number of farms and farmers continues to decrease, agriculture remains an important industry in Canada, accounting for about $12.1 billion in export sales in 1991. Crises in the agricultural sector, therefore, have significant implications not only for provinces and regions where agriculture is the predominant industry, but also for the Canadian economy. Consequently, agricultural and rural issues are important areas of study. The structural transformation of agriculture in the past few decades has produced social and economic contradictions that, along with related issues and problems, have been the focus of analysis in this chapter.

Capitalization, mechanization, and use of yield-enhancing technologies and chemicals have contributed to increased production and efficiency in agriculture. This has been accompanied by a decrease in the total number of farms, a corresponding increase in the size of the average farm holding, and rural depopulation.

Intensive farming and use of chemicals have led to a decline in soil quality and soil erosion. Agricultural land has been lost to urbanization. Other contradictions between productivity and the quality of the rural environment have emerged. While the use of chemicals has substantially increased productivity, it has also led to degradation of the environment. This has adverse consequences for the health of farmers and farm workers and has contaminated food, especially fruit and vegetable crops.

Rural depopulation has led to a decline in rural communities and rural services. The evidence presented here shows considerable inequality in the availability and accessibility of health services and educational opportunities for rural residents relative to urban dwellers.

Increasing competition in world markets for agricultural products and the cost–price squeeze pose threats to the very survival of the "family farm." This has forced many farmers and family members into off-farm work.

Agricultural labour is one of the most exploited segments of the working class. Where agricultural production is still labour-intensive, as in fruit and vegetable farming, this labour pool is primarily composed of racial minority workers. The survival of the small farms and the profits of the larger units depend on the availability of this labour. In addition to farm workers, other segments of the rural population (notably Native people) live in poverty. Poor housing is widespread. Rural crime is another problem deserving further study.

It is possible that the contradictions noted here may become even sharper in the agricultural sector under the North American Free Trade Agreement. Rather than opening new markets for agricultural products, the agreement threatens Canada's farm marketing boards with elimination because some of their practices "inhibit and distort" trade. Abolition of farm subsidies and tax rebates for gasoline and diesel fuel, an increase in grain freight rates, and the elimination of Canada's farm marketing boards would make it even more difficult for many farmers to survive. Under these conditions, many politicians and business groups are beginning to question the need to maintain anything but the most competitive farm operations under the argument that the "open market" should prevail. As farm residents become more dependent on off-farm work, and rural services further deteriorate in many regions, the extremes in rural conditions—represented by large agribusiness operations or luxury properties on the one hand and isolated pockets of poverty on the other—are likely to intensify.

Study Questions

1. If various attempts to increase productivity in the agricultural sector reduce the ability of the ecosystem to produce sufficient quantities of high-quality, safe, affordable food, what new agricultural policy initiatives should be taken to counter this tendency?

2. Despite some evidence that indicates the existence of a greater need for health care services in rural areas as compared to urban areas, fewer services are available. Why? What, if anything, can be done to create a more rational and equitable distribution of health care resources between urban and rural areas?

3. The paper argues that there is a basic contradiction between profits and labour costs. Discuss how this contradiction is manifested in the agricultural sector with respect to wage levels, working conditions, and health and safety standards.

4. Discuss why, despite the proliferation of poverty, crime, illness, lack of services, and poor working conditions in many rural areas, policy-makers tend to ignore rural problems.

5. Is there a distinct "rural" way of life? Discuss the relationship between rural issues and general social problems.

Recommended Reading

Basran, G.S. "The Rural Depopulation of the Prairies." In *Economy, Class, and Social Reality*, ed. John A. Fry. Toronto: Butterworths, 1979. 391–410.

Basran, G.S., and D.A. Hay, eds. *The Political Economy of Agriculture in Western Canada*. Toronto: Garamond Press, and Social Research Unit, 1988.

Bronson, Harold. "Multinational Corporations and Canadian Food Policy. In *Economy, Class, and Social Reality*, ed. John A. Fly. Toronto: Butterworths, 1979. 364–90.

Buttell, Fred, and Howard Newley, eds. *The Rural Sociologies of Advanced Societies: Critical Perspectives.* Montclair, NJ: Alanheld-Osmun, 1980.

Dillman, Don A., and Daryl J. Hobbs, eds. *Rural Society in the U.S.: Issues for the 1980s*. Boulder, CO: Westview Press, 1982.

Kent, George. *The Political Economy of Hunger*. New York: Praeger, 1984.

Murdoch, William W. *The Poverty of Nations: The Political Economy of Hunger and Population*. Baltimore: Johns Hopkins University Press, 1980.

Pugh, Terry, ed. *Fighting the Farm Crisis*. Saskatoon: Fifth House, 1987.

References

Adams, I., W. Cameron, B. Hill, and P. Prenz. 1971. *The Real Poverty Report*. Edmonton: Hurtig.

Agriculture Canada. 1989. *Growing Together: A Vision for Canada's Agri-Food Industry*. Ottawa: Supply and Services Canada.

Alberta Agriculture. 1982. *Safety Guide for Farming*. Edmonton.

———. 1983. *A Manager's Guide to Farm Safety*. Edmonton.

Anisef, P., M.-A. Bertrand, U. Hortian, and C. E. James. 1984. *Accessibility to Postsecondary Education in Canada: A Review of the Literature*. Ottawa: Department of the Secretary of State of Canada.

Arbab, D.M., B.L. Weidner. 1986. "Infectious Diseases and Field Water Supply and Sanitation Among Migrant Farm Workers." *American Journal of Public Health* 76, no. 6: 694–95.

Barthel, E. 1981. Increased Risk of Lung Cancer in Pesticide-Exposed Male Agricultural Workers." *Journal of Toxicology and Environmental Health* 8:1027–40.

Bird, P.M., and D.J. Rapport. 1986. *State of Environment Report for Canada*. Ottawa: Supply and Services Canada.

Bolaria, B.S. 1992. "From Immigrant Settlers to Migrant Transients: Foreign Professionals in Canada." In *Deconstructing a Nation: Immigration Multiculturalism and Racism in '90s Canada*, ed. Vic Satzewich. Halifax, N.S.: Fernwood Publishing. 211–28.

Bolaria, B.S., and P.S. Li. 1988. *Racial Oppression in Canada*. 2d ed. Toronto: Garamond Press.

Bollman, R.D., and P. Smith.1988. "Integration of Canadian Farm and Off-Farm Markets and the Off-Farm Work of Farm Women, Men, and Children." In *The Political Economy of Agriculture in Western Canada*, ed. G.S. Basran, and D.A. Hay. Toronto and Saskatoon: Garamond Press and Social Research Unit, Department of Sociology, University of Saskatchewan. 185–202.

Boydell, C.L. 1985. "Rural Justice: A Systems Analysis of Property Offences." *Canadian Journal of Criminology* 27, no. 3 (July): 289–97.

British Columbia Human Rights Commission. 1983. *What This Country Did to Us. It Did to Itself.* Report of the BC Human Rights Commission on Farmworkers and Domestic Workers. February.

Bull, D. 1982. *A Growing Problem: Pesticides and the Third World Poor*. Oxford: Oxfam.

Burawoy, M. 1976. "The Functions and Reproduction of Migrant Labour: Comparative Material from Southern Africa and the United States." *American Journal of Sociology* 81 (March): 1050–87.

Burmeister, L.F. 1985. "Cancer Mortality in Iowa Farmers." In *Health and Safety in Agriculture*, ed. J. Dosman. Saskatoon: University of Saskatchewan.

Campbell, I. 1986. "Health and Safety on the Farm." *At the Centre* 9, no. 3: 1, 5, 7.

Canada, Department of Manpower and Immigration. 1973. "The Seasonal Farm Labour Situation in Southwestern Ontario." Mimeograph.

Canada Employment and Immigration Commission. 1981. "Commonwealth Caribbean and Mexican Seasonal Agricultural Workers Program: Review of 1979 Payroll Records." Hull, PQ: Labour Market Planning and Adjustment Branch. Mimeographed.

Canadian Centre for Occupational Health and Safety. 1986. "Occupational Health and Safety in Agriculture." *At the Centre* 9, no. 3.

Canadian Council on Social Development. 1981. *Social Policy for the Eighties*. Ottawa: Canadian Council on Social Development.

Canadian Farmworkers' Union. 1980. *Support British Columbia Farm Workers*. Vancouver, B.C.

Chase, H.P., S. Barnett, N. Welch, F. Briese, and M. Krossner.1973. "Pesticides and U.S. Farm Labour Families." *Rocky Mountain Medical Journal* 70: 27–31.

Clement, W. 1984. "Canada's Coastal Fisheries: Formation of Unions, Cooperatives, and Associations." *Journal of Canadian Studies* 19, no. 1.

Cliff, K.S. 1981. "Agriculture: The Occupational Hazards." *Public Health* 95: 15–27.

Cogbill, T.H., H.M. Busch, and G.R. Stiers. 1985. "Farm Accidents in Children." *Pediatrics* 83: 267–71.

Coye, M.J. 1985. "The Health Effect of Agricultural Production: The Health of Agricultural Workers." *Journal of Public Health Policy* (September): 349–70.

Debertin, D.L., R.L. Clouser, and J.M. Huie. 1986. "Rural Poverty, Funding for Education and Public Policy." *The Policy Studies Journal* 15.2 (December): 327–38.

Denis, W.B. 1988. "Causes of Health and Safety Hazards in Canadian Agriculture." *International Journal of Health Services* 18, no. 3:419–36.

Dennis, C.A.R. 1969. *A Survey of the Hearing Levels of Saskatchewan Farmers.* Regina: Department of Public Health, Occupational Health Branch.

Department of Manpower and Immigration. 1973. "The Seasonal Farm Labour Situation in Southwestern Ontario: A Report." Mimeographed.

Dickinson, H.D., and G. Andre. 1989. *Rural Hospitals, Health Care Policy, and Public Opinions: Report of a Survey*. Saskatoon, SK: Sisters of St. Elizabeth.

Dickinson, H.D., and D.A. Hay. 1988. "The Structure and Cost of Health Care in Canada." In *Sociology of Health Care in Canada,* eds. B.S. Bolaria and H.D. Dickinson. Toronto: Harcourt Brace Jovanovich. 51–73.

Dickinson, H.D., P.S. Li, and W. Denis. 1988. "Respiratory Disease in Saskatchewan: Some Social and Regional Variations." In *The Political Economy of Agriculture in Western Canada*, ed. G.S. Basran and D.A. Hay. Toronto and Saskatoon: Garamond Press and Social Research Unit, Department of Sociology, University of Saskatchewan. 125–32.

Dosman, J., ed. 1985. *Health and Safety in Agriculture. Conference proceedings.* Saskatoon: University of Saskatchewan.

Doyal, L., and I. Pennell. 1979. The Political Economy of Health. London: Pluto Press.

Eitzen, D.S., and M.B. Zinn. 1989. *Social Problems*. 4th ed. Boston: Allyn and Bacon.

Engstad, P.A. 1980. "Environmental Opportunities and the Ecology of Crime." In *Crime in Canadian Society*, ed. R.A. Silverman and J.J. Teevan, Jr. 2d ed. Toronto: Butterworths, 203–19.

Environment Canada. 1986. *Canada's Environment: An Overview*. Ottawa: Supply and Services Canada.

Epstein, S. 1979. *The Politics of Cancer*. Garden City, NY: Anchor Books.

Eyer, J. 1984. "Capitalism, Health, and Illness." In *Issues in the Political Economy of Health Care*, ed. J.B. McKinley. New York: Tavistock Publications.

Field, W.E. and M.A. Purschwitz. 1987. "Cost of Farm and Rural Injuries. *Public Health Reports*, 102, (6), 642–44.

Fowke, V.C. 1978a. *Canadian Agricultural Policy: The Historical Pattern*. Toronto: University of Toronto Press.

———. 1978b. *The National Policy and the Wheat Economy*. Toronto: University of Toronto Press.

Freudenberg, N. 1989. "The Corporate Assault on Health." In *Perspectives in Medical Sociology*, ed. P. Brown. Belmont, CA: Wadsworth.

Gallagher, R.F., et al. 1985. "Cancer in Farmers and Farm Labourers in British Columbia." In *Health and Safety in Agriculture*, ed. J. Dosman. Conference proceedings. Saskatoon: University of Saskatchewan.

George, A. 1976. *Occupational Hazards to Women*. Ottawa: Advisory Council on the Status of Women. October.

Ghorayshi, P. 1987. "Canadian Agriculture: Capitalist or Petit Bourgeois?" *Canadian Review of Sociology and Anthropology* 24, no. 3: 358–73.

Gilbert, S. and B. Orok. 1993. "School Leavers." *Canadian Social Trends* 30 (Autumn), 2–7.

Goff, C.H., and C.E. Reasons. 1986. "Organizational Crimes Against Employees, Consumers and the Public." *The Political Economy of Crime*, ed. B. D. MacLean. Scarborough, ON: Prentice-Hall. 204–13.

Gordon, E. 1988. "Stress in the Farm Family: Implications for the Rural Human Service Worker." In *The Political Economy of Agriculture in Western Canada*, ed. G.S. Basran and D.A. Hay. Toronto and Saskatoon: Garamond Press and Social Research Unit, Department of Sociology, University of Saskatchewan. 143–51.

Government of Canada. 1993. *Leaving School: Results From a National Survey Comparing School Leavers and High School Graduates 18 to 20 Years of Age.* Ottawa: Supply and Services Canada.

Griffiths, C.T., and S.N. Verdun-Jones. 1989. *Canadian Criminal Justice.* Toronto: Butterworths.

Hagan, J. 1977. "Criminal Justice in Rural and Urban Communities: A Study of the Bureaucratization of Justice." *Social Forces* 55: 620–37.

Harding, J. 1988. "Environmental Degradation and Rising Cancer Rates: Exploring the Links in Canada." In *Sociology of Health Care in Canada*, ed. B.S. Bolaria and H.D. Dickinson. Toronto: Harcourt Brace Jovanovich. 411–25.

Hartnagel, T.F. 1987. "Correlates of Criminal Behaviour." *Criminology: A Canadian Perspective*, ed. Rick Linden. Toronto: Holt, Rinehart and Winston. 74–101.

Haughey, M.L., and P.J. Murphy. 1983. "What Rural Teachers Think of their Jobs." *Canadian School Executive* 2, no. 8 (Fall): 12–14.

Heyer, N.J., G. Franklin, F.P. Rivara, P. Parker and J.A. Haug. 1992. "Occupational Injuries Among Minors Doing Farm Work in Washington State: 1986 to 1989." *American Journal of Public Health* 82: 557–60.

Hussain, M. 1983. *Pesticide Safety Survey.* Edmonton: Alberta Agriculture.

Indian and Northern Affairs Canada. 1992. *Basic Departmental Data, 1992.* Ottawa: Supply and Services Canada.

Jasso, S., and M. Mazorra. 1984. "Following the Harvest: The Health Hazards of Migrant and Seasonal Farmworking Women." In *Double Exposure: Women's Health Hazards on the Job and at Home*, ed. W. Charkin. New York: Monthly Review Press.

Kahn, E. 1976. "Pesticide Related Illness in California Farm Workers." *Journal of Occupational Medicine* 18: 693–96.

Karlson, T., and J. Noren. 1979. "Farm Tractor Fatalities: The Failure of Voluntary Safety Standards." *American Journal of Public Health* 69:146–49.

Kelly, R. 1983. "Bitter Harvest." *New West Review* (November).

Kennedy, L.W., and H. Krahn. 1986. "Rural-Urban Origin and Fear of Crime: The Case for 'Rural Baggage'." In *Crime in Canadian Society*, ed. R.A. Silverman and J.J. Teevan, Jr. 3d ed Toronto: Butterworths, 283–91.

Labonte, R. 1980. "The Plight of the Farmworkers." *Vancouver Sun*, August 25.

———. 1982. "Racism and Labour: The Struggle of British Columbia's Farmworkers." *Canadian Forum* (June/July).

Lee, G.R. 1982. "Residential Location and Fear of Crime Among the Elderly." *Rural Sociology* 47, no. 4 (Winter): 665–69.

MacQueen, K. 1990. "Slim Pickings." *Vancouver Sun*, September 22, B1.

Matsqui, Abbotsford Community Services. 1982. "Agricultural Pesticide and Health Survey Results." Project of the Matsqui, Abbotsford Community Services. October, Abbotsford, British Columbia.

McMullan, J.L. 1992. *Beyond the Limits of the Law: Corporate Crime and Law and Order.* Halifax: Fernwood Books.

Mills, P.K., G.R. Newell, and D.E. Johnson. 1984. "Testicular Cancer Associated With Employment in Agriculture and Oil and Natural Gas Extraction." *Lancet* 1:207–10.

Milvey, T.H., and D. Wharton. 1980. "Epidemiological Assessment of Occupationally Related, Chemically Induced Sperm Count Suppression." *Journal of Occupational Medicine* 22: 77–82.

Mitchell, R. 1989. *Canada's Population from Ocean to Ocean.* Ottawa: Supply and Services Canada.

Moore, A. 184. "Study Shows at Least 7000 Farmers Poisoned by Pesticides Last Year." *Commonwealth* (March 15).

Nagy, P., D. Drost, and H. Banfield. 1985. "A Path Analytic Study of the Influence of Community Isolation on Student Achievement." *Alberta Journal of Educational Research* 31, no. 3 (Summer): 209–27.

National Council of Welfare. 1992. *Poverty Profile, 1980–1990.* Ottawa: Supply and Services Canada.

National Farmers' Union (NFLD). 1989. *Statement on the Subject of the Foreclosure of Farm Land in the Prairie Region.* Saskatoon: NFU.

Oberle, P.R. 1993. *The Incidence of Family Poverty on Canadian Indian Reserves.* Ottawa: Indian and Northern Affairs Canada.

Ontario Ministry of Agriculture and Food, and Ministry of Labour. 1985. *Report of the Task Force on Health and Safety in Agriculture.* Toronto.

Pierce, W.E., et al. 1985. "Prevention of Hearing Loss Among Animals." In *Health and Safety in Agriculture*, ed. J. Dosman. Saskatoon: University of Saskatchewan.

Porter, J., M. Porter, and B.R. Blishen. 1982. *Stations and Callings: Making It through the School System*. Toronto: Methuen.

Reasons, C.E., L. Ross, and C. Patterson. 1981. *Assault on the Worker*. Toronto: Butterworths.

Report of the Ontario Task Force. 1985. *Health and Safety in Agriculture*. Toronto: Ontario Ministries of Agriculture and Food and Labour.

Report of the Special Committee on Visible Minorities in Canadian Society. 1984. *Equality Now!* Ottawa: Supply and Services Canada.

Rivara, F.P. 1985. "Fatal and Nonfatal Farm Injuries to Children and Adolescents in the United States." *Pediatrics* 76:567–73.

Robertson, L. 1984. "It's Spring: The Farm Fatality Season." *Country Guide* 103, no. 5:20–22.

Rogers, E.M., R.J. Burdge, P.F. Horsching, and J.F. Donnemeyer. 1988. *Social Change in Rural Societies*. Englewood Cliffs, NJ: Prentice Hall.

Rust, G.S. 1990. "Health Status of Migrant Farmworkers: A Literature Review and Commentary." *American Journal of Public Health*, 80 (October 10): 1213–17.

Ryan, A., L. Sackney, and H. Birnie. 1981. *Program Delivery in the Small High School*. S.S.T.A. Research Centre report no. 76. Regina: Saskatchewan School Trustees' Association.

Sackney, L.E. 1983. "Program Delivery in Rural School Systems." *Canadian School Executive* 2, no. 8 (February): 9–11.

Sakala, C. 1987. "Migrant and Seasonal Farmworkers in the United States: A Review of Health Hazards, Status, and Policy." *International Migration Review* 21, no. 3: 659–87.

Salmi, L.R., H.B. Weiss, P.L. Peterson, R.F. Spengler, R.W. Sattin, and H.A. Anderson. 1989. "Fatal Farm Injuries Among Young Children." *Pediatrics* 83:267–71.

Sandborn, C. 1983. "Equality for Farmworkers: A Question of Social Conscience." Submission to the legislative caucus of the provincial New Democratic Party. B.C.

———. 1986. "DHS on the Canadian Farm: What is to be Done?" *At the Centre: Canadian Centre for Occupational Health and Safety* 9, no. 3 (July).

Sanderson, G. 1974. "The Sweatshop Legacy: Still With Us in 1974." *The Labour Gazette* 74: 400–417.

Saskatchewan Education. 1981. *Rural Education: Options for the 80s*. A Discussion Paper. Regina: Saskatchewan Education.

Satzewitch, V. and T. Wotherspoon. 1993. *First Nations: Race, Class, and Gender Relations*. Scarborough, ON: Nelson Canada.

Sharma. H. 1983. "Race and Class in British Columbia: The Case of B.C.'s Farmworkers." *South Asian Bulletin* 3: 53–69.

Sharma, S. 1982. "East Indians and the Canadian Ethnic Mosaic: An Overview." *South Asian Bulletin* 1: 6–18.

Simpson, S.G. 1984. "Farm Machinery Injuries." *The Journal of Trauma* 24, no. 2: 150–52.

Slesinger, D.P., B.A. Christenson and E. Cautley. 1986. "Health and Mortality of Migrant Farm Children." *Social Science and Medicine* 23, no. 1: 65–74.

Snider, L. 1993. *Bad Business: Corporate Crime in Canada*. Scarborough, ON: Nelson Canada.

Statistics Canada. 1984. *Urban Growth in Canada*. 1981 Census of Canada. (Cat. 99–942). Ottawa: Supply and Services Canada.

———. 1986a. *Census of Canada, 1986, Agriculture*. Ottawa: Supply and Services Canada.

———. 1986b. *Report of the Canadian Health and Disability Survey, 1983–1984*. Ottawa: Supply and Services Canada.

———. 1987. *Education in Canada. A Statistical Review for 1985–86*. (Cat. 81-229). Ottawa: Supply and Services Canada.

———. 1988. *Canadian Crime Statistics, 1987*. (Cat. No. 85-205). 0ttawa: Supply and Services Canada.

———. 1992a. *Agricultural Profile of Canada, Part I*. (Cat. 93-350). Ottawa: Supply and Services Canada.

———. 1992b. *Trends and Highlights of Canadian Agriculture and Its People*. (Cat. 96-303E). Ottawa: Supply and Services Canada.

———. 1993a. *Profile of Urban and Rural Areas, Part A: Canada, Provinces, and Territories*. (Cat. 93-339). Ottawa: Supply and Services Canada.

———. 1993b. *Advanced Statistics of Education, 1993–94.* Cat. No. 81-220. Ottawa: Minister of Industry, Science and Technology.

———. 1994a. *Household Facilities by Income and Other Characteristics.* (Cat. 13-218). Ottawa: Minister of Industry, Science and Technology.

———. 1994b. *Profile of Urban and Rural Areas, Part B.* (Cat. 93-340). Ottawa: Minister of Industry, Science and Technology.

———. 1994c. *Farming Facts 1993: Statistical Insights on Canadian Agriculture.* (Cat. 21-522E). Ottawa: Supply and Services Canada.

———. Various years. *List of Canadian Hospitals and Special Care Facilities.* Ottawa: Supply and Services Canada.

Stringini, P. 1982. "On the Political Economy of Risk: Farmworkers, Pesticides, and Dollars." *International Journal of Health Services* 12, no. 2: 263–92.

Stubbs, H.A., J. Harris, and R.C. Spear. 1984. "A Proportionate Mortality Analysis of California Agricultural Workers, 1978–79." *American Journal of Industrial Medicine* 6:305–20.

Swanson, J.A., M. Sachs, K.A. Dahlgren, and S.J. Tinguely. 1987. "Accidental Farm Injuries in Children." *American Journal of Diseases in Children* 141:1276–79.

Verdun-Jones, S.N., and G.K. Muirhead. 1982. "The Native in the Criminal Justice System: Canadian Research." In *The Canadian Criminal Justice System*, ed. C.L. Boydell and I.A. Connidis. Toronto: Holt, Rinehart and Winston. 266–81.

Waitzkin, H. 1983. *The Second Sickness.* New York: The Free Press.

Waldron, I., M. Nawotarski, M. Freimer, J. Henry. N. Post, and C. Wittin. 1982. "Cross-Cultural Variation in Blood Pressure: A Quantitative Analysis of the Relationships of Blood Pressure to Cultural Characteristics, Salt Consumption, and Body Weight." *Social Science and Medicine* 16: 419–30.

Weinberg, D.H. 1987. "Rural Pockets of Poverty." *Rural Sociology* 52, no. 3 (Fall): 398–408.

Winson, A. 1988. "Researching the Food-chain: The Case of Nova Scotia." *Canadian Review of Sociology and Anthropology* 25, no. 4: 520–59.

PART VI

Institutional Structures and Inequality

INTRODUCTION

While Canada is one of the richest countries in the world, these riches are unevenly distributed in the society. Inequalities of income produce differential opportunity structures and different life chances (material and social rewards) for individuals and social groups. These life chances are reflected in such measures as education, health, nutrition, and treatment by the justice system.

In his chapter, Leslie Samuelson discusses the unequal involvement and treatment of individuals in the justice system based upon their class, race, and gender.

He shows that the political–economic elite is able to influence the political–legal process so that corporate crimes (social, economic, and physical harms inflicted on society in the process of capital accumulation) are not treated very seriously, under either criminal or regulatory law, while the lower class is prosecuted quite severely for ordinary street crime. This is illustrated with data on the flouting of occupational health and safety laws, on price fixing, and on other illegal corporate activities. The evidence also strongly suggests class bias in policing and arrests, and in differential prosecution, sentencing, and granting of parole. Access to legal services follows the same pattern: low income individuals are less likely to retain private legal counsel to safeguard their legal rights.

Racial inequalities are evident in the overrepresentation of Native peoples in the criminal justice system. Samuelson argues that Native overrepresentation is but one manifestation of the destruction and dislocation of indigenous peoples that has taken place under colonialism, and of their continued disadvantaged position. They are subject to racial bias in policing, prosecution, sentencing, and incarceration. The problem of racism in policing is also manifest in the excessive use of force and the relatively high number of killings by police of racial minorities.

The treatment of women in the justice system has received considerable attention. The main issues in this area have been the biases, injustices, and ineffectiveness of the criminal justice system in dealing with women who have been the victims of domestic violence and sexual assault, and injustices and problems faced by incarcerated women.

In conclusion, Samuelson argues that liberal–critical initiatives aimed at the reform of laws and programs to suit the needs of Native and female offenders are desirable, and may have some success. But to reduce significantly the inequalities of class, race, and gender, the focus needs to be put on change in the structural and cultural condition and inequalities of power that lie at the centre of the problems.

Terry Wotherspoon discusses inequalities in educational opportunities and benefits by race, class, and gender. Wotherspoon examines recent attacks on Canada's education system, which are posed in the form of concern over educational excellence and proposals for "lifelong learning." Although the concerns and proposals are defined in a way that presents them as being in the national interest, he argues that they serve to advance specific business and political interests seeking profitable investment and a highly productive work force.

These debates have emerged at a time when the notion of equality of educational opportunity is being challenged as an organizing principle in Canadian education. The chapter shows that while the expansion of the educational system since the middle of the twentieth century has allowed greater opportunities for participation in formal education programs, different class, gender, and racial groups have experienced persistent inequalities in educational opportunities and benefits. In conclusion, Wotherspoon argues that the impact of recent attacks on the educational system is likely to increase educational selectivity and inequality to the detriment of disadvantaged persons.

Poverty, malnutrition, and hunger are generally thought of as problems of Third World countries. While the significance and concentration of these problems in the Third World cannot be overstated, the advanced capitalist countries have not eliminated them, either. The chapter entitled "Income Inequality, Poverty, and Hunger," by B. Singh Bolaria and Terry Wotherspoon, addresses these issues.

Inequalities of income produce inequalities of life chances—chances for material and social rewards. Poverty translates into homelessness, poor health, low life expectancy, malnutrition, hunger, and other hardships.

Income distribution in Canada—one of the dimensions of inequality—is highly skewed; there has been very little change over the past 35 years. The gap between the rich and the poor would be even wider were it not for government transfer payments. Poverty is a persistent phenomenon, affecting disproportionate numbers of certain social groups—women and the elderly, for example. Selected data on the linkages between income inequality and life chances are discussed in this chapter, with particular emphasis on the emergence and persistence of food banks as a response to hunger. In conclusion, the implications of food banks, a private, volunteer-based solution to a structural social problem produced by the contradictions of the capitalist economy, are explored in the context of the social welfare restraint being advocated to reduce federal and provincial deficits.

The last reading in this section, by Gary Teeple, examines the nature of the welfare state and discusses the common elements in the history of social reform and the significance of such policies in industrial nations. He pays particular attention to the development of the welfare state and social legislation in Canada. Teeple explores the reasons for the present decline in the welfare state and the consequences of this retrenchment in Canada, which are already very visible in a number of areas. The retrenchment of social programs is discussed in the context of the North American Free Trade Agreement. Teeple states that, concomitant with cutbacks to the public-sector provisions, private-sector provisions are growing, in the form of charitable donations or voluntary services (charities) and in the systematic privatization of services and programs. In general, Canada is moving away from the state provision of social services and programs, especially universal programs or those characterized as social rights. This undermines the principle that the state has a social responsibility to its citizens and puts an end to the principle and practice of social citizenship. Teeple argues that the interim goal of the provincial and federal retrenchment appears to be a minimalization of the state's social responsibilities;

for those aspects of the welfare state that are not yet abolished, the state is developing dual systems: private but publicly supported programs for the well-to-do and a degraded state program for those who cannot afford the "private." Teeple concludes that the forces of global capitalism that underlie this retrenchment are being resisted around the world. This resistance will continue to grow as economic inequality deepens and the ability of capitalism to provide for the material and human needs of the populace further declines.

CHAPTER 20

The Canadian Criminal Justice System: Inequalities of Class, Race, and Gender

Leslie Samuelson

Learning Objectives

The objective of this chapter is to teach students to think critically about the Canadian justice system. The rule of law posits formal equality, but the reality of the justice system is quite different. This chapter evaluates the nature and the extent of unequal involvement and treatment in the criminal justice system based on class, race, and gender. The likelihood of, and best venues for, progressive criminal justice are central issues that students should contemplate.

Introduction

In this chapter we provide a critical criminological analysis of the Canadian criminal justice system. We focus on three related issues, which we have separated for analytical purposes. These concern inequalities of race, class, and gender, in terms both of individuals' involvement in the justice system and of their treatment in it. We first outline the core of a critical criminological analysis of law and society, as well as some important developments within it.

The critical, or conflict, perspective in criminology emerged largely in the 1970s, and challenged conservative neoclassical and liberal pluralist conceptions of law and society (cf. Taylor, Walton, and Young 1973). The central focus for the emerging critical criminology was on how class-based inequality was enforced and legitimated by legal codes and state agencies of control. As Ratner and McMullan (1987, 10) note, conservative and liberal criminologists more or less tacitly accepted the bourgeois legal ideology that had evolved over the past two hundred years.

Here law is treated as relatively unproblematic. Citizens are expected to obey the law on the assumption that the legal system and the state are neutral institutions seeking to advance the common good (the conservative point of view) or the interests of successful competitors (the pluralist position) by rational and efficient means (Ratner and McMullan 1987, 10). As these and other critical criminologists point out, however, this ideology perpetuates an uncritical acceptance of the legal system and of the political–economic order that is both supportive of, and supported by, the legal system.

Early critical analyses of law, crime, and the state were however, criticized on several fronts. First, it was noted, they ignored gender. A range of analyses are emerging that focus on how criminal and civil law, and the treatment of women in the justice system, reinforce not only capitalist society with its inequalities, but also the patriarchal subjugation of women.[1]

Early critical criminology can also be criticized for its analysis of "race." In most early critical criminological research, such as that by Quinney (1970) and Chambliss and Seidman (1971), race is largely ignored as an issue in its own right; it appears mainly as a proxy indicator of social class status—the central concern of critical criminology (cf. Hawkins 1987).

Finally, Ratner and McMullan (1987) note that current conflict analyses of society must attempt to integrate substantive investigations into a general political economy of state control of social relations through law. As they point out, none of the conservative, liberal-pluralist, or early orthodox Marxist analyses of society offered any cohesive statement of the role of the state in the functioning of law and social control in capitalist society. The perspective advocated by Ratner and McMullen is particularly appropriate when analyzing state-sponsored legal reforms, such as victim–offender mediation programs and sentencing reforms.

The developments in critical criminological studies of society that address these criticisms have led us to organize this chapter as follows. We first present an analysis of inequalities of involvement and treatment of individuals in the justice system based upon class, race, and gender. Then we consider whether current and developing criminal justice policies are likely to produce any meaningful change in the structural–cultural conditions that are largely responsible for crime and inequalities of treatment within the justice system. This question is crucial. One of the central concerns confronting critical legal scholars is the extent to which laws and legal systems can be used to alter radically the current status quo.

Class

The central concern in critical criminological analyses has been to show the class-biased nature of law.[2] There are two basic dimensions here. One is what gets defined in legislation as crime, or is controlled through regulatory law. The second is differential processing of lower- and higher-class individuals in the criminal justice system for relatively ordinary "street crime."

Critical criminologists, who follow a political economy approach to the analysis of crime, hold that a relatively small group of individuals control a very large proportion of the wealth and political power in our society.[3] While not necessarily acting in unison, this elite is able to influence the political–legal process so that the social, economic, and physical harms they inflict on society in the process of capital accumulation are not treated very seriously under either criminal or regulatory law. By contrast, the crimes committed by lower-class people as a result of their economic and physical privations are prosecuted quite severely under law, with incarceration frequently being the result.

The main Canadian research in this area, pioneered by Goff and Reasons (1978) and Snider (1978), has established the failure to prosecute "corporate crime," even when the economic and physical costs of the crime, both to individuals and the environment, far exceed those of street crime. Corporate crime, or "suite crime," is defined as "crime" committed by a corporate official in the pursuit of organizational goals, usually profit. These acts are either illegal under criminal or regulatory law, or would be if we applied the criterion of economic and physical harm to society. This is ostensibly the core criterion of prohibitions and punishments in the Canadian Criminal Code.

Just how serious is corporate crime? Few criminologists, critical or otherwise, hold that crimes of the elite are less serious than street crime. Virtually no one disputes the fact that killing people is a serious criminal act. Much publicity has been given to the debate over whether or not we should inflict the death penalty for first-degree premeditated homicide. In Canada, one homicide occurs roughly every twelve hours. Even according to conservative estimates, however, a worker dies on the job from a generally preventable condition every six hours. Data from the Law Reform Commission (186, 5) show 854 fatal on-the-job accidents in Canada in 1982.

Moreover, in one of the most recent Canadian texts on corporate crime, McMullan (1992), cites data by Ellis (1986), which indicates that "If official statistics on work-related injuries are compared with statistics on criminal-code assaults in Canada, then the corporate assault rate is conservatively estimated to be 25 times greater than the conventional street-assault rate" (McMullan 1992, 24). Unfortunately, this statistic is much less publicized. Reasons, Ross, and Patterson (1986) stated that occupational hazards were the third-leading cause of death in Canada, preceded only by heart disease and cancer. Some data, moreover, indicate that Canada is one of the worst offenders in the Western world in this area.

In the 1991 update to their article, Reasons, Ross, and Patterson cite data from the 1988 *Year Book of Labour Statistics* that indicate that in many industries it appears to be safer to work in the United States than in Canada, especially in the mining industry, in which there were 900 fatalities in Canada in 1985 compared to 500 in the United States in a very similar time period in 1986. Reasons, Ross, and Patterson (1991) note, using American data, that at most only about one-third of all deaths and job injuries, can be related to worker carelessness. In the United States, about 40 percent of job injuries result from illegal working conditions. Legal but unsafe working conditions account for about another 25 percent. The high cost to Canadian society of worker injury was cast in economic terms by the former minister of Health and Welfare, Marc Lalonde, when he noted that time lost because of industrial accidents was 23 percent more than that lost during industrial disputes. Injured workers occupy 14 000 Canadian hospital beds every day, at a cost of about $750 million per year (cited in Glasbeek and Rowland 1986, 78).

It is well documented that corporate disregard for the health and safety of workers, coupled with extremely lax governmental control and sanctioning of corporate crime, is the basic cause of worker injuries and deaths (McMullan 1992; Snider 1988; Reasons, Ross, and Patterson 1986, 1991; Hagan 1985; Brannigan 1984). As one of the most prominent Canadian researchers on corporate crime noted, "Although there were 71 186 industrial accidents in Canada in 1973–74 and 62 fatalities, there were only 39 charges laid and a total of $38 100 in fines—an average of $976.92 per charge, or more pointedly $614.51 per death" (Snider 1988, 260). While there is a move to harsher penalties, even when charges were laid—which is not easy to do—most corporate officials pay more for a business suit than they do for the death of a worker. Why is this so?

Brannigan (1984) affixes blame, as does Mandel (1986), on the class bias in criminal law. Legal notions of culpability were established to prosecute individual offenders for street crime, not corporations or corporate officials for industry-related killings.

In one of the best analyses of this issue to date, McMullan (1992, 80) states that in Canada, prior to 1941, corporations were immune to any criminal liability because a corporation was deemed to have no mind of its own. Little progress was made in this area until the late 1970s and early 1980s. McMullan (1992) notes that cases heard before the Supreme Court of Canada, such as *Sault St. Marie* (1978), *The Canadian Dredge and Dock Co. Ltd.* (1985) and *Southam Inc.* v. *Hunter* (1983), have made some progress in fitting corporate offenders into an individualist model of liability, evidence, procedure, and sanction.

Importantly, however, he notes the dispute and confusion over whether or not the Canadian Charter of Rights is meant under S.7 and S.1(d), to enforce relatively rigid *mens rea* requirements for the prosecution of corporate offenders (under Section 7 and S.1[d]). Decisions at the provincial court of appeal have generally muted the penalty in corporate prosecutions by eliminating incarceration, as in civil proceedings. McMullan (1992) states, however, that, in the *Irwin Toy Ltd.* case, the Supreme Court of Canada (1989) ruled that a corporation could not avail itself of the protection provided by Section 7 of the Charter. McMullan (1992, 81) correctly concludes that the matter is somewhat up in the air, and, given previous Canadian judicial history, he is forced to side with Sargent (1989, 55), who states that, "Canadian Courts have remained reluctant to extend the scope of corporate criminal responsibility to include the illegal acts or omissions of a corporation's agents or employees." In addition to the problem of *mens rea*, corporations have been prosecuted almost exclusively for only regulatory violations, such as those governing health and safety, not for the consequences of those violations (Reasons, Ross, and Patterson 1986; McMullan 1992). As is well known, corporations give government frequent and vociferous input about the regulations governing them, generally under the guise of being enlisted to co-operate in creating "workable laws." The result is a lax system of regulation.

One of the most notable examples of this co-opting of the law by corporations is the Workers' Compensation scheme. Injured workers lost all rights of prosecution of, or compensation from, corporations covered by the scheme. The only source of redress, and right of appeal, is the compensation board (Reasons, Ross, and Patterson 1986, 124). Corporations were largely responsible for getting this corporate-friendly limitation on workers' rights enshrined in the act.

We could go on almost indefinitely on the injury and killing of both workers and consumers, as in the seventeen women killed by the Dalkon Shield birth control device (cf. Ermann and Lundman 1982). We will conclude this section, however, with an excerpt from McMullan (1992, 10) on the calculated Pinto design-flaw deaths—for which thc corporation budgeted:

> Corporate executives had full knowledge of these [Pinto] faults but deliberately decided not to correct them. They had calculated that they would save more than $85 million by delaying lifesaving correctives but would lose no more than $200,000 per death in legal suits. As a result, they chose to put profits before people. Here is how a company memorandum put it:
>
> **Benefits**
>
> | | |
> |---|---|
> | Savings: | 180 burn deaths, 180 burn injuries, 2,100 burned vehicles |
> | Unit Cost: | $200,000 per death, $67,000 per injury, $700 per vehicle |
> | Total Benefit: | (180 × $200,000) + (180 × $67,000) + (2,100 × $700) = $49.5 million |
>
> **Costs**
>
> | | |
> |---|---|
> | Sales: | 11 million cars, 1.5 million light trucks |
> | Unit Cost: | $11 per car, $11 per truck |
> | Total Cost: | (11 million × $11) + (1.5 million × $11) = $137 million |
>
> This cold calculus suggested that delaying action on car improvement and safety was cost-effective and therefore desirable, even if such safety standards and correctives would result in fewer auto fires and fewer burn deaths and injuries (McMullan 1992, 10).

Most critical criminologists would agree that the economic cost to society of corporate crime far exceeds that of street crime. Exact Canadian data are hard to come by, but the virtually undisputed figures cited by Conklin (1977) for the United States are $40 billion versus $4 billion annually, respectively, a difference of more than ten times. Moreover, McMullan (1992), citing U.S. data from Wheeler and Rothman (1982) and Cullen, Maakestadt, and Cavender (1987), indicates that the median economic loss for corporate crime was $387 274—about $8000 for individual white-collar offences—whereas the average economic loss per street crime was $689 for robbery and $900 for burglary. How does this large discrepancy arise?

Two primary dimensions of legal regulation, or more specifically the lack thereof, can be identified as being responsible for the high cost to society of corporate crime. First, corporations are often able to avoid prosecution for illegal activity. Second, even when they are prosecuted, the penalty is usually an inconsequential fine levied against the corporation, while individual corporate decision makers are not usually singled out, legally or publicly. Even when individual corporate offenders are singled out the penalties, both legal and social, are only nominal. Let us illustrate these dimensions with some notable Canadian examples.

The Bertrand Inquiry produced a seven-volume report in 1981 on illegal collusion on the part of large multinational oil companies in Canada to keep oil prices inflated. Bertrand was the chief investigator for the federal combines investigation branch, which investigated illegal business monopolies. According to Brannigan,

> Bertrand's investigation charged that Canadian subsidiaries of multinational companies paid too much for the imported oil bought from the mother companies and shipped to Canada for refining for the local market; that crude prices in Ontario were artificially enhanced; and that the major dealers systematically under-priced independent retailers of gasoline to squeeze them out of the market, even though this meant losses for the majors in the short run—and higher costs to consumers in the long run when the real competition is gone (1984, 111).

From 1958 to 1973, the estimated cost to consumers of this illegal activity was $12.1 billion. In 1981 dollars, this amounted to about $89.2 billion, or about $15 000 per family. No prosecution was forthcoming, even though under the Combines Investigation Act offenders may be prosecuted in criminal court (Brannigan 1984, 111).

Snider (1988) documents the extremely low rate of prosecution and nominal penalties under the Canadian Combines Investigation Act, one of four major forms of regulatory law ostensibly governing corporations. Over the recent 22-year period that Snider considered, only 89 prosecutions were initiated, with 57 offences deemed founded. Fines levied in these latter cases were small, averaging seven to eight thousand dollars per company, and no one went to jail. No one has ever gone to jail under this act, even though the costs to society are very high. In addition, Snider notes that the infrequent recommendations for prosecution from the conservative Restricted Trade Practices Commission may still be turned down by the Department of Justice. This occurred in over 10 percent of the cases. It appears that the legal–political system has little interest in prosecuting corporate crime.

But this is not real theft or fraud, you might say. Well, consider the following fraud—and thus theft—by one of Canada's corporate recidivists, cited in Hagan (1987, 327). It provides an interesting example of the common "cease and desist" orders frequently levied against illegal corporate activities, and disregarded, under Canadian regulatory law. It also emphasizes how minute are the penalties for corporate crime.

> CROWN SEEKS MILLION-DOLLAR FINE IN
> SIMPSONS-SEARS RING "RIPOFF"
>
> Toronto (CP)—The federal Justice Department has asked a Toronto judge to levy a $1-million fine against Simpsons–Sears Ltd. after the retailer was found guilty of false advertising.
>
> Crown counsel Rod Flaherty characterized the conduct of the company as "reprehensible" when it knowingly continued its "ripoff" of diamond-ring purchasers long after the federal combines branch informed the company it was breaking the law.

> Simpsons-Sears and H. Forth and Co. Ltd., a small jewelry appraiser, were found guilty of 12 counts of misleading advertising. Simpsons–Sears had *eight previous* false-advertising convictions.
>
> Flaherty said he asked Judge George Ferguson for the stiff fine because it would be the only sort of punishment which will make an impression on the company. Ferguson is to sentence the companies June 30.
>
> Defence lawyer R.G. Carter suggested a fine of $80,000 to $100,000. The previous record fine for the offence was $85,000.
>
> The charges stemmed from a highly successful advertising campaign which offered diamond rings at price reductions ranging from 33 to 50 per cent below "appraised values." Each customer received a free appraisal certificate showing carat weight, color and retail value.
>
> The company sold $7-million worth of the rings in the mid-1970s, all of which were improperly appraised by H. Forth with the knowledge of Simpsons–Sears officials.
>
> Some rings were mismatched with certificates as to size, clarity and color, the judge found. In fact, one ring sold as two diamonds sandwiching an emerald was in fact two diamonds sandwiching a piece of green glass.
>
> Ferguson said evidence indicated that "appraisal value" prices were fictitious ones agreed on by the companies.
>
> Flaherty said the company continued to sell the rings in this fashion despite its previous convictions and despite the fact that the combines branch was actively and visibly investigating the sales. (*Winnipeg Free Press* June 10, 1983; emphasis added).

Employees as well as consumers can be the target of corporate theft. Theft from employees appears to be a major business crime, especially in smaller businesses. Snider and West (1980) reported that in 1973–74 the Ontario Department of Labour alone had to assess employers $3 million for redress, as 37 000 employees were deemed defrauded by their employers (not paying for work done, not paying the minimum wage, and so forth). By way of comparison, Statistics Canada reported that, in 1970–72, 56 699 people were charged with theft. About 11 600 of these theft cases prosecuted under the criminal law were punished by incarceration (Snider 1988, 254). It is little wonder that our jails are disproportionately populated by individuals from the lower classes.

The general lack of sanctions against corporations is further demonstrated in those few cases where corporate actors are singled out for prosecution. Snider (1988) points out that ostensibly law-abiding Canada treats corporate crime, as compared to street crime, much less severely than the bastion of capitalism, the United States. She cites data from the United States, indicating that the average sentence for ordinary theft is 32.8 months; for income tax evasion, which generally involves much larger sums, the average sentence is 12.8 months. The discrepancy is even greater in Canada for two economic crimes with serious costs to society. Here the average prison sentence for robbery is 38.9 months, for income tax evasion, 1.4 months.

When it comes to parole, incarcerated corporate officials also appear to get very favourable treatment. In the famous scandal over the rigging of dredging and construction bids, the longest trial in Canadian history, two corporate executives and seven corporations were ultimately convicted. The officials were Harold McNamara of McNamara Corporation and Sydney Cooper of PITT Engineering (Brannigan 1984, 130). McNamara was sentenced to five years, and Cooper to three years in prison. The former was free in ten months and the latter in six. Citing Mandel's 1983 research, Brannigan points out that the criminals' return to their homes, as opposed to a half-way house, after one-sixth of their sentence was served, amounted to a full parole, which is usually only available after a full-third of a sentence is completed. As Brannigan notes, "the National Parole Board effectively cut the sentences in half by granting these particular criminals the widest possible interpretation of the parole regulations" (1984, 131).

This National Parole Board action was criticized for smacking of political favouritism to Liberal party supporters. The chairman of the National Parole Board, William Outerbridge, publicly defended the actions, in part because "the opprobrium attached to Mr. Cooper and Mr. McNamara during their trial and incarceration is the greatest deterrence to this type of non-violent crime" (Brannigan 1984, 131). This "opprobrium punishes sufficiently" thesis is a pervasive ideology in the prosecution of upper-class individuals for both corporate and street crime.

Snider indicates, however, that this statement is not empirically correct. This author cites data from Coleman (1985) that show that in 1972 the Ford Motor Company was fined a total of $7 million. In 1973, the salaries of all the chief executives—to whom apparently no very great amount of opprobrium attached—were increased. Moreover, she observes, Clinard and Yeager (1980) have found that if corporate executives do resign or get fired, they frequently get rehired very shortly, often as "consultants." Finally, Snider reports that an international study by Fisse and Braithwaite (1983) failed to find evidence that a company's "stock prices, reputations, sales or anything else suffered more than temporary embarrassment as a result of involvement in corporate crime" (Snider 1988, 261).

What we have here is major class bias in the application of criminal justice. It should not be hard to understand why Sutherland (1977) found, in his pioneering work on corporate crime, that 90 percent of the 70 largest corporations in the United States were habitual offenders, with an average of fourteen convictions per corporation (cf. also Clinard and Yeager 1980).

Whereas, Hagan (1992, 465) reported that more than half of Canada's largest corporations were recidivists, or had been convicted more than once, with an average of 3.2 decisions against them. Hagan notes, however, that the lenient attitude toward corporate and white-collar crime is hardening, socially and judicially.

In Canada, two of the strongest thrusts of this hardening are the 1987 replacement of the Environmental Contaminants Act with new legislation that provides for fines of up to $1 million per day and up to five years' imprisonment for guilty executives. In addition, Ontario has, Hagan (1992) notes, increased the fine for insider trading of securities from $25 000 to $1 million and increased the jail term to two years from one. Consistent with the global concern over our environment, the former legislative toughening is apparently beginning to take some effect in Canada, provincially and federally. For example, the Federal Environment Department prosecuted 22 corporate pollutors in 1991, compared with only 1 in 1987. In another example, the former president of Varnicolor Chemical Ltd. has recently been sentenced to eight months in jail for contaminating soil and ground water on company property in a southwestern Ontario town. This is likely the longest sentence ever for an environmental offence in Canada.

The second concern in critical legal studies dealing with class and law is that of class bias in the involvement and treatment of persons in the criminal justice system for "street" crime. The corporate crime dimension of class and crime is generally embedded in a fairly radical critique of the justice system and of the political–economic status quo. With street crime, however, we see more of a blending of liberal and radical legal research. Two interrelated central questions guide the research in this area.

Until the mid 1950s, official police statistics on crime were generally accepted as valid. These data indicated that street crime, the only type then really considered crime, was primarily engaged in by the lower class.[4] However, the self-report questionnaire on crime, specifically juvenile delinquency, introduced by Short and Nye (1957), appeared to indicate that the overinvolvement of lower-class youth in crime was nowhere near as great as official statistics indicated. Middle-class youth also appeared to be delinquent.

Out of this conundrum sprang two questions that would occupy many North American criminologists for the next three decades. First, was there really a strong social class-crime correlation? Second, to what extent was the contradiction between official and self-reported data on the class–crime relationship a result of the more frequent processing of lower-class people by the criminal justice system for criminal acts?

A history and summary evaluation of American and Canadian data on the class–crime correlation is well presented by Hartnagel (1987).[5] It is once again becoming accepted that in general, lower-class individuals are more frequently involved in street crime, especially when we consider relatively serious crimes and repeat offenders. This certainly conforms to the evidence of incarceration statistics. As Grainger noted, about 40 percent of offenders are unemployed when they commit a crime (1981, 3). Moreover, about 85 percent of all offenders are either unemployed or poorly employed at the time of their arrest. Occupational status is, as one might expect, a central measure of social class in this area of research.

Concern over the differential processing of different social classes, initially generated in North America by the discrepancy between official statistics and the self-reporting of crime, has emerged as a continuing criminological concern. Three strands of research can be separated in this area. The more liberal critical perspective has essentially been concerned with ascertaining whether "rich and poor alike are treated equally for sleeping under bridges." At the other conceptual pole, radical criminologists have been attempting to show how the class biased definition of laws and operation of the criminal justice system support the political–economic status quo in capitalist society (cf. Quinney 1977; Spitzer 1975, 1983). In the middle lies research based on labelling theory, generated largely in the early 1960s to mid-1970s (cf. LeBlanc, 1975).[6]

Unfortunately, empirical research on class biases in the application of criminal justice in Canada is relatively limited. West (1984), for example, argues that generalizing from the mainly American research on police discretion is problematic, for even within the United States, police discretion on whom to charge for what varies greatly from police force to police force, depending on a range of factors. A Canadian study by Conly (1977) showed wide community variation in the proportion of apprehended juveniles charged by police. For example, 17 percent of recorded youth contacts were charged with an offence in Hamilton, 30 percent in Edmonton, and 96 percent in Calgary.

However, other Canadian research by Nease (1968) and Frechette and LeBlanc (1979) is in accord with the seminal U.S. research on police discretion in charging assembled by Piliavin and Briar (1964). These studies indicate that the seriousness of an offence was the major criterion governing police decisions to arrest. Nonetheless, Piliavin and Briar did find that for less-serious offences, youths who did not display the appropriate "deference to authority demeanour" in dress and speech were more likely to be referred to juvenile court.

Given the similarity in police and policing between Canada and the United States, there is good reason to suspect that similar demeanour biases operate in the differential prosecution of lower-class individuals for relatively non-serious to moderately serious offences. Indeed, as West (1984) noted, Toronto police interviewed by Gandy (1967) admitted that they were more lenient in middle-class areas, thereby "overcharging" in working-class neighbourhoods. Given that many criminal offences, particularly youth offences, are not all that serious, this differential processing may create a sizable class bias in the administration of justice.

This dimension of the operation of the criminal justice system is certainly compounded by a well-established truism in criminology: you find crime where you look for it. Brannigan (1984) agrees with West that "with pressures to routinely maintain the public appearance of order, the police are concerned with disruptive displays on the street, exactly where minority and working-class youngsters [and often adults] are forced to 'hang out' as they lack other recreational places" (West 1984, 179). Indeed, Brannigan (1984) observes people in lower-class areas may treat the streets as their turf, or property. Police surveillance and intervention in relatively non-serious illegal acts (smoking a joint, public drinking and gambling, and so on) may be met with hostility, not deference to authority.

Brannigan (1984) presents data on the final, but very important, dimension of class bias in the criminal justice system to be considered here: the differential conviction and sentencing of lower- versus higher-class offenders for street crime. Given that the majority of people coming into the justice system are lower class—both males and females—obtaining a non–lower-class reference group is difficult. However, some information is available. Brannigan has stated that evidence shows that poor defendants are more likely to be judged guilty than wealthier defendants. This is true even when the individuals are charged with similar offences and have similar conviction records (1984, 103). Whether or not one can pay for a privately retained as opposed to a publicly paid lawyer is one major factor in this differential case outcome.

In Canada, defendants who cannot afford to retain a lawyer privately will usually be assigned a lawyer through legal aid programs. In some provinces, such as Ontario, duty counsel are located in the court. However, they generally give only interim advice and facilitate applications for legal aid that may take several weeks to process. Canadian lawyers thus operate both on a private and a legal aid basis. Differences in case outcome should thus generally be due not to differences in capability, but to the care, time, and legal resources allocated to cases (Brannigan 1984, 106).

Given the relatively low monetary return to lawyers from legal aid cases, lawyers may be more likely to advise their legal aid clients to plead guilty. U.S. data support this observation. Blumberg (1969) found that assigned counsel were almost twice as likely as privately retained lawyers to suggest a guilty plea in the initial client interview (60 percent opposed to 35 percent, respectively). The organizational and occupational similarities between U.S. and Canadian lawyers indicate that similar processes are likely to operate in Canada.

Canadian data assembled by Wilkins in *Legal Aid in the Criminal Courts* (1975) are, as Brannigan notes, certainly applicable here. One has to be very careful of the specific case outcomes considered here—for example, whether the defendant was found guilty on all accounts or on some. However, the Wilkins study did find that "the private lawyer experiences complete exoneration in 51% of the cases when pleading not guilty, compared to 31 % for the legal aid lawyer" (Brannigan 1984, 106).

One of the most notorious and contentious issues in Canadian criminal justice research is the relatively lenient sentencing of middle- and upper-class citizens for thefts, but more notably for sexual assaults. Much anecdotal information on the latter exists, to which Mandel (1983) has added a study of the class bias running systematically throughout Canadian cases involving middle- and upper-class offenders. The discussion earlier on, of the ideology that holds that social opprobrium punishes upper-class offenders sufficiently should be kept in mind as one reads the following account of Mandel's research by Brannigan.

> [The offender's] social history is used to justify keeping high status offenders out of jail. A good example of this is the case of *Regina* v. *A* (1976). A was a businessman who attacked and attempted to rape one of his female employees. She resisted vigorously and escaped. A was charged with attempted rape but was convicted of indecent assault. Throughout his brush with the law, A's identity remained unpublished. Upon conviction he received a suspended sentence and was put on probation for three years. One provision of his probation order called for A to pay $1,000 compensation to the victim. The court provided the following justification:
>
> Imprisonment would be of no assistance to the accused. It is likely it would ruin his one-man business. To him the conviction itself forms a substantial portion of the punishment.... While the solution I propose to follow here cannot be adopted in all cases, because the offender is usually without funds, here the offender is a man of modest means.... I propose to make compensation of the victim part of the process of rehabilitation. After all it has long been recognized that restitution for wrong done is rehabilitation (Brannigan 1984, 106–107).

Race

Canada is not alone in the overrepresentation of indigenous, or Native, peoples in its criminal justice system. For example, Australia and the United States have similar problems. This is not some accident of history, nor the result of a pathology of "lawlessness" among some non-European races of people. The overrepresentation of Native people in the Canadian justice system is but one manifestation of the destruction and dislocation of indigenous peoples that took place under European colonialism.

The European colonial political and economic subjugation of territories around the world has been rapidly diminishing, especially in past decades. However, it is largely the colonial population of European origin, and not the aboriginal inhabitants of these relatively new nations, who are enjoying freedom from colonialism and its exploitation and oppression. Essentially, aboriginal peoples are still treated as a colonial population, and Canada is no exception here. As Mikel has aptly noted,

> whenever Canada attacks Russia for the treatment of Jewish people, or Israel for the treatment of her Palestinian captives, in the United Nations, Canada is also universally condemned for the treatment of her Native peoples. Canada has kept its Indians in concentration camps, known as reserves, for about one hundred and twenty-five years and has regulated their behavior in all aspects of their lives (1979/80, 35).

LaPrairie (1988) and Verdun-Jones and Muirhead (1982) note that the over-involvement of Canadian Native peoples in crime and with the justice system can be fully understood only against this political, social, and economic context. Native overinvolvement in crime is but one of the social problems that have been generated for Native people by the relatively "passive genocide" perpetrated on them, largely under the rhetoric and guise of "assimilation."[7]

The common public perception of Native people as "drunks," "lazy," and "criminal" confuses symptoms with the underlying causes of these social problems (Hylton 1982, 125). Confusing symptom with cause is very convenient, for as we shall see, it allows for criminal justice policies and programs that address the "problem of crime" without seriously challenging the status quo of the current Canadian political economy. Of course, like most systems of domination from Roman slavery onward, those in power have generally developed strong ideologies and typifications that justify their control over subject populations.

We shall now document the extent and nature of the disproportionate involvement of Natives in the justice system, and the possibly biased application of criminal justice. Then we shall consider whether a spate of initiatives in this area dating from the mid-1970s has had any real impact.

Figures 20.1 and 20.2 show the most frequently analyzed dimension of the disproportionate involvement of Native people in the Canadian criminal justice system. The percentage of registered Indians in the population ranges from a low of less than 1 percent in the Maritimes, Quebec, and Ontario, to just over 20 percent in the Northwest Territories (see Figure 20.1). These figures must, of course, be

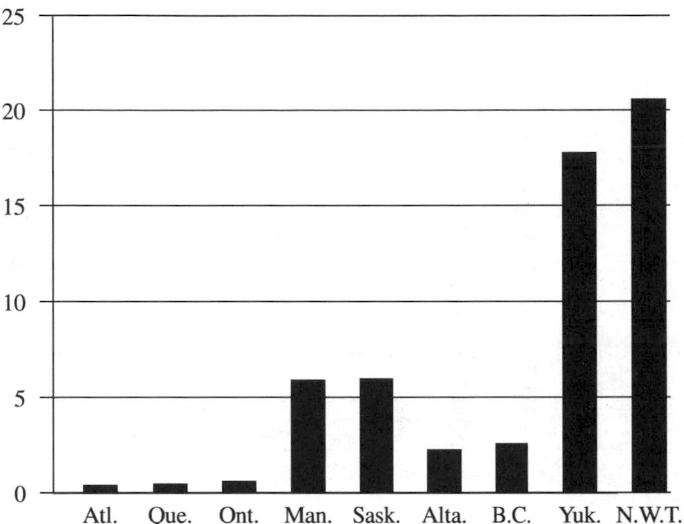

FIGURE 20.1: Registered Indians as a Percentage of Population, by Region 1991

Source: Statistics Canada, *Age and Sex - Aboriginal Data*, Cat. no. 94-327 (Ottawa: Minister of Industry, Science and Technology, 1993), p. 12. Reproduced by authority of the Minister of Industry, 1994.

increased by anywhere from 50 to 70% to take account of non-status Indians, Métis, and the Inuit. However, in virtually every province, Natives make up a far greater proportion of the prison population than their percentage in the general population would indicate (see Figure 20.2). The two most notable instances of this overrepresentation are in western and northern Canada. This is particularly true in the provincial institutions, where offenders serve time for offences that are generally less serious. This western and northern overrepresentation is even more pronounced for aboriginal women, who constitute up to 80 percent of inmates in provincial Prairie institutions (Satzewich and Wotherspoon, 1993).

A similar general overrepresentation of young aboriginal offenders has been documented in the *Cawsey Task Force Report on the Criminal Justice System in Alberta* (1992), and by a similar report of the *Saskatchewan Indian Justice Review Committee* (1992). The latter report found that, in June 1991, aboriginal youth constituted 45 percent of all Saskatchewan young offenders receiving some form of disposition under the Young Offenders Act. It is thus not surprising to find that data from the Alberta Task Force on aboriginal people and the justice system indicate that 78 percent of the aboriginal men surveyed reported having been arrested at some point in their lives (cited in Satzewich and Wotherspoon 1993).

While these data present a bleak enough picture, recent studies indicate that Native overrepresentation in the justice system is increasing rapidly. A recent critique of institutional programs for Native offenders by Bonta (1989) noted that in 1977 there were about eight hundred Native inmates in federal Canadian peniten-

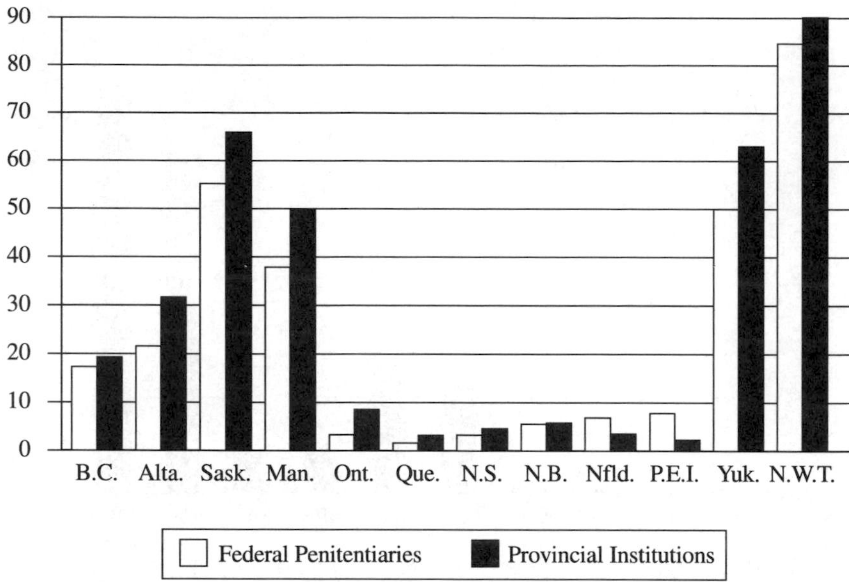

FIGURE 20.2: Natives as a Percentage of Sentenced Prison Population, 1991–1992

Source: Statistics Canada, *Adult Correctional Services in Canada, 1991-2*, Cat. no. 85-211 (Ottawa: Minister of Industry, Science and Technology, 1993), pp. 106, 119–120. Reproduced by authority of the Minister of Industry, 1994.

tiaries, while by 1987 that number had risen dramatically to twelve hundred—an increase of more than 50 percent.[8]

The 1988 *Final Report* of the Task Force on Aboriginal Peoples in Federal Corrections also documented recent increases in Native involvement in the justice system. In March 1983, aboriginal offenders comprised 27.3 percent of the federal inmate population in the Prairies; by March 1987 this figure had risen to 31 percent. Moreover, the percentage of Native offenders doing time in provincial institutions for federal offences rose from 17.3 percent to 24.7 percent in the same short period. Finally, Haveman et al. (1985) show that, from 1970–71 to 1980–81, Native overrepresentation in correctional institutions increased for all the jurisdictions they considered, except Alberta.

In order to understand Native peoples' overinvolvement in the justice system, we must consider the kinds of offences for which Natives are incarcerated. For practical purposes, this is important in designing immediate institutional and post-release programs for Native offenders. However, for the purpose of our analysis, it should provide us with a better understanding of the underlying cause of Native involvement in the criminal justice system. Boldt et al. (1983) state that, in general, the evidence indicates that most Native inmates have been incarcerated for relatively minor offences. The 1974 Law Reform Commission of Canada report, *The Native Offender and the Law*, concluded that Native offenders in provincial institutions were usually involved in less-serious crimes than non-Native offenders. However, Mikel (1979/80) indicated that for federally sentenced inmates, there was little difference between the types of offences committed by Native and non-Native inmates. In addition, Bonta (1989) cautions us that there is likely to be regional variation in the pattern of Native offences.

Nonetheless, Hylton's 1982 analysis of provincially incarcerated Native offenders in Saskatchewan stands as generally quite accurate. As he noted, 60 percent of these individuals had committed offences for which a sentence of 90 days or less was given, and fewer than 10 percent had committed offences against "the person." More typically, in nearly 50 percent of the cases, the offence was related to drinking or driving. A major piece of research by Hagan (1974) in western Canada indicated that default in payment of fines for minor, frequently alcohol-related, offences was one of the major reasons for Native incarceration. The rate of incarceration for Native offenders in default of fine payment was virtually double that for non-Native offenders (64 percent and 34 percent, respectively).

Verdun-Jones and Muirhead state: "Significantly, Hagan's data demonstrate the existence of a definite pattern of 'repeated involvement in minor (summary) offences, resulting in the sentencing options of fine or imprisonment, followed by racial differences in default and incarceration'" (1982, 272). In general, this has been termed the "revolving door" of Native incarceration. Here the Native "crime problem" is viewed as being the product of a relatively small number of Native offenders who are not seriously involved in crime. Instead, the problem is one of excessive, often public, drinking and disregard of bureaucratic rules, such as the Highway Traffic Act, and frequent defaulting on fines. There is some truth to this picture.

However, Hylton (1982) provides evidence that Native involvement in the justice system is much more pervasive than the revolving door perspective indicates. As Hylton stated,

> we were interested in knowing what the chance was of a 16-year-old male being admitted to a provincial correctional centre at least once by the age of 25. The age range of 16 to 25 was selected because it is one with a high risk of incarceration. We found that a male Treaty Indian turning 16 in 1976 had a 70% chance of at least one incarceration in a provincial correctional centre by the age of 25 ... for a non-Native male, the figure was 8% (1982, 124).

These data are quite important because they indicate that the social and economic conditions giving rise to aboriginal involvement in the justice system are pervasive in the lives of aboriginal people, and thus in our society. As Satzewich and Wotherspoon (1993) note, some of the most telling findings are surrounding aboriginal women. The Daubney (1988) report found, from an analysis of the offender profiles for women at Pine Grove Correctional Centre between April 1985 and April 1987, that 58.5 percent had at least one dependent child, 72 percent had Grade 9 education or less, 89.4 percent had been unemployed prior to incarceration, 55.2 percent had been victims of sexual abuse, and 79.3 percent admitted serious addictions problems. Hylton thus contends, and we concur, as would the recent Task

Force on Federally Sentenced Women (1990), that "traditionally conceived crime prevention programs are unlikely to have much positive impact on Native people because they fail to take account of the nature and extent of aboriginal involvement in the justice system and of the underlying reasons for this involvement" (Hylton 1982, 121).

As Ekstedt and Griffiths stated in their recent text, *Corrections in Canada* (1988), most of the fairly pervasive involvement of aboriginal people with the justice system is "more indicative of 'social' than that of 'criminal' problems" (331). Thus, the problems that society creates for aboriginal individuals, rather than any individualistic criminal pathology, are the most central social problems here. To make matters worse, Sugar and Fox (1989/90) and Satzewich and Wotherspoon (1993) concur that aboriginal women are one of the most oppressed groups in Canadian Society generally, but when incarcerated face several additional factors that impeded "healing instead of rage." As Satzewich and Wotherspoon (1993) state: "These include severely inadequate prison facilities and programs, cultural- and gender-biased assessment standards, failure to acknowledge and treat the realities of aboriginal women's abusive life histories, and unsympathetic prison regimes."

A recurrent theme in discussions of Native peoples and the law is that of prejudice and discrimination among Canadians generally and criminal justice personnel in particular (Boldt et al.1983). This concern has two basic dimensions. First, are Native people treated *differently* (usually more harshly) in the criminal justice system, when they shouldn't be? Second, are Native people treated *the same* as non-Natives when they shouldn't be? Each of these perspectives can be applied to the decision to arrest, in court disposition, institutional classification, length of sentence actually served, granting of parole, and finally, post-release processes.

In their important review of Native peoples and the justice system, Verdun-Jones and Muirhead (1982, 275) stated, "Clearly, the major thrust of Canadian research has been directed towards ascertaining the extent to which Native persons receive 'differential' treatment at the hands of decision-makers in the criminal justice system. " Several major pieces of research—including the early benchmark on this issue— have been conducted by Hagan (1974, 1975, 1977) in western Canada.

This research is generally accepted as indicating that there is no large-scale across-the-board differential sentencing of Native/non-Native offenders (Verdun-Jones and Muirhead 1982, 275). However, Hagan and other scholars show that certain forms and dimensions of inequality of treatment for Native people do exist in the justice system.

One of the most central dimensions of inequality of treatment of aboriginal people within the justice system centres not so much on overt discrimination, but on systemic discrimination (Stevens 1991). The administration of justice in geographically isolated northern communities is one notable example of systemic discrimination against aboriginal people. LaPrairie noted this concern within her analysis of aboriginal youth and the Young Offenders Act. She cites data by Kueneman et al. (1986), which found that some of the major problems were "(a) lack of criminal justice and social services; (b) lack of experienced legal counsel; (c) lack of local detention facilities; (d) too much work and too little time for court officials to handle cases most effectively; (e) lack of knowledge on the part of youth about the criminal justice system and/or youth's rights" (LaPrairie 1988, 163).

There is little reason to suspect that these concerns exist only for the young, as opposed to the majority of rural northern aboriginal peoples.

When it comes to getting released from the justice system, however, there is much less controversy over equality of treatment of Native offenders. As LaPrairie notes, a 1981 solicitor general's report on conditional release shows that Native offenders have a lower full-parole release rate from correctional institutions (1983, 342). The 1988 report of the Task Force on Aboriginal Peoples in Federal Corrections documents in detail a similar picture: in 1987, only about 18 percent of aboriginal releases were on full parole, compared to 42 percent for non-aboriginal offenders. While positive changes have taken place since then, differences still exist. Aboriginal offenders still serve greater proportions of their sentences.

The same study noted that for all offenders eligible for parole in 1980–81 to 1982–83, 16 percent of non-aboriginal offenders were released after serving 36 percent or less of their sentences, as compared to only 4 percent of aboriginal offenders. In large part, these differences exist not because fewer Native offenders apply for parole, but because of differences in the granting of parole; in 1986–87, 20.5 percent of aboriginal requests for parole were successful, compared to 38 percent for non-aboriginal offenders. An analysis of data for 1980–81 through 1982–83, moreover, shows that federal parole differences persisted regardless of the general category of offence considered.

LaPrairie states that racial differences in release processes may not be the result of blatant racism per se. Rather, release may be conditional upon factors such as employment prospects, social supports, and general community conditions. Unfortunately, as stated previously, the social and economic conditions under which Native people live make these release criteria more difficult for Native offenders. It may thus be the application of *equal* criminal justice system processes to a socially and economically disadvantaged Native population that results in these criminal justice system inequalities (LaPrairie 1983, 342).

The development of more appropriate programs, reflective of the past and present cultural and structural condition of Native peoples, has begun to receive more attention in the justice system since the mid-1970s. Ekstedt and Griffiths provide an excellent review and critique of the mostly federal justice initiatives in this area. Their list of initiatives is impressive and well worth noting, particularly in terms of the final outcome.

1. The National Conference and Federal–Provincial Conference on Native Peoples and the Criminal Justice System (Edmonton, 1975) which was attended by delegates from every major Native organization in Canada and by federal and provincial cabinet ministers and other government officials;
2. The Federal Advisory Council on Native People and the Criminal Justice System (1975) which was established at the Edmonton Conference and was composed of representatives from six national Native organizations and officials from five federal government departments;
3. The National Consultant on Natives and the Criminal Justice System (1976), which also was established in response to recommendations arising from the Edmonton Conference; and

4. The Métis and Non-Status Indian Crime and Justice Commission which was established in 1975 to study the Native inmate population and which reported to the Federal Department of Justice and the Solicitor General in 1977 (1988, 334).

Unfortunately, as these authors note, it is doubtful whether Native-based criminal policy initiatives have produced any substantive improvements. Particularly telling is research by Jolly, Peters, and Spiegel (1979), who surveyed government action on the 1975 Edmonton Conference. They found that many of the senior civil servants surveyed had not read the conference report and were not familiar with its recommendations. As well, "many of those who were aware of the recommendations of the conference expressed strong reservations regarding the creation of alternative justice structures for Native Indians" (Ekstedt and Griffiths 1988, 333).

More recent research by McCaskill (1985) has also noted a similar reluctance on the part of the Correctional Service of Canada to implement targeted reforms in correctional policies and programs for aboriginal peoples. Now we are faced with the monumental task of analyzing and implementing the changes in the criminal justice system and in society, as recommended by four major initiatives. The Marshall Commission (1990) investigated the wrongful conviction and eleven-year incarceration of Donald Marshall, Jr., a Mi'Kmag in Nova Scotia. The *Manitoba Aboriginal Justice Inquiry* (1991) was set up in the wake of the Winnipeg police shooting of J.J. Harper and the death of Helen Betty Osborne in The Pas, Manitoba, about which police took sixteen years before seriously pursuing the matter. The third major initiative, the *Justice on Trial Report of the Task Force on the Criminal Justice System and its Impact on the Indian and Métis People of Alberta* (1991) was followed by the *Reports of the Saskatchewan Indian and Métis Justice Review Committee* (1992).

The overall thrust of these reports, consistent with the move to aboriginal self-government, is toward criminal justice policies and programs formulated and run by the First Nations, along with cultural awareness training for non-Native criminal justice personnel. We will likely find a certain amount of reluctance, on the part of the existing justice system and society, in implementing the reforms proposed. Nonetheless, an additional, more-basic concern exists, which we raise in the final point of discussion in this section. Criminal justice system reforms cannot in and of themselves solve social justice concerns. The problem of racism in policing has emerged as an extremely important concern in the past several years. An important dimension of this concern is the relatively high number of killings by police of racial minorities.

Brannigan states, in his well-used text, *Crimes, Courts and Corrections* (1984), that recent data confirm that the unnecessary use of force by Toronto police is a substantial problem (58). He then cites Henshel, who showed that "for a ten-month period from mid-1978 to early 1979 there was almost a killing a month, mostly of members of minority groups" (1984, 58). The highly questionable use of deadly force against minorities was censured when a series of public protests culminated in the September 1979 vote of non-confidence in the Metropolitan Toronto Police Commission passed by Toronto City Council.

More recent killings by police of African-Canadians and Native people in very questionable circumstances have added much fuel to the fire now raging over racism in policing. Commissions have been struck to evaluate the problem. However, the poor implementation of Native justice program initiatives suggests there will be a great deal of difficulty in eliminating racist views among police and in putting curbs (such as independent review boards) on police practices. Reducing the involvement of Native people in the justice system in the first place is but half the problem.

One of the most important commissions has been the Manitoba aboriginal justice inquiry set up in the wake of the shooting by police in Winnipeg of Native leader J.J. Harper. The commission criticized racist police attitudes and punitive justice system reactions to the behaviour and lifestyles of structurally and cultural dislocated aboriginal people. It pointed out, however, that we cannot simply scapegoat the police. Other problems, such as the need for self-determination, the resolution of land claims, and the reconstruction of a viable modern society of First Nations within Canada are even more fundamental. Band-aid solutions to the overinvolvement and treatment of native peoples that ignore these larger concerns, are likely to achieve little.

This fact is particularly important when considering aboriginal women and society. Aboriginal women may retaliate against physical abuse by aboriginal men, who are frequently themselves living an economically and culturally marginalized existence. Or, these women may escape from such a situation by migrating to urban areas where, resulting from low levels of education and marketable skills, they face few, if any, legitimate economic opportunities. This, in turn, increases their susceptibility to involvement in alcohol or drug abuse and prostitution, and increases their likelihood of exposure to the police, who may be racially biased.

A study in Ontario concluded that "alcohol abuse, unemployment and poor living conditions were critical factors in the high incidence of arrest and incarceration of aboriginal people" (Johnson 1987, 42). The situation is even more aggravated for aboriginal women who suffer both racial and gender discrimination, as well as severe economic subordination in Canadian society.

Gender

Two central dimensions of concern with women and the justice system can be identified in the criminological literature. One focusses on the generally low criminal involvement rate of women relative to men. Particular attention has been paid to whether crime rates have been increasing faster for females than for males, and if so, why. The second central concern is with the treatment of women in the justice system, both as victims of crime, notably domestic violence and sexual assault, and as offenders, particularly for federally incarcerated women in the Kingston Penitentiary for Women—"P4W."

The starting point for empirical analyses of the involvement of women in crime is usually a statement of the generally low rate of female involvement in crime relative to men, followed by the presentation of statistics on recent increases in female involvement in certain offences (Hagan 1985; Hartnagel 1987). For example, in 1987 women accounted for only 10 percent of all adults charged with violent crimes in Canada; even their property crime statistic of 23 percent still indicated a reasonably large gender gap (Statistics Canada 1988). It is the increases in female criminality in the past decade and a half, however, that have caused the greatest stir.

Statistics Canada reported that between 1974 and 1983 the rate of increase of adult males charged for violent crime was about 25 percent, whereas the rate of increase for females charged was 65 percent. For property crimes, the rates of increase were about 50 percent and 61 percent, respectively. Society was thus said to be witnessing the rise of the "New Criminal Female," apparently a result of the encroachment of liberated females on a traditional male preserve (Adler 1975). Social roles for women were said to be changing, with women achieving greater equality of involvement in society generally, but also in the criminal justice system. This has been dubbed the *converging role* thesis.

In the late 1970s and early 1980s, much effort went into evaluating the criminal involvement of females. Hagan, Simpson, and Gillis (1979) developed a historical–theoretical argument based on Scull's 1976/77 article, which held that men tended to be the object of formal social controls such as the courts, as opposed to the informal "under the roof" social controls to which women were largely subjected. Fox and Hartnagel (1979) attempted to test empirically the converging roles explanation of female crime. In other research, official statistics were compared with self-reported data to try to get at the "real gender-based crime ratio" for varying types of crime and delinquency (LeBlanc 1983). Cautions on the implications of low base rates for evaluating increases in female crime were also forthcoming.

This literature is well summarized by Hartnagel (1987). He points out that an early report by the Canadian Committee on Corrections (1969) found that 80 percent of the increase in the female crime rate from 1960 to 1966 was due primarily to convictions of females for simple theft. A similar conclusion was made in a major review of studies on gender differences in crime by Smith and Visher (1980).

Steffensmeier (1980) builds upon these facts and concludes that "female experiences are not moving beyond traditional roles, either legitimate or illegitimate" (from Hartnagel 1987, 87). As Johnson noted in her article in the most extensive Canadian publication on women and the justice system to date, *Too Few to Count*, women's involvement in crime

> is consistent with their traditional roles as consumers, and increasingly, as low income, semi-skilled, sole support providers for their families. In keeping with the rapid increase in female-headed households and the stresses associated with poverty, greater numbers of women are being charged with shoplifting, cheque forging and welfare fraud (1987, 29).

While role convergence and a less "chivalrous" (read "paternalistic"—cf. Currie 1986) judicial system cannot totally be ruled out as factors in female criminal justice system involvement, a more fruitful explanation would lie elsewhere. Continuing extensive female job ghettoization (Krahn and Lowe 1988), the feminization of poverty (National Council of Welfare 1985), and the development of a youth consumer market (Greenberg 1977) frequently directed at teenage females, are all more basic to the understanding and modification of female patterns and rates of involvement in crime. A correctionalist criminology that focusses on changing the offender, or a liberal feminist criminology that stresses formal legal rights, or, to put it somewhat cynically, equalizing the gender ratio of dominators in capitalist society, can make very little contribution toward understanding or reducing female involvement in crime.

Unfortunately, analytically more comprehensive research has not yet made much impact on the analysis. We are here thinking of Currie's 1986 article on the historical evolution of the social control and subjugation of women under both capitalism and patriarchy, Adelberg and Currie's 1987 reader on women in conflict with the law, *Too Few to Count*, and the Status of Women Canada publication, *A Feminist Review of Criminal Law* (1985). Indeed, as we shall discuss in our analysis of the Federal Prison for Women in Kingston, P4W, outspoken liberal feminist correctional workers attempting to produce meaningful changes in the justice system's treatment of women have been fired (cf. Berzins and Hayes 1987).

The treatment by the justice system of women who have been the victims of crime has been the object of much very critical scrutiny in the past two decades. The main areas of concern have been biases, injustices, and ineffectiveness when dealing with women who have been the victims of domestic violence and sexual assault.

Domestic violence, largely against women, occurs in many Canadian families. MacLeod (1980) states, for example, that about 10 percent of women in Canada are battered by their partners each year. Unlike street crime, where victim and offender are overconcentrated in the lower socio-economic level of society, this violence is spread across all social classes. The police and criminal justice system have been heavily criticized for neglecting the problem.

Two of the most influential writers in this area, Dobash and Dobash (1979), state that research in the Hamilton–Wentworth area of Ontario found that 84 percent of family disputes actually entailed assaults, about 95 percent of which involved wife assault. As Burris and Jaffe (1983) note, past and current police policy in Canada frequently emphasizes minimal intervention on the part of police. Often they avoid laying assault charges in domestic assault situations. The same two authors, in an earlier study (Jaffe and Burris 1981), provide some of the most telling statistics in this area. They found that police laid assault charges in only 3 percent of all family violence cases, even though 20 percent of the victims were advised to seek medical treatment and 60 percent were told to lay their own charges.

However, one police force in Canada did undertake to correct this judicial neglect of violence against women. Burris and Jaffe (1983) note that, in May 1981, the London, Ontario, police force instituted a policy that encouraged officers to lay assault charges in cases of domestic violence. Here, officers were told that they did not have to witness the assault—they only needed to have reasonable and probable grounds to believe that an assault had occurred, for example, injury serious enough for them to advise the women to seek medical attention. In addition, the officers were told that if the couple were no longer living together then the matter should proceed to criminal court, not to family court.

Burris and Jaffe (1983) compared the police charges laid for approximately the first four months of this operation with a six-month period in 1979. With just this one directive, the number of charges of common assault laid by police rose from zero in the six-month 1979 period to thirty-six in the four-month period in 1981. Charges of assault causing bodily harm laid by police rose from six to thirty-six.

The problem of the victims' reluctance to press charges is frequently cited as a reason for police non-intervention in domestic violence. However, under this new policy, the number of private informations—where the victims had to press charges themselves—dropped substantially, from forty-six to thirteen. This indicates that many victims of domestic violence—who were almost exclusively female—wanted judicial action but were not getting it in a large number of cases.

In line with this initiative, and the data from the controversial 1981–82 Minneapolis policing experiment, which found that only 19 percent of arrested abusers repeated their crime, compared with 35 percent of cases dealt with by mediation only, in 1983 a national directive was implemented in Canada to encourage police to lay charges in wife-battering cases.[10] Canada was the first country to adopt such a nation-wide directive. As Comack (1992) notes, police training was upgraded to stress sensitive intervention in wife-assault cases and several provinces have established specialized courts to deal with domestic violence.

The product of these initiatives is that, as Comack (1992) also states, increasing numbers of abusive men are being dealt with by the courts. She states that "in the province of Manitoba alone, for example, the number of individuals (approximately 96% of whom were men) charged with spousal assault increased from 1136 in 1983 to 2035 in 1988/89" (Comack 1992, 43). Moreover, as MacLeod (1987) stated in her second Canadian Advisory Council on the Status of Women report, the number of transition houses providing shelter for battered women more than tripled from 85 shelters in 1982 to 264 in 1987.

However, much criticism and controversy exists over the "success" of these recent initiatives. Currie (1990) and Currie et al. (1992) state that socialist feminists have serious concerns over how the current focus on violence against women can feed into a reactionary law-and-order lobby, which MacLeod (1987) states even the victims may not overly advocate. Interwoven here is the concern that this institutionalization of women's issues fails to deal with the situation of unequal distribution of societal resources and power facing women. Currie et al. (1992, 29) frame the problem well: "Within a discourse that concerns legal rights, police protection, and criminal justice, this issue is transformed into a technical matter that can be safely met within the current system without any significant changes in relations of power."

However, Ursel (1991) states, in her analysis of the battered women's movement and the specialized Winnipeg spousal abuse court, that the positive dimensions of this state-sponsored approach to domestic violence must be recognized. She recognizes that "not all actors and agencies in the field will share the analysis of patriarchy common to the founders of the battered women's movement" (1991, 285). Nonetheless, she does find some progress: "It has been demonstrated that, as a result of state involvement, the number of services for wife abuse victims increased ten fold from 1982 to 1990" (Ursel 1991, 283). With just these two "camps" noted, one might be tempted to view current developments in this area as simply a double-edged sword. However, Comack (1992, 146–47) redirects us to the continued importance of radical transformation in our society, when she writes of the Montreal massacre at the École Polytéchnique:

> While the murder of fourteen women in Montreal has understandably received the attention and publicity it deserves, it is also noteworthy that the violence that women encounter at the hands of men has become "routine." In August 1990 alone, eleven women in Montreal were killed by their male partners, many of them estranged. Yet, two of every three women going to a shelter in Montreal are turned away because of lack of space.

Judicial biases against women who have been the victims of sexual assault is the next important concern. One of the most criticized has been the well-known ruling in *Pappajohn* v. *the Queen* (1980). In this case, the controversial decision given in *Morgan* (1975) was upheld. In *Pappajohn*, the Supreme Court of Canada held that an honest mistake of belief to consent was grounds for a defence to the charge of rape, whether there were reasonable grounds for that belief or not. The Supreme Court also made it clear that this defence was permitted only in circumstances where there was evidence to support such a belief. This "honest-mistake-of-fact" defence was allowed in *Pappajohn*, even though in the latter part of the alleged repeated raping the victim was bound to the bedposts and gagged. Perhaps Pappajohn's "mistake" arose because, as the accused stated to the police, the complainant did "not violently" object when they first went to bed and did not "resist very much" (*Pappajohn* v. *the Queen*, 481–82).

One of the best-known statistics in this area comes from the 1982 Canadian Urban Victimization Survey. This study elicited data on the number of victimizations for a sample of residents in seven major Canadian cities. Frequency estimates of a range of property and violent crimes were calculated from the sample results.

For present purposes, what is most noteworthy is that only 38 percent of the estimated 17 300 sexual assaults, primarily against females, in these cities were reported to police. While a third of the victims of sexual assault cited fear of revenge by the offender, 43 percent cited the attitude of the police or courts as the reason for not reporting the incident. Sexually assaulted women were generally more afraid of the additional suffering and humiliation that the justice system would be likely to inflict on them than they were of reprisals by the offender.

Efforts have been made in Canada to reduce the trauma visited upon sexually assaulted women in recent years. First, the legal charge of rape was abolished in a 1983 reform to the Criminal Code, and three levels of sexual assault based on the degree of violence were established (cf. Bill C-127, January 1983). The intent here was to reduce the stigma of rape and to emphasize, as many sociologists and feminists had strenuously contended, that rape was primarily a violent act of male domination in sexual form. The rape prohibition was, moreover, primarily a paternalistic, property form of social control against females, not protective legislation.

Changes have also been made in the procedural law governing the examination of persons alleging sexual assault and the rules of evidence in such cases. Prior to 1983, the testimony of the victim alleging rape had to be corroborated by other evidence. If not, the judge had to instruct the jury on the danger of convicting the accused based upon uncorroborated testimony (Brannigan 1984, 27–28).[11] However, no such warning had to be issued in criminal trials generally—for example, if the victim were identifying an individual who had stolen her purse. The extent to which the victim can be questioned about her previous sexual activity in a sexual assault trial has also been formally limited (cf. the 1985 Commission on the Status of Women publication, *A Feminist Review of Criminal Law*, 109–13).

Much scepticism existed right from the start over the extent to which these changes would produce any meaningful increase in the reporting of sexual assault by females, as well as in the judicial stereotyping and traumatization of sexually assaulted women. As Allison (1991, 2) noted, despite the legal reforms, many feminists maintained that "justice" would still be elusive for many victims of sexual violence, as "changing the content of the law does not ensure that implementation of the changes will reflect the objectives of the legislature." This scepticism was apparently warranted. In August 1991 the Supreme Court of Canada, in a 7-2 decision, struck down Section 246.6 of the Criminal Code, or the "rape shield provision." This section of the Code had been instituted in the 1983 reform with the aim of preventing a victim's sexual conduct from being used to discredit her. This 1991 ruling was justified on the basis that Section 246.6 could deny the accused the right to a fair trial, as enshrined in Sections 7 and 11(d) of the Charter.

Next, and finally, we turn to the injustices and problems faced by incarcerated women. Within this area three particular concerns need discussion. This is not so much because the concerns are unique to women but because they also exemplify the ideologies and social practices that are often central in the subjugation of females in paternalistic and capitalistic societies.

As Berzins and Cooper noted in their forceful critique of incarcerated females, "An historical review of the treatment of the federal female offender in Canada reveals a mixture of neglect, outright barbarism and well-meaning paternalism" (1982, 401). Currie (1986) would probably challenge the "well-meaning" dimension of paternalism they refer to; at most, it reflects the "helping" attitude that masks the social control and subjugation of women. More accurate is the statement by Ekstedt and Griffiths that "prison, as a microcosm of society, reflects all those inequalities which discriminate against women, be their source historical, social or administrative convenience" (1988, 337). These authors point out that this was the conclusion of the 1978 British Columbia Ministry of the Attorney General report on provincially incarcerated women. The truth of this statement, past and present, can be documented by looking at the three areas of female incarceration.

In *Young Offenders and the State* (1984), West cites research by Barnhorst (1980) as showing that, at least until the mid-1970s, young females with short delinquency records were more likely than adolescent males to be referred to court by police, and to receive harsher treatment when they got there. As Geller noted in her article in *Too Few to Count* (1987), research in Hamilton, Ontario, in the early 1970s found that after a finding of delinquency a greater proportion of young females than males were incarcerated in what were termed "training schools." Specifically, one female was brought to court for six males, yet one female for every three males was institutionalized.

West stated that three-quarters of young females incarcerated were deemed to be neglected or dependent, *not* delinquent. Here we find females whose "offences" consisted primarily of apparent early sexuality, truancy, disobedience, swearing, and running away. Yet research shows that young females are less sexually active than young males, and involved in very little serious delinquency. And as West noted, "Most of the training schools, despite slick promotional literature ... have usually been nothing more than custodial institutions" (1984, 189). Debilitating incarceration, not protection and training, are the daily norm in these institutions. West concurs with Geller (1987) that the youth court was more concerned, under the rhetoric of paternalism, with policing the boundaries of traditional gender stereotypes than it was with the protection of young females per se.

The old Juvenile Delinquency Act of 1908 has been replaced by the Young Offenders Act (YOA) (1981), which was phased in during the early 1980s. This new act was supposed to end the evils of the previous juvenile legislation. For example, juveniles can now no longer be formally prosecuted or incarcerated for "status offences," such as truancy and incorrigibility. As has been noted, however, the YOA is being used to bring more youth into court for minor and major offences.

For instance, increases of 150 percent in incarceration rates for youth have been noted in Manitoba since the introduction of the YOA, and youth are apparently being held in custody much longer (Getter 1987, 121). When one adds to this the fact that provinces are still able to adopt child protection legislation, the strong suspicion and fear arises that young offenders courts and youth protection agencies will continue to enforce gender-based inequalities in the treatment of young females. A similar conclusion surfaces when we consider the controversy over federally sentenced women.

Cooper analyzes the evolution of the Federal Prison for Women in Kingston. In 1934, P4W opened its doors across the road from the Kingston Penitentiary for Men, where federally sentenced women had previously been housed. The management of P4W continued to be the responsibility of the male penitentiary warden. Here all federally sentenced women were to be gathered from across Canada into a centralized institution, modelled generally after federal male penitentiaries. However, at P4W there were no gun towers. Nor, unfortunately, were there any outside windows, recreation grounds within the enclosure, provision for outdoor exercise of any kind, or educational facilities for the female prisoners (1987, 13).

It is thus not surprising that virtually every major commission investigating Canada's penal system, from Archambault (1938) onward—and there were many—severely criticized conditions at P4W and generally recommended its closure. The relatively small number of female prisoners should be housed, it was generally concluded, in their home provinces. Indeed, as Cooper (1987) noted, since 1968, no fewer than thirteen government studies, investigations, and private-sector reports reiterated this basic conclusion.

Women for Justice, seeing the lack of change that accompanied report after report, finally achieved a landmark 1981 Human Rights of Canada Commission decision. The commission ruled that the Correctional Services of Canada was discriminating against female prisoners at P4W. Berzins and Cooper (1982) note that, in particular, major deficiencies in facilities and programs compared to those available to federally incarcerated men were identified.

Federal penitentiaries for men are spread across the country, but the Kingston facility is the only federal institution for women. With only one facility, all federally sentenced women (except those sent to provincial institutions) are housed as maximum security prisoners, which also provides justification for limiting the quantity and quality of programs.

In a 1990 coroner's inquest into the death of Sandra Sayer, the high suicide rate of women at P4W, especially of Native women, most of whom are incarcerated far from home, has been clearly related to this type of systemic discrimination. Sayer, a 24-year-old Saulteaux, was found hanging from the bars of her cell less than two months before her expected release date. At P4W this was not unusual. In early February of 1991, a group of female prisoners at P4W barricaded themselves in the prison recreation room to protest the fourth aboriginal inmate suicide in sixteen months. The institution's response was to quell the protest by use of an assault team, dogs, and tear gas (*Star Phoenix*, February 13, 1991). One central concern at P4W was that no specialized psychiatric facilities were available for traumatized female inmates. At P4W, segregation facilities were used for this purpose. To make matters worse, these facilities have also been criticized as inferior to those in any male institution (Berzins and Cooper 1982, 406).

Another blatant discrimination, these authors note, is in the area of programs. Ekstedt and Griffiths (1988) discuss in detail the inadequacies and biases of programs at P4W and in provincial institutions, and provide a history of the criticism that has been levelled at them. Prison programs for women distinctly repeat, and attempt to reinforce, the stereotypical social and occupational roles of women in society. Working in the prison laundry, working in a beauty parlour, doing kitchen work, and learning sewing were cited in the 1978 Proudfoot Commission inquiry as typical correctional programs for women. Berzins and Hayes note that the epitome of education in P4W, newly introduced as a result of the Human Rights Commission decision, is the introduction of word processors. But women were to be taught keyboarding only, not programming, reinforcing their chances of experiencing poverty on their release and hence possibly starting the criminal cycle again (1987, 173).

The announcement has been made that P4W will be closed. Five new regional facilities, including a "healing centre" at Maple Creek, Saskatchewan, for aboriginal women, are to be built. It remains to be seen, however, how much these will improve the lives of incarcerated females. It certainly will do nothing to provide greater social justice for women. Indeed, with more space and a possible veneer of "easier time," the judiciary may be more inclined to sentence women to federal incarceration.

As stated at the beginning of this section, in order to move beyond limited piecemeal and partial socio-legal analyses of gender and social justice, it is necessary to develop a more comprehensive theoretical, analytical, and policy-based socialist–feminist critique of our so-called society. To quote Currie (1986, 237),

> What is necessary is a distinctly "feminist" criminology which can explain crime in general while studying women in particular. The goal of such an investigation should be not only to understand the involvement of women in officially recorded crime, but to understand the oppression of women, without this becoming a tool of oppression itself.

Gregory (198) concurs with Currie (1986) when the latter states that what is needed is a dynamic, integrated analysis of the interrelationships between patriarchy, capitalist society, and state control of women. Of course, critical criminologists have come to see ethnicity as an integral part of this project.

Conclusions

Is it likely that the unequal involvement and treatment of women and minorities in the justice system that we have described will be reduced significantly in the near future? Liberal–critical initiatives that seek to reduce the overuse of incarceration for relatively petty offences, to change sexual assault laws and in-court procedures, and to produce justice system programs better suited to the needs of Native and female offenders may have some possibility of success. These initiatives do not seriously threaten the current status quo in Canadian society.

In order to reduce significantly the inequities described in this chapter, however, we need to focus on the structural and cultural conditions and the distribution of power in society that lie at the centre of the problem.

Basic changes at this level, which radical–critical criminologists and sociologists have long argued for, are much more difficult to apply than liberal–critical solutions to inequalities of involvement and treatment in the justice system based upon class, ethnicity, and gender.

Study Questions

1. Critically evaluate the truth of the statement that "criminal law and the justice system protect us from serious economic and physical harm."

2. To what extent are upper-class individuals treated more favourably than lower-class people by the Canadian justice system?

3. Explain the nature of and reasons for the overinvolvement of Native people in the justice system.

4. Are women treated better by the justice system than men? Explain.

5. How likely is it that inequalities of involvement and treatment in the justice system based upon class, ethnicity, and gender will disappear in the near future?

Recommended Reading

Aboriginal Justice Inquiry of Manitoba. *The Justice System and Aboriginal People.* Report. Winnipeg: Supply and Services Canada, 1991.

Adelberg, Ellen, and Claudia Currie. *Too Few to Count: Canadian Women in Conflict with the Law*. Vancouver: Press Gang, 1987.

Brannigan, Augustine. *Crimes, Courts, and Corrections*. Toronto: Holt, Rinehart and Winston, 1984.

Currie, Dawn. "Female Criminality: A Crisis in Feminist Theory." In *The Political Economy of Crime*, ed. B. MacLean. Scarborough, ON: Prentice-Hall, 1986.

McMullan, John. *Beyond the Limits of The Law: Corporate Crime and Law and Order*. Halifax: Fernwood, 1992.

Snider, Laureen. "Commercial Crime." In *Deviance: Conformity and Control in Canadian Society*, ed. V. Sacco. Scarborough, ON: Prentice-Hall, 1988.

Notes

1. See Gregory (1986), Currie (1986), and Currie and MacLean (1986) for analyses of developments and problematic issues in feminist criminology.
2. In critical sociology, there has been much concern about how to conceptualize social class (Wight 1985). Specifying the exact dynamics of the relationship between an upper-class elite and the political–legal process has also been contentious (Brickley and Comack 1986, 17–21).
3. Wealth is very concentrated in Canada. The richest one-fifth of Canadians have 40 percent of the wealth, while the poorest fifth have about 6 percent nationally (National Council of Welfare 1985). Further, eight corporate conglomerates control about 30 percent of the 300 companies listed on the Toronto Stock Exchange (Forcese 1986, 60). Corporate tax revenue collected between 1971 and 1986 dropped slightly from $1.4 billion to $1.2 billion. In the same period, however, personal tax revenue levied jumped almost 900 percent, from $0.8 billion to $7.1 billion (Alberta Facts, 1988). Economic difficulties faced by individuals and families, and the intra-class street crimes that go with them, are thus partly engineered by government fiscal policy. In general, this shift of the tax burden from corporations to individuals since the early 1960s has had nation-wide effect. For a review of political economy perspectives in Canada, see Myles (1989) in the *Canadian Review of Sociology and Anthropology*, special issue, *Comparative Political Economy*.
4. Thus, most early criminological research was directed toward theorizing and investigating the specific factors in the lives of the lower class that could be responsible for lower-class criminal involvement.
5. See especially the critique by Hartnagel (1987, 99) of the measures of social class in the class-crime relationship,
6. See Downes and Rock (1982) for a good explanation and evaluation of labelling approaches to the study of deviance.
7. The cultural and structural dislocation of Native people in Canada has been well documented generally (Purich 1986; Czerny and Swift 1988), as well as for Native offenders specifically (Hylton 1982; LaPrairie 1988). Academic critiques of these conditions have, moreover, been amply supported by the 1980 Indian and Northern Affairs Canada publication, *Indian Conditions: A Survey*. Some basic facts about Native life: at age one year, Natives have a life expectancy approximately ten years less than other Canadians; the Native suicide rate is almost three times the national average; and for Natives fifteen to twenty-five years old, it is over six times the national average; as few as 10 percent of houses on reserves in Manitoba and Saskatchewan have running water and sewage disposal; Native retention to the end of secondary school is about 20 percent, as compared to a national average of 75 percent; only about 32 percent of working-age Natives are employed; welfare dependency often approaches 70 percent and has increased noticeably in certain areas in past years, for example among the Lubicon.
8. See Hylton (1982) for a discussion of the impact that demographic shifts in the Native versus non-Native population have on increases in Native incarceration rates.

References

Adelberg, E., and C. Currie, eds. 1987. *Too Few to Count: Canadian Women in Conflict With the Law*. Vancouver: Press Gang.

Adler, F. 1975. *Sisters in Crime*. New York: McGraw Hill.

Allison, M. 1991. "Judicious Judgements? Examining the Impact of Sexual Assault Legislation on Judicial Definitions of Sexual Violence." In *Criminal Justice: Sentencing Issues and Reforms*, ed. L. Samuelson and B. Schissel. Toronto: Garamond Press. 279–97.

Barnhorst, S. 1980. "Female Delinquency and Sex-Role Stereotype." LL.M. thesis. Queen's University.

Berzins, L., and S. Cooper. 1982. "The Political Economy of Correctional Planning for Women: The Case of the Bankrupt Bureaucracy." *Canadian Journal of Criminology* 24: 399–417.

Berzins, L., and B. Hayes. 1987. "The Diaries of Two Change Agents." In Adelberg and Currie, *Too Few*. 163–79.

Bienvenue, P., and A. Latif. 1974. "Arrests, Dispositions, and Recidivism: A Comparison of Indians and Whites." *Canadian Journal of Criminology and Corrections* 16: 105–16.

Blumberg, A. 1969. "The Practice of Law as Confidence Game: Organizational Cooptation of a Profession." In *Crime and the Legal Process*, ed. W. Chambliss. New York: McGraw Hill. 220–37.

Boldt, E., L. Hursch, S. Johnson and K. Taylor. 1983. "Presentence Reports and the Incarceration of Natives." *Canadian Journal of Criminology* 25: 269–76.

Bonta, J. 1989. "Native Inmates: Institutional Response, Risk, and Needs." *Canadian Journal of Criminology* 31: 49–62.

Brannigan, A. 1984. *Crimes, Courts, and Corrections*. Toronto: Holt, Rinehart and Winston.

Brickley, S., and E. Comack. 1986. *The Social Basis of Law*. Toronto: Garamond.

Burris, C., and P. Jaffe. 1983. "Wife Abuse as a Crime: The Impact of Police Laying Charges." *Canadian Journal of Criminology* 25: 309–18.

Canada. 1974. *The Native Offender and the Law*. Ottawa: The Law Reform Commission of Canada.

Canadian Committee on Corrections. 1969. *Toward Unity: Criminal Justice and Corrections*. Ottawa: Queen's Printer.

Chambliss, W., and R. Seidman. 1971. *Law, Order, and Power*. Reading, MA: Addison-Wesley.

Clinard, M., and P. Yeager. 1980. *Corporate Crime*. New York: The Free Press.

Coleman, J. 1985. *The Criminal Elite*. New York: St. Martin's.

Comack, E. 1992. "Women and Crime." In *Criminology: A Canadian Perspective,* 2d ed., ed. R. Linden. Toronto: Harcourt Brace Jovanovich. 127–62.

Conklin, J. 1977. *Illegal But Not Criminal*. New York: Spectrum.

Conly, D. 1977. *A Descriptive Analysis of Delinquency Patterns and Police Action in Twelve Major Metropolitan Canadian Cities During the Month of December, 1976*. Ottawa: Solicitor General.

Cooper, S. 1987. "The Evolution of The Federal Women's Prison." Adelberg and Currie. 127–44.

Cullen, F., W. Maakestadt, and G. Cavender. 1987. *Corporate Crime Under Attack: The Ford Pinto Case and Beyond.* Cincinnati: Anderson.

Currie, D. 1986. "Female Criminality: A Crisis in Feminist Theory," In *The Political Economy of Crime,* ed. B. MacLean. Scarborough, ON: Prentice-Hall.

———. 1990. "Battered women and the State: From a Failure of Theory to a Theory of Failure." *Journal of Human Justice* 1:77–96.

Currie, D., and B. MacLean. 1986. *The Administration of Justice*. Saskatoon: Social Research Unit, Department of Sociology, University of Saskatchewan.

Currie, D., B. MacLean, and D. Milovanovich. 1992. "Three Traditions of Critical Justice Inquiry: Class, Gender, and Discourse." In *Rethinking the Administration of Justice*, ed. D. Currie and B. MacLean. Halifax: Fernwood.

Czerny, M., and J. Swift. 1988. *Getting Started on Social Analysis in Canada*. Toronto:Between the Lines.

Daubney, D., chairman. 1988. *Taking Responsibility: Report of the Standing Committee on Justice and Solicitor General on Aspects of Corrections.* Ottawa: Supply and Services Canada.

Dobash, R., and R. Dobash. 1979. *Violence Against Wives: A Case Against the Patriarchy*. New York: The Free Press.

Downes, D., and P. Rock. 1982. *Understanding Deviance*. Oxford: Clarendon Press.

Ellis, D. 1986. *The Wrong Stuff.* Toronto: Collier McMillian.

Ermann, M., and R. Lundman. 1982. *Corporate Deviance*. New York: Holt, Rinehart and Winston.

Ekstedt, J., and C. Griffiths. 1988. *Corrections in Canada*. Toronto: Butterworths.

Fisse, B., and J. Braithwaite. 1983. *The Impact of Publicity on Corporate Offenders*. New York: State University of New York Press.

Forcese, D. 1986. *The Canadian Class Structure*. 3d ed. Toronto: McGraw-Hill Ryerson.

Fox, J., and T. Hartnagel. 1979. "Changing Social Roles and Female Crime in Canada." *Canadian Review of Sociology and Anthropology* 16: 96–104.

Frechette, M., and M. LeBlanc. 1979. *La Délinquence Cachée de l'Adolescente*. Montreal: Le Groupe de Recherche sur l'Inadaptation Juvénile, Université de Montreal.

Gandy, J. 1967. "The Exercise of Discretion by the Police in the Handling of Juveniles." D.S.W. thesis. Toronto: University of Toronto.

Geller, G. 1987. "Young Women in Conflict with the Law." In Adelberg and Currie, *Too Few*. 113–26.

Glasbeek, H., and S. Rowland. 1986. "Are Injuring and Killing in the Workplace Crimes?" In *The Social Basis of Law*, ed. N. Boyd. Scarborough, ON: Prentice-Hall. 66–85.

Goff, C., and C. Reasons. 1978. *Corporate Crime in Canada*. Scarborough, ON: Prentice-Hall.

Grainger, R. 1981. *Unemployment and Crime: A Critique of Methodology*. Ottawa: Solicitor General of Canada.

Greenberg, D. 1977. "Delinquency and the Age-Structure of Society." *Contemporary Crises* 1: 189–223.

Gregory, J. 1986. "Sex, Class, and Crime: Towards a Non-sexist Criminology." *The Political Economy of Crime*. Scarborough, ON: Prentice-Hall.

Hagan, J. 1974. "Criminal Justice and Native People: A Study of Incarceration in a Canadian Province." *Canadian Review of Sociology and Anthropology* (Special Issue) 220–36.

———. 1975. "Law, Order and Sentencing: A Study of Attitude in Action." *Sociometry* 38: 374–84.

———. 1977. "Criminal Justice in Rural and Urban Communities: A Study of the Bureaucratization of Justice." *Social Forces* 55: 597–612.

———. 1985. *Modern Criminology*. Toronto: McGraw-Hill.

———. 1987. "White-Collar and Corporate Crime." In *Criminology: A Canadian Perspective*, ed. R. Linden. Toronto: Holt, Rinehart and Winston. 320–36.

———. 1992. "White Collar and Corporate Crime." In *Criminology: A Canadian Perspective*, 2d ed., ed. R. Linden. Toronto: Harcourt Brace Jovanovich. 451–73.

Hagan, J., J. Simpson, and R. Gillis. 1979. "The Sexual Stratification of Social Control: A Gender Based Perspective on Crime and Delinquency." *British Journal of Sociology* 30: 25–37.

Hartnagel, T. 1987. "Correlates of Criminal Behavior." In *Criminology: A Canadian Perspective*, ed. R. Linden. Toronto: Holt, Rinehart and Winston. 74–101.

Haveman, P., K. Couse, L. Foster, and R. Matonvich. 1985. *Law and Order for Canada's Indigenous People*. Regina: School of Human Justice, University of Regina.

Hawkins, D. 1987. "Beyond Anomalies: Rethinking the Conflict Perspective on Race and Criminal Punishment." *Social Forces*. 65, no. 3: 719–45.

Hylton, J. 1982. "The Native Offender in Saskatchewan: Some Implications for Crime Prevention Programming." *Canadian Journal of Criminology* 24: 121–31.

Jaffe, P., and C. Burris. 1981. *An Integrated Response to Wife Assault: A Community Model*. Ottawa: Solicitor General of Canada.

Johnson, H. 1987. "Getting the Facts Straight: A Statistical Overview." In Adelberg and Currie, *Too Few*. 23–46.

Jolly, S., C. Peters, and S. Spiegel. 1979. *Progress Report on Government Action Taken Since the 1975 Federal-Provincial Conference on Native Peoples and the Criminal Justice System*. Ottawa and Toronto: Solicitor General of Canada and the Ontario Native Council on Justice.

Krahn, H., and G. Lowe. 1988. *Work, Industry, and Canadian Society*. Scarborough, ON: Nelson.

LaPrairie, C. 1983. "Native Juveniles in Court: Some Preliminary Observations." In *Deviant Designations*, ed. T. Fleming and L. Visano. Toronto: Butterworths. 337–50.

———. 1988. "The Young Offenders Act and Aboriginal Youth." In *Justice and The Young Offender in Canada*, ed. J. Hudson et. al. Toronto: Wall and Thompson, 1988: 159–68.

LeBlanc, M. 1975. "Upper Class vs. Working Class Delinquency." In *Crime in Canadian Society*, ed. R. Silverman and J. Teevan. Toronto: Butterworths. 102–18.

———. 1983. "Delinquency as an Epiphenomenon of Adolescence." In *Current Issues in Juvenile Justice*, ed. R. Corrado et al. Toronto: Butterworths. 31–48.

MacLeod, L. 1980. *Wife Battering in Canada: The Vicious Circle*. Ottawa: Canadian Advisory Council on The Status of Women, Minister of Supply and Services.

———. 1987. *Battered But Not Beaten ... Preventing Battering in Canada*. Ottawa: Canadian Advisory Council on the Status of Women.

McMullan, J. 1992. *Beyond the Limits of the Law: Corporate Crime and Law and Order*. Halifax: Fernwood.

Mandel, M. 1983. “Imprisonment, Class, and Democracy in Contemporary Canadian Capitalism.” Mimeograph. Toronto: Osgoode Hall Law School.

———. 1986. “Democracy, Class and Canadian Sentencing Law.” In *The Social Basis of Law,* ed. S. Brickey and E. Comack. Toronto, Garamond Press. 137–64.

McCaskill, D. 1985. *Patterns of Criminality and Correction Among Native Offenders in Manitoba: A Longitudinal Analysis*. Saskatoon: Correctional Service of Canada.

Mikel, D. 1979/80. “Native Society in Crisis.” *Crime and Justice* 617: 32–41.

Myles, J. 1989. “Introduction: Understanding Canada: Comparative Political Economy Perspectives.” *Canadian Review of Sociology and Anthropology* 26: 1–9.

National Council of Welfare. 1985. *Poverty Profile 1985*. Ottawa: Supply and Services Canada.

Nease, B, 1968. “Measuring Juvenile Delinquency in Hamilton.” In *Deviant Behaviour in Canada*, ed. W. Mann. Toronto: Social Science Publications. 43–54.

Pappajohn v. The Queen. 1980. *52 Canadian Criminal Cases*, 2d ed. 481–515

Piliavin, J., and S. Briar. 1964. “Police Encounters with Juveniles.” *American Journal of Sociology* 70: 206–47.

“Poverty in Our Province: Taxing the Poor.” *Alberta Facts*. (Edmonton Social Planning Council) 4 (1988).

Purich, D. 1986. *Our Land: Native Rights in Canada*. Toronto: James Lorimer.

Quinney, R. 1970. *The Social Reality of Crime*. Boston: Little, Brown and Company.

———. 1977. *Class, State, and Crime*. New York: David McKay.

Ratner, R., and J. McMullan. 1987. *State Control: Criminal Justice Politics in Canada*. Vancouver: University of British Columbia Press.

Reasons, C., L. Ross, and C. Patterson. 1991. “Your Money and Your Life: Workers Health in Canada.” In *The Social Basis of Law*, 2d ed., ed. S. Brickey and E. Comack. Toronto: Garamond Press. 131–41.

Sargent, N. 1989. “Law, Ideology, and Corporate Crime: A Critique of Instrumentalism.” *Canadian Journal of Law and Society* 4: 39–75.

Satzewich, V., and T. Wotherspoon. 1993. *First Nations: Race, Class, and Gender Relations*. Toronto: Nelson.

Scull, A. 1976–77. “Madness and Segregative Controls: The Rise of the Insane Asylum.” *Social Problems* 24: 337–51.

Short, J., and F. Nye. 1957. “Reported Behavior as a Criterion of Deviant Behavior.” *Social Problems* 5: 207–13.

Smith, D., and C. Visher. 1980. “Sex and Involvement in Deviance/Crime.” *American Sociological Review* 45: 691–701.

Snider, L. 1978. “Corporate Crime in Canada: A Preliminary Report.” *Canadian Journal of Criminology* 5: 142–68.

—. 1988. “Commercial Crime.” In *Deviance: Conformity and Control in Canadian Society*, ed. V. Sacco. Scarborough, ON: Prentice-Hall. 231–83.

Snider, L., and G. West. 1980. “A Critical Perspective on Law in the Canadian State: Delinquency and Corporate Crime.” In *Power and Change in Canada*, ed. R. Ossenberg. Toronto: McClelland and Stewart.

Spitzer, S. 1975. “Towards a Marxian Theory of Deviance.” *Social Problems* 22: 638–51.

———. 1983. “The Rationalization of Crime Control in Capitalist Society. “ In *Social Control and the State*, ed. S. Cohen and A. Scull. Oxford: Martin Robinson. 312–33.

Statistics Canada. 1988. *Canadian Crime Statistics*. Ottawa: Supply and Services Canada.

Steffensmeier, D. 1980. “Sex Differences in Patterns of Adult Crime, 1965–77.” *Social Forces* 58: 1080–108.

Stevens, S. 1991. “Aboriginal People and the Canadian Justice System.” In *Criminal Justice: Sentencing Issues and Reforms*, eds. L. Samuelson and B. Schissel. Toronto: Garamond Press.

Sugar, F., and L. Fox. 1989/90. “Nistum peyako sht’wawin iskwewak: Breakin Chains.” *Canadian Journal of Womens Law* 3:465–82.

Sutherland, E.H. 1977. “Crimes of Corporations.” In *White-Collar Crime: Offences in Business, Politics, and the Professions*, ed. G. Geis and R. Meier. New York: Free Press. 71–84.

Task Force on Aboriginal Peoples in Federal Corrections. 1988. Final Report. Ottawa: Supply and Services Canada.

Task Force on the Status of Women. 1985. *A Feminist Review of Criminal Law*. Ottawa: Supply and Services Canada.

Taylor, I., P. Walton, and J. Young. 1973. *The New Criminology: For a Social Theory of Deviance*. London: Routledge and Kegan Paul.

Ursel, J. 1991. "Considering the Impact of the Battered Women's Movement on the State: The Example of Manitoba." In *The Social Basis of Law*, 2d ed., ed. E. Comack and S. Brickey. Halifax: Garamond Press. 261–88.

Verdun-Jones, S., and G. Muirhead. 1982. "The Native in the Criminal Justice System: Canadian Research." In *The Canadian Criminal Justice System*, ed. C. Boydell and I. Connidis. Toronto: Holt, Rinehart and Winston. 266–81.

West, G. 1984. *Young Offenders and the State*. Toronto: Butterworths.

Wheeler, S., and M. Rothman. 1982. "The Organization as Weapon in White Collar Crime." *Michigan Law Review* 80, no. 7:1403–26.

Wilkins, J. 1975. *Legal Aid in the Criminal Courts*. Toronto: University of Toronto.

Wright, E. 1985. *Classes*. London: New Left Books.

Wynne, D., and T. Hartnagel. 1975. "Race and Plea Negotiation," *Canadian Journal of Sociology*. 1: 147–55.

CHAPTER 21

Transforming Canada's Education System: The Impact on Educational Inequalities, Opportunities, and Benefits

Terry Wotherspoon

Learning Objectives

The objective of this chapter is to make a clear distinction between the ideology and the reality of recent educational reforms. In particular, the student should contrast the notion of educational opportunity with the structured inequalities in education based especially on class, gender, and racial dimensions. Finally, the student should understand the process of educational transformation as a consequence of, as well as a contributing factor to, wider political and economic changes.

Introduction

"What's Wrong at School?" the headline screams from the feature story of the January 11, 1993, edition of *Maclean's* magazine. It is a question that, over the past decade, has been raised with increasing frequency by political and business leaders and through the mass media. From the high-profile report of the U.S. National Commission on Excellence in Education (1983), which stressed the urgent need to attack an apparent crisis of educational "mediocrity" in America, to repeated calls for "lifelong learning," "flexible" educational programs, and "core curricula" throughout Canada and elsewhere, there is a sense that something is amiss in school systems, and that it requires immediate and extensive repair. David Crombie, Canada's secretary of state in 1988, declared that "we must begin rebuilding our system of post-secondary education today if we are to give succeeding generations their 'fighting chance' tomorrow.... Certainly in the future, even more than today, education will be a life-long process and repeated retraining will be a routine matter for everyone" (Secretary of State 1988, 13–14). Investment in the learner is a "key to economic advancement" in an "increasingly tough world economy," according to the former Ontario premier, David Peterson, while a "loose and tight" school system "in which freedom exists within structure, in which the system's need for conformity and standardization is balanced by no less important needs for diversity and individualization" was advocated in a 1988 royal commission report on education in British Columbia (British Columbia 1988, 220; *Star–Phoenix* [Saskatoon] April 25, 1989: A14).

Surely most of us would readily agree with the sentiment that formal education should be made relevant to the changing needs of both the learner and society, since a stagnant education system offers few advantages to anyone. But what is the connection between the rhetoric and realities of educational transformation? Why has there been a resurgence of interest in the politics of education? Who is defining the issues, and what are the implications of educational structures and transformations for learners and other social groups? This chapter addresses these questions by considering the ways in which formal education contributes to social inequalities of class, gender, and race. The chapter contends that formal education operates in contradictory ways. While general trends to increase the provision of formal educational services have tended to expand opportunities for minority groups, education has also contributed to the subordination of these minorities. In this context, current debates around education are linked to the agendas of political and economic interests that seek to make education and its consequent inequalities more directly responsive to priorities determined by capitalist labour markets and the aggressive quest for new avenues of profitable investment.

The Politics of Educational Reform

From its inception, mass public schooling has been employed to integrate children into the fabric of social life. It is important to recognize, though, that the social "mainstream" is not a natural or given entity but rather is subject to different definitions and organizational forms advanced by persons who occupy distinct places within the social structure. The various perspectives that people employ to make sense of social reality affect not only where they stand on particular social or political issues, but also what phenomena they consider to be debatable issues. Our ability to understand the world always involves, of necessity, some selectivity. Not all positions, however, are considered valid in the context of politics, media, and other public discourse. In fact, one of the major consequences of modern education systems is to offer legitimacy to particular views of the world that correspond to dominant patterns of activity and belief, serving in the process to undermine or ignore alternatives (Apple 1988; Wotherspoon 1987).

For example, few people would disagree that high illiteracy rates pose a disturbing dilemma in an era in which nearly all individuals have access to at least ten years of free public schooling. Over the past few years, an extensive media blitz and a series of government-funded programs served to remind us how pressing a problem illiteracy was. They focussed on a 1987 national newspaper survey, which claimed that more than one in five Canadians lacked necessary skills in reading, writing, or computing to the extent that their ability to perform everyday work tasks was impaired. Yet, despite the high profile given the issue, few commentators challenged the timing of the sudden elevation to public consciousness of a phenomenon that had existed for decades. Even fewer sought to explain why something that was commonly seen as a social problem had been transformed into an economic matter that "cost" business "at least $4 billion a year in accidents, errors and lost productivity," with an estimated additional $6 billion lost annually in earnings, training, and other costs (Maynard 1989, 88). Individuals and schools were blamed for their failure to produce a literate population. Meanwhile, the possibility was ignored that illiteracy was in fact the product of a complex set of economic and social relationships that had for decades proven beneficial to groups such as employers of low-cost, poorly qualified labour power. At a more general level, the search for educational "excellence" and "quality" that characterized the war against illiteracy had a broad appeal that masked the real intentions of business interests to promote a type of "excellence" and "quality" that served their own particular purposes (Shor 1986).

Until the recent attacks on education systems, the most common way in which participation in education has been viewed in our society has been through a liberal orientation that addresses the rights and opportunities of individuals. The liberal perspective portrays formal education as a vehicle for nurturing the talents and capacities of each individual in harmony with his or her ability to contribute productively to social development. Such a view contends that to deny opportunity to individuals or groups of people is both morally unjust and counterproductive to the advancement of society, since industrial societies cannot afford to allow talent and brainpower to go to waste. The liberal orientation is often supported with reference to notions of a meritocracy in which social and economic rewards, such as prestige and wealth, are allocated to individuals as an incentive to maintain skilled and industrious performance in order to fulfil the most crucial social tasks (see Mazurek 1987).

Conceptions of equality of opportunity emphasize the need for fairness in social organization. Even the most ardent advocates of the liberal view acknowledge that there are several meanings to "equality of opportunity," ranging from simple assurances that all persons are allowed exposure to schooling and other common services to more active measures that attempt to equalize people's life chances (see Coleman 1968). Still, each of the liberal variants is premised on the assumption that individual differences are translated into unequal distributions of social rewards and outcomes without which society would be unable to function effectively and efficiently.

Despite the appeal for fairness and justice in liberal conceptions of equality of opportunity, and widespread public support for the sentiment that equality of opportunity should be a guiding principle in the organization of Canadian schools (Livingstone and Hart 1987, 21–22), several challenges to the notion have been mounted in recent years. As John Porter observed in 1977, "If the question were asked which of the major social innovations of the twentieth century had most failed in its mission a likely answer would be public education" (Porter 1987, 242). Both the political right and left have questioned the usefulness of equality of opportunity as an organizing principle in capitalist societies, the former because government efforts to maintain the rights of minority groups are seen as too costly to maintain and contrary to the principles of market-driven economies, and the latter because the promised opportunities have not been delivered for many persons in the form of substantial social advancement. This dissatisfaction is in part responsible for the emergence of contemporary debates over the future of education. On one side are proponents of a conservative view that schools are failing to teach the fundamental knowledge and skills required in a core area of academic subjects, while on the other are parents and employers who demand that schooling be made more directly responsive to labour-force requirements (Livingstone 1985). Regardless of the different positions on what schools should be doing, schooling is subject to the critique that whatever it is doing now is inadequate.

Unfortunately, most critics of public education's apparent failure tend to substitute a general discontent with formal educational institutions for a more sustained analysis of what schools do and why they operate as they do. An excessive faith in the ability of formal education systems either to overcome social and economic disparities or to match labour-force requirements is based on a misrepresentation of the history and practice of education. Education systems are not and cannot be an effective panacea for social and labour-market problems. In practice, as Carnoy and Levin (1985, 5) emphasize, formal systems of education in capitalist societies are driven by two contradictory dynamics. One is the thrust in liberal democracies toward greater equality of opportunity and participation in economic and political life for all members of society; the other is the fundamental conflict and inequality upon which a capitalist economy is based. In other words, while educational institutions are important mechanisms whereby persons are channelled into various positions within social divisions of labour governed by relations of domination, subordination, and exploitation, schools remain part of a public sphere of social life that is open to scrutiny and participation by a diverse, often conflicting, array of social groups.

The Dimensions of Educational Expansion in Canada

One of the major consequences of educational conflict and contradictions has been the massive expansion of the education sector within the welfare state. As the data in Table 21.1 indicate, annual educational expenditures in Canada have increased steadily since the Second World War, rising by a factor of more than 126 times between 1950–51 and 1993–94. The strongest growth has been at the university, community college, and trade/vocational training levels. The figures suggest a strong national commitment to educational expansion, especially as educational expenditures climbed to reach nearly one-tenth of Canada's gross national product (GNP) in 1970. Despite slower rates of growth in educational expenditures and their decreased proportion of the GNP from the late 1970s through the 1980s, the continuing high levels of fiscal support for education have opened opportunities for greater segments of the population to benefit from participation in educational programs.

Evidence of increased postwar educational enrollment is shown in Table 21.2, although it is clear that the rates of enrollment increase have been substantially

TABLE 21.1: Expenditures on Education in Canada, by Level, 1950–1993 $ million (% increase over preceding period in parentheses)

Year	Elementary/ Secondary	Trade/ Vocational	Non-university Postsecondary	University	Total	Total education expenditures as % of GDP[a]
1950–51	359.1	12.8	11.6	55.2	438.8	2.4
1955–56	674.4 (87.8)	19.2 (50.0)	31.0 (167.2)	104.4 (89.1)	829.0 (8.9)	2.9
1960–61	1 328.3 (97.0)	47.2 (145.8)	57.6 (85.8)	272.9 (161.4)	1 706.0 (105.8)	4.4
1965–66	2 410.8 (81.5)	153.4 (225.0)	98.8 (71.5)	736.6 (169.9)	3 399.6 (99.3)	6.1
1970–71	4 880.4 (102.4)	574.8 (274.7)	430.0 (335.2)	1 790.8 (143.1)	7 676.0 (125.8)	9.0
1975–76	8 433.8 (72.8)	841.8 (46.5)	975.7 (126.9)	2 760.5 (54.1)	13 011.8 (69.5)	7.8
1980–81	14 730.4 (74.7)	1 309.3 (55.5)	1 822.8 (86.8)	4 437.7 (60.8)	22 300.2 (71.4)	7.2
1985–86	21 946.6 (49.0)	2 832.9 (116.4)	2 783.9 (52.7)	7 000.6 (57.8)	34 564.0 (55.0)	7.2
1990–91	30 681.2 (39.8)	4 019.6 (41.9)	3 566.6 (28.1)	10 410.4 (48.7)	48 677.8 (40.8)	7.3
1993–94[b]	34 970.5 (14.0)	5 253.4 (30.2)	4 100.8 (15.0)	11 170.2 (7.3)	55 494.9 (14.0)	8.1[c]

Notes: [a]Figures from 1950–51 to 1975–76 are for gross national product, producing rates that tend to be slightly higher than for gross domestic product. [b]Figures for 1993–94 are estimates. [c]Figure for 1992.

Sources: **1950–51 to 1970–71:** Compiled from Statistics Canada, *Historical Compendium of Education Statistics*, Cat. no. 81-568 (Ottawa Minister of Supply and Services, 1978); **1974–75 to 1990–91:** Compiled from Statistics Canada, *Education in Canada*, (Annual series) Cat. no. 81-229 (Ottawa: Minister of Supply and Services); **1993–94:** Compiled from Statistics Canada, *Advance Statistics of Education 1993-94*, Cat. no. 81-220 (Ottawa: Minister of Industry, Science and Technology, 1993). Reproduced by authority of the Minister of Industry, 1994.

TABLE 21.2: Full-time Enrollment in Canada, by Level of Study, Selected Years, 1950–1993 (000s) (% increase over previous period in parentheses)

Year	Elementary/ Secondary		Non-university Postsecondary		University		Total	
1950–51	2 625		28		64		2 717	
1955–56	3 291	(25.4)	33	(17.9)	73	(14.1)	3 397	(25.0)
1960–61	4 204	(27.7)	49	(48.5)	114	(56.2)	4 367	(28.6)
1965–66	5 201	(23.7)	69	(40.8)	204	(78.9)	5 474	(25.3)
1970–71	5 888	(13.2)	166	(140.6)	310	(52.0)	6 364	(16.3)
1975–76	5 595	(–5.0)	222	(33.7)	371	(19.7)	6 188	(–2.8)
1980–81	5 106	(–8.7)	261	(17.6)	383	(3.2)	5 750	(–7.1)
1985–86	4 928	(–3.5)	322	(23.4)	467	(21.9)	5 717	(–0.6)
1990–91	5 141	(4.3)	325	(0.9)	532	(13.9)	5 998	(4.9)
1993–94[a]	5 363	(4.3)	365	(12.3)	585	(10.0)	6 314	(5.3)

Note: [a]Figures for 1993–94 are estimates.

Sources: **1950 to 1970:** Compiled from Statistics Canada, *Historical Compendium of Education Statistics*, Cat. no. 81-568 (Ottawa: Minister of Supply and Services, 1978); **1975–76 to 1990–91:** Compiled from Statistics Canada, *Education in Canada*, (Annual series) Cat. no. 81-229 (Ottawa: Minister of Supply and Services); **1993–94:** Compiled from Statistics Canada, *Advance Statistics of Education 1993–94*, Cat. no. 81-220 (Ottawa: Minister of Industry, Science and Technology, 1993). Reproduced by authority of the Minister of Industry, 1994.

lower than the rates of cost increase. At the non-university postsecondary (community college) level, for example, expenditures between 1950–51 and 1993–94 rose by a factor of 354 while enrollment increased 13 times; at the university level, costs over the same period increased by more than 200 times while enrollment increased by just over 9 times. It is clear that educational expansion and massive investment in education programs have made it increasingly possible for more people to attain both longer exposure to and higher levels of formal education. The rapid expansion of universities and the opening of community colleges in the 1960s allowed many to attain postsecondary credentials that previously had been limited to small sectors of the population. Between 1961 and 1991, the proportion of the population fifteen years of age and over who had less than Grade 9 declined from 44 percent to 14 percent, while the proportion who had received at least some postsecondary education rose from 13 percent to 43 percent (Mori and Burke 1989, 13; Statistics Canada 1993b, 1, 24).

Nonetheless, despite the general upgrading of educational credentials, it is important to recognize that considerable segments of the population continue to be excluded from postsecondary educational programs and other formal training opportunities beyond elementary and secondary school. In 1991–92, for example, slightly fewer than one-third of all persons in the 18 to 24 age group were enrolled in full-time postsecondary studies in Canada while 57 percent of the nation's adult population had no postsecondary education (Statistics Canada 1993b, 11; 1993c, 117). Part of the continuing debate over education concerns the extent to which these proportions should be altered to emphasize either greater accessibility or increasing selectivity with respect to opportunities for advanced education (see, e.g., Accessibility Task Force 1989; Bercuson, Bothwell, and Granatstein 1984).

A sense of urgency in determining educational priorities is heightened by the politics of educational finance. The rapid growth in educational expenditures has made education a visible target for governments preoccupied with deficit reduction and fiscal restraint. As the figures in Table 21.1 show, Canada has experienced declining rates of increase in expenditures on education and a reduction in the level of education spending in relation to other national expenditures since the 1970s. Schools, colleges, universities, and other educational institutions that had benefited from educational expansion in the 1960s and early 1970s have had to assess their priorities as they adopt cost-containment strategies and seek out new sources of revenue. The symptoms of educational reorganization are visible in a wide range of activities, including program cuts, curricular reorganization. teacher and faculty militancy, restrictions on student loans and bursaries, and closer working relationships between corporate and educational sectors (Livingstone 1987; Newson and Buchbinder 1988). In the process, education is being promoted by economic, political, and even educational leaders as a "commodity" that must be managed rationally in order to advance the national interest in increasingly competitive world markets driven by innovation, managerial flexibility, and high technology. Individuals who do not hold educational credentials are warned that they are at risk of losing out on the most lucrative and desirable labour market opportunities (Arnoti 1987, 31–32). We are left to conclude both that the education system cannot be maintained in its existing costly state and that an undereducated populace constitutes a barrier to the advancement of national productivity.

Ironically, exhortations that people must become educated in order to have labour-market success are emerging at a time when it is becoming increasingly difficult for many to continue into advanced education. Educational funding by sources other than provincial, territorial, municipal, and federal governments has increased from 7.6 percent of educational costs in 1975–76 to 9.8 percent in 1993–94 (Statistics Canada 1993a, 32). While the overall change does not seem to be that large, it becomes more significant when one considers that much of the additional burden of financing education has been placed on individuals. A 1983–84 National Post-Secondary Student Survey, for example, revealed that for full-time postsecondary students aged 30 years and under, contributions from parents increased from 47 percent of non-repayable funding of education in 1974–75 to 55 percent in 1983–84, while parents accounted for 20 percent of student-loan funding in 1983–84, up from 15 percent in 1974–75 (Porter and Jasmin 1987, 32). This means that access to formal education is increasingly subject to limitation based on the individual's or family's ability to pay, thereby contributing to educational inequalities. Before we consider the implications of challenges to the principle of equality of educational opportunity, however, it is important to examine the extent to which equal opportunity prevails in access to and attainment in education programs in Canada.

Inequalities of Educational Opportunities

While increasing numbers have benefited from exposure to formal educational programs since the Second World War, there are strong, persistent disparities in enrollment and attainment (years of schooling completed) patterns. This section examines inequalities along dimensions of class, gender, and ethnicity.

Data collected in a 1983–84 National Post–Secondary Student Survey, reproduced in Table 21.3, indicate that the incomes and occupations of students' parents have a strong impact on enrollment in postsecondary programs. One-half of students in graduate studies and just under one-half of undergraduates, compared to about one-quarter of college career students (registered in job-specific vocational or technical programs) and just over one-third of students in college programs where credit is obtained toward university standing, have fathers in managerial, semi-professional, and professional occupational categories. These proportions are nearly reversed for students with fathers in skilled and semi-skilled crafts and trades, who make up just under one-half of students in college career programs and about a quarter of university students. It is noteworthy that students whose fathers are in managerial, semi-professional, and professional occupations are overrepresented at all levels compared to the total proportion of the male work force in those occupations, while students whose fathers are in other occupational categories are underrepresented relative to the general male work force. Overall, based on the relationship between students' enrollment in postsecondary educational programs and their fathers' occupations, there is a strong likelihood that the occupational distribution will be reproduced from generation to generation. The same trends hold true with respect to the combined income of students' parents. While there are substantial numbers of students with parents in each income category represented in each type of educational program, there are some evident disparities. The greatest proportion of college career students are from lower-income families, while the highest income level ($45 000 and over) is the predominant category for students in university programs.

Several other studies have reported similar trends. Porter, Porter, and Blishen (1982) demonstrate in a survey of Ontario students that a student's socio-economic background is positively correlated with his or her educational aspirations and enrollment in educational programs, and influences even more strongly the student's eventual level of educational attainment. Social class has a higher impact on the likelihood of high school completion than does mental ability (Porter, Porter, and Blishen 1982, 288–89). Anisef and Okihiro (1982, 128), employing Ontario data from the 1970s, also show the strong influence of social class on educational attainment, particularly in universities, which tended to draw heavily from upper socio-economic strata; non-university postsecondary programs, by contrast, were attended by high numbers of students from both advantaged and disadvantaged groups. Similarly, Guppy, Mikicich, and Pendakur (1984) observe throughout the twentieth century a gradual decline in educational inequalities based on parental background, but they conclude that social origin continues to exert a strong influence on students' educational attainment, particularly for those students who attain a university education (see also Guppy and Arai 1993). Data from a 1988 national

TABLE 21.3: Full-time Students in Canada, 1983–1984: Type of Occupation of Father and Combined Income of Parents, by Type of Student

Type of student	TYPE OF OCCUPATION OF FATHER (PERCENT)						
	Managerial, semi-professional, professional	Clerical, sales, service	Skilled, semi-skilled, crafts and trades	Labourer	Other	Total[b]	Number of students
College career	26	21	46	3	4	100	130 049
College transfer	36	23	33	2[a]	6	100	50 657
Undergraduates	45	21	27	2	5	100	267 481
Graduate students	50	19	23	—[a]	6[a]	98	21 191
Total male labour force	25	27	48		—[a]	100	6 896 000

Type of student	Combined income of parents (in $000)					
	0–22	23–33	34–44	45+	Total[b]	Number of students
College career	33	27	21	19	100	122 657
College transfer	28	25	19	29	100	48 809
Undergraduates	26	21	18	35	100	253 905
Graduate students	31	20	16	33	100	22 726

Notes: [a]Numbers are too low or too unreliable to estimate. [b]Totals may not sum to 100 because of rounding.
Sources: Marion Porter and Gilles Jasmin, *A Profile of Post-Secondary Students in Canada* (Ottawa: Statistics Canada, 1987), pp. 22, 23; Statistics Canada, *The Labour Force*, Cat. no. 71-001 (January) (Ottawa: Minister of Supply and Services, 1984). Reproduced by authority of the Minister of Industry, 1994.

survey of persons who graduated from trade/vocational, college, and university programs in 1986 also reveal that an individual's likelihood of continuing to higher levels of postsecondary education increases with the amount of education attained by his or her parents (Clark 1991, 11).

Class and family background are not the only factors that influence educational opportunities and achievement. One of the most pervasive bases of social and educational inequality is gender. At first glance, it would appear that the importance of gender differences for education is diminishing. In the 1950–51 academic year, for example, female students constituted less than one-quarter (21.7 percent) of full-time university undergraduate students in Canada, while by 1993–94, that proportion had risen to more than one-half (53.8 percent); female students also accounted for over half (54.4 percent) of full-time community college enrollment in 1993–94 (Statistics Canada 1983, W341-2; Statistics Canada 1993a, 24–25). The proportions of female students are even higher when part-time students are taken into account. In 1993–94, for example, women constituted 63 percent of part-time university undergraduate and 52 percent of part-time graduate students (Statistics Canada 1993a, 26). Moreover, female students have moved into several non-traditional areas of study, particularly in the professions. Between 1970–71 and 1991–92, the proportion of women in full-time undergraduate studies in medicine increased from 18.1 to 45.2 percent; in law, the proportion rose from 12.7 to 51.2 percent, in dentistry and dental studies, from 5.6 to 40.3 percent, in commerce and business administration from 10.2 to 45.9 percent, and in agriculture from 10.5 to 45.5 percent (calculated from Statistics Canada 1977, 138–39; Statistics Canada 1993c, 84–88).

Despite these signs of greater gender equality in enrollment in postsecondary programs, gender segregation prevails throughout education programs at nearly all levels. As Gaskell (1981) emphasizes, women on the whole have at least as much formal education as men, but men and women tend to participate in different kinds of educational programs and receive different educational credentials. In 1993–94, the proportion of women in full-time studies was greater than that of men enrolled at all levels of post-secondary education except graduate studies; the proportion of women was 54.7 percent in community college career programs, 53.7 percent in community college university transfer programs, 53.8 percent in undergraduate studies, and 42.5 percent in graduate studies (Statistics Canada 1993a, 24–25). However, most disciplines of study have remained highly gender segmented. In 1991–92, women predominated in areas such as nursing (93.4 percent), household science (90.8 percent), and education (74.7 percent) in universities, and in health sciences (83.9 percent) and social services (85.2 percent) in community colleges, while men prevailed in such areas as physical sciences (75.4 percent) and engineering (84.0 percent) in universities, and in engineering technology (87.8 percent) and electronics and electrical technology programs (94.8 percent) in community colleges (Statistics Canada 1993c, 76–88). Gender segregation has also remained high in trades training programs outside of postsecondary institutions. The overall proportion of women in occupational, institutional, and apprenticeship training programs is very low, ranging from 4 to 30 percent; within these programs, women are concentrated in training for traditionally female occupations in the clerical and service sectors such as food and beverage services, hairdressing, and secretarial work, while men are concentrated in training for blue-collar occupations such as machining, work in construction trades, and product assembly or repair (Boothby 1986, 17–19).

Formal educational credentials at the highest level are held mostly by men. In 1991, 52.7 percent of the 17 989 master's degrees and 68.4 percent of the 2947 earned doctorates awarded in Canada went to men (Statistics Canada 1993c, 185). Men are also concentrated in programs that offer credentials oriented to specific careers, providing opportunities for direct access into labour-force positions that tend to offer relative job and wage security. The ratio of graduating males to females, for example, is 150 to 1 in construction electrician courses, 137 to 1 in courses in plumbing and pipe trades, and 40 to 1 in mechanical engineering degree programs (Mori and Burke 1989, 40). Although women, historically, have tended to predominate in programs that offer general certificates or degrees, such as general arts programs or broad vocational training programs that provide fewer job-specific work skills, there is some evidence that this trend is reversing (Boothby

1986, 17; Clark 1991, 60–61). Nonetheless, the general pattern is in some ways a reversal of what happens in high school, where girls are commonly prepared for specific vocational careers and boys are given more general training, which is later supplemented by paid training or apprenticeship for particular careers (Gaskell 1981). In short, there seems little likelihood that greater participation rates in formal education will automatically reverse women's traditional socio-economic disadvantages relative to men given pronounced differences in the patterns revealed by males' and females' programs of study and entry into labour markets.

Distinctions among ethnic groups constitute a further dimension of educational inequality. Based on an analysis of 1981 census data for Canadian labour force participants fifteen years and older, Li (1988, 76–79) identifies patterns of clearly differentiated educational attainment. Persons of Jewish and Chinese origin hold the strongest likelihood of having completed university education, while persons of southern European origin have the lowest attainment of university degrees and the highest likelihood of having less than secondary education. Overall, only a few groups, including persons of Jewish, British, northern and central European, African, and Chinese origin have attained more than the national average of 11.56 years of schooling. Some of the variability can be explained by such factors as age and immigration patterns. For example, according to the 1986 census, for persons aged 20 years and over, Canada's immigrant population had 12.4 median years of schooling compared with 12.3 for the non-immigrant population; the gap was widest for those aged 35 to 39 years, where the median years of schooling were 13.6 for immigrants and 12.7 for non-immigrants (Mori and Burke 1989, 21). A major reason for this variability lies in Canada's selective immigration policies, which since the 1960s have placed high value on formal education and skill training (Li 1988, 81).

It is more difficult to assess the direct impact of educational processes and institutions on opportunities and attainment for various ethnic groups. Nonetheless, it is clear that notable disparities do exist. The experience of Canada's aboriginal peoples, who have been consistently underrepresented in educational opportunities and achievement for several decades, strongly illustrates the nature of educational inequality in Canada. Data from the 1986 census show that, for the population fifteen years and over not attending school full-time, about one-quarter of the aboriginal population and 44.7 percent of Natives living on-reserve had less than Grade 9 education, compared with 17.1 percent of the total population. Of the aboriginal population, 31.8 percent had at least some postsecondary education, compared with 39.8 percent of the general population (Frideres 993, 184–87; Mori and Burke 1989; Statistics Canada 1989a). Trends associated with the educational attainment of younger cohorts appear to be more favourable. In 1991–92, 95.5 percent of Native children aged 4 to 18 living on-reserve were enrolled in schools; also that year, 53.6 percent of on-reserve students, compared with 19.6 percent in 1980–81 and 3.4 percent in 1960–61, remained in school continuously to Grade 12 (Department of Indian Affairs and Northern Development 1992, 35, 37). Among persons in the 17 to 34 year age cohort, in 1991–92, 8.1 percent of registered Indians participated in some form of postsecondary education, compared with a national rate of 10.7 percent (Indian and Northern Affairs Canada 1993, 2–47), although aboriginal people continue to be relatively more disadvantaged with regard to the kinds and levels of programs they are enrolled in. While recent First Nations initiatives such as band-controlled education and vocational programs have offered grounds for optimism that aboriginal peoples' educational status is likely to improve, there continue to be disturbing signs that such improvement may be limited (Satzewich and Wotherspoon 1993, 144–46). The federal government decision in the late 1980s to revoke the "E-12 guidelines" and restrict funding support for Native postsecondary education is an example of how a policy shift toward self-government may be more a manifestation of government cost-restraint than a show of true concern for the welfare of Canada's aboriginal peoples (Lanceley, 1991).

In summary, this section has examined several examples of inequality in educational opportunity and attainment according to the dimensions of class and socio-economic background, gender, and ethnicity. General historical trends reveal that the expansion of Canada's education system, in terms of both overall enrollment and increasing participation in postsecondary programs and vocational training, has allowed for extensive participation and achievement in formal education programs by groups such as women and Native people who previously had limited educational opportunities. Nonetheless, there is considerable evidence that persistent inequalities are deeply ingrained into the structure of Canada's education system. The next section discusses the major consequences of these disparities by examining inequalities in the distribution of benefits from education.

Inequality of Benefits from Formal Education

The importance of formal education as a mechanism for granting credentials in Canadian society, as in other industrialized democratic societies, relies upon a strong relationship between educational achievement and general economic and occupational opportunities. Overall, a person's likelihood of being employed and having a higher income increases with the level and amount of their formal educational credentials. In 1992, the unemployment rate for men with less than Grade 9 education was 16.3 percent, compared with 18.0 for men with some high school, 11.9 with some postsecondary, and only 5.6 with a university degree, while for women the corresponding unemployment rates were 15.7 percent for those with less than Grade 9, 16.7 for those with some high school, 10.9 with some postsecondary, and 5.4 with a university degree (Statistics Canada 1993e, B11). In 1992, the median income of families headed by a person with less than Grade 9 education was just under $31 500, much less than half the median income of over $72 000 for families headed by a university graduate (Statistics Canada 1993d, 71).

National surveys of persons who graduated from educational programs in 1982 and 1984 revealed that differences in benefits from education tended to be both immediate and compounded over time. Graduates from 1982 experienced an overall average increase in income of one-third between 1984 and 1987, compared to an average of 13 percent for all workers employed full-time on a full-year basis (Statistics Canada 1989b, 51). Table 21.4 illustrates the general tendency for average earnings to increase with higher levels of educational credentials with

TABLE 21.4: Estimated Median Annual Earnings of 1982 and 1986 Graduates, by Gender, Level, and Employment Status, 1984 and 1988

	1982 Graduates in 1984			1986 Graduates in 1988		
	Total	Men	Women	Total	Men	Women
	($ 000)			($ 000)		
Working full-time						
Trade/vocational	15	16	13	19	21	16
Career/technical	18	20	16	22	23	20
University	24	25	23	28	30	26
Bachelor's	23	24	22	27	28	26
Master's	32	35	30	38	40	36
Doctorate	34	35	31	39	40	38
Working part-time						
Trade/vocational	9	10	8	10	12	10
Career/technical	10	11	10	13	15	13
University	12	12	12	13	12	14
Bachelor's	12	12	12	13	12	13
Master's	15	14	16	15	12	16
Doctorate	15	16	13	20	16	24

Source: Warren Clark, *The Class of 1986: A Compendium of Findings of the 1988 National Graduates Survey of 1986 Graduates With Comparisons to the 1984 National Graduates Survey*, Cat. no. LM198E/1/92 (Ottawa: Employment and Immigration Canada, 1991) p. 42. Reproduced with the permission of Human Resources Development Canada and Supply and Services Canada, 1994.

persons who held postgraduate university degrees making on average about twice the earnings of persons with trade and vocational training.

It is important to note also the perpetuation of strong gender disparities. The figures in Table 21.4 reveal that women earned substantially less than men at all levels except for university graduates working part-time among those who graduated from postsecondary programs in 1982 and 1984. The highest gender gaps in average earnings, historically, have been among those with the lowest levels of educational credentials. Data from 1992 suggest that the wage gap is narrowing slowly, shifting in accordance with changes in work and labour markets. Among people who worked full-time on a full-year basis, women earned on average 71.8 percent of men's average earnings in 1992 compared to 63.7 percent in 1981. Among those with a university degree, the ratio of women's to men's average earnings in 1992 was 74.2 percent, while among those with some high school, the comparable figure was 67.3 percent; for those with less than a Grade 9 education, the ratio was 73.5 percent, suggesting the relatively poor occupational conditions for both men and women with low educational attainment (Statistics Canada 1994, 13).

These wage differentials can be explained, in part, by differences in the educational programs and career options available to or followed by men and women. For example, data collected on 1982 university bachelor's and first professional degree graduates working full-time in 1984 revealed that 32 percent of women compared with 13 percent of men were employed in teaching and related occupations. Women graduates had gone into such areas as health care (about 15 percent) and clerical work (10 percent), where numbers of men were low, and the male graduates had concentrated in areas such as engineering, natural sciences, and mathematics (23 percent), where there were few women employed (Picot, Wannell, and Lynd, 1987, 41–42).

Even in occupations where men and women are employed with equivalent educational credentials, wage gaps are apparent. Data from the 1986 census reveal, for example, that, in health diagnosing and treating occupations requiring university degrees (such as medicine, dentistry, and veterinary occupations), men earned on average $90 736 whereas women earned $53 300; male kindergarten and elementary school teachers with university degrees earned on average $37 110 and female kindergarten and elementary teachers with degrees $32 765; for bookkeepers and accounting clerks with trades certification, diplomas, or some postsecondary education, males earned on average $23 398 whereas females averaged $18 197; and for workers in food and beverage serving occupations who had less than Grade 9, men earned on average $15 706 compared with $11 066 for women (Statistics Canada 1989c).

Rates of unemployment are related closely to educational credentials. According to the survey of 1982 graduates, initially conducted during a major recession, 15 percent of graduates from trades and vocational programs were unemployed in 1987 compared to 24 percent in 1984; the proportion of college graduates who were unemployed in 1987 was 5 percent, half of the figure for 1984, and only 4 percent of university graduates were unemployed in 1987 compared with 9 percent in 1984 (Statistics Canada 1989b, 2). There is, however, evidence to indicate that shifting labour-force patterns are affecting different categories of graduates in particular ways. Among 1986 graduates surveyed, 16 percent of persons who graduated from trade/vocational programs were unemployed in 1988 compared with 7 percent of community college graduates and 9 percent of university graduates (Clark 1991, 20). Moreover, of those graduates who were unemployed, the duration of unemployment was associated with levels of education. In 1986, graduates from trades and vocational programs who experienced unemployment were out of work for an average of 25 weeks compared with an average of 18 weeks for unemployed college and university graduates (Statistics Canada 1989b, 3).

There continues to be a strong connection among educational opportunities and wider socio-economic opportunities amid important structural changes in labour markets. In the rise of the "service economy," new job creation is centred, on the one hand, around several higher-level jobs (characterized by relatively high wages, good working conditions, and requirements for advanced, specialized credentials) and massive growth, on the other hand, in the number of lower-level jobs (characterized by low wages, poorer working conditions, and little job-specific training). A corresponding decline in the proportion of jobs in intermediate categories (see, e.g., Economic Council of Canada 1991; Myles, Picot, and Wannell 1988) indicates that educational selectivity remains at the core of economic adjustment processes.

Education has implications for several forms of social opportunities in addition to employment and income. Such problems as poverty, criminality, illness, malnutrition, and racism have been linked by governments and researchers to low levels of educational attainment (Ghosh 1991; National Council of Welfare 1985). In short, education plays a major role either in shaping or reinforcing a person's social opportunities.

Conclusions

There are different ways in which we can interpret the trends presented in this chapter. With some exceptions, Canadian data reflect a general tendency for increased access to educational opportunities and a correlation between level of educational attainment and socio-economic benefits. On the basis of these trends, it is commonly concluded that the Canadian education system is essentially successful as a mechanism for ensuring fair and open competition for available life opportunities. It seems reasonable to make the conclusion that social success depends on a person's ability to gain strong educational credentials. Success or lack of success follows, apparently, as a consequence of individual capabilities and initiative. In other words, if a person is highly motivated to succeed, the educational opportunities are there to enable him or her to advance out of a cycle of poverty and low standard of living. From this viewpoint, that is represented in the quotations that were presented at the beginning of this chapter, the education system is judged to be a failure only when it reduces individuals' motivations to succeed. When students drop out of school before graduation or achieve low levels of formal certification, the losers are the individual who does not reap the benefits that education offers, as well as society as a whole, which suffers from the waste of talent. In a society characterized by rapid technological change and faced with the requisite to develop an increasingly productive work force under the challenge of strong international competition, it is, apparently, imperative that all individuals be driven to their highest levels of achievement for the common good. Within this context, critics of Canada's education system look enviously at nations such as Japan where a streamlined, highly competitive education system is assumed to be a fundamental engine of efficient productivity and massive economic growth (see, e.g., Maynard 1989).

It is instructive, however, to examine the trends using different sets of assumptions and points of emphasis. The data reveal that there are significant inequalities in educational enrollment and achievement that transcend individual differences and reflect instead the continuing importance of factors such as class, gender, and race. In other words, a person's prior place in the social structure influences both the opportunities for and benefits from education. Consequently, it is necessary to look at social, economic, and political structures rather than individual characteristics in order to explain social and educational failure and success.

There are several specific reasons why different persons and groups may fail or succeed in and out of school systems, constituting a complex equation that involves such factors as language, race, and gender stereotyping, parental background, student-teacher interaction, curriculum options, mental and verbal ability, and even "luck" (see, e.g., Martin and Macdonell 1982 for reviews of the literature). While it is important to look at the relative impact each of these variables has on people's life chances, it is also necessary to see these features as part of a totality that both reinforces and is produced by a social structure based on relations of inequality and of domination and subordination. Viewed in such terms, inequalities in educational opportunities and benefits are not merely unfortunate by-products of a formal education system, which requires some minor readjustments or repairs to stay in tune with social and technological change. To the contrary, the production of unequal social opportunities has been a systematic, regular feature of Canada's education system that has served to perpetuate the inequalities embedded within capitalist society. What is at issue in contemporary demands for "quality education," "lifelong learning," "flexibility," and "competitiveness" is not altruistic concern for the learner, but rather a direct response to capital's demands for an affordable, productive, and compliant work force. The shift has not been complete, but the terrain has clearly shifted away from an emphasis on participation, which did afford minority groups some opportunity for social advancement, to a more restrictive ethos defined by a small number of business and political leaders and driven by market competitiveness.

Study Questions

1. How has the concept of equality of opportunity been defined by different groups in Canada? Compare these definitions with the application of the principle to the organization of educational institutions.

2. Compare and contrast the major explanations of class, gender, and racial inequalities in educational opportunity and attainment.

3. Discuss how the concept of "educational excellence" is employed as an ideology. How is the concept related to contemporary changes in work and education?

4. To what extent can education be effective as a tool to reduce levels of social and economic inequality? Why?

5. Discuss the relationship between the trends in educational inequality emphasized in this chapter and significant developments in the history of Canadian education.

Recommended Reading

Aronowitz, Stanley, and Henry A. Giroux. *Education Under Siege: The Conservative, Liberal, and Radical Debate Over Schooling*. Boston: Bergin and Garvey, 1985.

Carnoy, Martin, and Henry M. Levin. *Schooling and Work in the Democratic State*. Stanford: Stanford University Press, 1985.

Gaskell, Jane, and Arlene McLaren, eds. *Women and Education*. 2d ed. Calgary: Detselig Enterprises, 1991.

Ghosh, Ratna, and Douglas Ray, eds. *Social Change and Education in Canada*. 2d ed. Toronto: Harcourt Brace Jovanovich, 1991.

Livingstone, D.W. *Social Crisis and Schooling*. Toronto: Garamond Press. 1985.

Wotherspoon, Terry, ed. *The Political Economy of Canadian Schooling*. Toronto: Methuen, 1987.

References

Accessibility Task Force. 1989. *Issues and Options Open to the Future: Accessibility. Equity, and Higher Learning for the People of Saskatchewan*. Saskatoon: University of Saskatchewan Accessibility Task Force.

Anisef, P., and N. Okihiro. 1982. *Losers and Winners: The Pursuit of Equality and Social Justice in Higher Education*. Toronto: Butterworths.

Apple, M.W. 1986. *Teachers and Texts: A Political Economy of Class and Gender Relations in Education*. New York: Routledge and Kegan Paul.

Arnoti, B. 1987. "Low Educational Attainment in Canada, 1975–1985." *Canadian Social Trends* (Spring): 28–32. (Cat. 11-008E).

Bercuson, D., R. Bothwell, and J. Granatstein. 1984. *The Great Brain Robbery: Canada's Universities on the Road to Ruin*. Toronto: McClelland and Stewart.

Boothby, D. 1986. *Women Re-entering the Labour Force and Training Programs: Evidence From Canada*. Study prepared for the Economic Council of Canada. Ottawa: Supply and Services Canada.

British Columbia. 1988. *A Legacy for Learners: The Report of the Royal Commission on Education*. Victoria: Province of British Columbia.

Carnoy, M., and H.M. Levin. 1985. *Schooling and Work in the Democratic State*. Stanford: Stanford University Press.

Clark, W. 1991. *The Class of 1986: A Compendium of Findings of the 1988 National Graduates Survey of 1986 Graduates With Comparisons to the 1984 National Graduates Survey*. Ottawa: Employment and Immigration Canada. (LM 198E/1/92).

Coleman, J. 1968. "The Concept of Equality of Educational Opportunity." *Harvard Educational Review*. 38, no. 1 (Winter, Special issue): 7– 22.

Department of Indian Affairs and Northern Development. 1992. *Basic Departmental Data, 1992*. Ottawa: Supply and Services Canada.

Devereaux, M.S., and D.J. Higgins. 1988. "Part-Time Adult Training." *Canadian Social Trends* 11 (Winter): 28–30. (Cat. 11–008E).

Economic Council of Canada. 1991. *Employment in the Service Economy*. Ottawa: Supply and Services Canada.

Frideres, J.S. 1993. *Native Peoples in Canada: Contemporary Conflicts*. 4th ed. Scarborough, ON: Prentice-Hall.

Gaskell, J.S. 1981. "Equal Educational Opportunity for Women." In *Canadian Education in the 1980's*, ed. J.D. Wilson. Calgary: Detselig Enterprises. 173–93.

Ghosh, R. 1991. "Social Change and Education: Evaluation and Prospects," in *Social Change and Education in Canada*, ed. R. Ghosh and D. Ray. Toronto: Harcourt Brace Jovanovich, 302–09.

Guppy, N., and A.B. Arai. 1993. "Who Benefits From Higher Education? Differences by Sex, Social Class, and Ethnic Background." In *Social Inequality in Canada: Patterns, Problems, Policies*, 2d ed., eds. J. Curtis, E. Grabb, and N. Guppy. Scarborough, ON: Prentice-Hall. 214–32.

Guppy, N., P.D. Mikicich, and R. Pendakur. 1984. "Changing Patterns of Educational Inequality in Canada." *Canadian Journal of Sociology* 9, no. 3 (Summer): 319–31.

Indian and Northern Affairs Canada and Polar Commission. 1993. *1993–1994 Estimates*. Part 3. Ottawa: Supply and Services Canada.

Lanceley, D. 1991. "The Post-Secondary Education Assistance Program for Indian Students: The Vehicle for the Voice of Opposition." In *Hitting the Books: The Politics of Educational Retrenchment*, ed. T. Wotherspoon. Toronto: Garamond Press and Social Research Unit. 235–48.

Li, P.S. 1988. *Ethnic Inequality in a Class Society*. Toronto: Wall and Thompson.

Livingstone, D. 1985. *Social Crisis and Schooling*. Toronto: Garamond Press.

———. 1987. "Crisis, Classes, and Educational Reform in Advanced Capitalism." In *The Political Economy of Canadian Schooling*, ed. T. Wotherspoon. Toronto: Methuen. 57–67.

Livingstone, D.W., and D. Hart. 1987. "The People Speak: Public Attitudes toward Schooling in Canada." In *Social Change and Education in Canada*, ed. R. Ghosh and D. Ray. Toronto: Harcourt Brace Jovanovich. 3–27.

Martin, W.B.W., and A.J. Macdonell. 1982. *Canadian Education: A Sociological Analysis*. 2d ed. Scarborough, ON: Prentice-Hall.

Maynard, R. 1989, "Look, Jane, Dick Can't Read," *Report on Business Magazine* (May): 87–96.

Mazurek, K. 1987. "Multiculturalism, Education, and the Ideology of the Meritocracy." In *The Political Economy of Canadian Schooling*, ed. T. Wotherspoon. Toronto: Methuen. 141–63.

Mori, G.A., and B. Burke. 1989. *Educational Attainment of Canadians*. (Cat. 98–134). Ottawa: Supply and Services Canada.

Myles, J., G. Picot, and T. Wannell. 1988. "The Changing Wage Distribution of Jobs, 1981–1986." *The Labour Force, October 1988*. Ottawa: Statistics Canada and Supply and Services Canada. 85–129.

National Commission on Excellence in Education. 1983. "A Nation at Risk: An Imperative for Educational Reform." *Education Week* April 27: 12–16.

National Council of Welfare. 1985. *Poverty Profile 1985*. Ottawa: Supply and Services Canada.

Newson, J., and H. Buchbinder. 1988. *The University Means Business: Universities, Corporations, and Academic Work*. Toronto: Garamond Press.

Parliament, J.-A. 1986. "Education in Canada: Selected Highlights." *Canadian Social Trends* (Autumn): 15–20. (Cat. 11-008E).

Picot, W.G., T. Wannell, and D. Lynd. 1987. "1976 and 1982 Postsecondary Graduates: Selected Highlights of their Labour Force Experience." *Canadian Social Trends* (Autumn): 38–42. (Cat. 11-008E).

Porter, J. 1987. "Education, Equality, and the Just Society." In *The Measure of Canadian Society: Education, Equality and Opportunity*, ed. J. Porter. Ottawa: Carleton University Press. 242–80.

Porter, J., M. Porter, and B.R. Blishen. 1982. *Stations and Callings: Making it Through the School System*. Toronto: Methuen.

Porter, M., and G. Jasmin. 1987. *A Profile of Post-Secondary Students in Canada: The 1983–1984 National Post-Secondary Student Survey: Summary National Data*. Ottawa: Secretary of State and Statistics Canada.

Satzewich, V., and T. Wotherspoon. 1993. *First Nations: Race, Class, and Gender Relations*. Scarborough, ON: Nelson.

Secretary of State. 1988. *Access to Excellence: Being Canadian ... Working Together for Post-Secondary Education: Federal–Provincial Initiatives*. Ottawa: Secretary of State of Canada.

Shor, I. 1986. *Culture Wars: School and Society in the Conservative Restoration, 1969–1984*. Boston: Routledge and Kegan Paul.

Statistics Canada. 1977. *Education in Canada 1976*. (Cat. 81-229). Ottawa: Supply and Services Canada.

———. 1978. *Historical Compendium of Education Statistics From Confederation to 1975*. Ottawa: Minister of Industry, Trade and Commerce.

———. 1983. *Historical Statistics of Canada*. 2d ed. Ottawa: Supply and Services Canada.

———. 1989a. *A Data Book on Canada's Aboriginal Population From the 1986 Census of Canada*. Ottawa: Aboriginal Peoples Output Program.

———. 1989b. "The Class of 82 Revisited." *Education Statistics: Service Bulletin* 11, no. 1 (February). (Cat. 81-002).

———. 1989c. *The Nation: Employment Income by Education*. (Cat. 93-116). Ottawa: Supply and Services Canada.

———. 1993a. *Advance Statistics of Education, 1993–1994*. (Cat. 81-220). Ottawa: Minister of Industry and Science Technology.

———. 1993b. *Educational Attainment and School Attendance, The Nation.* (Cat. 93-328). Ottawa: Minister of Industry and Science Technology.
———. 1993c. *Education in Canada, 1991–1992.* (Cat. 81-229). Ottawa: Minister of Industry and Science Technology.
———. 1993d. *Income Distributions by Size in Canada, 1992.* (Cat. 13-207). Ottawa: Minister of Industry and Science Technology.
———. 1993e. *Labour Force Annual Averages, 1992.* (Cat. 71-220). Ottawa: Minister of Industry and Science Technology.
———. 1994. *Earnings of Men and Women, 1992.* (Cat. 13-217). Ottawa: Minister of Industry and Science Technology.
Wotherspoon, T. 1987. "Conflict and Crisis in Canadian Education." In *The Political Economy of Canadian Schooling,* ed. T. Wotherspoon. Toronto: Methuen. 1–15.

CHAPTER 22

Income Inequality, Poverty, and Hunger

B. Singh Bolaria and Terry Wotherspoon

Learning Objectives

This chapter explores the linkages between income inequality and life chances, and discusses the emergence and persistence of food banks in Canada as a response to hunger. Over the last 35 years, there has been little change in Canada in income distribution, which continues to be highly skewed. Poverty, too, is persistent. Structural barriers put groups such as women and the elderly at a high risk of being poor, and that limits their life chances. The chapter also treats the implications of a private-voluntary solution (food banks) for a structurally produced social problem (poverty and hunger) in the context of the social welfare restraint currently being advocated to manage federal and provincial budgets. Students are encouraged to consider the questions of the persistence of income inequality and the linkages between inequality and life chances.

Introduction

Poverty, malnutrition, hunger, and disease have come to be identified with developing Third World countries. We see television images of famine and starvation in Africa and Asia almost daily. Charities constantly invoke images of frail, empty-bellied children to collect funds to help the famine-stricken populations in other countries. These images help reinforce the view that such problems exist only in Third World nations.

While the significance and concentration of poverty in the Third World cannot be overstated, neither have the advanced capitalist countries eliminated economic inequalities and poverty. The inequalities of wealth and income produce unequal life chances—that is, chances for material and social rewards. Poverty translates into homelessness, ill health, short life expectancy, malnutrition, and hunger, to mention only a few of its effects.

Canada is a highly stratified society. There are wide disparities in wealth, income, power, and prestige. These inequalities are not mere statistical categories used to classify people for social analysis; they have important implications for people's lives.

In this chapter we confine our discussion to only one dimension of inequality, disparities of income. Selective data are presented on the linkages between income inequalities and life chances. This chapter also explores the links between inequality, poverty, and hunger in this country, with particular emphasis on the emergence and persistence of food banks as a response to hunger. In the concluding section, the implications of this "private-voluntary solution" to a structurally produced social problem are explored in the context of the social expenditure restraint that is being advocated to eliminate budget deficits and to scale down the welfare state.

Income Inequality and Poverty

Income inequality is an important dimension of social stratification. An examination of income distribution data reveals wide income disparities among Canadians. These data also show the meagre extent of change in the share of income held by Canadians in different income categories over time (National Council of Welfare 1988; 1989; 1990; 1992). For instance, families in the lowest quintile had only 6.1 percent of the total income in 1951 and 6.3 percent in 1986. The corresponding figures for the highest quintile were 41.1 percent and 39.4 percent—over six times the lowest quintile's share. The figures for unattached individuals reveal that in 1986 the lowest quintile had 5.3 percent of the total income. In contrast, the highest quintile had 44.7 percent of the total income—over eight times the bottom group's share. The income distribution for unattached individuals was even more skewed in 1951 (National Council of Welfare 1988). Income inequalities continue to persist in Canada.

A significant number of Canadians live in poverty. The most common measure used to establish the poverty line is the low-income cutoffs used by Statistics Canada. These cutoffs are set at levels at which, on average, 58.5 percent of income is spent on the necessities of life: food, clothing, and shelter (National Council of Welfare 1989). There is no single cut-off line for all of Canada, because living costs vary by family size and place of residence. It should also be noted that "poverty lines only establish the upper limit of the low income population. Most poor Canadians live on incomes that are hundreds and more often thousands of dollars under the poverty line" (National Council of Welfare 1989, 5).

Poverty figures fluctuate with economic conditions. While poverty declined in Canada in the 1970s, it increased substantially during the first half of the 1980s as a result of the 1981–82 recession (National Council of Welfare 1988). Despite some movement, by the late 1980s the poverty rates had not returned to prerecession levels.

Table 22.1 shows national trends in poverty from 1980 to 1990. In 1980, the number of people living in poverty was little over 3.6 million and the poverty rate was just over 15 percent. Both the number of people who lived in poverty and the poverty rate fluctuated throughout the 1980s. These figures rose from 1982 to 1984, declined from 1985 till 1989, and rose again in 1990.

TABLE 22.1: Poverty Trends, All Persons, 1980–1992

Year	No. of persons living in poverty	Poverty rate (percent)
1980	3 624 000	15.3
1981	3 643 000	15.3
1982	3 951 000	16.4
1983	4 406 000	18.2
1984	4 397 000	18.1
1985	4 170 000	17.0
1986	3 976 000	16.0
1987	3 912 000	15.6
1988	3 744 000	14.8
1989	3 487 000	13.6
1990	3 821 000	14.6
1991	4 227 000	16.0
1992	4 320 000	16.1

Source: From *Poverty Profile 1980–1992*, Table 2, National Council of Welfare, 1993. Reproduced with permission of the Minister of Supply and Services Canada, 1994.

As Table 22.2 shows, child poverty figures followed the same general pattern as statistics for the general population. Child poverty increased in the early part of the 1980s, declined during the next few years and rose again in 1990. During the peak years of 1983 and 1984, well over 1.2 million children, or 19 percent, were living in poverty. Almost one in every five children was poor.

Certain groups face a high risk of poverty. These include families headed by women, unattached or elderly women, unemployed, and persons whose participation in the labour force is irregular, and those with low educational levels (National Council of Welfare 1992). Women overall face a much higher risk of poverty than men, a phenomenon that has come to be known as the "feminization of poverty" (National Council of Welfare 1990).

Because a vast majority of Canadians earn their income from wage employment, labour-market characteristics that determine which jobs are well paid are particularly important in any discussion of poverty. For instance, those in managerial and professional occupations and their families are unlikely to live in poverty, as compared to those in the service industries. Occupations with an above-average risk of poverty include farming, fishing, forestry, and services (National Council of Welfare 1992).

Income Inequality, Life Chances, and Consumption

Income inequality and poverty have an important influence on the lives of individuals. Max Weber saw class as closely linked to people's life chances, that is,

TABLE 22.2: Poverty Trends, Children Under 18, 1980–1992

Year	No. of Children under 18 living in poverty	Poverty rate (percent)
1980	984 000	14.9
1981	998 000	15.2
1982	1 155 000	17.8
1983	1 221 000	19.0
1984	1 253 000	19.6
1985	1 165 000	18.3
1986	1 086 000	17.0
1987	1 057 000	16.6
1988	987 000	15.4
1989	934 000	14.5
1990	1 105 000	16.9
1991	1 210 000	18.3
1992	1 218 000	18.2

Source: From *Poverty Profile 1980–1992*, Table 2, National Council of Welfare, 1993. Reproduced with permission of the Minister of Supply and Services Canada, 1994.

their chances to acquire material goods and other amenities (Gerth and Mills 1958). Economic and social inequalities produce inequality of opportunities and life chances, which are reflected in such measures as education, living standards, housing, health, and consumption patterns. A number of chapters in this volume attest to these inequalities and differential opportunity structures and life chances.

Most relevant to the discussion in this chapter is the link between income inequalities and consumption patterns. Chossudovsky points to "the dual and divided structure of social consumption and of consumer goods markets between necessary subsistence goods on the one hand and luxury and semi-luxury goods consumed by the privileged upper-income groups on the other hand.... This duality in the structure of social consumption, while more pronounced in peripheral social formations, is also present in the advanced capitalist countries" (1983, 76).

In addition to the differences in the goods they consume, persons with different income levels devote a different percentage of their money income to necessary subsistence goods. Families and unattached individuals in the lowest quintile spend 57.5 percent of their income on the necessities of life. The corresponding figure for the second-lowest quintile is 45.6 percent. With each higher quintile, the percentage of income spent on necessities is lower. The family units in the highest quintile spend 33 percent of their income on the necessities of life (National Council of Welfare 1989, 13). Data from the United States indicate that those in the lowest income decile spend over 40 percent of their income on food alone, as compared to only 11 percent for the highest decile (Blumberg 1980, 181).

Chossudovsky notes that "food is by far the most important component of necessary consumption." Adequate production and supply of food in themselves do not assure adequate levels of food consumption and nutrition. Consumption levels are influenced by the social distribution of food to different groups in the population (Chossudovsky 1983), which itself is a function of income distribution. A number of studies show the relationship between low incomes and inadequate diets (Nutrition Canada 1975; Myres and Kroetsch 1978; Reid and Miles 1977). Millions of poor Americans suffer from malnutrition and hunger (Kotz 1984; Physicians' Task Force on Hunger in America 1985; Wilkinson and Sidel 1986).

Poverty, nutrition, and hunger are also closely linked to health status (Epp 1986; Statistics Canada and Health and Welfare Canada 1981; Wilkins and Adams 1983; Wigle and Mao 1980). A report published by the Minister of Health revealed that "men in the upper income group live six years longer than men with a low income." The same report also indicated that "men in upper income groups can expect 14 more disability-free years than men with a low income; in the case of women, the difference is eight years" (Epp 1986, 398). Other evidence associates poverty with malnutrition, psychomotor and growth retardation, emotional disturbances, and visual difficulties. These problems are even more acute among Native people (Special Senate Committee on Poverty 1971; Shah and Farkas 1985).

The adverse health effects of poverty for children have their start during pregnancy; they have significant impact on complications during pregnancy, low birth weight of children, handicaps, poor growth, and intellectual and emotional disorders (National Council of Welfare 1975; Ross and Rutter 1978; Vernon 1979; Perkins 1974; Bradley, Ross, and Warnyca 1978; Brown 1978). Child mortality rates are higher for poor children than their wealthy peers (Fine 1989).

The cumulative effect of poverty, malnutrition, hunger, and ill health is the extensive reproduction of poverty. All of these things influence poor children's learning ability and performance in school (Chu 1989; National Council of Welfare 1975), which subsequently affect job prospects, employment patterns, and earnings. As a report by the National Council of Welfare (1975, 1) states: "To be born poor in Canada does not make it a certainty that you will live poor and die poor—but it makes it very likely."

Food Banks: Voluntary Response to a Public Problem

The contradictions associated with "hunger in the midst of plenty" are starkly illustrated by the rise of food banks across Canada in the 1980s. Since the first food bank opened in Edmonton in 1981, food banks and similar organizations have been established in many towns and cities across Canada (Canadian Association of Food Banks 1989; Riches 1986; Oderkirk 1992; Webber 1992). As Table 22.3 indicates, by 1984 there were 75 food banks in Canada, mostly in the western provinces. The number of food banks continued to increase through the 1980s. By 1991, there were 292 food banks in various parts of Canada. This growth is likely to continue as the economy further experiences the effects of economic recession.

It is estimated that two million Canadians used food banks in 1991. Children account for a large number of food-bank users. While 25 percent of the Canadian population was under age 18, nearly 40 percent of the food-bank beneficiaries in

TABLE 22.3: Food Banks in Canada, 1981–1991

	1981	1984	1988	1989	1990	1991
Newfoundland	0	0	1	1	1	17
Prince Edward Island	0	0	2	2	2	3
Nova Scotia	0	2	8	14	14	27
New Brunswick	0	2	27	34	35	40
Quebec	0	2	5	5	5	11
Ontario	0	4	19	33	35	88
Manitoba	0	1	1	3	3	4
Saskatchewan	0	5	5	5	8	11
Alberta	1	12	16	26	24	40
British Columbia	0	47	42	36	34	51
Canada	1	75	126	159	161	292

Note: Estimates from 1988 to 1991 from the Canadian Association of Food Banks do not include Salvation Army Family Services Divisions food banks. Growth during this period can be attributed to the creation of new food banks and to the registration of existing food banks with the association.
Source: J. Odekirk, "Food banks," *Canadian Social Trends*, Cat. no. 11-008, 24 (Spring 1992): 6–14. Reproduced by authority of the Minister of Industry, 1994.

1990 were in this age group (Canadian Association of the Food Banks, 1991, cited in Oderkirk 1992). For over two-thirds (68 percent) of the food-bank users, welfare was the primary source of income. It is evident that many Canadians depend upon food banks and other charitable meal operations for their daily food.

It is important to recognize that food-bank services operate separately from food hamper distribution and meal programs offered by other agencies such as soup kitchens, church and school programs, community friendship centres, and Salvation Army centres (Riches 1986, 13). Whereas the latter programs have operated for several decades, food-bank services constitute a relatively recent phenomenon. Charitable operations tend to serve a relatively specific clientele, such as older male indigents or children in low-income areas. By contrast, food banks do not usually target selected groups, but rather provide food parcels for any individuals and families who appear voluntarily or are referred by agencies when their cash or food supplies are inadequate. The very existence of food banks and their proliferation in food-producing regions of Canada indicate the extent to which hunger and poverty have become regular features of advanced industrial societies.

Food banks originated as an emergency response to a situation in which people did not have sufficient welfare and other income to provide food and necessities for themselves and family members. The guiding principle on which most food banks operate is summarized by the Greater Vancouver Food Bank Society (1989, 1–2) as follows: "The food bank does not represent a long-term solution to the problem of hunger in our community; rather we see ourselves as meeting a crisis situation when government aid to the needy is diminishing." Nonetheless, they are becoming more than a temporary reality.

In other words, food banks constitute a response to shifts in both the economy and state policy. They first appeared in western Canada during the severe economic crisis of the early 1980s, in which national unemployment rates nearly doubled from 7 percent in July 1981 to 12.8 percent in December 1982; the highest increases were in Alberta, British Columbia, and other parts of western Canada. At the same time, the adoption of neoconservative government policies hastened the diversion of state priorities and resources from social and human services to the enhancement of labour productivity and capital accumulation.

This constituted a reorganization of the state, one of whose consequences has been a sustained attack on welfare programs and social services. Business and political organizations claimed that welfare expenditures were contributing to government deficits and impeding individual initiative and labour productivity at a time when Canada needed to become more competitive internationally. In the 1980s, the federal and provincial governments began to overhaul welfare, unemployment insurance, and other social programs, imposing tighter eligibility requirements and spending ceilings. The theme that all Canadians must take greater individual responsibility for their own and their families' welfare, and that of the nation as a whole, resounded as a common refrain.

Through the ideology and practice of restraint, we have come to expect that employment discontinuities in the form of job losses or career shifts will accompany economic restructuring. Food banks are commonly accepted as one way of sharing the burden of temporary displacement through appeals to persons with steady incomes to donate food for distribution to those less fortunate than themselves. In this sense, food banks are seen as a temporary measure designed to alleviate crisis conditions for the hardest hit victims of recession and economic reordering. Their creation as voluntary organizations supported by contributions of food, money, and time from community members reinforces the notion that we all have a responsibility to others without placing excessive dependence on the state or other agencies.

At the same time, however, a victim-blaming ideology aligned with the emphasis on individual initiative implies that food-bank recipients are not merely innocent casualties of economic change. The attacks on welfare and the glorification of productive private enterprise are designed to leave the impression that persons who require social assistance and food-bank support have failed to contribute to the capitalist system, not that they have been failed by it. The criticism implies that it is not so much that food banks and meal-distribution programs are a necessary evil in Canada but that recipients are lazy, unmotivated, uneducated, or incapable of caring for themselves. The image that hunger is an anomaly in contemporary society is buttressed by statements from prominent public officials. The premier of British Columbia claimed that children were going to school hungry because their parents were playing bingo and drinking excessively; the minister of Families in Saskatchewan put it this way: "You're dealing with people, a lot of them are illiterate, as a result they don't know how to shop properly, they can't get the best buys on food. All that sort of thing" (Burton 1989).

A closer examination dispels the popular notion that food banks are a temporary measure to serve less-than-desirable segments of the population. Their number and the range of clients have grown substantially since programs began operation. In Vancouver, for example, the food bank provided food aid to up to three thousand households (about 8300 persons) per week in 1989, compared with two hundred households in 1982. In Nanaimo, British Columbia, the number of registered food-bank users in December 1989 was 5569, or nearly 11 percent of the city's population, and was expanding with an average of twenty new registrations per week. The Calgary Inter-Faith Food Bank distributed food hampers to 3175 recipients in November 1989, an increase of 22 percent from one year earlier. The Saskatoon food bank served 24 083 families in 1988 compared to 8724 in 1985. An average of 679 food hampers were distributed monthly in 1989 by an agency in the Kitchener-Waterloo area, compared to 409 per month in 1988; and in Metropolitan Toronto, the Daily Bread Food Bank served about 80 000 persons per month in 1989 compared to about 500 in 1984 (Braungart 1989; Greater Vancouver Food Bank Society 1989; Robinson 1989; *Star-Phoenix* [Saskatoon] December 15, 1989: D14; *Star-Phoenix* August 30, 1989).

Other charitable agencies have also supplied growing numbers of meals. In Regina, for instance, agencies that distribute several thousand meals and snacks to school children and adults monthly reported increases of between 20 and 33 percent in the use of their services between 1988 and 1989, while in several other cities, schools have begun or expanded regular meal and snack distribution to hungry children in recent years (Regina 1989, 9–10; York 1989). In all, based on data from March 1989, over 1.1 million meals were served that month by more than 1100 grocery programs and 400 meal programs across Canada. (Canadian Association of Food Banks 1989, 2–3). As noted above, two million Canadians used food banks in 1991.

In all cases—when supplies are available—food banks distribute parcels that include basic foods such as bread, peanut butter, canned meat and fish, powdered milk, pablum, and infant formula. In other words, they provide essential nutrition, not unnecessary or extravagant items. These foods cannot always be assured; food banks depend upon whatever food items are donated and what can be purchased with cash donations. Their ability to provide adequate services is reliant upon the success of regular appeals to the public and various agencies for food, resources, and volunteer labour. In several instances, they have had to turn away people seeking their services. Moreover, several thousand more potential recipients do not receive or are not able to receive food from food banks (Canadian Association of Food Banks 1989, 4; Regina 1989, 36).

Traditionally, soup kitchens and other charitable food services have catered to older men and transients, but food banks tend to have a younger, more diverse clientele, as shown by the food items they distribute. Data on food-bank recipients present a composite picture of persons who, in their prime working years and often supporting children, have limited access to jobs and labour-force income. In Toronto, the proportion of food-bank recipients who were employed increased from 13 percent in late 1987 to 18 percent in early 1989 (Stefaniuk 1989). In 1988–89, 40 percent of food-bank recipients across Canada, with little regional variation, were children under the age of eighteen (Canadian Association of Food Banks 1989, 2). As reported earlier, this proportion continued into 1990.

The overwhelming majority of food-bank users continue to be people on welfare. Many argue that these trends provide strong evidence that incompetent or unenterprising persons, most of them welfare recipients, are more inclined to squander their "unearned" money when they know that they can receive food handouts from volunteer agencies. But these people are by no means just lazy or irresponsible. Stated simply, people who receive food-bank services, with few exceptions, do so because they cannot survive in capitalist societies without those services. Officials with food banks and other charitable meal organizations are particularly concerned about the recent trend toward large numbers of "non-traditional unemployed" who have become reliant on welfare and food-bank services because jobs have disappeared in their white-collar occupations (Greater Vancouver Food Bank Society 1989, 3; York 1989). Although the measure of the poverty line must be interpreted with caution, as noted earlier in the chapter, one in seven Canadians lived below the poverty line in 1986. Nonetheless, welfare and social assistance rates are not keeping pace with increases in the cost of basic needs, including food, clothing, and shelter. Moreover, as the National Council of Welfare (1987, 49) observes, "In all provinces, the definition of basic requirements is so stringent that the welfare benefit levels calculated according to these standards permit only an impoverished existence." Cutbacks in social service expenditures, particularly for single employable persons, exacerbate personal crisis to the extent that, in order for recipients to pay for some minimal necessities such as rent, clothing, heating, and transportation, other necessities such as food often have to be forgone. Analysis by the Social Planning and Research Council of British Columbia (1989, 32), for example, reveals that persons in all categories receiving income assistance experience a shortfall in total income relative to daily living costs ranging from 29 percent monthly for a single parent with one child living in a one-bedroom apartment to 83 percent for a single male.

Changing employment patterns make it difficult, if not impossible, for many potential workers to find work; extensive unemployment, underemployment, and low-wage work make people reliant on welfare and other forms of social assistance; and restrictive social assistance practices and low rates force people to turn to food banks and other charitable support. These points are reinforced in an inquiry into hunger in Regina, which stresses that virtually all respondents, including food-bank agencies, recipients, community organizations, and public officials agree that hunger is caused by poverty, which in turn is associated with

- minimum wage rates that are too low;
- high unemployment and only low-paying or part-time jobs, particularly for certain categories of people such as youth, women with young children, people with mental illnesses, and Native people;
- high-cost, poor-quality housing which forces people to spend much of their income, sometimes 50 percent or more, on shelter;
- inadequate support services including child care, home economic skills, and supportive living facilities;
- inadequate welfare allowances and inadequate financial supports for the working poor (Regina 1989, 14).

These trends force us to rethink widely accepted notions that recipients are the major beneficiaries of food-bank services. It is important to stress that unlike relatively fixed costs, such as rent and utilities, for which non-payment makes persons subject to eviction or loss of services, food and other consumption purchases are more "voluntary" in the sense that they have attached to them no deadlines or compulsion by external agencies. In other words, people who turn to food banks when they have no income left for food have already spent their available funds on shelter and other necessary goods and services. Under these circumstances, it is rental unit owners, utility companies, and other businesses that are in a position to gain from the "subsidized" costs of food-bank services, which would otherwise have to be purchased by recipients. Food banks are not the only form of social assistance that benefits capital. As Swanson (1989) observes, welfare policy in general "can also help business by providing direct wage subsidies to employers and direct rent subsidies to landlords." In this way, programs that allegedly operate to alleviate hunger and poverty actually help perpetuate these phenomena by fuelling the conditions under which they are produced.

Because most public attention directed toward food banks emphasizes food donations and the needs of recipients, issues of hunger and food banks tend to be depoliticized. We think less in terms of structured inequalities and the systemic creation of poverty than of "fortune," with the "better-off" sectors of society being called on to help the "less fortunate." It is clear that food banks and other voluntary and charitable meal operations provide a valuable service by feeding people on a day-to-day basis and enlightening many persons, such as their volunteers who encounter directly the problems of hunger and its consequences. We must also recognize, though, that these solutions to immediate problems deflect attention away from the real causes of hunger and poverty and may actually encourage government and business to distance themselves further from taking an active role in promoting the welfare of the general population. As Riches (1986, 117) concludes, the issues associated with food banks cannot be divorced from the wider contradictory realities of the welfare state:

> On the one hand, food banks, like the welfare state, can be seen as meeting the needs of capital and the state by acting as a means of social control. On the other hand, they can be viewed as forms of voluntarist social endeavor which could, in a number of ways, act as catalysts for progressive change.

Conclusions

Wide income disparities continue to exist among Canadians. Many Canadians continue to live in poverty. Groups at a high risk of being poor include women, families headed by women, those with low educational levels, those working in the marginalized sector of the labour market, and part-time workers.

Although poverty has fluctuated with economic cycles, it is a constant presence in Canadian society. Income transfer payments and tax credit programs have helped mitigate the impact of poverty and inequality; still, they have done little to redistribute incomes in this country more equitably.

Economic and social inequalities produce inequality of opportunities, differential life chances, and different social consumption patterns. A duality of social consumption patterns is linked to income levels—while upper-income groups have disposable income for luxury and semi-luxury goods, at the other extreme, lower-income groups are often unable to purchase even necessary subsistence goods, including food. The malnutrition and hunger that are associated with poverty have serious effects on the health and performance of individuals. The emergence of food banks has alleviated hunger for thousands of Canadians, but any permanent and long-range solutions require the elimination of economic and social inequality and poverty. This in turn requires a consideration of the causes of inequality and poverty.

Why is there poverty in the midst of plenty? One answer blames the poor themselves for some personal deficiency, either innate (biological or intellectual) or cultural. Followers of the nineteenth-century sociologist Herbert Spencer, along with other Social Darwinists, have argued that the poor are poor because they are unfit; others argue that certain groups lack intellectual endowment, a trait that they claim is primarily inherited (Herrnstein 1971, 1973; Jensen 1969, 1980).

Irrespective of any flaws in their formulation and evidence, these perspectives have important social policy implications. In the case of Social Darwinism, the implication is that the poor should not be helped because that would interfere with "natural selection," while in the case of biological arguments, like those of Jensen and Herrnstein, the implication is that the poor cannot be helped since they are "uneducatable" (Eitzen and Zinn 1989, 178-79). The "culture of poverty" hypothesis locates poverty in poor people's "defective" cultural values, such as lack of motivation, low aspirations, inability to defer gratification, lack of moral values, and fatalism (Lewis 1966). Therefore, the poor are poor either because they are "defective individuals" or they have a "defective" way of life. In either case, they are the objects of what Ryan (1971) has called "blaming the victim." In contrast to the individual and cultural deficiency approaches, a structural explanation of poverty locates its cause in the social structural conditions of capitalism, which produce high unemployment, low-paying jobs, and unequal opportunity structures. The basic tenet of capitalism—the profit-motive—leads capitalists to use every means to reduce labour costs. They accomplish this by maintaining a surplus of labour, which depresses wages and allows employers to rotate their labourers and take other measures to benefit themselves (Eitzen and Zinn 1989, 185).

Because a vast majority of Canadians earn their income in a form of wages from employment, labour-market characteristics that determine which jobs are well paid are particularly important in any discussion of poverty (Osberg 1981). Consider the following:

- Families headed by persons in managerial and professional occupations are unlikely to live below the poverty line.
- Occupations with an above-average risk of poverty include farming, fishing, and services.
- The poverty rate for families headed by workers in service industries—a heavy employer of women—increased from 16.2 percent in 1980 to 19.6 percent in 1986. (National Council of Welfare 1988)

Because unemployment, underemployment, and marginalized jobs all contribute to inequality and poverty, the solution to poverty lies in the alteration of these conditions. However, the continuing high unemployment levels and labour-market segmentation do not lead to optimism. Not only are unemployment rates in Canada high, they are accompanied by increases in long-term unemployment (that is, lasting six months or longer). The number of Canadians experiencing long-term unemployment more than tripled between 1980 and 1983, and by 1985, 28 percent of unemployed Canadians were in the long-term unemployed category (Parliament 1987). Moreover, the Canadian labour market is segmented along occupational, gender, and ethnic lines. Many women and minorities end up in secondary and marginal sectors, which offer poor working conditions and low wages.

While the roots of poverty lie in the structural conditions just discussed, prominent sectors of the political and business elite continue to adhere to a victim-blaming strategy. The poor are blamed not only for their own poverty, but also for the fiscal crisis and budgetary deficits. It is argued that excessive social expenditures are responsible for deficits and need to be cut back in order to avert economic crisis. As Minkler (1983, 155) states, "A hallmark of the current politics of retrenchment has been the tendency by many policy makers to scapegoat the poor and the elderly as 'causes' of the 'fiscal crisis.'"

The scapegoating rhetoric has coincided with "a resurgence of the ideology that individuals create their own conditions and opportunities, and that they are to be held accountable for their predicament" (Estes 1982, 575). The rhetoric of victim blaming, fiscal crisis, and individual responsibility combine to justify cutbacks to welfare and other social programs. Large deficits are said to make it impractical to continue to support social expenditures—since we "cannot afford it," or there are "limits of the possible." As Piven and Cloward (1982, 134) state, "Fiscal austerity will not appear to be political: it will appear to be the inevitable adaptation of a responsible government to the constraints imposed by limited resources."

While "responsible governments" are implementing cutbacks in social expenditures that mostly affect the poor, public funds are being channel led to private-sector interests through the privatization of state services and other measures that strengthen the capitalist class and subsidize corporations. Concomitantly, we have seen the resurrection of the notion that individual-voluntaristic ameliorative programs, such as food banks, are the best way to help the unfortunate among us. This situation relieves the state of the responsibility to provide social assistance programs. Remaining public-sector assistance programs are explicitly targeted toward specific groups and specific problems and, therefore, tend to be "exceptionalistic" rather than "universalistic" in nature.

While transfer payments have not led to any redistribution of incomes, if it were not for state-provided social assistance programs, the gap between the rich and the poor would be even wider than it is now. Furthermore a majority of poor families now rely on government transfer payments for the major part of their income. Therefore, any reductions in social programs will adversely affect those who most need them.

In conclusion, voluntary programs, such as food banks, are simply treating the symptoms rather than the disease. In order to eliminate the basic causes of hunger, which are inequality and poverty, a basic alteration of the structural and social condition is required. In the absence of any fundamental transformation and in view of the current attacks on the welfare state, and proposals to restructure it, it appears that a large segment of the population is likely to have to manage on its own or depend on the charity and good will of individual voluntaristic assistance provided by the shrinking numbers of the "fortunate" among the population.

Study Questions

1. Discuss the linkages between income inequality and life chances. In your answer, include material from other chapters in this volume.

2. Discuss the relationships among inequality, poverty, hunger, and health.

3. "To be born poor in Canada does not make it a certainty that you will live poor and die poor but it makes it very likely." Discuss this statement.

4. From all evidence, there is no world-wide shortage of food. Why is it, then, that millions of people go hungry every day and thousands face famine and starvation?

5. Canada is one of the richest countries in the world, and it certainly produces abundant food. How, then, can we explain hunger in this country and the emergence and persistence of food banks?

6. Compare and contrast "victim-blaming" approaches with structural explanations of inequality, poverty, and hunger.

7. Identify and discuss the major contradictions associated with voluntary programs, such as food banks, that address hunger, and other social problems in this country.

Recommended Reading

Gunderson, Morley, and Leon Muszynski. *Women and Labour Market Poverty.* Ottawa: Canadian Advisory Council on the Status of Women, 1990.

Lappé, Frances Moore, and Joseph Collins. *World Hunger: Twelve Myths.* York: Gore Press, 1986.

Moscovitch, Alan, and Jim Albert, eds. *The "Benevolent" State: The Growth of Welfare in Canada.* Toronto: Garamond Press, 1987.

Oderkirk, J. "Food Banks." *Canadian Social Trends* 24, no. 6 (1992): 6–14.

Piven, F.F., and R.A. Cloward. *The New Class War: Reagan's Attack on the Welfare State and Its Consequences.* New York: Ballantine Press, 1982.

Riches, Graham. *Food Banks and the Welfare Crisis.* Ottawa: Canadian Council on Social Development. 1986.

Warnock, John W. *The Politics of Hunger.* Toronto: Methuen, 1987.

References

Blumberg, P. 1980. *Inequality in an Age of Decline.* New York: Oxford University Press.

Bradley, C.F., S.E Ross, and J.M. Warnyca. 1978. "Parent's Choice. A Comprehensive Perinatal Programme." Vancouver Perinatal Health Project, November.

Braungart, S. 1989. "Food Hampers Key to Survival for the Needy." *Calgary Herald* December 16, Al.

Bronson, H.E. 1984. "Multinational Corporations, Food, and Energy." In *Contradictions in Canadian Society*, ed. J.A. Fry. Toronto: John Wiley and Sons. 43–62.

Brown, J.C. 1978. *Prevention of Handicap: A Case for Improved Prenatal and Perinatal Care*. Ottawa: Canadian Institute of Child Health.

Burton, R. 1989. "Social Workers to Help Battle Hunger in Schools." *Star-Phoenix* (Saskatoon), December 2, A3.

Canadian Association of Food Banks. 1989. *Canadian Hungercount, 1989*. Summary. Toronto: Canadian Association of Food Banks.

Chossudovsky, M. 1983. "Underdevelopment and the Political Economy of Malnutrition and Ill Health." *International Journal of Health Services* 13, no. 1: 69–87.

Chu, C. 1989. "Malnutrition Affects Learning Ability of the Poor." *Star-Phoenix* (Saskatoon), November 7,: C4.

Eitzen, S., and M.B. Zinn. 1989. *Social Problems*. 4th ed. Boston: Allyn and Bacon.

Epp, J. 1986. "Achieving Health for All: A Framework for Health Promotion." *Canadian Journal of Public Health* 77, no 6: 393–407.

Estes. C.L. 1982. "Austerity and Aging in the United States: 1980 and Beyond." *International Journal of Health Services* 12, no. 4: 573–84.

Fine, S. 1989. "Poor Children More Likely to Die Than Wealthy Peers, Study Finds." *Globe and Mail*, July 25, A5.

Greater Vancouver Food Bank Society. 1989. "Food Bank Information Kit." Vancouver: Greater Vancouver Food Bank Society.

Herrnstein, R. 1971. "I.Q." *Atlantic* 228 (September): 43–64.

———. 1973. *I.Q. in the Meritocracy*. Boston: Little, Brown.

Jensen, A.R. "How Much Can We Boost IQ and Scholastic Achievements?" *Harvard Educational Review* 39 (Winter): 1–123.

———. 1980. *Bias in Mental Testing*. New York: The Free Press.

Kotz, N. 1984. "The Politics of Hunger," *New Republic* 190 (April): 19–23.

Lewis, O. 1966. *La Vida*. New York: Random House.

Minkler, M. "Blaming the Aged Victim: The Politics of Scapegoating in Times of Fiscal Conservatism." *International Journal of Health Services* 13, no. 1: 155–68.

Myres, A.W., and D. Kroetsch. 1978. "The Influence of Family Income on Food Consumption Patterns and Nutrition Intake in Canada." *Canadian Journal of Public Health* 69, no. 3: 208–21.

National Council of Welfare. 1975. *Poor Kids*. Ottawa. Supply and Services Canada.

———. 1987. *Welfare: The Tangled Safety Net*. Ottawa: Supply and Services Canada.

———. 1988. *Poverty Profile 1988*. Ottawa: Supply and Services Canada.

———. 1989. *Poverty Lines*. Ottawa: Supply and Services Canada.

———. 1990. *Women and Poverty Revisited.* Ottawa: Supply and Services Canada.

———. 1992. *Poverty Profile, 1980–1990. Ottawa: Supply and Services Canada.*

Nutrition Canada. 1975. Survey Report on Indians and Eskimos. Ottawa: Information Canada.

Oderkirk, I. 1992. "Food Banks." *Canadian Social Trends* 24, no. 6: 6–14.

Osberg, L. 1981. *Economic Inequality in Canada*. Toronto: Butterworths.

Parliament, J. 1987. "Increase in Long-Term Unemployment." *Canadian Social Trends* (Statistics Canada) (Spring): 8–11.

Perkins, S. 1974. "Malnutrition and Mental Development." International Union of Child Welfare Conference.

Physicians' Task Force on Hunger in America. 1985. *Hunger in America: The Growing Epidemic*. Middletown, CT: Wesleyan University Press.

Piven, F.F., and R.A. Cloward. 1982. *The New Class War: Reagan's Attack on the Welfare State and Its Consequences*. New York: Pantheon Books.

Regina Mayor's Board of Inquiry. 1989. *An Inquiry Into Hunger in Regina*. Regina: The Mayor's Board of Inquiry.

Reid, D.L., and J.E. Miles. 1977. "Food Habits and Nutrition Intakes of Non-Institutionalized Senior Citizens." *Canadian Journal of Public Health* 68, no. 2: 154–58.

Riches, G. 1986. *Food Banks and the Welfare Crisis*. Ottawa: Canadian Council on Social Development.

Robinson, A. 1989. "Richards Has to Face Burning Issue in New Job." *Star-Phoenix* (Saskatoon), September 25, A3.

Ross, S.E., and A.C. Rutter. 1978. "Healthiest Babies Possible: An Outreach Program." Vancouver Perinatal Health Project.

Ryan, W. 1971. *Blaming the Victim*. New York: Pantheon.

Shah, C.P., and C.S. Farkas. 1985. "The Health of Indians in Canadian Cities: A Challenge to the Health-Care System." *Canadian Medical Association Journal* 133: 859–63.

Social Planning and Research Council of British Columbia. 1989. *Regaining Dignity: An Examination of Costs and the Adequacy of Income Assistance Rates* (CAIN) in British Columbia. Vancouver: Social Planning and Research Council of British Columbia.

Special Senate Committee on Poverty. 1971. *Poverty in Canada*. Ottawa: Information Canada.

Statistics Canada and Health and Welfare in Canada. 1981. *The Health of Canadians: Report of the Health Survey*. (Cat. 82-538E). Ottawa: Supply and Services Canada.

Stefaniuk, W.1989. "More Working People Using Food Banks, Survey Finds." *Toronto Star*, March 22, A21.

Swanson, J. "If Welfare 'Helps,' Why Doesn't It Help the Poor?" *Vancouver Sun* November 18, B5.

Vernon, P.E. 1979. *Intelligence: Heredity and Environment*. San Francisco: W.H. Freeman.

Webber, M. 1992. *Food for Thought*. Toronto: Coach House Press.

Wigle, D.T., and Y. Mao. 1980. *Mortality by Income Level in Urban Canada*. Ottawa: Health and Welfare Canada.

Wilkins, R., and O. Adams. 1983. *Healthfulness of Life*. Montreal: Institute on Public Policy.

Wilkinson, W.H., and V.W. Sidel. 1986. "Hunger in America," *Social and Health Review* 3: 59–64.

York, G. 1989. "Soup Kitchens Try to Ease Hunger for Regina's Children of Poverty." *Globe and Mail*, October 9, A5.

CHAPTER 23

The Decline of the Canadian Welfare State: Policies and Implications of Retrenchment

Gary Teeple

Learning Objectives

This chapter[1] will examine the nature of the welfare state. It will delineate the common elements of the history of social reform and the significance of such policies in industrial nations. Particular attention will be paid to the development of social legislation in Canada.

The chapter will also explore the reasons for the current decline in the welfare state. The consequences of this retrenchment, already visible in this country, will be explored.

After reading this chapter, the student should have an understanding of the component elements, history, and rationale of the welfare state in general; the significance of social reform to Canadian life; and the reasons for the decline of the welfare state and the consequences thereof.

Introduction

Hardly any aspect of life in the modern industrial nation-state is not affected by the policies, programs, and regulations that make up the so-called welfare state. Indeed, so extensive are these reforms—yet so taken for granted—that few citizens of these countries realize how profoundly their lives are influenced by them.

"From the cradle to the grave" is the dusty cliché that was often employed to describe the extent of the influence. Merely to be born into a modern industrial nation-state is to become the recipient of numerous goods and services and the beneficiary of many standards and regulations, all associated with the welfare state. In one way or another these "reforms" have a profound impact all through one's life, and even beyond. And all for very important reasons, as we shall see below.

Since the late 1970s, a transformation of the welfare state has been underway. In virtually every country that claims to have extensive social reforms, governments have made conscious efforts to undermine, retract, retrench, or eliminate them (Mishra 1984; Banting 1987; Kamerman and Kahn 1989; Sulieman and Waterbury 1990). Nonetheless, despite more than a decade of these efforts and repeated declarations that "welfarism" has lost public favour, that "big government" must be cut back, that state regulations inhibit economic growth, and that neoliberalism[2] has created a new morality, the reforms that comprise the welfare state have maintained a remarkable level of popular support—everywhere (Mishra 1990, chap. 2; Navarro 1985/86; Therborn and Roebeck 1986).

That the majority of citizens continue to look positively on social policies, programs, and regulations should not be surprising. Imagine a society without these reforms. In the labour market, there would be no minimum wage, no limits to the working day, no employment or health or safety standards, no restrictions on hiring and firing, no unemployment or accident insurance, and so on. People would have to do without state pensions, social services, hospital and medical insurance, public education, and income supplements. This list could easily be extended. Such a state of affairs is difficult to imagine because these reforms have become part of an accepted standard of living: they are essential to the way of life that has come to be a norm in the industrial world.

Even in capitalist societies that have all these reforms, however, people live in fear, particularly of unemployment and of the financial consequences of illness, injury, childbirth and old age. This is because reforms are still just reforms; that is, they rarely provide more than minimal support and certainly give no guarantee that membership in society will bring employment, decent housing, accessible education, a living retirement pension or disability benefits, an unpolluted environment, employment standards, or freedom from poverty. For the most part, social reforms offer only limited security or standards for whatever need or issue they are intended to address; and while these "minimums" can be raised, they can also be lowered. Given rising unemployment and the present retrenchment of the welfare state, the above fears are becoming more deep-seated for growing numbers.

There can be little doubt about the consequences of cutbacks or elimination of social reforms. Capitalist societies with minimal or no reforms are close at hand. Here will be found workplaces without standards, child labour, high rates of illiteracy, environmental degradation and destruction, pervasive poverty, and enormous disparities in the wealth of citizens.

These social conditions appear to be typical of the direction in which industrial nations are moving. This places the question of the nature of the welfare state and the reasons for its decline at centre stage.

The Welfare State

What is the Welfare State?

Considerable debate has raged over the definition of the welfare state, and several authors have attempted to forge its many characteristics into a coherent concept (Titmuss 1958; Gough 1979; Carrier and Kendall 1986; Quadagno 1987; Esping-

Andersen 1989). It cannot be said, however, that any general agreement came out of this controversy. For our purposes the following definition will suffice: The welfare state refers to a capitalist society in which the state has intervened to determine the form of social policies, programs, standards, and regulations in order to mitigate class conflict *and* to provide for, answer, or accommodate certain social needs for which the capitalist mode of production in itself has no solution or provision.

The main elements of this definition, common to all welfare states, should be spelled out since they are important to an understanding of what the welfare state is, not to mention why it is being dismantled. First, it is a product of a capitalist society, which is characterized by commodity production, by contradictory interests (in particular between workers and the representatives of capital), and by the profit motive as the purpose of production. Second, the role of government, as the political embodiment of the system as a whole, has been to ensure its maintenance and reproduction. The government must fulfil this role because such a system has no inherent design, aside from the production of commodities for sale, for coping with potentially destabilizing social needs or class conflict. Third, the welfare state is delimited by the boundaries of the nation-state, the geographic territory under the jurisdiction of a given government.

The nature of the social reforms at the centre of this definition should be further specified. In general, these comprise state interventions in four key overlapping arenas of societal reproduction. The one most commonly associated with the welfare state is that of the physical propagation of the working class and its preparation for the labour market. Included herein are the health care and educational systems and many of the non-contributory social benefits (the largest recipients of which are women and children), which include subsidized day care, child/family allowance, food stamps, transfer payments to single mothers, and so on.

Another arena is the labour market and here the state has intervened not only to mitigate the extent of leverage that capital has over labour, but also to prepare fresh workers for the market and to ensure an "adequate" labour supply. Typically, this arena includes regulations on the minimum wage, hours of work, child labour, retirement age; education and training, injury insurance, immigration, and so on.

The third arena is the point of production, that is, the point of contact between workers and the representatives of capital, and the point where labour has submitted to the dictates of capital. Here the state intervenes to provide the institutional framework for class conflict (collective bargaining) and to protect the workers from the worst effects of exploitation by capital. Collective bargaining rights are central here, but employment and health and safety standards are also very important.

The fourth arena is the provision of income assurance for the "unproductive," in a word, retirement and other pensions and social assistance of all kinds for those unable, for whatever reason, to work in the system.

Just how these social reforms are carried into effect can be briefly categorized as follows. The most commonly recognized form of implementation would likely be the provision of services, such as education, health care, and child day care. The second most significant form of realizing these reforms is probably income transfers, such as pensions, unemployment or injury insurance, social security, and so on. In some countries the supply of "goods," for example in the form of public housing, comprises an important aspect of social reform. Lastly, there is the large category of laws, regulations, and standards that the state has promulgated in order to institutionalize inherent conflicts and to protect the disadvantaged in a system based on inequalities.

When State Intervention Becomes "The Welfare State"

If many of these social reforms, along with the modes of implementation, seem to have accompanied the long development of capitalism and the modern state, the question has arisen about just when a society can be defined as a welfare state. Is it the amount of reform or the sort of reform that is necessary for a regime to be so classified?

If it were possible to give a short answer, the following would likely suffice: When class conflict, reduced to the contest between workers and the representatives of capital, presents a chronic threat to the stability of the system and has to be institutionalized (i.e., placed within a legal framework of industrial relations) *and* when the majority of social needs pertaining to the reproduction of the working classes are addressed formally (i.e., by the state via "public" policies, etc.) rather than informally (i.e., via the community, family, friends), the welfare state has arrived. Such a definition, of course, leads one to question why and how this happens, not to mention when in history.

Why and How the Welfare State Comes About

The introduction of social reforms varies across nations in time, circumstances, and kind. While one cannot identify all the specific reasons and how they contribute to each case of the welfare state, one can isolate a common premise and other factors general to the development of all national reform programs in the nineteenth and twentieth centuries.

The shared premise of national reform programs was the development and rise to pre-eminence of industrial capitalism within the nation-state. It was the consequences of the breakdown of the old mode of production and the coming of this new one that laid the ground for the social reforms that followed sooner or later.

The fundamental outcome of the destruction of precapitalist modes of production was twofold: a) the creation of a capitalist labour market and working class, or the "freeing" of labour from its means of production and existing forms of bondage; and b) the breakdown of social institutions, labour processes, and communities that embodied to a considerable degree an integrated social, political, and economic life. The significance of this transformation was that it gave rise to objective needs that had formerly been integral to a way of life. It also created new needs and new problems, which arose from and were associated with the capitalist labour market, the "freedom" of the worker, and new labour processes. In itself, capitalism had no answers for these needs and problems aside from the wage relation and the purchase of commodities; the "answers" were to come as imposed reforms.

The "freed" working class, after it became entirely dependent on employment for its livelihood, found it necessary to defend itself against the depredations of the capitalist class and the vagaries of the labour market. The consequent organized resistance by sections of the working class brought trade unions into being, which were to become the principal force behind the introduction, defense, and extension of many social reforms. Class conflict of one sort or another, or its potential, has been the common context for all reform.

Far from homogeneous, however, the fragmented and stratified working class produced corresponding fractures in its organized representation. As a counter-force to capital, trade unions were perpetually weakened in most countries by irresolvable sectionalism and the narrow interests and cautiousness of unions representing certain strata. In part because of this lack of a militant, united, and class conscious trade union movement, class conflict, which is intrinsic to the system, was increasingly expressed in "gradualist" terms and the outcome limited to forms of compromise and accommodation (Kirk 1985).

This same organized resistance spurred the struggle for universal enfranchisement, and gave rise to political parties representative of certain strata of the working population. Such changes broadened the institutional political choices, allowing for a modicum of access to state power and the public purse, and for more political leverage for reform legislation. The number and inclusiveness of reforms owes much to these extra-parliamentary struggles and to the nature of political expression for the working class within the nation-state.

Out of the resistance to industrial capitalism came theories of socialist alternatives. The "spectre" of socialism or communism, a direct consequence of the coming of capitalism and the organized working class, has always been part of the motivation for the introduction of systematic reform programs (Mommsen 1981; Whitely 1981). All the industrial countries in the late nineteenth and early twentieth centuries had working-class parties and trade unions well versed in socialist theory and aware of the potential for revolution. Many actual attempts at revolution and numerous examples of general strikes appeared the world over. The success of the Bolshevik revolution was no minor inspiration to reforms in the West. Even after much of the political theory of the working class turned from revolution to reform and social democracy, spurs to reform included ongoing wars of liberation and the examples of the Soviet Union, China, and Cuba as "workers' states." In short, they served as reminders to the representatives of capital who might resist reforms.

Another consequence of industrial capitalism was increased productivity and the consequent need to expand overseas, producing colonial or imperial systems to "complement" the productivity of the industrial metropole. This expansion of capitalism brought with it the possibility to ameliorate its inherent conflicts. Among the effects of this export-led growth was the rapid increase in capital accumulation in the metropolitan countries. In turn, this allowed for a rise in the general standard of living. Capital accumulation expanded, confirming the legitimacy of the system and generating sufficient revenues for the creation of a "social wage,"[3] the fiscal foundation of modern social reforms.

By the late nineteenth century, new technology, increased productivity, and expanded markets had begun to increase the segmentation, stratification, and social mobility of the labour force. The resulting complex hierarchies and numerous strata created a multitude of varying immediate interests within the working class, many of which actually depended on the continuing expansion of capitalism. Divisions along many lines fractured the working population, and the grounding of the interests of some strata in capitalism itself made substantial sections of the class more amenable to reform than revolution.

With industrial capitalism also came the "business cycle": the periodic rise and fall of economic activity and employment. In times of economic slumps, the working population, with no alternative to employment for its livelihood, suffered profoundly. These periodic deprivations frequently produced civil unrest, threatened social stability, and at times even piqued the conscience of members of the middle-class and corporate leaders. Organized and unorganized social disruption (and, to a small degree, charitable sentiment) during recessions or depressions have been the motivation for some reforms.

Another general aspect to the origin of the welfare state is the concessionary and even promotional attitudes on the part of organized capital. The former is explained in part by the delimited national labour market and relative immobility of national capital in the relatively "closed" national economy prior to the 1970s. The latter is explained by the desire of the corporate sector to "socialize," and thereby limit, some of the costs to industry that are "incidental" to its operations. In various countries, the introduction of seniors' pensions, hospital insurance, and even public education are illustrative of this point. The origin of industrial accident insurance schemes, while not without the component of working-class demand, lies largely in the efforts by corporations to create a system both limiting their liability for industrial accidents and "socializing" the costs through industry-wide insurance premiums and chronically inadequate compensation to workers and their families (Tampke 1981; Lubove 1986).

Although these are the principal reasons for, and conditions underlying, the coming of the welfare state to all industrial countries, it is important to stress that they comprise a multidimensional rationale, in the context of the contradictions of nationally structured capitalism. While throughout the industrial world, reforms attempt to address broadly the same needs and problems intrinsic to capitalist society, the specific forms they take as "policy regimes," and when they develop, depend on a host of historically specific national factors. (There is a specific literature for each country. See Domhoff 1990; Rimlinger 1971; Kohler and Zacher 1982.)

By the first decade of the twentieth century, as a result of the forces outlined above, many of the reforms we now identify with the welfare state had been instituted in a limited way in most of the industrial nations. The reforms were not comprehensive because in these industrial countries large percentages of the labour force remained "on the land" outside the wage relation, and large-scale emigration and colonial expansion relieved much of the social pressure from "redundancies" in the labour force.

Only in the aftermath of the Second World War did all the conditions that underlie the modern welfare state fall into place, and the welfare state, as defined above, come into being.

The Modern Welfare State

In light of conditions in the post–Second World War period, the welfare state became a political and economic necessity. The industrial economies, with the exception of the United States, lay exhausted or in ruins, and the experience of the 1930s and the collective war effort made socialism an attractive alternative to the fear and indignity the working classes experienced in the capitalist labour market.

In order to reconstruct national capitalism in Europe and to resist widespread popular support for socialism in the industrial world, the state had to be employed (Hirschman 1988), to a degree not seen in earlier decades, to socialize the costs of reconstruction and to circumvent a repeat of the Depression and its consequent class struggles. So began almost three decades of unprecedented state intervention in the arenas comprising the relation between labour and capital.

The modern welfare state is often referred to as the Keynesian welfare state (KWS). The name derives in part from the economist, John Maynard Keynes, whose theories came to dominate in the industrial countries during and after the Second World War (Schott 1982). His principal assumption was the existence of a national economy, in which, he argued, the state could intervene to effect levels of investment and domestic income, and thereby partially regulate unemployment by these national "demand management" policies. Such intervention represented a certain socialization of the costs of production (state credits, guarantees, grants and concessions) and of working-class reproduction ("public works," and aspects of the welfare state), as part of a political compromise with the working classes. This compromise included the goals of moderating the business cycle (to prevent a repeat of the unrest of the 1930s), helping rebuild the war-destroyed economies of Europe (to ensure the re-establishment of capitalism), and containing or diminishing the growing interest in socialism stemming from the experience of the 1930s and the devastation of war (Winch 1969, 221, 349).

This rationale for state intervention in the economy was complemented by several other postwar developments, which combined to create the general conditions demanding and allowing for the construction of the welfare state in this period. These conditions were many and interrelated, but it is possible to identify and isolate some of the important ones.

The most significant was the persistence of the national state, the political counterpart to national corporate enterprise. Here lay the political and operational framework of the welfare state. That is, social reforms have been defined and administered as national programs. Social reforms have represented the political compromise between the power of a national capitalist class and resistance to its particular forms of exploitation by sections of a national working class or social movements. Social reforms have depended partly on the kind and degree of political alternatives historically evolved in particular nations.

The state's ability to finance the programs of the KWS rested on several economic prerequisites. Among them were massive state indebtedness and expenditures during and after the Second World War (Lend-lease for the war effort, the Marshall Plan for reconstruction, then the Korean and Vietnam wars, etc.); decolonization, which created new markets and cheap labour; and the "deepening of the domestic market," consumerism by another name, which depended on the vast expansion of ever-cheapening domestic commodities. In these ways, during this period, enormous surplus-value was generated, Gross National Products (GNPs) expanded relatively constantly, high wages could be paid, and, it followed, the tax-base in the industrial nations grew in concert.

Advanced Fordism[4] transformed the capitalist labour market, expanding and consolidating it with dramatic reductions in farm labour and the rapid growth of unproductive sectors. A relatively consistent high demand for labour and corresponding rises in wages and salaries in these postwar decades laid the basis for the growth in the number and size of trade unions. Accompanying this increasing union strength, there arose new and more comprehensive institutions of collective bargaining. The importance of collective bargaining for maintaining the system in the form of the nation-state, where the organized working class presents a threat to state power and capitalist hegemony, is much underrated (Harbison 1954).

The concomitant development of huge numbers and many layers of technical, para-professional, and administrative workers in both the private and public spheres substantially increased the strata of the working class, whose immediate interests rested on employment hierarchies, growth of the state sector, and national economic expansion. Here were the ingredients for the political platform promoted by social democracy as its vision of "reformed capitalism."

It is in this postwar period, then, that we find the culmination of social reform in the shape of the KWS. The overwhelming majority of the labour force had become working class, with sizeable percentages organized into trade unions. Class conflict now implied a chronic threat to the reproduction of the system and so had to be contained by institutionalized legal means. Moreover, with the transformation of the labour force and demise of precapitalist modes of production, the majority of social needs necessary to the reproduction of the working class (health, education, and social security) could only be met formally by the state through "public" policies, programs, and standards, that is, macroeconomic policies based on state indebtedness and the "social" wage.

Redistribution

Most aspects of the welfare state were designed to redistribute a portion of wages and salaries, collected by the state in the form of tax revenues, premiums, and deferred income. They were not intended to redistribute social wealth, the accumulated capital assets of society. To do this would have contradicted the essence of the system, the private accumulation of capital, and thereby challenged the powers vested in such private ownership.

In redistributing the "social wage," the function of the welfare state has actually rested on a prior distribution of total income, determined by existing property relations and by the ongoing struggle between the working class and the corporate sector over their respective shares of the social product. These shares are determined more specifically by a number of variable factors, namely, historical and current expectations, the legislated minimum wage, the supply and demand for labour, the degree of unionization, the restrictions on collective bargaining, the business cycle, and so on. Such factors determine the initial distribution of the social product, which takes the form of wages/salaries and profits. It is from a divided and distributed pie, then, that the state collects its tax revenues, premiums, and deferred income.

If we examine how components of the welfare state are financed, the nature of redistribution can be seen more clearly. Certain programs in Canada, such as workers' accident and hospital insurance, unemployment benefits, and pension plans, are state-run indemnity schemes financed by premiums or deferred income paid by the working class out of wages and salaries. Some costs are often shared in part by corporations, their portion of the premiums calculated as part of the wage bill or the *faux frais* of doing business, like fire and theft insurance. Other programs, such as public education facilities, family allowance or child benefits, social assistance, public housing, etc., are usually paid out of general revenue. but the lion's share of general revenue comes from taxes on wages and salaries.

It is possible, then, to say that the welfare state represents two forms of redistribution. One is the general redistribution of deductions from wages and salaries in the forms mentioned to pay for schemes that assist the working class to reproduce itself. The other is a certain redistribution of revenues upward in the social strata since the well-to-do make proportionally greater use of the more costly programs (for example, health care and public education) but contribute proportionately less income in their support because of the structure of the tax regimes.

It can be said, moreover, that the redistribution associated with the welfare state has had little effect on economic inequality, mainly because it was never intended to level economic differences. Although a degree of levelling may take place because of the "averaging" of a portion of labour income, it does as an unintended consequence of the principal goal of such programs, namely, to ameliorate the worst effects of economic inequality and to placate resistance to all the political and social implications of such inequality. A modicum of social security, certain minimum standards, and containment of class conflict, as opposed to economic equality, has been the intent of the welfare state. The existence of social policies and programs has not threatened the basis of inequality, namely, the structure of ownership and control, and it has not changed the necessity for workers to sell themselves in a competitive labour market.

Social Citizenship and Decommodification

If the foregoing is the negative evaluation of the impact of the welfare state, the positive evaluation must bring into focus the concept of social rights, or "social citizenship"[5] (Marshall 1963). Here is contained the notion that all members of society have an innate claim to certain social services and programs such as health care, education, seniors' pensions, unemployment insurance, and so on. The degree of universality of these reforms is the degree to which the concept has been realized. Social citizenship implies an equality of status in the social realm, in the same way that citizenship denotes equality in the political realm: just as there is universal enfranchisement, there has been, with conditions, universal entitlement to certain social guarantees with the welfare state.

Like the historical struggle for universal suffrage, driven by the aspiration of the working population to have control over their lives, so the demand for universal social security is the implicit desire of the working classes to be free from the insecurity of the labour market and the bondage of wage labour. The only recourse from the instability of the labour market and the servility of employment—in a word, to the commodification of labour power—is to organize into trade unions to secure concessions from corporations or to obtain, through protest, state-sponsored social and economic reform. Such reforms and union rights to bargain collectively, to strike and to organize, however are never more than conditional concessions against the insecurities of the competitive labour market. In other words, they represent a qualified decommodification of labour power. The degree to which the reliance on the labour market for one's livelihood is supplanted by reforms is the degree to which social rights have been established in labour law and social benefits. The less universal and less comprehensive the welfare state, the less social citizenship can be said to exist (Esping-Andersen and Korpi 1984).

In other words, decommodification, whatever its degree, runs counter to the principles of the capitalist labour market. The existence of a social net and union rights undermine the negative effects of competition, powerlessness, fear, and poverty for the working class, which are part and parcel of the labour market. To go further, social citizenship represents the highest development of the principle of welfarism or social reformism. Just as universal enfranchisement marks the completion of politics, the concept and limited achievement of social citizenship marks the completion of social welfare, that is, the final result of a citizenry's struggle to have social security and meaning in an alienated society. Within capitalist social relations, the working class can achieve no more.

The partial and conditional achievement of social citizenship in the Western welfare states, however, helps clarify the limits of reformism. Even in those countries in which social and union rights have gained wide application, they have always remained provisional. That is, first, they often do not apply to certain categories of the population outside the labour force or marginal to it. Second, the boundaries of application are continuously subject to a fluctuating balance of class power. Third, social citizenship is only a compromise offered by a state and capitalist class, in answer to the question of welfare reform. Fourth, it does not bring economic equality and presents no fundamental challenge to existing power relations. It rests, moreover, on several economic and political preconditions, which, as we shall argue, are rapidly disappearing.

This delineation of limitations is not intended to disparage legislative attempts at redistribution of income for economic security. In fact, it should be strongly asserted here that these are positive gains for the working class. They are not gifts from anyone, and, as such, they should be defended (and will have to be defended) as gains, however paradoxical their nature may be. We are simply attempting to uncover what "redistribution" is actually redistributing and to question the prevailing myth surrounding welfare-state expenditures. In a word, all of these programs, from unemployment insurance to state pensions to health care, are financed by deferred or diverted component parts of wage income, not by deductions from the profits of capital, although they do presume wages high enough to allow for deductions. They are forms of state-controlled redistribution of a portion of working-class income intended to facilitate the reproduction of wage-earners, to provide limited economic security, and to serve as emollients for the denial of economic privilege.

The Welfare State in Canada

Background

The history of social reform in Canada before the 1940s possesses no single moment of introduction and no developmental continuity or comprehensiveness. Many of the reforms that preceded the Second World War were specific and limited responses to trade union pressure, corporate desire to socialize costs, and the destabilizing effects of unemployment and worker unrest. The most significant arenas of state intervention throughout this period were in formal education and in relations between labour and capital at the point of production.

From the early 1870s the legislative results of pressure for educational reform begin to be seen. An Ontario act proclaiming compulsory education was promulgated in 1871 but its realization was limited. These nineteenth-century efforts to introduce state-sponsored elementary education came in response to the growth of industrial capitalism and to the need to prepare the working class for the factory work place. Literacy, numeracy, and respect for authority all had to be instilled at an early age. But the unintended consequences proved to be equally important to the system, namely, the provision of an "official" route for working-class upward mobility and legitimation for economic inequality and the role of the state (Spring 1972; Schecter 1976).

Also from the early 1870s, successive attempts were staged to restrain and contain the growing powers of the trade unions, to institutionalize class conflict[6] as it became more destabilizing (Logan 1956, 7–10; Woods and Ostry 1962, 18–87). To prevent, moreover, the utter degradation of workers in the factories of the late nineteenth century, several provincial Factory Acts were put in place attempting to regulate hours and conditions of work. Although varying considerably in their terms, they were similar in their lax enforcement (Kealey 1973).

Also from the late 1880s, limited efforts were made to introduce industrial accident insurance (workmen's compensation). For the most part, the intention of these acts was to limit the liability of corporations in the case of work-related injury, disease, or death. The level of compensation was dismally inadequate until their revision and standardization across Canada in the late 1920s. Industrial Standards Acts specifying minimum wages and hours of work, with designated boards and agents for enforcement, became a reality only in the second half of the 1930s.

With respect to the labour market, the state could not ignore the periodic rise of unemployment to levels that produced social unrest. Prior to the 1930s, high unemployment was dealt with primarily by means of increased "public works" and municipal relief payments (Struthers 1977). Unemployment insurance, although frequently a political issue from the turn of the century, was not to come into being until the 1940s (Cuneo 1979). What did come instead, in the depths of the Depression, were legislative and coercive suppression of unions, imprisonment of Communist party members, deportation of foreign-born militants; *and* in 1932 the "relief camps," established as a form of "workfare" for single, homeless, and unemployed young men. When closed down in 1936, these camps had "taken in" over 170 000 unemployed men (Liversedge 1973; Brown 1987).

Despite widespread unemployment and poverty, many demonstrations and strikes by workers, and numerous reform proposals from the business sector (not to mention legislative attempts) during the "dirty thirties," little was introduced by way of social reform aside from the "relief camps" (Finkel 1979).

Present Structure

The present structure of the welfare state in Canada has been described as a "'patch-work quilt' of programs" (Banting 1982) or as a "hodge-podge" of policies, programs, and laws and standards "that vary across political jurisdictions (federal, provincial and municipal), categories of people," and types of need (Ismael 1985; xi). This patch-like structure, not in itself different from most other welfare states, is indicative of the nature of these social reforms as national attempts to respond to developing social needs not met by the wage relation, to contain the class conflict that is inherent in this same relation, and to maintain a labour force available for capital.

Such a motley array of social reforms, however, makes a coherent description very difficult. They have been ranked by amount of expenditure, periodized by date of enactment, categorized by constitutional division, described by type of "delivery system," among other approaches (Armitage 1975). Probably the most common methods of grouping the programs are by a) the mode of financing and b) the nature of the recipient (Banting 1982).

Modes of Financing

The modes of financing social reform in Canada reflect the unsystematic introduction and nature of the reforms themselves. If the many forms of federal government funding have anything in common, it is that they represent attempts to moderate provincial disparities and maintain national standards across the country (Hess 1992).

One of the most important means by which Ottawa accomplishes these goals is through the transfer of funds in the form of equalization grants. These comprise unconditional payments given to "have not" provinces on an unconditional basis (the amount determined by a formula); they derive from general tax revenues and are intended to allow the same quality and kinds of public service across the country.

National standards in health care and postsecondary education, the two most expensive components of the welfare state, have been maintained since 1977 by a funding arrangement called "Established Programs Financing," sometimes referred to as block funding. This involves transfers to the provinces of federal funds, which were supposed to increase with the growth of population and GNP and are conditional on meeting certain criteria. In the terms of the Medical Care Act 1966), for instance, the provinces must meet five criteria for the funding; namely, accessibility, universality, portability, comprehensiveness, and public administration. Although intended to contribute to the financing of health care and education, these federal block grants are not program specific and therefore the provincial governments have had considerable leeway in their disposition.

National standards are also maintained in the sphere of welfare and social assistance by the funding arrangement known as the Canada Assistance Plan (CAP). Established in 1966, CAP is a cost-sharing system in which certain terms are specified for the social programs by the federal government and provinces meeting them can be reimbursed for half the cost. This system lies at the heart of what is colloquially known as welfare, the mainstay in the attempts by federal and provincial governments to ameliorate the worst effects of poverty.

Premium payments, which are deductions from income, usually "at source," represent a sizable source of funding for significant components of the welfare state. Under this category may be placed such programs as unemployment insurance, medicare, and the Canada Pension Plan. Such components may include funds from general tax revenue but for the most part they are financed by the premiums paid.

Federal grants for specific programs (concerning, for example, literacy, drugs, job strategies, etc.) also constitute a source of federal transfer payments, although not as large as the above transfers.

In addition, the income tax system is employed to finance social benefits through tax credits and deductions or exemptions, sometimes called "tax expenditures." The tax credits are intended to boost indirectly the income of those with children or of retirement age whose incomes are below certain levels. The exemptions and deductions, on the other hand, for the most part further the incomes of the relatively well-to-do, and properly belong to a hidden welfare system for the rich (NCW 1976, 1979), not to mention being in part a Trojan horse to the existing welfare state, as we shall see.

Despite the fact that these forms of funding of the welfare state in Canada have gone a long way to establishing a relatively unified set of national standards and programs, it cannot be said that there is a genuinely national system of social reform. The jurisdictional lines of governmental responsibility and the sources of funding have always been, and remain, divisive matters. The trade union movement has never been sufficiently united to wrest a more coherent system of reform or indeed a national system of industrial relations from the powers that be.

Categorizing social reform by the mode of financing reveals some essential features of the welfare state. It does not embrace certain arenas of the welfare state, however, such as the labour market, employment standards, or the volunteer sector. It remains, moreover, descriptive and offers no explanation for the motley nature of social reform, the varied forms of funding, or the present retrenchment of the welfare state.

The Nature of the Recipient

If we examine the nature of the recipient as the criterion for attempting a coherent description of social reform in Canada, we find that the following categories are usually employed: a) universal programs, or "demogrants," which apply to all individuals of a given unit (e.g., Old Age Security, Veterans Programs, public education, etc.); b) social insurance programs, which provide benefits to those who have made contributions or premium payments (e.g., Workers' Compensation,

Unemployment Insurance, Canada Pension Plan, medicare, etc.); and c) social assistance programs, which are based on needs or income assessment and provide income supplements to those whose income falls below a certain level (e.g., Guaranteed Income Supplement, Refundable Child Tax Credit, welfare, etc.).

This way of grouping the programs of the welfare state, however widely used, does have significant shortcomings, some similar to those of the mode of funding. First, the categories are usually restricted to income security systems, which do not usually include education or health care; or an array of social services, which do not easily fall into one of the categories; or those privately run programs encouraged by the state through income tax exemptions and deductions (in particular, pensions, but increasingly education and health); or those programs financed and run by the volunteer sector. Second, the categories do not include any of the broad range of reforms dealing with the labour market or the point of production, namely, minimum wages and hours, collective bargaining, employment standards, and so on. Third, the categories have no underlying rationale; they are essentially descriptive, and while they reveal roughly who gets what, there is no explanation of why these programs were implemented, what role they serve in the system as a whole, and why they now appear to be on the wane. The categories are not anchored in the nature of the system itself.

The Welfare State and the Capitalist Mode of Production

If we return to our definition of the welfare state, it becomes possible to relate its component parts to the capitalist mode of production and thereby introduce an element of explanation into the categorization. To recapitulate, the welfare state refers to a capitalist society in which the state has had to intervene to ameliorate the contradiction between labour and capital and to ensure the reproduction of the working class and of the system as a whole.

As we have seen, historically one of the earliest arenas of intervention was at the point of production, the most immediate sphere of class conflict between workers and the representatives of capital. There are two main elements to this arena, namely, the bargaining relation between the union and corporation, and the need to impose elementary standards on corporate power in the workplace. The first is institutionalized in industrial relations acts or labour codes, which set out the terms for collective bargaining, intended to reconcile unreconcilable differences (Weiler 1980). There are ten provincial codes and one federal code, which govern the structure of these relations in Canada (Sethi 1989). The second refers to those standards and regulations that are imposed by government on capital because of the unmitigated power it holds in the workplace. These would include health and safety standards, minimum wage and hours regulations, and other employment standards. All of these have both provincial and federal jurisdictions.

Aspects of these forms of intervention overlap in their implications with state activity in the arena of the labour market. Here the state is concerned in part with setting the broad parameters for the supply and demand of labour power; that is, of course, the supply *for* and the demand *by* capital. The parameters are established by immigration policies, which are used to add selectively to the labour force, and by numerous programs aimed at developing the skills, training and education, and mobility of the existing work force. Besides these boundaries to the labour market, the state must concern itself with the maintenance of the existing labour force, ensuring a constant and adequate supply of fresh workers for the market. Unemployment insurance, workers' compensation, and legislation covering statutory holidays, paid vacations, and other employment standards are the main forms of intervention here.

The existing labour force, however, must also be replenished with new generations of workers, and this necessity involves the propagation of the working class and its preparation for the labour market. One of the earliest forms of social reform falls into this category, namely, public education, which served to socialize the costs of training the working class to be literate, disciplined, and respectful of authority (Schecter 1977). Access to hospital and medical care was greatly increased in the late 1950s and 1960s (Swartz 1977, 1987) in an attempt to address the significant and growing problems of disease and injury resulting from the passive, consumerist society and the advanced Fordist mode of production. The supply of subsidized housing, a very important aspect of the welfare state in some countries, has always been limited mainly to the elderly and the lowest strata of the working class in Canada, but this amounts to about 15 percent of all households. Other means of supplementing wages that have been employed include offsetting the costs of maintaining a family with the "family allowance," the child tax credits, the child care expense deduction, and so on.

The fourth arena of intervention concerns the provision of income assurance for the "unproductive" (mainly the physically and mentally challenged and single mothers) and for people whose "productive" life is over. Most of the varied programs for the former are financed through the Canada Assistance Plan. For the latter, the Canada Pension Plan (premium financed in the main), Old Age Security (general

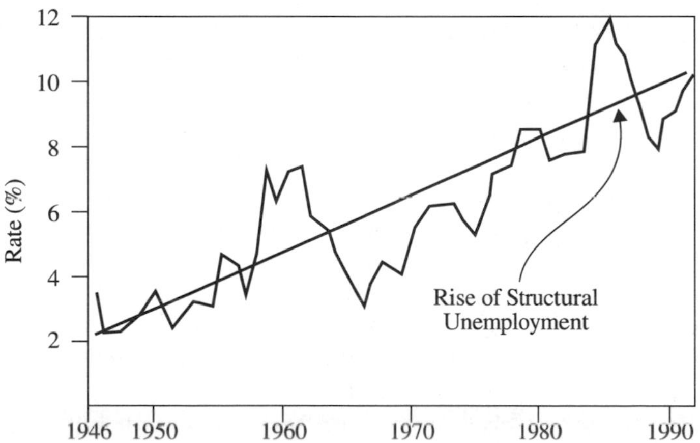

FIGURE 23.1: Unemployment Rates, 1946–1992

Sources: Statistics Canada, *Annual Labour Estimates*, 1946–1990, 1991, 1992 (Ottawa: Minister of Supply and Services); Statistics Canada, *Canadian Social Trends*, 20 (Spring): 30.

revenues), the Guaranteed Income Supplement (for those over 65 with very limited other income), and the tax-assisted Registered Retirement Pension Plans (RRSPs) are the principal means of providing for those past productive age as defined by the capitalist mode of production (Phillipson 1982). Despite these income security programs, a substantial percentage of the "old" and "unproductive" live in relative poverty with subsistence incomes, inadequate housing, and poor medical care.

Despite the relative comprehensiveness of the programs of the welfare state and the huge state bureaucracies dedicated to their functioning, poverty has never been eliminated and indeed is growing. Unemployment has risen inexorably since the 1960s to over 10 percent of the labour force, employment standards are being reduced, literacy rates are falling, demand for health care is expanding, the rates of certain chronic diseases increase, and on and on. In short, whatever amelioration of the worst effects of capitalism, redistribution of income, and containment of class conflict the welfare state may have proffered, it has neither changed the fundamental nature of the capitalist mode of production nor provided permanent immunity from its effects.

The Decline of the Welfare State

"Necessary" though it was, the KWS could only be developed after the Second World War under certain conditions, which have been briefly sketched above. Economic reconstruction carried out with advanced Fordism in national economies, a consistent demand for labour, rising real wages, expanding trade unions, and growing social state and employment hierarchies were some of these interrelated prerequisites. Here were the ingredients for widespread support among the representatives of labour and capital for state intervention in practice and even as a political philosophy in the form of social democracy.

All this began to change, however, in the early 1970s. The productive power of advanced Fordism had already long outgrown the national market, but now it was being replaced by computer-aided processes whose productive capabilities were far superior. In concert with these changes, the structure of capital itself began to shift from a national to an international base. Under the auspices of the General Agreement on Tariffs and Trade, the World Bank and the International Monetary Fund, systematic pressure was gradually applied to level national social and economic policies to facilitate world trade. Changes in the labour market followed, not so much for the workers, who remained restricted by national boundaries, but for capital, which now began to search for ways to escape the high wages necessary to maintain the KWS. As real wage rises began to stagnate and then to fall in the 1970s and 1980s, often owing to state intervention, trade union membership followed suit, also often "assisted" by restrictive government legislation. As national policies, regulations, and standards began to be usurped by their international counterparts, the sovereignty of the nation-state began to wane. Trade union leverage on the national state and capitalist class could no longer be maintained. "Real existing socialism," moreover, became exposed as corrupted state capitalist regimes, and so the socialist alternative to the capitalist mode of production could not longer be presented as a goal worth fighting for.

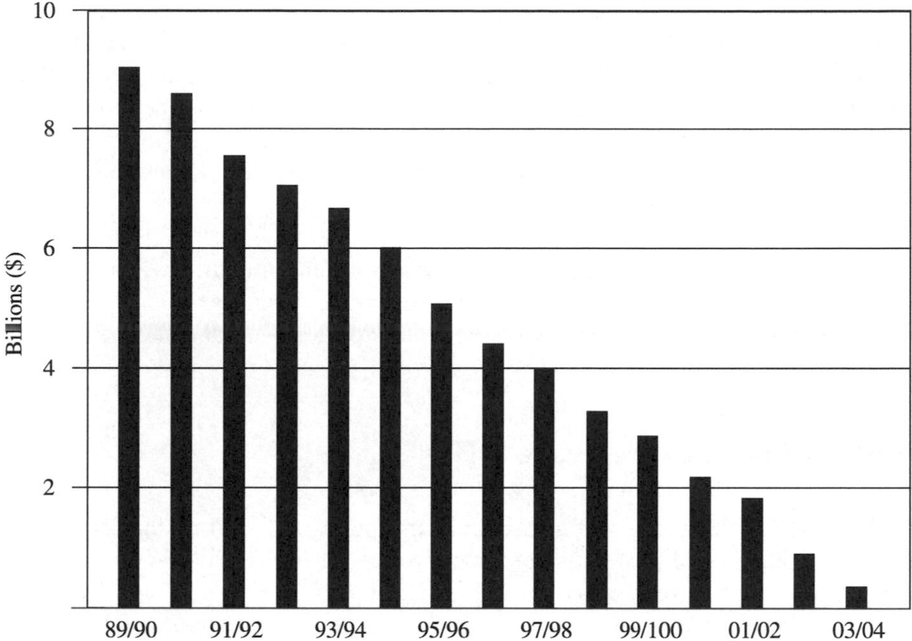

FIGURE 23.2: Federal Transfers to Provinces for Health and Education, 1989–2004

Source: Canadian Council on Social Development, "Canada's Social Programs Are in Trouble," *Newsletter for the Campaign Against Bill C-69* (Ottawa: CCSD, October 1990). Reprinted with permission.

Neoliberal policies, variously labelled as Thatcherism, Reaganism, neoconservatism, and the New Right Agenda, began to become visible by the mid-1970s and became formal government policy in many countries by the end of that decade. They were, we suggest, the policy side of the "new reality"; they represented the political requirements of capital internationalized, highly centralized, and global in perspective. In attempting to transform all forms of state intervention into market functions, these policies are intended to level national distinctions for global investment. They also represent the last truly national policies to be promulgated, the final act of the independent nation-state, because with their acceptance the economic and political barriers to production and distribution around the world will have been minimized. With their adoption they in effect harmonize the national with the global economy.

The possibility of national management of national economies is now increasingly abridged, and national forms of the welfare state are now more and more difficult to maintain. In all the industrial nations and in most of the developing nations, these neoliberal policies continue to be legislated, and with their promulgation social reform as we know it is being transformed. Social democracy as embodied in the New Democratic Party in Canada, it follows, is losing its meaning and purpose. All political parties, the social democrats included, increasingly find themselves obliged with greater or lesser resistance to carry out the agenda.

For Canada, as for all industrial countries, the coming of the global economy has meant relatively less corporate tax and declining wages and so a declining social wage. It has also meant less national sovereignty and so less union or political leverage over policy. Global corporate demands for access to the public sector and for the "level playing field" have come to prevail.

> "Treat us nice or kiss us goodbye," warns mining mogul. B.C. should give its mining companies a break or watch as they seek a warmer climate in countries like Chile, says Cominco Ltd. President. (*BC Business*, April 21, 1992).

North American Free Trade

Co-terminous with these global demands and policy reflections that are cutting back Canadian social programs are the pressures arising from the Canada-United States Free Trade Agreement (FTA) and the North American Free Trade Agreement (NAFTA). These treaties, which are intended to create a single continental economy, present two areas of threat to the Canadian welfare state. First, the treaties themselves contain no explicit safeguards for the multifaceted social programs and standards of this country. In light of the marketplace principles underlying the accords, all aspects of the welfare state may well be considered "unfair subsidies" or "barriers to trade." Under the terms of the FTA, furthermore, should the Canadian government wish to establish either new social programs that are universal or new Crown corporations, it must "notify and consult" the U.S. government. Not only, then, are the present programs unprotected, but also any possible extensions or new programs are made conditional on "consultations" with Washington.

Second, there are the broad implications of a unified economy: increasing pressure for the harmonization of all regulations, standards, laws, programs, policies, etc., which pertain to the labour market, the workplace, the reproduction of the labour force, and the "non-" or "unproductive," not to mention fiscal and monetary policies. Differences do exist and will persist among political jurisdictions, but where they create overriding economic disadvantages government will maintain higher-than-average standards and policies at the risk of declining investment and their own political doom. It is, to say the least, implausible that the Canadian welfare state can be maintained as we have known it in the face of these free trade agreements (Drover 1988).

The Decline of the Welfare State in Canada

By the late 1970s, the attack on the welfare state in the United Kingdom, the United States, and Canada had become visible, and by 1980 it had become government policy in the former two. As in these two countries, the dismantling of the welfare state in Canada went on in a patchwork manner throughout the 1980s; in the early

1990s, however, the Government of Canada passed Bill C-69, which began the progressive, systematic, and comprehensive withdrawal of federal monies from national social programs.

> Even when countries are not asking for financial aid, the IMF apparently gives unsolicited advice: "The International Monetary Fund secretly urged the Canadian government this year to freeze public servants' wages, slash unemployment insurance in poor regions, and stop protecting inefficient farmers, confidential documents ... reveal. In [the] report ... the UN agency also urged Ottawa to axe a staggering $6 billion from next year's projected $30.5 billion deficit" (*Vancouver Sun*, November 1991).

The earliest stages of retrenchment in Canada were most easily seen in the arena of state intervention at the point of production. In the 1970s the increasing use of back-to-work legislation and the Anti-Inflation Program of 1975–78, which enabled the federal government to roll back wage increases that went beyond certain guidelines, set the stage for a much more comprehensive assault on collective bargaining rights (Panitch and Swartz 1993). From the early 1980s on, the federal and provincial governments embarked on changes to labour legislation that were to diminish significantly the established rights of trade unions. Provincial wage restraint laws were also promulgated; the right to strike was restricted, and for some workers even eliminated; union organizing and certification regulations were everywhere made more difficult; and "right-to-work" (anti-union) laws began to make their appearance in several provinces.

Gradual improvement in employment standards came to a halt by the early 1980s and many began to be cut back. Hours of work, minimum wages, vacation time, termination regulations, restrictions on child employment, the right of appeal, and so on, all were subject to gradual retrenchment by provincial and federal governments (Fawkes 1983).

With respect to the labour market, two major programs have been undergoing curtailment for several years. Workers' compensation boards have allowed a relative decline in assessment rates for the corporate sector and have cut back on benefits and services to ill or injured workers. Less emphasis is being paid to prevention and monitoring, or inspection has been downgraded outright. Significant changes to the unemployment insurance system have been made since about the mid-1970s. In several stages, the qualifying periods have been lengthened, other eligibility criteria have been tightened, the benefits have been cut back, maximum time for benefits has been reduced, penalties for voluntary quitting have been introduced, the federal contribution has been withdrawn, some of the funds have been reallocated to wage subsidization, and the premiums paid by employees and employers have been raised. Increasingly severe restrictions continue to be legislated.

Of the welfare state, the principal component for preparing the working class for the labour market is the educational system. Primary and secondary education is funded provincially and all the provinces have engaged in cutbacks since at least the early 1980s. This has resulted in teacher salary freezes, program cuts, fewer extramural activities, and larger class sizes. Postsecondary education is financed under the block-funding arrangements mentioned above whereby the federal government has contributed according to a formula based on growth of the GNP and population. Since the mid-1980s, however, the formula has been cut back, the increases frozen, and the funding reduced annually.

These same retrenchments apply to the medical care system, which is financed in the same way and is central to the maintenance and propagation of the working class. The results are similar: national standards have declined as have the accessibility and comprehensiveness of the services offered.

Federal contributions to subsidized housing have also suffered cutbacks since the mid-1980s. During the latter half of this decade the overall funding was reduced, including finds for co-operative housing and "low-cost" rental shelter.

For those considered "unproductive" or "non-productive" in light of the capitalist mode of production, namely, those over 65 years old, those under employment age, and those receiving social assistance, the retrenchment has been similarly consistent over the past decade. Both the family allowance and Old Age Security were subject to clawbacks starting in 1989, so ending their universality in all but name. The Canadian Assistance Plan, the only shared-cost national program intended to alleviate poverty, has had limits put on increases to the three richest

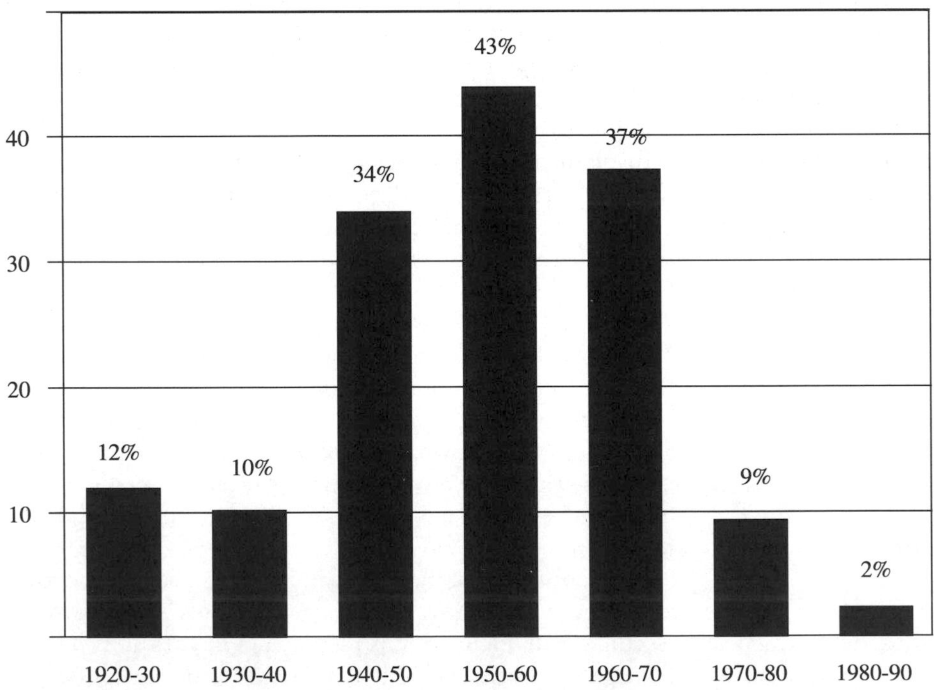

FIGURE 23.3: Real Annual Wage Increases, 1920–1990

Source: Statistics Canada, *Canadian Social Trends*, Cat. no. 11-008E, 32 (Spring 1994): 18. Reproduced by authority of the Minister of Industry, 1994.

provinces, Ontario, British Columbia, and Alberta, where it so happens that most of the poor in Canada live. It should not be forgotten that a sizable percentage of welfare recipients, about 40 percent, are children; they will experience the impact of these cuts most dramatically.

We have only touched on thc most significant cuts to the welfare state, but across the levels of government there has been a systematic divestment of the role and responsibilities previously assumed by the state. This divestment encompasses the increasing introduction of user fees, the reduction of subsidies and grants, disentitlement by the re-definition of state responsibilities, contracting out to private enterprise, and the cancelling of non-statutory services such as family support, child abuse programs, and so on (Ismael 1988).

Official Alternatives

Coincident with these cutbacks to the public-sector provision of all aspects of social welfare, has been the active encouragement of private-sector provision in the form of charitable donations or volunteer service and through privatization.

The Rise of Charities

There are many hundreds of "charities" in Canada and many more are added each year, including educational facilities, hospitals, and a range of social services previously funded by the state. The size and role of such umbrella organizations as the United Way has grown enormously since the late 1970s when this retrenchment first began to be felt.

Several important trends comprise the context for this vast growth since 1980 in size and number of charitable institutions and non-profit organizations, and for the conscious efforts by government and the corporate sector to promote it. One such trend has been the rapid increase in social needs, which has accompanied increasing long-term, structural unemployment, among other forms of social disintegration. Another has been the growing limits on further expansion of the social wage;[7] a third has been the planned reduction of the services of the welfare state. As these trends accelerate, the entire sphere of social reproduction, embracing all aspects of health, education, and social services, will increasingly be moved into the realm of the private market, one part of which takes the form of charities or trusts. The fostering of such institutions and agencies is but a means of "privatizing" public facilities; and their expansion is an attempt to shift the responsibility for the human costs of an inhuman system from the state to the individual, and to transfer the means of redress from the "social wage" to private "gifts."[8]

Although charitable donations at present comprise only a small fraction of state social expenditures, they play an increasingly larger role as the above trends continue to unfold. To the degree that they replace state provision, they make it evident that society as a marketplace does not provide for all of its members such basic elements of life as employment, housing, food, health care, and so on. It has no mechanism, aside from social reforms, charity, or volunteer work (i.e., anomalies to the system), to provide such "amenities" to those who are not working or, for that matter, even to the growing numbers of working poor. With the decline of the welfare state and the growth of charities, the marginalized will increasingly become dependent on the purported benevolence or good will of others; and this in a society which looks upon altruism as abnormal.

It also becomes clear that society as marketplace relies mainly on individual donations and tax revenues, that is, on deductions from the wages of those working, to shore up the chronic social destruction that takes place under capitalism. But now, increasingly in the form of charity, social redistribution becomes a voluntary matter and indeed tax deductible. This last point means that the more that is given to charity, the less goes to the state for redistribution. It is a planned paradox: charities are both a substitute for and an instrument in the decline of the welfare state.

To the degree that charitable institutions and non-profit or volunteer organizations become significant forms of social redistribution, moreover, the existing "social rights" and universal entitlements to state-funded social services will be narrowed. In part in the name of charity, the elements of "social citizenship," though never fully realized anywhere, have begun the process of erosion everywhere.

Systematic Privatization

Aside from the active promotion of charitable and volunteer organizations to compensate for the conscious discharging of the role and responsibility of the welfare state, policies of systematic privatization are becoming commonplace.[9]

The least visible and yet widely employed process of privatization is the policy of incremental degradation of benefits and services. Public services are increasingly restricted by rising eligibility criteria, cancellation, disentitlement, contracting out, redefinition, transferred responsibility, or declining quality. Income benefits are rolled back, taxed back, or allowed to fall behind the rate of inflation. The objective of such policies is that, over time, pressure to meet minimum standards or fill omissions will be met by the private sector. The public health care systems provide good examples of this form of privatization with the growth of user fees, deductibles, and restricted treatments, operations and facilities, while at the same time private insurance and medical treatments are encouraged by a variety of incentives.

Other examples can be found in social assistance programs and insurance for unemployed and injured workers, wherein qualifications and restrictions increase and payments do not keep pace with the cost of living. Government restrictions on grants to public schools have multiplied, while increasing government funding encourages the growth of private schools. Similarly, universities have experienced restrictions on grant increases, causing a rise in student fees, larger classes, declining facilities, restricted eligibility, and a need to pursue greater links with private enterprise.

In contrast to these undeclared policies of erosion, the government makes use of open incentive policies. The use of tax deductions is a widely employed form of inducement to move to the private provision of benefits, and the privatization of pension plans and medical insurance are the common objectives of such schemes.

Included here might also be the use of education vouchers, which can be used in the public or private schools, with the ultimate goal of undermining the public system and providing the private sector with state funding, making a universal social program of benefit to the private sector. These incentives all involve a form of subsidy to those who can afford private provision at the expense of those who are and will be completely reliant on state provision. They will, moreover, encourage existing two-tiered systems in which those who have the means to set aside money or afford private fees are assisted in doing so.

Implications

In general, society is moving away from state provision of social services and programs, especially those that are universal or characterized as social rights. In place of these "rightful" entitlements, government is re-instituting and reinforcing the principles of the "poor laws," the welfare schemes of pre-industrial times and the Third World (Midgley 1984). The current trends in Canada represent a revivification of the concept of the "deserving" versus the "undeserving" poor, and of the principles of means testing, of familial liability and responsibility, of qualifying moral conduct, of temporary benefits, of deterrent eligibility criteria, of "targeting the needy," and of the workhouse ("workfare"). The more that these principles come into practice, the more the principles of universality and social right are undermined, and the more the failures and omissions of the system are presented as the responsibility of the individual rather than of the state or the corporations—and the more every aspect of the welfare state can be made into an instrument of social control.[10]

There are many reasons for these changes in policy, for the encouragement of charities and the privatization of social services and benefits. Among them are the following political goals: to "downsize" the role of government by reducing state responsibilities and the number of employees; to "open up" state sectors to private accumulation; to divert the revenues spent on health, education, and welfare, which represent a large percentage of national budgets, to the private sector; and, not least, to attempt to "discipline" the working classes by undermining union achievements and eroding their social security in the face of rising permanent unemployment.

There are, of course, broader material causes behind these changes. The decline in state revenues, for instance, is no small factor, but this is only an immediate cause because it in turn is due mainly to chronic recession, the shift in tax burden, and greater demands from capital. The global context of these changes is the economic necessity to "harmonize" national social security reforms, which constitute barriers of varying degrees to the needs of the international market.

In a society that can now provide employment only for a diminishing number of its citizens and that has no inherent mechanism for providing for those without work, the rescinding and downgrading of those parts of the welfare state that offer a modicum of support have consequences that are now visible throughout Canada. Unemployment presently stands at about 10 percent with much higher rates in the Maritimes and Quebec; and, given free trade, new technology and global production, it is unlikely that this chronic rate will decrease. The demands on unemployment insurance will continue to rise and the welfare rolls increase: the system has no intrinsic morality: it sloughs off human beings as so much waste (Burman 1988) and, for a growing percentage of youth, provides no future. Today over two million Canadians receive social assistance payments (about 8 percent of the population), a figure that is growing and that does not include all those who could qualify for welfare, namely, the homeless, the working poor, among others.

Such social assistance, which does not even keep pace with the cost of living, is not extended to everyone without work or means of support. Over the past decade the need to supplement welfare and to provide for those who have no other means of income has given rise to food banks, an institution dependent on charitable, private donations. The first opened in Edmonton in 1981; by 1991 there were almost 300 of them across the country. In that year about two million individuals received food from a food bank at least once; about 600 000 were regular monthly recipients and the numbers have grown markedly every year (Oderkirk 1992; Riches 1986, 1987).

The past decade has also seen a large and growing number of homeless. Unemployment, welfare retrenchment, a shrinking rental market (especially in the low-end), abolished social programs, redefined state responsibilities, privatized social services (Ismael 1989), discharged mental patients without services or care (Ismael and Vaillancourt 1988) have all contributed to social disintegration. Far from seeking an answer to this problem, the federal government has continued to cut back its support of affordable housing. In 1990 it cut funds for low-cost housing; in 1992 it terminated the co-operative housing program; and in 1993 it froze expenditures for social housing at 1993 levels. Estimates of the number of homeless are difficult to make, but in 1986, almost a decade ago, it was estimated that between 130 000 and 250 000 people were homeless at any given time that year (Begin 1989).

Conclusions

Both of these developments, the privatization and the shifting of the social services and income security programs to charitable organizations, share a common rationale. They undermine the principle that the state has social obligations to its citizens, and they circumvent the existence and fulfillment of state social responsibilities. In short, they end the development of the principle and practice of social citizenship, the foremost achievement in the long attempt to reform capitalism. They also represent the progressive abandonment by the state of significant aspects of public "property" to the private sector. Both privatization and the encouragement of charities represent the systematic abolition of the forms of collective property represented by the welfare state and its limited achievement of social citizenship, replacing these with the principle and practice of private property.

The interim goal of provincial and federal retrenchment would appear to be a minimalization of the state's social responsibilities, achieved by the various means outlined above. For those aspects of the welfare state that are not abolished, dual systems are developing already, as well as private but publicly supported programs for the well-off, and a degraded state program for those who cannot afford the other.

As long as the welfare state remains relatively intact, providing a range of services and benefits, there remains a political aspect, albeit modest, to the determination of the kind and nature of these policies and to the disposal of the necessary public funds. With charities and a privatized system of welfare, this element of political determination is replaced in theory by moral sentiment (in a society whose highest virtues are egoism and selfishness) and market principles (impersonal, apolitical forces beyond the control of the state, especially when stripped of its economic management policies). Not only, then, does the goal of a privatized welfare system remove the future possibility of political control, it also makes the provision of essential aspects of the reproduction of the working class subject to the vagaries of market forces. As the market follows its booms and slumps, so too will rise and fall the benefits and services so necessary to a healthy working population. Just as stock markets can collapse, businesses go bankrupt, corporate theft and embezzlement on a grand scale continue, and unemployment remain chronically high, so will the elements of a privatized welfare system bear not only the consequences of the business cycle, but also those of a system of contradictory class interests.

The forces of global capitalism that underlie this retrenchment, however, are not the only forces presently at work. Numerous experiments in alternative modes of production and new forms of resistance to capitalist expansion have begun to develop around the world. In the industrial countries, the resistance appears in a number of forms as yet poorly organized and with consciousness limited to particular issues, but it is unmistakably there. The most prominent actions are those of the trade unions, the environmental organizations, aboriginal alliances, and the women's movement; but to these can be added consumer protection groups, old age advocacy coalitions, unions of the unemployed, cultural forms of protest, civil liberty associations, gay rights organizations, and antinuclear groups. In the Third World, organized armed resistance to repressive regimes is once again growing.

Resistance and co-operative alternatives will necessarily grow as economic inequality deepens and the ability of capitalism to provide for the material, let alone the human, needs of the populace declines and the experience and recognition of this inability expands.

Study Questions

1. What is the definition of the welfare state? At what historical moment can it be said to have come into existence, and why?

2. What are the general preconditions of the welfare state? What are the post–Second World War conditions of the modern welfare state?

3. What are the two most common ways of categorizing the Canadian welfare state? What are their shortcomings?

4. Why can we say that "social citizenship" "represents the highest development of the principle of welfarism"?

5. Describe the consequences of the decline of the welfare state and suggest what might be the logical conclusion of present developments.

Recommended Reading

Brown, M.K., ed. *Remaking the Welfare State: Retrenchment and Social Policy in America and Europe*. Philadelphia: Temple University Press. 1988.

Dickinson, J., and B. Russell, eds. *Family, Economy, and State.* Toronto: Garamond Press, 1986.

Guest, D. *The Emergence of Social Security in Canada.* Vancouver: University of British Columbia Press, 1985.

Hess, M. *The Canadian Fact Book on Income Security Programs.* Ottawa and Montreal: Canadian Council on Social Development. 1992.

Mishra, R. *The Welfare State in Capitalist Society.* Toronto: University of Toronto Press, 1990.

Moscovitch, A., and J. Albert, eds. *The Benevolent State: The Growth of Welfare In Canada.* Toronto: Garamond Press, 1987.

Notes

1. Parts of the argument of this paper are drawn from my forthcoming book, *Globalization and the Decline of Social Reform*, (Toronto): Garamond.
2. Neoliberalism is the name given to a comprehensive set of policies, presently being adopted by governments around the world, which seek to change every aspect of state intervention in society. What they all have in common is the goal to privatize all forms of property that embrace collective or co-operative elements. (For a comprehensive analysis of these policies, see my *Globalization and the Decline of Social Reform.*)
3. By "social wage" we refer to state-sponsored partial socialization of income from wages and salaries by means of premiums, taxes, and deferred income; the funds so created are used for redistribution from one strata to another through transfers such as pensions, income supplements, or social insurance schemes. The essence of the social wage was captured in the earlier phrase "averaging mechanisms." See P. Flora and A.J. Heidenheimer, "The Historical Core and Changing Boundaries of the Welfare State." in Flora and Heidenheimer 1984, 18–19.
4. Fordism arose out of the cauldron of the First World War to become the prevailing mode of production in the industrial world. It is generally seen as a system of production employing semi-automated assembly-lines and giving rise to rapidly expanding domestic and external markets for "cheapened" consumer goods, that is, a system of mass production and consumption. It is also associated with large production units and complex work hierarchies.

   Advanced Fordism arose out of the forced industrial growth of the Second World War. Here science and technology, once subordinated to capitalist production and increased automation, vastly expanded the quantities and improved the qualities of goods and services. It co-existed with a delimited national labour market, a protected product market, and growth based on extranational and domestic expansion. The resulting high standard of living in the industrial nations for the majority of the working class allowed for a grand compromise between the trade unions, corporations, and government, which took the form of the KWS.
5. The increase in these social rights, "the revolution of rising entitlements," as D. Bell put it, became an issue for debate and one of the reasons the Trilateral Commission raised the spectres of "excess democracy" and "ungovernability." D. Bell, "The Public Household: 'On Fiscal Sociology and the Liberal Society,'" *The Public Interest* (Fall 1974), 39.

6. The attention paid by the federal and provincial states to class conflict was far more extensive than that paid to any other arena of intervention. At the federal level the reforms began as early as 1872, with The Trade Union Act, then the Conciliation Act of 1900 and 1906, the Fair Wage Resolution, the Railway Labour Disputes Act of 1903, and the Industrial Disputes Investigation Act of 1907 (extended in 1916 and 1918). Very little changes until 1940 (PC2685) and 1944 (PC1003), which established the foundation of the modern labour relations system in Canada (Logan 1956).
7. The movement to "world wages" in the industrial nations means the gradual reduction of the "disposable" portion of income and of taxable portions, which in turn results in the decline of the social wage. Indeed, wages and salaries increasingly become sufficient only to reproduce labour power during periods of employment, leaving periods of unemployment, invalidity, old-age, maternity, and so on, with increasingly only private, limited resources.
8. The most significant umbrella charity in North America is the United Way. Promoted vigorously by corporations, its annual drive for funds amounts to another tax on the working class, while corporate donations remain *very* limited.

   Recognizing the decline in corporate tax revenue and its implications in declining social reforms, the corporate sector in Canada has initiated a Centre for Philanthropy and a program of corporate charity called "Imagine," intended to stimulate corporate but mainly employee donations of time and money to charitable and other non-profit organizations.
9. From the perspective of property rights, privatization is "a reassignment of claims to the control and use of [state] assets." In this sense, privatization undermines "the foundation of claims for public purpose and public service." P. Starr, "The Meaning of Privatization," in S. Kamerman and A. Kahn, eds., *Privatization and the Welfare State*, (Princeton: University of Princeton Press, 1989), 42.
10. The element of social control is not generally visible: deterrents to benefits can force people to work for subsistence or below subsistence wages; qualifications can counter the readiness to go on strike by making the benefits conditional on reasons for being out of work; conditions for benefits may include retraining, moving, menial work, or eventual acceptance of low-paid jobs; and so on.

References

Allen, R.C., and G. Rosenbluth, eds. 1986. *Restraining the Economy*. Vancouver: New Star Books.

Andrew, C. 1984. "Women and the Welfare State." *Canadian Journal of Political Science* 17, 667–83.

Aquan-Yuen, M. 1991. *Homelessness in Canada: A Selected Bibliography*. Waterloo: University of Waterloo Library.

Armitage, A. 1975. *Social Welfare in Canada*. Toronto: McClelland and Stewart.

Banting, K. 1982. *The Welfare State and Canadian Federalism*, Kingston: McGill–Queen's University Press.

———. 1987. "The Welfare State and Inequality in the 1980s." *Canadian Review of Sociology and Anthropology* 24, no. 3, 309–328.

Begin, P. 1989. *Homelessness in Canada*. Ottawa: Research Branch, Library of Parliament.

Briggs, A. 1967. "The Welfare State in Historical Perspective." In *The Welfare State*, ed. C.I. Schottland. New York: Harper and Row.

Brown, L. 1987. *When Freedom Was Lost*. Montreal: Black Rose.

Brown, M.K., ed. 1988. *Remaking the Welfare State: Retrenchment and Social Policy in America and Europe*. Philadelphia: Temple University Press.

Burman, P. 1988. *Killing Time, Losing Ground*. Toronto: Wall and Thompson.

Carrier, J., and I. Kendall. 1986. "Categories, Categorizations, and the Political Economy of Welfare." *Journal of Social Policy* 15, no. 3, 315–335.

Cuneo, C.J. 1979. "State, Class, and Reserve Labour: The Case of the 1941 Canadian Unemployment Insurance Act." *Canadian Review of Sociology and Anthropology* 16, no. 2, 147–170.

Dickinson, J., and B. Russell, eds. 1986. *Family, Economy, and State*. Toronto: Garamond Press.

Djao, A.W. 1983. *Inequality and Social Policy*. Toronto: John Wiley and Sons.

Domhoff, G.W. 1990. *The Power Elite and the State*, New York: Aldine De Gruyter.

Drover, G., ed. 1988. *Free Trade and Social Policy*. Ottawa: The Canadian Council on Social Development.

Esping-Andersen, G. 1989. "The Three Political Economies of the Welfare State." *Canadian Review of Sociology and Anthropology* 26, no. 1, 10–35.

Esping-Andersen, G., and W. Korpi. 1984. "Social Policy as Class Politics in Post-War Capitalism: Scandinavia, Austria, and Germany." In *Order and Conflict in Contemporary Capitalism*, ed. J.H. Goldthorpe. New York: Oxford University Press.

Fawkes, T. 1983. *Assault From the Right*. BC Federation of Labour and BC & Yukon Building Trades Council.

Finkel, A. 1977. "Origins of the Welfare State." In *The Canadian State*, ed. L. Panitch. Toronto: University of Toronto Press, 344–70.

———. 1979. *Business and Social Reform in the Thirties*. Toronto: James Lorimer.

Flora, P., and A.J. Heidenheimer, eds. 1984. *The Development of Welfare States in Europe and America*. New Brunswick, NJ: Transaction Books.

Gough, I. 1979. *The Political Economy of the Welfare State*. London: Macmilan.

Guest, D. 1985. *The Emergence of Social Security in Canada*. Vancouver: University of British Columbia Press.

Harbison, F. 1954. "Collective Bargaining and American Capitalism." In *Industrial Conflict*, ed. A. Kornhauser, R. Dubin, and A. Ross. New York: McGraw Hill, 270–79.

Hess, M. 1992. *The Canadian Fact Book on Income Security Programs*. Ottawa and Montreal: Canadian Council on Social Development.

Hirschman, A.O. 1988. "How Keynes Was Spread From America." *Challenge* (November-December, 4–7.

Ismael, J.S., ed. 1987. *The Canadian Welfare State*. Edmonton: University of Alberta Press.

Ismael, J.S., and Y. Vaillancourt, eds. 1988. *Privatization and Provincial Social Services in Canada*. Edmonton: University of Alberta Press.

Kamerman, S.B., and Kahn, A.J., eds. 1989. *Privatization and the Welfare State*. Princeton: Princeton University Press.

Kealey, G., ed. 1973. *Canada Investigates Industrialism*. Toronto: University of Toronto Press.

Kirk, N. 1985. *The Growth of Working Class Reformism in Mid-Victorian England*. London: Croom Helm.

Leseman, F. 1987. *Services and Circuses: Community and the Welfare State*. Montreal: Black Rose Books.

Lightman, E., and A. Irving. 1991. "Restructuring Canada's Welfare State."

Liversedge, R. 1973. *Recollections of the On to Ottawa Trek*. Toronto: McClelland and Stewart.

Logan, H.A. 1948. *Trade Unions in Canada*. Toronto: Macmillan.

———. 1956. *State Intervention and Assistance in Collective Bargaining*. Toronto: University of Toronto Press.

Lubove, R. 1986. *The Struggle for Social Security, 1900–1935*. Pittsburgh: University of Pittsburgh Press.

McLaughlin, M. 1987. *Homelessness in Canada: The Report of the National Inquiry*. Ottawa: Canadian Council on Social Development.

Magnusson, W., et al., eds. 1984. *The New Reality: The Politics of Restraint in British Columbia*. Vancouver: New Star Books.

Marsh, L. 1975. *Report on Social Security for Canada*. Toronto: University of Toronto Press.

Marshall, T.H. 1963. "Citizenship and Social Class." In *Sociology at the Crossroads*, T.H. Marshall. London: Heinemann.

Midgley, J. 1984. "Poor Law Principles and Social Assistance in the Third World: A Study in the Perpetuation of Colonial Welfare," *International Social Work* 27, no. 1.

Mishra, R. 1984. *The Welfare State in Crisis*. Brighton: Wheatsheaf Books.

———. 1990. *The Welfare State in Capitalist Society*. Toronto: University of Toronto Press.

Mommsen, W.J., ed. 1981. *The Emergence of the Welfare State in Britain and Germany, 1850–1950*. London: Croom Helm.

Moscovitch, A. 1986. "The Welfare State Since 1975." *Journal of Canadian Studies* 21, no. 2, 77–94.

Myles, J. 1988. "Decline or Impasse? The Current State of the Welfare State." *Studies in Political Economy* 26, 73–107.

National Council of Welfare NCW). 1976. *The Hidden Welfare System*. Ottawa: The Council.

———. 1979. *The Hidden Welfare System Revisited*. Ottawa: The Council.

Navarro, V. 1985/86. "The 1980 and 1984 U.S. Elections and the New Deal: An Alternative Interpretation." In *Socialist Register 1985/86*, ed. R. Miliband et al. 158–209.

Oderkirk, J. 1992. "Food Banks." *Canadian Social Trends*. 24 (Spring).

Offe, C. 1984. *Contradiction of the Welfare State*. Cambridge, MA: MIT Press.

Panitch, L. 1986. *Working Class Politics in Crisis*. London: Verso.

Panitch, L., and D. Swartz. 1993. *The Assault on Trade Union Freedoms*. Toronto: Garamond Press.

Phillipson, C. 1982. *Capitalism and the Construction of Old Age*. London: Macmillan.

Quadagno, J. 1987. "Theories of the Welfare State." *American Review of Sociology*. 13, 109–128.

Reasons, C.E., L.L. Ross and C. Paterson. 1981. *Assault on the Worker: Occupational Health and Safety in Canada*. Toronto: Butterworths.

Riches, G. 1986. *Food Banks and The Welfare Crisis*. Ottawa: Canadian Council on Social Development.

———. 1987. "Feeding Canada's Poor: The Rise of the Food Banks and the Collapse of the Public Safety Net." In Ismael, *Canadian Welfare State*.

Rimlinger, G.V. 1971. *Welfare Policy and Industrialization in Europe, America, and Russia*. New York: John Wiley and Sons.

Russell, B. 1984. "The Politics of Labour-Reproduction, Funding Canada's Social Wage, 1917–1946." *Studies in Political Economy* 14, 43–93.

Schecter, S. 1977. "Capitalism, Class, and Educational Reform in Canada." In *The Canadian State*, ed. L. Panitch.

Schott, K. 1982. "The Rise of Keynesian Economics: Britain 1940–1964." *Economy and Society* 11, no. 3. 292–316.

Sethi, A.S., ed. 1989. *Collective Bargaining in Canada*. Scarborough, ON: Nelson.

Splane, R. 1965. *Social Welfare in Ontario, 1791–1898*. Toronto: University of Toronto Press.

Spring, J. 1972. *Education and the Rise of the Corporate State*. Boston: Beacon Press.

Stafford, J. 1986. "Retirement Pensions: Reinforced Exploitation." In Dickinson and Russell, *Family*.

Struthers, J. 1977. "Prelude to Depression: The Federal Government and Unemployment." *Canadian Historical Review* 58, no. 3, 277–293.

———. 1983. *No Fault of Their Own: Unemployment and the Canadian Welfare State, 1914–1941*. Toronto: University of Toronto Press.

Sulieman, E.N., and J. Waterbury, eds. *The Political Economy of Public Sector Reform and Privatization*. Boulder: Westview Press.

Swartz, D. 1977. "The Politics of Reform: Conflict and Accommodation in Canadian Health Policy." In *The Canadian State*, ed. L. Panitch, 311–43.

———. 1987. "The Limits of Health Insurance." In *The "Benevolent" State*, ed. A. Moscovitch and J. Albert, 255–70.

Tampke, J. 1981. "Bismarck's Social Legislation: A Genuine Breakthrough?" In Mommsen, *the Emergence*.

Taylor, M.G. 1987. *Heath Insurance and Canadian Public Policy*. Kingston and Montreal: McGill-Queen's University Press.

Therborn, G., and J. Roebeck. 1986. "The Irreversible Welfare State." *International Journal of Health Services* 16, no. 3.

Titmuss, R.M. 1958. *Essays on "The Welfare State." London: Allen and Unwin.*

Torczyner, J. 1987. "The Canadian Welfare State: Retrenchment and Change." In Modern Welfare States, ed. R.R. Friedmann, N. Gilbert, and M. Sherer. Brighton: Wheatsheaf Books.

Wallace, E. 1950. "The Origins of the Social Welfare State in Canada, 1867–1900." *Canadian Journal of Economic and Political Science* 16, no. 4.

Warnock, J. 1988. *Free Trade and the New Right Agenda*. Vancouver: New Star Books.

Weiler, P. 1980. *Reconcilable Differences: New Directions in Canadian Labour Law*. Toronto: The Carswell Company.

Whitely, P. 1981. "Public Opinion and the Demand for Social Welfare in Britain." *Journal of Social Policy* 10, no. 4, 453–476.

Wilensky, H.L., and C.N. Lebeaux. 1965. *Industrial Society and Social Welfare.* New York: The Free Press.

Winch, D. 1969. *Economics and Policy.* London: Hodder and Stoughton.

Woods, H.D., and S. Ostry. 1962. *Labour Policy and Labour Economics in Canada.* Toronto: Macmillan.

PART VII

Conclusions

CHAPTER 24

Social Issues and Social Policy

B. Singh Bolaria

Introduction

In their study of social issues, generations of sociologists have not only focussed on different problems but have also used different conceptual frameworks and perspectives. Early sociologists, who were mainly concerned with issues of deviance and criminality, analyzed the pathologies of individuals. The organismic, order, and medical models of society dominated the analysis of societal ills, which was expressed in clinical language.

Now, the study of social issues encompasses a much wider range of topics. There has also been a shift, over time, in the conceptualization and analysis of social issues. These issues are no longer analyzed solely with reference to the personal pathologies of individuals. Sociologists with a critical orientation not only question the order and stability model of society (by positing conflict rather than order as the norm), but also tend to focus on the social structural conditions and institutional arrangements that produce social problems. This approach locates the cause of the problematic conditions in the "defective" system rather than in "defective" individuals and their "defective" way of life.

The distinction between "personal troubles" and "public issues" and the division of social analysis into an individualistic versus a structural dichotomy may be an oversimplification of a complex phenomenon, but it leads us to a different perspective and allows us to conceptualize problematic conditions in new ways. As well, it helps us distinguish between individualistic and structural explanations. This distinction also has important consequences for the individual. A "personal situation" is commonly defined as a consequence of one's own failure, and so one easily falls into self-blame and self-accusation; in that case, one is likely to accept the situation passively. A more detailed discussion of this topic was presented in the introductory pages of this book. This chapter examines the policy implications of interpreting and analyzing social issues within individualistic or structural frameworks. As the following discussion indicates, dramatically different solutions and policies flow from these analyses. A number of policy alternatives are discussed that are intended to help "manage" the contradictions. These include individualization of social problems, their medicalization, and the implementation of reforms that do not disrupt the existing power relationships.

Individualization of Problems

Whether such social issues as inequality, poverty, and hunger are interpreted and analyzed within an individualistic or structural framework has important consequences for their solutions.

Many people tend to individualize these issues as personal problems of the poor and unemployed by attributing them to the personal characteristics of individuals. The ideology of equality of opportunity for everyone in this society tends to promote the notion that success or failure depends on individual characteristics. Positive characteristics, such as hard work, competitiveness, and high motivation, are associated with success. Failure and poverty, on the other hand, are attributed to some personal deficiency such as intellectual inferiority, laziness, or low aspirations. Public opinion polls tend to confirm the popularity of these beliefs. A 1985 Gallup poll asked a national sample in the United States, "In your opinion, which is more often to blame if a person is poor—lack of effort on his part, or circumstances beyond his control?" Of the national sample, 33 percent responded with "lack of effort," 34 percent with "circumstances," and 31 percent felt that both lack of effort and circumstances were to blame (Gallup 1985, 24). In a 1986 *Maclean's*/Decima poll of 1575 Canadians, in response to a question about what it takes to be successful or get ahead, 82 percent replied hard work, 10 percent said luck, and 7 percent chose privilege (*Maclean's* January, 6 1986).

Refinements of these attitudes have been the Social Darwinism of the nineteenth century and more recent theories of biological causation that put the blame for failure on inherited physical or intellectual traits (Herrnstein 1971,1973; Jensen 1969,1980). These perspectives have important social policy implications. From Social Darwinism it follows that the poor *should not* be helped because that would interfere with "natural selection"; the implication of arguments such as those of Jensen and Herrnstein is that the poor *cannot* be helped—they are "uneducatable" (Eitzen and Zinn 1989, 178–79).

Biological, intellectual, and cultural deficiency theories of inequality and poverty support the status quo and promote a laissez-faire policy whereby individuals are left to fend for themselves. This focus on individuals tends to strengthen the ideology of individualism by which one is responsible for one's station in life; it justifies Social Darwinism and masks the social structural conditions in societies that produce inequality and poverty (Feagin 1975; Navarro 1978; Eitzen and Zinn 1989).

A strictly individualistic and "blaming the victim" approach absolves the state, its political-economic structure, and other institutions of any responsibility for these problems. Consequently, solutions are oriented toward changing the individuals and their "defective" ways of life. Ryan calls the "blaming the victim" ideology "a brilliant ideology for justifying a perverse form of social action designed to change, not society, as one might expect, but rather society's victim" (1971, 7). If the problems are defined as a result of personal pathologies, the "treatment" may involve individual counselling and psychotherapy (Eitzen and Zinn 1989).

As noted before, uncritical use of the socialization perspective in gender studies diverts attention from the structured inequalities of the system and ends up blaming women themselves for gender inequality. This displaces not only the cause of the problem but also the solutions. Peterson and Enarson (1974, 8) conclude, "Rather than directing efforts toward radical social change, the solution seems to be to change women themselves, perhaps through exhortation ('If we want to be liberated, we'll have to act more aggressive ...') or, for example, changing children's literature and mothers' child rearing practice."

Another illustration comes from the area of medical sociology. Individual lifestyles and consumption patterns are now widely invoked as explanations of the current increase in many chronic and degenerative diseases. I have discussed elsewhere the ideological and policy implications of individual lifestyle and self-care approaches in the area of health care (Bolaria 1988). Health promotion strategies and educational campaigns are primarily oriented toward changing individuals and their lifestyles. This obfuscates the social causes of disease, shifts responsibility for health and illness back onto the individual, individualizes what is essentially a social problem. As Berliner (1977, 119) has commented, "Focussing on lifestyles serves only to reify the lifestyles as an entity apart from the social conditions from which it arises." Berliner further argues, "Discussing changes in lifestyles without first discussing the changes in the social conditions which give rise to them, without recognizing that the lifestyle is derivative, is misleading and, in effect, is victim blaming."

The poor are blamed not only for their own poverty, lack of health and education, and so forth, but also, by extension, for fiscal crises and budgetary deficits. It is argued that excessive social expenditures are responsible for deficits and need to be cut back in order to avert economic crises. As Minkler (1983, 155) states, "A hallmark of the current politics of retrenchment has been the tendency by many policy makers to scapegoat the poor and the elderly as 'causes' of the fiscal crises."

The rhetoric of victim-blaming, fiscal crisis, and individual responsibility all combine to justify cutbacks to welfare and other social programs.

Medicalization of Problems

Historically, medical jurisdiction has expanded over a number of human conditions. Medicine's domain has been extended to such areas as family life, sexuality, addiction, fertility, domestic violence, problems related to work and the life cycle, and many other areas (Cooperstock and Parnele 1982; Crawford 1980; Conrad and Schneider 1980; Stark and Flitcraft 1982; Koumjian 1981; Waitzkin 1983). Medical vocabulary is used more and more to define and analyze social problems. Many of the human conditions that were once considered "bad" are now classified as "sick" (Conrad and Schneider 1980). Illich has referred to this extension of the medical domain as the "medicalization of life."

This medicalization has mixed effects. The medical vocabulary and the definition of behaviour in medical terms tend to create more humanitarian tolerance than its definition in criminal terms. Medicalization also has negative consequences. Medical language mystifies human conditions and problems and thus removes them from public debate (Conrad and Schneider 1980). It often categorizes problems that are basically social in origin as "biological or personal deficits" (Stark and Flitcraft 1982). Waitzkin (1983, 41) states,

> As medical professionals assume responsibility for managing problems beyond the illnesses of individuals, attention shifts away from the underlying structural conditions that often are sources of individual distress. By defining social problems as medical, medicine becomes an institution of social control. Through medicalization, the structural roots of personal distress become mystified and depoliticized.

As Waitzkin points out, occupational stress becomes classified as muscular tension, a worker with black lung disease is given a medical certificate of disability, a homemaker's emotional stress related to the demands of housework is given a prescription for a tranquillizer, or a poor woman who cannot support her family receives a physician's recommendation to be sterilized. The important point to be made here is that "in each instance ... a problem at the level of social structure—stressful work demands, unsafe working conditions, sexism, and poverty—is transformed into an individual problem under medical control" (Waitzkin 1983, 41).

Thus, medical "technological fixes" are used to "cure" a wide range of problems that are social in origin. The most frequent response to many socially induced psychological disorders may be pharmacological—antidepressants, anti-anxiety agents, stimulants, and tranquillizers (Waldron 1977; Stroufe and Stewart 1973; Fee 1977). These are generally prescribed to women, who consume large quantities of prescribed drugs (Cooperstock and Parnele 1982; Koumjian 1981; Harding, Wolf, and Chan 1977; Fee 1977).

Medicine is playing an important role in some other respects, in the area of occupational health. For instance, genetic screening is being done in some petrochemical industries in order to detect those workers whose genetic make-up may make them more susceptible than others to various toxins. The assumption made in genetic screening programs is that certain workers get ill because of their genetic background and structure rather than because of the general dangers posed by exposure to toxins at the workplace. This shifts responsibility for disease back onto the individual, promoting a victim-blaming epidemiology. Thus, medical "intervention" transforms a social issue—occupational diseases affecting a large segment of the labour force, with roots in the hazardous work environment—into an individual problem of the genetic heredity of the individual worker.

Structural Changes

Both the individualistic and medical models of social problems see the solution in changing individuals, through, respectively, social or medical intervention. Within the structural framework, however, the solutions are seen to lie in transforming the political-economic structures and other institutional arrangements that produce and reproduce deleterious social conditions. Its proponents argue that equality of class, race, and gender is not possible within the existing capitalist system. Substantial evidence supports this contention. A number of readings in this book show that many social groups continue to encounter unequal opportunities and differential life chances, correlated with gender, class, and race.

A structural explanation of poverty locates its causes in the structural conditions that produce unemployment, low-paying jobs, and unequal opportunity structures. The segmentation of the Canadian labour market along occupational, gender, ethnic, and racial lines is a structural source of inequality. Therefore, the solution to social inequality lies in the alteration of labour market inequalities rather than in changing the individuals. Individual solutions cannot solve structural problems. We conclude this discussion by quoting at length from C. Wright Mills:

> In so far as an economy is so arranged that slumps occur, the problem of unemployment becomes incapable of personal solution. In so far as war is inherent in the nation-state system and in the uneven industrialization of the world, the ordinary individual in his [or her] restricted milieu will be powerless—with or without psychiatric aid—to solve the troubles this system or lack of system imposes upon him [or her]. In so far as the family as an institution turns women into darling little slaves and men into their chief providers and unweaned dependents, the problem of satisfactory marriage remains incapable of purely private solution. In so far as the overdeveloped megalopolis and the overdeveloped automobile are built-in features of the overdeveloped society, the issues of urban living will not be solved by personal ingenuity and private wealth. (1959, 10)

Conclusions

Linking social issues and social problems to the basic underlying social contradictions also raises the question of political strategy. If various policies do not address the social roots of social problems, solutions will be piecemeal, limited, and unsatisfactory. Yet, in the absence of a radical transformation of society, these issues and problems need to be "managed," both from the point of view of the state to maintain legitimacy and social harmony and of the individuals and social groups affected by deleterious social conditions.

The state, through a number of strategies, has tried to manage these problems. These include appointments of royal commissions to further study the problem, parliamentary investigations, appointment of various committees composed of members representing various groups affected by the adverse conditions, and human rights commissions to oversee various programs.

While these strategies may give the appearance that "something is being done," the objective reality is that in spite of various royal commissions and Senate Committee reports, Status of Women committees, multicultural committees, and human rights commissions, women and racial minority groups continue to face economic, social and political inequality. Wide income disparities continue to exist among Canadians. The welfare state has not been able to solve these problems. This is because, as some have argued, the piecemeal and technocratic approaches to social problems have dominated the social policy decisions. As George and Wilding (1976, 17) state, "To see the eradication of social problems as depending upon a range of piecemeal welfare programmes is to cherish a comfortable illusion." The technocratic "approach assumes that if only we knew more about the causation of such problems and if there were the necessary resources, then these problems would be solved."

While piecemeal solutions may be ameliorative and provide immediate relief to individuals, they do not address the underlying social-structural causes of these problems. In fact, as some have argued, these reforms "may reinforce the *status quo* by reducing the potential for social conflict" (Waitzkin 1983, 42). The history of welfare reforms in capitalist countries shows that these reforms most often follow social unrest and protests, make incremental changes and improvements that do not alter overall patterns of inequality, and face retrenchment when social unrest and protests recede (Piven and Cloward 1971). Gorz's (1973) distinction of "Reformist reforms" and "Nonreformist reforms" may help to clarify this point. "A reformist reform is one which subordinates objectives to the criteria of rationality and practicality of a given system and policy.... [It] rejects those objectives and demands—however deep the need for them—which are incompatible with the preservation of the system." These reforms, by providing small material relief, reduce discontent and leave intact the current economic, political and social structures and obscure the basic sources of inequality. The "nonreformist reforms," on the other hand, expose the sources of exploitation and inequality and address the issues of fundamental structural changes in the system. This distinction is quite crucial because many programs, that on the surface may appear to be aimed at structural changes, are in reality "reformist reforms": they help sustain the current political, economic, and other structural sources of inequality.

These social policy issues will become even more prominent in the context of the current attacks on the welfare state and politics of retrenchment and deficit reductions and their impact on the lives of millions of Canadians. We need to continue to carefully examine various reforms and their direction and potential to challenge basic social contradictions and structural changes. To paraphrase Waitzkin (1983, 43), without a careful examination of the links between social problems and social structure "both problems and solutions will continue to float in a haze of confusion and mystification."

References

Berliner, H.S. 1977. "Emerging Ideologies in Medicine." *Review of Radical Political Economics* 9: 116–24.

Bolaria, B. 1988. "The Politics and Ideology of Self-Care and Lifestyles." In *Sociology of Health Care in Canada*, ed. B.S. Bolaria and H. Dickinson. Toronto: Harcourt Brace Jovanovich. 537–52.

Conrad, P., and J.W. Schneider. 1980. *Deviance and Medicalization: From Badness to Sickness*. St. Louis, MO: C.V. Mosby.

Cooperstock, R., and P. Parnele. 1982. "Research on Psychotropic Drug Use: A Review of Findings and Methods." *Social Science and Medicine* 16: 1179–96.

Crawford, R. 1980. "Healthism and the Medicalization of Everyday Life." *International Journal of Health Services* 10: 365–89.

Eitzen D.S., and M.B. Zinn. 1989. *Social Problems.* 4th ed. Boston: Allyn and Bacon.

Feagin, J.R. 1975. *Subordinating the Poor: Welfare and American Beliefs.* Englewood Cliffs, NJ: Prentice-Hall.

Fee, E. 1977. "Women and Health Care: A Comparison of Theories." In *Health and Medical Care in the United States: A Critical Analysis*, ed. V. Navarro. New York: Baywood Publishing. 115–32.

Gallup Report. 1985. "Poverty." No. 234 (March): 21–25.

George, V., and P. Wilding. 1976. *Ideology and Social Welfare.* London: Routledge and Kegan Paul.

Gorz, A. 1973. *Socialism and Revolution.* Garden City, NY: Anchor Books.

Harding, J., N. Wolf, and G. Chan. 1977. "A Socio-Demographic Profile of People Being Prescribed Mood-Modifying Drugs in Saskatchewan." Regina: Alcoholism Commission of Saskatchewan.

Herrnstein, R. 1971. "I.Q." *Atlantic* 228 (September): 43–64.

———. 1973. *I.Q. in the Meritocracy.* Boston: Littlewood.

Jensen, A.R. 1969. "How Much Can We Boost I.Q. and Scholastic Achievement." *Harvard Educational Review* 39 (Winter): 1–123.

———. 1980. *Bias in Mental Testing.* New York: The Free Press.

Koumjian, K. 1981. "The Use of Valium as a Force of Social Control." *Social Science and Medicine* 15E: 245–49.

Mills, C. 1959. *The Sociological Imagination.* New York: Oxford University Press.

Minkler, M. 1983. "Blaming the Aged Victim: The Politics of Scapegoating in Times of Fiscal Conservatism." *International Journal of Health Services* 13: 155–68.

Navarro, V. 1978. "The Crisis of the Western System of Medicine in Contemporary Capitalism." *International Journal of Health Services*, 8, no. 2.

———. 1986. *Crises, Health and Medicine.* New York: Tavistock Publications.

Peterson, L, and E. Enarson. 1974. "Blaming the Victim in the Sociology of Women: On the Misuse of the Concept of Socialization." Paper presented at the Pacific Sociological Association, San Jose, California, March; cited in Eitzen and Zinn, *Social Problems.*

Piven, F.F., and R.A. Cloward. 1971. *Regulating the Poor: The Functions of Public Welfare.* New York: Vintage Books.

Ryan, W. 1971. *Blaming the Victim.* New York: Pantheon.

Stark, E., and A. Flitcraft. 1982. "Medical Therapy as Repression: The Case of Battered Women." *Health and Medicine* 1: 29–32.

Stroufe, L.A., and M.A. Stewart. 1973. "Treating Children With Stimulant Drugs." *New England Journal of Medicine*, no. 291, 289–409.

Waitzkin, H. 1983. *The Second Sickness.* New York: The Free Press.

Waldron, 1. 1977. "Increased Prescribing of Valium, Librium, and Other Drugs: An Example of the Influence of Economics and Social Factors on the Practice of Medicine." *International Journal of Health Services* 7, no. 1: 37–62.

CONTRIBUTORS

B. Singh Bolaria is a professor in the Department of Sociology at the University of Saskatchewan. He has researched and published widely in the areas of racial and ethnic studies, migrant labour, and medical sociology. Most recently, he has co-edited *Contemporary Sociology* (1994) and *Health, Illness, and Health-Care in Canada* (1994). He also co-authored *Racial Oppression in Canada*, second edition (1988).

Harold E. Bronson has recently retired from the Department of Economics and Political Science at the University of Saskatchewan. His publications have included consideration of the issues and contradictions that have become more prominent as a result of the debates over the Canada–U.S. Free Trade Agreement. Four of his books in sequence have examined two decades of economic, political, and social developments. They are *The Prevention of World War III* (1971), *The Renegade Revolutionaries* (1975), *The Two Superpowers* (1980), and *The Profit Parasites* (1986). In addition, he has contributed chapters to a number of edited volumes.

William K. Carroll, a professor of Sociology, teaches in the graduate program in the Department of Contemporary Social and Political Thought at the University of Victoria. Among his publications are *Corporate Power and Canadian Capitalism* (1986), articles in the *Canadian Review of Sociology and Anthropology* (1987), *Capital and Class* (Summer 1989), and *Critical Sociology* (Summer 1989).

Michael Clow is a member of the Department of Social Science at St. Thomas University in Fredericton, New Brunswick. He has done research on resource management, particularly forest management, community development, and sociological theory. He is currently exploring the ways that critical sociological analysis can contribute to public as well as academic dialogues concerning sustainable development. He is currently completing a three-year study of sustainable forest development in New Brunswick.

Wilfrid B. Denis is a professor at St. Thomas More College, Saskatoon, where he has been teaching for about fifteen years. His areas of research include Francophone minorities, agriculture, and occupational health and safety. He has published widely in these areas and has contributed to *Studies in Political Economy* and other journals and edited volumes.

Harley D. Dickinson is currently a professor in the Department of Sociology at the University of Saskatchewan. His main research interests are in the areas of medical sociology and the sociology of work. He has recently authored a book entitled *The Two Psychiatries: The Transformation of Psychiatric Work in Saskatchewan* (1989), and co-edited (with B. Singh Bolaria) *Health, Illness, and Health-Care in Canada*, second edition (1994). He has also co-edited (with Bob Russell) *The Politics of Work in the West: Historical and Contemporary Perspectives* (1986).

Lawrence F. Felt is a member of the Department of Sociology at Memorial University of Newfoundland. He has written extensively in areas of rural development, occupations, and work and resource management. He is a co-author of a recent book entitled "Living on the Edge" (1994) along with Peter Sinclair. It examines how households and individuals respond to resource depletion in a fishing region with few alternative economic opportunities. He is presently working on a three-year grant to examine long-term survival strategies for communities in north-east Newfoundland faced with the collapse of their traditional fishing economies.

James S. Frideres has taught at a number of Canadian universities and is currently at the University of Calgary. He is a professor of Sociology and an associate dean of research in the Faculty of Social Sciences. His past research has focussed on ethnic relations in Canadian society, with an emphasis on Native people. He has carried out extensive research and written numerous articles on Native people, as well as a book, *Native Peoples in Canada*, which is in its third edition. His articles have appeared in respected academic journals. In addition, he has acted as a consultant for various Native organizations and for government.

Karen R. Grant is an associate professor of Sociology at the University of Manitoba. Her research interests and publications are in the areas of women's health, health care and aging, occupational health and safety legislation in Canada, and AIDS as a social phenomenon. In addition to her other publications, she has contributed to *Sociology of Health Care in Canada* (1988).

Alison Hayford is an associate professor and department head in the Department of Sociology and Social Studies, University of Regina. Her current research interests reflect an interdisciplinary approach to the study of urbanization and city life, gender roles, and the family. She has published extensively in her areas of specialization and has contributed to a number of edited volumes.

Leslie J. Miller is an associate professor of Sociology at the University of Calgary. Her research has appeared in the *Canadian Journal of Sociology* and in the *British Journal of Sociology*. She has also contributed to edited volumes.

Alicja Muszynski is an associate professor in the Department of Sociology and Social Studies at the University of Waterloo. Her previous research involved work on ethnicity, class, and gender relations among shore workers in the British Columbia fishing industry. It appeared in the *Canadian Journal of Sociology and Studies in Political Economy*. She is currently involved in an international study on the family farm, with researchers in Brazil, Poland, Tunisia, France, Quebec, and Saskatchewan.

Herbert C. Northcott is currently a professor of Sociology at the University of Alberta. He specializes in the sociology of health and the sociology of aging. He has published a number of journal articles and has recently written two books: *Changing Residence: The Geographic Mobility of Elderly Canadians* (1988) and, with G. Lowe, *Under Pressure: A Study of Job Stress* (1986).

Leslie Samuelson is an associate professor in the Department of Sociology, University of Saskatchewan. His primary interests are in the areas of criminology and the sociology of law. His secondary interests include crime and socio-economic conditions, as well as criminal justice administration and policy. His recent publications include a contribution to *Hitting the Books: The Politics of Educational Retrenchment* (1990).

Vic Satzewich is an associate professor of Sociology at the University of Lethbridge. He has published articles in *Canadian Ethnic Studies*, the *Canadian Journal of Sociology, Ethnic and Racial Studies, International Sociology*, and *Studies in Political Economy*. He is also the author of *Racism and the Incorporation of Foreign Labour* (1990), a study of postwar farm labour migration to Ontario.

Peter R. Sinclair is a professor of Sociology at Memorial University of Newfoundland, where he has worked since 1980. Major recent publications include *From Traps to Draggers* (1985), *State Intervention in the Newfoundland Fisheries* (1987), and *A Question of Survival: The Fisheries and Newfoundland Society* (1988), of which he was a contributing editor. His current research focusses mainly on regional development and on household organization and economic activity in northern Newfoundland.

James Stolzman is an associate professor in the Department of Sociology and Social Anthropology, Dalhousie University. His areas of academic interest are the sociology of mental disorders, social stratification, and social theory. He has published extensively in the area of mental health and was a contributor to *Sociology of Health Care in Canada* (1988).

Kathleen Storrie is an associate professor in the Department of Sociology, University of Saskatchewan. Her publications include "The Modern Movement for the Submission of Women," in *Canadian Woman Studies* 5, no. 2 (1983) and "Introduction: The Ecology of Gender," in *Women: Isolation and Bonding* (1987), which she also edited. She was co-author of *Violence Against Women* (1987).

Gary Teeple is an associate professor in the Department of Sociology and Anthropology at Simon Fraser University. Currently he is researching the areas of political sociology and the global division of labour. His publications include *Capitalism and the National Question in Canada (1972) for which he was editor; Marx's Critique* of Politics (1984); and the forthcoming *Globalism and the Decline of Social Reform.*

K. Victor Ujimoto is a professor and research associate at the Gerontology Research Center, University of Guelph. He has published numerous articles on Japanese

Canadians, multiculturalism, and aging ethnic minorities. He also co-edited, with G. Hirabayashi, *Visible Minorities and Multiculturalism: Asians in Canada* (1980). At present he is researching comparative aspects of aging in Asian Canadians.

Rennie Warburton is an associate professor in the Department of Sociology, University of Victoria. His most recent publication is *Workers, Capital, and the State in British Columbia* (1988) of which he was co-editor. He was also a contributor to *Sociology of Health Care in Canada* (1988).

Terry Wotherspoon is an associate professor and department head of Sociology at the University of Saskatchewan. He has recently edited *The Political Economy of Canadian Schooling* (1987) and *Hitting the Books: The Politics of Educational Retrenchment* (1990). He has also published articles on other aspects of education, including prison education and nursing education. His current research projects include work on teacher–state relations in British Columbia, Native education, and vocational education.

INDEX

Reader Reply Card

We are interested in your reaction to *Social Issues and Contradictions in Canadian Society*, by B. Singh Bolaria. You can help us to improve this book in future editions by completing this questionnaire.

1. What was your reason for using this book?

   ❑ university course ❑ college course ❑ continuing education course
   ❑ professional development ❑ personal interest ❑ other (specify) ________________

2. If you are a student, please identify your school and the course in which you used this book.

3. Which chapters or parts of this book did you use? Which did you omit?

4. What did you like best about this book?

5. What did you like least about this book?

6. Please identify any topics you think should be added to future editions.

7. Please add any comments or suggestions.

8. May we contact you for further information?

   Name: ________________________________

   Address: ________________________________

   ____

   Phone: ________________________________

(fold here and tape shut)

- -

Canada Post Corporation / Société canadienne des postes

Postage paid If mailed in Canada | **Port payé** si posté au Canada

Business Reply | **Réponse d'affaires**

0116870399 01

0116870399-M8Z4X6-BR01

Heather McWhinney
Publisher, College Division
HARCOURT BRACE & COMPANY, CANADA
55 HORNER AVENUE
TORONTO, ONTARIO
M8Z 9Z9